Handbook of
Relationship
Marketing

Handbook of
Relationship
Marketing

Jagdish N. Sheth
Atul Parvatiyar Editors

Sage Publications, Inc.
International Educational and Professional Publisher
Thousand Oaks ■ London ■ New Delhi

For information:

Sage Publications, Inc.
2455 Teller Road
Thousand Oaks, California 91320
E-mail: order@sagepub.com

Sage Publications Ltd.
6 Bonhill Street
London EC2A 4PU
United Kingdom

Sage Publications India Pvt. Ltd.
M-32 Market
Greater Kailash I
New Delhi 110 048 India

Printed in the United States of America

Library of Congress Cataloging-in-Publication Data

Main entry under title:

Handbook of relationship marketing/edited by Jagdish N. Sheth and Atul Parvatiyar.
    p. cm.
Includes bibliographical references and index.
   ISBN 0-7619-1810-8 (cloth)—
   1. Relationship marketing. I. Sheth, Jagdish N. II. Parvatiyar, Atul. III. Title.
   HF5415.55.H36 2000
   658.8—dc21   99-050408

This book is printed on acid-free paper.

00 01 02 03 04 05 06 7 6 5 4 3 2 1

Acquiring Editor:	Harry Briggs
Editorial Assistant:	MaryAnn Vail
Production Editor:	Wendy Westgate
Editorial Assistant:	Victoria Cheng
Typesetter:	Danielle Dillahunt
Indexer:	Juniee Oneida

To our wives,
Madhu Sheth and Divya Parvatiyar

Contents

PART II. CONCEPTUAL AND THEORETICAL FOUNDATIONS OF RELATIONSHIP MARKETING

PART III. PARTNERING FOR RELATIONSHIP MARKETING

Preface

The idea for this book originated as a result of a special session that we organized at the Academy of Marketing Science conference in 1994. In a very lively session, participants debated the idea of preparing a compendium of scholarly articles on the emerging topic of relationship marketing. Dave Cravens, a speaker at the session and editor of the *Journal of the Academy of Marketing Science (JAMS)*, took the initiative and invited the special session presenters to write position papers on different areas of relationship marketing. Thus a special issue of *JAMS* on this topic was published in fall 1995 and has had a significant impact on fostering research and scholarly work in relationship marketing. However, we soon realized that this subject needed a more comprehensive examination that goes beyond the articles published in *JAMS* and that is not bound by the page limitations of a standard academic journal.

Although in recent years there has been explosive growth in business practices and academic curiosity with respect to relationship marketing, no textbook is available that presents conceptual ideas on the subject in an organized fashion for use by students and faculty. For people already teaching relationship marketing courses or course modules, it is a challenge to develop relevant course material from many disparate sources. The purpose of this book is to fill this gap and provide a foundation for developing textbooks. It can be used by academic scholars and PhD students as a source of references and extant knowledge on the topic of relationship marketing. It can also serve as a textbook for courses on relationship marketing at the MBA level.

In many ways the development of this book and the subject area of relationship marketing mirrors the early stages of the development and growth of other subdisciplines of marketing, such as consumer behavior, channel management, product management, and marketing theory. All of these areas witnessed considerable academic interest and scholarship before they grew to become part of standard marketing course offerings at business schools. In fact, books written or edited by leading scholars facilitated the acceptance of certain topics as standard marketing courses and legitimate streams of doctoral research. For example, Stern and El-Ansary's (1977) book on channels and Engel, Kollat, and Blackwell's (1968) book may not have been written around existing course offerings in the marketing curriculum, but they eventually became textbooks as new courses were created on these topics in graduate and undergraduate programs at most institutions. Similarly, the early editions of marketing theory books such as that edited by Sheth and Garrett (1986), comprising articles by leading scholars, and that authored by Hunt (1983) provided useful teaching material on this subject in PhD programs. They also led to the development of other books by these scholars on the topic of marketing theory (Hunt, 1991; Sheth, Gardener, & Garrett, 1988).

Thus our intent here is to provide a comprehensive scholarly book to students and faculty interested in the area of relationship marketing. We have taken an inclusive rather than exclusive approach to this subject, including a broad coverage of topics, diverse perspectives, theoretical and conceptual paradigms, and scholarly representation. Instead of adopting a single view as to what constitutes relationship marketing or limiting ourselves to the North American viewpoint, we have included the viewpoints of scholars from other parts of the world, particularly Europe, where relationship marketing issues have been of interest to many scholars for several years now. We have attempted to include contributions of some of the best-known scholars on this subject by inviting them to write chapters specifically for this book.

This volume is organized into five parts. The first, consisting of five chapters, deals with the domain, evolution, and growth of relationship marketing. In Chapter 1, we define relationship marketing and discuss the antecedents to its emergence as a subdiscipline of marketing. We also present a relationship marketing process model to highlight the domains of current and potential academic inquiry into the subject matter. In Chapter 2, Adrian Payne provides an overview of the development of relationship marketing from the U.K. perspective. He presents a six-markets model as a framework for understanding relationship marketing practice and research domains. In Chapter 3, Håkan Håkansson and Ivan J. Snehota outline the history of the IMP (Industrial Marketing and Purchasing) Group perspective. They review its conceptual cornerstones and suggest future directions for research in business relationships. In Chapter 4, Christian Grönroos describes the Nordic school perspective on relationship marketing. He identifies the core processes of relationship marketing and discusses their application to the management and marketing of services. Finally, in Chapter 5, we trace the evolution of relationship marketing by comparing business practices during the preindustrial, industrial, and postindustrial eras. We also trace the development of marketing thought from the early 1900s to clarify the shifting paradigms that have led to the recent emergence of a relationship marketing viewpoint.

Part II addresses the conceptual and theoretical foundations of relationship marketing and primarily comprises the position papers that were published in the 1995 special issue of *JAMS* mentioned above. In Chapter 6, Leonard L. Berry discusses the imperative of relationship marketing in the services sector and its emerging perspectives. He presents his ideas on how relationships can be developed and promoted by service marketers and its consequent research implications. In Chapter 7, we discuss the antecedents and consequences of relationship marketing in consumer markets. We draw upon consumer behavior literature to understand why consumers reduce choice and thereby engage in relationships with marketers. Barton A. Weitz and Sandy D. Jap discuss the conceptual developments relating to distribution channel relationships and partnering behavior in Chapter 8. They provide an overview of the application of various theoretical perspectives, such as transaction cost, power dependence, and relational norms, in the study of distribution channel relationships. In Chapter 9, David T. Wilson provides an integrated model of buyer-seller relationships. He identifies current research on relationship marketing in the business-to-business context at the concept, model, and process levels and suggests directions for future research based on the integrated model of buyer-seller relationships. In Chapter 10, P. Rajan Varadarajan and Margaret H. Cunningham provide a synthesis of conceptual foundations of strategic alliances. Based on resource allocation theories, they recommend directions for future studies on strategic alliances. And in Chapter 11, we develop a typology of alliances by drawing upon the underlying themes of interorganization literature. Based on this typology and implied characteristics of different types of alliances, we develop theoretical propositions on business alliance formation.

Part III comprises chapters on partnering for relationship marketing. Several aspects of partnering that facilitates the development and implementation of customer relationships are addressed in this section. In Chapter 12, C. B. Bhattacharya and Ruth N. Bolton discuss relationship marketing in mass markets where there are potentially large numbers of customers. They address questions related to (a) the conditions under which relationship marketing will be effective in mass markets and (b) the marketing strategies most appropriate for influencing relationship processes and outcomes under these different conditions. In Chapter 13, Thomas W. Gruen proposes a model that provides a comprehensive set of constructs related to membership organizations and their relationship marketing practices. He outlines several avenues of additional research with respect to membership customers and relationship marketing. Vanitha Swaminathan and Srinivas K. Reddy provide a framework of affinity partnering relationships in Chapter 14. They develop a typology and present a conceptual model of affinity partnering strategies. Key account management (KAM) programs, as a means for engaging in relationship marketing with business customers, are Joseph P. Cannon and Narakesari Narayandas's focus in Chapter 15. They contrast traditional sales approaches with KAM and review the relevant issues as presented in the extant literature to point out opportunities for future research in key account management. In Chapter 16, David W. Cravens and Karen S. Cravens consider the context of horizontal alliance relationships and develop a process model for it. They also examine major constructs comprising the process model and explore emerging issues concerning the conceptualization of and research on horizontal alliances. And in Chapter 17, John T. Mentzer examines the potential of positional advantage involving value-added services through supplier partnering. He identifies 11 dimensions of supplier partnering and presents the apparent impetus for each dimension, along with the extant research and managerial thinking related to it.

The chapters in Part IV of this book concern the enablers of relationship marketing posture by firms. In Chapter 18, Robert M. Morgan discusses the evolution of relationship marketing strategy within an organization. He presents an expanded conceptualization of commitment-trust theory of relationships, develops an understanding of how firms combine and manage resources to achieve relationship-based competitive advantages, and introduces the concept of cooperative value nets to represent the highest level of sophistication of relationship marketing strategy. In Chapter 19, Ian Gordon provides a framework for organizational redesign so that an organization can better undertake the relationship marketing function. He reviews how relationship marketing can affect the enterprise and how a company could respond through new approaches to organizational design and meet those challenges. Rajendra S. Sisodia and David B. Wolfe, in Chapter 20, describe the role of information technology (IT) in building, maintaining, and enhancing customer relationships. They present a model that shows the symbiosis between IT and relationship marketing and discuss the characteristics and impact of technology-enabled relationship marketing. In Chapter 21, Kaj Storbacka presents a methodology for customer profitability analysis within the relationship marketing context. He also examines the issue of designing appropriate customer relationships based on current and potential profitability of customers and customer bases.

Finally, the chapters in Part V explore the research and educational implications of relationship marketing. In Chapter 22, Joseph P. Cannon and Jagdish N. Sheth provide a framework for developing curricula to enhance the teaching of relationship marketing. They describe the innovative curriculum and supporting structure developed at Emory Business School, which creates a three-way partnership among students, faculty, and the business community, in order to place a greater emphasis on relationship marketing. In Chapter 23, Sheth discusses the future of relationship marketing research and its potential for influencing a paradigm shift in marketing approach and theory.

We hope that this book will be of value to students, scholars, and practitioners interested in the conceptual foundations of relationship marketing. We wish to thank all of the authors who have contributed chapters; without their valuable contributions, we would not have been able to prepare this volume. We offer our special thanks to Naresh Malhotra, president of the Academy of Marketing Science, who suggested that we prepare this book on relationship marketing. We also wish to thank Sage Publications for agreeing to publish the book and to make it available to the academic and practitioner communities. In particular, we would like to thank

Harry Briggs at Sage Publications, for his support and help in the production of this volume. Finally, we thank our research assistants, Ron Bruno and Chitturi Suresh Rayudu, for helping us in assembling the manuscripts.

Jagdish N. Sheth
Atul Parvatiyar

References

Engel, J. F., Kollat, D. T., & Blackwell, R. D. (1968). *Consumer behavior.* New York: Holt, Rinehart & Winston.

Hunt, S. D. (1983). *Marketing theory: The philosophy of marketing science.* Homewood, IL: Richard D. Irwin.

Hunt, S. D. (1991). *Modern marketing theory: Critical issues in the philosophy of marketing science.* Cincinnati, OH: Southwestern.

Sheth, J. N., Gardner, D. M., & Garrett, D. E. (1988). *Marketing theory: Evolution and evaluation.* New York: John Wiley.

Sheth, J. N., & Garrett, D. E. (Eds.). (1986). *Marketing theory: Classic and contemporary readings.* Cincinnati, OH: Southwestern.

Stern, L. W., & El-Ansary, A. (1977). *Marketing channels.* Englewood Cliffs, NJ: Prentice Hall.

PART I

Domain, Evolution, and Growth of Relationship Marketing

Alternative Perspectives

1

The Domain and Conceptual Foundations of Relationship Marketing

ATUL PARVATIYAR
JAGDISH N. SHETH

In the current era of intense competition and demanding customers, relationship marketing has attracted the expanded attention of scholars and practitioners. Marketing scholars are studying the nature and scope of relationship marketing and developing conceptualizations regarding the value of cooperative and collaborative relationships between buyers and sellers as well as the relationships between different marketing actors, including suppliers, competitors, distributors, and internal functions in creating and delivering customer value. Many scholars with interests in various subdisciplines of marketing, such as channels, services marketing, business-to-business marketing, and advertising, are actively engaged in studying and exploring the conceptual foundations of relationship marketing.

However, the conceptual foundations of relationship marketing are not fully developed as yet. The current growth in the field of relationship marketing is somewhat similar to what was experienced in the early stages of the development of the discipline of consumer behavior. There is a growing interest in the subject matter, and many explorations are under way to establish its conceptual foundations. In the flood of knowledge, diverse perspectives are required for understanding this growing phenomenon. Each exploration offers a perspective that should help us to conceptualize further the discipline of relationship marketing. As Sheth (1996) has observed, for a discipline to emerge, it is necessary for scholars to build conceptual foundations and develop theory that will provide purpose and explanation for the phenomenon. This is how consumer behavior grew to become a discipline that now enjoys a central position in marketing knowledge. We expect relationship marketing to undergo a similar growth pattern and soon to become a discipline unto itself.

Our purpose in this chapter is to provide a synthesis of existing knowledge on relationship marketing by integrating diverse explorations. In the following section, we examine various perspectives on relationship marketing and offer a definition of relationship marketing. Subsequently, we trace the paradigmatic shifts in the evolution of marketing theory that have led to the emergence of a relationship marketing school of thought. We also identify the forces that have had impacts on the marketing environment in recent years, leading to the rapid development of relationship marketing practices. We present a typology of relationship marketing programs to provide a parsimonious view of the domain of relationship marketing practices. We then describe a process model of relationship marketing to delineate more clearly the challenges of relationship formation, its governance, its performance evaluation, and its evolution. Finally, we examine the domain of current relationship marketing research and the issues that researchers need to address in the future.

What Is Relationship Marketing?

Before we begin to examine the theoretical foundations of relationship marketing, it will be useful to define what the term *relationship marketing* means. As Nevin (1995) points out, this term has been used to reflect a variety of themes and perspectives. Some of these take a narrow functional marketing perspective, whereas others employ a view that is broad and somewhat paradigmatic in approach and orientation.

NARROW VERSUS BROAD VIEWS
OF RELATIONSHIP MARKETING

One example of a narrow perspective on relationship marketing is database marketing that emphasizes the promotional aspects of marketing linked to database efforts (Bickert, 1992). Another narrow, yet relevant, viewpoint considers relationship marketing only as customer retention, in which a variety of aftermarketing tactics are used for customer bonding or staying in touch after the sale is made (Vavra, 1992). A more popular approach with recent application of information technology is to focus on individual or one-to-one relationships with customers that integrate database knowledge with a long-term customer retention and growth strategy (Peppers & Rogers, 1993). Thus Shani and Chalasani (1992) define relationship marketing as "an integrated effort to identify, maintain, and build up a network with individual consumers and to continuously strengthen the network for the mutual benefit of both sides, through interactive, individualized and value-added contacts over a long period of time" (p. 44). Jackson (1985) applies the individual account concept in industrial markets to define relationship marketing as "marketing oriented toward strong, lasting relationships with individual accounts" (p. 2). In other business contexts, Doyle and Roth (1992), O'Neal (1989), and Paul (1988) have proposed similar definitions of relationship marketing.

McKenna (1991) offers a more strategic view of relationship marketing by putting the customer first and shifting the role of marketing from manipulating the customer (telling and selling) to genuine customer involvement (communicating and sharing the knowledge). Berry (1983), in somewhat broader terms, also has a strategic viewpoint on relationship marketing. He stresses that attracting new customers should be viewed only as an intermediate step in the marketing process. Developing closer relationship with these customers and turning them into loyal ones are equally important aspects of marketing. Thus he defines relationship marketing as "attracting, maintaining, and—in multi-service organizations—enhancing customer relationships" (p. 25).

Berry's notion of relationship marketing resembles that of other scholars studying services marketing, such as Grönroos (1983), Gummesson

(1987), and Levitt (1981). Although each of them espouses the value of interactions in marketing and its consequent impact on customer relationships, Grönroos (1990) and Gummesson (1987) take a broader perspective and advocate that customer relationships ought to be the focus and dominant paradigm of marketing. For example, Grönroos (1990) states: "Marketing is to establish, maintain, and enhance relationships with customers and other partners, at a profit, so that the objectives of the parties involved are met. This is achieved by a mutual exchange and fulfillment of promises" (p. 138). The implication of Grönroos's definition is that customer relationships are the raison de'être of the firm and marketing should be devoted to building and enhancing such relationships.

Morgan and Hunt (1994) draw upon the distinction made between transactional exchanges and relational exchanges by Dwyer, Schurr, and Oh (1987) to propose a more inclusive definition of relationship marketing. According to Morgan and Hunt, "Relationship marketing refers to all marketing activities directed toward establishing, developing, and maintaining successful relationships" (p. 22). Such a broadened definition has come under attack by some scholars. Peterson (1995) declares Morgan and Hunt's definition guilty of an error of commission and states that if their "definition is true, then relationship marketing and marketing are redundant terms and one is unnecessary and should be stricken from the literature because having both only leads to confusion" (p. 279). Other scholars who believe that relationship marketing is distinctly different from the prevailing transactional orientation of marketing may contest such an extreme viewpoint.

RELATIONSHIP MARKETING VERSUS
MARKETING RELATIONSHIPS

El-Ansary (1997) raises an interesting question as to what the difference is between "marketing relationships" and "relationship marketing." Certainly marketing relationships have existed and have been a topic of discussion for a long time. But what distinguishes marketing relationships from relationship marketing are their nature and specificity. Marketing relationships could take any form, including adversarial relationships, rivalry relationships, affiliation relationships, and independent or dependent relationships. However, relationship marketing is not concerned with all aspects of marketing relationships. The core theme of all

relationship marketing perspectives and definitions is a focus on cooperative and collaborative relationships between the firm and its customers
and/or other marketing actors. Dwyer et al. (1987) have characterized
such cooperative relationships as being interdependent and long-term
oriented rather than concerned with short-term discrete transactions.
The long-term orientation is often emphasized because it is believed that
marketing actors will not engage in opportunistic behavior if they have a
long-term orientation and that such relationships will be anchored in mutual gains and cooperation (Ganesan, 1994).

Thus the terms *relationship marketing* and *marketing relationships* are
not synonymous. *Relationship marketing* describes a specific marketing
approach that is a subset or a specific focus of marketing. However, given
the rate at which practitioners and scholars are embracing the core beliefs
of relationship marketing for directing marketing practice and research,
it has the potential to become the dominant paradigm and orientation of
marketing. As such, several authors have described the emergence of relationship marketing as a paradigm shift in marketing approach and orientation (e.g., Kotler, 1990; Parvatiyar & Sheth, 1997; Webster, 1992). In
fact, Sheth, Gardner, and Garrett (1988) have observed that the emphasis
on relationships as opposed to transaction-based exchanges is very likely
to redefine the domain of marketing.

DELIMITING THE DOMAIN
OF RELATIONSHIP MARKETING

For an emerging discipline, it is important to develop an acceptable
definition that encompasses all facets of the phenomenon and also effectively delimits the domain so as to allow focused understanding and
growth of knowledge in the discipline. Although Morgan and Hunt's
(1994) definition focuses on the relational aspects of marketing, it has
been criticized for being too broad and inclusive. They include buyer partnerships, supplier partnerships, internal partnerships, and lateral partnerships within the purview of relationship marketing. Many of these partnerships have been construed as being outside the domain of marketing,
and hence their inclusion risks diluting the value and contribution of the
marketing discipline in directing relationship marketing practice and research or theory development (Peterson, 1995).

Therefore, Sheth (1996) has suggested that we limit the domain of relationship marketing to only those cooperative and collaborative marketing actions that are focused on serving the needs of customers. That would be consistent with marketing's customer focus and the understanding of customers that made the discipline prominent. Other aspects of organizational relationships, such as supplier relationships, internal relationships, and lateral relationships, are aspects that are directly attended to by such disciplines as purchasing and logistics management, human resources management, and strategic management. Therefore, relationship marketing has the greatest potential for becoming a discipline and developing its own theory if it delimits its domain to the firm-customer aspect of the relationship. However, to achieve mutually beneficial relationships with customers, the firm may have to cooperate and collaborate with its suppliers, competitors, consociates, and internal divisions. The study of such relationships is a valid domain of relationship marketing as long as this study is conducted in the context of how relationship marketing enhances or facilitates customer relationships.

TOWARD A DEFINITION OF
RELATIONSHIP MARKETING

An important aspect of Berry's (1983), Grönroos's (1990), and Morgan and Hunt's (1984) definitions is that they all recognize the process aspects of relationship development and maintenance. Heide (1994) also identifies a set of generic processes of relationship initiation, relationship maintenance, and relationship termination. Heide claims that the objectives of relationship marketing are to establish, develop, and maintain successful relational exchanges. Wilson (1995) has developed a similar process model of buyer-seller cooperative and partnering relationships by integrating conceptual and empirical research conducted in this field. Thus a process view of relationship marketing currently prevails in the literature and indicates that the discipline is in its early stages of development, whereby marketing practice and research need to be directed to the different stages of the relationship marketing process.

In addition to the process view, there is general acceptance that relationship marketing is concerned with cooperative and collaborative relationships between the firm and its customers. Such cooperative and collaborative relationships are more than standard buyer-seller relationships, yet short of merger or acquisition relationships. They are formed between the firm and one or many of its customers, including end consumers, distributors or channel members, and business-to-business customers. Also, a prevailing axiom of relationship marketing is that cooperative and collaborative relationships with customers lead to greater market value creation and that such value will benefit both parties engaged in the relationship. Creation and enhancement of mutual economic value are thus the purposes of relationship marketing. Hence we define relationship marketing as *the ongoing process of engaging in cooperative and collaborative activities and programs with immediate and end-user customers to create or enhance mutual economic value at reduced cost.* There are three underlying dimensions of relationship formation suggested by this definition: purpose, parties, and programs. We use these three dimensions below to illustrate a process model of relationship marketing. Before we present this process model, let us examine the antecedents to the emergence of relationship marketing theory and practice.

The Emergence of the Relationship Marketing School of Thought

As is widely known, the discipline of marketing grew out of economics, and the growth was motivated by a lack of interest among economists in the details of market behavior and the functions of middlemen (Bartels, 1976; Sheth et al., 1988). Marketing's early bias toward distribution activities is evident in the fact that the first marketing courses (at the University of Michigan and Ohio State University) were focused on effective performance of the distributive task (Bartels, 1976). Early marketing thinking centered on efficiency of marketing channels (Cherrington, 1920; Shaw, 1912; Weld, 1916, 1917). Later, the institutional marketing thinkers, because of their grounding in institutional economic theory, viewed the phenomena of value determination as fundamentally linked to exchange (Alderson, 1954; Duddy & Revzan, 1947). Although institutional thought of marketing was later modified by the organizational dynamics viewpoint and marketing thinking was influenced by other social sciences, exchange remained the central tenet of marketing (Alderson, 1965; Bagozzi, 1974, 1978, 1979; Kotler, 1972).

SHIFT FROM DISTRIBUTION FUNCTIONS
TO UNDERSTANDING CONSUMER BEHAVIOR

The demise of the distributive theory of marketing began after World War II, as the focus began to shift from distributive functions to other aspects of marketing. With the advent of market research, producers, in an attempt to influence end consumers, began to direct and control the distributors regarding product merchandising, sales promotion, pricing, and so on. Thus repeat purchase and brand loyalty gained prominence in the marketing literature (Barton, 1946; Churchill, 1942; Howard & Sheth, 1969; Sheth, 1973; Womer, 1944). Also, market segmentation and targeting were developed as tools for marketing planning. Thus the marketing concept evolved and the consumer, not the distributor, became the focus of marketing attention (Kotler, 1972). And producers, in order to gain control over the channels of distribution, adopted administered vertical marketing systems (McCammon, 1965). These vertical marketing systems, such as franchising and exclusive distribution rights, permitted marketers to extend their representation beyond their own corporate limits (Little, 1970). However, marketing orientation was still transactional, as its success was measured in such transactional terms as sales volume and market share. Only in the 1980s did marketers begin to emphasize customer satisfaction measures to ensure that they were not evaluated purely on the basis of transactional aspects of marketing and that sales were not considered to be the culmination of all marketing efforts.

EARLY RELATIONSHIP MARKETING IDEAS

Although Berry formally introduced the term *relationship marketing* into the literature in 1983, several ideas of relationship marketing emerged much before then. For example, McGarry (1950, 1951, 1953, 1958) included six activities in his formal list of marketing functions: contactual function, propaganda function, merchandising function, physical distribution function, pricing function, and termination function. Of these, the contactual function falling within the main task of marketing reflected McGarry's relational orientation and his emphasis on developing cooperation and mutual interdependence among marketing actors. For example, he suggested the following (as cited in Schwartz, 1963):

1. Contactual function is the building of a structure for cooperative action.
2. Focus on the long-run welfare of business and continuous business relationship.
3. Develop an attitude of mutual interdependence.
4. Provide a two-way line of communication and a linkage of their interests.
5. Cost of dealing with continuous contact is much less than the cost of casual contacts; by selling only to regular and consistent customers, one can reduce costs by 10-20%.

McGarry's work has not been widely publicized, and his relational ideas did not lead to the same flurry of interest caused by Wroe Alderson's (1965) focus on inter- and intrachannel cooperation. Although the distributive theory of marketing no longer enjoys the central position in marketing, interest in channel cooperation has been sustained for the past three decades, and many relationship marketing scholars have emerged from the tradition of channel cooperation research (Anderson & Narus, 1990; Stern & El-Ansary, 1992; Weitz & Jap, 1995). They have contributed significantly to the development of relationship marketing knowledge and have been most forthcoming in applying various theoretical ideas from other disciplines, such as economics, law, political science, and sociology. We discuss these in more detail in other sections of this chapter.

Two influential writings in the 1960s and 1970s provided impetus to relationship marketing thinking, particularly in the business-to-business context. First, Adler (1966) observed the symbiotic relationships between firms that were not linked by the traditional marketer-intermediary relationship. Later, Varadarajan (1986) and Varadarajan and Rajaratnam (1986) examined other manifestations of symbiotic relationships in marketing. The second impetus was provided by Johan Arndt (1979), who noted the tendency of firms engaged in business-to-business marketing to develop long-lasting relationships with their key customers and their key suppliers rather than focusing on discrete exchanges and termed this phenomenon "domesticated markets." The impacts of these works spread across two continents. In the United States, several scholars began examining long-term interorganizational relationships in business-to-business markets, and in Europe, the Industrial Marketing and Purchasing (IMP)

Group laid emphasis on business relationships and networks (e.g., Anderson, Håkansson, & Johanson, 1994; Dwyer et al., 1987; Håkansson, 1982; Hallén, Johanson, & Seyed-Mohamed, 1991; Jackson, 1985). The Nordic school approach to services marketing has also been relationship oriented from its birth in the 1970s (Grönroos & Gummesson, 1985). Adherents of this school believe that for a company to achieve effective marketing and delivery of services, it needs to practice "internal marketing" and involve the entire organization in developing relationships with customers (Grönroos, 1981). Except for the greater emphasis placed on achieving marketing paradigm shift by the Nordic school, its approach is similar to relationship marketing ideas put forth by services marketing scholars in the United States (Berry, 1983, 1995; Berry & Parasuraman, 1991; Bitner, 1995; Czepiel, 1990). To a certain degree, recent scholars from the Nordic school have tried to integrate the network approach popular among Scandinavian and European schools with service relationship issues (Holmlund, 1996).

As relationship marketing grew in the 1980s and 1990s, several perspectives emerged. One approach that integrates quality, logistics, customer services, and marketing is found in the works of Christopher, Payne, and Ballantyne (1991) and Crosby, Evans, and Cowles (1990). Another approach that involves studying partnering relationships and alliances as forms of relationship marketing is observed in the works of Morgan and Hunt (1994), Heide (1994), and Varadarajan and Cunningham (1995). Similarly, conceptual and empirical papers have appeared on relationship-oriented communication strategies (Mohr & Nevin, 1990; Owen, 1984; Schultz, Tannenbaum, & Lauterborn, 1992), supply-chain integration (Christopher, 1994; Payne, Christopher, Clark, & Peck, 1994), legal aspects of relationship marketing (Gundlach & Murphy, 1993), and consumer motivations for engaging in relationship marketing (Sheth & Parvatiyar, 1995b).

The Emergence of Relationship Marketing Practice

As we have observed in previous work, relationship marketing has historical antecedents going back to the preindustrial era (Sheth & Parvatiyar, 1995a). Much of it was due to direct interaction between producers of agricultural products and their consumers. Similarly, artisans often developed customized products for each customer. This direct interaction led to relational bonding between the producer and the consumer. It was only after the industrial era's mass-production society created a need for middlemen that there were less frequent interactions between producers and consumers, and this led to transaction-oriented marketing. The production and consumption functions became separated, and this led to marketing functions being performed by the middlemen. And middlemen are in general oriented toward the economic aspects of buying, given that the largest cost is often the cost of goods sold.

In recent years, however, several factors have contributed to the rapid development and evolution of relationship marketing. These include the growing de-intermediation process taking place in many industries due to the advent of sophisticated computer and telecommunication technologies that allow producers to interact directly with end customers. For example, in many industries—such as air travel, banking, insurance, computer software, household appliance manufacture, and even consumables—the de-intermediation process is fast changing the nature of marketing and consequently making relationship marketing more popular. Databases and direct-marketing tools give these industries the means to individualize their marketing efforts. As a result, producers do not need those functions formerly performed by middlemen. Even consumers are willing to undertake some of the responsibilities of direct ordering, personal merchandising, and product-use-related services with little help from producers. The recent successes of on-line banking, Charles Schwab and Merrill Lynch's on-line investment programs, and direct sales of books, automobiles, insurance, and more on the Internet all attest to growing consumer interest in maintaining direct relationships with marketers.

The de-intermediation process and consequent prevalence of relationship marketing have also been influenced by the growth of the service economy. Because services are typically produced and delivered at the same institution, this minimizes the role of the middleman. A greater emotional bond between the service provider and the service user also develops the need to maintain and enhance that relationship. It is therefore not difficult to see that relationship marketing is important for scholars and practitioners of services marketing (Berry & Parasuraman, 1991; Bitner, 1995; Crosby et al., 1990; Crosby & Stephens, 1987; Grönroos, 1995).

Another force driving the adoption of relationship marketing has been the total quality movement. When companies embraced the total quality management (TQM) philosophy to improve quality and reduce costs, it became necessary for them to involve their suppliers and customers in implementing the program at all levels of the value chain. This required them to have close working relationships with customers, suppliers, and other members of the marketing infrastructure. Thus several companies, such as Motorola, IBM, General Motors, Xerox, Ford, and Toyota, formed partnering relationships with suppliers and customers to practice TQM. Other programs, such as just-in-time (JIT) supply and material requirements planning (MRP), have also made use of interdependent relationships between suppliers and customers (Frazier, Spekman, & O'Neal, 1988).

With the advent of digital technology and complex products, a systems selling approach became common. This approach emphasizes the integration of parts, supplies, and the sale of services along with the individual capital equipment. Customers liked the idea of systems integration, and sellers were able to sell augmented products and services to customers. The popularity of systems integration began to extend to consumer packaged goods as well as to services (Shapiro & Posner, 1979). At the same time, some companies started to insist upon new purchasing approaches, such as national contracts and master purchasing agreements, forcing major vendors to develop key account management programs (Shapiro & Moriarty, 1980). These measures created intimacy and cooperation in buyer-seller relationships. Instead of purchasing products or services, customers were more interested in buying a relationship with vendors. A key (or national) account management program designates account managers and account teams to assess the customer's needs and then husband the selling company's resources for the customer's benefit. Such programs have led to the establishment of strategic partnering relationship programs within the domain of relationship marketing (Anderson & Narus, 1991; Shapiro, 1988).

Similarly, in the current era of hypercompetition, marketers are forced to be concerned with customer retention and loyalty (Dick & Basu, 1994; Reichheld, 1996). As several studies have indicated, retaining customers is less expensive and perhaps a more sustainable competitive advantage than acquiring new ones. Marketers are realizing that it costs less to retain customers than to compete for new ones (Rosenberg & Czepiel, 1984). On the supply side, it pays more to develop closer relationships with a few suppliers than to develop more vendors (Hayes, Wheelwright, & Clark, 1988; Spekman, 1988). In addition, some marketers are concerned with keeping customers for life, rather than making one-time sales (Cannie & Caplin, 1991). In a recent study, Naidu, Parvatiyar, Sheth, and Westgate (in press) found that relationship marketing intensity increased in hospitals facing a higher degree of competition.

Also, customer expectations have changed rapidly over the past two decades. Fueled by new technology and the growing availability of advanced product features and services, customers' expectations are changing almost on a daily basis. Consumers are less willing to make compromises or trade-offs when it comes to product and service quality. In the world of ever-rising customer expectations, cooperative and collaborative relationships with customers seem to be the most prudent way to keep track of and appropriately influence those expectations (Sheth & Sisodia, 1995).

Today, many large internationally oriented companies are trying to become global by integrating their worldwide operations. To achieve this, they are seeking cooperative and collaborative solutions for global operations from their vendors instead of merely engaging in transactional activities with them. Such customers' needs make it imperative for marketers interested in the business of global companies to adopt relationship marketing programs, particularly global account management programs (Yip & Madsen, 1996). Global account management is conceptually similar to national account management, except that it is global in scope and thus more complex. Managing customer relationships around the world calls for external and internal partnering activities, including partnering across a firm's worldwide organization.

A Process Model of Relationship Marketing

Several scholars who have examined buyer-seller relationships have proposed relationship development process models (Borys & Jemison, 1989; Dwyer et al., 1987; Evans & Laskin, 1994; Wilson, 1995). Building on that work and anchored to our definition of relationship marketing as a *process* of engaging in cooperative and collaborative relationships with customers, we have developed a four-stage relationship marketing process model. The broad model suggests that the relationship marketing process comprises four subprocesses: formation process, management and governance process, performance evaluation process, and relationship evolution or enhancement process. The generic model is shown in Figure 1.1;

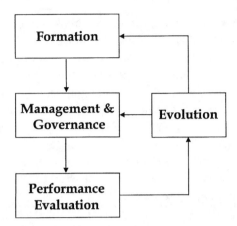

Figure 1.1. Relationship Marketing Process Framework

Figure 1.2 presents a more detailed illustration of the important components of the process model.

THE FORMATION PROCESS
OF RELATIONSHIP MARKETING

The formation process of relationship marketing involves the decisions that must be made regarding initiation of relationship marketing activities for a firm with respect to a specific group of customers or an individual customer with whom the company wishes to engage in a cooperative and collaborative relationship. In the formation process, three important decision areas relate to defining the *purpose* (or objectives) of engaging in relationship marketing, selecting parties (or customer partners) for relationship marketing, and developing programs (or relational activity schemes) for relationship marketing engagement.

Relationship Marketing Purpose

The overall purpose of relationship marketing is to improve marketing productivity and enhance mutual value for the parties involved in the

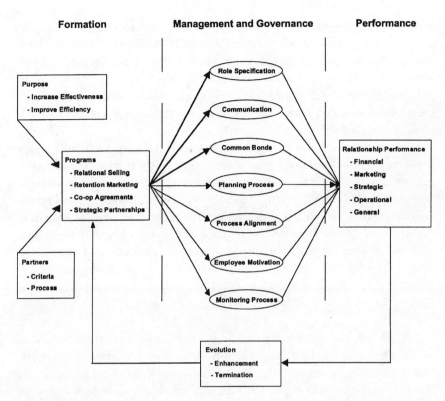

Figure 1.2. Formation Governance and Evaluation Model of Relationship Marketing

relationship. Relationship marketing has the potential to improve marketing productivity and to create mutual values by increasing marketing effectiveness and/or improving marketing efficiencies (Sheth & Parvatiyar, 1995b; Sheth & Sisodia, 1995). By seeking and achieving strategic marketing goals—such as entering new markets, developing new products or technologies, serving new or expanded needs of customers, and redefining the competitive playing field—firms can enhance their marketing effectiveness. Similarly, by seeking and achieving operational goals—such as the reduction of distribution costs, streamlining of order processing and inventory management, and reduction of the burden of excessive customer acquisition costs—firms can achieve greater marketing efficiencies. Thus stating objectives and defining the purpose of relationship marketing can help firms to clarify the nature of relationship marketing programs and activities that ought to be performed by the partners. Defining the purpose also helps firms to identify suitable relationship partners who have the necessary expectations and capabilities to fulfill mutual goals. It can further help firms to evaluate relationship marketing performance by comparing results achieved against objectives. These objectives could be specified as financial goals, marketing goals, strategic goals, operational goals, and general goals.

Similarly, in the mass-market context, consumers expect to fulfill their goals related to efficiencies and effectiveness in their purchase and consumption behavior. As we have noted previously, consumers are motivated to engage in relational behavior because of the psychological and sociological benefits associated with a reduction in choice decisions (Sheth & Parvatiyar, 1995b). In addition to their natural inclination to reduce choices, consumers are motivated to seek the rewards and associated benefits offered by companies' relationship marketing programs.

Relational Parties

The selection of customer partners (or parties with whom to engage in cooperative and collaborative relationships) represents another important decision to be made in the formation stage. Even though a company may serve all customer types, few have the necessary resources and commitment to establish relationship marketing programs for all. Therefore, in the initial phase, a company has to decide which customer types and specific customers or customer groups will be the focus of its relationship marketing efforts. Subsequently, when the company has gained experience and achieved successful results, it can expand the scope of relationship marketing activities to include other customers in the program, or it can engage in additional programs (Shah, 1997).

Although the selection of partners is an important decision for firms to make in achieving their relationship marketing goals, not all companies have formalized processes of selecting customers. Some follow the intuitive judgmental approach of senior managers in selecting customer partners; others partner with those customers who demand so. Yet other companies have formalized processes for selecting relational partners that involve extensive research and evaluation against particular criteria. The criteria for partner selection vary according to different companies' goals and policies. These range from a single criterion, such as revenue potential of the customer, to multiple criteria that may include several

TABLE 1.1 Types of Relationship Marketing Programs

	Customer Type		
Program Type	*Individual Consumers*	*Distributors/ Resellers*	*Institutional Buyers (Business to Business)*
Continuity marketing	loyalty programs	continuous replenishment and ECR programs	special supply arrangements (e.g., JIT, MRP)
Individual marketing	data warehousing and data mining	customer business development	key account management
Comarketing/partnering	cobranding	cooperative marketing	joint marketing and codevelopment

variables, such as customer commitment, resourcefulness, and management values.

Relationship Marketing Programs

A careful review of the literature and observation of corporate practices suggest that there are three types of relationship marketing programs: continuity marketing, one-to-one marketing, and partnering programs. These take different forms depending on whether they are meant for end consumers, distributor customers, or business-to-business customers. Table 1.1 displays the various types of relationship marketing programs that are prevalent among different types of customers. Obviously, marketing practitioners in search of new creative ideas develop many variations and combinations of these programs to build closer and mutually beneficial relationships with their customers.

Continuity marketing programs. Given the growing concern for retaining customers as well as the emerging knowledge about customer retention economics, many companies have developed continuity marketing programs that are aimed at both retaining customers and increasing their loyalty (Bhattacharya, 1998; Payne, 1995). For consumers in mass markets, these programs usually take the shape of membership and loyalty card programs in which consumers are often rewarded for their member and loyalty relationships with the marketers (Raphel, 1995; Richards, 1995). These rewards may range from privileged services to points for up-grades, discounts, and cross-purchased items. For distributor customers, continuity marketing programs take the form of continuous replenish-ment programs ranging from JIT inventory management programs to effi-cient consumer response initiatives that include electronic order process-ing and MRP (Law & Ooten, 1993; Persutti, 1992). In business-to-business markets, these may be in the form of preferred customer programs or spe-cial sourcing arrangements, including single sourcing, dual sourcing, net-work sourcing, and JIT sourcing arrangements (Hines, 1995; Postula & Little, 1992). The basic aim of continuity marketing programs is to retain customers and increase loyalty through long-term special services that have the potential to increase mutual value as the partners learn about each other (Shultz, 1995).

One-to-one marketing. The one-to-one or individual marketing approach is grounded in account-based marketing. Such programs are aimed at meeting and satisfying each customer's needs uniquely and individually (Peppers & Rogers, 1995). What was once a concept prevalent only in business-to-business marketing is now implemented in mass-market and distributor-customer contexts. In the mass market, the dissemination of individualized information on customers is now possible at low cost due to the rapid development in information technology and the availability of scalable data warehouses and data-mining products. By using on-line in-formation and databases on individual customer interactions, marketers aim to fulfill the unique needs of each mass-market customer. Informa-tion on individual customers is utilized to develop frequency marketing, interactive marketing, and aftermarketing programs in order to develop relationships with high-yielding customers (File, Mack, & Prince, 1995; Pruden, 1995). For distributor customers, these individual marketing pro-grams take the form of customer business development. For example, Procter & Gamble has established a customer team to analyze and pro-pose ways in which Wal-Mart's business could be developed. Thus, by bring-ing to bear its domain-specific knowledge from across many markets, Procter & Gamble is able to offer expert advice and resources to help build the business of its distributor customer. Such a relationship requires co-operative action and an interest in mutual value creation. In the context of business-to-business markets, individual marketing has been in place for

quite some time. In what are known as key account management programs, marketers appoint customer teams to husband company resources
according to individual customer needs. Often such programs require extensive resource allocation and joint planning with customers. Key
account programs implemented for multilocation domestic customers
usually take the form of national account management programs; for customers with global operations, these programs become global account
management programs.

Partnering programs. The third type of relationship marketing programs involves partnering relationships between customers and marketers to serve end-user needs. In the mass markets, two types of partnering
programs are most common: cobranding and affinity partnering (Teagno,
1995). In cobranding, two marketers combine their resources and skills
to offer advanced products and services to mass-market customers (Marx,
1994). For example, Delta Airlines and American Express have cobranded
the Sky Miles credit card for gains to consumers as well as to the partnering organizations. Affinity partnering programs are similar to cobranding
except that the marketers do not create new brands; rather, they use endorsement strategies. Usually, affinity partnering programs try to take advantage of customer memberships in one group to cross-sell other products
and services. In the case of distributor customers, partnering programs are
implemented through logistics partnering and cooperative marketing efforts. In such partnerships, the marketer and the distributor customers
cooperate and collaborate to manage inventory and supply logistics and
sometimes to engage in joint marketing efforts. For business-to-business
customers, partnering programs involving codesign, codevelopment, and
comarketing activities are not uncommon today (Mitchell & Singh, 1996;
Young, Gilbert, & McIntyre, 1996).

MANAGEMENT AND GOVERNANCE PROCESS

Once a relationship marketing program is developed and rolled out, the
program as well as the individual relationships within it must be managed
and governed. For mass-market customers, the degree to which there is
symmetry or asymmetry in the primary responsibility of whether the customer or the program sponsoring company will be managing the relationship varies with the size of the market. However, for programs directed at

distributors and business customers, the management of the relationship requires the involvement of both parties. The degree to which these governance responsibilities are shared or managed independently depends on the perception of norms of governance processes among relational partners given the nature of their relationship marketing program and the purpose of engaging in the relationship. Not all relationships are or should be managed alike; however, several researchers have suggested appropriate governance norms for different hybrid relationships (Borys & Jemison, 1989; Heide, 1994; Sheth & Parvatiyar, 1992).

Whether relational partners undertake management and governance responsibilities independently or jointly, they must address several issues. These include decisions regarding role specification, communication, common bonds, planning process, process alignment, employee motivation, and monitoring procedures. Role specification relates to the determination of the roles of partners in fulfilling the relationship marketing tasks as well as the roles of specific individuals or teams in managing the relationships and related activities (Heide, 1994). The greater the scope of the relationship marketing program and associated tasks, and the more complex the composition of the relationship management team, the more critical are role specification decisions for the partnering firms. Role specification also helps to clarify the nature of resources and empowerment needed by individuals or teams charged with the responsibility of managing relationships with customers.

Communication with customer partners is another necessary process of relationship marketing. It helps in relationship development, fosters trust, and provides the information and knowledge partners need to undertake the cooperative and collaborative activities of relationship marketing. In many ways, communication is the lifeblood of relationship marketing. By establishing proper communication channels for sharing information with customers, a company can enhance its relationships with those customers. In addition to communicating with customers, it is essential that a company establish intrafirm communication, particularly among all individuals and corporate functions that play direct roles in managing relationships with specific customers or customer groups.

Although communication between the firm and customer partners helps to foster relationship bonds, conscious efforts to create common bonds will have a more sustaining impact on relationships. In business-to-business relationships, social bonds are created through interactions; however, with mass-market customers, frequent face-to-face interactions between partners will be uneconomical. Thus marketers should create common bonds through symbolic relationships, endorsements, affinity groups, membership benefits, and the establishment of on-line communities. Whatever the chosen mode, the creation of value bonding, reputation bonding, and structural bonding is a useful way to institutionalize relationships with customers (Sheth, 1994).

Another important aspect of relationship governance is the process of planning, which includes decisions about the degree to which customers need to be involved in the planning process. Involving customers in the planning process can ensure their support in plan implementation and achievement of planned goals. All customers are not willing to participate in the planning process, however, nor is it possible to involve all customers in relationship marketing programs for the mass market. However, for firms to manage cooperative and collaborative relationships with large customers, the involvement of those customers in the planning process is desirable and sometimes necessary.

Executives are sometimes unaware, or they choose to ignore, at least initially, the nature of misalignment in operating processes between their company and customer partners, leading to problems in relationship marketing implementation. Several aspects of the operating processes need to be aligned, depending on the nature and scope of the relationship. For example, operating alignment is needed in order processing, accounting and budgeting processes, information systems, merchandising processes, and the like.

Several human resource decisions are also important in creating the right organization and climate for managing relationship marketing. It is important that firms train employees to interact with customers, to work in teams, and to manage relationship expectations. The creation of the right employee motivations through incentives, rewards, and compensation systems is also important for building stronger relationship bonds and customer commitment. Although institutionalizing the relationship is desirable for the long-term benefit of the company, personal relationships are nevertheless formed and have impacts on the institutional relationship. Thus firms need to train and motivate employees properly so that they can handle customer relationships professionally.

Finally, proper monitoring processes need to be in place to safeguard against failure and to manage conflicts in relationships. Such processes include periodic evaluations of goals and results; the initiation of changes in relationship structure, design, or governance process if needed; and the creation of a system for discussing problems and resolving conflicts. Good monitoring procedures help avoid relationship destabilization and the creation of power asymmetries. They also help to keep the relationship marketing program on track by making possible the evaluation of the proper alignment of goals, results, and resources.

Overall, the governance process helps in the maintenance, development, and execution aspects of relationship marketing. It also helps to strengthen relationships among relational partners, and if the process is satisfactorily implemented, it ensures the continuation and enhancement of relationships with customers. Relationship satisfaction for involved parties includes satisfaction with the governance process in addition to satisfaction with the results achieved in the relationship (Parvatiyar, Biong, & Wathne, 1998).

PERFORMANCE EVALUATION PROCESS

Companies need to undertake periodic assessment of the results of relationship marketing in order to evaluate whether or not programs are meeting expectations and whether or not they are sustainable in the long run. Performance evaluation is also useful because it allows firms to take corrective action in areas of relationship governance or to modify relationship marketing objectives and program features as needed. Without a proper performance metric against which to evaluate relationship marketing efforts, it is hard to make objective decisions regarding continuation, modification, or termination of relationship marketing programs. Developing a performance measure is always a challenging activity, as most firms are inclined to use existing marketing measures to evaluate relationship marketing. However, many existing marketing measures, such as market share and total volume of sales, may not be appropriate in the context of relationship marketing. Even when more relationship marketing-oriented measures are selected, these cannot be applied uniformly across all relationship marketing programs, particularly when the purposes of the programs are different. For example, if the purpose of a particular relationship marketing effort is to enhance distribution efficiencies by reducing overall distribution cost, measuring the program's impact on revenue growth and share of customer's business may not be appropriate. In this case, the program must be evaluated based on its impact on reducing distribution costs and other metrics that are aligned with that objective. When the objectives and performance measures are in harmony, one can expect to see more goal-directed managerial action taken by those involved in managing the relationship.

For the measurement of relationship marketing performance, a *balanced scorecard* that combines a variety of measures based on the defined purpose of each relationship marketing program (or each cooperative/collaborative relationship) is recommended (Kaplan & Norton, 1992). In other words, the performance evaluation measure for each relationship or relationship marketing program should mirror the set of defined objectives for the program. However, some global measures of the impacts of relationship marketing efforts of the company are also possible. Srivastava, Shervani, and Fahey (1998) recently developed a model to suggest the asset value of cooperative relationships of the firm. If the existence of cooperative and collaborative relationships with customers is treated as an intangible asset of the firm, one can assess that asset's economic value added using discounted future cash-flow estimates. In some ways, the value of relationships is similar to the concept of brand equity of the firm—hence many scholars have alluded to the term *relationship equity* (Bharadwaj, 1994; Peterson, 1995). Although a well-accepted model for measuring relationship equity is not available in the literature as yet, companies are trying to estimate the value of such equity, particularly for measuring the intangible assets of the firm.

Another global measure used by firms to monitor relationship marketing performance is relationship satisfaction. Similar to the measurement of customer satisfaction, which is now widely applied in many companies, the measurement of relationship satisfaction would help firms to determine to what extent relational partners are satisfied with their current cooperative and collaborative relationships. Unlike customer satisfaction measures that evaluate satisfaction on one side of the dyad, relationship satisfaction measures could be applied on both sides of the dyad. Both the customer and the marketing firm have to perform in order to produce results in a cooperative relationship, hence each party's relationship satisfaction could be measured (Biong, Parvatiyar, & Wathne, 1996). By measuring relationship satisfaction, one could estimate the propensity of either party's inclination to continue or terminate the relationship. Such propensity could also be evaluated indirectly through the measurement of customer loyalty (Reichheld & Sasser, 1990). Relationship satisfaction or loyalty measurement scales that are designed based on these antecedents could provide rich information on their determinants and thereby help companies identify those managerial actions that are likely to improve relationship satisfaction and/or loyalty.

EVOLUTION PROCESS OF
RELATIONSHIP MARKETING

Individual relationships and relationship marketing programs are likely to undergo evolution as they mature. Some evolution paths may be planned, whereas others will evolve naturally. In any case, the partners involved have to make several decisions about the evolution of their relationship marketing programs. These include decisions regarding the continuation, termination, enhancement, and modifications of the relationship engagement. Several factors could cause the precipitation of any of these decisions. Among these factors, relationship performance and relationship satisfaction (including relationship process satisfaction) are likely to have the greatest impact on the evolution of relationship marketing programs. When performance is satisfactory, partners would be motivated to continue or enhance their relationship marketing program (Shah, 1997; Shamdasani & Sheth, 1995). When performance does not meet expectations, partners may consider terminating or modifying their relationship. However, extraneous factors could also affect these decisions. For example, when companies are acquired, merged, or divested, many relationships and relationship marketing programs undergo changes. Also, when senior corporate executives and senior leaders in a company leave or change positions, relationship marketing programs undergo changes. Yet many collaborative relationships are terminated because they had planned endings. When companies can chart out their relationship evolution cycles and state the contingencies for making evolutionary decisions, they can engage in relatively systematic relationship marketing programs.

Relationship Marketing Research Directions

Wilson (1995) has classified the research directions taken in the area of relationship marketing into three levels: concept, model, and process research. At the concept level, he indicates the need to improve concept definitions and their operationalization. Concept-level research relates to identifying, defining, and measuring constructs that are either successful predictors or useful measures of relationship performance. Several scholars and researchers have recently enriched our literature with relevant relationship marketing concepts and constructs. These include such constructs as trust, commitment, interdependence, interactions, shared values, power imbalance, adaptation, and mutual satisfaction (Doney & Cannon, 1997; Gundlach & Cadotte, 1994; Kumar, Scheer, & Steenkamp, 1995; Lusch & Brown, 1996; Morgan & Hunt, 1994; Smith & Barclay, 1997).

At the model level, scholars are interested in presenting integrative ideas to explain how relationships are developed. Several integrative models have recently begun to emerge, providing us with richer insight into how relationships work and what affects relationship marketing decisions. The IMP interaction model is based upon insights developed through the study of more than 300 industrial marketing relationships (Håkansson, 1982). By identifying the interactions among actors, the IMP model traces the nature and sources of relationship development. The IMP model and its research approach have become a tradition for many scholarly research endeavors in Europe over the past 15 years or more. The network model of relationships uses social network theory to trace how relationships are developed among multiple actors and how relationship ties are strengthened through networks (Anderson et al., 1994; Iacobucci & Hopkins, 1992). Bagozzi (1995) makes a case for the need for more conceptual models to help us understand the nature of group influence on relationship marketing.

Integrative models that take a more evolutionary approach look at the process flow of relationship formation and development. Anderson and Narus (1991) and Dwyer et al. (1987), along with numerous other scholars, have contributed toward our understanding of the relationship process model. By looking at the stages of the relationship development process, one can identify which constructs will actively affect the outcome considerations at that stage and which will have latent influences (Wilson, 1995). The process model of relationship formation, relationship governance, relationship performance, and relationship evolution described in the previous section is an attempt to add to this stream of knowledge development on relationship marketing.

For practitioners, process-level research could provide useful guidelines for developing and managing successful relationship marketing programs and activities. Some research has now started to appear in the marketing literature on relationship marketing partner selection (Schijns &

Schroder, 1996; Stump & Heide, 1996). Mahajan and Srivastava (1992) recommend the use of conjoint analysis techniques for partner selection decisions in alliance-type relationships. Dorsch, Swanson, and Kelley (1998) propose a framework of partner selection based on the evaluation of customers' perceptions of the quality of their relationships with their vendors. At the program level, key account management programs and strategic partnering have been examined in several research studies (Aulakh, Kotabe, & Sahay, 1996; Nason, Melnyk, Wolter, & Olsen, 1997; Wong, 1998). Similarly, within the context of channel relationships and buyer-seller relationships, several studies have been conducted on relationship governance process (Biong & Selnes, 1995; Heide, 1994; Lusch & Brown, 1996). Also, research on relationship performance is beginning to appear in the literature. Kalwani and Narayandas (1995) examined the impact of long-term relationships among small firms on those firms' financial performance. Similarly, Naidu et al. (in press) examined the impact of relationship marketing programs on the performance of hospitals. Srivastava et al. (1998) studied the economic value of relationship marketing assets. However, not much research has been reported on relationship enhancement processes and relationship evolution. Although studies relating to the development of relationship marketing objectives are still lacking, the conceptual model on customer expectations presented by Sheth and Mittal (1996) could provide the foundation for research in this area. Overall, we expect future research efforts to be directed toward the process aspects of relationship marketing.

The Domain of Relationship Marketing Research

Several areas and subdisciplines of marketing have been the focus of relationship marketing research in recent years. These include issues related to channel relationships (El-Ansary, 1997; Robicheaux & Coleman, 1994; Weitz & Jap, 1995), business-to-business marketing (Dwyer et al., 1987; Hallén et al., 1991; Keep, Hollander, & Dickinson, 1998; Wilson, 1995), sales management (Boorom, Goolsby, & Ramsey, 1998; Smith & Barclay, 1997), services marketing (Berry, 1983, 1995; Crosby et al., 1990; Crosby & Stephens, 1987; Grönroos, 1995; Gwinner, Gremler, & Bitner, 1998), and consumer marketing (Gruen, 1995; Kahn, 1998; Sheth & Parvatiyar, 1995b; Simonin & Ruth, 1998). Marketing scholars interested in strategic marketing have studied the alliance and strategic partnering aspects

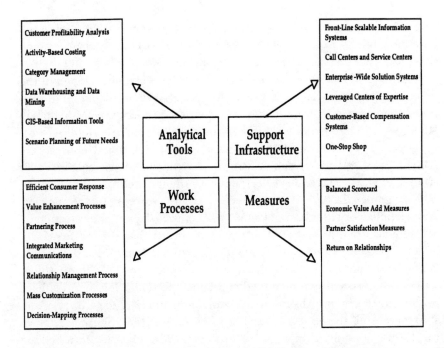

Figure 1.3. Tools and Work Processes Applied in Relationship Marketing

of relationship marketing (Bucklin & Sengupta, 1993; Sheth & Parvatiyar, 1992; Varadarajan & Cunningham, 1995). Gundlach and Murphy (1993) have provided a framework on public policy implications of relationship marketing. In the context of international marketing, relationship marketing concepts and models are used in the study of global account management programs (Yip & Madsen, 1996), export channel cooperation (Bello & Gilliland, 1997), and international alliances (Yigang & Tse, 1996).

Relationship marketing has also been converging with some other paradigms in marketing, including database marketing (Schijns & Schroder, 1996; Shani & Chalasani, 1992), integrated marketing communications (Duncan & Moriarty, 1998; Schultz et al., 1992; Zinkhan, Madden, Watson, & Stewart, 1996), logistics, and supply-chain integration (Christopher, 1994; Fawcett, Calantone, & Smith, 1997). Some of these are applied as tools and work processes in relationship marketing practice. Figure 1.3 illustrates the tools and work processes applied in relationship marketing. As more and more companies use these processes and other practical aspects such as TQM, process reengineering, mass customization, electronic data interchange, value enhancement, activity-based costing, and cross-functional teams, we are likely to see more and more convergence between these and related paradigms and relationship marketing.

A number of theoretical perspectives that have been developed in the fields of economics, law, and social psychology have been applied in relationship marketing. These include transaction cost analysis (Mudambi & Mudambi, 1995; Noordewier, John, & Nevin, 1990; Stump & Heide, 1996), agency theory (Mishra, Heide, & Cort, 1998), relational contracting (Dwyer et al., 1987; Lusch & Brown, 1996), social exchange theory (Hallén et al., 1991; Heide, 1994), network theory (Achrol, 1997; Walker, 1997), game theory (Rao & Reddy, 1995), interorganizational exchange behavior (Rinehart & Page, 1992), power dependency (Gundlach & Cadotte, 1994; Kumar et al., 1995), and interpersonal relations (Iacobucci & Ostrom, 1996). More recently, resource allocation and resource dependence perspectives (Lohtia, 1997; Varadarajan & Cunningham, 1995) and classical psychological and consumer behavior theories have been used to explain why companies and consumers engage in relationship marketing (Iacobucci & Zerillo, 1997; Kahn, 1998; Sheth & Parvatiyar, 1995b; Simonin & Ruth, 1998). Each of these studies has enriched the field of relationship marketing. As research moves forward, we expect to see more integrative approaches to the study of relationship marketing, as well as a greater degree of involvement of scholars from almost all subdisciplines of marketing. The appeal of relationship marketing is global—marketing scholars from around the world are interested in the study of this phenomenon, particularly in Europe, Australia, and Asia, in addition to North America.

Conclusion

The domain of relationship marketing extends into many areas of marketing and strategic decision making. Its recent prominence has been facilitated by the convergence of several other paradigms of marketing and by corporate initiatives that have been developed around the theme of cooperation and collaboration of organizational units and company stakeholders, including customers. The term *relationship marketing* refers to a conceptually narrow phenomenon of marketing; however, if the phenomenon of cooperation and collaboration with customers becomes the dominant paradigm of marketing practice and research, relationship marketing has the potential to emerge as the predominant perspective in marketing.

References

Achrol, R. S. (1997). Changes in the theory of interorganizational relations in marketing: Toward a network paradigm. *Journal of the Academy of Marketing Science, 25,* 56-71.

Adler, L. (1966). Symbiotic marketing. *Harvard Business Review, 45*(2), 59-71.

Alderson, W. (1954). Factors governing the development of marketing channels. In R. Clewett (Ed.), *Marketing channels for manufactured products* (pp. 5-34). Homewood, IL: Richard D. Irwin.

Alderson, W. (1965). *Dynamic marketing behavior: A functionalist theory of marketing.* Homewood, IL: Richard D. Irwin.

Anderson, J. C., Håkansson, H., & Johanson, J. (1994). Dyadic business relationships within a business network context. *Journal of Marketing, 58*(4), 1-15.

Anderson, J. C., & Narus, J. A. (1990). A model of distributor firm and manufacturer firm working partnerships. *Journal of Marketing, 54*(1), 42-58.

Anderson, J. C., & Narus, J. A. (1991). Partnering as a focused market strategy. *California Management Review, 33*(3), 95-113.

Arndt, J. (1979). Toward a concept of domesticated markets. *Journal of Marketing, 43*(4), 69-75.

Aulakh, P. S., Kotabe, M., & Sahay, A. (1996). Trust and performance in cross-border marketing partnerships: A behavioral approach. *Journal of International Business Studies, 27,* 1005-1032.

Bagozzi, R. P. (1974). Marketing as an organized behavioral system of exchange. *Journal of Marketing, 38*(4), 77-81.

Bagozzi, R. P. (1978). Marketing as exchange: A theory of transactions in the marketplace. *American Behavioral Scientist, 21,* 535-536.

Bagozzi, R. P. (1979). Toward a formal theory of marketing exchanges. In O. C. Ferrell, S. W. Brown, & C. W. Lamb, Jr. (Eds.), *Conceptual and theoretical developments in marketing* (pp. 431-447). Chicago: American Marketing Association.

Bagozzi, R. P. (1995). Reflections on relationship marketing in consumer markets. *Journal of the Academy of Marketing Science, 23,* 272-277.

Bartels, R. (1976). *The history of marketing thought* (2nd ed.). Columbus, OH: Grid.

Barton, S. G. (1946). The movement of branded goods to the consumer. In A. D. Blankenship (Ed.), *How to conduct consumer and opinion research* (pp. 58-70). New York: Harper & Bros.

Bello, D. C., & Gilliland, D. L. (1997). The effects of output controls, process controls and flexibility on export channel performance. *Journal of Marketing, 61*(1), 22-38.

Berry, L. L. (1983). Relationship marketing. In L. L. Berry, G. L. Shostack, & G. D. Upah (Eds.), *Emerging perspectives on service marketing* (pp. 25-38). Chicago: American Marketing Association.

Berry, L. L. (1995). Relationship marketing of services—growing interest, emerging perspectives. *Journal of the Academy of Marketing Science, 23,* 236-245.

Berry, L. L., & Parasuraman, A. (1991). *Marketing services: Competing through quality.* New York: Free Press.

Bharadwaj, S. G. (1994). The value of intangible firm assets: An empirical examination. In J. N. Sheth & A. Parvatiyar (Eds.), *Relationship marketing: Theory, methods and applications*. Atlanta, GA: Emory University, Center for Relationship Marketing.

Bhattacharya, C. B. (1998). When customers are members: Customer retention in paid membership contexts. *Journal of the Academy of Marketing Science, 26,* 31-44.

Bickert, J. (1992, May). The database revolution. *Target Marketing, 15,* 14-18.

Biong, H., Parvatiyar, A., & Wathne, K. (1996). Are customer satisfaction measures appropriate to measure relationship satisfaction? In A. Parvatiyar & J. N. Sheth (Eds.), *Contemporary knowledge of relationship marketing* (pp. 258-275). Atlanta, GA: Emory University, Center for Relationship Marketing.

Biong, H., & Selnes, F. (1995). Relational selling behavior and skills in long-term industrial buyer-seller relationships. *International Business Review, 4,* 483-498.

Bitner, M. J. (1995). Building service relationships: It's all about promises. *Journal of the Academy of Marketing Science, 23,* 246-251.

Boorom, M. L., Goolsby, J. R., & Ramsey, R. P. (1998). Relational communication traits and their effect on adaptiveness and sales performance. *Journal of the Academy of Marketing Science, 26,* 16-30.

Borys, B., & Jemison, D. B. (1989). Hybrid arrangements as strategic alliances: Theoretical issues in organizational combinations. *Academy of Management Review, 14,* 234-249.

Bucklin, L. P., & Sengupta, S. (1993). Organizing successful co-marketing alliances. *Journal of Marketing, 57*(2), 32-46.

Cannie, J. K., & Caplin, D. (1991). *Keeping customers for life.* Chicago: American Marketing Association.

Cherrington, P. T. (1920). *The elements of marketing.* New York: Macmillan.

Christopher, M. (1994). Logistics and customer relationships. *Asia-Australia Marketing Journal, 2*(1), 93-98.

Christopher, M., Payne, A., & Ballantyne, D. (1991). *Relationship marketing: Bringing quality, customer service and marketing together.* Oxford: Butterworth-Heinemann.

Churchill, H. L. (1942). How to measure brand loyalty. *Advertising and Selling, 35,* 24.

Crosby, L. A., Evans, K. R., & Cowles, D. (1990). Relationship quality in services selling: An interpersonal influence perspective. *Journal of Marketing, 54*(3), 68-81.

Crosby, L. A., & Stephens, N. (1987). Effects of relationship marketing and satisfaction, retention, and prices in the life insurance industry. *Journal of Marketing Research, 24,* 404-411.

Czepiel, J. A. (1990). Service encounters and service relationships: Implications for research. *Journal of Business Research, 20*(1), 13-21.

Dick, A. S., & Basu, K. (1994). Customer loyalty: Toward an integrated conceptual framework. *Journal of the Academy of Marketing Science, 22,* 99-113.

Doney, P. M., & Cannon, J. P. (1997). An examination of the nature of trust in buyer-seller relationships. *Journal of Marketing, 61*(2), 35-51.

Dorsch, M. J., Swanson, S. R., & Kelley, C. W. (1998). The role of relationship quality in the stratification of vendors as perceived by customers. *Journal of the Academy of Marketing Science, 26,* 128-142.

Doyle, S. X., & Thomas, R. G. (1992, February). Selling and sales management in action: The use of insight coaching to improve relationship selling. *Journal of Personal Selling and Sales Management, 12,* 59-64.

Duddy, E. A., & Revzan, D. A. (1947). *Marketing: An institutional approach.* New York: McGraw-Hill.

Duncan, T., & Moriarty, S. E. (1998). A communication-based marketing model for managing relationships. *Journal of Marketing, 62*(2), 1-13.

Dwyer, F. R., Schurr, P. H., & Oh, S. (1987). Developing buyer-seller relationships. *Journal of Marketing, 51*(2), 11-27.

El-Ansary, A. (1997). Relationship marketing: A marketing channel context. In J. N. Sheth & A. Parvatiyar (Eds.), *Research in marketing* (Vol. 13, pp. 33-46). Greenwich, CT: JAI.

Evans, J. R., & Laskin, R. L. (1994). The relationship marketing process: A conceptualization and application. *Industrial Marketing Management, 23,* 439-452.

Fawcett, S. E., Calantone, R., & Smith, S. R. (1997, September). Delivery capability and firm performance in international operations. *International Journal of Production Economics, 15,* 191-204.

File, K. M., Mack, J. L., & Prince, R. A. (1995). The effect of interactive marketing on commercial customer satisfaction in international financial markets. *Journal of Business and Industrial Marketing, 10*(2), 69-75.

Frazier, G. L., Spekman, R. E., & O'Neal, C. R. (1988). Just-in-time exchange relationships in industrial marketing. *Journal of Marketing, 52*(4), 52-67.

Ganesan, S. (1994). Determinants of long-term orientation in buyer-seller relationships. *Journal of Marketing, 58*(2), 1-19.

Grönroos, C. (1981). Internal marketing: An integral part of marketing theory. In J. H. Donnelly & W. R. George (Eds.), *Marketing of services* (pp. 236-238). Chicago: American Marketing Association.

Grönroos, C. (1983). *Strategic management and marketing in the service sector.* Cambridge, MA: Marketing Science Institute.

Grönroos, C. (1990). *Service management and marketing: Managing the moments of truth in service competition.* Lexington, MA: Lexington.

Grönroos, C. (1995). Relationship marketing: The strategy continuum. *Journal of the Academy of Marketing Science, 23,* 252-254.

Grönroos, C., & Gummesson, E. (1985). *Service marketing: A Nordic school perspective* (Research Rep.). Stockholm: Stockholm University.

Gruen, T. W. (1995). The outcome set of relationship marketing in consumer markets. *International Business Review, 4,* 447-469.

Gummesson, E. (1987). The new marketing: Developing long-term interactive relationships. *Long Range Planning, 20*(4), 10-20.

Gundlach, G. T., & Cadotte, E. R. (1994). Exchange interdependence and interfirm interaction: Research in a simulated channel setting. *Journal of Marketing Research, 31,* 516-532.

Gundlach, G. T., & Murphy, P. E. (1993). Ethical and legal foundations of relational marketing exchanges. *Journal of Marketing, 57*(4), 35-46.

Gwinner, K. P., Gremler, D. D., & Bitner, M. J. (1998). Relational benefits in service industries: The customer's perspective. *Journal of the Academy of Marketing Science, 26,* 101-114.

Håkansson, H. (Ed.). (1982). *International marketing and purchasing of industrial goods: An interaction approach.* Chichester: John Wiley.

Hallén, L., Johanson, J., & Seyed-Mohamed, N. (1991). Interfirm adaptation in business relationships. *Journal of Marketing, 55*(2), 29-37.

Hayes, R. H., Wheelwright, S. C., & Clark, K. B. (1988). *Dynamic manufacturing: Creating the learning organization.* New York: Free Press.

Heide, J. B. (1994). Interorganizational governance in marketing channels. *Journal of Marketing, 58*(1), 71-85.

Hines, P. (1995, Spring). Network sourcing: A hybrid approach. *International Journal of Purchasing and Materials Management, 31,* 18-24.

Holmlund, M. (1996). *A theoretical framework of perceived quality in business relationships* (Research Rep.). Helsinki, Finland: Swedish School of Economics and Business Administration.

Howard, J. A., & Sheth, J. N. (1969). *The theory of buyer behavior.* New York: John Wiley.

Iacobucci, D., & Hopkins, N. (1992). Modeling dyadic interactions and networks in marketing. *Journal of Marketing Research, 29,* 5-17.

Iacobucci, D., & Ostrom, A. (1996). Commercial and interpersonal relationships: Using the structure of interpersonal relationships to understand individual-to-individual, individual-to-firm, and firm-to-firm relationships in commerce. *International Journal of Research in Marketing, 13,* 53-72.

Iacobucci, D., & Zerillo, P. (1997). The relationship life cycle: 1) A network-dyad-network dynamic conceptualization, and 2) The application of some classic psychological theories to its management. In J. N. Sheth & A. Parvatiyar (Eds.), *Research in marketing* (Vol. 13, pp. 47-68). Greenwich, CT: JAI.

Jackson, B. B. (1985). *Winning and keeping industrial customers: The dynamics of customer relationships.* Lexington, MA: D. C. Heath.

Kahn, B. E. (1998). Dynamic relations with customers: High-variety strategies. *Journal of the Academy of Marketing Science, 26,* 45-53.

Kalwani, M. U., & Narayandas, N. (1995). Long-term manufacturer-supplier relationships: Do they pay off for supplier firms? *Journal of Marketing, 59*(1), 1-16.

Kaplan, R. S., & Norton, D. (1992). The balanced scorecard: Measures that drive performance. *Harvard Business Review, 70*(3), 71-79.

Keep, W. W., Hollander, S. C., & Dickinson, R. (1998). Forces impinging on long-term business-to-business relationships in the United States: An historical perspective. *Journal of Marketing, 62*(2), 31-45.

Kotler, P. (1972). A generic concept of marketing. *Journal of Marketing, 36*(2), 46-54.

Kotler, P. (1990, November). Speech presented at the Trustees Meeting of the Marketing Science Institute, Boston.

Kumar, N., Scheer, L. K., & Steenkamp, J.-B. E. M. (1995). The effects of perceived interdependence on dealer attitudes. *Journal of Marketing Research, 32,* 348-356.

Law, W. K., & Ooten, H. (1993, August). Material management practices and inventory productivity. *Hospital Material Management, 15,* 63-74.

Levitt, T. (1981). Marketing intangible products and product intangibles. *Harvard Business Review, 59*(5), 94-102.

Little, R. W. (1970). The marketing channel: Who should lead this extra-corporate organization. *Journal of Marketing, 34*(1), 31-38.

Lohtia, R. (1997). A transaction cost and resource-dependence based model of buyer-seller relations. In J. N. Sheth & A. Parvatiyar (Eds.), *Research in marketing* (Vol. 13, pp. 109-134). Greenwich, CT: JAI.

Lusch, R. F., & Brown, J. R. (1996). Interdependency, contracting, and relational behavior in marketing channels. *Journal of Marketing, 60*(4), 19-38.

Mahajan, V., & Srivastava, R. K. (1992, April). *Partner selection: A conjoint model application.* Paper presented at the First Research Conference on Relationship Marketing, Atlanta, GA.

Marx, W. (1994, November). A relationship marketing primer. *Management Review,* p. 35.

McCammon, B. (1965). The emergence and growth of contractually integrated channels in the American economy. In P. D. Bennett (Ed.), *Economic growth, competition, and world markets* (pp. 496-515). Chicago: American Marketing Association.

McGarry, E. D. (1950). Some functions of marketing reconsidered. In R. Cox & W. Alderson (Eds.), *Theory of marketing* (pp. 269-280). Homewood, IL: Richard D. Irwin.

McGarry, E. D. (1951, April). The contractual function in marketing. *Journal of Business, 24,* 93-105.

McGarry, E. D. (1953). Some viewpoints in marketing. *Journal of Marketing, 17*(3), 36-43.

McGarry, E. D. (1958). The propaganda function in marketing. *Journal of Marketing, 22*(4), 125-135.

McKenna, R. (1991). *Relationship marketing: Successful strategies for the age of the customer.* Reading, MA: Addison-Wesley.

Mishra, D. P., Heide, J. B., & Cort, S. G. (1998). Information asymmetry and levels of agency relationships. *Journal of Marketing Research, 35,* 277-295.

Mitchell, W., & Singh, K. (1996). Survival of businesses using collaborative relationships to commercialize complex goods. *Strategic Management Journal, 17,* 169-195.

Mohr, J., & Nevin, J. R. (1990). Communication strategies in marketing channels: A theoretical perspective. *Journal of Marketing, 54*(4), 36-51.

Morgan, R. M., & Hunt, S. D. (1994). The commitment-trust theory of relationship marketing. *Journal of Marketing, 58*(3), 20-38.

Mudambi, R., & Mudambi, S. M. (1995). From transaction cost economics to relationship marketing: A model of buyer-supplier relations. *International Business Review, 4,* 419-434.

Naidu, G. M., Parvatiyar, A., Sheth, J. N., & Westgate, L. (in press). Does relationship marketing pay? An empirical investigation of relationship marketing practices in hospitals. *Journal of Business Research.*

Nason, R. W., Melnyk, S. A., Wolter, J. F., & Olsen, C. P. (1997). Beyond strategic alliances: Fusion relationships. In J. N. Sheth & A. Parvatiyar (Eds.), *Research in marketing* (Vol. 13, pp. 135-156). Greenwich, CT: JAI.

Nevin, J. R. (1995). Relationship marketing and distribution channels: Exploring fundamental issues. *Journal of the Academy of Marketing Science, 23,* 327-334.

Noordewier, T. G., John, G., & Nevin, J. R. (1990). Performance outcomes of purchasing arrangements in industrial buyer-vendor relationships. *Journal of Marketing, 54*(4), 80-93.

O'Neal, C. R. (1989). JIT procurement and relationship marketing. *Industrial Marketing Management, 18,* 55-63.

Owen, W. (1984). Interpretative themes in relational communication. *Quarterly Journal of Speech, 70,* 274-287.

Parvatiyar, A., Biong, H., & Wathne, K. (1998, June). *A model of the determinants of relationship satisfaction.* Paper presented at the Fourth Research Conference on Relationship Marketing, Atlanta, GA.

Parvatiyar, A., & Sheth, J. N. (1997). Paradigm shift in interfirm marketing relationships. In J. N. Sheth & A. Parvatiyar (Eds.), *Research in marketing* (Vol. 13, pp. 233-255). Greenwich, CT: JAI.

Paul, T. (1988). Relationship marketing for health care providers. *Journal of Health Care Marketing, 8,* 20-25.

Payne, A. (1995, February 2). Keeping the faith. *Marketing,* p. xiii.

Payne, A., Christopher, M., Clark, M., & Peck, H. (1994). Relationship marketing and the relationship marketing chain. *Asia-Australia Marketing Journal, 2*(1), 81-91.

Peppers, D., & Rogers, M. (1993). *The one to one future: Building relationships one customer at a time.* Garden City, NY: Doubleday.

Peppers, D., & Rogers, M. (1995). A new marketing paradigm: Share of customer, not market share. *Managing Service Quality, 5*(3), 48-51.

Persutti, W. D., Jr. (1992, Winter). The single source issue: U.S. and Japanese sourcing strategies. *International Journal of Purchasing and Materials Management, 28,* 2-9.

Peterson, R. A. (1995). Relationship marketing and the consumer. *Journal of the Academy of Marketing Science, 23*, 278-281.

Postula, F. D., & Little, D. T. (1992, May). Dual sourcing to reduce aerospace hardware costs. *Cost Engineering, 34*, 7-14.

Pruden, D. R. (1995). There's a difference between frequency marketing and relationship marketing. *Direct Marketing, 58*(2), 30-31.

Rao, B. P., & Reddy, S. K. (1995). A dynamic approach to the analysis of strategic alliances. *International Business Review, 4*, 499-518.

Raphel, M. (1995). The art of direct marketing: Upgrading prospects to advocates. *Direct Marketing, 58*(2), 34-37.

Reichheld, F. F. (with Teal, T.). (1996). *The loyalty effect: The hidden force behind growth, profits, and lasting value.* Boston: Harvard Business School Press.

Reichheld, F. F., & Sasser, W. E., Jr. (1990). Zero defections: Quality comes to services. *Harvard Business Review, 69*(1), 105-111.

Richards, A. (1995, March 9). CU pioneers loyalty card for customers. *Marketing*, p. 1.

Rinehart, L. M., & Page, T. J., Jr. (1992). The development and test of a model of transaction negotiation. *Journal of Marketing, 56*(4), 18-32.

Robicheaux, R. A., & Coleman, J. E. (1994). The structure of marketing channel relationships. *Journal of the Academy of Marketing Science, 22*, 38-51.

Rosenberg, L. J., & Czepiel, J. A. (1984). A marketing approach to customer retention. *Journal of Consumer Marketing, 1*(2), 45-51.

Schijns, J. M. C., & Schroder, G. J. (1996, Summer). Segment selection by relationship strength. *Journal of Direct Marketing, 10*, 69-79.

Schultz, D. (1995, Summer). Understanding the new research needs. *Journal of Direct Marketing, 9*, 5-7.

Schultz, D. E., Tannenbaum, S. I., & Lauterborn, R. F. (1992). *Integrated marketing communications.* Lincolnwood, IL: NTC Business Books.

Schwartz, G. (1963). *Development of marketing theory.* Cincinnati, OH: Southwestern.

Shah, R. H. (1997). *All alliances are not created equal: A contingency model of successful partner selection in strategic alliance.* Unpublished doctoral thesis, University of Pittsburgh.

Shamdasani, P. N., & Sheth, J. N. (1995). An experimental approach to investigating satisfaction and continuity in marketing alliances. *European Journal of Marketing, 29*(4), 6-23.

Shani, D., & Chalasani, S. (1992). Exploiting niches using relationship marketing. *Journal of Consumer Marketing, 9*(3), 33-42.

Shapiro, B. P. (1988). *Close encounters of the four kinds: Managing customers in a rapidly changing environment* (Working Paper No. 9-589-015). Boston: Harvard Business School.

Shapiro, B. P., & Moriarty, R. T., Jr. (1980). *National account management.* Cambridge, MA: Marketing Science Institute.

Shapiro, B. P., & Posner, R. S. (1979). Making the major sale. *Harvard Business Review, 57*(4), 68-79.

Shaw, A. (1912). Some problems in market distribution. *Quarterly Journal of Economics, 26*, 706-765.

Sheth, J. N. (1973). A model of industrial buyer behavior. *Journal of Marketing, 37*(4), 50-56.

Sheth, J. N. (1994, July-August). A normative model of retaining customer satisfaction. *Gamma News Journal*, pp. 4-7.

Sheth, J. N. (1996). *Relationship marketing: Paradigm shift or shaft?* Paper presented at the annual meeting of the Academy of Marketing Science, Miami, FL.

Sheth, J. N., Gardner, D. M., & Garrett, D. E. (1988). *Marketing theory: Evolution and evaluation.* New York: John Wiley.

Sheth, J. N., & Mittal, B. (1996). A framework for managing customer expectations. *Journal of Market-Focused Management, 1,* 137-158.

Sheth, J. N., & Parvatiyar, A. (1992). Towards a theory of business alliance formation. *Scandinavian International Business Review, 1*(3), 71-87.

Sheth, J. N., & Parvatiyar, A. (1995a). The evolution of relationship marketing. *International Business Review, 4,* 397-418.

Sheth, J. N., & Parvatiyar, A. (1995b). Relationship marketing in consumer markets: Antecedents and consequences. *Journal of the Academy of Marketing Science, 23,* 255-271.

Sheth, J. N., & Sisodia, R. S. (1995). Improving marketing productivity. In J. Heilbrunn (Ed.), *Encyclopedia of marketing for the year 2000.* Chicago: American Marketing Association/NTC.

Simonin, B. L., & Ruth, J. A. (1998). Is a company known by the company it keeps? Assessing the spillover effects of brand alliances on consumer brand attitudes. *Journal of Marketing Research, 35,* 30-42.

Smith, J. B., & Barclay, D. W. (1997). The effects of organizational differences and trust on the effectiveness of selling partner relationships. *Journal of Marketing, 61*(1), 3-21.

Spekman, R. E. (1988, July-August). Strategic supplier selection: Understanding long-term buyer relationships. *Business Horizons,* pp. 75-81.

Srivastava, R. K., Shervani, T. A., & Fahey, L. (1998). Market-based assets and shareholder value: A framework for analysis. *Journal of Marketing, 62*(1), 2-18.

Stern, L. W., & El-Ansary, A. I. (1992). *Marketing channels* (4th ed.). Englewood Cliffs, NJ: Prentice Hall.

Stump, R. C., & Heide, J. B. (1996). Controlling supplier opportunism in industrial relationships. *Journal of Marketing Research, 33,* 431-441.

Teagno, G. (1995, June). Gelt by association. *American Demographics,* pp. 14-19.

Varadarajan, P. R. (1986). Cooperative sales promotion: An idea whose time has come. *Journal of Consumer Marketing, 3*(1), 15-33.

Varadarajan, P. R., & Cunningham, M. H. (1995). Strategic alliances: A synthesis of conceptual foundations. *Journal of the Academy of Marketing Science, 23,* 282-296.

Varadarajan, P. R., & Rajaratnam, D. (1986). Symbiotic marketing revisited. *Journal of Marketing, 50*(1), 7-17.

Vavra, T. G. (1992). *Aftermarketing: How to keep customers for life through relationship marketing.* Homewood, IL: Business One-Irwin.

Walker, O. C., Jr. (1997). The adaptability of network organizations: Some unexplored questions. *Journal of the Academy of Marketing Science, 25,* 75-82.

Webster, F. E., Jr. (1992). The changing role of marketing in the corporation. *Journal of Marketing, 56*(4), 1-17.

Weitz, B. A., & Jap, S. D. (1995). Relationship marketing and distribution channels. *Journal of the Academy of Marketing Science, 23,* 305-320.

Weld, L. D. H. (1916). *The marketing of farm products.* New York: Macmillan.

Weld, L. D. H. (1917). Marketing functions and mercantile organizations. *American Economic Review, 7,* 306-318.

Wilson, D. T. (1995). An integrated model of buyer-seller relationships. *Journal of the Academy of Marketing Science, 23,* 335-345.

Womer, S. (1944). Some applications of the continuous consumer panel. *Journal of Marketing, 8*(4), 132-136.

Wong, Y. H. (1998). Key to key account management: Relationships (*guanxi*) model. *International Marketing Review, 15*(3), 215-231.

Yigang P. & Tse, D. K. (1996). Cooperative strategies between foreign firms in an overseas country. *Journal of International Business Studies, 27,* 929-946.

Yip, G. S., & Madsen, T. L. (1996). Global account management: The new frontier in relation-
    ship marketing. *International Marketing Review, 13*(3), 24-42.
Young, J. A., Gilbert, F. W., & McIntyre, F. S. (1996). An investigation of relationalism across a
    range of marketing relationships and alliances. *Journal of Business Research, 35*(2),
    139-151.
Zinkhan, G. M., Madden, C. S., Watson, R., & Stewart, D. (1996). Integrated marketing com-
    munications and relationship marketing: Complementary metaphors for the twenty-
    first century. In A. Parvatiyar & J. N. Sheth (Eds.), *Contemporary knowledge of relation-
    ship marketing* (pp. 182-184). Atlanta, GA: Emory University, Center for Relationship
    Marketing.

2

Relationship Marketing

The U.K. Perspective

ADRIAN PAYNE

In the 1990s, the topic of relationship marketing has become one of great interest to both marketing scholars and marketing practitioners. In the increasingly mature and complex markets in which organizations are now operating, building relationships and sustaining them are frequently more important than customer acquisition. Much of the recent interest in relationship marketing has evolved from the work undertaken in industrial marketing and services marketing in the 1980s, although antecedents of relationship marketing can be traced back to ancient times.

Although the importance of the topic is now fairly widely accepted, the scope of relationship marketing, the discipline, is still under debate. Different groups of scholars argue as to which are the most relevant areas for progress and whether or not the domain of relationship marketing represents a new paradigm. With the academic output on relationship marketing rapidly increasing, Sheth (1996) has argued the need for relationship marketing to establish itself as a discipline: "Only when the [relationship marketing] domain becomes a discipline, [will it result] in a paradigm shift." Sheth proposes an eight-stage framework for achieving this, commencing with "delimiting the domain" and "agreeing on a definition" that will help ensure relationship marketing becomes a discipline.

The tasks of delimiting the domain and agreeing on a definition will be evolving processes. Coote (1994) identifies three approaches to relationship marketing, all of which have different emphases and scope. He terms these the "Nordic" approach, the "North American" approach, and the "Anglo-Australian" approach and seeks to identify the foundation theories associated with each. Although Coote's typology is incomplete and somewhat restrictive, it does illustrate some different approaches to the domain of relationship marketing and how it is defined that are being followed in different geographic regions.

My purposes in this chapter are to provide an overview of the development of the relationship marketing domain from the U.K. perspective and to enable comparison of this perspective with the North American, European, and Industrial Marketing and Purchasing (IMP) Group approaches, which are discussed in other chapters. This attempt to summarize all the academic work on relationship marketing from the U.K. perspective has involved some decisions regarding what to include and what to exclude. The increasing international collaboration in academic research has resulted in many researchers from different countries working together. This is best illustrated by the IMP Group, which initially involved cooperation among schools in five European countries but now involves academic colleagues from many other parts of the world, including the United States and Australia.

Inevitably, I have had to make some judgments as to what to include in this discussion of the U.K. perspective. Three decisions have determined the scope of this chapter. First, I have decided to exclude a detailed description of the IMP Group and related network research. This is an area of considerable importance, and one that has resulted in the publication of "many hundreds of journal articles and book chapters, and conference papers" (Easton & Håkansson, 1996), but is one that is addressed in a separate chapter in this book. Second, work under the broad heading of the Anglo-Australian approach is included, as much of the initial work was undertaken within the United Kingdom. Third, I have chosen to focus here on five themes to help structure the U.K. work in relationship marketing; these themes involve a broad view of (a) relationship marketing, (b) relationship marketing and customer markets, (c) relationship marketing and supplier markets, (d) relationship marketing and internal markets, and (e) relationship marketing and networks.

Although these represent only a small number of the dimensions that could be used to explore relationship marketing, I have chosen them because they represent much, although by no means all, of the current research focus in the United Kingdom. The study of other areas, such as commitment and trust, has been developed more extensively elsewhere, especially in the United States, and so I do not address that line of research in detail here. My objective is to review a representative selection of research on relationship marketing in the United Kingdom rather than to cover all contributions.

The chapter is structured as follows. First, I briefly discuss the context and evolution of relationship marketing and then provide a historical overview of U.K. relationship marketing. I then examine each of the five areas of research outlined above, after which I offer brief reviews of some relevant books and other published works. Finally, I offer some concluding comments.

Relationship Marketing: Context and Evolution

In the United Kingdom, the interest in relationship marketing evolved from research carried out in the United States and elsewhere in Europe. In this section I review the context and evolution of relationships as a background for a discussion of relationship marketing in the United Kingdom.

It has been argued that the emergence of relationship marketing in the 1980s was not so much a discovery as a rediscovery of an approach that has long proved to be the cornerstone of many successful businesses. Relationship marketing has been described as a "new-old concept" (Berry, 1995), and there are many historical antecedents of modern relationship marketing. For example, Grönroos (1994, 1996) describes ancient Chinese and Middle Eastern stories that demonstrate relational approaches, and many authors have pointed to earlier works that emphasize the need to market to existing customers (Berry, 1995; Sheth & Parvatiyar, 1995).

However, although many of the ideas behind relationship marketing have been addressed previously, but not under the modern title of *relationship marketing*, the topic of relationships has been underemphasized in the pre-1990s marketing literature. Berry (1995) has described how relationship marketing is now moving to the forefront of marketing practice and academic marketing research after being "on marketing's back burner for so many years." Although researchers and practitioners from all sectors are now embracing relationship marketing, it is in the areas of industrial and services marketing that it has its recent origins. The use of the term *relationship marketing* can be traced to the industrial and services marketing literature of the 1980s.

In the industrial marketing literature, the early work of Levitt (1983) focused on the notion that the real value of a relationship between a customer and a supplier occurs after the sale. Levitt argued that the supplier's emphasis needs to shift from closing a sale to delivering superior customer satisfaction throughout the lifetime of the supplier-customer relationship. Further work by Jackson (1985) was among the early literature to differentiate between transaction marketing and relationship marketing. Jackson outlined the importance of relationships and how the context of the industrial sale set the scene for the type of relationship that is possible. She argued that building and enhancing long-term customer relationships involves concentrating on a number of things that have to be executed over long periods and in a consistent manner. Her work was based on organizations operating in the shipping, communications, and computer industries.

In the services area, researchers at Texas A&M University started to study the applicability of relationship marketing to services. Berry's (1983) landmark paper was one of the earliest to define relationship marketing as "attracting, maintaining, and . . . in multi-service organizations . . . enhancing customer relationships." His work drew attention to the importance of internal marketing's role in creating an organizational climate that supports external marketing activities. He also drew attention to a number of relationship-building strategies that an organization could use.

Although work on relationship marketing in the United States continued to develop over the balance of the 1980s, it has been in the 1990s that we have seen the greatest level of activity. Research output has increased significantly, several academic journals have published special issues on relationship marketing, and the Center for Relationship Marketing, led by Sheth and Parvatiyar, has been established at Emory University and has hosted several research conferences on relationship marketing.

Within Europe, the research of Scandinavian academics, including Grönroos, Gummesson, and a number of their colleagues, working at the Swedish School of Economics and Business Administration in Finland,

Stockholm University in Sweden, and other institutions, has become widely known. The work of these researchers on relationship marketing draws strongly on their earlier work in services marketing and service quality (e.g., Grönroos, 1989, 1991; Gummesson, 1987).

In other parts of Europe, the work of the Industrial Marketing and Purchasing Group has been highly influential. This group, which originally consisted of 12 researchers from Germany, France, Italy, Sweden, and the United Kingdom, is concerned with networks, interactions and relationships in the setting of industrial markets. Since the 1980s, the IMP Group has made a considerable contribution to the literature on industrial markets. A number of books have summarized this work, including publications by Turnbull and Cunningham (1981), Håkansson (1982), Ford (1990), Axelsson and Easton (1992), and Ford et al. (1997). The IMP work has attracted special attention because of its equal emphasis on the characteristics of the buyer and the seller.

The studies undertaken by the researchers mentioned above have had significant influence on a number of other groups within the United Kingdom, Europe, and the United States. By the early 1990s, a number of further groups of researchers had started to pursue separate but related work in relationship marketing. In an effort to characterize some of these approaches, Coote (1994) has identified three broad approaches to relationship marketing: the Anglo-Australian approach, the Nordic approach, and the North American approach. The first, according to Coote, is based on the work of Christopher, Payne, and Ballantyne (1991) and emphasizes the integration of quality management, services marketing concepts, and customer relationship economics. The second approach derives from the work of Scandinavian academics such as Grönroos (1989, 1990, 1991). Coote suggests that the foundations of the Nordic approach include the interactive network theory of industrial marketing, services marketing concepts, and customer relationship economics. The North American approach emphasizes the relationship between the buyer and seller in the context of the organizational environment; it is characterized by the work of Berry (1983), Levitt (1983), and Perrien, Filiatrault, and Ricard (1993).

Although useful for drawing attention to different groups of researchers working within the relationship marketing area, Coote's description is incomplete in at least two aspects. First, the characterization, by some academics, of such bodies of work as separate "schools" is somewhat misleading. (It should be noted that Coote does not use the term *school*.

However, a number of other academics have used this term during confer-ences to refer to his three classifications.) Not only is there considerable overlap among them, but the state of development of these approaches has not reached the point where any of them could be appropriately de-scribed as a school. Second, Coote's scheme ignores a significant body of literature, including the IMP research, that has been published in both the United States and elsewhere.

Such classifications are, however, helpful in putting some of the differ-ent perspectives of relationship marketing under scrutiny and creating a platform for debate regarding the appropriate definition of the domain of relationship marketing. In the balance of this chapter, I examine the U.K. perspective on relationship marketing.

A Historical Overview of
U.K. Relationship Marketing

EARLY DEVELOPMENTS AND CONFERENCE ACTIVITY

Before I present an examination of the literature on relationship mar-keting, it is appropriate to discuss briefly the early developments in rela-tionship marketing in the United Kingdom. During the 1980s, most of the U.K. researchers with an interest in relationships were working within the IMP Group. It was not until the late 1980s that other researchers in the United Kingdom started to develop an interest in relationship marketing from a more strategic perspective. This interest was driven by concerns about the traditional marketing approach and the recognition of the im-portance of relationships in contemporary markets.

Excluding the IMP research, much of the early work involved the coop-eration of a number of academics from Cranfield University in England and, later, from Monash University in Australia. This work commenced in 1989, and the results of the work were presented at a number of confer-ences in Europe and Australia between 1991 and 1993, including the U.K. Marketing Education Group's annual conference, the annual conference of the British Academy of Management, the Australia-New Zealand Man-agement Educators conference, and the International Quality in Services conference. Some of the early work in this area was summarized in a book by Christopher et al. (1991); it is this ongoing work at the Centre for

Relationship Marketing and Service Management at Cranfield University that Coote has characterized as the Anglo-Australian approach.

By 1993, academic interest in relationship marketing was increasing at a rapid rate within the United Kingdom and elsewhere. This interest led to the First International Colloquium in Relationship Marketing, held by Monash University in Melbourne, Australia, in 1993. The colloquium was chaired by Ballantyne, who had recently moved from the United Kingdom to Australia. The papers presented reflected not only the Anglo-Australian and Nordic work but also the work of researchers from the United States and the IMP Group. This colloquium has now become an annual event: The Second International Colloquium was held at Cranfield, England, in 1994; the Third International Colloquium in Melbourne, Australia, in 1995; and the Fourth International Colloquium in Helsinki, Finland, in 1996.

Other major international conferences were also being run in other countries in parallel with these events. The IMP Group has held annual research conferences for many years, and Emory University in Atlanta, Georgia, has held three major research conferences on relationship marketing, in 1992, 1994, and 1996. These three regular conference and research events for relationship marketing are becoming increasingly international and are attended by academics with a wide range of relationship-based research interests.

Relationship marketing is now firmly on the agendas at marketing and management conferences within Europe. The number of papers on relationship issues is increasing at conferences such as those held by the U.K. Marketing Education Group (now the Marketing Academy of the United Kingdom) and the British Academy of Management, and at the European Marketing Academy Conference (EMAC). As at major U.S. conferences, such as that of the American Marketing Association (AMA), increasingly special topic theme meetings are being held on relationship marketing. Also, in the AMA's Education Division, the Relationship Marketing Special Interest Group is one of the top five special interest groups in membership.

PUBLICATION WITHIN JOURNALS
AND BOOKS

Work in relationship marketing draws heavily on research in services marketing. Some of the early work undertaken in services research had relational themes, although the researchers did not specifically use the term *relationship marketing*. Work within the services sector with relational themes can be found as early as 1981 in such U.K. journals as the *Journal of Service Industry Management*. Research on relationship marketing is increasingly being published in U.K. and European marketing and management journals, including the *Journal of Marketing Management, European Journal of Marketing, International Journal of Service Industry Management, Journal of Marketing Practice,* and *Management Decision*. In May 1995, the *International Journal of Service Industry Management* published a special issue devoted to relationship marketing. This pattern of special issues devoted to relationship marketing is reinforcing the importance of the domain. Special issues on relationship marketing have been published in the *Journal of the Academy of Marketing Science* (fall 1995), the *Asia-Australia Marketing Journal* (issue 1, 1994, and issue 1, 1997), *Industrial Marketing Management* (issue 2, 1997), and the *European Journal of Marketing* (issue 2, 1997).

A further measure of the increasing significance of relationship marketing in the United Kingdom is the extent to which books and edited works on the topic have appeared. A total of seven edited and authored works on relationship marketing have been published (Buttle, 1996; Christopher et al., 1991; Cram, 1994; Payne, 1995; Payne, Christopher, Clark, & Peck, 1995; Peck, Payne, Christopher, & Clark, 1997; Stone & Woodcock, 1995). Although a number these include chapters by authors from outside the United Kingdom or are practitioner oriented, the contributors to the Payne (1995) and Buttle (1996) books are principally U.K. researchers. The contributors include academics working at Manchester Business School, University College Salford, University of Nottingham, Surrey University, Manchester Metropolitan University, University of Warwick, Staffordshire University, Cranfield University, and the University of Buckingham. This work reflects the wide range of academic institutions in the United Kingdom where research is being undertaken in the relationship marketing field. In the following sections, I explore this work in more detail. I begin with the development of a broader view of relationship marketing, and then discuss research dealing with relationship marketing and customer markets, relationship marketing and supplier markets, relationship marketing and internal markets, and relationship marketing and networks.

A Broader View of Relationship Marketing: Addressing Multiple Markets

Concerns regarding the validity of the traditional marketing approach and recognition of the increasing importance of relationships in the complex and mature markets of the past decade have been widespread. These concerns have been voiced by many within the United Kingdom and the rest of Europe in the work of Christopher et al. (1991), Grönroos (1994), and Gummesson (1994). They have also been raised by consulting firms such as McKinsey and Co. (George, Freeling, & Court, 1994).

In the United Kingdom, these concerns have led to a broadened view of relationship marketing. This view has been summarized as follows:

- ▓ A move from functionally based marketing to cross-functionally based marketing
- ▓ An approach that addresses a total of six key market domains, not just the traditional customer market
- ▓ A shift from marketing activities that emphasize customer acquisition to marketing activities that emphasize customer retention as well as acquisition (Payne, 1995, p. 30)

I discuss the first two of these elements in this section and the third element of customer retention in the next section of this chapter.

The shift to cross-functional marketing reflects the difficulties encountered by traditional hierarchically structured and functionally oriented organizations that adopt a departmental or functional approach to marketing. This new view of relationship marketing emphasizes the organization of marketing activities around cross-functional processes as opposed to organizational functions. This view is consistent with that of Ostroff and Smith (1992), who argue the need for a horizontal mode of organization in which cross-functional, end-to-end work flows link internal processes with the needs and capabilities of both suppliers and customers. This suggests the need for a coordinated approach to relationships with other groups or "markets," including suppliers and internal staff as well as customers, to maximize relational value.

A number of authors have suggested an expanded perspective on marketing. For example, Kotler (1972) has argued for a broadening of

Figure 2.1. The Six-Markets Model
SOURCE: Payne (1997).

perspective to take into account the relationships between an organization and its publics—a view he later extended (Kotler, 1992). Gummesson
(1994, 1995) takes this further, to include 30 relational forms. Other
models advocating multiple markets have been suggested in the United
States (Morgan & Hunt, 1994) and in the United Kingdom (Doyle, 1995).
Sharma and Sheth (1997) suggest a framework for value creation through
supplier partnering, alliance partnering, and customer partnering. The
contributors to Buttle's (1996) edited volume also point to the importance of relationship marketing in the context of multiple markets, including regulatory bodies and advisory boards.

   In the United Kingdom, a framework that illustrates this expanded perspective of relationship marketing is the six-markets model, which identifies the six key "markets" or "market domains" where organizations may
consider directing their marketing activities and where detailed marketing plans and strategies can be developed—plans and strategies that ultimately have impacts on the development of enhanced relationships with
customers. I developed the first version of this model (Payne, 1991), which
was later published in Christopher et al. (1991). The original model has
been slightly amended over time, following experience in using it with a

large number of organizations; the latest version is shown here in Figure 2.1.

The six markets or market domains in the model include customer markets (including existing and prospective customers as well as intermediaries), referral markets (these include two main categories: existing customers who recommend their suppliers to others and referral sources, or "multipliers," such as an accounting firm that may refer work to a law firm), influence markets (which may include financial analysts, shareholders, the business press, the government, and consumer groups), recruitment markets (which are concerned with attracting the right employees to the organization), supplier/alliance markets (these include traditional suppliers as well as organizations with which the firm has some form of strategic alliance), and internal markets (the organization, including internal departments and staff). Peck (1996) provides a brief history of the six-markets model and suggests a further variant based on her work in specific industry sectors.

Some comment should be made on the distinctions among these relationship *markets* or *market domains,* the term *publics* as it is used in public relations, and the term *stakeholders* as it is used in strategy and corporate affairs. There are marked differences in relational emphasis among these terms; addressing these groups as markets involves the use of marketing techniques such as segmentation, positioning, and the development of rigorous marketing strategies and plans to achieve specific strategic objectives. This market-based approach is fundamentally different, in the manner in which it is managed, from the influencing of or communicating to these groups as suggested by public relations.

Not all of these markets require the same degree of attention and resources. Decisions regarding the appropriate level of attention required for each market can be determined through identification of key groups or segments within each market domain, determination of expectations and requirements of these key groups, review of the current and proposed level of attention and resources that need to be applied to each market, and the formulation of a marketing strategy and—where appropriate—a marketing plan for each marketing domain (Payne, 1995). The six-markets model recognizes that an organization must balance its activities and aim at developing appropriate relationships with each of the market domains. I have developed a relationship marketing network diagram, or "spidergram," for use in identifying an organization's present emphasis on each market; the spidergram can also be used to plot the desired emphasis and to illustrate the gap between these two positions (Payne, 1993). This diagram can be developed by a jury of management opinion or can be based on a much more detailed evaluation of the "segments" within each of the six markets and a determination of the current emphasis and desired emphasis on a more rigorous quantified basis.

Within the broadened approach to markets there is also a developing interest in the impact of organizational culture on relationship marketing. Palmer and Hodgson (1996) suggest that organizations can be characterized as exhibiting either predominantly transactional or predominantly relational behavior in their interactions, and these share similarities with characteristic gender differences in buyer-seller behavior. Using the six-markets model, they have developed a gender orientation matrix that allows the organizational positioning to be plotted for each market. This matrix plots exchange relationships in terms of transactional versus relational ones and company value orientation in terms of cooperation and conflict resolution (feminine) and aggression and confrontation (masculine).

Much of the research on relationship marketing in the United Kingdom has been concentrated on three markets: customer markets, supplier markets, and internal markets. In the next section, I review some of the research that has been carried out in each of these areas.

Relationship Marketing and Customer Markets

THE RELEVANCE AND APPLICABILITY
OF RELATIONSHIP MARKETING

A considerable amount of work has focused on the relevance and applicability of relationship marketing to all customers and suppliers as well as the limitations of relationship marketing. Although a long-term relationship focus may be desirable in many business contexts, such a focus may not be appropriate with all customers in every situation. Blois (1996) examines the conditions under which a customer is willing to become involved in and then to continue a relationship. Building on the work of Oliver (1990), Blois considers the factors that affect the development of a supplier-customer relationship. Assessment of these factors allows a supplier to determine the level of resources the supplier may need to develop a particular customer relationship. Blois points out that a customer will also assess the value of entering into and developing a relationship; there are costs incurred by the customer, such as those involved in mutual learning across supplier-customer relationships. The customer must be convinced of the overall benefits of the relationship, so that the advantages outweigh the costs of obtaining similar supplies through discrete transactions. Blois concludes that building a long-term relationship is appropriate only in circumstances where both the customer and the supplier are convinced of the profitability of the relationship.

Some researchers have questioned whether relationship marketing practices benefit both customer and supplier. Worthington and Horne (1996) consider whether relationship marketing operates in a mutually beneficial way across customer-supplier relationships with reference to the affinity card industry. Their research suggests that these are not mutual wins across the triangular relationship of card issuer, the affinity organization, and the card user; the weakest gains are made between the affinity organization and the card user. They conclude that it is possible to identify whether or not all parties gain in a supplier-customer relationship, and this will provide evidence of whether relationship marketing supports a reciprocity of benefits between supplier and customer or acts to gain a closer grip on the customer.

Other researchers, such as Murphy (1996), have examined the financial services industry and found that both customers and suppliers benefit from relationship marketing; for the customer a long-term relationship helps reduce perceived risk in purchasing financial services, whereas for the supplier it allows enhanced retention rates and therefore improved profitability. Foxall (1996) also considers whether relationship marketing implies reciprocity of benefits for both customer and supplier. He examines the nature of marketing organizations, which, he argues, exist in order to reduce the costs involved for firms in finding and retaining customers. As market relationships operate in a competitive environment, consumers can choose the suppliers they wish to purchase from. Foxall concludes that this implies that, in free market economies, relationships are adopted only by mutual consent—that is, where there is a win-win situation. Other academic work by Palmer (1994) explores the role of relationship marketing in the marketing curriculum and the alternative perspectives of relationship marketing held by a sample of U.K. managers (Palmer & Mayer, 1996).

LEVELS OF RELATIONSHIPS
AND CUSTOMER LOYALTY

Achieving a balance between marketing efforts directed at existing and new customers is essential. Frequently, existing customers do not receive sufficient attention. A simple conceptual framework is the relationship marketing ladder of customer loyalty (Christopher et al., 1991). Models that include ladders of loyalty have been used by practitioners in charity marketing and sales management for many years. This version of the ladder follows closely that developed by Raphel and Raphel (1995) but has more stages, including a final stage of partnership.

The relationship with a customer is considered as a number of stages that can be seen as a ladder of customer loyalty. A "prospect" is defined as a potential customer who has no direct relationship with a prospective supplier; however, a prospect will have some expectations and perceptions of the supplier that are based on knowledge acquired in the marketplace. The relationship can progress to the point that the prospect becomes a "customer," which is defined narrowly as someone who has had *one* direct encounter with the organization. A "client" is defined as a customer who has had repeated transactions with the supplier, but is neutral or negative toward the supplier. This is contrasted with a "supporter," who has positive commitment to the relationship, and an "advocate," who actively promotes the company by positive word-of-mouth marketing. The final step on the ladder is "partnership," when both customer and supplier are linked through mutually beneficial exchanges—for example, information exchanges of customer sales that speed up order and delivery time while also giving the supplier better knowledge of customer requirements.

The relationship marketing ladder of loyalty is a useful tool for enhancing awareness of customer segmentation opportunities; for example, the emphasis on different elements of the marketing mix may vary for customers on different steps of the ladder. In addition, there is a recognition that not all customers are suited to the higher rungs of the ladder; customers with low profit potential are not necessarily suitable candidates for the investment that may be needed to take them to the level of advocates or partners.

Palmer and Bejou (1994) extend the concept of the relationship ladder and present evidence of a buyer-seller relationship life cycle. In their examination of investment services organizations, they identify how the elements binding buyer and seller change as a relationship progresses. They identify sales orientation/selling pressure, ethics, and empathy as different constructs that have differing importance at various stages of the relationship life cycle. The findings of this research imply that a firm should seek to move customers rapidly through the stages of relationship development, as too much selling pressure may deter adoption of mutual understanding. Palmer and Bejou acknowledge that the relative importance of various constructs will differ across customer segments; therefore, sellers must tailor their sales messages according to the needs of the different segments, which are related to the duration of the buyer-seller relationship.

Understanding factors affecting customer loyalty in the retail sector is the focus of interest for a number of U.K. researchers. Knox and Denison (1995) undertook an empirical study of consumer loyalty in five retail sectors, examining the extent to which store loyalty is associated with level of consumer spending. They investigated the effect of loyalty in a broad range of retail sectors, including gasoline, groceries, "do it yourself," mixed retail, and department stores. They used a composite index, the Enis-Paul measure, to measure loyalty; this index considers the mean of consumer store patronage, propensity to switch, and total budget allocated to first-choice stores. Knox and Denison compared their results with those of similar studies conducted in the United States in the 1960s (e.g., Enis & Paul, 1970) and found that U.K. consumers are relatively less loyal to their first-choice stores; this suggests that recent trends in retailing, such as higher mobility levels and more impersonal sales systems, have contributed to lower customer loyalty. The results indicate that different retail sectors typically demonstrate differing levels of customer loyalty, with do-it-yourself and department stores scoring the lowest.

In other work, Knox and Walker (1997) have looked at brand loyalty. They identify four consumer purchasing styles: "loyals," "habituals," "variety seekers," and "switchers." These segments distinguish involved purchasing behavior from routinized purchasing behavior. Know and Walker conclude that behavioral elements characterized by commitment and support of a brand are necessary for brand loyalty to exist.

CUSTOMER RETENTION

The rising interest in relationship marketing in the early 1990s acted as a catalyst to work on customer retention—in particular, the impact of customer retention on profitability. In their pioneering work, Reichheld and Sasser (1990) found a high correlation between customer retention and profitability in a range of industries. Based on a survey of the literature on customer retention, Clark and Payne (1994) identify some key concepts for retention improvement. Drawing on this work and our experience with a number of services organizations, we propose a three-stage framework for retention improvement that involves three sequential steps: customer retention measurement, identification of causes of defections and key service issues, and corrective action to improve retention. The first stage, customer retention measurement, is of considerable interest to both academics and managers. In particular, practicing managers are excited about prospects for profit improvement in their businesses; however, they are unsure about the profit improvement they might expect in their particular businesses and in market segments within those businesses.

Up to the mid-1990s, most of the research results on retention had shared a number of characteristics (Payne & Rickard, 1996): They were based on company-specific examples from consulting work, they were descriptive and based on confidential work assignments, they included a limited specification of variables, and not all the factors identified were supported by strong empirical evidence. To address this gap, Payne and Rickard (1996) developed a mathematical model of customer retention with the objective of enabling a trade-off to be made in the allocation of scarce marketing resources between strategies concerned with retaining existing customers and those concerned with attracting new customers. The model permits the calculation of the impact on profitability of a number of factors related to customer retention and acquisition, including the customer retention rate, the number of existing customers, the acquisition target for new customers, the cost of acquiring each customer, and the profit per customer per period. This model has been used in a number of industries to examine how changes in the above variables affect customer segment and company profitability.

Payne and Frow (in press) used this model to examine the impacts of marketing programs aimed at retaining existing customers and acquiring new customers for a major U.K. electricity supplier. This is a sector that presents special relationship marketing challenges. In 1998, competition would enter the U.K. residential electricity supply market, and suppliers would face, for the first time, the challenge of keeping their existing customers, who would now be open to competitive attack from electricity suppliers beyond their geographic boundaries, as well as the task of acquiring new customers in the geographic territories of their new competitors. Based on the results of a segmentation study of 2,000 residential customers, Payne and Frow modeled long-term profitability within four key market segments. We concluded that retention strategies needed to be based on an understanding of the relative profitability of different segments and microsegments, and that former mass- marketing strategies would need to be replaced by marketing strategies based on identifiable value propositions and retention management programs aimed at specific segments.

Ennew and Binks (1996) examine the links between customer retention/defection and service quality in the context of the U.K. banking sector and the banks' relationships with small business customers. They develop a framework for examining satisfaction and retention and present the results of some empirical research. They find support for the hypothesis that loyalty/retention is influenced by service quality and customer relationships, and they find that trust in the banking relationships has the largest impact on potential defection.

Other work on customer retention has been undertaken by Page, Pitt, Berthon, and Money (1996), who developed a quantitative approach to analyzing defections and their impacts by using case studies. They explore the role of customer defection probability and customer contribution as a function of age and then use sensitivity analysis to investigate the impact on contribution and market share sensitivity of two different strategies: reduction in defection rate and improvement in new customer acquisition. They then address different potential marketing mix strategies for new and existing customers. In common with others, such as Blattberg and Deighton (1996), Page et al. conclude that the cost of retaining customers is generally much less than the cost of acquiring new customers.

Relationship Marketing and Supplier Markets

The management of supplier markets, one of the six markets described earlier, has been a topic of considerable interest to U.K. researchers. Building successful relationships with suppliers is recognized as critical to the success in customer markets. Since the late 1980s, several authors have focused on strategic supply-chain management, recognizing that organizations that develop appropriate relationships in this market can reap significant advantages. Scott and Westbrook (1990) set out a model for integrating the supply chain. They point out that although examples of good supply-chain management demonstrate significant benefits in terms of costs, quality, delivery lead time, and reliability, remarkably few organizations have successfully pursued a strategic approach to managing their supplier relationships. Scott and Westbrook set out three analytic steps that help this process: mapping the supply pipeline to identify lead times and inventory levels and comparing these with those of competitors, positioning the organization in terms of the relations it currently has with suppliers, and then selecting appropriate actions to enhance supply-chain effectiveness.

Lamming, Cousins, and Hotman (1995) have developed a technique, the Relationship Assessment Programme (RAP), for use in assessing the relationships between customers and suppliers. They point out that many traditional systems for evaluating suppliers access only one side of the supplier-customer relationship, although it is the overall health of the interaction that should be assessed. RAP stresses the sharing of information and collaboration between supplier and customer in order that mutually beneficial improvements can be made. Lamming et al. note that many suppliers regard vendor assessment programs as part of a coercive strategy on the part of customers and not as developmental exercises. For a successful supplier-customer relationship to develop, there must be mutual understanding of the two sides' various influences on each other. These include competitive pressures, internal relationships, and purchasing and marketing abilities. Lamming et al. suggest that "relationship enabling factors" need to be mutually developed and then managed within the context of the relationship. RAP stresses that both parties share responsibility for developing a successful relationship and need both the willingness and the resources to invest.

Other recent research has looked at the nature of supplier partnerships and has sought to understand how these evolve. Sinclair, Hunter, and Beaumont (1996) discuss the different types of trading relationships and explore whether the process of development has any impact on the closeness between organizations. They suggest three progressive stages along which closer supplier collaboration may develop, the overall benefit being reduction of risk to both parties. These three stages are represented as three models: (a) the demands model, in which customers are largely concerned with technical issues relating to empathy; (b) the audit model, in which customers assess supplier performance using their own auditing procedures; and (c) the supplier development model, in which customers actively seek to assist improvement in supplier performance through a range of activities. These three models represent a progressive pursuit of risk reduction, with the ultimate objective of partnership. Using this model, Sinclair et al. examined a number of manufacturing organizations and found that although many firms believe they have partnerships with suppliers, few demonstrate collaborative management of their relationships. In particular, few customers are actively concerned with people management strategies in supplier organizations.

Jüttner and Peck (1996) have also examined supply chains in the context of the relationship marketing and strategy interfaces. They look at two issues: the degree of collective supply-chain strategizing and organizational beliefs. They distinguish two feedback loops, integrating relationship nature and strategic flexibility, as two further constructs that need investigation.

Relationships and Internal Marketing

Internal marketing is an area that has attracted considerable interest around the world—especially in the United States, the Nordic region, and the United Kingdom. Research on internal marketing has a longer history than some other areas within relationship marketing. Researchers working within the services marketing area, such as Grönroos (1981) and Berry (1983), have long been interested in internal marketing. In even earlier work, Kotler (1972) discussed "employee directed marketing." However, Rafiq and Ahmed (1993) conclude that although the need for internal marketing is well understood, the reality is that very few organizations actively apply the concept in practice.

Within the United Kingdom there has been relatively little empirical work on internal marketing. Helman and Payne (1992) conducted a pilot survey of internal marketing in U.K. organizations and found that formalized internal marketing programs rarely exist in U.K. companies; however, internal marketing is "implicit in quality initiatives, customer service programs and broader business strategies." In a survey of 100 U.K. organizations, Thomson (1990) found that internal marketing was largely

associated with motivational campaigns by personnel and human resource management practitioners. Piercy and Morgan (1989), who surveyed 200 businesses in the United Kingdom, found little recognition of
internal marketing activity.

Varey (1994) has explored internal marketing's linkages with a number
of areas, including service quality, marketing orientation and marketing
strategy, total quality management, organizational development and
change management, internal service productivity, innovation, corporate
image, and the firm's perspective as an internal integrator. He has also developed a model of internal marketing. His ongoing work includes empirical testing of his model.

Some work has focused on the marketing of functional departments
within organizations. Collins and Payne (1991) have explored internal
marketing from the perspective of a human resource department's internal
marketing activities within the firm. Holland (1994) has outlined a six-step
process for marketing the marketing function within the organization.

Other internal marketing research has focused on organizational issues. Piercy (1995) addresses the issue of customer satisfaction and the
internal market. After examining the role of customer satisfaction and the
literature relating to it, he discusses the organization as an internal marketplace and looks at the implementation problem as an internal marketing issue in which customer satisfaction needs to be positioned and marketed in a strong and positive way in order to achieve implementation of
customer satisfaction management. Ballantyne (1995) has explored the
internal and external market dimensions in marketing planning, especially emphasizing his concept of "code breaking, border-crossing and en-
ergising activities."

Work by Reynoso and Moores (1996) has contributed toward identifying internal service quality criteria and linking these to quality dimensions used by customers. In their study of employees in health care organizations, Reynoso and Moores were able to identify and evaluate quality
dimensions that the employees used to assess internal quality received
from other parts of the organization. The dimensions these authors identify are similar to those found in the SERVQUAL instrument developed by
Parasuraman, Zeithaml, and Berry (1988), emphasizing the linkage between internal and external quality management. Reynoso and Moores's
work reinforces the view that organizations wishing to improve customer
relationships need to focus on internal as well as external quality
enhancement.

Relationship Marketing and Networks

Much of the work on networks in the relationship marketing literature has been conducted in the context of the IMP Group's research, which is addressed by Håkansson and Snehota in Chapter 3 of this volume. However, there are some aspects related to networks that I should comment on here—the concepts of the network and virtual organization and the form of network marketing practiced by organizations such as Amway and Tupperware.

Several authors have examined the concept of the network organization. Piercy and Cravens (1995) consider the shift from functional marketing to a customer-focused process adopted across an organization and the problem of how this process should be organized and managed. They identify four types of network organizations that characterize different forms that companies have adopted to manage their organizational relationships (see also Cravens, Piercy, & Shipp, 1996). Each is appropriate to different market circumstances. The "hollow network" is typical of highly volatile environments where there are frequent changes in market needs; it relies on transactional relationships that link customers to supplies of products and services, and often these are contracted from other suppliers. The "flexible organization" is also typical of volatile environments, but it sustains collaborative, long-term links within the network; this organization provides a flexible stream of products and services to customers, using its knowledge and long-term relationships with suppliers. The "value-added network" uses a global network of suppliers but maintains internal operations focused on innovation and product design; this network is typical of markets (such as apparel manufacturing) that have no need for sophisticated technologies or product customization. This contrasts with the "virtual network," where the long-term needs of different market segments are met through the formation of collaborative relationships between network members and customers. The virtual network organization retains core competencies but also develops appropriate enduring, external relationships; it is typical of markets that experience stable market environments so that long-term needs of customers can be assessed.

Christopher (1997) examines the role of strategic marketing networks and in particular how the roots of competitive advantage lie in the relationships that exist within a wider network of suppliers, intermediaries, and customers. He identifies a range of key network management issues and process management issues that are essential for firms to identify appropriate partners, join them within strategic networks, and develop enduring relationships with them.

Croft and Woodruffe (1996) use data based on Amway's recent Pacific Rim flotations to assess the concept of network marketing against six strategic criteria for channel management. They investigate the Japanese retail market and conclude that network marketing has both strengths and weaknesses in international marketing. They suggest that it has potential in countries where there are strong social and family bonds, where retailing is characterized by large numbers of small independent outlets lacking specialist skills, and where imported consumer goods have a high perceived value. They conclude that the approach to network marketing channels must be integrated with every other aspect of marketing management.

Books and Other Published Work

A number of edited and authored books on relationship marketing have been published in the United Kingdom. I provide brief descriptions of some of these below, in chronological order, as some are practitioner oriented, cover work outside the United Kingdom, or otherwise do not fit within the topics discussed earlier.

The first book on relationship marketing, *Relationship Marketing: Bringing Quality, Customer Service and Marketing Together* (Christopher et al., 1991), summarizes some of the early work done at Cranfield University. Its chapters focus on relationship marketing, developing a relationship strategy, quality as a competitive strategy, monitoring service quality performance, the transition to quality leadership, and managing relationship marketing. This book also includes five case studies on quality leadership.

Cram's book *The Power of Relationship Marketing* (1994) is influenced by the work of McKenna (1991). The book is practitioner oriented and is organized around seven key themes: loyal staff, loyal customers, the learning organization, relationship pricing, communications, staff training, and relationship management.

Relationship Marketing for Competitive Advantage: Winning and Keeping Customers (Payne et al., 1995) consists of texts and readings in relationship marketing. The book is divided into a number of specific areas, including key concepts in relationship marketing, industrial perspectives of relationship marketing, service perspectives of relationship marketing, culture and climate, achieving employee commitment, delivering customer satisfaction, generating customer commitment, and planning and developing relationship strategies. It contains 21 readings, including many of the early groundbreaking papers on relationship marketing. This book includes North American, Nordic, IMP, and U.K. work.

Relationship Marketing, by Stone and Woodcock (1995), is aimed at practitioners and vocationally oriented students. The principal focus is on such key issues as customer retention and loyalty, integration of marketing strategies, people and processes, and the role of customer database management in relationship marketing.

Advances in Relationship Marketing (Payne, 1995) is an edited work that draws together some earlier conference papers and academic journal articles. Most of the work is from Cranfield academics, but the book also includes work from elsewhere within Europe. The 14 chapters are divided into five parts that address relationship marketing and customer retention; internal marketing; managing relationships before, during, and after the sale; service quality themes in relationship marketing; and value creation through relationship marketing.

Relationship Marketing: Theory and Practice (Buttle, 1996) is an edited collection of work on relationship marketing. The 16 chapters describe, analyze, and critique relationship marketing in a number of organizational settings and industries. Some chapters focus on specific market areas, such as supply-chain relationships, principal-agent relationships, business-to-business relationships, and internal relationships. The volume also includes contributions that focus on specific industrial sectors, such as retail banking, corporate banking, credit cards, financial advisers, airlines hospitality, advertising agents, and the not-for-profit sector.

Relationship Marketing: Strategy and Implementation (Peck et al., 1997) presents text and case studies on relationship marketing. Using the six-markets model, the book is divided into sections addressing the six-markets framework, customer and intermediary markets, supplier and alliance markets, referral and influence markets, internal and recruitment markets, and integration of the six markets. The cases cover consumer, industrial, service, and not-for-profit organizations. Both European and North American case studies are included.

Concluding Comments

From the U.K. perspective, relationship marketing has moved to a position of high interest for both academics and practitioners. In the early part of the 1980s, most of the researchers in the United Kingdom who had an interest in relationships were working as members of the Europe-wide IMP Group. By the late 1980s, a further handful of researchers at Cranfield University and elsewhere developed an interest in what could be described as *strategic* relationship marketing. By the late 1990s, a large number of academics in the United Kingdom had commenced work in this area. This high level of interest in relationship marketing is evidenced by the increasing flow of conference papers and publications in academic journals by U.K. academics, the wide-ranging academic affiliations of the authors working in the area, and the increasing number of people attending conferences and research seminars on relationship marketing.

Although it is a simplification to classify all contributions to the wide range of research being carried out in relationship marketing as falling into one or the other of the U.K., Nordic, IMP, or Anglo-Australian approaches, this classification does highlight differences in definition and focus. Currently there are wide variations in definitions of and approaches to relationship marketing. However, one of the central issues is the breadth of the domain. Some see it as solely concerned with the customer-supplier dyad, others as extending beyond customer relationships to include other specific markets or stakeholders. In general, the Anglo-Australian and Nordic groups define relationship marketing more broadly, whereas the North American group argues for a narrow definition at the customer-supplier dyad level.

The discussion on the domain and definition of relationship marketing is reminiscent of the debate that followed publication of Kotler and Levy's article "Broadening the Concept of Marketing" (1969) and the response initiated by Luck's article "Broadening the Concept of Marketing—Too Far" (1969). This debate on relationship marketing should be viewed as a useful and constructive one, as it focuses attention and thought on what constitutes the relevant domain of marketing and may create appropriate and more specific definitions. My own view is that it is necessary for researchers to adopt commonly agreed-upon terminology to differentiate between these broad and narrow approaches; I suggest the use of *customer relationship marketing* (a term increasingly employed in Europe) in reference to relationships with customers and *relationship marketing* in reference to the broader definition.

As the previous sections of this chapter illustrate, the past six years of U.K. work in relationship marketing have been largely concerned with the development of conceptual thought and theory in relationship marketing. The British and European research tradition has tended to emphasize this approach rather than an empirical positivist approach. Gummesson (1996) has pointed to some of the origins of this approach, which is drawn from inductive research methods and particularly "grounded theory."

Within the United Kingdom there is now an opportunity to develop further many of the research areas discussed in this chapter and to concentrate more on empirically based research relating to them. Of these, I suggest four areas as illustrations of where some of this work can be extended. First, within the six-markets framework, research has focused on three market domains: customer markets, supplier markets, and internal markets. In terms of the other three markets—referral markets, influence markets, and recruitment markets—relatively little work has been done, either in the United Kingdom or elsewhere. Tuominen's (1997) work on "investor relationship" marketing provides a good example of how relationship marketing can be applied to these other market domains. Second, the area of customer retention and customer acquisition trade-offs is one of considerable importance. Further empirical work on the profit impact of alternative marketing strategies on customer lifetime value, based on rigorous segmentation, is critical to extending our understanding of retention economics and its impact on maximizing profitability. Third, the area of customer loyalty has much potential. In particular, segmentation on the basis of loyalty has particular appeal. Knox and Denison (1995) have examined the retailing sector; their approach could be utilized in comparative work across a wide range of industry settings. And fourth, further work needs to be done in operationalizing the relationship marketing ladder of loyalty concept. This concept has been used extensively by one British-based market research agency. Empirically based work on this topic will yield insights into the levels of relationships and degrees of loyalty and retention associated with them.

Following the rapid growth of work in relationship marketing around the world, an enormous range of further research opportunities are apparent. However, it could be argued that now is the time for reflection, assessment, and consolidation of work to date, in order that we may develop a more coherent research agenda for the future. Sheth (1996) argues that to shift relationship marketing toward the status of a discipline, researchers must take specific steps. Following the development of the domain and agreement upon a definition, his agenda involves the development of measures, the development of explanatory theory, the building of a respected database, the use of longitudinal research methods, and the creation of a profile through publication in high-quality journals and involvement by respected scholars. There is now an opportunity for scholars to work more closely, on an international basis, to assess the work to date and then address these steps.

References

Axelson, B., & Easton, G. (Eds.). (1992). *Industrial networks: A new view of reality*. London: Routledge.

Ballantyne, D. (1995). *Relationship marketing management: The internal and external market dimensions in marketing planning*. Paper presented at the Industrial Marketing and Purchasing Conference, Manchester Business School.

Berry, L. L. (1983). Relationship marketing. In L. L. Berry, G. L. Shostack, & G. D. Upah (Eds.), *Emerging perspectives on service marketing* (pp. 25-38). Chicago: American Marketing Association.

Berry, L. L. (1995). Relationship marketing of services—growing interest, emerging perspectives. *Journal of the Academy of Marketing Science, 23*, 236-245.

Blattberg, R., & Deighton, J. (1996). Managing marketing by the customer equity criterion. *Harvard Business Review, 74*(6), 136-144.

Blois, K. (1996). Relationship marketing in organizational markets: When is it appropriate? *Journal of Marketing Management, 12*, 161-173.

Buttle, F. (Ed.). (1996). *Relationship marketing: Theory and practice*. Liverpool: Paul Chapman.

Christopher, M. (1997). *Strategic marketing networks* (Working paper). Cranfield, England: Cranfield University, School of Management.

Christopher, M., Payne, A., & Ballantyne, D. (1991). *Relationship marketing: Bringing quality, customer service and marketing together*. Oxford: Butterworth-Heinemann.

Clark, M. K., & Payne, A. (1994, July). *Achieving long-term customer loyalty: A strategic approach*. Paper presented at the annual meeting of the Marketing Education Group.

Collins, B., & Payne, A. (1991). Internal marketing: A new perspective for HRM. *European Management Journal, 9*, 261-270.

Coote, L. (1994). Implementation of relationship marketing in an accounting practice. In J. N. Sheth & A. Parvatiyar (Eds.), *Relationship marketing: Theory, methods and applications*. Atlanta, GA: Emory University, Center for Relationship Marketing.

Cram, T. (1994). *The power of relationship marketing*. London: Pitman.

Cravens, D., Piercy, N., & Shipp, S. H. (1996). New organization forms for competing in highly dynamic environments: The network paradigm. In A. Parvatiyar & J. N. Sheth (Eds.),

Contemporary knowledge of relationship marketing. Atlanta, GA: Emory University, Center for Relationship Marketing.

Croft, R., & Woodruffe, H. (1996). Network marketing: The ultimate in international distribution. *Journal of Marketing Management, 12,* 201-214.

Doyle, P. (1995). Marketing in the new millennium. *European Journal of Marketing, 29*(13), 23-41.

Easton, G., & Håkansson, H. (1996). Markets as networks: Editorial introduction. *International Journal of Research in Marketing, 13,* 407-313.

Enis, B. M., & Paul, G. W. (1970). Store loyalty as a basis for market segmentation. *Journal of Retailing, 46*(3), 42-56.

Ennew, C. T., & Binks, M. R. (1996). The impact of service quality and service characteristics on customer retention: Small businesses and their banks in the UK. *British Journal of Management, 7,* 219-230.

Ford, D. (Ed.). (1990). *Understanding business markets: Interaction, relationships, networks.* London: Academic Press.

Ford, D., Gadde, L.-E., Håkansson, H., Lundgren, A., Snehota, I., Turnbull, P., & Wilson, D. (1997). *Managing business relationships.* Chichester: John Wiley.

Foxall, G. (1996). *The marketing firm* (Working paper). Birmingham, England: University of Birmingham.

George, M., Freeling, A., & Court, D. (1994). Reinventing the marketing organisation. *McKinsey Quarterly, 4.*

Grönroos, C. (1981). Internal marketing: An integral part of marketing theory. In J. H. Donnelly & W. R. George (Eds.), *Marketing of services* (pp. 236-238). Chicago: American Marketing Association.

Grönroos, C. (1989). Defining marketing: A market-oriented approach. *European Journal of Marketing, 23*(1), 52-60.

Grönroos, C. (1990). Marketing redefined. *Management Decision, 27*(1), 5-9.

Grönroos, C. (1991). The marketing strategy continuum: A marketing concept for the 1990s. *Management Decision, 29*(1), 7-13.

Grönroos, C. (1994). From marketing mix to relationship marketing: Towards a paradigm shift in marketing. *Management Decision, 32*(2), 4-20.

Grönroos, C. (1996). Relationship marketing: Strategic and tactical implications. *Management Decision, 34*(3), 5.

Gummesson, E. (1987). The new marketing: Developing long-term interactive relationships. *Long Range Planning, 20*(4), 10-20.

Gummesson, E. (1994). Making relationship marketing operational. *International Journal of Service Industry Management, 5*(5), 5-20.

Gummesson, E. (1995). *Relationship marketing: From 4Ps to 30Rs.* Malmö, Sweden: Liber-Hermods.

Gummesson, E. (1996). *Toward a theoretical framework of relationship marketing.* Paper presented at the International Conference on Relationship Marketing, Berlin.

Håkansson, H. (Ed.). (1982). *International marketing and purchasing of industrial goods: An interaction approach.* New York: John Wiley.

Helman, D., & Payne, A. (1992). *Internal marketing: Myth versus reality* (Working paper). Cranfield, England: Cranfield University, School of Management.

Holland, K. A. (1994). How to sell marketing to your company. *Marketing Intelligence and Planning, 12*(11), 22-25.

Jackson, B. B. (1985). *Winning and keeping industrial customers: The dynamics of customer relationships.* Lexington, MA: D. C. Heath.

Jüttner, U., & Peck, H. (1996). *Strategy and relationships in supply chains.* Paper presented at the International Conference on Relationship Marketing, Berlin.

Knox, S., & Denison, T. (1995). Pocketing the change from loyal shoppers: The double indemnity effect. In M. Kirkup et al. (Eds.), *Proceedings on emerging issues in marketing* (pp. 221-233). Loughborough, England: Marketing Education Group Conference.

Knox, S., & Walker, D. (1997, May). *New empirical perspectives on brand loyalty: Implications for segmentation strategy and equity.* Paper presented at the 26th Annual European Marketing Academy Conference, Warwick, England.

Kotler, P. (1972). A generic concept of marketing. *Journal of Marketing, 36*(2), 46-54.

Kotler, P. (1992). Its time for total marketing. *Business Week Advance,* Executive Brief, p. 2.

Kotler, P., & Levy, S. J. (1969). Broadening the concept of marketing. *Journal of Marketing, 33*(1), 10-15.

Lamming, R., Cousins, P., & Hotman, D. (1995). *Relationship Assessment Programmes: Developing a new management look-work-in-progress.* Paper presented at the Industrial Marketing and Purchasing Conference, Manchester Business School.

Levitt, T. (1983). After the sale is over. *Harvard Business Review, 62*(1), 87-93.

Luck, D. (1969). Broadening the concept of marketing—too far. *Journal of Marketing, 33*(3), 53-54.

McKenna, R. (1991). *Relationship marketing: Successful strategies for the age of the customer.* Reading, MA: Addison-Wesley.

Morgan, R. M., & Hunt, S. D. (1994). The commitment-trust theory of relationship marketing. *Journal of Marketing, 58*(3), 20-38.

Murphy, J. A. (1996). Retail banking. In F. Buttle (Ed.), *Relationship marketing: Theory and practice.* Liverpool: Paul Chapman.

Oliver, C. (1990). Determinants of interorganizational relationships: Integration and future directions. *Academy of Management Review, 15,* 241-265.

Ostroff, F., & Smith, D. (1992, Winter). The horizontal organization. *McKinsey Quarterly,* pp. 148-167.

Page, M., Pitt, L., Berthon, P., & Money, A. (1996). Analyzing customer defections and their effects on corporate performance: The case of Indco. *Journal of Marketing Management, 12,* 617-627.

Palmer, A. J. (1994). Relationship marketing: Back to basics? *Journal of Marketing Management, 10,* 571-579.

Palmer, A. J., & Bejou, D. (1994). Buyer-seller relationships: A conceptual model and empirical investigation. *Journal of Marketing Management, 10,* 495-512.

Palmer, A. J., & Hodgson, M. (1996). *An analysis of the congruence of gender effects on relationship marketing strategy.* Paper presented at the International Conference on Relationship Marketing, Berlin.

Palmer, A. J., & Mayer, R. (1996). A conceptual evaluation of the multiple dimensions of relationship marketing. *Journal of Strategic Marketing, 4,* 207-220.

Parasuraman, A., Zeithaml, V. A., & Berry, L. L. (1988). SERVQUAL: A multiple theme scale for measuring consumer perceptions of service quality. *Journal of Retailing, 64,* 12-40.

Payne, A. (1991). *Relationship marketing: The six markets framework* (Working paper). Cranfield, England: Cranfield University, School of Management.

Payne, A. (1993). *The essence of services marketing.* Hemel Hempstead: Prentice Hall.

Payne, A., Christopher, M. G., Clark, M. K., & Peck, H. (Eds.). (1995). *Relationship marketing for competitive advantage: Winning and keeping customers.* Oxford: Butterworth-Heinemann.

Payne, A. (Ed.). (1995). *Advances in relationship marketing.* London: Kogan Page.

Payne, A. (1997). *Relationship marketing—the six markets framework: A review and extension* (Working paper). Cranfield, England: Cranfield University, School of Management.

Payne, A., & Frow, P. E. (in press). Relationship marketing: Key issues for the utilities sector. *Journal of Marketing Management.*

Payne, A., & Rickard, J. (1996). *Relationship marketing, customer retention and firm profitability* (Working paper). Cranfield, England: Cranfield University, School of Management.

Peck, H. (1996). *Towards a framework for relationship marketing: The six markets model revisited and revised.* Paper presented at the Marketing Education Group Conference, Strathclyde, Scotland.

Peck, H., Payne, A., Christopher, M. G., & Clark, M. K. (1997). *Relationship marketing: Strategy and implementation.* Oxford: Butterworth-Heinemann.

Perrien, J., Filiatrault, P., & Ricard, L. (1993). The implementation of relationship marketing in commercial banking. *Industrial Marketing Management, 22,* 141-148.

Piercy, N. F. (1995). Customer satisfaction and the internal market. *Journal of Marketing Practice: Applied Marketing Science, 1*(1), 22-44.

Piercy, N. F., & Cravens, D. W. (1995). The network paradigm and the marketing organization. *European Journal of Marketing, 29*(3), 7-34.

Piercy, N. F., & Morgan, N. A. (1989). Internal marketing strategy: Managing the corporate environment for marketing. In *Proceedings of the annual Marketing Education Group Conference* (pp. 404-424). Glasgow: Marketing Education Group.

Rafiq, M., & Ahmed, P. K. (1993). The scope of internal marketing: Defining the boundary between marketing and human resource management. *Journal of Marketing Management, 9,* 219-232.

Raphel, M., & Raphel, N. (1995). *Up the loyalty ladder.* Dublin: O'Brien.

Reichheld, F. F., & Sasser, W. E., Jr. (1990). Zero defections: Quality comes to services. *Harvard Business Review, 69*(1), 105-111.

Reynoso, J., & Moores, B. (1996). Internal relationships. In F. Buttle (Ed.), *Relationship marketing: Theory and practice.* Liverpool: Paul Chapman.

Scott, C., & Westbrook, R. (1990). New strategic tools for supply chain management. *International Journal of Physical Duration and Logistics Management, 21*(1), 23-33.

Sharma, A., & Sheth, J. N. (1997). Relationship marketing: An agenda for inquiry. *Industrial Marketing Management, 26*(2), 87-90.

Sheth, J. N. (1996). *Relationship marketing: Paradigm shift or shaft?* Paper presented at the annual meeting of the Academy of Marketing Science, Miami, FL.

Sheth, J. N., & Parvatiyar, A. (1995). The evolution of relationship marketing. *International Business Review, 4,* 397-418.

Sinclair, D., Hunter, L., & Beaumont, P. (1996). Models of customer-supplier relations. *Journal of General Management, 22*(2), 56-75.

Stone, M., & Woodcock, N. (1995). *Relationship marketing.* London: Kogan Page.

Thomson, K. M. (1990). *The employee revolution: The rise of corporate internal marketing.* London: Pitman.

Tuominen, P. (1997, May). *Investor relationship marketing: A theoretical framework and empirical evidence.* Paper presented at the 26th Annual European Marketing Academy Conference, Warwick, England.

Turnbull, P. W., & Cunningham, M. T. (1981). *International marketing and purchasing.* London: Macmillan.

Varey, R. (1994). Internal marketing: A review and some interdisciplinary research challenges. *International Journal of Service Industry Management, 6*(1), 40-63.

Worthington, S., & Horne, S. (1996). Relationship marketing: The case of the university alumni affinity credit card. *Journal of Marketing Management, 12,* 189-199.

3

The IMP Perspective

*Assets and Liabilities of
Business Relationships*

HÅKAN HÅKANSSON
IVAN J. SNEHOTA

A keynote speaker addressing some 200 participants from more than 15 countries at the 12th annual conference of the Industrial Marketing and Purchasing (IMP) Group at the University of Karlsruhe in Germany in the fall of 1996 declared the IMP to be "a well-known trademark that has been around for 20 years and yet [it is] impossible to define what it stands for." Indeed, looking back at the fertile stream of IMP research, we can see that it consists of many different strands, with findings reported in numerous publications over a long period of time. However, what an outsider such as the speaker quoted above may consider a weakness of this research tradition is probably one of its main strengths. The IMP is a prime example of what it is also studying—a flexible network organization with floating boundaries but built around some strong relationships that connect and permit cross-fertilization of various streams of ideas and research. The IMP research program has been productive not because of a clearly defined core but because it has brought together quite different kinds of knowledge in new ways. It springs from some shared basic empirical findings and onto-logical assumptions, but it is spinning in numerous different directions, as do its implications.

The variety of projects that are part of IMP research may make it diffi-cult for some to grasp the main findings and propositions of this research and to assess its implications for management and for further studies. Having taken part in it for two decades, we will in this chapter offer our pic-ture of the essence of the IMP. We will attempt to outline briefly the history of the IMP, to review its conceptual cornerstones, and to discuss the main implications of the IMP findings both for management and for the future directions of research. Although the picture we offer is probably shared by most of our IMP colleagues, we know for sure that some of them would em-phasize other aspects. The IMP has various facets and shows different ones depending on the angle from which it is approached. Indeed, although its origins and its center of gravity are in the marketing discipline, it has fac-ets that touch on organization theory, theory of international business, and studies of technical development, to mention a few.

The IMP Story

One way to describe what the IMP stands for is to explain how it has evolved. The IMP began in the mid-1970s and later developed along many different trails. In hindsight, we can see that it consists of three inter-twined parts that have evolved over about two decades. Two of these parts are large international research projects (IMP1 and IMP2), and the third, running in parallel with the first two, is the formation of a research net-work connecting researchers scattered in several countries. The history of the IMP is about bringing together, confronting, and cross-fertilizing vari-ous pieces of research and conceptual development.

IMP1

The first project of the IMP is the International/Industrial Marketing and Purchasing Project (later called IMP1), initiated in 1976 and carried out until about 1982. The key notion of this project is relationship interaction. The antecedents of IMP1 were studies conducted in Swedish export industries (Johanson, 1966), distribution systems in the United Kingdom (Ford, 1976), industrial purchasing (Håkansson & Wootz, 1975), and marketing in Sweden, the United Kingdom, and Germany (Cunningham & White, 1974; Håkansson & Östberg, 1975; Kutchker, 1975). The researchers who conducted these and other studies at that time observed the existence of lasting buyer-seller relationships in business markets and pointed out severe shortcomings of the marketing theory at hand to capture and explain this phenomenon (e.g., Arndt, 1979; Twedt, 1964).

Shared interest in industrial markets and dissatisfaction with the available marketing concepts led a group of junior researchers in several European countries to establish contacts that resulted in the design of IMP1. The research backgrounds and interests of those joining the project involved issues ranging from purchasing and industrial marketing to internationalization. However, all were focused on the role of buyer-seller relationships between companies. Relationships and interaction thus became the research object on which they converged.

Despite their heterogeneous backgrounds, the members of the group that gathered around the project had two traits in common: empirical research orientation and familiarity with emerging organization theory at that time. Their empirical orientation made the joining researchers aware of the difficulties in using mainstream analytic concepts in marketing for interpretation of the phenomena encountered in industrial markets. Certain strands of organization theory (in particular the works of Cyert & March, 1963; March & Simon, 1958; Thompson, 1967) and the emergent interorganizational theory (e.g., Aiken & Hage, 1968; Blau, 1964) provided an intellectually stimulating theoretical source. The researchers found it fruitful to borrow some of the concepts of these theories to develop interpretative schemes regarding some of the phenomena they observed in business relationships.

The initial purpose of IMP1 was empirical. The researchers were to collect descriptive data about buyer-seller relationships in industrial markets in five European countries, with the aim of creating a large database. The hypothesis underlying the project, based on previous research, was that the content of supplier-customer relationships is broader than simple economic exchanges. The project was designed, in particular, to capture elements of social exchange, interaction in customer-supplier relationships, and the variation in the content and duration of relationships for different types of companies.

The data were collected and elaborated jointly by cooperating research groups in five European countries. Data were gathered on more than 1,000 customer-supplier relationships through structured interviews, about half of which were conducted with buyers and half with sellers. Some 80% of the relationships studied were cross-border—that is, international—relationships. More than 20 researchers from France, Germany, Italy, Sweden, and the United Kingdom took part in the project. The initial empirical thrust and international scope of IMP1 have come to characterize much of the subsequent IMP research.

The outcomes of IMP1 were both empirical and theoretical. A broad and rather rich empirical descriptive database was produced regarding the features of buyer-seller relationships in industrial markets. Along with the aggregated structured database, a number of in-depth cases describing relationship processes were elaborated. The main empirical findings were reported in several publications (Cunningham, 1980; Håkansson, 1982; Hallén, 1980; Kutchker & Kirsch, 1978; Perrin, 1979; Turnbull & Cunningham, 1980; Turnbull & Valla, 1985).

The theoretical outcome of IMP1 came from an intense effort to develop interpretative schemes and conceptual frames to capture the features and processes at work in buyer-seller relationships in industrial markets. These efforts resulted in elaboration of "the interaction model of buyer-seller relationships" (Håkansson, 1982). The interaction model then became a base for further elaboration of conceptual frameworks and propositions with regard to international purchasing (Hallén, 1980), marketing communication, and international industrial marketing strategies (Hallén, Johanson, & Seyed-Mohamed, 1989; Turnbull & Valla, 1985).

IMP2

IMP2, the IMP project started in 1986, represents the second part of the IMP. It originated in the empirical findings and conceptual achievements of IMP1, but it brought in other researchers, interests, and strands of research. The key notion of this part was the network form. It was inspired by indications of interdependencies in and between buyer-seller relationships and the resulting concept of the network form of business markets (Hägg & Johanson, 1982; Hammarkvist, Håkansson, & Mattsson, 1982). Building on the evidence of the existence of strong buyer-seller relationships in industrial markets, the focus of IMP2 was on interdependencies in and between the relationships and the effects of interdependencies on the companies involved. Networks of relationships thus became of main empirical and conceptual interest for IMP2.

Methodologically similar to the first project, IMP2 involved structured interviews with both buyers and sellers, having as objects both specific customer-supplier relationships and company case studies. Researchers from Australia (Wilkinson & Young, 1994), Japan (Teramoto, 1990), and the United States (Anderson & Narus, 1990; Wilson & Mummalaneni, 1986) joined IMP2, along with most of the researchers from IMP1, and brought in some new interests, evidence, and ideas. Standardized data about buyer-seller relationships have been collected and combined with a number of in-depth company cases.

The main outcomes of IMP2 are again both empirical and conceptual. The project has led to further elaboration of the concept of business networks and refinement of the conceptual frame of business relationships (Anderson, Håkansson, & Johanson, 1994; Axelsson & Easton, 1992; Håkansson & Snehota, 1995). More extensive empirical descriptions and interpretative schemes of the interaction processes in buyer-seller relationships have been produced and reported in several publications (Blankenburg & Johanson, 1990; Blankenburg Holm, 1996; Havila, 1996). Empirical studies of business networks have addressed the issue of connectedness in business relationships and the effects of interdependencies.

THE RESEARCH COMMUNITY

The third part of the IMP has been the organization of a research network that connects various streams of research with different topics (purchasing, marketing, technical development, internationalization) and different methodologies (qualitative as well as quantitative). A forum has emerged where a successively broadening research community, sharing concerns with business relationships and networks, can meet and confront community members' findings and propositions.

A visible manifestation of this forum took the form of the first annual IMP conference, held at University of Manchester in 1984; an IMP conference has been held every year since that time. From 50 to 100 working papers are produced and presented each year; these appear in the conference proceedings but also in a steady stream of other publications (e.g., Cavusgil & Sharma, 1993; Ford, 1990, 1997; Gemunden, Ritter, & Walter, 1998;

Hallén & Johanson, 1989; Turnbull & Paliwoda, 1986; Wilson & Möller, 1995).

This part of the IMP, which is still going on, reflects the increasing differentiation and heterogeneity of the various strands of research spurred by the previous findings. It meets the researchers' need to explore further the impacts of buyer-seller relationships on various aspects of business management and on the functioning of business markets. It coincides with the broadening of the scope of the IMP research and with continuing conceptual development. The empirical base underlying the IMP conferences is extensive. It is a blend of case studies and quantitative analyses of firms, networks, and business relationships.

The empirical thrust of the IMP has gone hand in hand with efforts to interpret observed phenomena and to develop adequate analytic concepts. The efforts toward conceptual development have been inspired by impulses from various disciplines of management. Although rooted in marketing, the scope of the conceptual development is broader than marketing management—it involves the market process and its overall impact on business organizations. It has thus been inspired, as recurrent references indicate, by the more institutional marketing theory (e.g., Alderson, 1957, 1965; Arndt, 1979; Reve & Stern, 1979; Sheth, Gardner, & Garrett, 1988), which deals with the working of the market system rather than only with marketing management, and some developments within industrial marketing area in the United States (Sheth, 1978; Sheth & Parvatiyar, 1992; Spekman, 1988; Webster, 1992). Other sources of inspiration often referred to are certain strands of sociology (e.g., Burt, 1982, 1992; Cook & Emerson, 1978, 1984; Granovetter, 1985; Nohria & Eccles, 1992), organization theory (Aldrich, 1979; Ebers, 1997; Grabher, 1993; Weick, 1969), industrial organization (Bain, 1968; Scherer, 1970), transaction cost theory (Reve, 1990; Williamson, 1975, 1985), business strategy (Lorenzoni & Ornati, 1988; Porter, 1980, 1985), and evolutionary economics (Dosi, Freeman, Nelson, Silverberg, & Soete, 1988; Nelson & Winter, 1982).

Conceptual Cornerstones of the IMP

Although the IMP research has evolved organically, with hindsight it is possible to identify some of its important cornerstones. As these have emerged gradually, the relative importance of each has shifted over time and for individual researchers. We discuss four such cornerstones below. The first two come from major empirical findings, and they are therefore concepts shared by most of the researchers; the other two are hypotheses regarding general explanations of these findings, and thus are more questionable and personal.

The first cornerstone is the discovery and empirical findings regarding relationships between buyers and sellers in business markets:

1. *Between buyers and sellers exist relationships.* These are built from interaction processes in which technical, social, and economic issues are dealt with. Relationships are organized patterns of interaction and interdependence with their own substance. They are an important phenomenon in the business landscape and have to be recognized and handled by management both as problems in themselves and as marketing or purchasing means. They are as often problems as they are solutions.

The importance of business relationships is both an empirical finding and a discovery. We were looking for decisions regarding single market exchange episodes when we first noticed these relationships. We could not find the discrete decisions, and when we found them, they seemed not to be related to important or interesting issues. Instead, we found that companies were dealing with each other in ways that could be characterized as relationships—that is, they were acting and reacting based on each others' acts over time and with specific considerations for their counterparts. There were interaction processes in which reactions were as important as actions, listening was as important as talking, and mutuality seemed to be a necessary condition for both parties to reach their goals. Thus the existence of relationships and their substance is an empirical finding. Clearly, some companies also tried to use relationships as marketing or purchasing means, but this seemed not to be without problems. The relationships seemed to be so heavy that they were not easily redirected in specific ways.

In the studies, three different types of issues often came into focus in the relationships: technical, social, and economic issues. This signaled the existence of three types of problems in relationships, but also indicated that the relationships could have functions in those three dimensions.

TECHNICAL CONTENT

In many cases, interactions between buyers and sellers have a technical content—at least in industrial markets. The relationship is a way of building together the technical resources of one company with the technical resources of the counterpart. Again and again, the relationship between customer and supplier turns out to be one of the most important ways a company can develop its products and production processes. At the same time, the relationship also creates technical problems within the companies involved.

The technical content in the relationship becomes manifest in a number of ways. One is that technicians often play an important role in the contacts between companies. Even if sales representatives and purchasing people have the most frequent contacts, technicians have a key role. That role can be as in one Swedish company, where the marketing manager did not like the results of market research showing that the R&D manager was perceived by key customers as the most important individual in the interaction. Technicians have a direct role as they solve the technical problems appearing over time, but they also gain knowledge about how products and production processes are combined. The existence of these contacts can be used as a means to develop the relationship, but it can also make the relationship more difficult to control.

A second way that technical content is apparent in the interaction is through the products or services. Their technical content must be in accordance with the technical parameters of the user and, at the same time, with the seller's technical features, if they are to be produced and sold in an economical way. Sometimes two parties are lucky and find a perfect fit just by chance, but in most situations the two companies have to go through a more or less continuous learning process in order to find and keep a structural fit from a technical point of view. The relationship must be fitted into two different technical systems, both of which are always changing; thus there is need for a continuous technical adaptation process. Again, this can be used in a positive way by one or both of the counterparts, but it also will be a source of difficulties and irritations.

A third way the technical content becomes apparent is through special projects performed by either of the two parties. Interaction with external parties can be an important ingredient in specific development projects, and interaction in these cases becomes part of "larger" constellations or projects. This can cause problems with integration and confrontation in technical terms. Both can be valuable, but the problems must certainly be taken care of.

SOCIAL CONTENT

The interaction between customer and supplier almost always has a social content. It is performed by individuals who, through the interaction, get the opportunity to develop social relationships. Social content is an important ingredient in several respects. One is related to trust, another to commitment, and a third to influence/power. Each of these can be used in a positive way but also will create problems.

Uncertainty is a prevailing condition in typical exchange situations, and therefore the parties have to trust each other. The uncertainty exists in different dimensions; on the buying side, for example, it is possible to distinguish among need, market, and transaction uncertainty (Håkansson, Johanson, & Wootz, 1976). Uncertainty cannot be reduced simply through increased information, as it has to do with future events; instead, the parties have to learn to trust each other. Trust is built up over time in a social exchange process whereby the parties learn, step by step, to trust each other.

Commitment is related to trust but has a specific content. A high degree of trust can exist between parties without there being much feeling of commitment. Commitment has to do with priorities and can be built up between two parties over time if they have demonstrated that they give each other a certain level of priority. Positive interactions give the parties a feeling of being related, of belonging to a high-priority group. Consequently, there can be certain feelings of responsibility for or commitment to each other. The logic behind this is that everyone has to act in relation to individual counterparts—the environment will develop a social structure that always includes some differentiation in importance. As soon as there is a structure, there are preferences. Again, commitment can have both positive and negative effects. The term *commitment* connotes the positive aspects, whereas *obligation* indicates some of the negative. In certain situations an actor has to comply; the actor cannot comply only when he or she wants to. In all relationships, there is this question of what we can demand of our counterparts and what we have to do for them.

The third aspect of social content relates to power/influence. In a group of social actors who give each other different priorities—that is, where there is a certain structure—there will always be a certain "power of influence" related to different positions. Relationships entail such positions and thus also become means for gaining and exercising influence over others.

ECONOMIC CONTENT

Interactions in business relationships have economic consequences and are subject to an economic logic. A relationship is costly to develop and involves a flow of activities/resources with substantial economic consequences. Three different and distinct economic aspects can be identified. The first is that single relationships are quite important in terms of cost and revenue volume. The 10 most important relationships with customers or suppliers often account for a large share of a company's turnover. The economic consequences of breaking one of these relationships can be very severe and might also affect other relationships for each of the two counterparts.

The second economic aspect has to do with the costs of developing and handling relationships. A relationship can be costly, as it might involve a number of persons putting in a lot of time in order to handle the technical, economic, and social aspects described above. It can entail a lot of traveling as well as many technical contacts and projects, as there might be technical adaptations and other changes. The time and cost involved in changing from one counterpart to another can thus be substantial. Some consultancies claim that the cost ratio between keeping a customer and getting a new is 1 to 10. A consequence is that there are reasons to rationalize the handling of relationships—that is, to find ways to reduce unnecessary costs.

A relationship can be seen as an asset and a market investment. This is the third economic aspect of relationships. Looking at relationships as investments is the classical economic way of trying to evaluate substances (i.e., resources that have certain life spans). For established companies, some of their largest resources are their existing relationships. Capturing this substance is probably a common motive when companies buy into other companies in approaching new markets. One consequence of viewing relationships as market investments is the realization that they have to be in balance and coordinated with investments in other internal assets of the company.

The existence of business relationships and their technical, social, and economic content make them important economic phenomena. They are important marketing means for companies, but they are also one of the largest sources of both strategic and tactical problems.

The second cornerstone of the IMP, another empirical finding, can be summarized in the following way:

2. *Business relationships are connected.* That makes them elements of a wider economic organization that takes a network form. Companies are embedded in multidimensional ways into their counterparts—into their counterparts' contexts. This embeddedness affects companies' discretion in contradictory ways. First, it provides serious limitations; any company can only pursue things that are accepted by a number of its counterparts. However, it also offers a company the opportunity to influence its counterparts, and that can be done in a number of dimensions both directly and indirectly.

Through empirical observation, we know that single relationships are difficult to understand on their own merits, without any context. Company representatives often refer to other relationships when explaining their behavior: Acquiring new customers can reduce costs for other customers, getting new customers depends on existing relationships, and so on. The IMP researchers found that relationships were connected to each other in a number of ways, and these connections gave them a very distinct feature. They were related and therefore also relative. They were all parts of something larger and therefore all interactions were in some ways mirrors of the context. The interaction could be understood only when it was put into this context. One critical consequence is that it becomes impossible to evaluate or understand a relationship/interaction disconnected from others. Every relationship has to be seen and judged in relation to the connected relationships that either of the two counterparts has with others and, in some situations, in relation to relationships between third parties.

Whereas the first findings lead to the conclusion that relationships have their own substance, these findings indicate that every relationship is also a part of something larger; it is an integrator of surrounding relationships. This has two obvious consequences: First, the value and content of a relationship can be changed without any action within that relationship, through changes in some related relationships; second, when a change is made within a relationship, some other relationships will be influenced. Every relationship is not only a bridge between two actors but also a reflector or a projection of other relationships. It includes history and environment, still very specific and unique. This is probably the reason so many authors have spent so many pages analyzing how single relationships are influenced by the development of others.

These connections are important in all of the three dimensions—technical, social, and economical. The technical content in the interaction has to mirror all the interdependencies existing among products, production processes, and use of resources. Technological systems cut across the networks of companies in different ways, and the corresponding technical connections have to be addressed within the relationships. In the same way, individuals within companies are members of social structures with special social roles and functions, such as professional associations, school alumni groups, boards in other companies or organizations, and social clubs. Again, companies cut across these structures and the interactions between companies are also part of these structures, benefiting or being hurt by existing structures. Finally, every element—whether technical items such as products or social elements such as trust, commitment, and power—of the single business relationship is a piece of an economic puzzle for which the final outcome depends on how these pieces are related to each other. Networking, as a concept, has in this context a much deeper meaning.

The existence of business relationships and their connectedness are empirical phenomena that ought to be important also from a more general economic viewpoint. The IMP research has come up with different suggestions, hypotheses, and theory fragments that we will summarize in two propositions, which are our third and fourth cornerstones. The first of these can be summarized as follows:

3. *A relationship is a combination.* It affects productivity and efficiency in firms and can therefore be used to exploit complementarities between activities performed by different companies and their resources. At the same time, it is subject to interdependencies. Through relationships, economic benefits can be captured by technical, administrative, or temporal connections.

Traditionally, the economic organization of production activities is described in economics in terms of a dichotomy between market and hierarchy. From such a perspective buyer-seller relationships appear as market imperfections—a way to create monopolistic market situations. Transaction cost theory has shown that relationships are important in situations when the market fails to provide efficient coordination. The IMP research has moved one step further, claiming that relationships are a unique third type of coordination that includes elements of both market and hierarchy but also has its own specific features. Interaction relationships appear as an efficient coordination mechanism when there are multiplex and changing interdependencies. Thus relationships can be used to link activities to each other, combining individual adaptations and scale-effective production.

There are opportunities to take advantage of interdependencies among activities performed within the company and its customers, its customers' customers, its customers' suppliers, its own suppliers, its suppliers' suppliers, its suppliers' customers, and so on, depending upon how business relationships are designed (Dubois, 1998). Connections to suppliers and customers can be differentiated, and operations can still take advantage of important scale effects. There are also negative effects, as relationships will lock the company into a given structure, which will lead to rigidity in certain dimensions and thus to vulnerability to external changes.

The indications from IMP research are that in many industrial settings business relationships are a key mechanism of efficiency. Such relationships are important for the single company and for its counterparts. This gives relationships a hard core of economics; relationships can be a way to reach a higher level of efficiency in the combination of production and transactions. These ideas are consistent with various findings on positive economic effects of quasi-integration arrangements described by concepts such as just-in-time inventory management, time-based management, and total quality control.

It is important to note that we have used here the word *can*. Relationships can be used to link activities and tie resources, but all relationships do not automatically lead to that. Relationships create a context in which this potential exists, but very few companies work in a systematic way to capture these benefits. There are certainly also some problems with relationships, as all links between customer and supplier activities make it more difficult for both parties to establish alternative links and ties as the companies become embedded into specific others.

The discussion of relationships as ways of combining activities, resources, and individual actors has some similarities and can be seen as complementary to corresponding analysis made by economists such as Williamson (1975, 1985), Richardson (1972), and Chandler (1990).

The fourth cornerstone of IMP is the second proposition regarding the economic effects of relationships and their implications for the utilization of resources:

4. *Relationships are confrontation.* They are a way to create a confrontation of the two parties' knowledge, which affects resource development and thus innovativeness. Knowledge is often developed in the border zone between different knowledge areas. In more general terms, relationships can be means for tying resources to each other in such a way that some of their heterogeneity is utilized—that is, different dimensions of the resources are partly unknown, and through "interaction" these dimensions are identified and utilized.

Industrial companies generally have substantial resources in the forms of technical facilities, raw materials, people, knowledge, and established positions in relation to different counterparts. The importance of these for the single company's competitiveness and development is generally recognized. A relationship can be used by the two parties to activate, develop, and direct resources toward each other. This directing can include learning that will give both parties opportunities to find new and better ways to tie the resources together. Technical development within and through relationships becomes an interesting opportunity.

There are two main reasons for using relationships in this way. One has to do with the opportunity to confront and use knowledge from quite different sources in order to find new solutions. The other has to do with the interactive effect. Knowledge is often developed in the border zone between established knowledge areas. If two actors with different knowledge try to combine and confront each other's resources, there is a possibility that they will develop new knowledge.

Technical development therefore mostly takes place in the interface between companies as they represent different resources or knowledge areas. Relationships can be a crucial means to increase a company's ability to innovate and to take part in technological development. Again we use the word *can*. Relationships create a context where it is possible to develop this kind of process, but there is no simple mechanism that triggers it. Many relationships are used the other way around—to block changes. This can be an efficient strategy for a single company, but it will certainly decrease the company's speed of development.

The analysis of the developmental effects of business relationships has driven IMP research in the direction of work by researchers such as von Hippel (1988), Hughes (1983, pp. 404-460), Teece (1980), Nelson and Winter (1982), Rosenberg (1982), Dosi et al. (1988), and Storper and Walker (1989).

Pertinence for Management Action

Because dissatisfaction with marketing theory at the time gave birth to IMP research, the issue of normative implications is important for the IMP. The dissatisfaction was focused on the positive foundations of the normative recommendations, which, in particular in the field of industrial marketing, were based on a very limited understanding of how industrial markets work. Such recommendations are not only meaningless, they are outright bad for practice. The IMP reflects the conviction that if we are to improve the practice of marketing we need first of all a better understanding of the marketing process in industrial markets. In light of our findings, that still remains a valid point. Researchers and companies still have the need for better understanding—that is, a better positive theory. All positive theories are also normative. Because we feel that the IMP Group has advanced our understanding of the marketing process, we are convinced that its findings and resulting propositions offer fruitful ground for normative recommendations for management practice.

However, there are some problems in formulating clear normative implications. One is that the main findings of the IMP research point to and confirm the complexity of relationship consequences and the risks of acting on oversimplified assumptions. The uniqueness of relationships, an empirical fact, makes the mechanical transfer of successful practices among different companies dubious at best. Another problem is that the normative implications of the findings are broad and far-reaching. They can hardly be confined to changes in techniques or methods, nor can they be limited to the domain of marketing management. They are "managerial" in a broad sense. They shed new light on some traditional problems of business management but also suggest some new problems to be considered.

Although the main empirical findings and hypotheses regarding the substance of the business relationships and the network form of business markets deserve to be tested further, once we accept them their implications are numerous and profound. Those that have been outlined and explored within the IMP regard such different areas of management as purchasing (e.g., Gadde & Håkansson, 1992; Pedersen, 1996; Torvatn, 1996), strategy development (e.g., Gadde & Mattsson, 1987; Håkansson & Snehota, 1989, 1995; Henders, 1992; Johanson & Mattsson, 1994; Kock,

1991), internationalization of the firm (e.g., Forsgren & Johanson, 1992; Halinen, 1997; Hallén et al., 1989; Herz, 1993; Pardo & Salle, 1994; Salmi, 1995; Turnbull & Valla, 1985), technological strategy in business (e.g., Biemans, 1992; Ford, 1988; Håkansson, 1987, 1989; Laage-Hellman, 1997; Lundgren, 1995; Raesfeld Meijer, 1997; Waluszewski, 1990), and organization (Havilia, 1996; Tunisini, 1997). Aside from these, there have been publications covering more general aspects of marketing management, such as the work of Easton (1996), Ford (1990, 1997), Iacobucci (1996), and Wilson and Möller (1995).

The implications of the IMP findings and propositions for marketing management contrast with those of the more traditional marketing management theory. The relationship phenomenon and interaction as a core process change the nature of the marketing problem. The existence of relationships points to the importance of specific mutual interdependencies. In a relationship the outcome of a course of action by one party will reflect the acts and counteracts of the counterpart rather than the course of action as such. This means that outcomes and consequences of behaviors depend on a series of interactions too complex to be planned or even thought through beforehand. The three traditional areas of marketing management—market analysis, market strategy options, and implementation—will all get new faces. They will also get another sequence. It becomes natural to start with the ongoing processes—that is, in the implementation.

IMPLEMENTATION

From an interaction perspective, we have to start with the existing processes, at what is generally seen as the "end"—the implementation. The interaction process in relationships makes the very notion of implementation questionable, sometimes even unsuitable and misleading. Customer-supplier relationship interaction consists of a series of acts and counteracts through which the situations to be acted upon continuously evolve. The requests of the customer or supplier regarding various arrangements are met in different ways, which produce new situations that have to be handled. The goals and the alternative means of the involved companies become as much results of the interaction as preconditions. In a true interaction, the involved parties have to accept that they are being transformed.

An important consequence is that extensive interaction processes are difficult to monitor and impossible to predict or plan. Both the content of the relationship (products and services rendered) and the interaction pattern of the individuals involved tend to evolve organically. In this process, choices are being made—implemented—often without having been previously conceived and considered as choice situations. In customer relationships things are being undertaken because circumstances call for solutions that are being offered by either of the two parties. The outcomes of a company's behavior in such a market reflect the interaction more than any formal plan.

The strength of a relationship and its consequences change as mutual activity coordination is tightened up or loosened, as reciprocal adaptations in resources are made, and as individuals engage in interpersonal interaction. This process is vital given the consequences, not the least economic, of activity links, resource ties, and actor bonds for the companies involved. Choices in fact are made in interaction with others, and are at best dependent on how the emerging situations are framed and made sense of.

High-involvement relationships with some strong links, ties, or bonds can be valuable assets for a company, but they always also are a heavy liability. Balance is often perceived as needed but can generally be achieved only temporarily and for a certain area. Companies have to live with imbalances and demanding relationships; they have to accept the burdens. The problem becomes how to activate and motivate the counterparts on a continuous basis—how to take part in development processes without any final state. The scope for planning of market activities becomes very limited—often reduced to a ritual whose importance is primarily symbolic.

In light of the IMP findings, the very notion of implementation becomes irrelevant because it assumes planned action. As mutual conforming is the essence of relationship, implementation has meaning only as "mediated" action. Unilaterally controlled relationships are pathological; they are not the typical case. Business markets are in that sense conceivable as "life game" situations.

The main consequence is that instead of implementing preplanned marketing activities, the company has to be an intelligent interaction partner. Key attributes become sensitivity, flexibility, and reflection. The company has to learn from what is going on, learn about the counterparts but also about itself, to learn about when and how the own company performs as an efficient interaction partner. Experimentation is important for companies that want to develop efficient ways to interact.

MARKET STRATEGY OPTIONS

Two features of customer-supplier relationships and networks become strategically relevant. Relationship interaction is costly, and, especially when new relationships are established, the returns lag. At the same time, the interaction mechanism and the difficulties of monitoring an adaptation's coordination and contacts tend to produce another phenomenon: Interacting with others tends to pull the company in different directions, often mirroring the development of the single counterparts.

The centrifugal force of relationship interaction leads to the need to reconsider the issue of "differentiation." Differentiation of the offering is in the network context a fact, and limiting the extent of differentiation is the issue. Strategy options emerge as interactive choices aggregate to patterns that can be given meaning. Options are tried out and interpreted rather than conceived a priori.

The economy cycle in customer relationships—or what we may call their *investment logic*—also has important consequences. Balancing efforts between the existing and new customer relationships and prioritizing customer relationships that compete for limited managerial attention and capacity constitute another strategic issue. A focus on the existing set of relationships as a platform for possible development is unavoidable.

Both features converge on the need for account management logic—that is, differentiation of the roles of the different customer relationships. Not every relationship needs to be economically profitable in the short or long run. Account management (i.e., dealing with each relationship as a distinct entity) reflects the need to keep in consideration the complementary and combinatory effects of relationships. Most important is that whereas relationships are a given, the type of relationship, in terms of high and low involvement, is a variable. Some relationships over time offer new possibilities, whereas inevitably others become a burden. There is nothing intrinsically positive about high-involvement relationships; they are assets to the extent that use can be made of them and liabilities at the same time if their usefulness is not perceived. The two are different sides of the same coin.

MARKET ANALYSIS

The purpose of market analysis is to gain understanding of the context of the marketing action. The question raised by the IMP findings is, What is an appropriate scope of analysis to gain that understanding? The IMP findings imply that we cannot limit market analysis to an abstract product demand analysis if we are to achieve understanding. Mapping the existing customer relationships of the company and of possible interdependencies (i.e., of the relevant network) becomes a necessary first step. The network of buyer-seller relationships rather than the product market becomes the relevant unit of analysis. The difference becomes particularly significant when we deal with companies that are not one-product firms.

Mapping the relevant business network amounts to answering questions such as the following: How large a portion of our overall business do major customers account for? How is that changing? What is the product breakdown? What are the reasons for the changes? What relationships do the customers have to their customers, suppliers, and third parties? It means anchoring the market analysis strictly in the relevant customer context.

Understanding the market context requires focusing the analysis on the customer/buyer (the one who pays for performance) rather than simply on the customer/end user (who often is the customer of the customer). Although understanding the latter remains important, understanding the former is crucial. The definition of *customer* may be tricky and deserves attention.

Mapping the network is but a first step in gaining understanding. Next is understanding the individual account (customer). Understanding the customer-buyer requires assessment not only of its buying behavior but also of the impact of supplier relationships on its operations and on its business. In practice, this amounts to assessment of the share of the customer needs and of the development and outlook of its business, and not only of its purchasing behavior. It entails assessment of the individual customer's share of the company's business and how it has developed and can develop. Knowing the principles of customer operations and their business outlook is critical to understanding their interaction behavior.

It is impossible to forecast how a network will develop, as it is always the result of unique interactions. Rather than attempting to foresee, a company needs to direct its efforts toward understanding the forces that form the network and shape its development. That cannot be accomplished without an understanding of the cliques in the network that correspond to shared interests.

Domains to Explore

Reviewing the IMP research to date, we find that it stands out clearly as more basic than applied research. We believe that this is not likely to change anytime soon, as, in our opinion, the mainstream theory development in marketing is close to a paradigm shift, and we are only at the beginning of it. Future research directions are difficult to predict, as they will flow from stepwise discovery and achievements. If we were to suggest some future research directions, they would stem from three considerations.

First, there is an obvious need to increase further the empirical understanding of business relationships and networks. In particular, we believe that the variety in relationship substance has to be examined in more depth. Other areas that need further empirical investigation are the links that join relationship interaction to company performance and the dynamics of the evolution of business networks. Current classification schemes with respect to the substance of relationships offer a starting point for assessing the impacts on both network and company development, but these can be elaborated more extensively.

Second, conceptual development is in no way yet accomplished. We still need more precision in concepts—more effective language—to gauge the processes and in particular the effects and consequences. Concepts such as activity links, resource ties, and actor bonds need more precision as well as clarification of how they relate to each other and how they produce economic consequences (e.g., Håkansson & Snehota, 1995). There is a need to gain insight into the dynamics of business networks and thus deepen the understanding of the forces shaping the context of business. Concepts such as network position, internationalization, change in distribution networks, and network organization are about to be developed more fully, but the remaining path is uphill. The current state is more one of a conceptual frame than of a consistent theory.

Third, the conceptual development resulting from the IMP research is but part of a broader development of thought about the economic organization that springs from numerous sources. It is thus related to developments in economics, economic sociology, and economic history, and the link becomes interesting. The IMP findings so far point also to some more fundamental issues, such as the autonomy of action and the meaning of economic and social rationality.

References

Aiken, M., & Hage, J. (1968). Organizational interdependence and intra-organizational structure. *American Sociological Review, 33*, 912-930.

Alderson, W. (1957). *Marketing behavior and executive action: A functionalist approach to marketing theory*. Homewood, IL: Richard D. Irwin.

Alderson, W. (1965). *Dynamic marketing behavior: A functionalist theory of marketing*. Homewood, IL: Richard D. Irwin.

Aldrich, H. E. (1979). *Organizations and environments*. Englewood Cliffs, NJ: Prentice Hall.

Anderson, J. C., Håkansson, H., & Johanson, J. (1994). Dyadic business relationships within a business network context. *Journal of Marketing, 58*(4), 1-15.

Anderson, J. C., & Narus, J. A. (1990). A model of distributor firm and manufacturer firm working partnerships. *Journal of Marketing, 54*(1), 42-58.

Arndt, J. (1979). Toward a concept of domesticated markets. *Journal of Marketing, 43*(4), 69-75.

Axelson, B., & Easton, G. (1992). *Industrial networks: A new view of reality*. London: Routledge.

Bain, J. S. (1968). *Industrial organization* (2nd ed.). New York: John Wiley.

Biemans, W. G. (1992). *Managing innovation within networks*. London: Routledge.

Blankenburg, D., & Johanson, J. (1990). Managing network connections in international business. *Scandinavian International Business Review, 1*(1), 5-19.

Blankenburg Holm, D. (1996). *Business networks connections and international business relationships*. Unpublished doctoral dissertation, Uppsala University.

Blau, P. M. (1964). *Exchange and power in social life*. New York: John Wiley.

Burt, R. S. (1982). *Toward a structural theory of action: Network models of social structure, perception and action*. New York: Academic Press.

Burt, R. S. (1992). *Structural holes: The social structure of competition*. Cambridge, MA: Harvard University Press.

Cavusgil, S., & Sharma, D. (1993). *Advances in international marketing: Vol. 5. Industrial networks*. London: JAI.

Chandler, A. D., Jr. (with Hikino, T.). (1990). *Scale and scope: The dynamics of industrial capitalism*. Cambridge, MA: Belknap.

Cook, K. S., & Emerson, R. M. (1978). Power, equity and commitment in exchange networks. *American Sociological Review, 43*, 721-739.

Cook, K. S., & Emerson, R. M. (1984). Exchange networks and the analysis of complex organizations. In S. B. Bacharach & E. J. Lawler (Eds.), *Research in the sociology of organizations* (Vol. 3, pp. 1-30). Greenwich, CT: JAI.

Cunningham, M. (1980). International marketing and purchasing: Features of a European research project. *European Journal of Marketing, 14*(5-6), 5-21.

Cunningham, M., & White, J. G. (1974). The behavior of industrial buyers in their search for suppliers of machine tools. *Journal of Management Studies, 11*(2), 115-128.

Cyert, R. M., & March, J. G. (1963). *A behavioral theory of the firm.* Englewood Cliffs, NJ: Prentice Hall.

Dosi, G., Freeman, C., Nelson, R., Silverberg, G., & Soete, L. (Eds.). (1988). *Technical change and economic theory.* London: Pinters.

Dubois, A. (1998). *Organizing industrial activities across firm boundaries.* London: Routledge.

Easton, G. (Ed.). (1996). Markets as networks [Special issue]. *Journal of Research in Marketing, 13*(5).

Ebers, M. (1997). *The formation of inter-organizational networks.* Oxford: Oxford University Press.

Ford, D. (1976). *An analysis of some aspects of the relationships between companies in channels of distribution.* Unpublished doctoral dissertation, University of Manchester.

Ford, D. I. (1988). Develop your technology strategy. *Long Range Planning, 21*(5), 85-95.

Ford, D. I. (Ed.). (1990). *Understanding business markets.* San Diego, CA: Academic Press.

Ford, D. I. (Ed.). (1997). *Understanding business markets* (2nd ed.). London: Dryden.

Forsgren, M., & Johanson, J. (Eds.). (1992). *Managing networks in international business.* Philadelphia: Gordon & Breach.

Gadde, L.-E., & Håkansson, H. (1992). *Professional purchasing.* London: Routledge.

Gadde, L.-E., & Mattsson, L.-G. (1987). Stability and change in network relationships. *International Journal of Research in Marketing, 4,* 29-41.

Gemunden, H. G., Ritter, T., & Walter, A. (Eds.). (1998). *Relationships and networks in international markets.* London: Elsevier.

Grabher, G. (Ed.). (1993). *The embedded firm: On the socioeconomics of industrial networks.* London: Routledge.

Granovetter, M. (1985). Economic action and social structure: The problem of embeddedness. *American Journal of Sociology, 91,* 481-510.

Hägg, I., & Johanson, J. (1982). *Foretag i natwork. Ny syn pa konkurrenskraft* [Enterprise in networks: New perspective on competitiveness]. Stockholm: SNS.

Håkansson, H. (Ed.). (1982). *International marketing and purchasing of industrial goods: An interaction approach.* New York: John Wiley.

Håkansson, H. (Ed.). (1987). *Industrial technological development: A network approach.* London: Croom Helm.

Håkansson, H. (1989). *Corporate technological behavior: Cooperation and networks.* London: Routledge.

Håkansson, H., Johanson, J., & Wootz, B. (1976). Influence tactics in buyer-seller processes. *Industrial Marketing Management, 5,* 319-332.

Håkansson, H., & Ostberg, K. (1975). Industrial marketing: An organizational problem? *Industrial Marketing Management, 4,* 113-123.

Håkansson, H., & Snehota, I. (1989). No business is an island. *Scandinavian Journal of Management, 5*(3), 187-200.

Håkansson, H., & Snehota, I. (1995). *Developing relationships in business networks.* London: Routledge.

Håkansson, H., & Wootz, B. (1975). Supplier selection in an international environment: An experimental study. *Journal of Marketing Research, 12,* 46-51.

Halinen, A. (1997). *Relationship marketing in professional services: A study of agency-client dynamics in the advertising sector.* London: Routledge.

Hallén, L. (1980). *Sverige på Europamarknaden. Åsikter om inköp och marknadsföring* [Sweden on the European Market: Opinions about purchasing and marketing]. Lund: Studentlitteratur.

Hallén, L., & Johanson, J. (Eds.). (1989). *Networks of relationships in international industrial marketing.* Greenwich, CT: JAI.

Hallén, L., Johanson, J., & Seyed-Mohamed, N. (1989). Relationships and exchange in international and domestic business. In L. Hallén & J. Johanson (Eds.), *Networks of relationships in international industrial marketing* (pp. 7-25). Greenwich, CT: JAI.

Hammarkvist, O., Håkansson, H., & Mattsson, L.-G. (1982). *Marknadsföring för konkurrenskraft* [Marketing for competitive strength]. Lund: Liber.

Havila, V. (1996). *International business-relationships triads: A study of the changing role of the intermediating actor.* Unpublished doctoral dissertation, Uppsala University.

Henders, B. (1992). *Position in industrial networks: Marketing newsprint in the UK.* Unpublished doctoral dissertation, Uppsala University.

Herz, S. (1993). *The internationalization process of freight transport companies.* Unpublished doctoral dissertation, Stockholm School of Economics.

Hughes, T. P. (1983). *Networks of power: Electrification in Western society, 1880-1930.* Baltimore: Johns Hopkins University Press.

Iacobucci, D. (Ed.). (1996). *Networks in marketing.* Thousand Oaks, CA: Sage.

Johanson, J. (1966). *Svenskt specialstål på utländska marknader* [Swedish special steel on foreign markets]. Unpublished doctoral dissertation, Uppsala University, Sweden.

Johanson, J., & Mattsson, L.-G. (1994). The market-as-networks traditions in Sweden. In G. Laurent, G. Lilien, & B. Pras (Eds.), *Research traditions in marketing.* Boston: Kluwer Academic.

Kock, S. (1991). *A strategic process for gaining external resources through long-lasting relationships.* Unpublished doctoral dissertation, Swedish School of Economics and Business Administration, Helsinki, Finland.

Kutchker, M. (1975). *Rationalität und Entschedungskriterien komplexer Investitionsentscheidungen—ein empirischer Bericht* [Rationality and decision parameters in complicated investment decisions]. Unpublished doctoral dissertation, University of Mannheim.

Kutchker, M., & Kirsch, W. (1978). *Verhandlungen auf dem Markt fur Investitionsguter* [Bargaining in the market for investment goods] (Research Rep.). Munich.

Laage-Hellman, J. (1997). *Business networks in Japan: Supplier-customer interaction in product development.* London: Routledge.

Lorenzoni, G., & Ornati, J. P. (1988). Constellations of firms and new ventures. *Journal of Business Venturing, 3*(1), 41-57.

Lundgren, A. (1995). *Technical innovation and industrial evolution.* London: Routledge.

March, J. G., & Simon, H. A. (1958). *Organizations.* New York: John Wiley.

Nelson, R. R., & Winter, S. G. (1982). *An evolutionary theory of economic change.* Cambridge, MA: Belknap.

Nohria, H., & Eccles, R. G. (Eds.). (1992). *Networks and organizations: Structure, form and action.* Boston, MA: Harvard Business School Press.

Pardo, C., & Salle, R. (1994). Strategic interplays of an actor in a relationship with a distributor. *Industrial Marketing Management, 23,* 403-418.

Pedersen, A.-C. (1996). *Utvikling av leverandorrelasjoner i industriella netverk* [Development of supplier relationships in industrial networks: A study of connections between relationships]. Unpublished doctoral dissertation, Norwegian School of Technology, Trondheim.

Perrin, M. (1979). *Les entreprises francaises de biens industriels face à la concurrence sur cinq marche's européens.* Paris: Centre Francais du Commerce Extérieur.

Porter, M. E. (1980). *Competitive strategy: Techniques for analyzing industries and competitors.* New York: Free Press.

Porter, M. E. (1985). *Competitive advantage: Creating and sustaining superior performance.* New York: Free Press.

Raesfeld Meijer, A. von. (1997). *Technological cooperation in networks: A socio-cognitive approach.* Unpublished doctoral dissertation, Twnte University.

Reve, T. (1990). The firm as a nexus of internal and external contracts. In M. Aoki, B. Gustafsson, & O. E. Williamson (Eds.), *The firm as a nexus of treaties* (pp. 133-161). London: Sage.

Reve, T., & Stern, L. W. (1979). Interorganizational relationships in marketing channels. *Academy of Management Review, 4,* 405-416.

Richardson, G. B. (1972). The organization of industry. *Economic Journal, 82,* 883-896.

Rosenberg, N. (Ed.). (1982). *Inside the black box: Technology and economics.* Cambridge: Cambridge University Press.

Salmi, A. (1995). *Institutionally changing business networks.* Unpublished doctoral dissertation, Swedish School of Economics and Business Administration, Helsinki, Finland.

Scherer, F. M. (1970). *Industrial market structure and economic performance.* Chicago: Rand McNally.

Sheth, J. N. (1978). Recent developments in organizational buying behavior. *P.U. Management Review, 1*(1), 65-91.

Sheth, J. N., Gardner, D. M., & Garrett, D. E. (1988). *Marketing theory: Evolution and evaluation.* New York: John Wiley.

Sheth, J. N., & Parvatiyar, A. (1992). Towards a theory of business alliance formation. *Scandinavian International Business Review, 1*(3), 71-87.

Spekman, R. E. (1988, July-August). Strategic supplier selection: Understanding long-term buyer relationships. *Business Horizons,* pp. 75-81.

Storper, M., & Walker, R. (1989). *The capitalist imperative.* New York: Basil Blackwell.

Teece, D. J. (1980). Economies of scope and the scope of enterprise. *Journal of Economic Behavior and Organizations, 1*(1), 233-247.

Teramoto, Y. (1990). *Network power.* Tokyo: NTT.

Thompson, J. D. (1967). *Organizations in action: Social science bases of administrative theory.* New York: McGraw-Hill.

Torvatn, T. (1996). *Productivity in industrial networks: A case study of the purchasing function.* Unpublished doctoral dissertation, Norwegian School of Technology, Trondheim.

Tunisini, A. (1997). *The dissolution of channels and hierarchies: An inquiry into the changing customer relationships and organization of the computer companies.* Unpublished doctoral dissertation, Uppsala University.

Turnbull, P. W., & Cunningham, M. (1980). *International marketing and purchasing: A survey among marketing and purchasing executives in five European countries.* London: Macmillan.

Turnbull, P. W., & Paliwoda, S. J. (Eds.). (1986). *Research in international marketing.* London: Croom Helm.

Turnbull, P. W., & Valla, J.-P. (Eds.). (1985). *Strategies for international industrial marketing.* London: Croom Helm.

Twedt, D. (1964). How stable are advertiser-advertising agency relationships? *Journal of Marketing, 28*(3), 83-84.

von Hippel, E. A. (1988). *The sources of innovation.* New York: Oxford University Press.

Waluszewski, A. (1990). Framväxten av en ny massateknik–en utvecklingshistoria [The development of a new pulp process technology]. *Acta Universitatis Upsaliensis, Studia Oeconomia Negotiorum, 21.*

Webster, F. E., Jr. (1992). The changing role of marketing in the corporation. *Journal of Marketing, 56*(4), 1-17.

Weick, K. (1969). *The social psychology of organizing*. Reading, MA: Addison-Wesley.

Wilkinson, I. F., & Young, L. (1994). Business dancing: An alternative paradigm for relationship marketing. *Asia-Australia Marketing Journal, 2*(1), 67-80.

Williamson, O. E. (1975). *Markets and hierarchies: Analysis and antitrust implications*. New York: Free Press.

Williamson, O. E. (1985). *The economic institutions of capitalism: Firms, markets, and relational contracting*. New York: Free Press.

Wilson, D. T., & Möller, K. (Eds.). (1995). *Business marketing: An interaction and network perspective*. Boston: Kluwer Academic.

Wilson, D. T., & Mummalaneni, V. (1986). Bonding and commitment in supplier relationships: A preliminary conceptualization. *Industrial Marketing and Purchasing, 1*(3), 44-58.

4

Relationship Marketing

The Nordic School Perspective

CHRISTIAN GRÖNROOS

The Nordic school is a marketing school of thought that originally grew out of the research into services marketing in Scandinavia and Finland and quickly became an internationally recognized approach to services marketing research (see Berry & Parasuraman, 1993; Grönroos & Gummesson, 1985). In the 1990s it has been developing into a relationship marketing school of thought. From the beginning, the Nordic school researchers emphasized the long-term relational nature of services marketing (e.g., the buyer-seller interaction wheel in Gummesson, 1977, and the marketing and need-adaptation circle in Grönroos, 1980), but without using the term *relationship marketing*. Instead, they used terms such as *buyer-seller interactions* and *interactive marketing* (Grönroos, 1980), *customer relationship life cycle* (Grönroos, 1983), *the new marketing concept* (Gummesson, 1983), *phases of the service consumption process* (Lehtinen, 1984), and *interactive relationships* (Gummesson, 1987) to indicate the relational nature of the marketing of services.

The term *relationship marketing* was first introduced in the literature by Berry (1983) in a conference paper. Although services marketing, according to the Nordic school approach, has always been relationship oriented, this term was not used by Nordic school researchers until the end of the 1980s (e.g., Grönroos, 1989). One of the major reasons for this was the then growing interest in understanding services of the manufacturing sector, especially those of manufacturers of industrial goods. This trend was growing stronger during the latter part of that decade. Nordic school researchers realized that the introduction of services marketing concepts and models into business relationships (industrial marketing) was the beginning of a major shift in the general marketing paradigm far beyond the services marketing sphere (e.g., Blomqvist, Dahl, & Haeger, 1993; Grönroos, 1989; Gummesson, 1987, 1991; Holmlund, 1996). According to the Nordic school of thought, this paradigm shift is predominantly but of course not solely growing out of services marketing.

Another very similar line of development also emanating from Scandinavia is the growth of the interaction and network approach to the management of business relationships (the IMP Group), which, from a start in the 1970s in Sweden in the following decade and even more so in the 1990s, has become a marketing school of thought that stresses the importance of relationships in business networks (e.g., Håkansson, 1982; Håkansson & Snehota, 1995). According to this approach, networks of companies are the dominant concept, with relationships as a subconcept that explains the development and management of networks. Mattsson (1997) discusses the similarities and differences between relationship marketing studies in the Nordic school tradition and IMP studies. In a study of business relationships, Holmlund (1996) has integrated the network approach with the Nordic school of thought in a perceived quality context, whereas Brodie, Coviello, Brookes, and Litle (1997) suggest a continuum of relational approaches.

Services in Relationship Marketing

It is not difficult to see how services marketing has become a pillar of relationship marketing. An integral part of services marketing is the fact that the consumption of a service is *process consumption* rather than *outcome consumption*, where the consumer or user perceives the service production process as part of the service consumption and not only the outcome of that process, as in traditional consumer packaged goods marketing. Thus service consumption and production have interfaces that are always critical to the consumer's perception of the service and to his or her long-term purchasing behavior. The management of these interfaces is called *interactive marketing* in the services marketing literature, and this concept has been used in the relationship marketing literature as well (see Bitner, 1995). The service provider almost always has direct contact with its customers. In these contacts relationships may easily start to develop, and if the simultaneous consumption and production processes turn out well, an enduring relationship may follow.

When manufacturers of industrial goods and equipment turn their interest from single transactions with their customers to doing business on a long-term basis, the nature of consumption changes from pure outcome consumption to ongoing process consumption or usage. In this process the customer consumes or uses the outcomes of the manufacturer's production processes (goods, equipment) that are exchanged between the parties in the relationship as well as a number of service processes that are produced and consumed or used before, during, and in between the exchanges of outcomes. The nature of this process becomes very similar to the process consumption characteristic of services.

From a marketing point of view this change of the nature of consumption or usage is emphasized even more when the outcomes (goods and equipment) constantly become more similar as competition increases. In most cases even continuous product development does not lead to a sustainable competitive advantage anymore, and hence only services—such as tailor-made design, deliveries, just-in-time logistics, installation of equipment, customer training, documentation of goods, maintenance and spare part service, customer-oriented invoicing, the handling of inquiries, service recovery and complaints management, and pricing below the market standard—are left for the marketer to use. If one does not want to use the price variable, which seldom creates a sustainable competitive advantage, only services are left for developing such an advantage.

Hence, according to the Nordic school approach, managing services is at the core of relationship building and maintenance, although relationship marketing also is supported by other factors, such as the building of networks (Håkansson & Snehota, 1995), the establishment of strategic alliances and partnership agreements (Hunt & Morgan, 1994), the development of customer databases (Vavra, 1994), and the management of relationship-oriented integrated marketing communications (Schultz,

1996; Schultz, Tannenbaum, & Lauterborn, 1992). In other approaches to relationship marketing, other elements or phenomena are seen as the primary pillars, as in the network approach or the strategic alliance and partnership approaches. It all depends on the perspective of the researcher.

There is also another characteristic of the Nordic school approach to services marketing that fits relationship building and maintenance as a marketing strategy, and that is the fact that marketing is seen more as market-oriented management than as a task for marketing specialists only, which means that marketing is viewed more as an overall process than as a separate function (Grönroos & Gummesson, 1985). Of course, transaction marketing may be justified in some cases, but as the work of Reichheld and Sasser (1990), Reichheld (1993), and Storbacka (1994) demonstrates, long-term customer relationships form a base for profitable business in a growing number of situations.

In order to implement relationship marketing, companies require a shift of focus regarding key areas of marketing. In the following sections, I discuss three such areas that are vital for the successful execution of a relationship strategy: an *interaction process* as the core of relationship marketing, a *dialogue process* supporting the development and enhancement of relationships, and a *value process* as the output of relationship marketing. First, however, I will address the service focus of relationship marketing as this is developed in the Nordic school of marketing thought.

Relationship Marketing and Service Competition

According to the Nordic school approach, marketing from a relational perspective has been defined as *the process of identifying and establishing, maintaining, enhancing, and when necessary terminating relationships with customers and other stakeholders, at a profit, so that the objectives of all parties involved are met, where this is done by a mutual giving and fulfillment of promises* (Grönroos, 1997). This definition bears clear similarities to Berry's (1983) services marketing definition from a relationship perspective and to more recently offered definitions by Hunt and Morgan (1994), Sheth and Parvatiyar (1994), and Christopher, Payne, and Ballantyne (1991). For example, marketing has been defined as the

understanding, explanation, and management of the ongoing collaborative business relationship between suppliers and customers. Another
well-known Nordic school definition, by Gummesson (1995), states that
relationship marketing is *marketing seen as interactions, relationships,
and networks.*

Both the Nordic school definitions, my own explicitly and Gummesson's implicitly, emphasize that relationship marketing is first and fore-
most a *process*. Most other definitions that have been offered also imply
this nature of marketing. All activities that are used in marketing have to
be geared toward the management of this process. Hence no marketing
variables are explicitly mentioned in these definitions. According to my
definition, the process moves from identifying potential customers to establishing a relationship with them, and then to maintaining the relationship that has been established and enhancing it so that more business as
well as good references and favorable word of mouth are generated. Finally, if necessary, relationships that are not profitable, even in the long
run, should be terminated. As Gummesson's definition implies, this process includes interactions that form relationships that may be developing
in networks of suppliers, distributors, and consumers or end users.

The *focal relationship* is the one between a supplier or provider of goods
or services in consumer or business markets and a buyer and consumer or
user of these goods or services. Relationship marketing is first and fore-
most geared toward the management of this relationship. However, in order to facilitate this, other stakeholders in the process may have to be involved. Other suppliers, partners, distributors, financing institutions, and
sometimes even political decision makers may have to be included in the
management of the relationship if marketing is to be successful (compare
Gummesson, 1995).

A shift of focus in marketing decision making from the transaction toward a process in which a relationship is built and maintained has important effects on central marketing areas (Grönroos, in press). As this process becomes as important for the customer as the outcomes, for
example, in the form of goods and equipment, the nature of the product
concept changes. The product as the outcome of a production process is
basically a transaction-oriented construct. In a relationship perspective,
physical goods and equipment (products) become a part of the process,
together with other elements such as a host of services. In the best case
these services enhance the value of the products, as with just-in-time

deliveries, prompt service and maintenance, and customer-oriented and timely service recovery. In the worst case they damage or altogether destroy their value, as with delays in deliveries, unsuccessful maintenance, and unclear documentation about the use of equipment that has been purchased.

Customers do not look only for goods or services; they demand a much more holistic offering, including everything from information about the best and safest way to use a product to delivery, installation, updates, repairs, maintenance, and correct solutions for what they have bought. And they demand that all this, and much more, be provided in a friendly, trustworthy, and timely manner. Moreover, the core product is less often the reason for dissatisfaction than are the elements surrounding the core. As Webster (1994) has noted, "The automobile purchaser is unhappy with the car because of lousy service from the dealer; the insurance customer has problems with the agent, not with the policy" (p. 13). What Levitt (1983) concluded in the early 1980s about what should accompany the sale of the mere product—"Having been offered these extras, the customer finds them beneficial and therefore prefers to do business with the company that supplies them" (quoted in Webster, 1994, pp. 9-10)—is even more true today. By and large, customers are more sophisticated and better informed than ever and therefore more demanding, and increasing global competition offers customers more alternatives than ever before.

In a customer relationship that goes beyond a single product transaction, the outcomes themselves—including goods, services, and industrial equipment—become just one element in the *total ongoing service offering.* For a manufacturer, the physical good is a core element of this service offering, of course, because it is a prerequisite of a successful offering. However, what counts is the ability of the firm to manage the additional elements of the offering better than its competitors. The supplier has to truly *serve* its customers (Grönroos, 1996).

The product seen as a total service offering thus becomes a service including tangible elements such as physical goods and equipment and intangible elements such as a host of various types of services. In long-term relationships, firms face a competitive situation for which, in another context, I have coined the term *service competition* (Grönroos, 1996). When service competition is the key to success for practically everybody and the product has to be defined as a service, *every business is a service business* (Webster, 1994).

Shift in Focus of Central Marketing Areas

The product in a transaction-oriented approach to marketing has to be replaced with a long-term construct that fits the requirement of service competition in relationship marketing. *Interaction* is such a concept; it has been developed as one key construct in services marketing and is taken over by relationship marketing, as the Gummesson definition explicitly states. In the network approach to industrial marketing, the interaction construct has been developed as a key concept in business relationships as well (see Håkansson, 1982; Håkansson & Snehota, 1995). Thus, as the exchange of a product is the core of transaction marketing, the management of an *interaction process* is the core of relationship marketing. In this process, a supplier of goods or a service firm represented by people, technology and systems, and know-how interacts with its customer represented by everything from a single consumer to a group of buyers, users, and decision makers in a business relationship. Sometimes more parties in a network may be involved in the interactions (Grönroos, 1996; Gummesson, 1996).

In transaction marketing, marketing communication including sales is a central part of marketing. Marketing communication is predominantly mass marketing, but with a growing element of direct marketing. Sales, where appropriate, is a directly interactive element of the communication process. In the field of marketing communication, a new trend has emerged in the 1990s toward integrating communication elements such as advertising, direct marketing, sales promotion, and public relations into a two-way *integrated marketing communications* (Schultz, 1996; Schultz et al., 1992; Stewart, 1996). Also, in the Nordic school research this holistic view of marketing communication was studied to a limited extent in the mid-1980s (Grönroos & Rubinstein, 1986). This view of marketing communication was called *total communication*. Contrary to the new approach of the 1990s, it also integrated the communication effects of, for example, customer service with the effects of traditional communications media. Integrated marketing communications is clearly influenced by the relationship perspective in marketing. "As we are committed to two-way communication, we intend to get some response from those persons to whom the integrated marketing communications program has been directed. . . . We adapt the customer's or prospect's communication wants or needs and begin the cycle all over again. This is truly relationship marketing at its best" (Schultz et al., 1992, p. 59).

Sometimes communications researchers seem to give the impression that integrated marketing communications using various means of communications in an integrated manner is almost or totally synonymous with relationship marketing. However, in transaction marketing effective marketing communication about a bad or inappropriate product does not lead to a good result. By the same token, effective integrated marketing communications, as a purely communications program, does not develop successful and lasting relationships if the interaction process is bad. Integrated marketing communications is not the same as relationship marketing, but clearly it is an important part of a relationship marketing strategy. A two-way or dialogue marketing communication approach is needed to support the establishment, maintenance, and enhancement of the interactions process if relationship marketing is to be successful. Hence the management of a two-way communications process, or a *dialogue process,* is required in relationship marketing. It is the communications aspect of relationship marketing.

One of the most recent research streams within the Nordic school of marketing thought is related to customer perception of value created in ongoing relationships (Ravald & Grönroos, 1996). The importance of adding a relationship aspect to studies of customer value has also been demonstrated by Lapierre (1997) in Canada. In the interaction process value is transferred to and also partly created for the customer. In the dialogue communication process this creation and transfer of value should be supported before and during the interaction process of the relationship. Finally, a *value process* is needed to demonstrate how the customer indeed perceives the creation and transfer of value over time. When all three processes are in place and well understood, we have a good part of a theory of relationship marketing, or actually a theory of marketing based on a notion that the ultimate objective of marketing is to "manage the firm's market relationships" (see Grönroos, 1996, p. 11).

The Core: The Interaction Process of Relationship Marketing

As noted in the preceding section, successful marketing requires a good enough solution for the consumer or user. In transaction marketing of consumer goods, this solution is a product in the form of a physical good.

In relationship marketing the solution is the relationship itself and how its functions lead to need satisfaction for the customer. As I have concluded previously, the relationship includes the exchange or transfer of physical goods or service outcomes, but also a host of service elements without which the goods or service outcomes may be of limited value or without value for the customer. For example, delayed deliveries, late service calls, badly handled complaints, lack of information, or unfriendly personnel may destroy an otherwise good solution.

The relationship, once it has been established, proceeds in an interaction process where various types of contacts between the supplier or service firm and the customer occur over time. These contacts may be very different depending on the type of marketing situation—some contacts are between people, some are between customers and machines and systems, and some are between systems of the supplier and customer, respectively. In this context, I will not be discussing the differing nature of these contacts in the interaction process depending on whether consumer goods, services, or business relationships are studied. Instead, I will examine more closely the nature of the interaction process. In the Nordic school of marketing thought this issue has been studied to some extent.

In order to understand—and, in practical marketing situations, to analyze and plan—the interaction process, one must divide it into logical parts. In the context of services, the interaction process has been studied in terms of acts, episodes, and relationships (Liljander, 1994; Liljander & Strandvik, 1995; see also Stauss & Weinlich, 1995; Storbacka, 1994; Strandvik & Storbacka, 1996). According to Liljander and Strandvik (1995), an episode is, for example, a visit to a bank office to discuss a loan, whereas an act would be the meeting with the loan officer during the visit. In the context of business relationships, IMP researchers have traditionally offered a two-level approach including short-term episodes (such as exchange of goods and services, information, and financial and social aspects) and long-term processes leading to adaptation and institutionalization of roles and responsibilities (Håkansson, 1982; Möller & Wilson, 1995). In a more generic relationship marketing context, Holmlund (1996) has recently developed the understanding of the interaction process further, in order to achieve an extended analytic depth in the analysis of relationships. In Figure 4.1, the interaction process of the ongoing relationship is divided into four levels of aggregation: the act, episode, sequence, and relationship levels.[1] Holmlund also suggests a fifth level of aggregation, a partner level, for situations in which network partners are

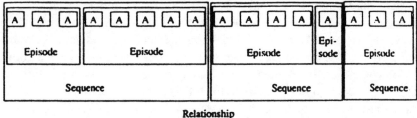

Figure 4.1. Different Interaction Levels in a Relationship

SOURCE: Holmlund (1996, p. 49). Reprinted by permission of the author and of the Swedish School of Economics and Business Administration, Helsinki, Finland.

required in a business relationship. This level is omitted here because it is specific to business-to-business relationships, whereas the four others are applicable to the analysis of relationships in general.

Acts are the smallest unit of analysis in the interaction process, such as phone calls, plant visits, service calls, and hotel registration. In the service management literature, acts are often called "moments of truth." Acts may be related to any kind of interaction elements, physical goods, services, information, financial aspects, or social contacts. "Individual act[tion]s are connected to other act[ion]s and may be analysed accordingly. Interrelated act[ion]s may therefore be grouped into interactions on a higher . . . level, which corresponds to episodes" (Holmlund, 1996, p. 49).

Hence interrelated acts form a minor natural entity in a relationship, an *episode* such as a negotiation, a shipment of goods, or dinner at a hotel restaurant during a stay at that hotel. Every episode includes a series of acts. For example, "a shipment may include such act[ion]s as the placement of an order by telephone, assembling and packing the products, transporting, . . . unpacking, making a complaint, and sending and paying an invoice" (Holmlund, 1996, p. 49).

Interrelated episodes form the next level of analysis in the interaction process, a *sequence*. According to Holmlund (1996), a sequence can be defined in terms of a time period, an offering, a campaign or a project, or a combination of these. "This implies that the analysis of a sequence may contain all kind of interactions related to a particular year, when a particular project . . . has been carried out. Sequences may naturally overlap" (pp. 49-50). To take another type of example, in a restaurant context a sequence comprises everything that takes place during one visit to a particular restaurant.

The final and most aggregated level of analysis is the *relationship*. Several sequences form the relationship. Sequences may follow each other directly, may overlap, or may follow at longer or shorter intervals, depending, for example, on the type of business. This way of dividing the interaction process into several layers on different levels of aggregation gives the marketer, and the researcher, an instrument detailed enough to be used in the analysis of interactions between supplier or service firms and their customers. All different types of elements in the interaction process—goods and services outcomes, service processes, information, social contacts, financial activities, and so on—can be identified and put into correct perspective in the formation of a relationship over time.

The Dialogue Process of Relationship Marketing

According to the total communication concept of the 1980s, in addition to pure marketing communication activities, all contacts that a customer has with another party include a communicative element. Goods, service processes, administrative routines, invoicing, and the like communicate something about the solution and the firm offering this particular solution. However, in this context I follow the view of the integrated marketing communications concept of the 1990s regarding what is part of the communication process—that is, only communicative activities that are more or less purely marketing communication, such as traditional advertising, direct response, public relations, and also sales activities (see the definition of integrated marketing communications of the American Association of Advertising Agencies' Integrated Marketing Communications Committee, as quoted in Reitman, 1994; see also Frischman, 1994). Other than communications elements are included only if they become transparent and merge with the communications elements, as distribution and communication become the same in the case of direct-response marketing (Stewart, 1996; Stewart, Frazier, & Martin, 1996).

The characteristic aspect of marketing communication in a relationship marketing context is an attempt to create a two-way or sometimes even multiway communication process. Not all activities are directly two-way communication, but all communication efforts should lead to a response of some sort that maintains and enhances the relationship. One effort, such as a sales meeting, direct-mail letter, or information package, should be integrated into a planned ongoing process. Therefore, this communication support to relationship marketing is called a dialogue process. This process includes a variety of elements that, for example, can be divided into sales activities, mass communication activities, direct communication (other than sales efforts where a direct response is sought), and public relations (adapted from Grönroos & Rubinstein, 1986). Any other number or type of categories could of course also be used, and the suggested groups naturally include a number of subgroups. Mass communication includes traditional advertising, brochures, sales letters for which no immediate response is sought, and other similar activities, whereas direct communication includes personally addressed letters including offers, information, recognition of interactions that have taken place, and requests for data about the customer. Here a more direct response is sought in the form of feedback from previous interactions, requests for more information or an offer, data about the customer, purely social responses, and the like.

In Figure 4.2 the dialogue process is illustrated as a circle that parallels the interaction process, which includes a number of episodes consisting of individual acts. For the sake of illustration, various types of communication efforts are depicted throughout the ongoing dialogue process. As the figure shows, the dialogue process starts before the interaction process. This is, of course, the stage in which the relationship is established. From the point where the two processes go together, the relationship is maintained and further enhanced. At some point the relationship may be broken or terminated. The dialogue and interaction processes indeed parallel each other, which means that they should support and not counteract each other. The two-way arrows between the two circles in the figure indicate this. An activity in the dialogue process, a sales meeting or a personally addressed letter, creates an expectation, and the interaction process must follow up on this expectation. If, for example, only the dialogue process is considered part of relationship marketing, negatively perceived acts or episodes in the interactions process easily destroy the initially good impression of a communication effort, and no relationship building takes place.

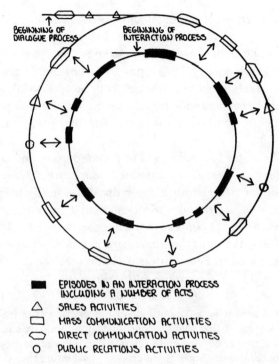

Figure 4.2. The Interaction and Dialogue Processes of Relationship Marketing

In conclusion, just planning and managing marketing communication, even as a dialogue process, is not relationship marketing, although the communication efforts may look relational, such as personally addressed letters. Only the integration of the dialogue and the interaction processes into one strategy that is systematically implemented creates relationship marketing.

The Value Process of Relationship Marketing

Clearly, relationship marketing takes more effort than transaction marketing. Therefore, a relationship marketing strategy must create more value for the customer or for some other party, such as a retailer, than the value of the mere transactions of goods or services in single episodes. The customer has to perceive and appreciate this value that is created in the ongoing relationship. Because a relationship is a process over time, value for customers is also emerging in a process over time. I refer to this as a *value process*. If relationship marketing is to be successful and accepted as meaningful by the customer, there must be such a value process paralleling the dialogue and interaction processes that is appreciated by the customer.

Traditionally, *value* has been used in the marketing and consumer behavior literature as "the value of customers for a firm." Only to some extent has "value for the customer" been discussed in the literature (e.g., Peter & Olson, 1993; Zeithaml, 1988), and then it has more or less been in a transaction marketing context. For example, Zeithaml (1988) defines customer perceived value as the consumer's overall assessment of the utility of a product based on a perception of what is received and what is given. However, as Ravald and Grönroos (1996) note:

> The relational aspect as a constituent of the offering is not taken into account. . . . We suggest that the relationship itself might have a major effect on the total value perceived. In a close relationship the customer probably shifts the focus from evaluating separate offerings to evaluating the relationship as a whole.
>
> The core of the business, i.e. what the company is producing, is of course fundamental, but it may not be the ultimate reason for purchasing from a given supplier. (p. 23; see also Lapierre, 1997)

One can also imagine that even if the solution in terms of goods and services is not the best possible, the parties involved may still find an agreement if they consider the relationship valuable enough. "Value is considered to be an important constituent of relationship marketing and the ability of a company to provide superior value to its customers is regarded as one of the most successful strategies for the 1990s. This ability has become a means of differentiation and a key to the riddle of how to find a sustainable competitive advantage" (Ravald & Grönroos, 1996, p. 19; see also Heskett, Jones, Loveman, Sasser, & Schlesinger, 1994; Nilson, 1992; Treacy & Wiersema, 1993).

If transactions are the foundation for marketing, the *value* for customers is more or less totally embedded in the exchange of a product (a physical good or a service) for money in an episode. The perceived sacrifice equals the price paid for the product. However, if relationships are the base of marketing, the role of the product becomes blurred. In the case of industrial robots, to take an example from business relationships, delivery, customer training, maintenance and spare part service, information and documentation about the use of a robot, claims handling and perhaps joint development of the final robots, and a number of other activities are necessary additions to the core solution—the robot—if the customer is to be satisfied with the purchase. It is easy to see how the value of the core of the offering becomes highly questionable if the additional services are missing or not good enough. The role of the core product in the value perception of customers is indeed very much blurred in a case like this. Without the value-adding additional services, it is highly questionable whether the core product, in this case the industrial robot, has any value at all. Similar examples can easily be found in consumer and industrial services and even in consumer goods.

In a relationship context the offering includes both a *core product* and *additional services* of various kinds (as demonstrated by the example of the industrial robot). The sacrifice includes a price and also additional costs for the customer that result from the fact of being in a relationship with another party. In a relationship context such additional sacrifice can be called *relationship costs* (Grönroos, 1997). Such costs follow from the decision to go into a relationship with a supplier or service firm. Relationship costs may increase if the customer, for example, has to keep larger inventories than necessary because of the delivery policy of the supplier or suffer from higher standstill costs than expected because of delayed repair and maintenance service.

Another way of looking at value for customers is to distinguish between the core value of an offering and the added value of additional elements in the relationship. Hence *customer perceived value* in a relationship context can be described with the following two equations:

[1]
$$\text{Customer Perceived Value (CPV)} = \frac{\text{Core Solution} + \text{Additional Services}}{\text{Price} + \text{Relationship Costs}}$$

[2] $\text{Customer Perceived Value (CPV)} = \text{Core Value} \pm \text{Added Value}$

In a relationship, customer perceived value is developing and perceived over time. In Equation 1, the price has a short-term notion; in principle it is paid upon delivery of the core product. However, relationship costs occur over time as the relationship develops, the usefulness of the core solution is perceived, and the additional services are experienced in sequences of episodes and single acts. In Equation 2, a long-term notion is also present. The added-value component is experienced over time as the relationship develops. However, here it is important to observe the double signs. Often added value is treated as if something is always indeed added to a core value. This is clearly not the case, because the added value can also be negative. For example, a good core value of a machine can be decreased or even destroyed by untimely deliveries, delayed service, lack of necessary information, bad management of complaint handling, unclear or erroneous invoices, or the like. The additional services do not add a positive value; instead, they subtract from the basic core value—that is, they provide a *negative added value* or *value destruction*.

In situations with negative added value, creating added value for customers does not require the addition of new services to the offering. Instead, the firm must improve existing services in the relationship, such as deliveries, service and maintenance, and invoicing, in order to reduce or altogether eliminate the negative added value—or, rather, value destruction of these services. Probably this is a faster and more effective way of creating added value in most relationships than would be the addition of new services. When appropriate, new services can of course be included in the offering. However, firms should always remember that the value-enhancing effect of new services is counteracted and sometimes even offset by the value destruction of existing services that the customer perceives in a negative way.

The core solutions and additional services provided in the sequences of episodes in the interaction process should create a perceived value for the customer on an ongoing basis. The core value should not be counteracted by the negative added value of badly handled or untimely services. Simultaneously, the communication activities in the dialogue process should support this value process and not counteract or destroy it.

In conclusion, as is illustrated in Figure 4.3, a successful relationship marketing strategy requires that all three processes discussed above be taken into account in relationship marketing planning. The *interaction process* is the core of relationship marketing, the *dialogue process* is the communications aspect of relationship marketing, and the *value process*

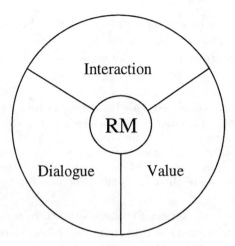

Figure 4.3. The Triplet of Relationship Marketing

is the outcome of relationship marketing. If the customer value process is not carefully analyzed, wrong or inadequate actions may easily be taken in the interaction process. If the dialogue process is not integrated with the interaction process, the value process may easily take a negative turn, because customers may get conflicting signals and promises may not be fulfilled. Interaction, dialogue, and value indeed form a triplet. If any one of them is not analyzed and planned carefully, the implementation of relationship marketing may suffer.

Future Research Agenda

Relationship marketing is a new area in marketing research. Although relationship aspects of marketing have been studied within the Nordic school approach for about 20 years, first within the context of services marketing and later in a more general context, the area is still new, and many research opportunities present themselves. In this final section, I point out some areas for future research.

Customer interest in relationship marketing. In the literature, relationship marketing is offered as a solution for all customers in all situations where such an approach is suitable. This is probably not at all the case.

Some customers may be willing to accept relational contact with a firm, whereas others may want to be in purely transactional contact. Moreover, a person may be interested in a relationship in one situation and not interested in another.

> Thus, in a given marketing situation the consumer (or user in a business-to-business relationship) is either in a *relational mode* or in a *transactional mode*. Furthermore, consumers in a relational mode can be either in an *active* or *passive* relational mode. . . . Consumers or users in an active mode seek contact, whereas consumers in a passive mode are satisfied with the understanding that if needed the firm will be there for them. (Grönroos, 1997, p. 409)

There have been some suggestions in the literature as to why customers choose to enter a relational mode and react favorably to a relationship marketing approach (e.g., Bagozzi, 1995; Sheth & Parvatiyar, 1995), but so far there has been almost no empirical research in this area. Specific research questions to be explored include the following: Why do customers choose to be in active or passive relational modes? What makes a customer move from a passive to an active mode? What types of core solutions (consumer goods or consumer services, goods and services to organizational users, and so on) tend to require a relationship marketing approach more then others? What are the exogenous conditions that trigger the choice of a passive or active relational mode? What types of activities in the interaction and dialogue processes, respectively, are suitable for various types of core solutions, markets, relational modes, and individual customers?

Internal marketing. The need for internal marketing has been recognized in the services marketing literature since the 1970s (see Grönroos, 1978). In interactions with customers, a large number of employees who do not belong to marketing departments have profound impacts on the quality perceptions and future purchasing behaviors of consumers and users. Turning these employees into true *part-time marketers* (Gummesson, 1991) is a demanding task.[2] Internal marketing is as important in relationship marketing as in services marketing. If the part-time marketers are not capable of and prepared to take their role in marketing, the interaction process will fail and the value process will be hurt. Regardless of how good the dialogue process is, marketing will be less successful, perhaps will fail altogether. However, internal marketing has been vastly neglected in academic research, partly because of its multidisciplinary nature (see Cahill, 1996; George, 1990). Cross-disciplinary research including marketing and human resource management would seem appropriate. Specific research questions would include these: What type of corporate culture nurtures a motivation among employees for relationship marketing? What types of internal activities, including training, communication, rewarding, and management guidance and support, make employees committed to relationship marketing? What is the role of top management in internal marketing? What type of external marketing communication has a positive internal effect on employees?

Organizing marketing. As the normal way of organizing marketing, traditional marketing departments may not be the best solution in relationship marketing. This area, too, has been neglected in marketing research. From the area of services marketing, one early study indicates that traditional marketing departments easily may be a hindrance to successful marketing in service firms (Grönroos, 1983; see also Piercy, 1985). The reasons for this are partly real and partly psychological. If marketing is concentrated within a marketing department only, the part-time marketers are not managed from a customer perspective. Moreover, a dominating marketing department becomes a psychological problem, because it signals to the rest of the organization that "marketing" is the same as the marketing department. Incidentally, this is also the way marketing is treated in most standard textbooks. The term *marketing department* is often used interchangeably with *marketing function.* However, if a substantial part of the marketing impact is a result of activities outside the marketing department, new organizational innovations are needed to support successful relationship marketing. Some specific research questions include the following: What type of organizational structures support the internal processes needed to implement the interaction process successfully and integrate it with the dialogue process? What is the role of marketing and sales departments in relationship marketing? How can and should customers be integrated into the organization?

Marketing planning. Marketing planning is traditionally considered the task of the marketing department. However, if a large number of vital marketing activities take place outside this department and are the responsibility of other departments, traditional marketing planning is not enough anymore. Relationship marketing requires new planning procedures. Some specific research questions: What is the relationship between corporate planning and the planning of relationship marketing? How is a customer focus included in planning routines throughout the organization? What is the role of top management in the planning of relationship marketing?

Pricing. Traditional pricing strategies and models are based on a transaction marketing approach. Prices are set on goods and services that are exchanged in transactions. However, in an ongoing relationship price is only part of the customer's total sacrifice. The price paid in the moment of exchange can be high or low; what should count for the customer is the total sacrifice over time—that is, price and relationship costs. A lower price can be offset by higher relationship costs over time, and a higher price can be well compensated by lower relationship costs. Relationship pricing is an area where much research is needed. Specific research questions to be explored include the following: What is the relationship between price and relationship costs in various situations? How should the impact of relationship costs be calculated and included in relationship pricing? What does relationship pricing require of the accounting systems of firms?

Relationship buying. Implementing a relationship marketing strategy is difficult, but buying solutions based on a relationship approach is equally difficult. It requires a long-term cost notion, where the price as well as additional costs over the expected lifetime of the solution have to be calculated and taken into account, for example, as a net present value of lifetime use of the solution. Today there is a lack of research on relationship buying. Some suggested questions for research include these: How does one incorporate price and additional lifetime costs of a solution into one total cost measure for purchasing decisions? What changes in the purchasing routines are required in order to facilitate relationship buying? How can buyers be motivated to engage in relationship buying?

Notes

1. Holmlund (1996) uses the term *action,* but here I use the word *act,* as originally suggested by Liljander and Strandvik (1995), to describe the smallest unit of analysis in an interaction.

2. Part-time marketers are people who are not part of a marketing (or sales) department, whose main task is something other than a marketing-related one and who normally are not trained in marketing skills but who, when performing their tasks, directly or indirectly influence customer satisfaction and the future purchasing behavior of customers (Gummesson, 1991).

References

Bagozzi, R. P. (1995). Reflections on relationship marketing in consumer markets. *Journal of the Academy of Marketing Science, 23*, 272-277.

Berry, L. L. (1983). Relationship marketing. In L. L. Berry, G. L. Shostack, & G. D. Upah (Eds.), *Emerging perspectives on service marketing* (pp. 25-38). Chicago: American Marketing Association.

Berry, L. L., & Parasuraman, A. (1993). Building a new academic field: The case of services marketing. *Journal of Retailing, 69*(1), 13-60.

Bitner, M. J. (1995). Building service relationships: It's all about promises. *Journal of the Academy of Marketing Science, 23*, 246-251.

Blomqvist, R., Dahl, J., & Haeger, T. (1993). *Relationsmarknadsföring. Strategi och metod för servicekonkurrens* [Relationship marketing: Strategy and methods for service competition]. Göteborg, Sweden: IHM Förlag.

Brodie, R. J., Coviello, N. E., Brookes, R. W., & Litle, V. (1997). Towards a paradigm shift in marketing? An examination of current marketing practices. *Journal of Marketing Management, 13*, 383-406.

Cahill, D. J. (1996). *Internal marketing: Your next stage of growth.* New York: Haworth.

Christopher, M., Payne, A., & Ballantyne, D. (1991). *Relationship marketing: Bringing quality, customer service and marketing together.* Oxford: Butterworth-Heinemann.

Frischman, D. E. (1994). A voice of reality. In C. Faure & L. Klein (Eds.), *Marketing communications strategies today and tomorrow: Integration, allocation, and interactive technologies* (pp. 35-36). Cambridge, MA: Marketing Science Institute.

George, W. R. (1990). Internal marketing and organizational behavior: A partnership in developing customer-conscious employees at every level. *Journal of Business Research, 20*(1), 63-70.

Grönroos, C. (1978). A service-oriented approach to the marketing of services. *European Journal of Marketing, 12*, 588-601.

Grönroos, C. (1980, April). Designing a long range marketing strategy for services. *Long Range Planning, 13*, 36-42.

Grönroos, C. (1983). *Strategic management and marketing in the service sector.* Cambridge, MA: Marketing Science Institute.

Grönroos, C. (1989). Defining marketing: A market-oriented approach. *European Journal of Marketing, 23*, 52-60.

Grönroos, C. (1996). Relationship marketing logic. *Asia-Australia Marketing Journal, 4*(1), 1-12.

Grönroos, C. (1997). Value-driven relational marketing: From products to resources and competencies. *Journal of Marketing Management, 13*, 407-420.

Grönroos, C. (in press). Relationship marketing: Challenges for the organization. *Journal of Business Research.*

Grönroos, C., & Gummesson, E. (1985). The Nordic school of service marketing. In C. Grönroos & E. Gummesson (Eds.), *Service marketing: A Nordic school perspective* (Research rep., pp. 6-11). Stockholm: Stockholm University.

Grönroos, C., & Rubinstein, D. (1986). *Totalkommunikation. Analys och planering av företags marknadskommunikation* [Total communication: Analysis and planning of the marketing communication of firms]. Stockholm: Liber and Marketing Technique Center.

Gummesson, E. (1977). *Marknadsföring och inköp av konsulttjänster* [Marketing and purchasing of professional services]. Stockholm: Marketing Technique Center/ Akademilitteratur.

Gummesson, E. (1983). *A new concept of marketing.* Paper presented at the annual European Marketing Academy Conference, Institute d'Etudes Commerciales de Grenoble, France.

Gummesson, E. (1987). The new marketing: Developing long-term interactive relationships. *Long Range Planning, 20*(4), 10-20.

Gummesson, E. (1991). Marketing-orientation revisited: The crucial role of the part-time marketer. *European Journal of Marketing, 25*(2), 60-74.

Gummesson, E. (1995). *Relationsmarknadsföring. Från 4P till 30R* [Relationship marketing: From 4P to 30R]. Malmö, Sweden: Liber-Hermods.

Gummesson, E. (1996). Relationship marketing and imaginary organizations: A synthesis. *European Journal of Marketing, 30*(2), 31-44.

Håkansson, H. (Ed.). (1982). *International marketing and purchasing of industrial goods: An interaction approach.* New York: John Wiley.

Håkansson, H., & Snehota, I. (1995). *Developing relationships in business networks.* London: Routledge.

Heskett, J. L., Jones, T. O., Loveman, G. W., Sasser, W. E., & Schlesinger, L. A. (1994). Putting the service-profit chain to work. *Harvard Business Review, 72*(1), 164-174.

Holmlund, M. (1996). *A theoretical framework of perceived quality in business relationships* (Research rep.). Helsinki, Finland: Swedish School of Economics and Business Administration.

Hunt, S. D., & Morgan, R. M. (1994). Relationship marketing in the era of network competition. *Marketing Management, 3*(1), 19-28.

Lapierre, J. (1997). *Development of measures to assess customer value in a business-to-business context* (Rep. No. EPM/RT 97/20). Montreal: École Polytechnique Montréal.

Lehtinen, J. R. (1984). *Asiakasohjautuva palveluyritys* [Customer-oriented service firm]. Espoo, Finland: Weilin+Göös

Levitt, T. (1983). After the sale is over. *Harvard Business Review, 62*(1), 87-93.

Liljander, V. (1994). Introducing deserved service and equity into service quality models. In M. Kleinaltenkamp (Ed.), *Dienstleistungsmarketing—Konzeptionen und Anwendungen* (pp. 1-30). Berlin: Gabler Edition Wissenschaft.

Liljander, V., & Strandvik, T. (1995). The nature of customer relationships in services. In D. Bowen, S. W. Brown, & T. A. Swartz (Eds.), *Advances in services marketing and management* (Vol. 4, pp. 141-167). Greenwich, CT: JAI.

Mattsson, L.-G. (1997). "Relationship marketing" and the "markets-as-networks approach": A comparison analysis of two evolving streams of research. *Journal of Marketing Management, 13,* 447-461.

Monroe, K. B. (1991). *Pricing: Making profitable decisions.* New York: McGraw-Hill.

Möller, K., & Wilson, D. (1995). Business relationships: An interaction perspective. In K. Möller & D. Wilson (Eds.), *Business marketing: An interaction and network perspective* (pp. 23-52). Boston: Kluwer Academic.

Nilson, T. H. (1992). *Value-added marketing: Marketing for superior results.* London: McGraw-Hill.

Peter, J. P., & Olson, J. C. (1993). *Consumer behavior and marketing strategy* (3rd ed.). Homewood, IL: Richard D. Irwin.

Piercy, N. (1985). *Marketing organisation: An analysis of information processing, power and politics.* London: George Allen & Unwin.

Ravald, A., & Grönroos, C. (1996). The value concept and relationship marketing. *European Journal of Marketing, 30*(2), 19-30.

Reichheld, F. F. (1993). Loyalty-based management. *Harvard Business Review, 71*(4), 64-73.

Reichheld, F. F., & Sasser, W. E., Jr. (1990). Zero defections: Quality comes to services. *Harvard Business Review, 69*(1), 105-111.

Reitman, J. (1994). Integrated marketing: Fantasy or the future? In C. Faure & L. Klein (Eds.), *Marketing communications strategies today and tomorrow: Integration, allocation, and interactive technologies* (Rep. No. 94-109, pp. 30-32). Cambridge, MA: Marketing Science Institute.

Schultz, D. E. (1996). The inevitability of integrated communications. *Journal of Business Research, 37*(3), 139-146.

Schultz, D. E., Tannenbaum, S. I., & Lauterborn, R. F. (1992). *Integrated marketing communications.* Lincolnwood, IL: NTC Business Books.

Sheth, J. N., & Parvatiyar, A. (Eds.). (1994). *Relationship marketing: Theory, methods and applications.* Atlanta, GA: Emory University, Center for Relationship Marketing.

Sheth, J. N., & Parvatiyar, A. (1995). Relationship marketing in consumer markets: Antecedents and consequences. *Journal of the Academy of Marketing Science, 23,* 255-271.

Stauss, B., & Weinlich, B. (1995). *Process-oriented measurement of service quality by applying the sequential prevention technique.* Presentation made at the Fifth Workshop on Quality Management in Services, EIASM, Tilburg, Netherlands.

Stewart, D. W. (1996). Market-back approach to the design of integrated communications programs: A change in paradigm and a focus on determinants of success. *Journal of Business Research, 37*(3), 147-154.

Stewart, D. W., Frazier, G., & Martin, I. (1996). Integrated channel management: Merging the communications and distributions functions of the firm. In E. Thorson & J. Moore (Eds.), *Integrated marketing and consumer psychology.* Hillsdale, NJ: Lawrence Erlbaum.

Storbacka, K. (1994). *The nature of customer relationship profitability: Analyses of relationships and customer bases in retail banking.* Helsinki, Finland: Swedish School of Economics and Business Administration.

Strandvik, T., & Storbacka, K. (1996). *Managing relationship quality.* Paper presented at the QUIS 5 Quality in Services Conference, University of Karlstad, Sweden.

Treacy, M., & Wiersema, F. (1993). Customer intimacy and other value disciplines. *Harvard Business Review, 71*(3), 84-93.

Vavra, T. G. (1994). The database marketing imperative. *Marketing Management, 3*(1), 47-57.

Webster, F. E., Jr. (1994). Executing the new marketing concept. *Marketing Management, 3*(1), 9-18.

Zeithaml, V. A. (1988). Consumer perceptions of price, quality and value: A means-end model and a synthesis of evidence. *Journal of Marketing, 52*(3), 2-22.

5

The Evolution of Relationship Marketing

JAGDISH N. SHETH
ATUL PARVATIYAR

Although marketing practices can be traced back as far as 7000 B.C. (Carratu, 1987), marketing thought as a distinct discipline was born out of economics around the beginning of the 20th century. As the discipline gained momentum and developed through the first three-quarters of the century, the primary focus was on transactions and exchanges. However, the development of marketing as a field of study and practice is undergoing a reconceptualization in its orientation from transactions to relationships (Kotler, 1990; Webster, 1992). The emphasis on relationships as opposed to transaction-based exchanges is very likely to redefine the domain of marketing (Sheth, Gardner, & Garrett, 1988). Indeed, the emergence of a relationship marketing school of thought is imminent given the growing interest of marketing scholars in the relational paradigm.

In this chapter, we observe that the paradigm shift from transactions to relationships is associated with the return of direct marketing in both

---

NOTE: This chapter is reprinted from *International Business Review,* vol. 4, Jagdish N. Sheth and Atul Parvatiyar, "The Evolution of Relationship Marketing," pp. 397-418, Copyright 1995, with permission from Elsevier Science.

business-to-business and business-to-consumer markets. As in the preindustrial era (characterized by direct-marketing practices of agricultural
and artifact producers) once again direct marketing, albeit in a different
form, is becoming popular, and consequently so is the relationship orientation of marketers. When producers and consumers deal directly with
each other, there is a potential for emotional bonding that transcends economic exchange. The parties can understand and appreciate each other's
needs and constraints better, are more inclined to cooperate with one another, and, thus, become more relationship oriented. This is in contrast to
the exchange orientation of the middlemen (sellers and buyers). To the
middlemen, especially the wholesalers, the economics of transactions are
more important; therefore, they are less emotionally attached to products. Indeed, many middlemen do not physically see, feel, or touch products; they simply act as agents and take title to the goods for financing and
risk sharing.

The separation of the producers from the users was a natural outgrowth
of the industrial era. On the one hand, mass production forced producers
to sell through middlemen, and on the other, industrial organizations, due
to specialization of corporate functions, created specialist purchasing departments and buyer professionals, thus separating the users from the
producers. However, with today's technological advancements that permit producers to interact directly with large numbers of users (for example, Levi's making custom products directly for the users), and because of
a variety of organizational development processes, such as empowerment
and total quality programs, direct interface between producers and users
has returned in both consumer and industrial markets, leading to a
greater relational orientation among marketers. Academic researchers
are reflecting these trends in marketing practice and searching for a new
paradigm of the discipline that can better describe and explain it.

As with each new shift in the focus of marketing, there are advocates
and critics of the *relationship focus* in marketing. However, in the same
way Kotler (1972, p. 46) has observed about other shifts in marketing, we
believe that the emergence of a relationship focus will provide a "re-
freshed and expanded self-concept" to marketing. Our optimism stems
from at least four observations:

1. Relationship marketing has caught the fancy of scholars in many parts of the
    world, including North America, Europe, Australia, and Asia, as is evident

from the participation in some of the recent conferences held on the subject (see Sheth & Parvatiyar, 1994).

2. The scope of relationship marketing is wide enough to cover the entire spectrum of marketing's subdisciplines, including channels, business-to-business marketing, services marketing, marketing research, customer behavior, marketing communication, marketing strategy, international marketing, and direct marketing.

3. Like other sciences, marketing is an evolving discipline and has developed a system for extending, revising, and updating its fundamental knowledge (Bass, 1993).

4. Scholars who at one time were leading proponents of the exchange paradigm, such as Bagozzi (1974), Kotler (1972), and Hunt (1983), are now intrigued by the relational aspects of marketing (Bagozzi, 1994; Kotler, 1994; Morgan & Hunt, 1994).

In the context of these developments, our purposes in this chapter are to trace the evolution of relationship marketing and to identify its antecedents. We plan to demonstrate that although the relationship focus in the postindustrial era is a clear paradigm shift from the exchange focus of the industrial era, it is really a rebirth of marketing practices of the preindustrial age, when the producers and users were also sellers and buyers and engaged in market behaviors that reduced the uncertainty of future supply and demand, assurances that could not be otherwise guaranteed due to the unpredictability of weather, raw materials, and customers' buying power. Our approach mirrors the activities recommended by Savitt (1980) as the appropriate methodology for conducting historical research.

Axioms and Purpose of Relationship Marketing

Relationship marketing attempts to involve and integrate customers, suppliers, and other infrastructural partners into a firm's developmental and marketing activities (McKenna, 1991; Shani & Chalasani, 1991). Such involvement results in close interactive relationships with suppliers, customers, or other value-chain partners of the firm. Interactive relationships between marketing actors are inherent compared with the arm's-length relationships implied under the transactional orientation (Parvatiyar, Sheth, & Whittington, 1992). An integrative relationship assumes overlap in the plans and processes of the interacting parties and suggests close economic,

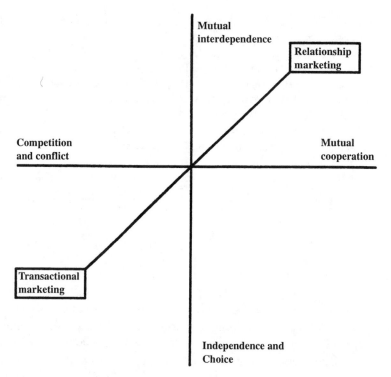

Figure 5.1. Axioms of Transactional Marketing and Relationship Marketing

emotional, and structural bonds among them. It reflects interdependence rather than independence of choice among the parties, and it emphasizes cooperation rather than competition and consequent conflict among the marketing actors. Thus development of relationship marketing points to a significant shift in the axioms of marketing: *competition and conflict* to *mutual cooperation* and *choice independence* to *mutual interdependence,* as illustrated in Figure 5.1.

One axiom of transactional marketing is the belief that competition and self-interest are the drivers of value creation. Through competition, buyers can be offered a choice, and this choice of suppliers motivates marketers to create higher-value offerings in their own self-interest. This axiom of competition is now challenged by the proponents of relationship marketing, who believe that mutual cooperation, as opposed to competition and conflict, leads to higher value creation (Morgan & Hunt, 1994). In fact, some social psychologists have gone so far as to suggest that competition is inherently destructive and mutual cooperation inherently more productive (Kohn, 1986).

The second axiom of transactional marketing is the belief that independence of choice among marketing actors creates a more efficient system for creating and distributing marketing value. Maintaining an "arm's-length relationship" is considered vital for marketing efficiency. Industrial organizations and government policy makers believe that independence of marketing actors provides each actor the freedom to choose his or her transactional partners on the basis of preserving his or her own self-interests at each decision point. This results in the efficiency of lowest-cost purchases through bargaining and bidding. However, this belief has also been challenged in economics (Williamson, 1975). It has been argued that every transaction involves transaction costs in search, negotiation, and other associated activities, which add to, rather than reduce, the cost and thus lead to inefficiencies instead of efficiencies for the firms engaged in exchange transactions. Relationship marketers, therefore, believe that interdependencies reduce transaction costs and generate higher quality while keeping governance costs lower than does exchange marketing (Heide & John, 1992; Williamson, 1985). In short, better quality at a lower cost is achieved through interdependence and partnering among the value-chain actors.

The purpose of relationship marketing, therefore, is to enhance marketing productivity by achieving efficiency and effectiveness (Sheth & Sisodia, 1995). Several relationship marketing practices can help achieve efficiency, such as customer retention, efficient consumer response, and the sharing of resources between marketing partners. Each of these activities has the potential to reduce operating costs of the marketer. Similarly, greater marketing effectiveness can be achieved because it attempts to involve customers in the early stages of marketing program development, facilitating the future marketing efforts of the company. Also, through individualized marketing and adoption of mass customization processes, relationship marketers can better address the needs of each selected customer, making marketing more effective.

To what extent is the above-described purpose of relationship marketing a totally new phenomenon? And haven't these objectives always been important in marketing? If yes, how is relationship marketing different from exchange marketing? We will try to address these questions by first agreeing that marketing has indeed always been concerned with retaining profitable customers and with facilitating future marketing activities.

However, marketing practices that were adopted to achieve these objectives have changed over a period of time. The reasons for this change can be attributed to the prevailing context and conditions of each time period and their influence on marketing thought. In the subsequent sections of this chapter, we examine the causes of marketing practices during the preindustrial, industrial, and postindustrial eras.

Shifts in Marketing's Orientation

As is widely known, the discipline of marketing grew out of economics, and that growth was motivated by lack of interest among economists in the details of market behavior, especially those related to the functions of middlemen (Bartels, 1976; Houston, Gassenheimer, & Maskulka, 1992; Hunt & Goolsby, 1988). It coincided with the growth in the number of middlemen and the importance of distribution during the industrial era. The first courses offered on the subject area of marketing—at the University of Michigan in 1902 and at Ohio State University in 1906—therefore focused on the interrelationships among marketing institutions and among various divisions of the firm in performing the distributive task (see Bartels, 1976, pp. 22-23).

Unlike mainstream economists of the late 19th century, who were preoccupied with public policy and economic effects of market institutions, early marketing thinkers had operational interests (Bartels, 1976). Most of these interests centered on efficiency of marketing channels and the services performed by them in transporting and transforming the goods from the producers to the consumers (Shaw, 1912; Weld, 1916, 1917). The process of marketing was thought to generate additional forms of utility—including time, place, and possession utilities—to the consumer (Macklin, 1924).

Thus marketing as a discipline was organized around the institutional school of thought, and its main concerns centered on the functions performed by wholesalers and retailers as marketing institutions (Sheth et al., 1988). The founders of institutional marketing justified the need for the independent middleman role on the grounds of specialization and division of labor, although both producers and consumers believed that middlemen received higher margins than they deserved. Thus middlemen were perceived as adding no value and creating economic inefficiencies by having location monopolies. Weld (1916) addressed this issue of marketing efficiency:

> When the statement is made that there are too many middlemen, it may mean one of the two things: either that the process of subdivision already described has gone too far so that there are too many successive steps, or there are too many of each class, such as too many country buyers, too many wholesalers, or too many retailers.
>
> The discussion in the preceding paragraphs bears directly on the question as to whether there are too many successive steps, and this is what most people mean when they glibly state that there are too many middlemen. It was pointed out that such subdivision is merely an example of the well-known doctrine of division of labor, and that the economies result from specialization by functions. . . . Those who have really made firsthand studies of the marketing system in an impartial and unprejudiced way realize that on the whole the system of marketing that has developed is efficient, rather than "extremely cumbersome" and wasteful, and that there are very good practical reasons for the form of organization that has developed. It is necessary to realize these fundamental facts before the reader can approach a study of the marketing problem with a sane point of view. (pp. 21-22)

Other authors of that period belonging to the institutional school of marketing thought, such as Butler (1923), Breyer (1934), Converse and Huegy (1940), and Alderson (1954), also espoused the value and functions of middlemen in achieving marketing efficiency. They utilized economic theories to design effective and efficient institutional frameworks. Because of their grounding in economic theory, institutional marketing thinkers viewed the phenomenon of value determination as fundamentally linked to exchange (Duddy & Revzan, 1947). Alderson (1954) elaborated on this institutional thinking by placing the intermediaries at the center of exchange and marketing:

> The justification for the middleman rests on specialized skill in a variety of activities and particularly in various aspects of sorting. The principle of the discrepancy of assortments explains why the successive stages in marketing are so commonly operated as independent agencies. While economists assume for certain purposes that exchange is costless, transactions occupy time and utilize resources in the real world. Intermediary traders are said to create time, place and possession utility because transactions can be carried out at lower cost through them than through direct exchange. In our modern economy, the distribution network makes possible specialized mass production on the one hand and the satisfaction of the differentiated tastes of consumers on the other. (pp. 13-14)

Although the institutional thought of marketing was later modified by the organizational dynamics viewpoint, and marketing thinking was influenced by other social sciences, such as psychology, sociology, and anthropology, exchange remained and still remains the central tenet of marketing (Alderson, 1965; Bagozzi, 1974, 1978, 1979; Houston, 1994; Kotler, 1972). Formal marketing theory developed around the idea of exchange and exchange relationships, and placed considerable emphasis on outcomes, experiences, and actions related to transactions (Bagozzi, 1979).

Recently, several scholars have begun to question the exchange paradigm and its ability to explain the growing phenomena of relational engagement of firms (e.g., Grönroos, 1990; Sheth et al., 1988, Webster, 1992). In the recent past, researchers have tried to develop frameworks for relational engagement of buyers and sellers, often contrasting it with the exchange mode inherent in transactions (Arndt, 1979; Ganesan, 1994; Lyons, Krachenberg, & Henke, 1990).

Business practice exhorts both customer and supplier firms to seek close, collaborative relationships with each other (Copulsky & Wolf, 1990; Goldberg, 1988; Katz, 1988). This change in focus from value exchanges to value-creation relationships has led companies to develop a more integrative approach to marketing, one in which other firms are not always competitors and rivals but are considered partners in providing value to the consumer. This has resulted in the growth of many partnering relationships, such as business alliances and cooperative marketing ventures (Anderson & Narus, 1990; Johnston & Lawrence, 1988). Close, cooperative, and interdependent relationships are seen to be of greater value than purely transaction-based relationships (Kalwani & Narayandas, 1995). However, the relationship orientation of marketing is not an entirely new phenomenon. If we look back to the practice of marketing before the 1900s, we find that relationship orientation to marketing was quite prevalent. Although the history of marketing thought dates back to only the early 1900s (Bartels, 1962), marketing practices existed in history, even to prehistory (Nevett & Nevett, 1987; Pryor, 1977; Walle, 1987). During the agricultural era, the concept of "domesticated markets" and relationship orientation were equally prevalent. In short, the current popularity of relationship marketing is a reincarnation of the marketing practices of the preindustrial era, when producers and consumers interacted directly with each other and developed emotional and structural bonds in their economic market behaviors.

ORIENTATION OF MARKETING PRACTICE
IN THE PREINDUSTRIAL ERA

Preindustrial society was based largely on agricultural economy and the trade of art and artifacts. During the agricultural days, most farmers sold their produce directly in bazaars. Similarly, artisans sold their art and artifacts at these markets. Consumers and producers gathered together face-to-face to trade products. The role of the producer was not separated from that of the trader, and producers functioned as both "manufacturers" and "retailers" of their own products. Also, producers and consumers developed strong relationships that led to the production of customized products made by artisans for individual customers.

Similarly, relational bonding between traders was also quite prevalent, partly because of the need to do business with others one could trust. Thus ongoing trade relationships were a critical element of business practices in the preindustrial era, when ownership was linked with the management of business. Most traders of Africa traded only with selected clans on a regular basis. So important was the element of trust in these clan trade relationships that outsiders could rarely enter into the system (Mwamula-Lubandi, 1992).

The evidence of such clan-based trading exists even today within the clan-oriented network of traders in diamonds and precious metals. For example, the Palanpuri clan (from Gujurat, India) has dominated the trade of diamonds all over the world, along with Orthodox Jews (Rothermund, 1988). Economic and anthropological studies indicate that the Jews were not really outcasts left to perform trading activities; rather, they chose to control trade among themselves as they could trust no others (Sombart, 1951). Such clan-oriented trading developed a network of partnerships as the trading activities extended internationally, with the network partners often coming from the same or related clans with whom ongoing business could be conducted.

Similar evidence of ongoing business relationships can be found in the economic history of the old "silk route" that flourished during precolonial times in China, India, and Afghanistan. Economic history books narrate the vigorous efforts of Chinese silk producers toward market development and promotion of ongoing trade activity along the silk trade route (Feltwell, 1991; Li, 1981). Relationships between customers and suppliers of silk were vital, because Indian weavers and silk craftsmen depended heavily on the supply of Chinese silk to produce garments and artifacts required by local kings and nobles. Such relationships once again reflect the interdependencies among these marketing actors. In order to facilitate future trade, some traders cooperated with weavers and designers in India, providing them with contemporary designs from China. The influence of Chinese designs in the early arts of India bears clear evidence of the cultural exchange in the interest of promoting future trade of Chinese silk.

Retaining customers, influencing repeat purchases, fostering trust, and facilitating future marketing were also concerns of marketers in the preindustrial era. The development of "branding" as a marketing practice can be cited as the best evidence of these concerns. Although the history of branding can be traced back for many centuries, the term was derived from the marking of livestock (Carratu, 1987). Owners of livestock started branding their cattle in order to distinguish theirs from other cattle when they brought them to the market for sale. As this system evolved, family names were used as brands, not only to identify the products, but to give consumers the satisfaction of knowing that products carrying such names had a certain "warranty" of quality because the producers were willing to ascribe their family names to those products (Room, 1987). Branding became a method of providing quality assurance to the buyer, a system to promote repeat purchase, and a method to facilitate future marketing (Crone, 1989).

Even the development of open-air markets or bazaars in the preindustrial period was aimed at facilitating ongoing business and trade. Not only did such marketing venues provide a common arena for buyers and sellers to meet, they aimed at minimizing nomadic trade, whereby traders could swindle their customers and escape any form of retribution. Urban trade privileges and guild regulations (DeVries, 1976) in Europe restricted the "hit and run" sellers from becoming a part of the market system. Those who participated in the market knew and trusted each other (MacKenney, 1987), once again providing continuity and security for the repeat purchaser. Producers established permanent retail shops at the marketplace where they could make and sell their goods on a daily basis (Cundiff, 1988). As a consequence, consumers and producers had direct relationships with each other.

We can see that a relationship orientation in marketing was evident during the preindustrial era. Direct interaction between producers and consumers necessitated cooperation reliance, and trust among marketing actors. Evidence suggests that these relationships sometimes continued for generations, as producers and consumers trusted each other's families and clans (Kingson, Hirshorn, & Cornmarn, 1986).

The relationship orientation in marketing and trade continued into the early years of the Industrial Revolution and the emergence of capitalism. Fullerton (1988) describes some of the efforts adopted by marketers during this period to build and maintain relationships with buyers. Market development efforts were complemented by close cooperation between business and government, which helped develop markets among the nobility, the high clergy, and the growing urban bourgeoisie (Fullerton, 1988). Merchants of this period established fixed-location retail shops in cities throughout Europe. This represented their desire to build and retain customers. Fixed-location retail outlets meant that local buyers could come back time and again, allowing producers and consumers to establish long-term relationships for repeat purchases over the long term. This also meant that both producers and consumers were directly accountable for their actions.

Marketing practices during early industrialization were also highly individualized, relationship oriented, and customized. Many products were manufactured on a custom basis for rich individuals or industrial customers. The design and tailoring of clothes and the creation of jewelry, watches, home furnishings, and other consumer products were customized. Marketers rarely had to consider inventories of finished products, and publishers sold textbooks for which demand already existed (Febvre & Martin, 1958/1976). Such production, based primarily on customer request and demand, did not require marketing activities such as advertising or price competition. Relationships between customers and suppliers were critical because customers depended on manufacturers or traders to make goods available to them as per specifications and expectations. Consumers' making commitments to buy based on the trustworthiness and commitment of the marketers was critical. Reciprocally, producers relied on the creditworthiness of consumers and took the risk of making custom products.

Branding became even more popular during this period, as producers and merchants began to attach their own family names to the products they offered, in great symbolic gestures, assuring their personal commitment to their products' quality. This practice of branding based on family names continued in the early years of the industrial era in Europe (Philips, Fiat, Daimler-Benz) and North America (Eli Lily, Ford, Johnson &

Johnson, Kellogg's, Procter & Gamble), and also in Japan (Toyota, Honda, Matsushita).

ORIENTATION OF MARKETING PRACTICE
IN THE INDUSTRIAL ERA

It was with the advent of mass production and mass consumption that marketers began to adopt a more transactional approach. The emergence of mass production and mass consumption resulted in key consequences. First, people moved away from small subsistence farms to jobs in industrial towns and needed retailers to supply an assortment of the basic conveniences of food, shelter, and clothing (Cundiff, 1988). Second, manufacturers were motivated to produce in mass quantities given the associated economies of scale. On the one hand, economies of scale helped these manufacturers to lower the cost of goods, and hence the prices of the products they sold; on the other hand, mass production increased their need to find markets for their products. Unable to sell their entire stocks of produced goods, producers were confronted with increased inventories of finished products. These market conditions gave rise to aggressive selling and the development of marketing institutions that were willing to bear the risks and costs of inventory ownership and storage. Wholesalers, distributors, and other marketing intermediaries assumed the role of middlemen who, on the one hand, stored the excess production of manufacturers, and, on the other, helped in locating and persuading more buyers to purchase goods and services. So crucial became this function that early marketing thought was developed on the concept of distribution and the creation of time and place utilities. Early marketing thinkers, such as E. D. James, Simon Lifman, and James Hagerty, concentrated on these distributive elements of marketing (Bartels, 1965). This period also gave rise to such modern marketing practices as sales, advertising, and promotion, for the purpose of creating new demand to absorb the oversupply of goods that were being produced. Ralph Butler was among the first scholars to articulate this promotional concept of marketing (Bartels, 1965).

Thus emerged the transactions orientation of marketing, whereby marketers became more concerned with sales and promotion of goods and less with building ongoing relationships. This shift was further accentuated during the Great Depression of 1929, when the oversupply of goods in the

system heightened the pressure on marketers to find and persuade customers to buy their products. Thus the transactions orientation has been
a major influence in marketing thought and academic research throughout the industrial era.

During the height of the industrial period, marketing practices were
aimed at promoting mass consumption. Developed out of the need to support the mass-production machinery, the emphasis was placed on increasing the sales of products. Both personal and impersonal manifestations of
the selling "force" were found increasingly in business, supported by other
activities such as advertising and promotion. Marketing was considered
successful only when it resulted in sales. Measures of marketing performance were linked, as is still the practice today in many companies, to sales
and market share. Some marketers resorted to extreme practices of persuasive selling, including deceptive advertising and false claims.

As competition intensified with excess capacity, sales transactions further increased. Many engaged in aggressive selling and competitive war-
fare. A short-term orientation dominated marketing practices; the desire
to maximize profit in the short run was accentuated as the uncertainties
of the future market appeared perilous, given the rise in competition and
its consequent effect on industry mortality. Some marketers relented and
looked for innovative ways to protect their markets.

Aided by the managerial school of marketing thought, two important
developments occurred in the later period of the industrial era. The first
was the marketer's realization that repeat purchase by customers was
critical, making it necessary to foster brand loyalty. Several marketing
scholars also became interested in repeat-purchase and brand-loyalty behavior as early as World War II (Barton, 1946; Churchill, 1942; Patterson &
McAnally, 1947; Womer, 1944). This research was further advanced in the
buyer behavior theory of Howard and Sheth (1969), who closely examined
repeat-purchase behavior and brand loyalty. In companies' attempts to
achieve brand image, brand differentiation, and effective advertising, certain marketing techniques emerged. Market segmentation and targeting
became important tools for marketing planning. In the face of competition, marketers realized the benefits of focusing on specific groups of customers for whom they could tailor their marketing programs and successfully differentiate themselves from their competitors (Peterson, 1962).
The brand marketing that grew during this period supported the philosophy that the retailer was not the salesman for the manufacturer but rather
the buyer for the consumer. Some marketers read this change and shifted

focus from discrete, one-time sales to ongoing, repeat-purchase possibilities.

The second significant change was the development of administered vertical marketing systems (McCammon, 1965), whereby marketers not only gained control over channels of distribution but developed effective means of blocking competitors from entering into these channels. Vertical marketing systems such as franchising and exclusive distribution rights permitted marketers to extend their representation beyond their own corporate limits to reach final customers (Little, 1970). In many ways, the development of vertical channels was a reversal of the practice of separating producers from the consumers.

These developments represented the reemergence of direct marketing and the philosophy of maintaining long-term relationships with consumers. Yet the orientation of the industrial era was largely transactional, as can be gauged by the standard measures used to evaluate marketing performance: market shares, sales revenues, and profitability per brand, territory, and segments (see PIMS database). Such measures reflect the concern for competition and its consequent effects on profits.

In industrial marketing, the transactional approach was further compounded by the practice of competitive bidding. On one hand, users of industrial products were separated from the purchasing function, given specialist procurement departments in most industrial and business organizations. On the other, competitive bidding processes forced industrial marketers to prepare bid documents for each transaction. Every transaction became important, and it was necessary for firms to outsmart other competitors in such bids so that they could win the customer orders. Although "reciprocity" was practiced to facilitate future sales, the emphasis remained on discrete transactions.

However, not all firms were happy concentrating on discrete transactions. Several industrial buyers and sellers began to develop longer-term contracts for supplies and service, creating ongoing interactive relationships between themselves (Håkansson, 1982). Some of them engaged in long-term partnerships and formed alliances with other companies. For example, partnering types of relationships have existed between Whirlpool and Sears and between McDonald's and Coca-Cola for more than 50 years. Similarly, Mitsubishi Electric and Westinghouse Electric have been engaged in an alliance-type relationship for more than 60 years, as have Philips and Matsushita (Business International Corporation, 1987).

ORIENTATION OF MARKETING PRACTICE
IN THE POSTINDUSTRIAL ERA

The postindustrial era has seen substantial development toward relationship marketing, both in practice and in managerial thinking. Marketers started realizing the need to supplement a transaction orientation
with an orientation that shows more concern for customers. This began
with the advent of complex products, which gave rise to the systems selling approach. This approach emphasizes the integration of the sales of
parts, supplies, and services with the individual capital equipment. Customers liked the idea of systems integration, and sellers were able to sell
augmented products and services to customers. The popularity of system
integration began to extend to consumer packaged goods, as well as to
services (Shapiro & Posner, 1979).

At the same time, some companies started to insist upon new purchasing approaches, such as national contracts and master purchasing
agreements, forcing major vendors to develop key account management
programs (Shapiro & Moriarty, 1980; Shapiro & Wyman, 1981). These
measures forced intimacy and permanence into buyer-seller relationships.
Instead of purchasing a product or service, customers were more interested in buying a relationship with a vendor. The key (or national) account
management program designates account managers and account teams
that assess the customer's needs and then husband the selling company's
resources for the customer's benefit. Still considered a boundary-
spanning sales activity, key account programs reflect higher commitment
of selling organizations toward their major customers. Such programs,
concurrently, led to the foundation of the strategic partnering relationships that have emerged under relationship marketing (Anderson & Narus, 1991; Shapiro, 1988).

The growth of a relationship orientation of marketing in the postindustrial era is the rebirth of direct marketing between producers and consumers. Several environmental and organizational development factors are responsible for this rebirth of direct relationships. At least five
macroenvironmental forces can be identified: (a) rapid technological advancements, especially in information technology; (b) the adoption of total quality programs by companies; (c) the growth of the service economy;
(d) organizational development processes leading to empowerment of

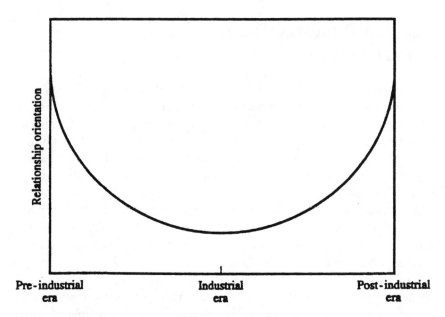

Figure 5.2. Evolution of Relationship Orientation

individuals and teams; and (e) an increase in competitive intensity leading to concern for customer retention. These forces are reducing the reliance of producers, as well as consumers, on middlemen for effecting the consummation and facilitation processes. We briefly discuss below how these forces are encouraging more direct interactions between producers and consumers of goods and services as well as the growth of relationship marketing.

The impact of the technological revolution is changing the nature and activities of marketing institutions. The current development and introduction of sophisticated electronic and computerized communication systems into our society is making it easier for consumers to interact directly with producers. Producers are also becoming more knowledgeable about their consumers by maintaining and accessing, at very low cost, sophisticated databases that capture information related to each interaction with individual consumers. This gives them the means through which they can practice individual marketing. As a result, the functions formerly performed by middlemen are now being undertaken by either consumers or producers. Producers are building systems that allow them to respond quickly with regard to manufacturing, delivery, and customer service, eliminating the need for inventory management, financing, and order processing through middlemen. Also, consumers have less time and thus reduced inclination to go to stores for every purchase. They are willing to undertake some of the responsibilities of direct ordering, personal merchandising, and product-use-related services with little help from the producers.

Hence, given the recent technological strides and consumer attitudes, some functions performed by middlemen may be entirely eliminated. For instance, just-in-time (JIT) inventory systems, made possible by the real-time transportation and communication systems now available, allow producers to eliminate the need for intermediate inventory holding institutions between themselves and consumers or suppliers (Sheth et al., 1988). Other technological systems, such as flexible manufacturing, are being used by some to mass customize their offerings for individual consumers.

Rapid technological developments have also increased the costs of research and development. The window of time in which it is possible to recover R&D costs has also shortened. This has forced companies to work together in joint research projects and joint product development programs. Similarly, the rapid convergence of technologies—in computers and other electronics as well as home appliances—mandates that companies in such industries work on joint projects to leverage their combined resources and share risks. Thus interfirm partnering and alliances are becoming popular.

Another major force driving the adoption of relationship marketing is the total quality movement, which recently revolutionized industry's perspectives regarding quality and cost. Most companies saw the value of offering quality products and services to customers at the lowest possible prices. When companies began to embrace total quality management (TQM) to improve quality and reduce costs, it became necessary to involve suppliers and customers in implementing the program at all levels of the value chain. This required the companies to build close working relationships with customers, suppliers, and other members of the marketing infrastructure. Thus several companies, such as Motorola, IBM, Xerox, Ford, AT&T, and Toyota, formed partnering relationships with suppliers and customers in order to practice TQM. Other programs, such as JIT supply and material requirements planning, also make use of the interdependent relationships between suppliers and customers (Frazier, Spekman, & O'Neal, 1988).

The third force ushering in relationship marketing has been the growth of the service economy, especially in advanced countries. As more and more organizations depend upon revenues from the service sector, relationship marketing becomes prevalent. One reason for this is that services are typically produced and delivered by the same institution; that is, service providers are usually involved in the production and delivery of their services. For instance, in the case of personal and professional services, such as haircutting, maid services, consulting services, accounting services, and legal services, the individual producer of the service is also the service provider. In much the same way, the users of these services are directly engaged in obtaining and using the services, thus minimizing the role of the middleman, if any. In such a situation, a greater emotional bond develops between the service provider and the service user, and thus the need for maintaining and enhancing the relationship. It is therefore evident that relationship marketing is important for scholars and practitioners of services marketing (Berry, 1983; Crosby, Evans, & Cowles, 1990; Crosby & Stephens, 1987).

Certain organizational changes have facilitated the growth of relationship marketing, among which the most significant is the role definition of the members of the organization. Through a variety of changes in organizational processes, companies are now directly involving users of products and services in purchase and acquisition decisions. For a considerable time, these functions were managed by procurement departments as a specialized function, with little or no input from the actual users of the products and services. Thus the separation that existed between the producer and the user due to the existence of user middlemen, acting as gatekeepers, is potentially bridged in many cases. Wherever such changes are being made, direct interactions and cooperative relationships between producers and users develop.

Finally, in the postindustrial period the increase in competitive intensity has forced marketers to be concerned with customer retention. As several studies have indicated, retaining customers is less expensive and perhaps a more sustainable competitive advantage than acquiring new customers. Marketers are realizing that it costs less to retain customers than to compete for new ones (Rosenberg & Czepiel, 1984). On the supply side, it pays more to develop closer relationships with a few suppliers than to develop more vendors (Hayes, Wheelwright, & Clark, 1988; Spekman,

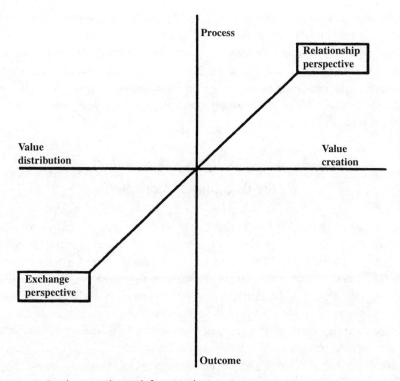

Figure 5.3. The Paradigm Shift in Marketing Orientation

1988). In addition, several marketers are also concerned with keeping customers for life, rather than merely making one-time sales (Cannie & Caplin, 1991).

In summary, the relationship orientation in marketing has staged a comeback. It was only during the peak of industrialization that marketing's orientation shifted toward a transactional approach. With the advent of middlemen and the separation of producers and users, there was a greater transactional orientation. Industrialization led to a reversal in the relationship between supply and demand when, due to mass production efforts, producers created excess supplies of goods and services and were themselves preoccupied with achieving production efficiencies. Thus they needed middlemen to service their customers. The middlemen in turn adopted a transactional approach, as they were more interested in the economic benefits of exchange than in the value of production and/or consumption. Although efficiencies in product distribution were achieved through middlemen, effectiveness was not always accomplished, as is evident from the literature on channel conflict.

Now with a one-to-one connection between the producer and the user, relationship orientation in marketing has returned. Figure 5.3 depicts the changes in the relationship orientation of marketing during the preindustrial, industrial, and postindustrial eras.

Consequences of the Relational Paradigm for the Discipline of Marketing

The advent of the relational paradigm is likely to alter the basic foundations of marketing anchored in exchange theory. Several marketing scholars are questioning the sufficiency of the exchange paradigm to explain emerging relationship marketing practices (Cannon & Sheth, 1994; Christopher, Payne, & Ballantyne, 1991; Grönroos, 1994; O'Neal, 1989). Some of these criticisms are based on the outcome orientation of the exchange paradigm, in which, these scholars argue, concern for quality, customer service, and customer retention is lacking.

Although the exchange paradigm has been very useful in the development of marketing theory, it has outlived its utility. Born out of the transactions focus, the exchange paradigm serves the purpose of explaining *value distribution* among marketing actors. In the industrial era, when only manufacturers created value through their developmental and production activities and middlemen shared the risk of ownership and provided the time and place utility, the exchange paradigm was a useful way to study value distribution among these marketing actors. Consumers derived a surplus and utility from this exchange, but they could not contribute as much in value creation.

However, where consumers are involved in coproduction and have interdependent relationships with producers, the concern for *value creation* is paramount. For example, in home building, buyers become involved in and emotionally attached to the home-building process as they seek to create value for themselves. The nature of the interaction between builder and home buyer is not related to the exchange as much as it is aimed at creating a dream home for the buyer. Although the exchange paradigm may explain the transaction in the sale of an existing home, where value distribution is being undertaken, in the home-building case, and in other situations where consumers are directly involved as coproducers, codesigners, or comarketers, there is a need for an alternative paradigm of marketing.

There are implied assumptions in exchange theory that the seller and the buyer (marketing actors) have well-defined roles, that they independently create values, and that there is a place and time of transaction that can be easily articulated for exchange. However, in the era of relationship marketing, the roles of producers, sellers, buyers, and consumers are blurring. Consumers are increasingly becoming coproducers. Not only is there less need for middlemen in the process, there is less of a boundary between producers and consumers. In many instances, market participants jointly participate in design, development, production, and consummation of goods and services. They do not seek any particular exchange; rather, they seek the creation of a greater market value for both through the relationship. Sometimes these relationships and activities become so enmeshed that it is difficult to separate the marketing actors from one another.

There is also a blurring of time and place boundaries between the producer and the consumer. For example, Procter & Gamble has assigned 20 of its employees to live and work at Wal-Mart's headquarters to improve the speed of delivery and reduce the cost of supplying P&G goods to Wal-Mart's branch stores (Kotler, 1994). It is therefore hard to distinguish the elements as well as the times of occurrence of exchange. In relationship marketing, organizational boundaries are hard to distinguish as companies are more likely to be involved in shared relationships with their marketing partners. Some of these activities relate to joint planning, coproduction, comarketing, cobranding, and so on, where the parties in the relationship bring their resources together to create greater market value. The boundaries of time, place, and transaction are unclear in many relational arrangements. For example, in the world of bits and bytes, where electronic data interchanges are becoming common, payments transfers are not linked to transactions anymore. Payment flows, goods and services flows, and knowledge flows between marketing actors are becoming less anchored to exchange.

Although some authors still label this type of cooperation a form of exchange, calling it "relational exchange" (Dwyer, Schurr, & Oh, 1987; Gundlach & Murphy, 1993; Morgan & Hunt, 1994), the cooperative relationships among marketing actors are not always for the purpose of exchange. As several of these researchers show, the marketing actors cooperate to share resources and engage in joint value creation, such as coproduction, research and development partnering, and comarketing. In these arrangements, exchange, if any, is incidental. The primary activity relates to value creation through joint action by participants in a relational engagement (Heide & John, 1990). The outcome of this engagement is not necessarily an exchange of values; it is instead a process of value creation through cooperative and collaborative effort.

Therefore, an alternative paradigm of marketing is needed, a paradigm that can account for the continuous nature of relationships among marketing actors. It might be better for the continuous development of the discipline to give up the sacred cow of exchange theory in search of some other paradigm. What the nature of this alternative paradigm would be is not clear, but, as many scholars are trying to argue, such a paradigm ought to be based on value creation instead of value distribution and should focus on the processes of relationship engagement and not on the outcomes or consequences of the relationship (Figure 5.3). In other words, we need to explain the conditions that encourage marketing actors to enter relationships, the purposes of engaging in such relationships, the processes of managing such relational engagements, the processes of evaluating the performance of such relational engagements, the processes and conditions of terminating the relationships, and the processes of enhancement of the relationships.

Conclusion

In this chapter we have attempted to trace the evolution of relationship marketing. We have observed that a relational orientation to marketing existed until the early years of industrial development. It was only when mass production led to an oversupply of goods that marketers became transaction oriented. However, this transactional orientation in marketing is giving way to the return of a relationship orientation in marketing. Beginning with interests in repeat purchase and brand loyalty, the number of scholars studying ongoing marketing relationships is growing. This reemergence of relationship marketing has the potential to lead to a new "general theory of marketing" (Sheth et al., 1988), as its fundamental axioms explain marketing practice better than do other theories.

The reemergence of the relational perspective in marketing has been caused primarily by the return of direct producer-to-consumer marketing. This requires a change in the paradigm of marketing theory. The exchange paradigm is insufficient to explain the continuous nature of relationships between marketing actors. It is anchored in value distribution and outcomes of exchange, and hence is insufficient to explain marketing relationships that focus on value creation and in which the process of relationship engagement is equally as important as, if not more important than, the outcomes of the exchange.

References

Alderson, W. (1954). Factors governing the development of marketing channels. In R. Clewett (Ed.), *Marketing channels for manufactured products* (pp. 5-34). Homewood, IL: Richard D. Irwin.

Alderson, W. (1965). *Dynamic marketing behavior: A functionalist theory of marketing.* Homewood, IL: Richard D. Irwin.

Anderson, J. C., & Narus, J. A. (1990). A model of distributor firm and manufacturer firm working partnerships. *Journal of Marketing, 54*(1), 42-58.

Anderson, J. C., & Narus, J. A. (1991). Partnering as a focused market strategy. *California Management Review, 33*(3), 95-113.

Arndt, J. (1979). Toward a concept of domesticated markets. *Journal of Marketing, 43*(4), 69-75.

Bagozzi, R. P. (1974). Marketing as an organized behavioral system of exchange. *Journal of Marketing, 38*(4), 77-81.

Bagozzi, R. P. (1978). Marketing as exchange: A theory of transactions in the marketplace. *American Behavioral Scientist, 21*, 535-536.

Bagozzi, R. P. (1979). Toward a formal theory of marketing exchanges. In O. C. Ferrell, S. W. Brown, & C. W. Lamb, Jr. (Eds.), *Conceptual and theoretical developments in marketing* (pp. 431-447). Chicago: American Marketing Association.

Bagozzi, R. P. (1994). Interactions in small groups: The social relations model. In J. N. Sheth & A. Parvatiyar (Eds.), *Relationship marketing: Theory, methods and applications.* Atlanta, GA: Emory University, Center for Relationship Marketing.

Bartels, R. (1962). *The development of marketing thought.* Homewood, IL: Richard D. Irwin.

Bartels, R. (1965). Development of marketing thought: A brief history. In G. Schwartz (Ed.), *Science in marketing* (pp. 47-69). New York: John Wiley.

Bartels, R. (1976). *The history of marketing thought* (2nd ed.). Columbus, OH: Grid.

Barton, S. G. (1946). The movement of branded goods to the consumer. In A. D. Blankenship (Ed.), *How to conduct consumer and opinion research* (pp. 58-70). New York: Harper & Bros.

Bass, F. M. (1993). The future of research in marketing: Marketing science. *Journal of Marketing Research, 30*, 1-6.

Berry, L. L. (1983). Relationship marketing. In L. L. Berry, G. L. Shostack, & G. D. Upah (Eds.), *Emerging perspectives on service marketing* (pp. 25-38). Chicago: American Marketing Association.

Breyer, R. F. (1934). *The marketing institution*. New York: McGraw-Hill.

Business International Corporation. (1987). *Competitive alliances: How to succeed at cross-regional collaboration*. New York: Author.

Butler, R. S. (1923). *Marketing and merchandising*. New York: Alexander Hamilton Institute.

Cannie, J. K., & Caplin, D. (1991). *Keeping customers for life*. Chicago: American Marketing Association.

Cannon, J. P., & Sheth, J. N. (1994, Summer). Developing a curriculum to enhance teaching of relationship marketing. *Journal of Marketing Education, 16,* 3-14.

Carratu, V. (1987). Commercial counterfeiting. In J. M. Murphy (Ed.), *Branding: A key marketing tool*. London: Macmillan.

Christopher, M., Payne, A., & Ballantyne, D. (1991). *Relationship marketing: Bringing quality, customer service and marketing together.* Oxford: Butterworth-Heinemann.

Churchill, H. L. (1942). How to measure brand loyalty. *Advertising and Selling, 35,* 24.

Converse, P. D., & Huegy, H. (1940). *The elements of marketing*. New York: Prentice Hall.

Copulsky, J. R., & Wolf, M. J. (1990, July-August). Relationship marketing: Positioning for the future. *Journal of Business Strategy, 11,* 16-20.

Crone, P. (1989). *Pre-industrial societies*. Cambridge, MA: Basil Blackwell.

Crosby, L. A., Evans, K. R., & Cowles, D. (1990). Relationship quality in services selling: An interpersonal influence perspective. *Journal of Marketing, 54*(3), 68-81.

Crosby, L. A., & Stephens, N. (1987). Effects of relationship marketing and satisfaction, retention, and prices in the life insurance industry. *Journal of Marketing Research, 24,* 404-411.

Cundiff, E. W. (1988). The evolution of retailing institutions across cultures. In T. Nevett & R. A. Fullerton (Eds.), *Historical perspectives in marketing: Essays in honor of Stanley C. Hollander* (pp. 149-162). Lexington, MA: Lexington.

DeVries, J. (1976). *Economy of Europe in an age of crisis 1600-1700*. Cambridge: Cambridge University Press.

Duddy, E. A., & Revzan, D. A. (1947). *Marketing: An institutional approach*. New York: McGraw-Hill.

Dwyer, F. R., Schurr, P. H., & Oh, S. (1987). Developing buyer-seller relationships. *Journal of Marketing, 51*(2), 11-27.

Febvre, L., & Martin, H. J. (1976). *The coming of the book* (D. Gerard, Trans.). London: NLB. (Original work published 1958)

Feltwell, J. (1991). *The story of silk*. New York: St. Martin's.

Frazier, G. L., Spekman, R. E., & O'Neal, C. R. (1988). Just-in-time exchange relationships in industrial marketing. *Journal of Marketing, 52*(4), 52-67.

Fullerton, R. A. (1988). Modern Western marketing as an historical phenomenon: Theory and illustration. In T. Nevett & R. A. Fullerton (Eds.), *Historical perspectives in marketing: Essays in honor of Stanley C. Hollander* (pp. 71-89). Lexington, MA: Lexington.

Ganesan, S. (1994). Determinants of long-term orientation in buyer-seller relationships. *Journal of Marketing, 58*(2), 1-19.

Goldberg, B. (1988). Relationship marketing. *Direct Marketing, 51*(6), 103-105.

Grönroos, C. (1990). Relationship approach to marketing in service contexts: The marketing and organizational behavior interface. *Journal of Business Research, 20*(1), 3-11.

Grönroos, C. (1994, June). *European perspectives on relationship marketing*. Paper presented at the American Marketing Association's Fourteenth Faculty Consortium on Relationship Marketing, Atlanta, GA.

Gundlach, G. T., & Murphy, P. E. (1993). Ethical and legal foundations of relational marketing exchanges. *Journal of Marketing, 57*(4), 35-46.

Håkansson, H. (Ed.). (1982). *International marketing and purchasing of industrial goods: An interaction approach.* New York: John Wiley.

Hayes, R. H., Wheelwright, S. C., & Clark, K. B. (1988). *Dynamic manufacturing: Creating the learning organization.* New York: Free Press.

Heide, J. B., & John, G. (1990). Alliances in industrial purchasing: The determinants of joint action in buyer-supplier relationships. *Journal of Marketing Research, 27,* 24-36.

Heide, J. B., & John, G. (1992). Do norms matter in marketing relationships? *Journal of Marketing, 56*(2), 32-44.

Houston, F. S. (1994). *Marketing exchange relationships, transactions, and their media.* Westport, CT: Quorum.

Houston, F. S., Gassenheimer, J. B., & Maskulka, J. (1992). *Marketing exchange transactions and relationships.* Westport, CT: Quorum.

Howard, J. A., & Sheth, J. N. (1969). *The theory of buyer behavior.* New York: John Wiley.

Hunt, S. D. (1983). General theories and the fundamental explananda of marketing. *Journal of Marketing, 47*(4), 9-17.

Hunt, S. D., & Goolsby, J. (1988). The rise and fall of the functional approach to marketing: A paradigm displacement perspective. In T. Nevett & R. A. Fullerton (Eds.), *Historical perspectives in marketing: Essays in honor of Stanley C. Hollander.* Lexington, MA: Lexington.

Johnston, R., & Lawrence, P. R. (1988). Beyond vertical integration: The rise of the value-adding partnership. *Harvard Business Review, 66*(4), 94-101.

Kalwani, M. U., & Narayandas, N. (1995). Long-term manufacturer-supplier relationships: Do they pay off for supplier firms? *Journal of Marketing, 59*(1), 1-16.

Katz, M. (1988). Understanding customer relationships: Marketing CIF. *Bank Systems and Equipment, 25*(4), 62-65.

Kingson, E. R., Hirshorn, B. A., & Cornmarn, J. M. (1986). *Ties that bind: The interdependence of generations.* Cabin John, MD: Seven Locks.

Kohn, A. (1986). *No contest: The case against competition.* Boston: Houghton Mifflin.

Kotler, P. (1972). A generic concept of marketing. *Journal of Marketing, 36*(2), 46-54.

Kotler, P. (1990, November). Speech presented at the Trustees Meeting of the Marketing Science Institute, Boston.

Kotler, P. (1994). *Marketing management: Analysis, planning, implementation, and control.* Englewood Cliffs, NJ: Prentice Hall.

Li, L. M. (1981). *China's silk trade: Traditional industry in the modern world 1842-1937.* Cambridge, MA: Harvard University Press.

Little, R. W. (1970). The marketing channel: Who should lead this extra-corporate organization. *Journal of Marketing, 34*(1), 31-38.

Lyons, T. F., Krachenberg, A. R., & Henke, J. W., Jr. (1990). Mixed motive marriages: What's next for buyer-supplier relations? *Sloan Management Review, 31*(3), 29-36.

MacKenney, R. (1987). *Tradesmen and traders: The world of the guilds in Venice and Europe, c.1250-c.1650.* London: Croom Helm.

Macklin, T. (1924). *Efficient marketing for agriculture.* New York: Macmillan.

McCammon, B. (1965). The emergence and growth of contractually integrated channels in the American economy. In P. D. Bennett (Ed.), *Economic growth, competition, and world markets* (pp. 496-515). Chicago: American Marketing Association.

McKenna, R. (1991). *Relationship marketing: Successful strategies for the age of the customer.* Reading, MA: Addison-Wesley.

Morgan, R. M., & Hunt, S. D. (1994). The commitment-trust theory of relationship marketing. *Journal of Marketing, 58*(3), 20-38.

Mwamula-Lubandi, E. D. (1992). *Clan theory in African development studies.* New York: University Press of America.

Nevett, T., & Nevett, L. (1987). The origins of marketing: Evidence from classical and early Hellenistic Greece (500-300 B.C.). In T. Nevett & S. Hollander (Eds.), *Marketing in three eras: Proceedings of the Third Conference on Marketing History* (pp. 13-22). East Lansing: Michigan State University.

O'Neal, C. R. (1989). JIT procurement and relationship marketing. *Industrial Marketing Management, 18,* 55-63.

Parvatiyar, A., Sheth, J. N., & Whittington, F. B. (1992). *Paradigm shift in interfirm marketing relationships: Emerging research issues* (Working Paper No. CRM 92-101). Atlanta, GA: Emory University, Center for Relationship Marketing.

Patterson, D. D., & McAnally, A. J. (1947, October). The family panel: A technique for diagnosing sales ills. *Sales Management, 59,* 134-136.

Peterson, P. G. (1962). Conventional wisdom and the sixties. *Journal of Marketing, 26*(2), 63-67.

Pryor, F. L. (1977). *The origins of the economy.* New York: Academic Press.

Room, A. (1987). History of branding. In J. M. Murphy (Ed.), *Branding: A key marketing tool.* London: Macmillan.

Rosenberg, L. J., & Czepiel, J. A. (1984). A marketing approach to customer retention. *Journal of Consumer Marketing, 1*(2), 45-51.

Rothermund, D. (1988). *An economic history of India.* New York: Croom Helm.

Savitt, R. (1980). Historical research in marketing. *Journal of Marketing, 44*(4), 52-58.

Shani, D., & Chalasani, S. (1992). Exploiting niches using relationship marketing. *Journal of Consumer Marketing, 9*(3), 33-42.

Shapiro, B. P. (1988). *Close encounters of the four kinds: Managing customers in a rapidly changing environment* (Working Paper No. 9-589-015). Boston: Harvard Business School.

Shapiro, B. P., & Moriarty, R. T., Jr. (1980). *National account management.* Cambridge, MA: Marketing Science Institute.

Shapiro, B. P., & Posner, R. S. (1979). Making the major sale. *Harvard Business Review, 57*(4), 68-79.

Shapiro, B. P., & Wyman, J. (1981). New ways to reach your customer. *Harvard Business Review, 59*(6), 103-110.

Shaw, A. (1912). Some problems in market distribution. *Quarterly Journal of Economics, 26,* 706-765.

Sheth, J. N., Gardner, D. M., & Garrett, D. E. (1988). *Marketing theory: Evolution and evaluation.* New York: John Wiley.

Sheth, J. N., & Parvatiyar, A. (Eds.). (1994). *Relationship marketing: Theory, methods and applications.* Atlanta, GA: Emory University, Center for Relationship Marketing.

Sheth, J. N., & Sisodia, R. S. (1995). Improving marketing productivity. In J. Heilbrunn (Ed.), *Encyclopedia of marketing for the year 2000.* Chicago: American Marketing Association/NTC.

Sombart, W. (1951). *The Jews and modern capitalism.* Glencoe, IL: Free Press.

Spekman, R. E. (1988, July-August). Strategic supplier selection: Understanding long-term buyer relationships. *Business Horizons,* pp. 75-81.

Walle, A. (1987). Import wine at a budget price: Marketing strategy and the Punic Wars. In T. Nevett & S. Hollander (Eds.), *Marketing in three eras: Proceedings of the Third Conference on Marketing History.* East Lansing: Michigan State University.

Webster, F. E., Jr. (1992). The changing role of marketing in the corporation. *Journal of Marketing, 56*(4), 1-17.

Weld, L. D. H. (1916). *The marketing of farm products.* New York: Macmillan.

Weld, L. D. H. (1917). Marketing functions and mercantile organizations. *American Economic Review, 7,* 306-318.

Williamson, O. E. (1975). *Markets and hierarchies: Analysis and antitrust implications.* New York: Free Press.

Williamson, O. E. (1985). *The economic institutions of capitalism.* New York: Free Press.

Womer, S. (1944). Some applications of the continuous consumer panel. *Journal of Marketing, 8*(4), 132-136.

PART II

Conceptual and Theoretical
Foundations of Relationship Marketing

6

Relationship Marketing of Services

Growing Interest, Emerging Perspectives

LEONARD L. BERRY

Relationship marketing is a new-old concept. The idea of a business earning customers' favor and loyalty by satisfying their wants and needs was not unknown to the earliest merchants. Grönroos (1994) cites this Middle Eastern proverb from ancient trade: "As a merchant, you'd better have a friend in every town" (p. 18). Yet the blossoming of relationship marketing, the creation of a conceptual framework for understanding its properties and studying its possibilities, was slow to develop. Until recently, marketing's focus was *acquiring* customers. Formally marketing to existing customers to secure their loyalty was neither a top priority of most businesses

NOTE: This chapter is reprinted from Leonard L. Berry, "Relationship Marketing of Services—Growing Interest, Emerging Perspectives," *Journal of the Academy of Marketing Science*, vol. 23, no. 4, pp. 236-245, copyright © 1995 by the Academy of Marketing Science. Reprinted by permission.

nor a research interest of marketing academics. As Schneider wrote in 1980:

> What is surprising is that (1) researchers and businessmen have concentrated far more on how to attract consumers to products and services than on how to retain those customers, (2) there is almost no published research on the retention of service consumers, and (3) consumer evaluation of products or services has rarely been used as a criterion or index of organizational achievements. (p. 54)

The phrase *relationship marketing* appeared in the services marketing literature for the first time in a paper I published in 1983 (Berry, 1983; see also Barnes, 1994; Grönroos, 1994). In that paper, I defined relationship marketing as "attracting, maintaining and—in multi-service organizations—enhancing customer relationships" (p. 25). I stressed that the attraction of new customers should be viewed only as an intermediate step in the marketing process. Solidifying the relationship, transforming indifferent customers into loyal ones, and serving customers as clients also should be considered as marketing. I outlined five strategy elements for practicing relationship marketing: developing a core service around which to build a customer relationship, customizing the relationship to the individual customer, augmenting the core service with extra benefits, pricing services to encourage customer loyalty, and marketing to employees so that they, in turn, will perform well for customers (Berry, 1983).

Although relationship marketing terminology in the services literature can be traced back to 1983, recognition of the need to market formally to existing customers appeared earlier. Ryans and Wittink suggested in 1977 that many service firms pay inadequate attention to encouraging customer loyalty. Levitt emphasized the need for firms marketing intangible products to engage in constant reselling efforts in 1981. George (1977), Grönroos (1981), and I (Berry, 1980, 1981) all wrote about improving the performance of service personnel as a key to retaining customers.

Today, relationship marketing is at the forefront of marketing practice and academic marketing research. The concept of marketing to existing customers to win their continuing patronage and loyalty is becoming well integrated into the various subdisciplines of marketing, as this volume attests. On marketing's back burner for so many years, relationship marketing now sits on the front burner. My purpose in this chapter is to explore the state of relationship marketing in services marketing. I discuss reasons for the growing interest in relationship marketing and emerging themes in the literature. I conclude with a list of future research topics.

Relationship Marketing in Services: In the Growth Phase

Using product life-cycle terminology, relationship marketing in both practice and research is beyond the introduction stage and on a growth curve toward becoming a mature concept. What accounts for the accelerated interest in relationship marketing in services? Four convergent influences have propelled the current focus on relationship marketing: the maturing of services marketing, increased recognition of potential benefits for the firm *and* the customer, and technological advances.

THE MATURING OF SERVICES MARKETING

The implications of marketing a *performance* rather than an object are well understood today. The reality of many services being rendered on an ongoing or periodic basis coupled with the reality of customers forming relationship with people rather than goods paves the way for relationship marketing. Repeated contact between customers and service providers facilitates relationship marketing. Moreover, product intangibility often requires reselling efforts. As Levitt (1981) has noted:

> The most important thing to know about intangible products is that the customers usually don't know what they're getting until they don't get it. Only then do they become aware of what they bargained for; only on dissatisfaction do they dwell. . . . in keeping customers for intangibles, it becomes important regularly to remind and show them what they're getting so that occasional failures fade in relative importance. (p. 100)

The core subject as the services marketing field has developed—service quality—also has stimulated interest in relationship marketing. The object of improving service quality, after all, is to engender customer loyalty. A natural extension of the strong interest in service quality is growing interest in relationship marketing. Effective relationship marketing should help a company capitalize on its investment in service improvement.

BENEFITS TO THE FIRM

The development of services marketing was itself fueled by intensifying intratype and intertype competition in the late 1970s and early 1980s, including the deregulation of banking, airline, trucking, and other service industries (Berry & Parasuraman, 1993). Service industry competition has never been more fierce than it has been in the mid- to late 1990s. AT&T and MCI are continually raiding each other's customer bases, supermarkets are competing with warehouse clubs such as Sam's Club and Price/Costco, discount broker Charles Schwab is attracting millions of investment dollars from full-service brokerages and commercial bank accounts every week, and airlines have implemented lower-cost service strategies (United Express) to try to stem the tide of price leader Southwest Airlines. In the late 1990s, marketing to protect the customer base has become an imperative.

Reichheld and Sasser (1990) have demonstrated across a variety of service industries that profits climb steeply when a company successfully lowers its customer defection rate. Based on an analysis of more than 100 companies in two dozen industries, these researchers found that the firms could improve profits from 25% to 85% by reducing customer defections by just 5%. Not only do loyal customers generate more revenue for more years, the costs to maintain existing customers frequently are lower than the costs to acquire new customers. An analysis of a credit card company showed that lowering the defection rate from 20% to 10% doubled the longevity of the average customer's relationship from 5 years to 10 and more than doubled the net present value of the cumulative profit streams for this customer from $135 to $300. If the defection rate declines another 5%, the duration of the relationship doubles again, and profits increase 75%—from $300 to $525 (Reichheld & Sasser, 1990).

BENEFITS TO THE CUSTOMER

Relationship marketing benefits the customer as well as the firm. For continuously or periodically delivered services that are *personally important, variable in quality,* and/or *complex,* many customers will desire to be "relationship customers." High-involvement services also hold relationship appeal for customers. Medical, banking, insurance, and hairstyling services illustrate some or all of the significant characteristics—importance, variability, complexity, and involvement—that would cause many customers to desire continuity with the same providers, a proactive service attitude, and customized service delivery. All are potential benefits of relationship marketing.

The intangible nature of services makes them difficult for customers to evaluate prior to purchase. The heterogeneity of labor-intensive services encourages customer loyalty when excellent service is experienced. Not only does the auto repair firm want to find customers who will be loyal, but customers want to find an auto repair firm that evokes their loyalty.

In addition to the risk-reducing benefits of having a relationship with a given supplier, customers can reap social benefits. Barlow (1992) points out that "it fundamentally appeals to people to be dealt with on a one-on-one basis" (p. 29). Jackson (1993) argues that relationship marketing addresses the basic human need to feel important. Czepiel (1990) writes that because service encounters also are social encounters, repeated contacts naturally assume personal as well as professional dimensions.

Relationship marketing allows service providers to become more knowledgeable about the customer's requirements and needs. Knowledge of the customer combined with social rapport built over a series of service encounters facilitate the tailoring or customizing of service to the customer's specifications.

Parasuraman, Berry, and Zeithaml (1991) report that customers' desires for more personalized, closer relationships with service providers are evident in transcripts of interviews with customers for both ongoing services (e.g., insurance, truck leasing) and services provided intermittently (e.g., hotel, repair services). The following customer comments illustrate many that were expressed in a series of 16 focus group sessions in five cities (Parasuraman et al., 1991, p. 43):

> They should be a partner and more actively give me advice on what my calculated risks are. When they are a partner our money is their money too. (business insurance customer)
>
> I would like them to be a distant extension of my company. They should take care of the details. (truck leasing customer)
>
> You need to know the service tech. I should be able to call him directly. I want to know the tech on a one-to-one basis. (business equipment repair customer)
>
> Agents should come back to you and ask you if you need more coverage as your assets increase. (auto insurance customer)
>
> When employees remember and recognize you as a regular customer you feel really good. (hotel customer)

Relationship marketing does not apply to every service situation, as Barnes (1994) emphasizes. However, for services distinguished by the characteristics discussed above, it is a potent marketing strategy.

TECHNOLOGICAL ADVANCES

Relationship marketing appears to be an expensive alternative to mass marketing. Thus marketers are likely to become interested in relationship marketing only if they deem it to be affordable and practical. Rapid advances in information technology are decreasing the costs and increasing the practicality of relationship marketing at the same time its potential benefits are becoming better known.

Information technology enhances the practical value of relationship marketing through the *efficient* performance of key tasks:

- Tracking the buying patterns and overall relationships of existing customers
- Customizing services, promotions, and pricing to customers' specific requirements
- Coordinating or integrating the delivery of multiple services to the same customer
- Providing two-way communication channels: company to customer, customer to company
- Minimizing the probability of service errors and breakdowns
- Augmenting core service offerings with valued extras
- Personalizing service encounters as appropriate

The United Services Automobile Association (USAA), Walgreen, and Bradys illustrate these applications of technology to relationship marketing.[1] USAA is a San Antonio-based insurer primarily serving a military clientele who are "members" of the "association." USAA has invested heavily in automating insurance policy writing, member inquiries, claims, and billing, among other processes. Building a computerized, integrated member database was a pivotal step. By 1994, USAA had information on more than 2.6 million members and associate members (members' children and grandchildren) in its database. Although USAA's military clients are spread throughout the world and change locations frequently, policy changes are a simple matter. In one brief phone call, a member can insure a new car, add a driver, change an address, or effect any number of other changes. The member's file is consolidated. No handoffs to other departments are necessary. In a one-stop process, the transaction is completed, and the new or changed policy is mailed the next morning.

One of USAA's most important technology investments is an electronic imaging system. The more than 30,000 pieces of daily mail never leave the mail room. Instead, correspondence is scanned onto optical disk and inserted into appropriate members' policy service files, which are accessible electronically to 2,500 service representatives. The service representative who takes Colonel Smith's phone call and answers his questions about his recent correspondence is positioned to customize and personalize the service encounter. Colonel Smith's recent letter, plus the rest of his file, is accessible to the representative on his or her IMAGE terminal.

Walgreen, the nation's largest drugstore chain, filling 7% of all prescriptions in the United States, also uses information technology at the heart of its relationship marketing strategy. Intercom is a satellite-based computer system that links all Walgreens stores in 30 states plus Puerto Rico—more than 2,000 stores in 1994.[2] The system maintains customers' prescription records for timely use in emergencies. Where state laws allow, customers can obtain refills at Walgreens stores in different states. Walgreens customers can reach a pharmacist 24 hours a day via a toll-free telephone number, and the company will send prescriptions by overnight mail. Through Intercom, Walgreens can provide a patient's prescription records to hospital emergency rooms 24 hours a day, 7 days a week. Intercom can supply customers with printouts of their prescription purchases for their tax and insurance records.

Bradys, a San Diego chain of men's clothing stores, uses a personal computer system to capture customer information such as demographics, clothing size and style preferences, purchasing history, and hobbies. Through this database, the company customizes and personalizes service. For example, Bradys mails personalized letters at the start of each month to clients having birthdays that month. A 15% discount coupon is included for any merchandise in the store. Regular customers are notified a week before a sale is publicly announced, allowing them the first look at the sale merchandise. If overstocked in certain sizes, Bradys writes and calls clients to invite them to the store for discounts on their sizes (Zielinski, 1994).

In effect, information technology advances are creating the opportunity for firms to move from segmenting markets by groups to segmenting by individual households. From *Business Week* comes this comment:

In ever-expanding processing power, marketers see an opportunity to close the gap that has widened between companies and their customers with the rise of mass markets, mass media, and mass merchants. Database marketing, they believe, can create a silicon simulacrum of the old-fashioned relationship people used to have with the corner grocer, butcher, or baker. ("A Potent New Tool," 1994, p. 58)

Emerging Perspectives

Accelerating interest and research are deepening and extending understanding of relationship marketing. In this section, I explore some of these emerging perspectives. Building on my 1983 definition of relationship marketing as attracting, maintaining, and enhancing customer relationships, Grönroos (1990) adds the perspectives of noncustomer partnerships, mutual benefit, promise keeping, and profitability: "Marketing is to establish, maintain, and enhance relationships with customers and other partners, at a profit, so that the objectives of the parties involved are met. This is achieved by a mutual exchange and fulfillment of promises" (p. 138). Grönroos emphasizes the *promise concept*, articulated by Calonius (1988), as integral to the practice of relationship marketing. Calonius argues that *keeping* promises, rather than *making* them, is the key to maintaining and enhancing customer relationships.

Czepiel (1990) notes that relationship marketing involves the mutual recognition of a special status between exchange partners. Thus, for a relationship to exist, it has to be mutually perceived and mutually beneficial (Barnes, 1994).

Hunt and Morgan (1994), in the spirit of Grönroos (1990), broaden the scope of relationship marketing to include all forms of relational exchange, not solely customer relationships: "Relationship marketing refers to all marketing activities directed at establishing, developing, and maintaining successful relational exchanges in . . . supplier, lateral, buyer, and internal partnerships" (p. 23).

TARGETING PROFITABLE CUSTOMERS

Some customers typically are far more profitable to a firm than others. Some customers actually may be unprofitable to serve. Some customers may be loyalty-prone, hoping to find a supplier that will effectively deliver the desired service and intending to stay with that supplier. Other customers may be deal-prone, receptive to better offers from competitors, or even seeking out such offers.

Relationship marketing involves fixed- and variable-cost investments during the customer-"attracting" phase to create an opportunity for "maintaining and enhancing" customer relationships—which offers the most profit potential. Accordingly, the idea of targeting the "right customers" for relationship marketing has emerged in the literature. Reichheld (1993) is a vigorous proponent of this view, stressing that companies aspiring to practice relationship marketing should make formal efforts to identify those customers who are most likely to be loyal and develop their overall strategies around delivering superior value to these customers. He points out that USAA could not have achieved a 98% retention rate in automobile insurance for its military clientele (a group known for its frequent moves) without its integrated, centralized database and telephone sales force that members can access worldwide. Those who may have been the "wrong" customers for some auto insurers—mobile military personnel—are highly profitable to USAA, which is positioned to provide superior value to them.

Targeting profitable customers for relationship marketing involves study and analysis of loyalty- and defection-prone customers, searching for distinguishing patterns in why they stay or leave, what creates value for them, and who they are. Relationship marketing firms need to determine which types of customer defectors they wish to try to save (e.g., price, product, or service defectors) and create value-adding strategies that fit their requirements and strengthen their bonds with loyalty-prone customers.

Importantly, some customers may be profitable as transactional customers, even if they are not profitable as relationship customers. Thus certain companies may wish to mount dual strategies: relationship marketing for some market segments, transactional marketing for other segments. The emerging focus on relationship profitability should not be interpreted by marketers as a mandate to forfeit customers lacking relationship potential. The healthier interpretation is that relationship marketing is not an appropriate strategy for all customers, but other strategies may be appropriate. Moreover, multiple relationship marketing strategies may be necessary for different market segments. Walgreen might design one relationship marketing strategy for moderate and heavy prescription drug users who prefer coming to the store, another relationship marketing

TABLE 6.1 Three Levels of Relationship Marketing

Level	Primary Bond	Degree of Service Customization	Potential for Sustained Competitive Advantage	Examples
1	financial	low	low	American Airlines AAdvantage program
2	social	medium	medium	Harley-Davidson Harley Owners' Group (HOG)
3	structural	medium to high	high	Federal Express Powership program

SOURCE: Adapted from Berry and Parasuraman (1991).

strategy for regimen pharmacy customers who find mail order more cost-effective and convenient, another relationship marketing strategy for prescribing physicians, and a convenience-based transactional strategy for customers who primarily purchase merchandise other than prescription drugs. Whereas a pure service company like USAA with a sharply focused customer niche likely would strive to build profitable relationships with all customers falling within the niche. Walgreen—with its goods-service mix, chain of stores, and large, heterogeneous customer base—would appropriately stress the profitable attraction, retention, and enhancement of some customers (relationship marketing) as well as the performance of profitable, independent transactions with others.

MULTIPLE LEVELS OF RELATIONSHIP MARKETING

Relationship marketing can be practiced on multiple levels, depending on the type of bond(s) used to foster customer loyalty. Relatively recent literature in relationship marketing distinguishes among types of linkages or bonds and their relative effects (e.g., Berry & Parasuraman, 1991; Turnbull & Wilson, 1989); these distinctions are not stressed in the earlier literature. As shown in Table 6.1, the higher the level at which relationship marketing is practiced, the greater its potential for sustained competitive advantage.

Level 1 relationship marketing relies primarily on pricing incentives to secure customers' loyalty. Higher interest rates for longer-duration bank accounts, a free video rental after 10 paid rentals, and frequent-flier points illustrate level 1 relationship marketing. Unfortunately, the potential for sustained competitive advantage from this approach is low because price is the most easily imitated element of the marketing mix. Within 3 years of American Airlines's establishment of its AAdvantage frequent-flier program, 23 other airlines offered their own frequent-flier programs (Stephenson & Fox, 1987). Moreover, customers most interested in pricing incentives are particularly vulnerable to competitor *promotions* and may well flunk the profitability test discussed in the preceding section. Marketers seeking to establish the strongest possible relationships typically must be more than price competitors.

Level 2 relationship marketing relies primarily on social bonds, although aggressive pricing may be a vital element of the marketing mix. Level 2 relationship marketers attempt to capitalize on the reality that many service encounters also are social encounters (Czepiel, 1990; McCallum & Harrison, 1985). Social bonding involves personalization and customization of the relationship—for example, communication with customers regularly through multiple means, referring to customers by name during transactions, providing continuity of service through the same representative, and augmenting the core service with educational or entertainment activities such as seminars or parties.

Harley-Davidson has forged a powerful relationship marketing strategy on the foundation of its Harley Owners' Group (HOG). Each Harley-Davidson dealership has its own local HOG chapter. Harley-Davidson pays the first year's membership dues for customers who buy one of its motorcycles. The underlying purpose of HOG is to help buyers enjoy and use their motorcycles. Thus the company and its dealer network sponsor and facilitate weekend riding rallies, training sessions, and other events that bring like-minded people together. Harley-Davidson mails a bimonthly magazine to HOG members that lists regional, national, and international riding events. Most dealers distribute local chapter newsletters. With more than 250,000 members, HOG is level 2 relationship marketing at its best. Michael Keefe, director of the HOG program, refers to the process as "customer bonding. If people use the motorcycle, they'll stay involved. If there's nowhere to ride, no place to go, the motorcycle stays in the garage, the battery goes dead, and a year from now, they just sell it" (quoted in "A Potent New Tool," 1994, p. 59).

Although social bonding normally cannot overcome a noncompetitive core product (Crosby & Stephens, 1987), it can drive customer loyalty when competitive differences are not strong. A social relationship also may prompt a customer to be more tolerant of a service failure or to give a company an opportunity to respond to competitor entreaties. Crosby, Evans, and Cowles (1990) found a significant effect of life insurance salesperson relational selling behaviors (staying in touch with clients; personalizing the relationship by confiding in clients and sending cards and gifts; demonstrating a cooperative, responsive service attitude) on relationship quality (client trust in and satisfaction with the salesperson). Relationship quality, in turn, had a significant positive influence on clients' anticipation of future interactions with the salesperson.

Level 3 relationship marketing relies primarily on structural solutions to important customer problems. When relationship marketers can offer target customers value-adding benefits that are difficult or expensive for customers to provide and that are not readily available elsewhere, they create a strong foundation for maintaining and enhancing relationships. If the marketers also are using financial and social bonds, the foundation is even more difficult for competitors to penetrate.

At level 3, the solution to the customer's problem is designed into the service delivery system rather than being dependent upon the relationship-building skills of individual service providers. The problem solution is "structural" and thus binds the customer to the company instead of—or in addition to—an individual service provider who may leave the firm.

Federal Express's Powership program, which installs computer terminals in the offices of high-volume customers, illustrates level 3 relationship marketing. Powership comprises a series of automated shipping and invoicing systems that save customers time and money while solidifying their loyalty to Federal Express. The systems are scaled to customers' usage. Customers receive free an electronic weighing scale, a microcomputer terminal with modem, a bar-code scanner, and a laser printer. Powership rates packages with the correct charges, combines package weights by destination to provide volume discounts, and prints address labels from the customer's own database. Users can automatically prepare their own invoices, analyze their shipping expenses, and trace their packages through the Federal Express tracking system (Lovelock, 1994, p. 275). By 1994, Federal Express was processing close to 60% of its volume through more than 60,000 Powership systems deployed at customer sites (Miller, 1994).

MARKETING TO EMPLOYEES
AND OTHER STAKEHOLDERS

The idea of marketing to service employees to improve their performance with customers predates the first papers on relationship marketing.
George (1977), Grönroos (1978, 1981), and I (Berry, 1981, 1983) were
early, ardent proponents of service firms' practicing internal marketing to
improve external marketing. Internal marketing is included as an emerging perspective nonetheless because of its increasingly sophisticated
treatment in the literature, including its linkage to relationship marketing, and because its maturation as a construct has provided a natural path
to relationship building with multiple stakeholder groups.

Internal marketing has been emphasized in the services marketing literature because the services product is a performance and the performers
are employees. Thus service firms must focus attention and resources on
"attracting, developing, motivating, and retaining qualified employees
through job-products that satisfy their needs" (Berry & Parasuraman,
1991, p. 151). Only when service providers perform well does the likelihood of customers' continuing to buy increase (Berry, 1983).

Gummesson (1981, 1987) coined the phrase *part-time marketer* to
stress the critical marketing role performed by customer-contact employees in service organizations, a theme of Grönroos's work from his earliest
publications on services marketing to his most recent works. In a 1994 article, Grönroos underscores the limitations of the traditional marketing
mix paradigm for relationship marketing:

> For a firm applying a relationship strategy the marketing mix often becomes
> too restrictive. The most important customer contacts from a marketing suc-
> cess point of view are the ones outside the realm of the marketing mix and the
> marketing specialists. The marketing impact of the customer's contacts with
> people, technology and systems of operation and other non-marketing func-
> tions determines whether he or she (or the organizational buyer as a unit) will
> continue doing business with a given firm or not. All these customer contacts
> are more or less interactive. . . . In relationship marketing interactive market-
> ing becomes the dominating part of the marketing function. (pp. 10-11)

Attracting employees with the potential to be part-time marketers, developing their marketing skills and knowledge, and building an

organizational climate for marketing will fail to deliver intended results if employees constantly turn over and customers continually must deal with different—or inexperienced—service providers. Recent contributions to the literature position employee retention as an antecedent of customer retention. Schlesinger and Heskett (1991) view high employee turnover as a central factor in what they label "the cycle of failure." High employee turnover discourages management from investing much in hiring, training, and other commitment-building activities; this, in turn, leads to ineffective performance and/or the perception of dull or dead-end work, which feeds employee turnover. High employee turnover negatively affects service quality and customer retention, thus hurting profitability and further reducing the resources available to invest in employees' success.

Reichheld (1993) argues that the longer employees stay with a company, the better able they are to serve their customers. Long-term employees know more about the business and have had more opportunity to develop bonds of trust and familiarity with customers. Reichheld writes, "Just as it is important to select the right kinds of customers before trying to keep them, a company must find the right kind of employees before enticing them to stay" (p. 68). He suggests that companies analyze the cases of former employees who defected early, looking for patterns. He also recommends that companies that typically rotate managers through a series of branch offices reconsider this practice, which has the effect of discouraging the long-term perspective required in relationship marketing.

Starbucks Coffee Company is one of the fastest-growing companies in the United States. The centerpiece of its growth strategy is an innovative, comprehensive internal marketing strategy that includes health care benefits, stock options, in-depth training, career counseling, and product discounts for all employees, including part-time workers. Chief executive officer and president Howard Schultz has been quoted as saying that the quality of Starbucks's workforce is what makes and keeps the company competitive. He believes in the necessity of creating pride in, and giving workers a stake in, the company, so that workers perceive both financial and spiritual ties to their jobs (Rothman, 1993, p. 59).

Starbucks's stock option plan, called Bean Stock, is designed to reduce employee turnover and instill the pride of ownership. The plan is structured on a 5-year vesting period. It starts a year after the option is granted, and then vests the employee at 20% each year. Every employee also receives a new stock-option grant each year, initiating a new vesting period.

The percentage of the grant is linked to the company's profitability (Rothman, 1993).

Conceptualizing effective internal marketing as a prerequisite of effective external marketing reveals relationship marketing in a means-end context. In effect, companies must establish relationships with noncustomer groups (the means) to establish successful relationships with customers (the end). Internal relationship marketing to pave the way for external relationship marketing is an example. As mentioned earlier, Hunt and Morgan (1994) extend relationship marketing to include internal, supplier, and lateral partnerships, as well as buyer partnerships. In an economic era characterized by more prevalent strategic network competition (networks of independent entities collaborating as partners and competing against other such networks), Hunt and Morgan stress that cooperation is increasingly necessary for competition. Gummesson, in a 1994 paper, proposes 30 potential types of relationships, including those of a company with customers, employees, investors, suppliers, mass media, and government; frontline personnel with customers; and full-time marketers with part-time marketers. He suggests that managers need to establish the mix of relationships essential to the company's success, as not all relationships are important to all companies all the time.

TRUST AS A MARKETING TOOL

For a strong relationship to exist, it must be mutually beneficial (Czepiel, 1990). The good intentions of partners in a relationship cannot be in doubt. Communications must be open, honest, and frequent. Similar values must prevail. Partners must be willing to give, not just get.

Relationship marketing is built on the foundation of trust, as accumulating research demonstrates (e.g., Crosby et al., 1990; Morgan & Hunt, 1994; Parasuraman et al., 1991). Trust is "a willingness to rely on an exchange partner in whom one has confidence" (Moorman, Deshpandé, & Zaltman, 1993, p. 3). It is critical to the formation of service-based relationships because of the intangibility of services. Most services are difficult to evaluate prior to one's purchasing and experiencing them, and some services remain difficult to evaluate even after they have been performed. These latter services, labeled "black box" services by van't Haaff (1989), are typically technical in nature, such as automobile repair, or are performed away from the customers' view, such as restaurant meals. Customers purchasing black-box services are particularly vulnerable because they have less knowledge than the supplier about what actually transpired in the service performance.

Under the best of circumstances, customers using a specific service supplier for the first time generally feel some uncertainty and vulnerability. As discussed earlier, these feelings are likely to be heightened for services that are personally important to customers, require considerable involvement, are heterogeneous, or are complex (black box). Customers who develop trust in service suppliers based on their experiences with them—especially suppliers of services with these significant characteristics—have good reasons to remain in these relationships: They reduce uncertainty and vulnerability.

The inherent nature of services, coupled with abundant mistrust in U.S. society, positions trust as perhaps the single most powerful relationship marketing tool available to a company. Yankelovich Partners has documented an erosion of trust among American consumers in its annual monitor study of consumer attitudes and lifestyles. Barbara Caplan (1993), a senior researcher at Yankelovich Partners, writes:

> How people are feeling and thinking speaks to a national mood of skepticism. Distrust permeates the very fabric of American life. . . . There is a sense that integrity, credibility, and competence are lacking. Consumers are wary of misrepresentation, exaggeration and hype and are determined to stamp deception out. (p. 1)

How can relationship marketers demonstrate their trustworthiness?

Opening lines of communication. Forthright, frequent, two-way communications clearly are important. Maritz Marketing Research surveyed consumers about being contacted by a company and found that 80% of those sampled felt it was important for a company to keep in touch with its customers; 87% indicated they would buy from a company that had a reputation for keeping in touch (Cottrell, 1994). Lexus, consistently ranked first by American consumers in J. D. Power research in both product quality and dealer service, offers free 1,000- and 7,500-mile maintenance checkups to owners even though the company's engineers say the checkups are unnecessary. The rationale is to increase personal contact between the customer and the dealer (Illingworth, 1991). Two-thirds of Lexus buyers today have bought a Lexus before, the highest repeat-purchase rate in the luxury car market (Henkoff, 1994).

Parasuraman et al. (1991) report that the automobile insurance customers they interviewed expressed strong resentment and mistrust of their insurance companies because they believed these firms were price gouging, were making false promotional promises (such as lower premiums for safe drivers), and were prone to cancel their insurance if they had an accident. Based on these findings, the researchers advise auto insurers to communicate with their policyholders more openly, regularly, and creatively about the rationale for rate hikes, their criteria for canceling insurance, and other sensitive subjects. Parasuraman et al. suggest that insurance companies sponsor education seminars and "town hall" meetings in local markets as well as other communication initiatives.

Regular, open, two-way communication conveys the firm's interest in the customer's welfare—what PHH Corporation calls its "Evergreen Philosophy" in its 1993 annual shareholders report. Communication leads to trust, and trust to relationship commitment (Morgan & Hunt, 1994). Communication intensity also can encourage customer perceptions of "special status" (Czepiel, 1990) and "closeness" (Barnes, 1994) that are indicative of true relationships, plus allow marketers the opportunity to "resell" intangible services continually (Levitt, 1981).

Communication effectiveness in building trust can have implications for organizational structure, especially in companies typically serving customers through different representatives at each service contact. Warner Corporation, a large heating, ventilation, and air-conditioning company in Washington, D.C., and surrounding markets, reorganized its service delivery system so that each technician is responsible for a specific geographic area. Instead of making service calls throughout the trade area and rarely seeing the same customers twice, the technician focuses on one or several zip codes. Called an "area technical director," each technician is expected to build a business in the assigned area. A new incentive system developed concurrently with the restructuring encourages the technician's staying in touch with customers and making sure they are satisfied with the service. One area technical director said that he goes so far as to give his pager number to his customers (Finegan, 1994, p. 66).

Delivering services through cross-functional teams also fosters service continuity and communication with customers. Customers are served by a team for most or all of their service requirements, giving a big company the opportunity to deliver a level of personalized service more characteristic of a small company (Berry, 1995).

Guaranteeing the service. Service guarantees are another means to build trust. Dissatisfied customers can invoke the guarantee and receive compensation for the burden they have endured. When executed well, service guarantees can symbolize a company's commitment to fair play with customers and facilitate competitive differentiation. Guarantees also force the organization to improve service to avoid the cost and embarrassment of frequent payouts.

A service company should never implement a service guarantee without a thorough analysis of its purpose and risks. Guaranteeing a poor service is always a mistake. Firms delivering poor service first should significantly improve their service quality. Then they can consider guarantees that will help facilitate further improvement.

When Bank One acquired a failed Texas bank in 1989, it found itself in the unusual situation of needing to start a trust banking division, because the failed bank's trust department had been sold. New management faced the daunting challenge of dislodging prospective clients from their existing institutions. Today, Bank One's Texas Trust Division is among the fastest-growing trust companies in the United States, with more than 4,500 accounts. An unconditional service guarantee anchors the trust division's market-entry and continued positioning strategy of service excellence.

The guarantee is simple. Clients dissatisfied with the service need not pay the fee. Given to every new client, the written guarantee reads: "If you are not satisfied with our service quality in any given year, we will return to you the fees paid, or any portion thereof you feel is fair." Customers wishing to invoke the guarantee must inform the bank in writing within 90 days of the end of the account year. Four clients invoked the guarantee during the first 4 years of operation. According to management, all the claims were justified and were for the same reason: overpromising.

A higher standard of conduct. Companies seeking to build genuine relationships with customers must be willing to operate with a higher standard of conduct than just legality. Corporate practices that rob customers of self-esteem or justice may be legal, but they destroy trust and consequently the potential for relationship building. Relationship marketers must be prepared to subject every policy and strategy to a fairness test.

They must be willing to level the playing field. They must be willing to ask not only "Is it legal?" but also "Is it right?" (Berry & Parasuraman, 1991, p. 145).

Going Forward

Relationship marketing's time has come. Marketing practitioners and academics are interested in its possibilities as never before, and for good reasons. Virtually all market offerings have a service component (from manufactured goods to pure services), and relationship marketing fits the salient characteristics of services. Both company and customer benefit from effective relationship marketing. Advances in information technology are making relationship marketing programs more affordable, feasible, and powerful.

Growing interest and active research in relationship marketing of services are bringing newer, more sophisticated perspectives to the subject. These include focusing on profitable relationships, recognizing multiple levels of relationship marketing with different effects, practicing relationship marketing with noncustomers such as employees and strategic alliance partners to serve customers better, and leveraging an old-fashioned idea—trust—as a central relationship building block.

Although relationship marketing in services is developing, it is far from mature. Here is a baker's dozen of issues requiring more research:

- What types of customers are most receptive to relationship marketing?
- What service characteristics increase or decrease the appeal of relationship marketing to customers?
- What are the common characteristics of successful relationship marketing programs?
- What drives customer loyalty for services?
- What are the antecedents of customer trust in service providers, and how do these rank for different types of services?
- Does the number of services a customer uses from a single company source affect future retention?
- Does duration of a customer's relationship with a company affect future retention?
- What are the implications of relationship marketing for organizational structure?
- What are the implications of relationship marketing for technology?

- What is the role of pricing in relationship marketing?
- What is the role of advertising in relationship marketing?
- What is the association between employee turnover and customer defection in different types of service companies?
- What are the different types of membership programs marketers can consider, and what are their strengths and limitations?

Service firms can increase market share three ways: They can attract more new customers, do more business with existing customers, and reduce the loss of customers. By directing marketing resources to existing customers, relationship marketing directly addresses two of these opportunities: expanding relationships and reducing customer defections. Because many customers want to be relationship customers, relationship marketing also can help firms attract more new customers. Relationship marketing is a potent strategy for today and tomorrow; it warrants the attention it is now receiving in the discipline.

Notes

1. These examples, and several others used in this chapter, are based on material appearing in Berry (1995).
2. The reader may wonder about the use of both *Walgreen* and *Walgreens*. Walgreen is the company name, and Walgreens is the store name.

References

Barlow, R. G. (1992, March). Relationship marketing: The ultimate in customer services. *Retail Control*, pp. 29-37.
Barnes, J. G. (1994, October). *The issues of establishing relationships with customers in service companies: When are relationships feasible and what form should they take?* Paper presented at the Frontiers in Services Conference, American Marketing Association and Vanderbilt University Center for Services Marketing.
Berry, L. L. (1980, May-June). Services marketing is different. *Business, 30*, 24-29.
Berry, L. L. (1981, March). The employee as customer. *Journal of Retail Banking*, pp. 33-40.
Berry, L. L. (1983). Relationship marketing. In L. L. Berry, G. L. Shostack, & G. D. Upah (Eds.), *Emerging perspectives on service marketing* (pp. 25-38). Chicago: American Marketing Association.
Berry, L. L. (1995). *On great service: A framework for action*. New York: Free Press.
Berry, L. L., & Parasuraman, A. (1991). *Marketing services: Competing through quality*. New York: Free Press.
Berry, L. L., & Parasuraman, A. (1993). Building a new academic field: The case of services marketing. *Journal of Retailing, 69*(1), 13-60.

Calonius, H. (1988). A buying process model. In K. Blois & S. Parkinson (Eds.), *Innovative marketing: A European perspective* (pp. 86-103). Bradford, England: University of Bradford, European Marketing Academy.

Caplan, B. (1993, July). The consumer speaks: Who's listening? *Arthur Andersen Retailing Issues Letter, 5,* 1-5.

Cottrell, R. J. (1994, March). Proactive versus reactive customer contact. *Mobius,* pp. 25-28, 39.

Crosby, L. A., Evans, K. R., & Cowles, D. (1990). Relationship quality in services selling: An interpersonal influence perspective. *Journal of Marketing, 54*(3), 68-81.

Crosby, L. A., & Stephens, N. (1987). Effects of relationship marketing and satisfaction, retention, and prices in the life insurance industry. *Journal of Marketing Research, 24,* 404-411.

Czepiel, J. A. (1990). Service encounters and service relationships: Implications for research. *Journal of Business Research, 20*(1), 13-21.

Finegan, J. (1994, August). Pipe dreams. *Inc., 16,* 64-70.

George, W. R. (1977, Fall). The retailing of services: A challenging future. *Journal of Retailing, 53,* 85-98.

Grönroos, C. (1978). A service-oriented approach to the marketing of services. *European Journal of Marketing, 12,* 588-601.

Grönroos, C. (1981). Internal marketing: An integral part of marketing theory. In J. H. Donnelly & W. R. George (Eds.), *Marketing of services* (pp. 236-238). Chicago: American Marketing Association.

Grönroos, C. (1990). *Service management and marketing: Managing the moments of truth in service competition.* Lexington, MA: Lexington.

Grönroos, C. (1994). From marketing mix to relationship marketing: Towards a paradigm shift in marketing. *Management Decision, 32*(2), 4-20.

Gummesson, E. (1981). Marketing cost concept in service firms. *Industrial Marketing Management, 10,* 175-182.

Gummesson, E. (1987). The new marketing: Developing long-term interactive relationships. *Long Range Planning, 20*(4), 10-20.

Gummesson, E. (1994, May). *Is relationship marketing operational?* Paper presented at the annual European Marketing Academy Conference, Maastricht, Netherlands.

Henkoff, R. (1994, June 27). Service is everybody's business. *Fortune,* pp. 48-60.

Hunt, S. D., & Morgan, R. M. (1994). Relationship marketing in the era of network competition. *Marketing Management, 3*(1), 19-28.

Illingworth, J. D. (1991, Fall). Relationship marketing: Pursuing the perfect person-to-person relationship. *Journal of Services Marketing, 5,* 49-52.

Jackson, D. (1993, March). The seven deadly sins of financial services marketing . . . and the road to redemption. *Direct Marketing,* pp. 43-45, 79.

Levitt, T. (1981). Marketing intangible products and product intangibles. *Harvard Business Review, 59*(5), 94-102.

Lovelock, C. (1994). *Product plus: How product + service = competitive advantage.* New York: McGraw-Hill.

McCallum, R. J., & Harrison, W. (1985). Interdependence in the service encounter. In J. A. Czepiel, M. R. Solomon, & C. F. Surprenant (Eds.), *The service encounter: Managing employee/customer interaction in service businesses* (pp. 35-48). Lexington, MA: Lexington.

Miller, B. (1994, October). *Information technology: The competitive edge.* Paper presented at Frontiers in Services Conference, American Marketing Association and Vanderbilt University Center for Services Marketing.

Moorman, C., Deshpandé, R., & Zaltman, G. (1993). *Relationships between providers and users of market research: The role of personal trust* (Working paper). Cambridge, MA: Marketing Science Institute.

Morgan, R. M., & Hunt, S. D. (1994). The commitment-trust theory of relationship marketing. *Journal of Marketing, 58*(3), 20-38.

Parasuraman, A., Berry, L. L., & Zeithaml, V. A. (1991). Understanding customer expectations of service. *Sloan Management Review, 32*(3), 39-48.

A potent new tool for selling database marketing. (1994, September 5). *Business Week,* pp. 56-62.

Reichheld, F. F. (1993). Loyalty-based management. *Harvard Business Review, 71*(4), 64-73.

Reichheld, F. F., & Sasser, W. E., Jr. (1990). Zero defections: Quality comes to services. *Harvard Business Review, 69*(1), 105-111.

Rothman, M. (1993, January). Into the black. *Inc., 15,* 58-65.

Ryans, A. B., & Wittink, D. R. (1977). The marketing of services: Categorization with implications for strategy. In B. Greenberg & D. Bellenger (Eds.), *Contemporary marketing thought* (pp. 312-314). Chicago: American Marketing Association.

Schlesinger, L. A., & Heskett, J. L. (1991, Spring). Breaking the cycle of failure in service. *Sloan Management Review, 32*(3), 17-28.

Schneider, B. (1980). The service organization: Climate is crucial. *Organizational Dynamics, 9*(2), 52-65.

Stephenson, F. J., & Fox, R. J. (1987, Fall). Corporate attitudes toward frequent flyer programs. *Transportation Journal,* pp. 10-22.

Turnbull, P. W., & Wilson, D. T. (1989). Developing and protecting profitable customer relationships. *Industrial Marketing Management, 18,* 233-238.

van't Haaff, P. A. (1989). Top quality: A way of life. In E. E. Scheuing & C. H. Little (Eds.), *Distinguished papers: Service quality in the 1990s.* New York: St. John's University, Business Research Institute, World Future Society.

Zielinski, D. (1994, February). Database marketing: With costs down, more use it to pinpoint promotions, create customer bonds. *Service Edge, 7,* 1-3.

7

Relationship Marketing in Consumer Markets

Antecedents and Consequences

JAGDISH N. SHETH
ATUL PARVATIYAR

Several areas of marketing have recently been the focus of relationship marketing, including interorganizational issues in the context of a buyer-seller partnership (Dwyer, Schurr, & Oh, 1987; Johanson, Hallén, & Seyed-Mohamed, 1991), network structures and arrangements (Anderson, Håkansson, & Johanson, 1994), channel relationships (Boyle, Dwyer, Robicheaux, & Simpson, 1992; Ganesan, 1994), sales management (Swan &

NOTE: This chapter is reprinted from Jagdish N. Sheth and Atul Parvatiyar, "Relationship Marketing in Consumer Markets: Antecedents and Consequences," *Journal of the Academy of Marketing Science,* vol. 23, no. 4, pp. 255-271, copyright © 1995 by the Academy of Marketing Science. Reprinted by permission.
AUTHORS' NOTE: We gratefully acknowledge the helpful comments of Rick Bagozzi, Joe Cannon, Banwari Mittal, Bob Peterson, and the editor of the *Journal of the Academy of Marketing Science,* Dave Cravens, on previous versions of this chapter.

Nolan, 1985), services marketing (Berry, 1983; Crosby, Evans, & Cowles, 1990; Crosby & Stephens, 1987), and business alliances (Bucklin & Sengupta, 1993; Heide & John, 1990; Sheth & Parvatiyar, 1992). Researchers have also focused on developing a theory of successful and efficient management of relationships (see Heide & John, 1992; Morgan & Hunt, 1994). These and other studies have significantly contributed to our knowledge of relationship marketing. However, the subject of relationship marketing is still nascent and in its very early stages of development.

Particularly lacking are studies on relationship marketing in consumer markets, especially for consumer products as opposed to consumer services. Whatever limited literature exists has been written to advise practitioners on how to improve relationship marketing practice (Christopher, Payne, & Ballantyne, 1991; Copulsky & Wolf, 1990; Illingworth, 1991). Moreover, much of the current literature considers relationship marketing, especially in consumer markets, to be a completely new phenomenon. Examples include database marketing, affinity marketing, and regional marketing practices focused on building ongoing relationships with consumers. Academic scholars (for example, at meetings of the American Marketing Association) have challenged this contention by suggesting that the direct buyer-seller relationship is actually an old-fashioned way of doing business. Indeed, in an earlier article, we tried to document that relationship marketing has strong historical antecedents from the preindustrial era, and only its form and practice have changed (Sheth & Parvatiyar, 1993; see also Chapter 5, this volume). In this chapter, we extend that argument to suggest that the antecedents of relationship marketing can also be found in early theories of consumer behavior.

As far as a firm's motivation to engage in relationship marketing is concerned, several arguments have been proposed based on either superior economics of customer retention (Reichheld & Sasser, 1990; Rosenberg & Czepiel, 1984; Rust & Zahorik, 1992) or the competitive advantage that relationship marketing provides to the firm (McKenna, 1991; Nauman, 1995; Vavra, 1992). These arguments are presumed valid and are generally not contested. However, we believe that such advantages of relationship marketing can accrue to a firm if, and only if, consumers are willing and able to engage in relationship patronage. If relationship marketing connotes an ongoing cooperative market behavior between the marketer and the consumer (Grönroos, 1990; Shani & Chalasani, 1992), it reflects some sort of a commitment made by the consumer to continue patronizing the particular marketer despite numerous choices that exist for him or her. In other words, marketers' motivation to engage in relationship marketing is tempered by consumers' motivation to reduce their choice set to be in relationship with a firm or a brand. Being in a relationship over time construes brand, product, or service patronage, and unless consumers are motivated to reduce their choice set, they will not be inclined to manifest brand, store, or product/service loyalty. Hence taking the consumer perspective, and understanding what motivates consumers to become loyal, is important.

Consumer Choice Reduction as the Basic Tenet of Relationship Marketing

The fundamental axiom of relationship marketing is, or should be, that consumers like to reduce choices by engaging in ongoing loyalty relationships with marketers.[1] This is reflected in the continuity of patronage and maintenance of ongoing connectedness over time with marketers. It is a form of commitment made by consumers to patronize selected products, services, and marketers rather than to exercise market choices. When consumers make such commitments, they repeatedly transact with the same marketers or purchase the same brands of products or services. In doing so, consumers forgo the opportunity to choose other marketers or products and services that would also serve their needs. Engaging in relationships, therefore, essentially means that consumers, even in situations where there is choice, purposefully reduce their choices, especially when they engage in choice situations, such as buying and consuming foods, beverages, and convenience products in general. Thus, from a consumer perspective, reduction of choice is the crux of relationship marketing behavior. We will henceforth refer to this purposeful choice reduction behavior of consumers as *relational market behavior.*

Reducing choices and thereby engaging in relational market behavior is a prevalent, natural, and normal consumer practice.[2] Consumers consistently demonstrate preferences to buy the same products or services, patronize the same stores, use the same processes of purchase, and visit the same service providers again and again. It is estimated that as much as 90% of the time, consumers go to the same supermarkets or the same shopping malls to purchase products and services. Thus a vast array of academic literature in consumer behavior has grown on repeat-purchase behavior and customer loyalty (Dick & Basu, 1994; Enis & Paul, 1970; Howard & Sheth, 1969; Jacoby & Chestnut, 1978; Sheth, 1967). As Jacoby and Kyner (1973) argue, "Brand loyalty is essentially a *relational* phenomenon" (p. 2). The same is also true of store loyalty, person loyalty, process loyalty, and other forms of committed behavior (Sheth, 1982).

When a product or service and its provider are inseparable, such as health care and doctors, or haircuts and barbers, consumers also develop relationships with the product-service providers. Similarly, where direct contact between consumers and marketers is unlikely, consumers develop relationships with products or their symbols. Brand loyalty and brand equity are, therefore, primarily measurements of the relationships that consumers develop with a company's products and symbols.

The question is, Why do consumers engage in relational market behavior? We postulate that consumers engage in relational market behavior to achieve greater efficiency in their decision making, to reduce the task of information processing, to achieve more cognitive consistency in their decisions, and to reduce the perceived risks associated with future choices. Consumers also engage in relational market behavior because of the norms of behavior set by family members, the influence of peer groups, government mandates, religious tenets, employer influences, and marketer-induced policies. In fact, these postulations are supported by the consumer behavior literature, which explicitly or implicitly explains how, why, and in what contexts consumers reduce choices. In the following sections, we draw on the consumer behavior literature to develop insights into why consumers engage in relational market behavior.

Before we examine the consumer behavior literature, it is important that we acknowledge that relationship marketing goes beyond repeat-purchase behavior and inducements. As Webster (1992) points out, repeated transactions are only a precursor of relationships; perhaps greater and more valuable relationships develop between consumers and marketers when consumers become actively involved in the decisions of the company. Any relationship that attempts to develop customer value through partnering activities is, therefore, likely to create greater bonding between consumers and marketers (their products, symbols, processes, stores, and people). The greater the enhancement of the relationship through such bonding, the more committed the consumer becomes to the relationship and hence the less likely he or she is to patronize other marketers.

Relational Market Behavior
and Consumer Behavior Theories

In the subsections that follow, we draw on consumer behavior theories that help us understand consumer motivations to engage in relational market behavior. We first look at the theoretical propositions and constructs of consumer behavior theories that are anchored to personal factors influencing consumer behavior, such as consumer learning, memory and information processing, perceived risk, and cognitive consistency. Next we draw on theories that explain sociological influences on consumer behavior, such as family, social class, and reference group theories. Finally, we examine institutional influences that suggest consumers reduce their choices to comply with the norms of institutions such as religion, government, employers, and marketers.

PERSONAL MOTIVATIONS TO ENGAGE
IN RELATIONAL MARKET BEHAVIOR

Consumer Learning Theories and
Relational Market Behavior

Several consumer behavior models that are anchored to learning theories have focused on how consumers make choice decisions over time (Andreasen, 1965; Engel, Blackwell, & Miniard, 1986; Hansen, 1972; Howard & Sheth, 1969; Nicosia, 1966). In essence, these models try to explain how consumers, over time, reduce choices regarding purchase and consumption. As originally proposed by Howard and Sheth (1969), consumers like to simplify their extensive and limited problem-solving situations into routinized behavior by learning to reduce the number of products and brands under consideration into an evoked set, which is a fraction of the alternatives available and familiar to the consumer (Reilly & Parkinson, 1985). The underlying motive for reducing choices into an evoked set is the consumer's desire to reduce the complexity of the buying situation. Limiting the choice to the evoked set allows easy information processing and, therefore, simplifies the task of choosing (Hoyer, 1984; Shugan, 1980). In addition, consumers also routinize other shopping and consuming tasks, such as where to shop, how to pay for what they buy, where and when to consume what they buy, how to reorder, and so on. The routinization of tasks results in habitual action and loyalty behavior. Consequently, consumers become more efficient in dealing with the buying task. Thus the following proposition:

P1: In buying and consuming situations, wherever there is a greater need to routinize choices because of the efficiency potential, consumers will engage in relational market behavior.

Paradoxically, although consumers seek routinization of the choice process, they also deliberately try to seek variety by exiting the relationship if they become bored or satiated. This is referred to as the "psychology of complication" in Howard and Sheth's (1969) theory. In these situations, consumers would seek additional alternatives and information and change their relationships, either into new forms and processes or with new parties. For example, consumers change the ways they buy from the same marketer by using different buying or paying systems, or they may look for additional variety in the offerings of the same marketer or engage in new relationships with other marketers altogether. Routinization and variety-seeking behavior become cyclical over time, but the cycles are asymmetric in favor of longer duration of routinized behavior (McAlister & Pessemier, 1982; Raju, 1980; Sheth & Raju, 1973). Hence:

P2: When consumers are satiated due to lack of novelty or variety in the relationship, they will disengage from the relational market behavior, including exiting the relationship.

Conditioning as a form of learning has been the subject of consumer behavior investigation over the past several decades (for a review of research in this area, see McSweeney & Bierley, 1984; see also Shimp, 1991). In relational market behavior, ongoing transactions with the same marketers provide consumers with learned experiences that they can store, process, and retrieve to use in subsequent problem situations and other similar situations. Repeated learning episodes condition consumers in stimulus generalization and stimulus discrimination (Berlyne, 1960). They learn to generalize from the stimulus and respond effectively to similar purchase and consumption circumstances. They also develop an ability to discriminate from other stimuli they may receive in the future and respond accordingly.

Thus, in conditions that offer a greater potential for response generalization, consumers will exhibit relational market behavior. For example, when companies offer one-stop shopping, consumers will be more inclined to engage in and maintain relationships with these companies. Hence:

P3: The greater the opportunity for consumers to generalize responses to other purchase and consumption situations, the greater will be consumer propensity to engage in relational market behavior.

Although modern conditioning studies have taken a significantly different route to suggest that conditioning is cognitive associative learning (Dawson, Schell, Beers, & Kelly, 1982), the focus on repeated learning episodes has other powerful implications for explaining consumer motivation for relational market behavior. In particular, in instrumental conditioning or operant conditioning (Skinner, 1953), where intermittent reinforcements are promised and provided, such as frequent-flier programs, consumers show a strong form of conditioning that persists for long periods of time. Thus the consumer's motive to engage in relationships with marketers is the consumer's expectation of future positive reinforcements that such relationships are likely to bring.

P4: The greater the expectations for future positive reinforcements, the greater will be consumer propensity to engage in relational market behavior.

Conditioning also creates consumer inertia. The concept of consumer inertia suggests that consumers are unwilling to switch to other choices because of inertia. This inertia stems either from the low valence of motivational intensity for change, given the conditioned behavior, or from the low level of consumer involvement in a decision process (Jacoby & Chestnut, 1978). Under such situations, consumers are not stimulated enough to exercise available choices. Therefore, marketers often create environments for increasing consumer inertia by providing conveniences and process simplification to minimize consumers' desire to seek other alternatives. Examples include home delivery by Domino's Pizza, package pickup service by Federal Express, and automatic teller machines established by banks. Thus we make the following proposition:

P5: The greater the potential for consumer inertia, the greater will be consumer propensity to engage in relational market behavior.

Information Processing, Memory, and Relational Market Behavior

Consumer decision-making efficiency also improves when the information-processing task is simplified and bounded. By invoking the concept of "bounded rationality," Simon (1955) has argued that decision makers have limitations on their abilities to process information. This results in satisficing, as opposed to maximizing self-interest. Several consumer behavior researchers have drawn upon this concept to study how consumers process information to make choice decisions (for a review of research in this area, see Bettman, Johnson, & Payne, 1991). The central argument of these theories is that consumers, due to limited capacity for information processing, use a variety of heuristics to simplify their decision-making tasks and manage information overload (Bettman, 1979; Jacoby, Speller, & Kohn, 1974). One of these simplification processes is the use of memory, which stores information for subsequent decisions (Biehal & Chakravarti, 1986). Given that the size of human memory (in particular working or short-term memory) is limited in capacity, consumers typically retain a few attributes and alternatives in memory to be retrieved for future choices (Miller, 1956; Simon, 1974). Not all that is stored in the memory may be invoked for inclusion in a consideration set in every purchase or consumption decision, but, as Alba, Hutchinson, and Lynch (1991) observe, memory plays an important role in the formation of the consideration set.

The role of memory in consumer decision making is well established. Memory is that part of the cognitive system that stores a consumer's prior experiences and prior knowledge. There is a good deal of evidence in the consumer behavior literature that previous experience, prior knowledge, and expertise have considerable effects on consumer choice decisions (Bettman & Park, 1980). Consumers rely on well-rehearsed memory to process information, because in addition to limitation of memory size, capacity to retain information over time is also limited (Murdock, 1961). Unless rehearsed again and again, information in memory slowly decays and fades away. One would therefore expect the consumer to maintain a continuity of relationship with a marketer (or a product) so as to use memory in future decision making. The task of information processing is minimized through short-circuiting.[3] Continuity of relationship helps consumers to rehearse their memory, to develop expertise with that decision problem, to become skilled at using retrieval cues, and, thereby, to manage all future decisions (Katona, 1975; Keller, 1987).

P6: The greater the need for information, knowledge, and expertise in making choices, the greater will be consumer propensity to engage in relational market behavior.

Perceived Risk and Relational Market Behavior

Consumer behavior is also motivated by the reduction of risk (Bauer, 1960; Taylor, 1974). Perceived risk is associated with the uncertainty and magnitude of outcomes. Consumers develop a variety of strategies to reduce perceived risk. Of these, the two most general strategies consumers adopt are as follows: (a) They engage in external searches for information, especially through word-of-mouth communication, and develop greater confidence in their own ability to judge and evaluate choices (Beatty & Smith, 1987; Cox, 1967; Dowling & Staelin, 1994); and (b) they become loyal to brands, products, stores, or marketers (Howard, 1965; Locander & Hermann, 1979).

Several empirical studies have shown that in cases of certain products and services, consumers find brand loyalty to be the best risk reducer (Derbaix, 1983; Punj & Staelin, 1983). It has also been demonstrated that the greater the customer satisfaction with past buying or consuming experiences, the lower the probability of customers' searching for external information in future similar circumstances (Kiel, 1977). Developing self-confidence regarding purchasing or consumption is a natural human tendency, although this confidence may also be achieved from external sources of information or from the promises made by marketers. However, experiences and ongoing interactions with marketers are a more reliable foundation for the development of self-confidence. By engaging in relational market behavior, consumers learn about marketers, their products and services, and the circumstances under which the marketers operate to fulfill their needs effectively. Paradoxically, if the perceived risk of making choices is reduced by an industry through service guarantees, quality assurance, and customer integrity, this is likely to encourage transactional behavior (Shimp & Bearden, 1982). Witness the recent experiences in the switching behavior of consumers concerning credit cards and long-distance telephone services.

> P7: The greater the perceived risk in future choice making, the greater will be consumer propensity to reduce choices and engage in relational market behavior. However, as the perceived risk reduces over time with increased self-confidence, consumer propensity to manifest transactional market behavior will increase.

Cognitive Consistency Theories and Relational Market Behavior

Cognitive consistency theories, such as balance theory (Heider, 1946) and congruity theory (Osgood & Tannenbaum, 1955), suggest that consumers strive for harmonious relationships in their beliefs, feelings, and behaviors (McGuire, 1976; Meyers-Levy & Tybout, 1989). Inconsistency in this cognitive system is presumed to generate psychological tension. Therefore, consumers avoid choosing alternatives or information that would be inconsistent or dissonant with their current belief systems. Indeed, in perceptual vigilance, consumers will selectively pay more attention to products, information, and persons toward which they have favorable attitudes. This phenomenon has been the subject of investigation under confirmation-disconfirmation theory of consumer attitudes (Oliver, 1993; Stayman, Alden, & Smith, 1992).

According to studies conducted by Fazio and Zanna (1981), descriptive beliefs, which are a result of direct experience with an object, are often held with much certainty and predict behavior relatively well. Other studies have confirmed that consumers are likely to act in consonance with their descriptive beliefs, shaped by their direct experiences with products, services, persons, or processes (Bagozzi, Baumgartner, & Yi, 1992; Mano & Oliver, 1993; for a review of studies, see Sheppard, Hartwick, & Warshaw, 1988). As long as they have positive experiences, and hence positive descriptive attitudes, consumers are more satisfied and more likely to engage in relational market behavior (Westbrook & Oliver, 1991). Such cognitively consistent behavior is believed to reduce consumers' psychic tension.

> P8: The greater the potential for market choice to upset cognitive consistency, the greater will be consumer propensity to engage in relational market behavior with choices that are consistent with their current belief systems.

A popular cognitive consistency theory in consumer behavior has been cognitive dissonance theory (Festinger, 1957), the primary implication of which is that consumers rationalize their choices by enhancing the positive aspects of the chosen alternatives and suppressing their negative aspects (Mazursky, LaBarbera, & Aiello, 1987). Similarly, consumers enhance the negative aspects and suppress the positive aspects of rejected alternatives. Therefore, consumers restructure their cognitions to be consistent with their behavior, including actively searching for information after making their choices (Hunt, 1970). This theory also explains the overwhelming empirical evidence that advertising appeals to predisposed consumers.

> P9: The greater the potential for postpurchase rationalization, the greater will be consumer propensity to engage in relational market behavior.

In essence, consumer decision, learning, information-processing, and cognitive consistency theories support our contention that consumers are naturally inclined to reduce choices and engage in ongoing relationships. This is so because (a) reduction of choices helps reduce perceived risks associated with future decisions, (b) consumers like to optimize their learning experiences and reward themselves with reinforced positive behavior, (c) reduction of choices reduces psychological tension and cognitive dissonance, and (d) consumers expect future gains from reinforced behavior.

SOCIOLOGICAL REASONS TO ENGAGE
IN RELATIONAL MARKET BEHAVIOR

The influence of society, family, and reference groups on consumer behavior is profound (Coleman, 1983; Levy, 1966; Nicosia & Mayer, 1976; Sheth, 1974b; Stafford & Cocanougher, 1977). Through the process of socialization, consumers become members of multiple social institutions and social groups (Moschis & Churchill, 1978; Ward, Klees, & Robertson, 1987). These social institutions and groups have powerful influences on consumers in terms of what they purchase and consume. Conforming to such social influences and pressures, consumers consciously reduce their choices and continue to engage in certain types of consumption patterns that are acceptable to the social groups to which they belong (Park & Lessig, 1977). Such group influences are also captured in the normative component in attitude-behavior models (Miniard & Cohen, 1983; Ryan, 1982; Sheth, 1974a; Sheth, Newman, & Gross, 1991).

The Influence of Family and Social Groups

Among the various social institutions that influence consumer behavior, family appears to be very important. As the basic sociological unit, the family determines and shapes the entire social viewpoints and perceptions of all of its members, including their purchase and consumption behavior. Family influences on consumer behavior have been the subject of investigation by many marketing scholars (Childers & Rao, 1992; Corfman & Lehmann, 1987; Sheth, 1974b). Studies have indicated that key family consumption roles are played by either a single member or several family members, varying across families and products. However, whoever may make the decisions or be the final users, family interests and norms are accounted for. For shared consumption, the choices for products or services to be consumed are reduced to those that will have greatest appeal among all consuming members of the family. Family norms and values, therefore, direct individual choices.

Conforming to norms and limiting choices to those that are appropriate within the social sphere to which the individual belongs are the underlying phenomena of the influence of social groups on consumers (Coleman, 1983). The key question is, Why do consumers comply with group and social influences? According to the theories of social exchange and interaction (Blau, 1964; Homans, 1961; Nisbet, 1973), there are at least four influencing factors: power, conflict, social exchange, and cooperation. Families and social groups have a greater level of power than do their individual members. Some of this power is legitimated in the form of authority, and some may be exercised through means of group rewards, coercion, and expertise. Individuals are subject to such power and also often possess it over others. Some of this power has perceived rewards and punishments associated with it, and individuals comply either to receive benefits or to avoid punishments.

A related aspect of power is conflict, which consumers like to avoid under normal circumstances. The concept of conflict is closely linked to that of psychological tension, discussed earlier. Consumers inherently like to avoid conflict and thus resort to more cooperative behavior. *Cooperation* here refers to joint efforts or behavior used to achieve a common goal. By yielding to or accepting social norms, consumers agree to cooperate with the interests of other members of the family and/or social group. According to social exchange theory, members usually expect reciprocal benefits when they act according to social norms. These could be in the form of personal affection, trust, gratitude, and sometimes economic returns. Other theories of group influence processes suggest that individuals are influenced by groups in ways that go beyond the use of power (Goodwin, 1987; Kelman, 1958). They propose that individuals have a desire to be closely identified with particular groups, and in order to attain such close relationships, individuals will adopt the behavioral norms of groups, irrespective of the level of the importance of the decision to the individuals. In other cases, individuals agree that the group's beliefs and norms are appropriate for the individuals as well, and hence the individuals internalize those norms.

> P10a: The greater the social orientation of the consumer, the greater will be consumer propensity to accept family and social norms with respect to relational market behavior.
>
> P10b: The intergeneration pattern of relational market behavior will be more prevalent among family-oriented consumers.

The Influence of Reference Groups and Word-of-Mouth Communication

Identification and internalization are also key constructs within reference group theory, as propounded by Herbert Hyman (1942). According to this theory, individuals compare themselves with a reference group to whom they look for guidance for their own behavior. Consumers may not necessarily be members of the group or be in physical contact with it, yet by referring to the group and its normative practices, individuals develop values and standards for their own behavior (Bearden & Etzel, 1982; Childers & Rao, 1992; Stafford & Cocanougher, 1977). Some of this behavior may be aspirational in nature (i.e., wanting to appear to be in a higher social class than one's own) or even dissociative (i.e., acting in a way deliberately opposite to the behavior of the selected group). The influences of reference groups on consumption behavior are quite common and are abundantly seen, for example, in celebrity advertisements, testimonials, and endorsements employed in modern advertising. Youngsters, in particular, are known to flock to celebrity-endorsed sportswear.

The two underlying motivational dimensions of reference-group-related consumer behavior are human aspirations and reduction of perceived risk (Bearden, Netemeyer, & Teel, 1989; Kelley, 1966). By adopting behavior similar to that of reference groups, individual consumers are fulfilling their aspirations. By rejecting the behavior of certain reference groups (those groups that are perceived negatively), consumers seek to lower their perceived risk. Consumers' motivations for reducing choices are therefore guided by what they would like to accomplish and what they would like to avoid.

> P11: The greater the potential of a market choice to fulfill social aspirations or reduce social risks, the greater will be consumer propensity to adopt relational market behavior.

Social group influences are coupled with powerful word-of-mouth communication (Arndt, 1967). Consumers either actively seek information and experiences of other consumers or overhear from other consumers their experiences regarding certain consumption situations. The influence of these sources of information has been extremely potent. Several researchers have found that individuals' perceptions and behavior are influenced by those of others, particularly in high perceived-risk situations (Grewal, Gotlieb, & Marmorstein, 1994). Generally called *informational social influence,* word-of-mouth communication can lead consumers to favorable acceptance of products and marketers or can repel them. The pioneering studies of Everett Rogers (1962) on the diffusion of innovation suggest that opinion leaders, through word-of-mouth communication, can exert direct influence on other consumers to adopt innovation.

There are two central constructs underlying word-of-mouth communication behavior: the source credibility of the communicator and the network through which the communication travels (Gatignon & Robertson, 1985; Zaltman & Stiff, 1973). When there is high source credibility and the connectedness among members in the referral network is high, word-of-mouth communication has greater influence (Brown & Reingen, 1987; Dholakia & Sternthal, 1977). Why are consumers influenced by word-of-mouth communication? They are influenced because (a) they have an inherent desire to be socially integrated, and (b) they would like to reduce their perceived risk (Herr, Kardes, & Kim, 1991; Richins, 1983). Thus connectedness and reliability are key issues in consumer behavior and choice reduction.

P12: Consumers will have a greater propensity to engage in relationships with market choices that are recommended by opinion leaders of referral networks.

In conclusion, sociological theories of consumer behavior suggest that consumers reduce choice to comply with group norms. Such compliance is motivated by consumers' desire to develop close relationships with the group, to attain the benefits of socialization and the rewards associated with social compliance, and to avoid conflict and punishments associated with noncompliance to norms. Consumers also reduce choice in order to fulfill aspirations and reduce perceived risk. They have a desire to be socially connected and give credence to information that has strong social ties. Those who have strong social orientations are likely to be more relationship-conscious than others.

However, a somewhat opposite view has been developed under reactance theory (Clee & Wicklund, 1980; Lessne & Venkatesan, 1989). Assuming that consumers are accustomed to having freedom of choice most of the time, reactance theorists have attempted to explain why consumers react against social pressures. Their contention is that when freedom of choice exerts significant pressure, consumers tend to react. It is possible that when group pressures exceed the limits of acceptable freedom, consumers may exhibit reactionary behavior. The implication of this is that although consumers are naturally inclined toward reducing choice, when forced to forgo all choices, or when they feel excessive pressure to conform to the beliefs of others, consumers react against that pressure. This theory may also be applicable in the area of relationship marketing practices, in that if marketers create excessive barriers, or create high switching costs, customers are likely to react negatively.

P13: The greater the sociological orientation of consumers, the greater will be their propensity to reduce choice and engage in relationships. However, there will be greater potential for revolt by consumers when such norms are excessively emphasized.

INSTITUTIONAL REASONS TO ENGAGE
IN RELATIONAL MARKET BEHAVIOR

There are at least four institutions that influence consumer behavior and play active roles in reducing consumer choice: government, religion, employers, and marketing. Each of these adopts a variety of explicit and implicit processes and person mechanisms to reduce consumer choice.

The Influence of Government

Governments around the world, in varying degrees of control, restrict consumers' choices. Through regulatory policies, governments specify norms, rules, regulations, technical standards, and the extent of public consumption. For example, governments have laws regarding minimum ages for automobile driving and alcohol consumption, impose restrictions on the sale of prescription drugs, prescribe limitations on the number of utility companies that can operate in a city, and create zoning laws that define where residential structures can be built. In addition to regulations, governments use participatory and promotional mechanisms to influence consumer behavior. For example, in several countries, governments directly purchase and distribute certain types of food grains, own and manage broadcast media and public transportation systems, provide incentives such as income tax deductions for home mortgages to promote home ownership, and run advertising campaigns to promote family planning. Consumers have to restrict their choices of products and services to those that are within government policy guidelines or, in some cases, to alternatives that are offered by the government (Sheth & Frazier, 1982). Such policies, although formed in the best interests of the citizens of the society, are essentially a choice reduction mechanism. Our purpose here is not to question the appropriateness of such government policies and regulations, but rather to seek an explanation of why consumers abide by these regulations.

There are three underlying theories to explain consumers' abidance by government regulations: social and civic responsibility theory (McNeill, 1974), compliance theory (Asch, 1953; Brockner, Guzi, Kane, Levine, & Shaplen, 1984), and welfare theory (Kamakura, Ratchford, & Agrawal, 1988). According to civic and social responsibility theory, in abiding by the laws of the government, consumers are generally meeting their civic responsibilities. It is assumed that citizens are conscious of their enlightened self-interest and believe that by following all rules and regulations they will help in making a better society. Under this assumption, consumers believe that the government has good reasons for forming certain policies and that the government has in mind the best interests of its citizens.

The consumers are thus self-convinced of the benefits of reduction of choice for themselves.

A similar but slightly different viewpoint is held under welfare theory. According to this theory, citizens yield to government policies, even though those policies may not be favorable to their personal interests, because they believe that governments are responsible for the welfare of all citizens and such policies are likely to benefit the needy segments of the society. The assumption here is that consumers are generally willing to make sacrifices regarding personal choices if other segments of the society can potentially benefit from their sacrifices (Corfman & Lehmann, 1993).

Compliance theory argues that consumers comply with government regulations to avoid punishments. Governments have coercive power that can be exercised to penalize offenders of the law. Thus even if consumers do not like certain rules and regulations, they can hardly afford to ignore them and consequently end up abiding by them. In essence, compliance theory is based on the concept of perceived risk, wherein noncompliance is associated with the risk of punishment.

P14: Consumers are more likely to maintain relationships with those market choices that are mandated by the government, especially if those choices also serve consumers' self-interests.

Religion and Relational Market Behavior

Although consumer behavior in the context of religious influences and mandates has not been studied extensively (some exceptions being Delener & Schiffman, 1988; Hirschman, 1988; McDaniel & Burnett, 1988), the influence of religion on the behavior of individuals is profound. Not only are symbolic and ritualistic consumption behaviors directed by religion, but moral training and spiritual education provided by religious institutions have behavioral impacts on individuals' use (consumption) of products, services, institutions, places, and time. For example, patronage of Catholic schools, religious hospitals, and religion-specific newspapers is common all over the world. There are three reasons that individuals comply with religious mandates and influences. One is the faith they have in religion and its doctrines. Strong faith develops strong beliefs and attitudes and thus influences individuals' worldviews, and when such persons are presented with choice alternatives in accordance with their faith, their responses are favorable. Not until their faith is shaken are individuals likely to act in a manner contrary to religious teachings.

The second reason consumers yield to the influence of religion is self-efficacy. Adopting moral values can lead to self-efficacy. When consumers follow religious teachings and doctrines, they have a sense of fulfillment and gratification. Recently there has been some attempt to incorporate self-efficacy in models of consumer behavior (Bagozzi & Warshaw, 1990).

Fear is the final reason many individuals accept the mandates of religious institutions. It is not uncommon for some religions to raise consumers' fears of the consequences of particular courses of action. If individuals do not respond to religious mandates, they are threatened with serious consequences.

> P15: Consumers are more likely to maintain relationships with those market choices that their religious institutions have identified as important, so as to maintain faith in their religions and enhance self-interest.

Employer Influence

Although consumer behavior studies have not focused on the influence of employers in the personal consumption of products and services, a lot of anecdotal evidence exists on employers' influence in reducing the choices of consumers. In addition to prescribing guidelines for employee usage of products and services within their organizations, employers influence employees concerning what they purchase and consume and use for their own personal or family purposes (Whyte, 1961). This influence includes norms that relate to employees' activities outside the organization, such as neighborhoods in which employees are expected to live, the types of automobiles they are expected to drive, social recreation behavior, and so on. In addition, employers limit employees' choices among fringe benefit items that are offered for personal consumption. For example, individual employees' choices are limited to the health plans offered by the company, the kind of telephone services available for use at the workplace, the food available in the cafeteria or vending machines, the office dress code, and so on. Company policy becomes almost as strong an influence as church and state. Consumers accept the limited choice of personal consumption at their workplaces because of the power of the institution and the impracticability of engaging in conflict with the hierarchy. The perceived risks of such conflict are usually extremely high, as the institution can end an individual's membership and thus deprive the person of various economic and noneconomic benefits. Some reference group arguments also apply here, in that individuals follow the consumption patterns of coworkers and supervisors because they serve as the reference group for the individual.

> P16: Consumers are more likely to engage in relational market behavior with those market choices that are formally or informally patronized by their employers.

Marketers' Influence on Relational Market Behavior

Marketers limit the purchase and consumption choices available to consumers. For example, in the case of a variety of stores, restaurants, and other service organizations, the hours of business impose limitations on available consumer options. Similarly, consumer options are restricted by marketers' decisions regarding the locations of businesses, the products they carry and offer for sale, the terms of payment (e.g., lease or purchase on credit), and so on. In general, whatever marketers do in terms of when, where, how, what, and who can engage in purchase or consumption inherently limits consumer choices. The marketing management literature illustrates how marketers influence consumers to reduce their choices through the use of advertising, pricing, merchandising, and other marketing mix variables (see Kotler, 1994).

> P17: Consumers will be more willing to accept marketer-induced choice reduction when marketer policies are positively balanced toward meeting the consumers' personalized needs.

In general, all four types of institutions discussed above influence consumers to reduce choice and to engage in relationships with marketers. However, institutions naturally differ in their influence, so that for some consumers government is most influential and for others religion, employers, or marketers themselves are. Although risk-reduction or compliance mechanisms may initiate a favorable response from consumers, ultimately consumers will not accept these institution-mandated choice reductions unless they perceive the limitations to be in their own self-interest.

P18: The greater the power of the institution to reduce consumer choices, the greater will be consumer propensity to engage in relational market behavior, as long as choice reduction is not capricious and against the interests of consumers.

In conclusion, psychological, sociological, and institutional theories of consumer behavior indicate that individual consumers are constantly facing limitations of choice that they normally yield to and accept. Consumers accept these limitations because they reduce perceived risk and uncertainty, psychological tension, and limitations of consumers' memory and information-processing capabilities; they promise rewards or threaten punishments; they have the potential to build expertise and confidence and to optimize decision making; they fulfill social and esteem needs, self-efficacy, faith, and fear; and they instill aspirations for a superior lifestyle. It is interesting to note that institutional and social influences are greater than personal influences of choice reduction. That is, consumers often comply with institutional mandates and social norms, even in situations in which they may think that the group norms or institutional mandates are against their own self-interests. Thus the proposition:

P19: Institutional forces will have greater influence on consumer propensity for relational market behavior than will social and personal forces. Personal forces will have the least influence on consumer propensity to engage in relational market behavior compared with institutional and social forces.

WHAT WE HAVE LEARNED
ABOUT CONSUMER BEHAVIOR

The established theories of consumer behavior suggest the following conclusions:

1. Contrary to expectations of microeconomic theory, consumers have a natural tendency to reduce choices, and, actually, consumers like to reduce their choices to a manageable set.
2. Reduction of choice does not necessarily mean a choice of one. It may result in choice among a few alternatives—usually not more than three (an evoked set).
3. Society is organized to reduce choices; that is, reducing choices for individuals is the norm for society.

4. Institutions such as government, religion, and employing organizations are actively engaged in systematically influencing choice reduction for individual consumers.

5. Institutions are the most powerful mechanisms for generating relationship behavior in consumers because they have legitimated power to reward and punish certain types of behavior. Reference groups, including cohorts such as coworkers, are the next most powerful influencing body. Their influences are both aspirational and coercive.

6. Individuals, although personally inclined toward being in relationships, are the least powerful influencers of such behavior. That is, societal and institutional motivations for relationship formation and maintenance are stronger than individual motivations. Therefore, we predict that relationship marketing activities that are more institutionally based will be more stable than those based on individuals.

7. There are several circumstances under which consumers terminate relationships:
   a. Satiation—that is, consumers seek novelty due to boredom with the current consumption.
   b. Dissatisfaction—this may occur if suppliers fail to match their offerings to rising customer expectations. As we know, consumer expectations rise with every level of satisfaction achieved, and when their expectations remain unfulfilled, consumers will terminate the relationship with that marketer.
   c. Superior alternatives—that is, an alternative has a higher perceived value.
   d. Conflict—that is, disagreement with the existing marketer.
   e. High exit barriers—if consumers experience high exit barriers, there is likely to be consumer revolt. Thus it is important for marketers to provide consumers the opportunity to voice their concerns, especially when choice is not available or is restricted.

Consequences of Relationship Marketing

In this section, we focus on some of the likely consequences of relationship marketing in consumer markets. It is our belief that relationship marketing will lead to greater marketing productivity by making marketing more effective and efficient. This in turn will lead to a greater willingness and ability among marketers to engage in and maintain long-term relationships with consumers. It is also our belief that these partnering relationships will be judged favorably by public policy and social critics as long as marketers or consumers do not abuse the relationships.

IMPROVEMENT IN MARKETING PRODUCTIVITY

Marketing productivity has come under critical scrutiny by the chief executives of companies and other business experts (Sullivan, 1991). The major criticisms have centered on the unnecessary marketing expenditures, ill focus, and overindulgence of the competitive pricing and advertising wars, as well as on the lack of innovative marketing practices (Sheth & Sisodia, 1995). Relationship marketing has the potential to improve marketing productivity by making marketing more effective and efficient. With one-to-one marketing practices and an increase in customer involvement in the organizational functions of design, development, and sales, relationship marketing will be more effective than other forms of marketing in meeting consumer needs. Similarly, by reducing some of the wasteful marketing practices associated with competitive mass marketing, and by letting the consumer become a partial producer, relationship marketing will help achieve greater marketing efficiency.

Achieving Marketing Effectiveness

The focus of relationship marketing is on establishing and enhancing a long-term, mutually beneficial relationship between the consumer and the marketer. Such a relationship assumes that the marketer is oriented toward customer retention and the development of a unique relationship with each individual customer, and is interested in involving the customer in the design, development, and marketing processes of the company (see McKenna, 1991; Peppers & Rogers, 1993; Sheth & Parvatiyar, 1993). Consequently, relationship marketing is likely to make marketing practices more effective because, on the one hand, the individual customer's needs are better addressed, and, on the other, consumer involvement in the development of marketing processes and practices leads to greater consumer commitment to the marketer's programs.

Individual Marketing

Marketing effectiveness is accomplished through the appropriate direction of marketing resources toward those areas that provide the greatest value to consumers. Implicit in the idea of relationship marketing are consumer focus and consumer selectivity—that is, all consumers do not need to be served the same way. In fact, it may not be feasible or worthwhile to develop long-term relationships with all consumers. Anticipation and recognition of different customer values, and appropriate company responses to service them individually, will make marketing more effective (Sheth & Mittal, 1995). Mass marketing is incapable of accommodating the diversity of consumers.

To a large extent, such individualized marketing is being facilitated by "mass customization" processes and their enabling technological advances. The most relevant of these advances are information technology and flexible manufacturing. Information technology now allows for interactive integration of customers with the business firm. With the interactive information technology available today, marketers can create and maintain organizational memory on each individual consumer, his or her preferences, behavior patterns, and many other characteristics (Sheth & Sisodia, 1993). Similarly, flexible manufacturing systems permit mass customization or mass-scale customized production of items to suit each individual consumer's specific requirements without significantly affecting economies of scale. The application of flexible manufacturing processes and mass customization is evident in, for example, the manufacture of pagers by Motorola, the printing of Hallmark greeting cards, and newsmagazine publication by Time Inc. Information technology and mass customization can be used cost-effectively to perpetuate relationships with customers (Sheth, 1994).

Consumer Involvement

A second reason relationship marketing leads to increased marketing effectiveness is consumer involvement in the design, development, and marketing processes of the company. With relationship marketing strategies that promote the early involvement of consumers in new product design and development processes, in training and compensation of employees, and in reviewing marketing or sales strategies, marketers can build rewarding relationships with consumers who not only provide invaluable information to the company but are themselves more committed to the company's market offerings. Thus customer involvement will increase marketing effectiveness.

Minimization of the Negative Image of Marketing

Finally, marketing effectiveness is also achieved through relationship marketing's minimization of the side effects or the negative public image of marketing practices. Many public policy and opinion leaders think that marketing practices are designed to manipulate consumers and, therefore, that consumer protection and vigilance are critical to balance the abusive powers of marketers. Similarly, many unenlightened marketers think of consumers as a "bloody nuisance" with an "entitlement" mind-set who are not willing to pay for the value offered by marketers. Indeed, many marketers fear that bogus lawsuits and allegations are put forward, especially in health care, as a way to exploit the underdog's rights and privileges. This acrimonious and nontrusting relationship and its costs to society can be mitigated by relational market behavior. In relationship marketing, instead of negotiations centered only on price, consumers are treated more like partners in business, and their role changes from passive recipient of marketing practices to interactive coproducer of marketing practices. This should remove some of the negative images of marketing and thereby enhance marketing effectiveness.

Achieving Marketing Efficiency

Three important aspects of relationship marketing lead to greater marketing efficiency. First, "customer retention economics" suggests that when marketers direct greater efforts toward retaining customers, it should be less expensive to do business. Second, with cooperative and efficient consumer response, marketers will be able to reduce many unproductive marketing resources that are wasted in the system. And third, as cooperation develops between the consumer and the marketer, the consumer will be willing to undertake some of the value-creation activities currently being performed by the marketer, such as self-service, self-ordering, and coproduction.

Customer retention. A fundamental aspect of long-term relationships between marketers and consumers is the encouragement of customer retention. It has been demonstrated that it is far less expensive to retain a customer than it is to acquire a new one (Reichheld & Sasser, 1990). Also, the longer the customer stays in the relationship, the more profitable this becomes to the marketer. For example, data from the banking industry indicate that a customer who has been with a bank for 5 years is far more profitable than a customer who has been with the bank for 1 year. Likewise, it has been estimated that automobile insurance policies must be in force for 7 years before they become profitable (Sheth & Sisodia, 1995). Therefore, when marketing dollars are spent more on retaining customers under the relationship marketing strategy, this is likely to make marketing more efficient.

Making resources more productive. A significant number of marketing activities generate wasteful expenditures. For example, it has been established that the average yield on 200 billion coupons distributed in the United States is no more than 2%. Given the massive efforts involved in large-scale printing and distribution of coupons, much of this seems to be wasted effort. Similarly, due to failure in proper forecasting and coordination of distribution logistics, a massive amount of inventory sits idle in the marketing system. One result of this overstocking in distribution channels is the increased pressure that marketers and middlemen exert on consumers to move some of the inventory. A lot of advertising dollars are spent in transferring some of this inventory from the marketer to the consumers. Given the expensive nature of mass advertising and the low yield it produces, marketing inefficiencies are common. Additionally, consumption-oriented mass marketing also generates a lot of waste in the form of excessive products, packaging, and so on, making marketing activities unsustainable for the society (Sheth & Parvatiyar, 1995).

Consumer-marketer partnering could bring about quick responses by marketers, leading to greater efficiency. The apparel and grocery industries have already initiated "quick response" schemes to reduce inventory in the system. A report on efficient consumer response (ECR) by Kurt Salmon Associates (1993) for the Food Marketing Institute found that the grocery industry had the potential to reduce inventory by 41% and to save $30 billion a year by adopting ECR. The ECR system is based on timely, accurate, and paperless information flow among suppliers, distributors, retail stores, and consumer households. Its objective is to provide a continual product flow matched to consumption. When consumers and marketers have good relationships and cooperate with each other, such flow can be more easily accomplished.

Asking consumers to do marketers' work. Consumers, in general, are more satisfied when they themselves can perform certain tasks that marketers would normally do for them. In a relationship, consumers are provided the opportunity to perform some of their own tasks, such as order processing, designing products, and managing information. They feel more empowered and hence more satisfied. However, not all consumers are willing to perform the same tasks. Individual consumers have their own abilities and requirements. Relationship marketing acknowledges this and allows individual consumers the flexibility to choose their own tasks. By letting consumers undertake some tasks, marketers reduce their own costs associated with these tasks, leading to greater efficiency. For example, stocks are purchased electronically with flat commissions, public phone services are automated, and banking services are performed through ATMs.

The Future of Relationship Marketing in Consumer Markets

Relationship marketing practices in consumer markets will grow in the future. Consumers have always been interested in relationships with marketers. In the future, marketer-initiated approaches to relationship marketing will become more prevalent and their frequency will rise sharply. Technological advances are making it possible and affordable for marketers to engage in and maintain relationships with customers. Marketers now have both the willingness and the ability to engage in relational marketing. The willingness has come from enlightened self-interest and the understanding that customer retention is economically more advantageous than constantly seeking new customers. The ability to engage in relationship marketing has developed primarily because of technological advances that are facilitating the process of engaging in and managing relationships with individual consumers.

Marketers are also likely to undertake efforts to institutionalize relationships with consumers—that is, create corporate bonding instead of bonding between a frontline salesperson and consumer alone. Corporate bonding would extend beyond single levels of the relationship to multiple levels. For instance, instead of sales personnel being the only ones responsible for creating and maintaining relationships with consumers, it is quite likely that other professionals in the company will also be able to interact directly and develop psychological bonds with consumers. Similarly, marketers would extend relationships to consumers' family members and friends. MCI's Friends and Family program is a good example of how one marketer has broadened the relationship with the larger social group. Once again, technology is the prime facilitator of such bonding. We are likely to see electronic frontline "intelligent agent" systems that can interface and become relationship managers for individual accounts. However, human backup to such technological systems is likely to continue, given consumers' desire for personal interaction with their marketers.

There will also be some fundamental changes in relationship marketing as a consequence of information technology. Technology will not only assist in relationship formation, it will help in the enhancement, and even termination, of relationships. Through the use of information technology, consumers can enhance relationships with marketing organizations. For example, when a bank or credit card company establishes a Web site, consumers learn about other offerings of the marketer and patronize multiple services, resulting in one-stop service. Consumers may not only conduct transactions and other business over these interactive networks, they may provide and obtain additional information from the marketers. Similarly, using such interactive systems, consumers can terminate their relationships with marketers if they so desire. It will become easier for consumers to leave membership programs when they can simply inform the marketers by e-mail.

Technologies such as electronic bulletin boards and integrated data interchange will facilitate group and institutional influence on consumers to engage in or terminate certain relationships. Already we are aware of the formation of interest groups that share views about products and marketers on electronic bulletin boards. Many institutions, such as churches, employers, and marketers, are using these forums to shape consumer choices and expectations. The U.S. Internal Revenue Service and the Department of Commerce effectively use electronic forms for filing tax returns and import-export applications, respectively. These agencies induce compliance with their rules through the wide dissemination of their forms. Several companies have begun to use fax broadcasts, voice-mail broadcasts, and electronic bulletin boards to influence existing and potential customers to engage in relationships.

Recently in consumer marketing, the focus has shifted from creating brand and store loyalties through mass advertising and sales promotion programs toward developing direct one-to-one relationships. These relationship marketing programs include frequent-user incentives, customer referral benefits, preferred customer programs, aftermarket support, use of relational databases, mass customization, and consumer involvement in company decisions. In most cases, consumers are also willing to accept such relationships with marketers. Evidence for this is found in the growth of membership in airline and hotel frequent-user programs, the use of store membership cards, direct inquiries, and registration with customer service hot lines established by manufacturers.

Our contention is that the more marketers try to develop relationships directly with their consumers (as opposed to through middlemen), the better will be the response and commitment from consumers. This is because middlemen do not have the same emotional bonds to what they offer as do manufacturers or service creators. Middlemen tend to be more transaction oriented, as they have neither the emotional attachment of producers nor the involvement of consumers with regard to consuming products and services. They derive their profits from transactions and not from production of products or services. In fact, one of the reasons marketing became more transaction oriented in the industrial era was the advent and later prevalence of middlemen (Sheth & Parvatiyar, 1993). As our society has become more service oriented, we have seen a shift toward direct marketing that bypasses the middlemen. As producers and consumers interact more directly, we expect that the relationship approach to market behavior will become increasingly prevalent.

APPENDIX Consumer Behavior Theories and Relational Market Behavior

Theoretical Approaches	Illustrative Works	Problems Explained	Relevance to Relational Market Behavior
Buyer behavior theory	Engel, Blackwell, and Miniard (1986); Howard and Sheth (1969); Nicosia (1966)	Consumer problem-solving behavior	Consumers reduce choice through use of evoked set. Desire for simplification and routinization of task drive relational behavior.
Learning/ conditioning theories	Berlyne (1960); Dawson, Schell, Beers, and Kelly (1982); Shimp (1991); Skinner (1953)	How consumer behavior is conditioned over time	Learned experiences help in stimulus generalization. Expectations of positive reinforcements induce relational market behavior.
Information processing and memory	Alba, Hutchinson, and Lynch (1991); Bettman (1979); Keller and Staelin (1987); Miller (1956); Simon (1955)	Consumer ability to process information	Relational market behavior helps rehearse memory and simplifies the information-processing task.

Theoretical Approaches	Illustrative Works	Problems Explained	Relevance to Relational Market Behavior
Perceived risk	Bauer (1960); Beatty and Smith (1987); Cox (1967); Derbaix (1983); Dowling and Staelin (1994); Kiel (1977); Taylor (1974)	Consumer risk-reduction behavior	Consumers become brand loyal—a manifestation of relational market behavior—to reduce perceived risk. Relational behavior develops self-confidence in consumers.
Cognitive consistency: balance theory, congruity theory, confirmation-disconfirmation theory of attitudes, cognitive dissonance theory	Bagozzi, Baumgartner, and Yi (1992); Fazio and Zanna (1981); Festinger (1957); Heider (1946); Hunt (1970); McGuire (1976); Oliver (1993); Osgood and Tannenbaum (1955)	How consumers' beliefs and feelings affect their behavior	Relational market behavior reduces psychological tension by creating more consistency in the cognitive system and reduces the potential for cognitive dissonance.
Family buying behavior	Childers and Rao (1992); Corfman and Lehmann (1987); Sheth (1974b)	The influence of family on consumer behavior	Consumers engage in relational market behavior to conform to family norms and interests, given the power of the family over the individual.
Social groups/social exchange theory/group influence processes	Blau (1964); Coleman (1983); Goodwin (1987); Homans (1961); Levy (1966); Nisbet (1973); Ward, Klees, and Robertson (1987)	The influence of social groups on consumer behavior	Consumers engage in relational market behavior by conforming to group norms in order to avail themselves of the benefits of socialization and to avoid conflict.
Reference group theory and word-of-mouth communication	Arndt (1967); Bearden and Etzel (1982); Brown and Reingen (1987); Herr, Kardes, and Kim (1991); Hyman (1942); Kelley (1966); Richins (1983); Rogers (1962)	How consumer behavior is influenced by reference groups and word-of-mouth communication	The motive to be socially integrated drives consumers to engage in relational market behavior, in accordance with the reference groups and word-of-mouth communication from opinion leaders.

Theoretical Approaches	Illustrative Works	Problems Explained	Relevance to Relational Market Behavior
Government: civic responsibility theory, compliance theory, welfare theory	Asch (1953); Brockner, Guzi, Kane, Levine, and Shaplen (1984); Corfman and Lehmann (1993); Kamakura, Ratchford, and Agrawal (1988); McNeill (1974)	Why consumers abide by government mandates	Consumers engage in relational market behavior when mandated by the government because of civic responsibilities, welfare expectations, and fear of legal action.
Religion: patronage theory, self-efficacy theory	Bagozzi and Warshaw (1990); Delener and Schiffman (1988); Hirschman (1988); McDaniel and Burnett (1988)	How religion and moral values influence consumer behavior	Strong faith, self-efficacy, and fear of negative consequences motivate consumers to engage in relational market behavior in such cases where choice is associated with religion.
Employers: organizational influence	Whyte (1961)	How employer organizations influence the personal lives of individuals	Consumers patronize those market behavior choices that are formally or informally patronized by their employers.

Notes

1. We use the term *axiom* here to describe our belief as to what constitutes a relationship. We use it in the same sense Milton Friedman (1953) uses it to describe "critical assumptions." Our axiom of consumer choice reduction in a relationship is selected on the grounds of "intuitive plausibility." It serves the purpose described by Brodbeck (1968), that axioms are "laws whose truth is, temporarily at least, taken for granted in order to see what other empirical assertions—the theorems—must be true if they are" (p. 10). Hunt (1991) summarizes the debate on axioms: "Axioms are true for the purpose of constructing theory rather than for the purpose of evaluating theory" (p. 131). However, the axioms in one theory could be theorems in another (Brodbeck, 1968).

2. As an intuitive observation, we know that human beings and primates are inclined to be in relationships with other human beings and primates. The disciplines of sociology and anthropology are essentially based on this premise. In personal relationships, people constantly forgo the opportunity to exercise continual choice and instead commit themselves to particular persons for relationships over time. This is true in dating, in marriage, and, in fact, in commitments to best friends, mentors, apprentices, and so on.

3. This is also the essence of learning behavior. Memory as a relevant construct of relationship marketing is applicable both from a consumer's perspective and from a marketer's

perspective. Madhavan, Shah, and Grover (1994) argue that a key characteristic of relation-ship marketing is organizational memory, in which a firm retains all relevant information about consumers and uses it to guide future interactions with them. The essence of a learn-ing organization is the creation and effective use of organizational memory (Senge, 1990).

References

Alba, J. W., Hutchinson, J. W., & Lynch, J. G., Jr. (1991). Memory and decision making. In T. S. Robertson & H. H. Kassarjian (Eds.), *Handbook of consumer behavior* (pp. 1-49). Engle-wood Cliffs, NJ: Prentice Hall.

Anderson, J. C., Håkansson, H., & Johanson, J. (1994). Dyadic business relationships within a business network context. *Journal of Marketing, 58*(4), 1-15.

Andreasen, A. R. (1965). Attitudes and customer behavior: A decision model. In L. E. Preston (Ed.), *New research in marketing* (pp. 1-16). Berkeley: University of California, Institute of Business and Economic Research.

Arndt, J. (1967). *Word of mouth advertising: A review of the literature.* New York: Advertising Research Foundation.

Asch, S. E. (1953). Effects of group pressure upon the modification and distortion of judg-ments. In D. Cartwright & A. Zander (Eds.), *Group dynamics* (pp. 189-200). New York: Harper & Row.

Bagozzi, R. P., Baumgartner, H., & Yi, Y. (1992). State versus action orientation and the theory of reasoned action: An application to coupon usage. *Journal of Consumer Research, 18,* 505-518.

Bagozzi, R. P., & Warshaw, P. R. (1990). Trying to consume. *Journal of Consumer Research, 17,* 127-140.

Bauer, R. A. (1960). Consumer behavior as risk taking. In R. S. Hancock (Ed.), *Dynamic mar-keting for a changing world* (pp. 389-398). Chicago: American Marketing Association.

Bearden, W. O., & Etzel, M. (1982). Reference group influence on product and brand purchase decisions. *Journal of Consumer Research, 9,* 183-194.

Bearden, W. O., Netemeyer, R., & Teel, J. (1989). Measurement of consumer susceptibility to interpersonal influence. *Journal of Consumer Research, 15,* 473-481.

Beatty, S. E., & Smith, S. M. (1987). External search effort: An investigation across several product categories. *Journal of Consumer Research, 14,* 83-95.

Berlyne, D. E. (1960). *Conflict, arousal, and curiosity.* New York: McGraw-Hill.

Berry, L. L. (1983). Relationship marketing. In L. L. Berry, G. L. Shostack, & G. D. Upah (Eds.), *Emerging perspectives on service marketing* (pp. 25-38). Chicago: American Mar-keting Association.

Bettman, J. R. (1979). *An information processing theory of consumer choice.* Reading, MA: Addison-Wesley.

Bettman, J. R., & Park, C. W. (1980). Effects of prior knowledge and experience and phase of the choice process on consumer decision processes: A protocol analysis. *Journal of Con-sumer Research, 7,* 234-248.

Bettman, J. R., Johnson, E. J., & Payne, J. W. (1991). Consumer decision making. In T. S. Rob-ertson & H. H. Kassarjian (Eds.), *Handbook of consumer behavior* (pp. 50-84). Engle-wood Cliffs, NJ: Prentice Hall.

Biehal, G., & Chakravarti, D. (1986). Consumers' use of memory and external information in choice: Macro and micro perspectives. *Journal of Consumer Research, 12,* 382-405.

Blau, P. (1964). *Exchange and power in social life.* New York: John Wiley.

Boyle, B., Dwyer, F. R., Robicheaux, R. A., & Simpson, J. T. (1992). Influence strategies in marketing channels: Measures and use in different relationship structures. *Journal of Marketing Research, 29*, 462-473.

Brockner, J., Guzi, B., Kane, J., Levine, E., & Shaplen, K. (1984). Organizational fundraising: Further evidence on the effect of legitimizing small donations. *Journal of Consumer Research, 11*, 611-614.

Brodbeck, M. (1968). *Readings in the philosophy of social sciences.* New York: Macmillan.

Brown, J. J., & Reingen, P. (1987). Social ties and word of mouth referral behavior. *Journal of Consumer Research, 14*, 350-362.

Bucklin, L. P., & Sengupta, S. (1993). Organizing successful co-marketing alliances. *Journal of Marketing, 57*(2), 32-46.

Childers, T. L., & Rao, A. R. (1992). Influence of familial and peer-based reference groups on consumer decisions. *Journal of Consumer Research, 19*, 198-211.

Christopher, M., Payne, A., & Ballantyne, D. (1991). *Relationship marketing: Bringing quality, customer service and marketing together.* Oxford: Butterworth-Heinemann.

Clee, M. A., & Wicklund, R. A. (1980). Consumer behavior and psychological reactance. *Journal of Consumer Research, 6*, 389-405.

Coleman, R. P. (1983). The continuing significance of social class to marketing. *Journal of Consumer Research, 10*, 265-280.

Copulsky, J. R., & Wolf, M. J. (1990, July-August). Relationship marketing: Positioning for the future. *Journal of Business Strategy, 11*, 16-20.

Corfman, K. P., & Lehmann, D. (1987). Models of cooperative group decision-making and relative influence: An experimental investigation of family purchase decisions. *Journal of Consumer Research, 14*, 1-13.

Corfman, K. P., & Lehmann, D. (1993). The importance of others' welfare in evaluating bargaining outcomes. *Journal of Consumer Research, 20*, 124-137.

Cox, D. F. (Ed.). (1967). *Risk taking and information handling in consumer behavior.* Boston: Harvard University, Graduate School of Business Administration, Division of Research.

Crosby, L. A., Evans, K. R., & Cowles, D. (1990). Relationship quality in services selling: An interpersonal influence perspective. *Journal of Marketing, 54*(3), 68-81.

Crosby, L. A., & Stephens, N. (1987). Effects of relationship marketing and satisfaction, retention, and prices in the life insurance industry. *Journal of Marketing Research, 24*, 404-411.

Dawson, M. E., Schell, A. M., Beers, J. R., & Kelly, A. (1982). Allocation of cognitive processing capacity during human autonomic classical conditioning. *Journal of Experimental Psychology: General, 3*, 273-295.

Delener, N., & Schiffman, L. G. (1988). Family decision making: The impact of religious factors. In G. Frazier et al. (Eds.), *1988 AMA educators' proceedings* (pp. 80-83). Chicago: American Marketing Association.

Derbaix, C. (1983, January). Perceived risk and risk relievers: An empirical investigation. *Journal of Economic Psychology, 3*, 19-38.

Dholakia, R. R., & Sternthal, B. (1977). Highly credible sources: Persuasive facilitators or persuasive liabilities? *Journal of Consumer Research, 3*, 223-232.

Dick, A. S., & Basu, K. (1994). Customer loyalty: Toward an integrated conceptual framework. *Journal of the Academy of Marketing Science, 22*, 99-113.

Dowling, G., & Staelin, R. (1994). A model of perceived risk and intended risk-handling activity. *Journal of Consumer Research, 21*, 119-134.

Dwyer, F. R., Schurr, P. H., & Oh, S. (1987). Developing buyer-seller relationships. *Journal of Marketing, 51*(2), 11-27.

Engel, J. F., Blackwell, R. D., & Miniard, P. W. (1986). *Consumer behavior* (5th ed.). Chicago: Dryden.

Enis, B. M., & Paul, G. W. (1970). Store loyalty as a basis for market segmentation. *Journal of Retailing, 46*(3), 42-56.

Fazio, R. H., & Zanna, M. P. (1981). Direct experience and attitude-behavior consistency. In L. Berkowitz (Ed.), *Advances in experimental social psychology* (Vol. 14, pp. 162-202). New York: Academic Press.

Festinger, L. (1957). *A theory of cognitive dissonance*. Stanford, CA: Stanford University Press.

Friedman, M. (1953). The methodology of positive economics. In M. Brodbeck (Ed.), *Essays in positive economics* (pp. 508-528). Chicago: University of Chicago Press.

Ganesan, S. (1994). Determinants of long-term orientation in buyer-seller relationships. *Journal of Marketing, 58*(2), 1-19.

Gatignon, H., & Robertson, T. S. (1985). A propositional inventory for new diffusion research. *Journal of Consumer Research, 11,* 849-867.

Goodwin, C. (1987). A social-influence theory of consumer cooperation. *Advances in Consumer Research, 14,* 378-381.

Grewal, D., Gotlieb, J., & Marmorstein, H. (1994). The moderating effects of message framing and source credibility on the price-perceived risk relationship. *Journal of Consumer Research, 21,* 145-153.

Grönroos, C. (1990). Relationship approach to marketing in service contexts: The marketing and organizational behavior interface. *Journal of Business Research, 20*(1), 3-11.

Hansen, F. (1972). *Consumer choice behavior: A cognitive theory*. New York: Free Press.

Heide, J. B., & John, G. (1990). Alliances in industrial purchasing: The determinants of joint action in buyer-supplier relationships. *Journal of Marketing Research, 27,* 24-36.

Heide, J. B., & John, G. (1992). Do norms matter in marketing relationships? *Journal of Marketing, 56*(2), 32-44.

Heider, F. (1946). Attitudes and cognitive organization. *Journal of Psychology, 21,* 107-112.

Herr, P. M., Kardes, F., & Kim, J. (1991). Effects of word of mouth and product attribute information on persuasion: An accessibility-diagnosticity perspective. *Journal of Consumer Research, 17,* 454-462.

Hirschman, E. C. (1988). The ideology of consumption: A structural-syntactical analysis of *Dallas* and *Dynasty. Journal of Consumer Research, 15,* 344-359.

Homans, G. (1961). *Social behavior: Its elementary forms*. New York: Harcourt Brace & World.

Howard, J. A. (1965). *Marketing theory*. Boston: Allyn & Bacon.

Howard, J. A., & Sheth, J. N. (1969). *The theory of buyer behavior*. New York: John Wiley.

Hoyer, W. D. (1984). An examination of consumer decision making for a common repeat purchase product. *Journal of Consumer Research, 11,* 822-828.

Hunt, S. D. (1970). Post-transaction communications and dissonance reduction. *Journal of Marketing, 34*(3), 46-51.

Hunt, S. D. (1991). *Modern marketing theory*. Cincinnati, OH: Southwestern.

Hyman, H. (1942). The psychology of status. *Archives of Psychology, 38*(269).

Illingworth, J. D. (1991, Fall). Relationship marketing: Pursuing the perfect person-to-person relationship. *Journal of Services Marketing, 5,* 49-52.

Jacoby, J., & Chestnut, R. W. (1978). *Brand loyalty measurement and management*. New York: John Wiley.

Jacoby, J., & Kyner, D. B. (1973). Brand loyalty vs. repeat purchasing behavior. *Journal of Marketing Research, 10,* 1-9.

Jacoby, L. L., Speller, D. E., & Kohn, C. A. (1974). Brand choice behavior as a function of information load. *Journal of Marketing Research, 11,* 63-69.

Johanson, J., Hallén, L., & Seyed-Mohamed, N. (1991). Interfirm adaptation in business relationships. *Journal of Marketing, 55*(2), 29-37.

Kamakura, W. A., Ratchford, B. T., & Agrawal, J. (1988). Measuring market efficiency and welfare loss. *Journal of Consumer Research, 15,* 289-302.

Katona, G. (1975). *Psychological economics.* New York: Elsevier.

Keller, K. L. (1987). Memory factors in advertising: The effect of advertising retrieval cues on brand evaluations. *Journal of Consumer Research, 14,* 316-333.

Keller, K. L., & Staelin, R. (1987). Effects of quality and quantity of information on decision effectiveness. *Journal of Consumer Research, 14,* 200-213.

Kelley, H. H. (1966). Two functions of reference groups. In H. Proshansky & B. Seidenberg (Eds.), *Basic studies in social psychology* (pp. 210-214). New York: Holt, Rinehart & Winston.

Kelman, H. C. (1958). Compliance, identification, and internalization: Three processes of attitude change. *Journal of Conflict Resolution, 2*(2), 51-60.

Kiel, G. C. (1977). *An empirical analysis of new car buyers' external information search behavior.* Unpublished doctoral dissertation. University of New South Wales, Kensington, Australia.

Kotler, P. (1994). *Marketing management: Analysis, planning, implementation, and control.* Englewood Cliffs, NJ: Prentice Hall.

Kurt Salmon Associates. (1993). *Efficient consumer response: Enhancing consumer value in the grocery industry.* Washington, DC: Food Marketing Institute.

Lessne, G., & Venkatesan, M. (1989). Reactance theory in consumer research: The past, present, and future. *Advances in Consumer Research, 16,* 76-78.

Levy, S. J. (1966). Social class and consumer behavior. In J. W. Newman (Ed.), *On knowing the consumer* (pp. 146-150). New York: John Wiley.

Locander, W. B., & Hermann, P. W. (1979). The effect of self-confidence and anxiety on information seeking in consumer risk reduction. *Journal of Marketing Research, 16,* 268-274.

Madhavan, R., Shah, R. H., & Grover, R. (1994). Relationship marketing: An organizational process perspective. In J. N. Sheth & A. Parvatiyar (Eds.), *Relationship marketing: Theory, methods and applications.* Atlanta, GA: Emory University, Center for Relationship Marketing.

Mano, H., & Oliver, R. L. (1993). Assessing the dimensionality and structure of the consumption experience: Evaluation, feeling, and satisfaction. *Journal of Consumer Research, 20,* 451-466.

Mazursky, D., LaBarbera, P. A., & Aiello, A. (1987, Spring). When consumers switch brands. *Psychology and Marketing, 4,* 17-30.

McAlister, L., & Pessemier, E. (1982). Variety seeking behavior: An interdisciplinary review. *Journal of Consumer Research, 9,* 311-322.

McDaniel, S. W., & Burnett, J. J. (1988). Consumer religious commitment and retail store evaluative criteria [abstract]. In G. Frazier et al. (Eds.), *1988 AMA educators' proceedings.* Chicago: American Marketing Association.

McGuire, W. J. (1976). Some internal psychological factors influencing consumer choice. *Journal of Consumer Research, 2,* 302-319.

McKenna, R. (1991). *Relationship marketing: Successful strategies for the age of the customer.* Reading, MA: Addison-Wesley.

McNeill, J. (1974). Federal programs to measure consumer purchase expectations, 1946-1973: A post-mortem. *Journal of Consumer Research, 1*(3), 1-10.

McSweeney, F. K., & Bierley, C. (1984). Recent developments in classical conditioning. *Journal of Consumer Research, 11,* 619-631.

Meyers-Levy, J., & Tybout, A. (1989). Schema congruity as a basis for product evaluation. *Journal of Consumer Research, 16,* 39-54.

Miller, G. A. (1956). The magical number seven, plus or minus two: Some limits on our capacity for processing information. *Psychological Review, 63,* 81-97.

Miniard, P. W., & Cohen, J. (1983). Modeling personal and normative influences on behavior. *Journal of Consumer Research, 10,* 169-180.

Morgan, R. M., & Hunt, S. D. (1994). The commitment-trust theory of relationship marketing. *Journal of Marketing, 58*(3), 20-38.

Moschis, G. P., & Churchill, G. (1978). Consumer socialization: A theoretical and empirical analysis. *Journal of Marketing Research, 15,* 599-609.

Murdock, B. B., Jr. (1961). The retention of individual items. *Journal of Experimental Psychology, 62,* 618-625.

Nauman, E. (1995). *Creating customer value: The path to sustainable competitive advantage.* Cincinnati, OH: Thompson Executive.

Nicosia, F. M. (1966). *Consumer decision processes: Marketing and advertising implications.* Englewood Cliffs, NJ: Prentice Hall.

Nicosia, F. M., & Mayer, R. N. (1976). Toward a sociology of consumption. *Journal of Consumer Research, 3,* 65-75.

Nisbet, R. A. (1973). Behavior as seen by the actor and as seen by the observer. *Journal of Personality and Social Psychology, 27,* 154-164.

Oliver, R. L. (1993). Cognitive, affective and attribute bases of the satisfaction response. *Journal of Consumer Research, 20,* 418-430.

Osgood, C., & Tannenbaum, P. H. (1955). The principle of congruity in the production of attitude change. *Psychological Review, 62,* 42-55.

Park, C. W., & Lessig, V. P. (1977). Students and housewives: Differences in susceptibility to reference group influence. *Journal of Consumer Research, 4,* 102-110.

Peppers, D., & Rogers, M. (1993). *The one to one future: Building relationships one customer at a time.* Garden City, NY: Doubleday.

Punj, G. N., & Staelin, R. (1983). A model of consumer information search behavior for new automobiles. *Journal of Consumer Research, 9,* 366-380.

Raju, P. S. (1980). Optimum stimulation level: Its relationship to personality, demographics, and exploratory behavior. *Journal of Consumer Research, 7,* 272-282.

Reichheld, F. F., & Sasser, W. E., Jr. (1990). Zero defections: Quality comes to services. *Harvard Business Review, 69*(1), 105-111.

Reilly, M., & Parkinson, T. L. (1985). Individual and product correlates of evoked set size for consumer package goods. *Advances in Consumer Research, 12,* 492-497.

Richins, M. L. (1983). Negative word-of-mouth by dissatisfied consumers: A pilot study. *Journal of Marketing, 47*(1), 68-78.

Rogers, E. M. (1962). *Diffusion of innovations.* New York: Free Press.

Rosenberg, L. J., & Czepiel, J. A. (1984). A marketing approach to customer retention. *Journal of Consumer Marketing, 1*(2), 45-51.

Rust, R., & Zahorik, A. (1992). *A model of the impact of customer satisfaction on profitability: Application to a health service provider* (Working paper). Nashville, TN: Vanderbilt University.

Ryan, M. J. (1982). Behavioral intention formation: The interdependency of attitudinal and social influence variables. *Journal of Consumer Research, 9,* 263-278.

Senge, P. M. (1990). *The fifth discipline.* Garden City, NY: Doubleday.

Shani, D., & Chalasani, S. (1992). Exploiting niches using relationship marketing. *Journal of Consumer Marketing, 9*(3), 33-42.

Sheppard, B. H., Hartwick, J., & Warshaw, P. (1988). The theory of reasoned action: A meta-analysis of past research with recommendations for modifications and future research. *Journal of Consumer Research, 15,* 325-343.

Sheth, J. N. (1967, August). Review of buyer behavior. *Management Science Series B,* pp. B718-B756.

Sheth, J. N. (1974a). A field study of attitude structure and the attitude-behavior relationship. In J. N. Sheth (Ed.), *Models of buyer behavior: Conceptual, quantitative, and empirical* (pp. 242-268). New York: Harper & Row.

Sheth, J. N. (1974b). A theory of family buying decisions. In J. N. Sheth (Ed.), *Models of buyer behavior: Conceptual, quantitative, and empirical* (pp. 17-33). New York: Harper & Row.

Sheth, J. N. (1982). An integrative theory of patronage, preference and behavior. In W. Darden & R. Lusch (Eds.), *Patronage behavior and retail management* (pp. 9-28). New York: Elsevier North-Holland.

Sheth, J. N. (1994, July-August). A normative model of retaining customer satisfaction. *Gamma News Journal,* pp. 4-7.

Sheth, J. N., & Frazier, G. L. (1982). A model of strategy mix choice for planned social change. *Journal of Marketing, 46*(1), 15-26.

Sheth, J. N., & Mittal, B. (1995). *A framework for managing customer expectations* (Working Paper No. CRM-WP-94-106). Atlanta, GA: Emory University, Center for Relationship Marketing.

Sheth, J. N., Newman, B. I., & Gross, B. L. (1991). *Consumption values and market choices.* Cincinnati, OH: Southwestern.

Sheth, J. N., & Parvatiyar, A. (1992). Towards a theory of business alliance formation. *Scandinavian International Business Review, 1*(3), 71-87.

Sheth, J. N., & Parvatiyar, A. (1993, May). *The evolution of relationship marketing.* Paper presented at the Sixth Conference on Historical Thoughts in Marketing, Atlanta, GA.

Sheth, J. N., & Parvatiyar, A. (1995). Ecological imperatives and the role of marketing. In M. J. Polonsky & A. T. Mintu-Wimsatt (Eds.), *Environmental marketing: Strategies, practice, theory, and research* (pp. 3-20). New York: Haworth.

Sheth, J. N., & Raju, P. S. (1973). Sequential and cyclical nature of information processing in repetitive choice behavior. In S. Ward & P. Wright (Eds.), *Advances in consumer research* (pp. 348-358). Urbana, IL: Association for Consumer Research.

Sheth, J. N., & Sisodia, R. (1993). The information mall. *Telecommunications Policy, 17,* 376-389.

Sheth, J. N., & Sisodia, R. S. (1995). Improving marketing productivity. In J. Heilbrunn (Ed.), *Encyclopedia of marketing for the year 2000.* Chicago: American Marketing Association/NTC.

Shimp, T. A. (1991). Neo-Pavlovian conditioning and its implications for consumer theory and research. In T. S. Robertson & H. H. Kassarjian (Eds.), *Handbook of consumer behavior* (pp. 162-187). Englewood Cliffs, NJ: Prentice Hall.

Shimp, T. A., & Bearden, W. O. (1982). Warranty and other extrinsic cue effects on consumers' risk perceptions. *Journal of Consumer Research, 9,* 38-46.

Shugan, S. M. (1980). The cost of thinking. *Journal of Consumer Research, 7,* 99-111.

Simon, H. A. (1955). A behavioral model of rational choice. *Quarterly Journal of Economics, 69,* 99-118.

Simon, H. A. (1974, February). How big is a chunk? *Science, 183,* 482-488.

Skinner, B. F. (1953). *Science and human behavior.* New York: Free Press.

Stafford, J. E., & Cocanougher, A. B. (1977). Reference group theory. In R. Ferber (Ed.), *Selected aspects of consumer behavior: A summary from the perspective of different disciplines* (pp. 361-379). Washington, DC: National Science Foundation.

Stayman, D., Alden, D., & Smith, K. (1992). Some effects of schematic processing on consumer expectations and disconfirmation judgments. *Journal of Consumer Research, 19,* 240-255.

Sullivan, M. P. (1991, January 7). CEOs are asking about declining productivity in marketing. *American Banker,* p. 4.

Swan, J. E., & Nolan, J. K. (1985, November). Gaining customer trust: A conceptual guide for the salesperson. *Journal of Personal Selling and Sales Management, 5,* 39-48.

Taylor, J. W. (1974). The role of risk in consumer behavior. *Journal of Marketing, 38*(2), 54-60.

Vavra, T. G. (1992). *Aftermarketing: How to keep customers for life through relationship marketing.* Homewood, IL: Business One-Irwin.

Ward, S., Klees, D. M., & Robertson, T. S. (1987). Consumer socialization in different settings: An international perspective. *Advances in Consumer Research, 14,* 468-472.

Webster, F. E., Jr. (1992). The changing role of marketing in the corporation. *Journal of Marketing, 56*(4), 1-17.

Westbrook, R. A., & Oliver, R. (1991). The dimensionality of consumption emotion patterns and consumer satisfaction. *Journal of Consumer Research, 18,* 84-91.

Whyte, W. F. (1961). *Men at work.* Homewood, IL: Richard D. Irwin.

Zaltman, G., & Stiff, R. (1973). Theories of diffusion. In S. Ward & T. S. Robertson (Eds.), *Consumer behavior: Theoretical sources* (pp. 416-468). Englewood Cliffs, NJ: Prentice Hall.

8

Relationship Marketing and Distribution Channels

BARTON A. WEITZ
SANDY D. JAP

Channel management research and practice have long recognized the importance of managing relationships between the people and firms performing distribution functions—functions that create value by making products and services available to customers in appropriate form at the right places and times. However, the growing interest in relationship marketing suggests a shift in the nature of general marketplace transactions from discrete to relational exchanges—from exchanges between parties with no past history and no future to exchanges between parties who have an exchange history and plans for future interactions.

As Macneil (1980, p. 60) indicates, pure discrete transactions are rare in business exchanges. Almost all channel transactions have some

NOTE: This chapter is reprinted from Barton A. Weitz and Sandy D. Jap, "Relationship Marketing and Distribution Channels," *Journal of the Academy of Marketing Science*, vol. 23, no. 4, pp. 305-320, copyright © 1995 by the Academy of Marketing Science. Reprinted by permission.

relational elements that can be used to coordinate channel activities and manage relationships between channel members (for reviews, see Frazier, 1983; Gaski, 1984; Hunt, Ray, & Wood, 1985; Reve & Stern, 1979).[1] Thus relationship marketing is not a new concept in the practice and study of channel management. However, the interests of both practitioners and academics have shifted from approaches used by one firm, typically the manufacturer, to coordinate channel activities to approaches for stimulating cooperative efforts between independent channel members.

Our objectives in this chapter are to outline the nature of the shift in channel research attention and to review some of the key issues related to this new direction. We focus on research associated with relationships between suppliers and intermediaries such as wholesalers and retailers. Other contributors to this volume discuss direct relationships between suppliers and end users, either consumers or business firms.

In the next section, we present a framework for categorizing relationship-oriented channel management research and use it to highlight the shift in focus that has occurred. After offering some thoughts on why this shift has occurred, we review some directions for future research in channel relationships. Our purpose in this chapter is to identify key unresolved issues in channel relationship management, not to provide a detailed literature review or a comprehensive theory on the development and maintenance of channel relationships.

Framework for Channel Relationship Management Research

Table 8.1 offers an approach for classifying channel relationship management research based on the methods or mechanisms used to control and coordinate the channel activities performed by people and firms in *ongoing* relationships. The framework is based on control mechanisms because the method used to control and coordinate channel activities is a fundamental decision variable for managing the distribution channel.

The two columns in the table indicate the contexts in which the control mechanisms are used—a vertically integrated, corporate channel and a conventional channel composed of independent firms.[2] This ownership distinction is critical because there are inherent conflicts of interest in

TABLE 8.1 Channel Relationship Management Research

Control/ Coordination Mode	Corporate Channel —Vertical Integration	Independent Firms Performing Channel Functions
Authoritative	Rules, policies, supervision	Power
Contractual	Incentive compensation	**Terms and conditions, franchising**
Normative	Organization culture	**Relationship norms—trust**

NOTE: Terms in boldface type indicate relationships in conventional channels that involve contractual and normative control mechanisms.

conventional channels. Each firm in a conventional channel has a fiduciary responsibility to maximize its stockholder value. Although a channel member may consider the interests of other parties in making its decisions, ultimately each channel member's stockholders will require the firm's managers to focus on the firm's long-term financial performance. In corporate channels, employees and departments performing the various activities might have different personal goals, but they have a common set of stockholders and thus a common corporate objective.

CONTROL MECHANISMS

The rows in the matrix in Table 8.1 identify three control mechanisms used to coordinate activities in corporate and conventional channels: authoritative, contractual, and normative. These control mechanisms parallel the three basic intraorganizational mechanisms suggested by Ouchi (1979): hierarchical, market, and clan.[3]

Authoritative Control

The authoritative mechanism involves one party in the relationship using its position or power to control the activities of the other party. In a corporate channel, the nature of the employment contract legitimates the use of this authoritative control mechanism. The firm and its managers have a right to control the activities of subordinates by initiating policies and using supervision to ensure that the policies are implemented. Examples of research examining authoritative control in a corporate (intraorganizational) setting are the use of promotion-from-within staffing policies (Ganesan & Weitz, 1994) and the use of various supervision styles (Teas & Horell, 1981) to control salespersons' activities.

In a conventional channel setting, one party controls channel functions by controlling the activities of the other party through the use of power. The opportunity to control other channel members arises from an imbalance in resources—the more powerful channel member has greater resources that are highly valued by the less powerful channel member. There is an extensive body of research on the use of authoritative control and power in a conventional (interorganizational) context (see Gaski, 1984).

Contractual Control

The contractual control mechanism involves an agreement by the parties in a relationship on terms that define their responsibilities and rewards for performing channel activities. These contractual terms can be established by one party or through a negotiation process involving both parties. The terms are defined a priori and can be accepted or rejected by the parties involved. They may also be changed during the contract period when circumstances change.[4] Agency theory offers a perspective on how such contractual terms should be developed under conditions commonly encountered in channel relationships such as uncertainty, differential information, and risk preferences (Bergen, Dutta, & Walker, 1992).

Incentives based on performance (see Coughlan & Senn, 1989; John & Weitz, 1989) represent the use of a contractual control mechanism in a corporate setting, whereas research on franchise agreements (see LaFountaine, 1992; Lal, 1990) and vertical market restraints such as territory exclusivity (Desiraju, 1994) are examples of research examining this control mechanism in a conventional channel setting. In both of these contexts, the parties agree on the sets of activities that each will perform, policies and procedures to which they will adhere, and the rewards they will receive for performing these activities and following these policies.

Normative Control

Normative control involves a shared set of implicit principles or norms that coordinate the activities performed by the parties and govern the relationship. In an intraorganizational context, these norms constitute a firm's organization culture. The activities of the employees are coordinated through shared beliefs. Employees learn about these norms and are encouraged to conform with them through informal communications with fellow employees. Deshpandé and Webster (1992) outline some research questions and issues concerning normative control in a corporate channel context.

A similar control mechanism operates in conventional channel contexts. Norms governing relationships in a conventional channel are learned through past interactions and marketplace reputations. For example, these norms might indicate how the parties will make trade-offs between long- and short-term profit opportunities (long-term orientation norm), the degree to which the other parties' interests are considered in decision making (fairness norm), the nature and quantity of proprietary information exchanged (openness norm), and the conditions under which prior commitments can be altered (flexibility norm). Although the impacts of relationship norms have been examined in an industrial buying context (Heide & John, 1992), research concerning this control mechanism needs to be conducted in channel relationships.

Unilateral and Bilateral Control

Heide (1994) makes a distinction between unilateral and bilateral control or governance mechanisms based on whether both parties participate in making decisions concerning the relationship. Using this distinction, the authoritative control mechanism in Table 8.1 involves unilateral control by definition. Power is typically defined as the degree to which one party can influence another party to undertake an action that the second party would not otherwise have done.

The exercise of power does not always have negative consequences for the less powerful party. The more powerful party might undertake actions that improve coordination and thus result in benefits for both parties, but the less powerful must rely on the more powerful party to share the increased benefits fairly.

The contractual control mechanism involves aspects of both unilateral and bilateral control. It is unilateral in the sense that one party, typically the manufacturer or franchisor, establishes the contractual terms governing the relationships. However, it is bilateral in the sense that both parties

accept the initial terms and negotiate any changes in terms occurring during the relationship.

Normative control is clearly bilateral in that the norms are accepted
and adhered to by both parties. Each party in the relationship may not adhere to the same norms, but there are some metanorms outlining the
norms to which each party will adhere.

Use of Multiple Control Mechanisms

Typically, multiple control mechanisms are used to coordinate the activities in actual channel relationships. Multiple mechanisms are needed
because each mechanism has unique positive and negative effects on a relationship. For example, the authoritative control mechanism, the use of
power, can be very effective in communicating the specific activities that
need to be done and how they should be done. But the unidirectional nature of the communications can also cause conflict because the needs of
the party receiving the direction may not be adequately considered. On
the other hand, the normative control mechanism typically involves the
consideration of both parties' needs and mutual acceptance of norms governing behavior in the relationship. However, because these norms are not
codified, there may be ambiguity in the expectations concerning activities
to be undertaken by the parties. These ambiguities may result in inefficient coordination due to miscommunication.

Due to the differential impacts of these control mechanisms, firms may
use multiple mechanisms to manage relationships more effectively. For
example, the negative aspects of the use of power may be dampened by the
development of relationship norms outlining the appropriate use of
power, such as the specific activities over which the party wielding the
power will influence the activities of the other party and the degree to
which the more powerful party will act unilaterally in matters affecting the
financial performance of the weaker party.

Research on channel relationship control mechanisms typically focuses
on one of the six cells in Table 8.1. The research examines either a conventional or a corporate channel context and draws on theoretical developments and empirical findings uniquely associated with one of the three
control mechanisms. This focusing on a single mechanism is consistent
with the need to narrow the range of a research project in order to examine

the mechanism of interest in sufficient depth. Research is needed to improve our understanding of the trade-offs associated with each of these control mechanisms and how these mechanisms are, and can be, used in tandem to improve short- and long-term relationship performance.

Shifting Focus of Channel Relationship Research

In the mid-1960s, considerable attention was directed toward the concept of vertical marketing systems (Bucklin, 1970). A vertical marketing system is a "centrally programmed network [that is] preengineered to achieve operating economies and maximum market impact" (McCammon, 1970, p. 43). Coordination is achieved through a plan developed by the executive responsible for channel management in a vertically integrated firm or by a channel leader or captain in a conventional channel. Typically, the channel leader is the most powerful party in the channel and uses its power to ensure that its plan is implemented. Thus vertical marketing systems focus on a control mechanism associated with centralized planning and decision making in a corporate channel or on the use of an authoritative control mechanism in a conventional channel (nonbold terms in Table 8.1).

The focus of channel relationship management practice and research is shifting away from vertical market systems and authoritative control toward examining relationships in conventional channels that involve contractual and normative control mechanisms (bold terms in Table 8.1). Three factors have contributed to this shift: (a) the growing disenchantment with vertical integration, (b) the consolidation and increasing power of intermediary channel firms (retailers and wholesalers), and (c) the recognition of opportunities to gain strategic advantage through the management of channel activities.

INEFFICIENCIES IN VERTICAL INTEGRATION

In the 1960s, it was fashionable for businesses to increase sales through unrelated diversification. For example, Sears expanded by acquiring real estate and stock brokerage firms. With increased international competition and stockholder demands for improved returns, firms began to refocus their attention on their core business and to "stick to their knitting" (Peters & Waterman, 1982). They could achieve greater financial returns by exploiting unique sources of competitive advantage than they could by managing portfolios of unrelated businesses.

This focus on core competencies was extended to a reexamination of which channel functions should be performed by a firm and which should be procured from independent firms (Anderson & Weitz, 1986; Mallen, 1973). The resulting interest in "outsourcing," using conventional channel structures to perform channel functions, has increased as firms recognize the inefficiencies in managing activities for which they lack adequate scale or distinctive competencies. For example, Kmart uses independent trucking firms to ship merchandise between its suppliers and its warehouses and stores. The trucking firms have unique expertise in managing transportation activities and greater opportunities to reduce costs through back loads. Although Kmart sacrifices some coordination opportunities by using independent trucking firms, the benefits of better coordination through vertical integration may not be great with respect to the performance of this channel activity.

Thus channel management attention has shifted from corporate to conventional channels. Retailers are less interested in backward integration into manufacturing, and manufacturer interest in forward integration into retailing has also diminished. Rather than relying on vertical integration to coordinate channel activities, firms are exploring approaches for managing channel activities performed by independent firms in conventional channels.

In addition to an increasing interest in examining relationship management in conventional channels, we need to develop a better understanding of the strategic implications of the trend toward outsourcing. Marketing scholars have examined the vertical integration issue in channels, but little attention has been directed toward these outsourcing issues. Researchers need to identify the nature of the value-added activities that are most appropriate for outsourcing and the advantages and disadvantages of outsourcing. For example, are network organizations such as Nike, which are characterized by heavy outsourcing except for a few key activities, likely to be winners due to their flexibility, or will they have difficulty developing a strategic advantage due to their inability to have exclusive control over key activities that create value for their customers?

POWER OF INTERMEDIARY CHANNEL FIRMS

The use of an authoritative control mechanism, power, has been the primary management approach examined in marketing research for achieving coordination in conventional channels. Research has identified different types of power and has explored the functional and dysfunctional effects of power. However, the use of power as a coordinating mechanism is limited to asymmetric relationships—relationships in which one channel member is more powerful than another.

Although there are examples of retailers and wholesalers using authoritative control mechanisms, in general, manufacturers, through their size and scale economies, have assumed the leadership role in managing conventional channels. Most channel management research has taken the manufacturer's perspective and examined the impact of manufacturer policies and behaviors on channel operations and performance. However, this manufacturer-dominated perspective needs to change.

Much has been written about the shift in power from the manufacturer to the retailer in the consumer packaged-goods channel. Ten years ago, if a supermarket chain executive wanted to speak to someone from Procter & Gamble other than a salesperson, he or she flew to P&G's corporate headquarters in Cincinnati. Now P&G executives regularly visit Wal-Mart's headquarters in Bentonville, Arkansas, where 50 P&G employees are permanently stationed.

The growing importance of retailers, and wholesalers in some industries, reflects a consolidation of the distributive trades made possible by new information, communication, and transportation technologies. Traditionally, the retailers and wholesalers have focused on local or regional markets surrounding their outlets or warehouses. In contrast to manufacturing, economies of scale were limited and the industries were highly fragmented. Even large retailers such as Sears and Federated adopted a very decentralized management approach. However, the development of mass media, new transportation methods, and sophisticated management information systems has enabled retailers and wholesalers to achieve scale economies through more centralized management. These scale economies have led to the rise of national retail chains and wholesalers that are large enough to challenge the dominance of manufacturers over the distribution channel.

In addition to the increasing power balance in channel relationships, there is some evidence that asymmetrical relationships are inherently unstable (Anderson & Weitz, 1989) and less profitable for one party in the relationship (Buchanan, 1992). When channel members are not able to realize an adequate financial return due to the unilateral control exercised by the channel leader, they are less committed to the relationship and seek alternative, more rewarding relationships.

Thus manufacturers may no longer be able to rely on the use of an authoritative control mechanism to coordinate channel activities. The increased power of channel intermediaries has shifted attention from unilateral to bilateral control mechanisms for managing symmetrical relationships between powerful, independent channel members (Heide, 1994).

STRATEGIC ADVANTAGE THROUGH
CHANNEL RELATIONSHIP MANAGEMENT

Manufacturers, distributors, and retailers have recognized that the management of distribution channel activities offers significant opportunities for firms to create strategic advantage and achieve extraordinary financial performance. Channel activities are a major source of valued-added benefits to end users—greater than the value added by other marketing activities. Due to this substantial added-value potential, firms can develop competitive advantage by reducing the costs of performing these activities or using distribution activities to differentiate their offerings.

Recent reports suggest that inventories in the packaged goods/supermarket value distribution channel can be reduced by $30 billion through the improvement of the information exchange and coordination in this conventional channel (McAlister, 1994). In light of this substantial potential cost reduction, it is surprising that marketing scholars and other academics have devoted so little attention to understanding the benefits of relationship marketing in this channel context. The primary investigators of the implications of improving coordination in this channel have been consulting companies. Reminiscent of the total quality movement, marketing scholars have been watching the world evolve rather than leading or even participating in the evolution.

In addition to developing relationships to improve channel efficiency, a number of firms that have traditionally focused on research and development (R&D) and production to gain strategic advantage are recognizing that channel management offers a basis of advantage. Dell Computer, the fifth-largest designer and manufacturer of personal computers, considers its direct-mail distribution skills to be its key source of competitive advantage—not its new product development and manufacturing capabilities.

In 1994, three giant pharmaceutical manufacturers—Merck, Smith-Kline Beecham, and Eli Lilly—spent more than $12 billion to purchase three mail-order distributors—Medco, Diversified Pharmaceutical Services, and the PCS Division of McKesson, respectively. These channel intermediaries have unique resources, the most important of which are their exceptional information systems, which contain databases linking patients, physicians, managed-care organizations, pharmacies, third-party payers, and pharmaceuticals prescribed. Merck, SmithKline Beecham, and Eli Lilly have historically been R&D-oriented companies. The acquisitions demonstrated each company's conclusion that distribution holds the key to its future. The acquisitions also signaled that each company felt it was unable to meet the challenges of the emerging health care environment on its own—that is, that its existing distribution skills were inadequate.

These two examples of creating strategic advantage through channel management involve vertical integration. Dell and the pharmaceutical companies decided to manage the development, production, and distribution functions under their corporate umbrellas. Previously, we suggested that attention is shifting from such corporate channels to conventional channel management. However, these examples raise an important issue: To what extent can firms go beyond increasing efficiency to develop competitive advantage by managing relationships in conventional channels?

The ultimate impact of relationship marketing in a channel context may differ from its impact in supplier-manufacturer, manufacturer-consumer, or strategic alliance contexts. In these other contexts, exclusive relationships commonly occur. Manufacturers have sole-source relationships with key suppliers, and consumers are loyal to one brand in a product category. However, assortment is a key benefit offered by retailers and wholesalers, and thus these channel members usually deal with multiple competitive suppliers in a product category to satisfy the needs of their customers.[5] Hence, even though P&G has a "partnering" relationship with Wal-Mart, the relationship will not develop to the point that Wal-Mart offers only laundry detergents made by P&G or that P&G sells its packaged goods only through Wal-Mart.

Problems can arise when channel firms attempt to enter into multiple relationships with competitive suppliers.[6] Suppliers may be concerned about sharing sensitive information with other channel firms, even if the information is useful in coordinating activities, fearing that the information will be revealed to competitors. Thus the need to provide assortment might limit the degree to which trusting and committed relationships can develop and strategic advantage can be achieved through relationships in conventional channels.

In the preceding pages, we have presented a scheme for categorizing channel relationship management research. We have used this scheme, based on control mechanisms, to describe the evolving interests of business and academics and to discuss some factors driving this evolution. In the following sections, we examine channel research findings and directions for future research related to the boldface terms in Table 8.1—channel relationships governed predominantly by mutually accepted explicit contractual terms or implicit norms as opposed to relationships governed by the use of authoritative control.

Research on Bilateral Control in Channel Relationships

THEORETICAL RESEARCH

Conceptual research has identified a set of dimensions characterizing business relationships in general (Dwyer, Schurr, & Oh, 1987; Macneil, 1980) and, more specifically, channel relationships governed by authoritative (unilateral) versus normative (bilateral) control (Heide, 1994). In addition, researchers have suggested the stages in the development of business relationships and how the natures of relationships change during this evolutionary process (Dwyer et al., 1987; Frazier, 1983).

Although this theoretical research provides a broad conceptual framework that identifies relationship characteristics and development stages, we need to build on this base to develop and test theories that provide prescriptive insights concerning the development and maintenance of bilateral relationships and relationship norms. Theoretical research needs to examine the potential unique aspects of channel relationships in contrast to the other types of interorganizational relationships discussed in this volume. Can theoretical developments related to interorganizational relationships be applied to channel relationships? What, if any, alterations need to be made or additional factors need to be considered in the adaptation of these broad theoretical developments to channel relationships? For example, previously we suggested that the need to deal with competing suppliers to provide assortments may differentiate channel relationships from other forms of interorganizational business relationships.

Limitations of Economic Theories

As discussed by Heide (1994), theoretical perspectives developed in economics, transaction cost analysis (TCA), and agency theory may not be useful in providing new insights on these issues. Both TCA and agency theory are narrowly focused, addressing a limited set of control and coordinating actions affecting channel relationships. In addition, both theories focus on one firm making decisions to maximize its profits (unilateral control) rather than two firms working together to maximize the profit generated by the relationship as well as their individual profits (bilateral control).

TCA, in a channel management context, is primarily concerned with defining the role of transaction-specific investments in determining whether a channel activity will be most efficiently performed in a corporate versus conventional channel structure. The theory ignores interdependencies between the firms and takes the perspective of minimizing transaction costs incurred by a single firm, not the costs incurred by both firms in the transaction (Zajac & Olsen, 1993).

The primary contribution of TCA to developing and maintaining relationships in conventional channels is the use of idiosyncratic investments to commit the parties to maintaining the relationship (Williamson, 1983). These mutual idiosyncratic investments, or exchange of "hostages," provide an economic incentive to maintain the value of these assets through preservation of the relationship. However, channel research has identified additional factors that serve to preserve relationships such as trust and commitment (Anderson & Weitz, 1992; Morgan & Hunt, 1994), contractual terms, relationship history, and reputation (Anderson & Weitz, 1989; Heide & John, 1990).

Agency theory focuses on the use of contractual terms to control and coordinate channel relationships. The principal-agent structure implies the use of unilateral control by the principal versus bilateral control in which both parties participate. For example, in some agency theory models, the principal offers a menu of contracts to the agent. The selection made by the agent reveals information not possessed by the principal— information that is used to maximize the profits of the principal, not both parties in the relationship.

Given the narrow, unilateral focus of TCA and agency theory, we need to explore other avenues for theory development concerning channel relationships. In the following subsection, we suggest the consideration of theories concerning interpersonal relationships and the development of theory based on the observation of channel relationships.

Theories of Interpersonal Relationships

Research on the development, maintenance, and dissolution of interpersonal relationships might provide useful insights for developing theories concerning channel relationships. For example, the stages in interorganization relationships discussed by Dwyer et al. (1987) are based on research investigating the development of interpersonal relationships.

As with all analogies, interpersonal and interorganizational channel relationships are similar in some respects and differ in others. For example, the general objective of parties in interpersonal and interorganizational relationships is to derive benefits from the relationships that they would not be able to achieve on their own. However, the specific objective of participants in channel relationships is to maximize long-term financial returns for their stockholders, whereas the parties in interpersonal relationships seek to maximize their utility, which can include noneconomic rewards and even altruistic rewards derived from increasing their partners' utility. Simply identifying the similarities and dissimilarities might lead to some insights into the nature of conventional channel relationships and the norms governing these relationships. Below, we suggest some specific research findings on interpersonal relationships that may be useful for developing a better understanding of channel relationships.

The theoretical and empirical research on interpersonal relationships is extensive (see Blieszner & Adams, 1992; Cate & Lloyd, 1992; Duck, 1994a, 1994b). Although there are some problems in applying interpersonal relationship research in an interorganizational domain, the interpersonal relationship research certainly is applicable to the relationships between the boundary-spanning employees involved in channel relationships—interpersonal relationships that have an important impact on the nature of interorganizational relationships (Larson, 1992).

Grounded Theory

Descriptive information about channel relationships in the real world offers an important source of data for theory development that has not been exploited. We need to develop a better understanding of what firms are doing to manage channel relationships effectively. After all, most of the innovative channel coordination mechanisms, such as franchising, were developed by managers searching for solutions to problems, not by academics. Competition in the marketplace has sorted out the good and poor solutions to channel coordination issues.

It is disappointing that qualitative research in marketing has focused primarily on consumer behavior and has not examined marketing activities within a firm or the relationships between firms (for an exception, see Workman, 1993). Such research can be very valuable for identifying the norms that support conventional channel relationships (see Larson, 1992). Similarly, descriptive information on the situations in which specific contractual terms and vertical market restraints are used in governing channel relationships could be the basis for developing theory concerning the use of these control mechanisms.

EMPIRICAL RESEARCH

The limited empirical research on conventional channel relationships involving bilateral control mechanisms suggests that (a) trust, commitment, and idiosyncratic investments and other pledges play an important role in the governance of conventional, bilateral channel relationships; and (b) communications, negotiations, and the use of influence strategies differ in bilateral (equal power or dependency, goal congruence) versus unilateral (unequal power or dependency) relationships.

Trust, Idiosyncratic Investments, and Commitment

Empirical research suggests that channel members who are committed to a relationship perceive the relationship to be characterized by trust, commitment, and idiosyncratic investments as well as perceived benefits, good communication, satisfactory prior interactions, shared values and goals, functional conflict, balanced power or dependency, and limited opportunistic behavior (Anderson & Weitz, 1989, 1992; Anderson & Narus, 1990; Ganesan, 1994; Heide & John, 1988; Morgan & Hunt, 1994).[7] Although this research appears to suggest a causal ordering among these constructs, the research results just describe the characteristics of committed relationships between conventional channel members. For example, one could argue that cooperation is an antecedent to, rather than a consequence of, trust and commitment (Morgan & Hunt, 1994) or that commitment and a long-term orientation lead channel members to make transaction-specific investments rather than investments causing commitment (Anderson & Weitz, 1989, 1992; Ganesan, 1994).

This uncertainty about causal ordering arises because these empirical studies have collected cross-sectional data examining a relationship at one point in time. But, as we will discuss later, relationships probably develop incrementally. For example, a small investment in the relationship by one party might increase the trust of the other party. With greater trust, the other party makes a larger investment, which in turn increases the trust of the first party.

Thus the empirical research on channel relationships characterizes these relationships at one point in time but does not provide much insight into the factors leading to the development of relationships or the effectiveness of the relationships. Only two studies, those conducted by Heide and John (1988) and Buchanan (1992), have investigated the performance of conventional channel relationships, and both of these focused on the impact of dependency balancing as opposed to the impact of relational norms and attitudes on relationship performance.

Communications, Use of influence Strategies, and Negotiations

The research on communication processes in channel relationships suggests that the nature of the communication strategies used by a channel member is reciprocated by the other channel member in the relationship. For example, the use of noncoercive strategies by one party creates a supportive atmosphere in the relationship that leads the other party to use noncoercive influence strategies. Even in channels in which one party is more powerful, there is a tendency for the powerful channel member to use collaborative communication strategies characterized by greater frequency, bidirectionality, informality, and noncoerciveness; however, this use of collaborative strategies increases as the relationship becomes more balanced (i.e., more equal in terms of dependency; Frazier, Gill, & Kale, 1989; Frazier & Rhody, 1991; Frazier & Summers, 1984, 1986; Ganesan, 1993; Mohr, Fisher, & Nevin, 1994).

Most of this research does not explicitly examine the impact of control mechanisms or attitudes toward the relationships or the communication patterns in the relationship. However, Ganesan (1993) examined the nature of negotiations as a function of the long-term orientation of the channel toward the relationship. He found that a long-term orientation reduces the use of active aggressive negotiating strategies; however, the impact of a long-term orientation on the use of problem-solving strategies is moderated by the level of conflict and the importance of the issue being negotiated.

Although the extant research provides insights into the characteristics of committed conventional channel relationships and the nature of communications in channel relationships, it does not provide much information about how or why these relationships develop, how they are maintained, and what the performance consequences of using relational norms as a control mechanism are. Some questions concerning bilateral channel relationships that need to be addressed are the following: Why and when should a firm attempt to develop long-term channel relationships? What norms can be established to govern continuing relationships in conventional channels? With whom should firms seek to develop relationships? How should a firm initiate long-term channel relationships and develop norms? What behaviors can a firm undertake to maintain channel relationships and strengthen the development of relationship norms? What is the role of contractual terms such as territory exclusivity and exclusive dealing in initiating and maintaining channel relationships? Why and when should these contractual terms be used? To what extent can a truly strategic relationship develop in a conventional channel context? Why do channel relationships dissolve? Does the use of norms to control a channel relationship increase the financial performance of the relationship and the performance of the individual parties? In the following section, we discuss some issues related to these research questions.

Research Issues in the Coordination
and Control of Bilateral Relationships

Some potential areas for future research on bilateral channel relationship research addressed in this section are the motivation for developing relationships, the selection of partners, the role of idiosyncratic assets and strategic relationships, and the development and maintenance of relationships. We conclude the section with a discussion of some methodological issues concerning channel relationship research.

MOTIVATION FOR DEVELOPING RELATIONSHIPS
AND SELECTING PARTNERS

Channel members make risky investments to develop conventional channel relationships. These investments are the human capital, the time and effort of employees required to develop the mutually accepted control norms and tangible assets, which we discuss below.

Returns for Channel Relationships

Channel members make investments in relationships with the expectation of realizing fair, risk-adjusted returns. These returns may involve increased profits for the channel members through the provision of superior value to end users and/or reduction of the risks confronted by the parties in the relationships.

Risk reduction is a potential benefit of channel relationships (Achrol & Stern, 1988). However, the use of a normative control mechanism to establish long-term channel relationships might increase uncertainty in returns because it reduces flexibility. The norms governing the relationship commit the parties, and thus one of the parties might face an opportunity loss by not being able to alter its relationships in response to a change in its environment.

Channel members face two sources of uncertainty or risk in making these relationship investment decisions (e.g., Helper & Levine, 1992). First, the parties in the relationship might not realize a fair return on their investment. The relationship might not increase profits by reducing the cost or increasing the benefits to end users or reduce uncertainty in supply or distribution. Second, even if the investments increase channel effectiveness, a specific channel member might not receive its fair share of the increased risk-adjusted returns. The first source of uncertainty is associated with the "size of the pie" produced by the relationship, whereas the second source of uncertainty is associated with "how the pie will be divided" between the parties in the relationship.

Selecting Channel Partners

When selecting a relationship partner, a channel member needs to consider both the potential increase and certainty in the profits realized through the relationship and the certainty of receiving a fair share of the increased profits. Two key factors associated with increasing profits due to the relationship are the degree to which the partners have synergistic capabilities and the potential for exploiting these capabilities.

The rationale for a relationship is the potential for earning returns that could not be achieved without engaging in the relationship. Thus we would expect relationships to develop between channel members possessing unique capabilities that enable the channel members to provide superior value to end users toward whom they are both targeting their offering. For example, a manufacturer of high-quality jewelry would be motivated to develop a relationship with a jewelry retail chain with stores that complement the manufacturer's image and employ sales associates who provide the service expected by the manufacturer's target market. The relationship is synergistic in that it combines the supplier's capability in designing merchandise and developing a high-quality brand name with the retailer's capability to offer a high-quality jewelry assortment that attracts customers and provides appropriate services for these customers.

> P1: A channel member will seek to develop relationships with firms offering synergistic capabilities that it does not possess.

In addition to complementary capabilities, channel members need to select partners with whom they can work effectively. If the parties do not possess similar values, beliefs, and practices, they will be less likely to exploit the potential synergies in their capabilities. In the previous example, if the jewelry manufacturer has a hierarchical organizational culture and the jewelry retailer has a participative organizational culture, the firms may have difficulty working together and accepting norms to govern their relationship.

P2: A channel member will seek to develop relationships with firms having values, beliefs, and operating practices similar to the channel member's own.

A final consideration in selecting a partner is the confidence the channel member has in receiving a fair share of increased profits generated by the relationship. Confidence is a function of the trust the channel member has in the partner. This trust is based on the partner's reputation and past interactions with the channel member. For an interesting discussion of fairness norms in relationship development, see Ring and Van de Ven (1994).

P3: A channel member will seek to develop relationships with firms that have reputations and histories of fairness and consideration.

Idiosyncratic Investments

A major contribution of transaction cost economics is the identification of problems that arise when idiosyncratic, or transaction-specific, investments are involved in an exchange relationship. Idiosyncratic assets resulting from these investments are specific to a relationship. The key feature of these assets is that they are not fully fungible. They cannot be redeployed easily to another channel relationship, and thus their value decreases if the relationship does not continue. Some examples of these idiosyncratic investments in channel relationships are training personnel to sell and service the unique features of a supplier's product, designing an information and distribution "quick response" system that minimizes the inventory a retailer needs to have in stock and minimizes stock outs, and linking a supplier and retailer in the end user's mind through common advertising and promotion.

Transaction cost economics has focused on the potential costs that can occur in channel relationships involving such idiosyncratic investments. When a distributor makes an idiosyncratic investment in a supplier's product line, the distributor is committed to the relationship. The supplier might take advantage of this situation by raising its price or reducing its service. The distributor will tolerate some increases in its cost because it realizes that discontinuing the relationship will reduce the value of its idiosyncratic assets.

This focus on cost increases fails to recognize the potential value created by these idiosyncratic investments (Zajac & Olsen, 1993), which can create synergies that can result in strategic advantage for the channel members in the relationship over competing channel relationships. For example, by making investments to learn each other's businesses and link their information systems, JCPenney and Levi Strauss can offer jeans at lower cost with higher quality and fewer stock outs than can Lee selling through Sears.

Although idiosyncratic investments in channel relationships have the potential to increase the size of the pie, problems arise in the allocation of increased profits generated by the investments. If the idiosyncratic investments are asymmetrical, the party making the lowest investment has less stake in the relationship and an opportunity to extract greater profits by threatening to discontinue the relationship. Such uncertainties in the division of the increased profits may lead parties in conventional channels to be overly cautious in making idiosyncratic investments (Helper & Levine, 1992). The transaction cost economics solution to this problem is vertical integration, in that the division of the pie is not a problem when the parties performing channel functions are owned by the same corporation (Williamson, 1985).

However, firms in conventional channel relationships do make idiosyncratic investments in the relationships. We need to develop a better understanding of how firms deal with the uncertainties and potential opportunistic behaviors that go with making these decisions. Heide and John (1988) have examined one approach used by channel members to safeguard idiosyncratic investments, but more research is needed.

RELATIONSHIP DEVELOPMENT

As noted earlier, much of the empirical channel research to date has focused on identifying important characteristics of bilateral control: trust, commitment, idiosyncratic investments, and characteristics of effective communication. An important direction for future research in advancing our understanding of bilateral control mechanisms would be to investigate the processes that lead to relationships characterized by these constructs. To date, there has been little empirical investigation into how intentions, expectations, and information are communicated within a channel dyad, aside from direct influence attempts.

It is only within the past 15 years that researchers have begun to de-velop conceptual frameworks of how channel relationships develop. Dwyer et al. (1987) and Frazier (1983) draw heavily on the channels literature and social exchange theory to posit a process by which channel relation-ships are formed and dissolved. More recent attempts have employed qualitative, inductive approaches to gain insight into the relationship pro-cess (e.g., Larson, 1992; Shapiro & Byrnes, 1991). Essentially, the concep-tualizations and qualitative studies indicate that channel relationships move through a series of phases: awareness, exploration, expansion, com-mitment, and dissolution. The problem with this sequential stage ap-proach is that there is a tendency to ignore at an individual level the strategies, mechanisms, and behaviors employed in actually bringing about movement from one stage to the next. One researcher notes:

> Those who treat close relationships as constituting merely a succession of states, of causal events, have failed to recognize its nature as a formative move-ment, of which Plato (in Phaedrus) was already shrewdly aware—"a cause whereby anything proceeds from that which is not, into that which is." . . . It is a creative process involving novelties. . . . It is the imaginative order and its func-tion in producing "images," "paradigms," and "figures" in terms of which to give form to one's feelings, and the use of such forms in guiding the develop-mental movements involved in personal (and social) transformations that are ignored, derided and ultimately repressed by current empirical approaches aimed at understanding (for the purpose of their management) interpersonal relations. (Shotter, 1987, p. 234)

Given the limited research in marketing on channel relationship pro-cesses, one way to begin stimulating thought in this area is to consider re-search that has already been accomplished on similar processes in other contexts. Because interorganizational relationships are composed of boundary-spanning individuals who interact and communicate on a regu-lar basis, examining interpersonal relationship developmental processes is a logical place to begin thinking about interfirm relationship dynamics.

A number of different conditions can initiate interpersonal and interor-ganizational relationships. These relationships may start with chance in-teractions between boundary-spanning employees, preexisting friend-ships, or active searches to locate firms possessing needed resources (Oliver, 1990). The potential relationship starting points are associated with different levels of information about the parties—information that is needed to form relationship norms and trust.

P4: Channel relationships will develop more quickly when the parties have prior economic and social ties.

A relationship between parties that are strangers develops incrementally. The relationship begins with informal communications that may lead to small exchanges of sensitive information or a minor economic transaction. Trust plays a minor role in these early stages because little risk is involved (Van de Ven, 1976).

In the early stages of a channel relationship, norms, rules, and other understandings are established that help to build a form of "metacommunication" (Bateson, 1972), an understanding of how messages should be received, filtered, and understood within the dyad. Individuals follow implicit rules that allow them to communicate their desire to continue the relationship, allow it to develop further, and allow the partner to respond in kind.

During these early phases, parties in channel relationships concentrate on assessing the potential transaction growth that might occur as a result of working closely together (Larson, 1992). By following implicit rules about dyadic behavior, the parties are able to distinguish between and develop different types of relationships at very early stages.

Communication

Parties communicate interest and assess partner worthiness by means of active (direct) and passive (indirect) strategies, depending on the efficiency of the strategy and its social appropriateness (Berger, 1979; Berger & Bradac, 1982; Berger & Calabrese, 1975; Berger, Gardner, Parks, Schulman, & Miller, 1976). Active strategies may take the form of question asking, disclosure, and relaxation of the other party. As the parties sense potential for a more strategic relationship, the topic of discussion typically moves away from superficial matters toward idiosyncratic domains such as attitudes, future goals, and intentions (see Baxter & Wilmot, 1985). This process allows the parties to develop dyadic norms and interaction styles that will enable them to communicate very efficiently in the future and provides a basis for the development of trust. A number of studies on marketing research users and providers indicate that as trust and involvement between the parties increase, the information shared becomes more comprehensive, accurate, and timely (Bialeszewski & Giallourakis, 1985;

Dwyer et al., 1987; Moorman, Zaltman, & Deshpandé, 1992; Schurr & Ozanne, 1985; Zand, 1972).

Although a relationship's development may feature selective instances of direct communication between the partners, these instances are embedded in—and rely heavily on—a dominant pattern of indirect, or passive, communication that allows the parties to gather information in an unobtrusive manner. This mode of communication affords efficiency in achieving goals with minimized threat to the face of the user; it allows the parties to play a delaying, holding game that enables them to determine what is acceptable behavior while simultaneously perpetuating the illusion of agreement until the relationship is on firmer ground and able to cope with difference and conflict.

Partners can communicate their attitudes and feelings with regard to the relationship's development indirectly through their actions in addition to their verbal behaviors. For example, channel members who seek to make a relationship increasingly strategic are likely to engage in extensive planning of meetings, attend a higher frequency of meetings, and use more inference, interpretation, and comparison of new information with existing information (see Miell & Duck, 1986). Additionally, a partner might communicate trust by engaging in confiding behavior, keeping confidences, expressing similarity in agreement, and adapting to the other partner by keeping conversational rules and allowing the other partner to control the conversation as appropriate (Bell & Daly, 1984). Alternatively, channel members who seek to restrict the relationship's development would tend to act in a restrained, polite manner, restrict the range of topics appropriate for discussion, and limit the frequency of meetings.

Baxter and Wilmot (1984) have identified "secret tests" in an interpersonal context that allow one party to test the other's feelings concerning the worth of relationship investment. In a channel relationship, a buyer might use an "endurance" test, such as a decrease in purchases, to gauge the depth of the distributor's commitment. Alternatively, the buyer might use a "triangle" test, in which a situation is created that involves a real or hypothetical alternative supplier that could replace the present supplier. This test allows the buyer to assess the supplier's loyalty to the relationship. A "separation" test may occur when the buyer discontinues contact for a period of time in order to monitor whether and when the supplier initiates interaction with the buyer. Information about the other party's attitudes toward the relationship might also be obtained through observation of the other party in situations involving various contexts, expectations, and pressures (Berger, 1979; Berger & Calabrese, 1975).

P5: In early stages of the relationship, channel members communicate interest and assess partner worthiness by engaging in direct or indirect strategies.

P5a: Active strategies such as question asking and disclosure are used initially to assess the other member's interest in a future relationship and the relationship's potential.

P5b: Indirect strategies such as observation and endurance, triangle, and separation tests are employed to gauge the partner's commitment, loyalty, and initiating responses.

Norms

Norms are expectations about behavior that are at least partially shared by a group of decision makers (Gibbs, 1981; Moch & Seashore, 1981; Thibaut & Kelley, 1959). Relationship norms are critical to establishing dyadic metacommunication because they help foster the enactment of predictable, interaction scripts. In the early stages of a relationship, the parties may follow universal norms of politeness, conflict avoidance, and the exchange of superficial information (Altman & Taylor, 1973; Clark & Mills, 1979). In discrete exchange, norms contain expectations of individualist or competitive interaction between members.

Over time, norms of fairness and honesty can help to develop and stabilize an interorganizational relationship such that the relationship's exchange norms include expectations of mutual interest and joint welfare (Larson, 1992). In this way, the relationship may come to be governed by norms of good faith, implying that members are obligated to accept benefits that are less valuable than those given, keep less accurate counts of returns, and forgive instances in which the other partner has forgotten to repay debts or failed to help. Hence norms help to curtail behaviors that promote individual goal attainment over relationship goals.

However, norms can also lead to false conclusions concerning the other party and less effective outcomes during early stages of the relationship. For example, Longley and Pruitt (1980) show that agreements reached in the early stages of a relationship's development are typically less integrative than agreements reached in later stages or in relations between people who do not know each other. This is because parties in a relationship who are attracted to each other but distrustful of each other's feelings tend to operate under a norm of conflict avoidance, which in turn creates a sense of false cohesiveness. Fry, Firestone, and Williams (1979) also provide evidence for this notion among dating couples.

> P6: Norms are used to provide a context for how verbal messages should be filtered, received, and understood in the developmental stages of the channel relationship, and they serve as a general protective device against opportunistic behavior.

RELATIONSHIP MAINTENANCE

Once channel members have established a relationship of frequent, ongoing exchange, the next challenge is to maintain or increase the level of rewards and benefits received from the relationship into the future. Institutionalization is the process that develops norms and values between the parties and permits the relationship to endure beyond the action of specific individuals involved. As relationships become institutionalized, (a) multiple personal relationships become more important than individual role relationships (e.g., purchasing agent and salesperson), (b) psychological contracts replace formal legal contracts, and (c) formal agreements mirror informal understandings and commitments (Ring & Van de Ven, 1994). The institutionalization of the relationship requires active attention and participation by both parties if the relationship is to endure in the long run. Several communication ethnographers, in their work on individual relationships, have noted the salience of a "work" metaphor (Katriel & Philipsen, 1981; Owen, 1984); respondents often make references about "working on" their relationships or "making their relationships work."

Conflict Management

Conflict exists when one partner perceives the other partner to be impeding the attainment of goals or some other function of concern (Etgar, 1979; Stern & El-Ansary, 1988; Thomas, 1979). Although conflict can have negative effects on relationships (Anderson & Weitz, 1992), it does not necessarily have to be destructive or disruptive to the relationship's development (Morgan & Hunt, 1994), nor need it be interpreted as an indication that the relationship lacks the interdependence that characterizes close, strategic relationships (Braiker & Kelley, 1979). Instead, conflict can often act as a source of novelty for the relationship, forcing it into new terrains that, if handled successfully, can strengthen the interpersonal relationship and cultivate greater trust, communication, relationship satisfaction, stability, and personal growth (Canary & Cupach, 1988; Deutsch, 1973; Lott & Lott, 1965). Although constructive conflict is not always guaranteed to "save" a troubled relationship, it can reveal incompatible values or changes in commitment that might otherwise go undetected.

Parties in a relationship are more likely to engage in constructive conflict resolution when they are equal in power; if power is imbalanced in the dyad, then the more powerful party has little incentive to engage in joint problem solving (Bach & Wyden, 1968; Thibaut & Faucheux, 1965). Even when balanced power exists, confrontation is never comfortable because both parties are usually motivated by the importance of the conflict and sensitivity between the pair is heightened.

Integrative resolutions are facilitated if the parties understand each other's motivational structure. Understanding can be developed by both explicit (direct talk) and implicit (indirect reference) exchange concerning member motives (Kimmel, Pruitt, Magenau, Konar-Goldband, & Carnevale, 1980; Pruitt et al., 1978). Explicit motivation exchange is more likely to lead to joint profit when both parties are high in cognitive complexity (Pruitt & Lewis, 1977), possess an orientation that seeks maximization of joint benefit (Deutsch, 1973), and reduce social distance (and hence greater trust) between the members. Implicit motivation exchange may take on several forms. For example, one channel member (the initiator) might offer directional information, such as statements concerning how the other channel member (the target) might improve his or her position through specific changes on dimensions with regard to a particular matter, or the initiator might make statements of preference that give the target insight into the initiator's priorities.

Successful conflict handling does not necessarily mean that every conflict situation must be dealt with immediately. Postponement or even long-term avoidance of conflict confrontation does not always hold negative consequences (Fitzpatrick, 1988); sometimes, by delaying discussion, the dyad is able to be in a better position (i.e., in terms of time and energy) to deal with the conflict effectively (see Bach & Wyden, 1968). Conflict theorists have noted that under certain conditions, ill-timed discussions can intensify, rather than reduce, conflict levels in a relationship (e.g., Hawes & Smith, 1973; Krauss & Deutsch, 1966).

P7: Constructive conflict resolutions are more likely to occur when (a) power is balanced within the dyad and (b) individual members are oriented toward maximization of mutual benefit, are high in cognitive complexity, and trust each other and understand each other's motivational structure.

Communication

Much of the research on relationship maintenance points to two critical aspects that facilitate successful relationships in the long run: extended interaction and active listening. In a study of married couples, Baxter and Wilmot (1985) found that the most frequent maintenance strategies employed in their sample included increased interaction and time spent together. In mature relationships, couples strive to execute their role obligations more responsibly than in the beginning of the relationship, introduce novelty in order to offset the routine aspects of the relationship, and strategically avoid direct talk about the status of the relationship. A similar process is likely to occur between channel members. Once the dyad has established a metacommunication structure that includes shared norms and expectations, the members are likely to work toward executing aspects of their relationship more efficiently. As the relationship develops over time, interaction is likely to involve a wider range of topics discussed at a deeper level (Miell & Duck, 1986). This not only strengthens dyadic trust (Samter & Burleson, 1984) but expands the parties' knowledge of each other's competencies, goals, and future expectations, which could potentially lead to joint innovations, novel solutions to problems, and so on.

P8: Communication that helps to maintain the relationship over time involves increased interaction and time spent together relative to early stages of the relationship. Topics of discussion are of a wider variety and deeper level than earlier in the relationship.

P9: Members in mature relationships are skilled active listeners, able to communicate correct understanding of the messages and emotions underlying posed questions.

ROLE OF PEOPLE

Along with the growing interest in relational norms as a governance form, there has been an interest in the role of personal relationships between boundary-spanning members in the conventional channel. Personal relationships have been found to shape economic outcomes in interorganizational exchange in a number of contexts: the publishing industry (Coser, Kadushin, & Powell, 1982), international joint ventures (Doz, 1988; Håkansson & Johanson, 1988; Walker, 1988), and small to midsize textile firms in Italy (Lorenzoni & Ornati, 1988).

In an inductive field study of dyadic relationships in high-growth entrepreneurial firms, Larson (1992) found that personal relationships shaped the context for new exchanges between firms by reducing risks and uncertainty about the motives and intentions of the other member. She also found that individual and firm reputations were important considerations in parties' decisions regarding whether or not to develop the interorganizational exchange relationship. Companies and individuals saw themselves as members of an inner circle or network within a broader industry circle. As a result, credibility and a positive reputation—for business and performance—were important attributes for coordinating exchange between firms. Hence social factors such as personal relationships and reputations (personal trust), coupled with a knowledge of the firm's skills and capabilities (economic trust), were prime considerations in interorganizational exchange.

> P10: Personal relationships and reputations between boundary-spanning members play an important role in facilitating and enhancing interorganizational exchange.

The role of people and their importance in the governance of interorganizational exchange is virtually ignored by economic theories of exchange, such as TCA (Bradach & Eccles, 1989; Granovetter, 1985; Maitland, Bryson, & Van de Ven, 1985; Perrow, 1981). More work is needed that expands our understanding of how individual boundary-spanning members enhance or impede interorganizational outcomes. For example, one issue that has not been addressed is the effect of turnover among boundary-spanning members on interorganizational exchange. In industries such as insurance and financial services, individual relationships between representatives and customers may supplant customer ties to the firm. If representatives are fired or switch firms, sales may be lost permanently or transferred to competitors. To date, there has been little work addressing how firms can balance the need for personal relationship development between reps and customers as a means to attract and keep new business and the need for firms to keep from becoming too dependent on individual sales reps. Heide and John (1988) have discussed how sales representatives balance their dependency on the principal firm, but the converse has not been examined.

METHODOLOGICAL ISSUES

With the increasing interest in channel relationships, interorganizational characteristics of these relationships, such as channel member commitment to the relationship rather than to the actions and beliefs of individual parties, play a central role in theory development and testing. This interest in relationship constructs at the interorganizational level presents some difficult methodological issues.

Numerous academics have called for the collection of data from multiple informants to be used in the assessment of organizational constructs, and for the collection of dyadic data from both participants in channel relationships. Some daunting practical problems arise in the collection of these types of data and in using them to develop measures of constructs. First, collecting such extensive data is very difficult. The failure of some respondents to provide data can dramatically reduce the sample size of relationships that can be examined. Second, real problems arise when the responses by key informants in one firm do not agree with each other. These problems are amplified when the responses from two channel members differ about the nature of their relationship. For example, consider a study examining the relationship between mutual commitment and performance of the channel relationship. What should a researcher do when there is a difference of opinion between the respondents from the two parties about the degree of mutual commitment in the relationship? Should the researcher assess the degree of mutual commitment by averaging the two sets of responses, by assuming one set of respondents is more accurate than the other, or by discarding all observations for which there is disagreement on the assessment of mutual commitment? Sound arguments can be made for rejecting all of these approaches in the development of a good measure of mutual commitment. The use of covariance structure analysis is not a solution to this problem—such analysis simply offers a method for identifying when the problem arises.

In light of these problems, empirical research on channel relationships involving dyadic data typically has developed construct measures using data collected from only one party. Then relationships between these measures are estimated for each type of partner (suppliers and distributors) in the relationship using separate (see Anderson & Narus, 1990) or combined (Anderson & Weitz, 1992) analyses. We suspect that these methodological problems will impede empirical research on channel relationships.

Summary

Although relationships have always played an important role in channel management, the nature of the control mechanisms used to coordinate activities in these relationships is changing. Practitioners are placing more emphasis on using relational norms and attitudes, such as trust and commitment, to maintain continuity rather than using authoritative control mechanisms or vertical integration.

Although conceptual and theoretical research on channel relationships has provided insights into the nature of effective relationships, we need to develop a better understanding of how these relationship develop, how they are maintained, and how members in conventional relationships deal with the uncertainties inherent in making idiosyncratic investments. In addition, we need to consider the unique nature of channel relationships and the needs of intermediaries in working with competing suppliers to offer assortments. This factor may limit the degree to which truly strategic relationships can develop in channel relationships.

Finally, research on channel relationships requires a refocusing of attention from the individual channel member to both parties in the relationship and the nature of the relationship. The use of dyadic data and relationship constructs raises some challenging issues in terms of research methodology.

Notes

1. In terms of channel activities, discrete transactions may occur in providing transportation and warehousing services. However, as we discuss in this chapter, even these services are moving toward relational exchanges.

2. The traditional taxonomy used to describe channel structures is corporate, administered, and conventional. However, these categories are not precisely defined so that each relationship can be uniquely classified. For example, relational exchanges that do not have a contractual basis are difficult to classify. The examples of administered channels usually involve well-defined programs or contractual (franchising) relationships. On the other hand,

some authors equate conventional channels with discrete transactions. We use the term *conventional channels* simply to indicate that the firms in the channels are independent businesses. The relationships between firms in conventional channels may be governed by the use of power, contractual terms, and/or relational norms.

3. This parallelism between intra- and interorganizational control mechanisms is discussed in Heide (1994).

4. This perspective on contractual relationships involving predetermined, explicit terms and conditions reflects a classical view of contracts. The relational contracting perspective develop by Macneil (1980) can be viewed as an approach for codifying the relational norms associated with a normative control mechanism discussed in the next section.

5. In some channel relationships, the channel members agree to contractual terms such as exclusive dealing or adapt relational norms to minimize these problems.

6. See Vilas-Boas (1994) for a discussion of this issue in the context of advertising agencies representing competing firms.

7. In this abbreviated literature review, we have considered only research involving relationships with channel intermediaries and ignored research on direct buyer-seller relationships in business-to-business marketing relationships.

References

Achrol, R. S., & Stern, L. W. (1988). Environmental determinants of decision-making uncertainty in marketing channels. *Journal of Marketing Research, 25,* 36-50.

Altman, I., & Taylor, D. A. (1973). *Social penetration: The development of interpersonal relations.* New York: Holt, Rinehart & Winston.

Anderson, E., & Weitz, B. A. (1986). Make-or-buy decisions: Vertical integration and market productivity. *Sloan Management Review, 27*(3), 3-19.

Anderson, E., & Weitz, B. A. (1989). Determinants of continuity in conventional industrial channel dyads. *Marketing Science, 8,* 310-323.

Anderson, E., & Weitz, B. A. (1992). The use of pledges to build and sustain commitment in distribution channels. *Journal of Marketing Research, 29,* 18-34.

Anderson, J. C., & Narus, J. A. (1990). A model of distributor firm and manufacturer firm working partnerships. *Journal of Marketing, 54*(1), 42-58.

Bach, W., & Wyden, P. (1968). *The intimate enemy.* New York: William Morrow.

Bateson, G. (1972). *Steps to an ecology of mind.* New York: Ballantine.

Baxter, L. A., & Wilmot, W. W. (1984). Secret tests: Social strategies for acquiring information about the state of the relationship. *Human Communication Research, 11,* 171-201.

Baxter, L. A., & Wilmot, W. W. (1985). Taboo topics in close relationships. *Journal of Social and Personal Relationships, 9,* 253-275.

Bell, R. A., & Daly, J. A. (1984). The affinity-seeking function of communication. *Communication Monographs, 51,* 91-115.

Bergen, M., Dutta, S., & Walker, O., Jr. (1992). Agency relationships in marketing: A review of the implications and applications in agency related theories. *Journal of Marketing, 56*(3), 1-24.

Berger, C. R. (1979). Beyond initial interaction: University, understanding, and the development of interpersonal relationships. In H. Giles & R. St. Clair (Eds.), *Language and social psychology* (pp. 122-144). Oxford: Basil Blackwell.

Berger, C. R., & Bradac, J. J. (1982). *Language and social knowledge: Uncertainty in interpersonal relations.* London: Edward Arnold.

Berger, C. R., & Calabrese, R. J. (1975). Some explorations in initial interaction and beyond: Toward a developmental theory of interpersonal communication. *Human Communication Research, 1,* 99-112.

Berger, C. R., Gardner, R. R., Parks, M. R., Schulman, L., & Miller, G. R. (1976). Interpersonal epistemology and interpersonal communication. In G. R. Miller (Ed.), *Explorations in interpersonal communication* (pp. 149-171). Beverly Hills, CA: Sage.

Bialeszewski, D., & Giallourakis, M. (1985). Perceived communication skills and resultant trust perceptions within the channel of distribution. *Journal of the Academy of Marketing Science, 13,* 206-217.

Blieszner, R., & Adams, R. G. (Eds.). (1992). *Adult friendships.* London: Sage.

Bradach, J. L., & Eccles, R. G. (1989). Price, authority, and trust: From ideal types to plural forms. *Annual Review of Sociology, 15,* 97-118.

Braiker, H. B., & Kelley, H. H. (1979). Conflict in the development of close relationships. In R. L. Burgess & T. L. Huston (Eds.), *Social exchange in developing relationships.* New York: Academic Press.

Buchanan, L. (1992). Vertical trade relationships: The role of dependence and symmetry in attaining organizational goals. *Journal of Marketing Research, 29,* 65-75.

Bucklin, L. P. (Ed.). (1970). *Vertical marketing systems.* Glenview, IL: Scott, Foresman.

Canary, D. J., & Cupach, W. R. (1988). Relational and episodic characteristics associated with conflict tactics. *Journal of Social and Personal Relationships, 5,* 305-325.

Cate, R. M., & Lloyd, S. A. (Eds.). (1992). *Courtship.* London: Sage.

Clark, M. S., & Mills, J. (1979). Interpersonal attraction in exchange and communal relationships. *Journal of Personality and Social Psychology, 37,* 12-24.

Coser, L. A., Kadushin, C., & Powell, W. W. (1982). *The culture and commerce of publishing.* New York: Basic Books.

Coughlan, A., & Senn, S. (1989). Salesforce compensation: Theory and managerial implications. *Marketing Science, 8,* 267-291.

Deshpandé, R., & Webster, F. (1992). Organizational culture and marketing: Defining the research agenda. *Journal of Marketing, 53*(1), 3-15.

Desiraju, R. (1994). *Exclusivity and resale price maintenance in channel of distribution* (Working paper). Newark: University of Delaware, College of Business.

Deutsch, M. (1973). *The resolution of conflict: Constructive and destructive processes.* New Haven, CT: Yale University Press.

Doz, Y. L. (1988). Technology partnerships between larger and smaller firms: Some critical issues. *International Studies of Management and Organization, 17*(4), 31-57.

Duck, S. W. (Ed.). (1994a). *Dynamics of relationships.* London: Sage.

Duck, S. W. (1994b). *Meaningful relationships: Talking sense and relating.* London: Sage.

Dwyer, F. R., Schurr, P. H., & Oh, S. (1987). Developing buyer-seller relationships. *Journal of Marketing, 51*(2), 11-27.

Etgar, M. (1979). Channel domination and countervailing power in distribution channels. *Journal of Marketing Research, 16,* 254-262.

Fitzpatrick, M. A. (1988). *Between husbands and wives: Communication in marriage.* Newbury Park, CA: Sage.

Frazier, G. L. (1983). Interorganizational exchange behavior in marketing channels: A broadened perspective. *Journal of Marketing, 47*(4), 68-78.

Frazier, G. L., Gill, J., & Kale, S. (1989). Dealer dependence levels and reciprocal action in a channel of distribution in a developing country. *Journal of Marketing, 53*(1), 50-69.

Frazier, G. L., & Rhody, R. (1991). The use of influence strategies in interfirm relationships in industrial product channels. *Journal of Marketing, 55*(1), 52-69.

Frazier, G. L., & Summers, J. (1984). Interfirm influence strategies and their applications within distribution channels. *Journal of Marketing, 48*(3), 43-55.

Frazier, G. L., & Summers, J. (1986). Perceptions of interfirm power and its use within a franchise channel of distribution. *Journal of Marketing Research, 23*, 169-176.

Fry, W. R., Firestone, I. J., & Williams, D. (1979). *Bargaining process in mixed-singles dyads: Loving and losing.* Paper presented at the annual meeting of the Eastern Psychological Association, Philadelphia.

Ganesan, S. (1993). Negotiation strategies and the nature of channel relationships. *Journal of Marketing Research, 30*, 183-202.

Ganesan, S. (1994). Determinants of long-term orientation in buyer-seller relationships. *Journal of Marketing, 58*(2), 1-19.

Ganesan, S., & Weitz, B. A. (1994). *The impact of staffing policies on marketing employee job attitudes and behaviors* (Working paper). Gainesville: University of Florida, College of Business Administration.

Gaski, J. (1984). The theory of power and conflict in channels of distribution. *Journal of Marketing, 48*(3), 9-28.

Gibbs, J. P. (1981). *Norms, deviance, and social control: Conceptual matters.* New York: Elsevier.

Granovetter, M. (1985). Economic action and social structure: The problem of embeddedness. *American Journal of Sociology, 91*, 481-510.

Håkansson, H., & Johanson, J. (1988). Formal and informal cooperation strategies in international and industrial networks. In F. J. Contractor & P. Lorange (Eds.), *Cooperative strategies in international business* (pp. 369-379). Lexington, MA: Lexington.

Hawes, L. C., & Smith, D. H. (1973). A critique of assumptions underlying the study of communication in conflict. *Quarterly Journal of Speech, 62*, 423-435.

Heide, J. B. (1994). Interorganizational governance in marketing channels. *Journal of Marketing, 58*(1), 71-85.

Heide, J. B., & John, G. (1988). The role of dependence balancing in safeguarding transaction-specific assets in conventional channels. *Journal of Marketing, 52*(1), 20-35.

Heide, J. B., & John, G. (1990). Alliances in industrial purchasing: The determinants of joint action in buyer-supplier relationships. *Journal of Marketing Research, 27*, 24-36.

Heide, J. B., & John, G. (1992). Do norms matter in marketing relationships? *Journal of Marketing, 56*(2), 32-44.

Helper, S., & Levine, D. (1992). Long-term supplier relations and product-market structure. *Journal of Law, Economics, and Organization, 8*, 561-582.

Hunt, S. D., Ray, N., & Wood, V. (1985). Behavioral dimensions of channels of distribution: Review and synthesis. *Journal of the Academy of Marketing Science, 13*, 1-14.

John, G., & Weitz, B. A. (1989). Salesforce compensation: An empirical investigation of factors related to the use of salary vs. incentive compensation. *Journal of Marketing Research, 26*, 1-14.

Katriel, T., & Philipsen, G. (1981). What we need is communication: "Communication" as a cultural category in some American speech. *Communication Monographs, 48*, 301-317.

Kimmel, M. J., Pruitt, D. G., Magenau, J. M., Konar-Goldband, E., & Carnevale, P. J. D. (1980). Effects of trust, aspiration, and gender on negotiation tactics. *Journal of Personality and Social Psychology, 38*, 9-23.

Krauss, R. M., & Deutsch, M. (1966). Communication in interpersonal bargaining. *Journal of Personality and Social Psychology, 4*, 572-577.

LaFountaine, F. (1992). Agency theory and franchising: Some empirical results. *RAND Journal of Economics, 23*, 263-283.

Lal, R. (1990). Improving channel coordination through franchising. *Marketing Science, 9,* 299-318.

Larson, A. (1992). Network dyads in entrepreneurial settings: A study of the governance of exchange relationships. *Administrative Science Quarterly, 37,* 76-104.

Longley, J., & Pruitt, D. G. (1980). A critique of Janis' theory of groupthink. In L. Wheeler (Ed.), *Review of personality and social psychology* (Vol. 1). Beverly Hills, CA: Sage.

Lorenzoni, G., & Ornati, O. (1988). Constellations of firms and new ventures. *Journal of Business Venturing, 3,* 41-57.

Lott, A., & Lott, B. (1965). Group cohesiveness as interpersonal attraction: A review of relationships between antecedent and consequent variables. *Psychological Bulletin, 64,* 259-309.

Macneil, I. (1980). *The new social contract.* New Haven, CT: Yale University Press.

Maitland, I., Bryson, J., & Van de Ven, A. H. (1985). Sociologists, economists, and opportunism. *Academy of Management Review, 10,* 59-65.

Mallen, B. (1973). Functional spin-off: A key to anticipating change in distribution structure. *Journal of Marketing, 37*(3), 18-25.

McAlister, L. (1994, June). *Overview of industry changes.* Paper presented at the Marketing Science Institute Conference on the Changing Landscape in Grocery Retailing: The Information Highway Reaches the Trading Post, Atlanta, GA.

McCammon, B., Jr. (1970). Perspective on distribution programming. In L. P. Bucklin (Ed.), *Vertical marketing systems* (pp. 2-48). Glenview, IL: Scott, Foresman.

Miell, D., & Duck, S. W. (1986). Strategies in developing friendships. In V. J. Derlega & B. A. Winstead (Eds.), *Friendship and social interaction.* New York: Springer-Verlag.

Moch, M., & Seashore, S. E. (1981). How norms affect behaviors in and of corporations. In P. C. Nystrom & W. H. Starbuck (Eds.), *Handbook of organizational design* (pp. 210-237). New York: Oxford University Press.

Mohr, J., Fisher, R., & Nevin, J. R. (1994). *The role of communication strategy in channel member performance: Is more collaborative communications better?* (Working Paper No. 94-119). Cambridge, MA: Marketing Science Institute.

Moorman, C., Zaltman, G., & Deshpandé, R. (1992). Relationships between providers and users of market research: The dynamics of trust within and between organizations. *Journal of Marketing Research, 29,* 314-328.

Morgan, R. M., & Hunt, S. D. (1994). The commitment-trust theory of relationship marketing. *Journal of Marketing, 58*(3), 20-38.

Oliver, C. (1990). Determinants of interorganizational relationships: Integration and future directions. *Academy of Management Review, 15,* 241-265.

Ouchi, W. (1979). A conceptual framework for the design of organizational control mechanisms. *Management Science, 25,* 833-848.

Owen, W. (1984). Interpretative themes in relational communication. *Quarterly Journal of Speech, 70,* 274-287.

Perrow, C. (1981). Markets, hierarchies, and hegemony. In A. H. Van de Ven & W. F. Joyce (Eds.), *Perspectives on organization design and behavior* (pp. 371-386). New York: John Wiley.

Peters, T. J., & Waterman, R. H., Jr. (1982). *In search of excellence: Lessons from America's best-run companies.* New York: Harper & Row.

Pruitt, D. G., & Lewis, S. A. (1977). The psychology of integrative bargaining. In D. Druckman (Ed.), *Negotiations: A social psychological perspective.* Beverly Hills, CA: Sage-Halsted.

Pruitt, D. G., Kimmel, M. J., Britton, S., Carnevale, P. J. D., Magenau, J. M., Peragallo, J., & Engram, P. (1978). The effect of accountability and surveillance on integrative bargaining. In H. Sauermann (Ed.), *Bargaining behavior.* Tubingen, NY: Mohr.

Reve, T., & Stern, L. W. (1979). Interorganizational relationships in marketing channels. *Academy of Management Review, 4,* 405-416.

Ring, P. S., & Van de Ven, A. H. (1994). Developmental processes of cooperative interorganizational relationships. *Academy of Management Review, 19,* 80-118.

Samter, W., & Burleson, B. R. (1984). *When you're down and troubled . . . have you got a friend? Effects of cognitive and motivational factors on spontaneous comforting in a quasi-natural situation.* Paper presented at the annual meeting of the International Communication Association, San Francisco.

Schurr, P. H., & Ozanne, J. L. (1985). Influences on exchange processes: Buyers' preconceptions of a seller's trustworthiness and bargaining toughness. *Journal of Consumer Research, 11,* 939-953.

Shapiro, R. D., & Byrnes, J. (1991). *Intercompany operating ties: Unlocking the value in channel restructuring* (Working paper). Boston: Harvard Business School, Division of Research.

Shotter, J. (1987). The social construction of an "us": Problems of accountability and narratology. In R. Burnett, P. McGhee, & D. Clarke (Eds.), *Accounting for relationships: Explanation, representation, and knowledge* (pp. 225-247). London: Methuen.

Stern, L. W., & El-Ansary, A. I. (1988). *Marketing channels* (3rd ed.). Englewood Cliffs, NJ: Prentice Hall.

Teas, K., & Horell, J. (1981). Salesperson satisfaction and performance feedback. *Industrial Marketing Management, 10,* 49-57.

Thibaut, J. W., & Faucheux, C. (1965). The development of contractual norms in a bargaining situation under two types of stress. *Journal of Experimental Social Psychology, 1,* 89-102.

Thibaut, J. W., & Kelley, H. H. (1959). *The social psychology of groups.* New York: John Wiley.

Thomas, K. W. (1979). Organizational conflict. In S. Kerr (Ed.), *Organization behavior* (pp. 151-181). New York: John Wiley.

Van de Ven, A. H. (1976). On the nature, formation, and maintenance of relations among organizations. *Academy of Management Review, 1,* 24-36.

Vilas-Boas, J. M. (1994). Sleeping with the enemy: Should competitors share the same advertising agency? *Marketing Science, 13,* 190-202.

Walker, G. (1988). Network analysis for cooperative interfirm relationships. In F. J. Contractor & P. Lorange (Eds.), *Cooperative strategies in international business* (pp. 227-240). Lexington, MA: Lexington.

Williamson, O. E. (1983). Credible commitment: Using hostages to support exchange. *American Economic Review, 73,* 519-540.

Williamson, O. E. (1985). *The economic institutions of capitalism: Firms, markets, and relational contracting.* New York: Free Press.

Workman, J. (1993). Marketing's limited role in new product development in computer system firms. *Journal of Marketing Research, 30,* 405-421.

Zajac, E., & Olsen, C. (1993, January). From transaction cost to transaction value analysis: Implications for the study of interorganizational relations. *Journal of Management Studies, 30,* 131-145.

Zand, D. E. (1972). Trust and managerial problem solving. *Administrative Science Quarterly, 17,* 229-239.

9

An Integrated Model of
Buyer-Seller Relationships

DAVID T. WILSON

Buyer and seller relationships have become an integral part of business-to-business operating strategies over the past 15 years. Academics have developed reasonably well supported models that define many of the relevant variables that influence success or failure in a relationship (Anderson, Lodish, & Weitz, 1987; Anderson & Weitz, 1989; Anderson & Narus, 1984, 1990; Hallén, Johanson, & Seyed-Mohamed, 1991; Han & Wilson, 1993; Morgan & Hunt, 1994; Wilson & Moller, 1991). We have less empirical knowledge about the process of relationship development. Dwyer, Schurr, and Oh (1987) and Wilson and Jantrania (1993) have suggested conceptual process models of relationship development, but these models do not integrate the existing knowledge about the variables that make for a successful relationship. A next logical step is to create a model that integrates

NOTE: This chapter is reprinted from David T. Wilson, "An Integrated Model of Buyer-Seller Relationships," *Journal of the Academy of Marketing Science*, vol. 23, no. 4, pp. 335-345, copyright © 1995 by the Academy of Marketing Science. Reprinted by permission.

the variables of the empirical "success" models with the stages in the relationship process models.

My objective in this chapter is to develop an integrated model that blends the empirical knowledge about successful relationship variables with the conceptual process models. Most relationship studies have been cross-sectional in design, which limits the extent to which the impacts of situational variables are captured. In addition, the influence of the different stages of the relationship development process are not accounted for within a cross-sectional design. I have conducted several cross-sectional studies and believe that some of the richness in the real world is lost in such studies. Although many variables have been used in modeling relationships, some variables are strong candidates for core relationship building blocks. When we look at relationships in cross section, we lose the insights that emerge from looking at the process of relationship development. I propose to integrate the knowledge we have gained from the empirical studies that have been done with the conceptual models of relationship development process. The result is a model that argues that many of the variables are active at different stages and become latent in others.

Because my focus is on buyer-seller relationships in business marketing situations, I first present the argument that relationships are likely developed in high-impact areas in the buying area. Next, I review the substantial body of literature on relationships, partnerships, strategic alliances, and joint ventures to create a list of relationship success variables that should be included in the model. A five-stage process model emerges from the literature and is the framework for the development of an integrated model. I argue that variables are the focus of the partners' attention in some stages and are latent in other stages. A variable is latent when it is in the background of the current interaction between the partners but is not receiving their attention. I conclude the chapter with a discussion of the need for future research to reflect situational factors.

The Context of Buyer-Seller Relationships

Relationships between buyers and sellers have existed since humans began trading goods and services. These relationships developed in a natural way over time as the buyers and sellers developed trust and friendships supported by good-quality products and services. Today these relationships have become "strategic" and the process of relationship development is accelerated as firms strive to create relationships to achieve their goals. In this stressful environment of relationship acceleration, there is less time for participants to explore carefully the range of long-term relationship development. The expectations of performance have increased, making the development of satisfactory relationships even more difficult.

An important phenomenon related to buyer-seller relationships is that many buyers are developing single-source suppliers because of pressures to increase quality, reduce inventory, develop just-in-time (JIT) systems, and decrease time to market. The intensity of contact needed to accomplish high quality, implement JIT, and reduce time to market cannot be achieved with multiple sources of supply. The ultimate goal in developing these capabilities is to reduce costs. These cost reductions can be obtained through one of two models. In an adversarial model, buyers pit suppliers against each other to achieve lower costs. In a cooperative model, both parties achieve lower costs by working together to lower both buyer's and seller's operating costs. This reduction is accomplished through better inventory management and elimination of unnecessary tasks and procedures.

Not all suppliers are appropriate partners for the type of cooperative relationship that is the focus of this chapter. Figure 9.1 presents a simple 2-by-2 table useful for categorizing those suppliers' buyers who are candidates for in-depth relationships. The horizontal scale is the amount of value that the supplier adds to the product that the buyer is producing. The vertical scale is the degree of operating risk associated with using the firm as a supplier. *Operating risk* refers to the risk that a buyer incurs because of supplier failure to produce quality goods, on-time delivery, or any of the other things that can go wrong and cause difficulties for the buying organization.

The firms that fall into the upper-right quadrant of Figure 9.1 add value to the firm's product and have low operating risks as partners. The high value added makes them important to the firm, and their low operating risks make them candidates for relationship development. A supplier who adds value to a buyer's product increases the eventual value added at the market level. These value-added purchases tend to affect operating costs and/or the ability to achieve a higher level of market price. For example, Briggs & Stratton provides high-name-recognition engines for lawn mowers and snow throwers that add significant value to these products. These are the prime types of buyer-seller relationships that are the focus of this discussion.

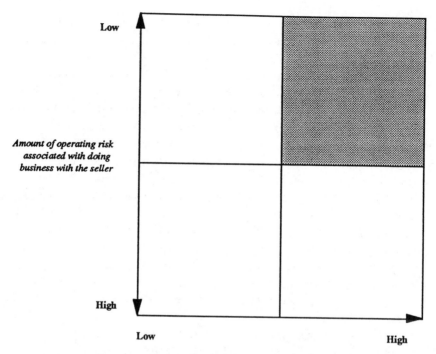

Figure 9.1. Classifying Potential Partners

Empirical Models of
Buyer-Seller Relationships

The basic elements of relationships to be addressed here come from an examination of the literature aimed at determining those variables that have been successful predictors of relationship performance in empirical studies. Although my focus is on buyer-seller relationships, I draw upon channel relationship and strategic alliance research to develop a set of constructs that seem to define the outcomes of relationships.

The Industrial Marketing and Purchasing (IMP) Group, using an ethnographic methodology, has developed an "interaction approach." The organization's members interviewed 878 buyers and sellers from 318 firms in France, Italy, West Germany, Sweden, and the United Kingdom. The IMP Group researchers came to believe that a model based upon buyer-seller cooperation was a better representation of the data they had collected than was the traditional view of buyers and sellers as adversaries. They conceptualized buyer-seller interaction as dyadic interaction at both the firm and individual levels, with the interaction influenced by the atmosphere—a multidimensional construct involving power/dependence, cooperation, expectations, and closeness—and the environment of the interaction (Ford, 1990; Håkansson, 1982; Håkansson & Wootz, 1979; Turnbull & Paliwoda, 1986). IMP Group members believe that interaction is a series of short-term social interactions that are influenced by the long-term business processes that bind the firms together.

Both individual buyers and sellers are influenced by traditional firm and individual variables, such as organizational structure, technology levels of the firm, and available resources. The individuals' attitudes, goals, and experiences influence their behavior within the interchange episodes. The atmosphere of the relationship can be thought of as hybrid culture that develops between the buying and selling firms and reflects elements of both firms' cultures but is different from either firm's culture. I have liberally interpreted the atmosphere concept, which is loosely defined within the IMP literature. The IMP Group model provides a rich view of buyer-seller relationships, which the group has continued to sharpen and develop.

There have been few empirical studies of buyer-seller relationships (Hallén et al., 1991; Han, 1992; Han & Wilson, 1993; Heide & John, 1990; Mummalaneni & Wilson, 1991; Noordewier, John, & Nevin, 1990; Wilson, Soni, & O'Keeffe, 1995), but those that have been undertaken share many variables in common. Indeed, models of channel relationships also use many of the same variables to predict channel relationships (Anderson et al., 1987; Anderson & Weitz, 1989; Anderson & Narus, 1984, 1990; Heide & John, 1990, 1992).

Wilson and Moller (1988, 1991) have assembled a list of variables that have been used with success in modeling different relationship situations. The original set of variables was culled from a survey of the relationship literature that in 1988 was heavily conceptual, with notable exceptions in the channels area (Anderson et al., 1987; Anderson & Narus, 1984). The core set of variables that I use in this chapter comes from Han and Wilson (1993), who drew upon the Wilson and Moller work previously cited for their study. I have enriched the original variable set with variables used in recent studies that proved to have both theoretical and empirical support. This list of variables (Table 9.1) is not exhaustive, as more variables could

TABLE 9.1 Extended List of Relationship Variables

Commitment
Trust
Cooperation
Mutual goals
Interdependence/power imbalance
Performance satisfaction
Comparison level of the alternative
Adaptation
Nonretrievable investments
Shared technology
Summative constructs
Structural bonds
Social bonds

be added by other researchers to reflect situational factors. Out of the many possible variables, I have selected a set that represents those variables that have both theoretical and empirical support. Given situational factors, one might add to or delete from the list to capture the relationship situation. Discussion of these variables follows.

COMMITMENT

Commitment is the most common dependent variable used in buyer-seller relationship studies (Anderson et al., 1987; Anderson & Weitz, 1989; Dwyer et al., 1987; Jackson, 1985; Moorman, Zaltman, & Deshpandé, 1992). Commitment is an important variable in discriminating between "stayers and leavers" (Mummalaneni, 1987). It is the desire to continue the relationship and to work to ensure its continuance. I agree with Dwyer et al.'s (1987) view that commitment is an "implicit or explicit pledge of relational continuity between exchange partners" (p. 19). In a similar vein, Moorman et al. (1992, p. 316) define commitment as an enduring desire to maintain a valued relationship.

Commitment implies importance of the relationship to the partners and their desire to continue the relationship into the future. Hardwick and Ford (1986) point out that commitment assumes that the relationship will bring future value or benefits to the partners. There is little doubt that commitment is a critical variable in measuring the future of a relationship.

TRUST

Trust is a fundamental relationship model building block and as such is included in most relationship models. Most definitions of trust involve a belief that one relationship partner will act in the best interests of the other. Following are four of the most often cited definitions of trust:

1. A willingness to rely on an exchange partner in whom one has confidence (Moorman et al., 1992)
2. The belief by one party that its needs will be fulfilled in the future by actions taken by the other party (Anderson & Weitz, 1989)
3. A party's expectation that another party desires coordination, will fulfill obligations, and will pull its weight in the relationship (Dwyer et al., 1987)
4. The belief that a party's word or promise is reliable and the party will fulfill its obligations in an exchange relationship (Schurr & Ozanne, 1985)

The theoretical justification for the above and other definitions of trust is drawn from literature outside the marketing domain (Deutsch, 1958; Pfeffer & Salancik, 1978; Williamson, 1975, 1985; Zand, 1972). The concept of trust is included in marketing studies based upon common sense, reports from both practitioners and marketers, and a vigorous literature detailing trust research. The inclusion of trust as a variable does not always work the way one might predict (Anderson & Narus, 1990; Ganesan, 1994; Han & Wilson, 1993), which may be part of the difficulty in defining trust within studies. Anderson and Narus (1990) point out that "when asked about their perceptions of their firm's trust in a working relationship, informants give a *present state* report; that is, they answer on how much their firm trusts the partner's firm at the current point in time" (p. 54). Time is only one of many elements that needs to be accounted for when trust is used as a variable in relationship research. Nevertheless, for current purposes, I believe that trust is a critical variable in relationship research.

COOPERATION

Cooperation has been defined as "similar or complementary coordinated actions taken by firms in interdependent relationships to achieve mutual outcomes or singular outcomes with expected reciprocation over time" (Anderson & Narus, 1990, p. 45). Morgan and Hunt (1994) seem to accept this definition of cooperation but continue to expand it by emphasizing the proactive aspect of cooperation versus coercion to take interdependent actions. The interaction of cooperation and commitment results in cooperative behavior allowing the partnership to work, ensuring that both parties receive the benefits of the relationship.

MUTUAL GOALS

I define the concept of mutual goals as the degree to which partners share goals that can be accomplished only through joint action and the maintenance of the relationship. These mutual goals provide a strong reason for relationship continuance. It has been suggested that mutual goals influence performance satisfaction, which, in turn, influences the level of commitment to the relationship (Wilson et al., 1995).

Shared values is a similar but broader concept. Morgan and Hunt (1994) define shared values as "the extent to which partners have beliefs in common about what behaviors, goals and policies are important, unimportant, appropriate or inappropriate, and right or wrong" (p. 25). Although the wider concept of shared values has some appeal, it seems too broad to be operationalized effectively. Norms are the rules by which values are operationalized. Heide and John (1992) suggest that norms differ in their prescribed behavior toward collective versus individual goals. Individual goals create norms of competitive behavior, whereas "relational exchange norms are based on the expectation of mutuality of interest, essentially prescribing stewardship behavior, and are designed to enhance the well being of the relationship as a whole" (p. 34). Most likely, mutual goals encourage both mutuality of interest and stewardship behavior that will lead to the achievement of mutual goals. Perhaps it is easier to measure the degree to which the partners share the same goals than it is to measure values and norms.

INTERDEPENDENCE AND POWER

Interdependence and power imbalance are important relationship variables. The power of the buyer or seller is closely tied to the interdependence of the partners in a relationship (Anderson et al., 1987; Anderson & Narus, 1984, 1990; Dwyer et al., 1987; Ganesan, 1994; Heide & John, 1988). Anderson and Weitz (1989) define power imbalance as the ability of one partner to get the other partner to do something he or she would not normally do. Power imbalance is directly related to the degree of one partner's dependence on the other partner. Power and dependence have been focal issues in traditional and relational channel research. Han, Wilson, and Dant (1993) found that both buyers and sellers in their study saw the need to increase interdependence between the partners.

PERFORMANCE SATISFACTION

Because we are discussing business relationships, performance satisfaction is a critical variable. Partners, especially sellers, must deliver high-level satisfaction on the basic elements of the business transaction. Buyers need to satisfy their partners' business needs or they risk becoming marginalized. General Motors's purchasing in 1992-1993 under the leadership of Jose Ignacio Lopez de Arriortua took a very hard line on price negotiations. The results were large savings for General Motors and battered suppliers. The detrimental cost to General Motors might be in having sellers only quote to specifications and not invest in developing new products with General Motors. One consultant has suggested that major suppliers will not take new designs to General Motors because they fear GM will give their designs to the lowest bidder. He asserts that the drying up of innovation will, over time, make General Motors less competitive (Taylor, 1994).

I define performance satisfaction as the degree to which the business transaction meets the business performance expectations of the partner. Performance satisfaction includes both product-specific performance and nonproduct attributes.

STRUCTURAL BONDS

The concept of structural bonds is the vector of forces that create impediments to the termination of the relationship. Although individual constructs (nonretrievable investments, Cl_{alt}, shared technology, and adaptations) tend to either strengthen or weaken a relationship, their interaction may be greater than the sum of their parts in creating a force to hold a relationship together. Structural bonds develop over time as the level of investments, adaptations, and shared technology grows until a point is reached when it may be very difficult to terminate a relationship. Firms with high levels of structural bonding have been found to have higher levels of commitment to the continuance of relationships than firms with lower levels of structural bonding (Han & Wilson, 1993).

COMPARISON LEVEL OF THE ALTERNATIVES

Drawing upon the work of Thibault and Kelley (1959), Anderson and Narus (1984, 1990) define the comparison level of alternatives (Cl_{alt}) as the quality of the outcome available from the best available relationship partner. They note that quality of the outcome when judged against alternatives is a measure of the dependence of one partner on the other. If there is a wide array of high-quality partners, dependence will be low, but if the level of Cl_{alt} is low, the partner will be less likely to leave the relationship because the alternative partners are not as attractive as the current partner. Anderson and Narus (1990) and Han and Wilson (1993) support the influence of Cl_{alt} in relationship research.

ADAPTATION

Adaptation occurs when one party in a relationship alters its processes or the item exchanged to accommodate the other party (Håkansson, 1982; Han & Wilson, 1993). Hallén et al. (1991) found that both buyer and seller make adaptations to the other. They expect that adaptation behavior will vary over the life of the relationship. In the early stages it will be a means to develop trust, and in the mature stage it will expand and solidify the relationship. Adaptations tend to bond the buyer and seller in a tighter relationship and create barriers to entry for competing suppliers (Hallén et al., 1991; Hallén, Seyed-Mohamed, & Johanson, 1988).

NONRETRIEVABLE INVESTMENTS

Nonretrievable investments are defined as the relationship-specific commitment of resources that a partner invests in the relationship. These nonretrievable investments (capital improvements, training, and equipment) cannot be recovered if the relationship terminates. The existence not only of these nonretrievable investments but also of the amount at stake creates a hesitancy within the parties to terminate the relationship. This hesitancy is directly related to the transaction-specific investments described by Williamson (1975, 1985). The assumption of economic opportunism is inherent in transaction cost analysis, in that a partner who has made a substantial nonretrievable investment may be at risk if appropriate safeguards are not developed to stop exploitation of the at-risk partner by the other partner.

SHARED TECHNOLOGY

Shared technology is the degree to which one partner values the technology contributed by the other partner to the relationship. It may range from product-level technology to the linking of computer systems. The creation of shared technology has been found to strain a relationship in the early stages of the development of the technology, but inevitably it contributes to a stronger relationship when the technology is up and working (Vlosky & Wilson, 1994). It has been found that technology contributes to increasing the parties' commitment to the relationship (Han & Wilson, 1993).

SOCIAL BONDS

Social psychologists have used social bonding to investigate friendships, sexual relationships, and family and group interactions (Johnson, 1978; McCall, 1970; Turner, 1970). Personal social bonds develop through subjective social interaction. Individuals may develop strong personal ties that tend to hold relationships together. It has been found that buyers and sellers who have strong personal relationships are more committed to maintaining their relationships than are less socially bonded partners (Mummalaneni & Wilson, 1991; Wilson & Mummalaneni, 1986). In a more complex buying situation, Han and Wilson (1993) found that social bonding did not contribute to buyer-seller commitment. I define social bonding as the degree of mutual personal friendship and liking shared by the buyer and seller.

The Process Model

I will now develop a process model that builds on the work of Dwyer et al. (1987) with the hybrid concept of Borys and Jemison (1989) by integrating the constructs listed in Table 9.1 with the relationship development stages of the model. Relationship research tends to be cross-sectional in nature and likely captures relationships at different stages of development. I believe that the constructs have both an active phase, during which they are the center of the relationship development process, and a latent phase, during which they are still important but not under active consideration in relationship interaction. Changes in environmental forces or relationship participants may activate a construct. For example, trust may be very active in the early stages of the process but may then become latent until an incident, such as a change in managers, makes it active again. I define an active construct as one that receives a great deal of manager time and energy. A latent construct is one in which the main issues have been settled to the manager's satisfaction and so do not receive time or attention. The latent construct has become part of the operating environment.

A hybrid relationship is a composite of the cultures of the buying and selling firms. It straddles the space between the firms with a unique blend of the cultures of the firms. Williamson (1991) describes hybrids in relationship to the polar modes of markets and hierarchies, with hybrids being in the middle between the two forms of governance structures. Hybrids have also been described as organizational networks that straddle markets and hierarchies. Hybrids use networks of relationships based on power and trust to exchange either influence or resources.

Borys and Jemison (1989) define hybrids as "organizational arrangements that use resources and/or governance structures from more than one existing organization" (p. 235). This broad definition covers a wide range of organizational forms, making it difficult to define and analyze hybrids precisely. Borys and Jemison also suggest that a theory of hybrids should "address the multiplicity of issues raised by hybrids, and it should integrate previous research in these areas into a theoretical whole. Existing theory fails on these counts" (p. 235). Their model has four stages: (a) defining the purpose of the relationship, (b) setting the boundaries of the relationship, (c) value creation, and (d) hybrid stability. I add the search for and selection of an appropriate partner as the preliminary stage in the process, to create a five-stage model.

The partner search and selection stage is more active than is implied by the "awareness" stage in Dwyer et al.'s (1987) model, which they define as "Party A's recognition that party B is a feasible exchange partner" (p. 15). In many instances, the buyer already may be purchasing products or services from the seller but decides to move to a deeper relationship with a

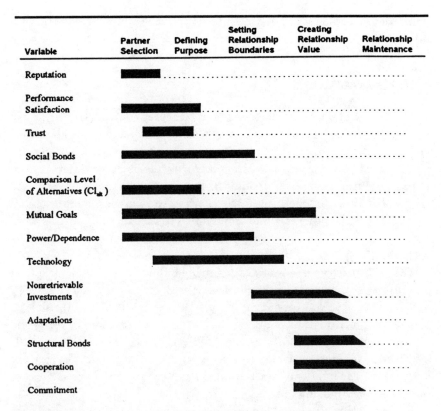

Variable	Partner Selection	Defining Purpose	Setting Relationship Boundaries	Creating Relationship Value	Relationship Maintenance
Reputation					
Performance Satisfaction					
Trust					
Social Bonds					
Comparison Level of Alternatives (CI_{alt})					
Mutual Goals					
Power/Dependence					
Technology					
Nonretrievable Investments					
Adaptations					
Structural Bonds					
Cooperation					
Commitment					

Figure 9.2. Integrating the Relationship Variables and the Relationship Development Process

supplier to accomplish internal goals such as lowering costs through a total quality management and JIT system.

Borys and Jemison (1989) developed their hybrid model to address organizational problems that arise in mergers, acquisitions, and joint ventures. Although they discuss supplier and buyer issues only briefly, their concept of an emerging hybrid structure of two organizations joining together in an intimate relationship is powerful and compelling. I extend their concept by merging the work on modeling relationships with the five-stage model of relationship development.

Figure 9.2 displays the stages and times when constructs may become active and/or latent. Below, I describe each stage in the relationship development process and then give my rationale for placing the active construct in that stage. Finally, I present a brief argument for the five-stage model.

SEARCH AND SELECTION

Finding an appropriate partner is a critical step in the relationship development process. Performance satisfaction, Cl_{alt}, and trust are the active constructs. If the buyer is personally acquainted with the potential partner, it is easier for the buyer to assess performance on these variables than if the potential partner is unknown. Reputation for performance and trustworthiness become the measures when the partner is an untested commodity. It is difficult, if not impossible, to measure Cl_{alt} at this early stage. A risk-reduction strategy would be to have preliminary discussions with multiple potential partners.

The pressure to partner quickly in many industries can make the trial and testing activities very difficult. Dwyer et al. (1987) suggest that these activities occur in an exploration stage. A concept similar to performance satisfaction, verification, is defined as "the amount of effort to verify the supplier's ability to perform as expected" (Heide & John, 1990, p. 25). Verification increases joint action between buyers and sellers. The process of assessing the quality of a potential partner seems to begin the process of hybrid development.

It is likely that the social bonding process begins when buyers and sellers interact in the early stages. This initial interaction may begin the development of mutual trust. Although uncertainty is high, trust begins as one partner earns the respect and trust of the other.

DEFINING PURPOSE

The balance between shared goals and individuals goals can make conflict resolution and maintenance of harmony in relationships very difficult if the individual goals dominate the mutual goals. Mutual goals are the glue that holds a relationship together in times of stress. Defining the purpose of the relationship will help the partners clarify their mutual goals.

The absence of a common culture, combined with the fact that the partners may not recognize the importance of this initial stage in relationship creation, makes this a critical time in the process. Most organizations "do not share a common environment or domain and, thus, lack a foundation for generating a set of common understandings about the purpose of the hybrid and the process by which that purpose can be achieved" (Borys & Jemison, 1989, p. 237). Purpose needs to provide organizational sanctioning of the relationship that gives legitimacy both between the partners and within each partnering organization.

The breadth of purpose or scope of the goals is a critical decision. If the scope is too broadly defined, there may not be enough detail to make decisions between issues. Probably it is better to start with a narrowly defined purpose and let success broaden the purpose of the relationship.

An agreed-upon set of mutual goals and objectives, the furthering of social bonding, and trust development are the ideal outcomes of the defining purpose stage. If these outcomes are not obtained, the relationship may fail. In describing failures in strategic alliances, Lorange and Roos (1991) suggest that major reasons for failure are related to a "lack of trust" or "incompatible personal chemistry." Less obvious pitfalls occur when managers find it difficult to work in relationships that require give-and-take or when managers rush into relationships only to find that their management styles, motivations, or commitment are not compatible with their partners' expectations (Levine & Byrne, 1986). It is clear that the purpose stage lays the groundwork for success only if the outcomes are achieved.

As I have noted in previous work, the initial stages in dyadic interaction involve source legitimation and information exchange (Wilson, 1978). In these interactions, the partners become acquainted and seek common ground on which to build social bonds and a trusting relationship. All relationships do not need to be founded on close personal ties, but they need to reach a business friendship level. Anderson and Narus (1990), Anderson et al. (1987), and Dwyer et al. (1987) employ a construct called *communication* within their models. Communication is a necessary process throughout all the stages of a relationship, but the content of the communication activities changes as the stages in the process change. In the relationship definition stage, I would expect the focus to be on establishing performance satisfaction, Cl_{alt}, and trust. The interaction process helps to establish social bonding, and the actions of the partners begin to define the level of trust that will shape the future of the relationship.

The relationship is at a fragile stage; both parties have limited commitment and can end the relationship relatively easily (Dwyer et al., 1987). Cl_{alt} begins to clarify as the buyer gains insight into the contribution the supplier will make to the relationship relative to alternative suppliers. At this stage in the relationship, perhaps Cl_{alt} is driven by the performance satisfaction measures. Later in the relationship, Cl_{alt} may be driven by expectations of strategic gains through joint activities that improve strategic efforts, such as time to market new products. If the supplier's Cl_{alt} is high compared with that of other potential suppliers, then structural bonding may be beginning as the buyer may work harder to build trust through better communication and improved social bonding.

BOUNDARY DEFINITION

Boundary definition answers two questions: (a) Where does each partner's organization end and the hybrid begin? (b) What is the hybrid's legitimate claim upon the resources of the partners? Joint ventures have clear legal boundaries, but other forms of relationships, such as strategic partnerships, buyer-supplier relationships, and channel partnerships, seldom have legal structures that define their boundaries. A powerful new way in which to view these forms of relationships is to consider a hybrid to be an informal organization developing a governance structure that draws on, but is not governed by, the structure of the parent organization. Boundary definition clarifies the degree to which each partner penetrates the other organization and achieves joint action (Heide & John, 1990).

The individuals who compose the hybrid team in a buyer-seller relationship acquire assets from their parent organizations as partners need to commit resources and people to the relationship. If the buyer-seller team members have developed strong mutual goals, trust, and social bonding, they will want their firm to commit appropriate resources to complete the task. As the team fights for resources to do this, resource negotiation will take place not only between the partner firms but between the firm's hybrid team members and their colleagues. The involvement in the hybrid is likely a function of mutual goals, trust, social bonding, and Cl_{alt}. For example, a single-source supply relationship will require the supplier to dedicate product and delivery resources to the relationship at the same time the buyer commits production resources to the relationship. Both organizations may alter their own accounting and billing procedures to accommodate their partners. A new set of informal rules develops, defining how much each partner may call upon the resources of the other and creating a governance structure for the relationship. In this scenario, we see the beginning of the adaptation of processes and products or services to accommodate the partner.

Hallén et al. (1988, 1991) have found that the adaptation construct from the IMP model contributes to relationship development. They state:

> Reciprocal adaptation also implies cost. The mutual investments in positions with the other firm may be difficult to transfer to other uses. However, as these investments tie the firms together in strong customer-supplier relationships, they form the basis for both business expansion and for securing current sales or supply sources. (Hallén et al., 1991, p. 35)

This adaptation process develops over time and usually involves a number of small steps, so that it is hard to pinpoint a clear investment decision. Dwyer et al. (1987) suggest a form of adaptation when they state, "By looking for or granting accommodation within a current rather than a new exchange association, the buyer and seller verify their mutual investment in the relationship" (p. 17).

As Borys and Jemison (1989) note, boundary definition has "two important effects. First it determines both resources available to the hybrid and the legitimacy of the partner's claims on those resources, thus affecting its purpose. It also affects the cohesiveness of hybrid members and thus, the hybrid's ability to achieve a given purpose" (p. 242). Failures in relationships are likely to be highly correlated with a lack of understanding of the interaction between purpose and boundary definition. If the two parties do not have strong common goals, they have little incentive to commit resources and to build a governance structure to make the relationship viable.

The level of performance satisfaction in the relationship is determined by the resources committed to the partnership and by the degree of commitment of the people involved. Boundary definition makes clear the resources available to create value in the relationship.

CREATING RELATIONSHIP VALUE

Value creation is the process by which the competitive abilities of the hybrid and the partners are enhanced by being in the relationship. It is a joint effort, founded on the hybrid structure that has evolved from the earlier stages. Value, created by the synergistic combination of the partners' strengths, allows each of them to gain from the relationship. Not all relationships are symmetrical, but for the relationship to flourish, each partner needs to see some benefit beyond what it would receive by working independently.

How to share between the partners the value created in the relationship is a major issue. Value comes in many forms, including in technology, market access, and information. Lower prices and operating costs for the buyer and lower operating costs for the seller can also be viewed as value. Knowledge gained by a partner in the relationship may be the most valuable output of the partnership, but it is also likely to be the most difficult to measure. As Badaracco (1991) states, "For one organization to acquire knowledge embedded in the routines of another, it must form a complex, intimate relationship with it" (p. 12). The acquisition of embedded knowledge can have enormous value to a firm. If Kmart could acquire with ease the embedded knowledge that Wal-Mart possesses in the operation of its distribution systems, Kmart could gain great cost reductions in its distribution system.

Value is created in many ways. Sometimes the partners will adapt their processes and products or specialize their investments. If an innovative technology is used, the partners will increase their structural bonds. As the firms increase the customizing of the hybrid relationship, the gap Cl_{alt} with alternative suppliers increases as it becomes more difficult to replace the current supplier.

Kalwani and Narayandas (1995), in a study of smaller firms (mean sales of $57 million), found that the value developed in long-term relationships was created through better cost management, not only in manufacturing costs but in all aspects of the firms' operations. The relationship firms, having lower prices than the firms using traditional buying methods, had higher profits. The nonaccounting value created in relationships is seldom measured, as it is difficult to place a value on concurrent engineering activities, technology improvement, and other high levels of value creation.

The sharing of value is likely a function of the power/dependence relationship modified by the degree of structural bonding present in the relationship. A partner with power may be able to extract value-sharing concessions, but this may be at the expense of trust and cooperation. In a balanced power/dependence relationship, commitment to the relationship and cooperation likely increase as the partners create more value.

The balanced relationship implies that both partners are willing to be reasonable in sharing a growing value pie, as they have limited ability to coerce more than a "fair share" from their partners. Pushing too hard may damage the relationship and risk the value being created. The basic assumption stated earlier, that relationships are "business" partnerships where enlightened self-interest operates, means that both partners will press hard to obtain advantage but will stay within the bounds of the trust compact they have developed.

Both parties make nonretrievable investments to increase value creation and help build stronger structural bonds. Value creation may involve more units and levels of the firms and an increase in both social and structural bonding. For example, concurrent engineering (CE) and early supplier involvement (ESI) involve engineers within both firms who are responsible for designing and manufacturing at the earliest design stage. CE and ESI seek to design products that can be manufactured and serviced with the highest quality at the lowest cost. According to a 1990 article in *Business Week,* NCR used CE to design a new terminal that was designed in half the time and had 85% fewer parts than its predecessor and could be assembled in one-fourth the time. By being part of the design team, suppliers add value to the relationship and build both structural and social bonds.

HYBRID STABILITY

Hybrid stability is a function of the success the partners in the relationship have had in creating positive outcomes for the key variables in the previous stages. A commitment to the buyer-seller relationship develops if the performance is achieved on combinations of these key variables (Han & Wilson, 1993; Heide & John, 1990; Morgan & Hunt, 1994; Mummalaneni & Wilson, 1991).

There has been little theoretically based research on the management of stable relationships. Several issues warrant more study, including the following: What is the best reward system to support relationship development? What is the impact on a relationship of the negotiation process and strategy? How do firms expend and renew relationships over time? What causes hybrid organizations or relationships to destabilize or dissolve?

It is likely that variables such as trust, performance, and satisfaction become latent in the maintenance of the relationship phase. It is not that

these variables are unimportant, but rather that they are issues that have
been or do not need the active involvement of those who manage the
relationship.

When a relationship is operating smoothly, working in the hybrid space
between the firms may be akin to working in one's own company, because
the social bonding, trust, cooperation norms, and commitment have created a stable atmosphere. Economic issues may arise, but these may be
seen as no different from dealing with another part of the internal organization. There is little awareness of the positive aspects of operating in a
stable, thriving relationship because most of the literature covers negative "war stories" from businesspeople or the business press.

Research Directions

CONCEPT LEVEL

Our knowledge about relationships is at an early stage. We need to improve our concept definitions and how we operationalize the concepts. For
example, a powerful variable such as trust does not always have the predicted effect in empirical studies because many times researchers do not
carefully capture the complexities of the trust concept in the measurement phase of the research. Having been guilty of this error in measuring
trust, I am aware of the problem. The list of concepts gathered from relationship papers and used in my earlier work (Wilson & Moller, 1988, 1991)
includes many that are described using similar words but that can be seen
to be quite different in the detailed explanations given. Many concepts
have strong similarities but some significant differences. As we progress
in relationship research, we have the opportunity to clarify and develop
scales to measure the key concepts outlined above.

MODEL LEVEL

The IMP interaction model (Håkansson, 1982) is based upon the insights gained from 878 interviews with 318 buyer and seller firms. Dwyer
et al. (1987) have given us another conceptual model of the relationship
process, and numerous others have contributed to our knowledge about
how relationships develop. Each of the models allows us some insight into

how relationships work, but we have not been sensitive to the situational factors that may determine the critical variables in individual relationship situations. Examples of situational factors are found in the contexts of relationships: whether the relationship is buyer-seller, channel, or strategic alliance; the time available to develop a relationship; the experience of the partners in relationships. Each situational factor will influence how the relationship model should be conceptualized.

The combination of the process model and the variables presented as an integrated model may help scholars to model relationships in different situations. The causal path to commitment that describes a channel partnership may be quite different from the causal path for a buyer-seller relationship. Although many of the variables in the two models will be the same, how they are operationalized and connected in the models will vary depending upon the situation. Situational variables, such as time pressures to develop a relationship, company cultures, and experience of potential partners, will influence how the partners move through the stages of relationship development and the variables that will be active in influencing dependent variables such as commitment and cooperation. We have an opportunity to explore how well these models work in different situations. Examining the differences among channel relationships, strategic alliances, and buyer-seller relationships in the levels of intensity of activities necessary to sustain committed relationships may provide us with some insights into how relationships work. Many of the empirical studies cited earlier in this chapter examined channel relationships, which are quite different from buyer-seller relationships. If the concepts and measurements were more compatible, we could compare the models to see the impacts of the different concepts.

PROCESS RESEARCH

Tracking the processes of relationships is a daunting task; it will be time-consuming and difficult. However, the payoff may be outstanding. We may fare better by focusing on the different stages to gain a better understanding of how relationships progress. There is no doubt that they are moved through people interacting within a series of episodes (Håkansson, 1982). There is a rich world to explore. How might a firm change to accommodate the different needs that a relationship may impose on it? What are the different roles that evolve in firms as they maintain relationships? What is the impact on a relationship when the key initiators move on to other tasks—will the relationship survive and grow, or will it drift toward failure, and why? These are challenging questions for scholars to address.

Managerial Implications

Global businesses are forging multiple relationships, ranging from buyer-seller partnerships to joint ventures, at an increasing rate. The basic premise of competitive adversarial buying, where cost improvements come from lower prices, is being slowly replaced by a cooperative model in which savings accrue through cost reductions in total operations, not just price reductions. Figure 9.1 suggests that although all buyer-seller situations do not need to be deep hybrid relationships, many buyers and sellers can benefit from developing hybrid single-source transactional relationships where the goal is to reduce the total costs of acquiring goods or services.

Buying centers and choice models are alive and well because hybrid relationships are still an emerging way of exchanging goods and services. One of the largest barriers to adoption of the relationship model is the organizational reward system, which encourages buyers to drive for lower prices and salespeople to sell, not manage a relationship, maintaining an adversarial environment. Senior managers often talk relationships while the managers charged with implementation operate in a transactional mode, which makes trust development and the achievement of mutual goals difficult if not impossible. Implementation of relationships requires changes in corporate cultures and reward systems to reinforce the behaviors that generate trust, mutual goals, adaptation, and other critical variables in the creation of a strong hybrid relationship.

Looking to the future, individual buyer-seller relationships are becoming part of competitive systems or networks as firms strive to create competitive advantage by developing sets of relationships that create value and are difficult to duplicate (Anderson, Håkansson, & Johanson, 1994; Cravens, Shipp, & Cravens, 1994). These networks seem to be organized by one firm that seeks to build an interlocked set of relationships that in their totality give the network competitive advantage over other sets of nonnetworked firms. For example, the Bombay Company has organized a network of designers, manufacturers, and shipping firms to create a substantial competitive advantage at the retail level over traditional methods of designing, manufacturing, and selling furniture (Finegan, 1993). The Bombay Company is the network driver and has a number of focal relationships with other network members. The Bombay Company manages the activities of the network members through coordination of the dyadic and triadic relationships between the company and its designers, manufacturers, and shippers. This network of relationships creates competitive advantage for the Bombay Company because it is very difficult for competitors to replicate.

Further work is required to conceptualize how a set of buyer and seller relationships becomes a powerful competitive network. The strategic role that relationships play, both at the dyad level and as part of value-creating networks, is a topic of concern for both managers and scholars. It is clear that the future will not be based solely upon a competitive model at the level of the firm; rather, it will be shaped by a firm's ability to operate at all levels of the new competitive paradigm. A firm may be called upon to operate in some segments under an adversarial competitive model while in other segments it may have dyadic relationships with suppliers or customers, and in still others it may operate as a key player in a network of firms that competes against another network. The development of a network from dyadic relationships is beyond the scope of this chapter; however, as a first step, the integrated model offers a way of studying these relationships and exploring the network as a series of dyads.

References

Anderson, E., Lodish, L. M., & Weitz, B. A. (1987). Resource allocation behavior in conventional channels. *Journal of Marketing Research, 24,* 85-97.

Anderson, E., & Weitz, B. A. (1989). Determinants of continuity in conventional industrial channel dyads. *Marketing Science, 8,* 310-323.

Anderson, J. C., Håkansson, H., & Johanson, J. (1994). Dyadic business relationships within a business network context. *Journal of Marketing, 58*(4), 1-15.

Anderson, J. C., & Narus, J. A. (1984). A model of the distributor's perspective of distributor-manufacturer working relationships. *Journal of Marketing, 48*(4), 62-74.

Anderson, J. C., & Narus, J. A. (1990). A model of distributor firm and manufacturer firm working partnerships. *Journal of Marketing, 54*(1), 42-58.

Badaracco, J. L., Jr. (1991). *The knowledge link: How firms compete through strategic alliances.* Boston: Harvard Business School Press.

Borys, B., & Jemison, D. B. (1989). Hybrid arrangements as strategic alliances: Theoretical issues in organizational combinations. *Academy of Management Review, 14,* 234-249.

Cravens, D. W., Shipp, S. H., & Cravens, K. S. (1994, July-August). Reforming the traditional organization: The mandate for developing networks. *Business Horizons,* pp. 19-28.

Deutsch, M. (1958). Trust and suspicion. *Journal of Conflict Resolution, 2,* 265-279.

Dwyer, F. R., Schurr, P. H., & Oh, S. (1987). Developing buyer-seller relationships. *Journal of Marketing, 51*(2), 11-27.

Finegan, J. (1993, December). Survival of the smartest. *Inc.,* pp. 78-88.

Ford, D. (Ed.). (1990). *Understanding business markets: Interaction, relationships, networks.* London: Academic Press.

Ganesan, S. (1994). Determinants of long-term orientation in buyer-seller relationships. *Journal of Marketing, 58*(2), 1-19.

Håkansson, H. (Ed.). (1982). *International marketing and purchasing of industrial goods: An interaction approach.* New York: John Wiley.

Håkansson, H., & Wootz, B. (1979). A framework for industrial buying and selling. *Industrial Marketing Management, 8,* 28-39.

Hallén, L., Johanson, J., & Seyed-Mohamed, N. (1991). Interfirm adaptation in business relationships. *Journal of Marketing, 55*(2), 29-37.

Hallén, L., Seyed-Mohamed, N., & Johanson, J. (1988). Adaptations in business relationships. In P. W. Turnbull & S. J. Paliwoda (Eds.), *Research developments in international marketing.* Manchester, England: IMP Group.

Han, S.-L. (1992). *Antecedents of buyer-seller long-term relationships: An exploratory model of structural bonding and social bonding* (Working Paper No. 6-1992). University Park: Pennsylvania State University, Institute for the Study of Business Markets.

Han, S.-L., & Wilson, D. T. (1993). *Antecedents of buyer commitment to a supplier: A model of structural bonding and social bonding.* Unpublished manuscript, Pennsylvania State University, Marketing Department.

Han, S.-L., Wilson, D. T., & Dant, S. (1993). Buyer-seller relationships today. *Industrial Marketing Management, 22,* 331-338.

Hardwick, B., & Ford, D. (1986). Industrial buyer resources and responsibilities and the buyer-seller relationships. *Industrial Marketing and Purchasing, 1,* 3-25.

Heide, J. B., & John, G. (1988). The role of dependence balancing in safeguarding transaction-specific assets in conventional channels. *Journal of Marketing, 52*(1), 20-35.

Heide, J. B., & John, G. (1990). Alliances in industrial purchasing: The determinants of joint action in buyer-supplier relationships. *Journal of Marketing Research, 27,* 24-36.

Heide, J. B., & John, G. (1992). Do norms matter in marketing relationships? *Journal of Marketing, 56*(2), 32-44.

Jackson, B. B. (1985). *Winning and keeping industrial customers: The dynamics of customer relationships.* Lexington, MA: D. C. Heath.

Johnson, M. P. (1978). Personal and cognitive features of the dissolution of commitment to relationships. In S. W. Duck (Ed.), *Personal relationships: Dissolving personal relationships.* London: Academic Press.

Kalwani, M. U., & Narayandas, N. (1995). Long-term manufacturer-supplier relationships: Do they pay off for supplier firms? *Journal of Marketing, 59*(1), 1-16.

Levine, J. B., & Byrne, J. A. (1986, July 21). Corporate odd couples. *Business Week,* pp. 100-105.

Lorange, P., & Roos, J. (1991, January-February). Why some strategic alliances succeed and others fail. *Journal of Business Strategy, 12,* 25-30.

McCall, G. J. (1970). The social organization of relationships. In G. J. McCall, M. M. McCall, N. K. Denzin, G. D. Suttles, & S. B. Kurth (Eds.), *Social relationships.* Chicago: Aldine.

Moorman, C., Zaltman, G., & Deshpandé, R. (1992). Relationships between providers and users of market research: The dynamics of trust within and between organizations. *Journal of Marketing Research, 29,* 314-328.

Morgan, R. M., & Hunt, S. D. (1994). The commitment-trust theory of relationship marketing. *Journal of Marketing, 58*(3), 20-38.

Mummalaneni, V. (1987). *The influence of a close personal relationship between the buyer and the seller on the continued stability of theory role relationships.* Unpublished doctoral dissertation, Pennsylvania State University.

Mummalaneni, V., & Wilson, D. T. (1991). *The influence of a close personal relationship between a buyer and seller on the continued stability of their role relationship* (Working Paper No. 4-1991). University Park: Pennsylvania State University, Institute for the Study of Business Markets.

Noordewier, T. G., John, G., & Nevin, J. R. (1990). Performance outcomes of purchasing arrangements in industrial buyer-vendor relationships. *Journal of Marketing, 54*(4), 80-93.

Pfeffer, J., & Salancik, G. R. (1978). *The external control of organizations: A resource dependence perspective.* New York: Harper & Row.

Schurr, P. H., & Ozanne, J. L. (1985). Influences on exchange processes: Buyers' preconceptions of a seller's trustworthiness and bargaining toughness. *Journal of Consumer Research, 11,* 939-953.

Taylor, A., III. (1994, September 5). The auto industry meets the new economy. *Fortune,* pp. 52-60.

Thibaut, J. W., & Kelley, H. H. (1959). *The social psychology of groups.* New York: John Wiley.

Turnbull, P. W., & Paliwoda, S. J. (Eds.). (1986). *Research in international marketing.* London: Croom Helm.

Turner, R. H. (1970). *Family interaction.* New York: John Wiley.

Vlosky, R. P., & Wilson, D. T. (1994). Technology adoption in channels. In J. N. Sheth & A. Parvatiyar (Eds.), *Relationship marketing: Theory, methods and applications.* Atlanta, GA: Emory University, Center for Relationship Marketing.

Williamson, O. E. (1975). *Markets and hierarchies: Analysis and antitrust implications.* New York: Free Press.

Williamson, O. E. (1985). *The economic institutions of capitalism: Firms, markets, and relational contracting.* New York: Free Press.

Williamson, O. E. (1991). Comparative economic organizations: The analysis of discrete structural alternatives. *Administrative Science Quarterly, 36,* 269-296.

Wilson, D. T. (1978). Dyadic interactions: Some conceptualizations. In T. V. Bonoma & G. Zaltman (Eds.), *Organizational buying behavior.* Chicago: American Marketing Association.

Wilson, D. T., & Jantrania, S. A. (1993). *Understanding the value of a relationship.* Paper presented at the International Colloquium on Relationship Marketing, Monash University, Melbourne.

Wilson, D. T., & Moller, K. K. (1988). *Buyer-seller relationships: Alternative conceptualizations* (Working Paper No. 10-1988). University Park: Pennsylvania State University, Institute for the Study of Business Markets.

Wilson, D. T., & Moller, K. K. (1991). Buyer-seller relationships: Alternative conceptualiza-
    tions. In S. J. Paliwoda (Ed.), *New perspectives on international marketing* (pp. 87-107).
    New York: Routledge.
Wilson, D. T., & Mummalaneni, V. (1986). Bonding and commitment in supplier relationships:
    A preliminary conceptualization. *Industrial Marketing and Purchasing, 1*(3), 44-58.
Wilson, D. T., Soni, P. K., & O'Keeffe, M. (1995). *Modeling customer retention as a relationship
    problem* (Working Paper No. 1995-13). University Park: Pennsylvania State University,
    Institute for the Study of Business Markets.
Zand, D. E. (1972). Trust and managerial problem solving. *Administrative Science Quarterly,
    17,* 229-239.

10

Strategic Alliances

A Synthesis of Conceptual Foundations

P. RAJAN VARADARAJAN
MARGARET H. CUNNINGHAM

Marketing, defined as building satisfying exchanges, rests on the establishment of relationships (Dwyer, Schurr, & Oh, 1987). The study of the major facets and nuances of both intraorganizational and interorganizational relationships has a long and rich tradition in the marketing discipline. For instance, the deterrents to, and the determinants of, cooperation between marketing and other functional areas within the organization (e.g., research and development [R&D] and manufacturing) have been studied extensively in reference to marketing research, innovation, and new product

NOTE: This chapter is reprinted from P. Rajan Varadarajan and Margaret H. Cunningham, "Strategic Alliances: A Synthesis of Conceptual Foundations," *Journal of the Academy of Marketing Science*, vol. 23, no. 4, pp. 282-296, copyright © 1995 by the Academy of Marketing Science. Reprinted by permission.

development (Gupta, Raj, & Wilemon, 1986; Ruekert & Walker, 1987). Similarly, the antecedents and outcomes of cooperation among the strategic business units of a diversified multibusiness firm have been researched by marketing scholars (Buzzell & Gale, 1987; Wells, 1984). Arndt (1979) has noted the tendency of firms engaged in business-to-business marketing to develop long-lasting relationships with their key customers and key suppliers rather than focusing on discrete exchanges and has termed this phenomenon "domesticated markets." Adler (1966) focused on interorganizational relationships between firms other than those linked by the traditional marketer-marketing intermediary relationships and termed this phenomenon "symbiotic marketing." Other manifestations of interorganizational relationships examined in the marketing literature include cause-related marketing (cooperation between a for-profit firm and a not-for-profit institution; see Varadarajan & Menon, 1988) and joint sales promotion (cooperation between firms within the confines of the sales promotion component of the marketing mix; see Varadarajan, 1986).

Building on this tradition, marketing scholars have evinced a growing interest in the study of an even broader array of intra- and interorganizational relationships. For instance, Morgan and Hunt (1994) identify as many as 10 distinct forms of intra- and interorganizational relationships pertinent to the study of relationship marketing:

1. *Buyer partnerships* with (a) intermediate customers and (b) ultimate customers
2. *Supplier partnerships* with (a) goods suppliers and (b) services suppliers
3. *Lateral partnerships* with (a) competitors, (b) nonprofit organizations, and (c) government
4. *Internal partnerships* among (a) the various business units, (b) functional departments, and (c) employees of the firm

Strategic alliances, a manifestation of interorganizational cooperative strategies, entail the pooling of skills and resources by the alliance partners in order to achieve one or more goals linked to the strategic objectives of the cooperating firms. Parkhe (1993) defines strategic alliances as "relatively enduring interfirm cooperative arrangements, involving flows and linkages that use resources and/or governance structures from autonomous organizations, for the joint accomplishment of individual goals linked to the corporate mission of each sponsoring firm" (p. 794). Table 10.1 provides illustrative examples of strategic alliances, including their motives and the

TABLE 10.1 Pooling of Skills and Resources for Competitive Advantage: An Exposition

Alliance Partners	Alliance Purpose	Key Resources and Skills Pooled in Strategic Alliance		Remarks	Source(s)
		Alliance Partner A	Alliance Partner B		
A. General Mills Inc. B. Nestle S.A.	To market General Mills brand cereals first in Western European countries, with future expansion plans into Asian, African, and Latin American countries	*Resources:* cereal brand names—Cheerios, Golden Grahams, etc.; proprietary cereals manufacturing equipment *Skills:* product innovation, development, and marketing skills specifically related to cereals	*Resources:* corporate name—Nestle—with widespread recognition in Europe, Asia, Africa, and Latin America. Network of manufacturing plants with spare capacity to undertake manufacturing of cereals. Sales force and distribution infrastructure. Access to and clout with retailers in Western European countries. Rights to use Walt Disney characters in Nestle products throughout Europe and the Middle East	Cereal boxes bear the Nestle label in addition to the General Mills cereal brand names. Excluded from the scope of the alliance are the North American markets in which General Mills is already established.	"Cafe au Lait" (1992), Gibson (1990), Knowlton (1991)
A. Ford Motor Company B. Mazda Motor Corp.	*Product development:* Styling of outside by Ford and engineering of inside by Mazda. *Production by proxy:* Ford supplies to Mazda cars and trucks assembled at some of its facilities for marketing under the Mazda label through the Mazda dealership network, and vice versa. *Marketing support:* Ford cars and trucks assembled in the United States are distributed by Mazda in Japan through Mazda's network of Autorama showrooms.	*Resources:* manufacturing facilities, brand name, distribution network *Skills:* exterior styling, international marketing, finance	*Resources:* manufacturing facilities, brand name, distribution network *Skills:* manufacturing, product development	Ford has a 25% equity interest in Mazda; Mazda has a 39% equity and Ford a 34% equity in Autorama, the network of showrooms in Japan through which automobiles of Mazda, Ford, and the makes of Mazda's other joint-venture partners are sold.	"How Ford and Mazda Shared" (1992), "The Partners" (1990), Rapoport (1990)

273

key resources and skills of the partners pooled in these alliances. Researchers who have studied the many facets of strategic alliances have used such terms as *symbiotic marketing, business alliances, strategic alliances, strategic partnerships, strategic networks, interorganizational linkages, interfirm cooperation, collaborative agreements, quasi-integration strategies, cooperative strategies, coalition strategies, collective strategies,* and *corporate linkages,* to list a few (see Badaracco, 1991; Bleeke & Ernst, 1991; Cravens, Shipp, & Cravens, 1993; Day & Klein, 1987; Ghemawat, Porter, & Rawlinson, 1986; Harrigan, 1984, 1988; Jarillo, 1988; Ohmae, 1985, 1987, 1989; Porter & Fuller, 1986; Sheth & Parvatiyar, 1992; Varadarajan & Rajaratnam, 1986).

At one extreme, a strategic alliance between two firms can encompass all of the functional areas; at the other extreme, it may be limited in scope to a single functional area or value activity (e.g., symbiotic marketing; see Adler, 1966; Varadarajan & Rajaratnam, 1986). Of late, the study of symbiotic marketing seems to have been largely subsumed under the rubric of the much broader and more encompassing business phenomenon commonly referred to as *strategic alliances.* Such developments raise important and intriguing questions regarding the role of marketing in the formulation and implementation of strategic alliances and the nature of research questions that merit exploration in marketing literature. Against this backdrop, our objective in this chapter is to provide a review and synthesis of the conceptual foundations of strategic alliances. The discussion is organized as follows:

- *Conceptualization and delineation:* What forms of interorganizational cooperation fall within the domain of strategic alliances?
- *Motives:* Why do firms enter into strategic alliances?
- *Scope:* In what alternative forms do/can strategic alliances exist?
- *Drivers:* What are some of the environmental, industry, and organizational factors that affect the propensity of firms to enter into strategic alliances?
- *Outcomes:* Under what conditions can strategic alliances enable cooperating firms to achieve a competitive positional advantage in the marketplace?
- *Role of marketing in strategic alliances:* What factors influence the role of marketing in strategic alliances?
- *Limitations and research directions:* What are some costs that a firm might incur as a partner in a strategic alliance? What are some research questions that merit investigation?

Conceptualization and Delineation

Consistent with the emerging consensus in favor of a broader construal of strategic alliances (see, e.g., Spekman & Sawhney, 1990; Terpstra & Simonin, 1992), we view as falling within the domain of strategic alliances a number of forms of interorganizational cooperation that vary in the degree of rigidity of the cooperative arrangement. Thus a strategic alliance could be structured as either (a) a distinct *corporate* entity to which the alliance partners commit agreed-upon skills and resources and in which each of the alliance partners holds an equity position (i.e., an equity joint venture) or (b) a distinct *interorganizational* entity to which the alliance partners commit agreed-upon skills and resources (e.g., a nonequity venture such as a joint technology development center or joint product development team).

In effect, although some types of strategic alliances will have finite life spans by definition (e.g., a joint product development *project*), other forms of strategic alliances, such as equity joint ventures, can theoretically exist in perpetuity. Alliances that do not involve shared equity are less rigid and may be easier to revise, reorganize, or terminate than strategic alliances that entail equity sharing in a joint venture. As a result, when unstable market conditions prevail, such as is the case when the technological base of an industry is evolving rapidly, the flexibility and adaptability offered by less rigid forms of alliances may be viewed favorably.

Interorganizational cooperative relationships can exist between two firms whose primary economic commitments are to the same set of value-chain activities (e.g., between Ford and Mazda; between Wal-Mart and Dillards) or between two firms whose primary economic commitments are to adjacent stages of the value chain (such is the case in supplier-manufacturer alliances, e.g., between Ford Motor Company and its auto parts suppliers). The former is illustrative of a *horizontal* interorganizational cooperative relationship, and the latter of a *vertical* interorganizational cooperative relationship.

Although interorganizational cooperation is a key facet of strategic alliances, this is by no means their only defining characteristic. Because the purpose of strategy is to achieve sustainable competitive advantage, an interorganizational partnership can realistically be viewed as a strategic alliance only if it would enable the cooperating firms to achieve competitive advantage in the marketplace. As Sheth and Parvatiyar (1992) point out, the primary purpose underlying close cooperation between organizations could be either *strategic* (e.g., entry into a new product-market domain) or *operational* (e.g., streamlining operations activities such as automatic reordering and invoicing through electronic data interchange systems). Thus, although the terms *strategic partnership, strategic partnering,* and *strategic alliances* are sometimes used to describe close cooperation between manufacturers and retailers in areas such as the development of systems for electronic data interchange (EDI) and procedures for efficient consumer response, these relationships are primarily operations oriented. They do not evidence important characteristics of strategic alliances, such as exclusivity and nonimitability, and therefore cannot result in a sustainable competitive advantage. Often, they are replicated by the manufacturer's competitors and its retail partners. For example, an EDI system linking Procter & Gamble and Wal-Mart is duplicated by similar ones between Wal-Mart and Procter & Gamble's chief rivals (i.e., Lever Brothers and Wal-Mart, Colgate-Palmolive and Wal-Mart). Moreover, Procter & Gamble, Lever Brothers, and Colgate-Palmolive have similar relationships with Wal-Mart's major competitors, Kmart and Target. In other words, given that the three competing manufacturers have similar cooperative arrangements with the three competing retailers, these partnerships cannot be instrumental in helping either an individual firm or a partnership enhance its competitive position over the others. Hence characterizing such relationships between manufacturing firms and marketing intermediaries as strategic alliances is questionable. They are more often a cost associated with doing business with particular firms and/or competing in certain industries.

Forming Strategic Alliances: Underlying Motives

Building on Ansoff's (1957) conceptualization of major growth alternatives available to a firm, the motives underlying a firm's entry into strategic alliances can be broadly characterized as attempts to capitalize on opportunities for sales and/or profit growth by doing the following:

- Promoting its *present* product offerings in its *present* served markets
- Developing *new* markets for its *present* products
- Developing *new* products for its *present* served markets
- Entering into *new* product-market domains that are either related to or unrelated to its *present* product-market domain

TABLE 10.2 Motives Underlying Entry of Firms Into Strategic Alliances

---

Motives related to market entry and market position
    Gain access to new international markets
    Circumvent barriers to entering international markets posed by legal, regulatory, and/or
        political factors
    Defend market position in present markets
    Enhance market position in present markets

Motives related to product
    Fill gaps in present product line
    Broaden present product line
    Differentiate or add value to the product

Motives related to product/market
    Enter new product/market domains
    Enter or maintain the option to enter evolving industries whose product offerings may
        emerge as either substitutes for or complements to the firm's product offerings

Motives related to market structure modification
    Reduce potential threat of future competition
    Raise or erect entry barriers
    Alter the technological base of competition

Motives related to market entry timing
    Accelerate pace of entry into new product-market domains by accelerating pace of R&D,
        product development, and/or market entry

Motives related to resource-use efficiency
    Lower manufacturing costs
    Lower marketing costs

Motives related to resource extension and risk reduction
    Pool resources in the face of large resource outlays required, technological uncertainties,
        market uncertainties, and/or other uncertainties

Motives related to skills enhancement
    Learn new skills from alliance partners
    Enhance present skills by working with alliance partners

Table 10.2 provides a more detailed exposition of the motives underlying the entry of firms into strategic alliances. The motives listed, however, are neither mutually exclusive nor collectively exhaustive. Illustrative of the motives' not being mutually exclusive is the case of an alliance partner's product offerings enabling the focal firm to broaden its product line or fill gaps in its product line. Such an alliance would also play a key role in enabling the firm to realize its market-position-related objectives, such as defending or enhancing market position in the markets it currently serves.

Furthermore, either a single important objective or a multiplicity of inter-related objectives may underlie a firm's decision to enter into strategic alliances. A more detailed discussion of some of the motives underlying entry of firms into strategic alliances follows.

MOTIVES UNDERLYING ALLIANCE FORMATION

Enter new international markets. Firms seeking to enter new international markets in their quest for growth and profitability have historically pursued different entry strategies, such as internal development, acquisitions, mergers, and joint ventures. In recent years, however, the growing recognition of the importance of entering and achieving viable market position in all of the major world markets seems to have provided the impetus for an ever-increasing number of firms to examine more closely the desirability of entering into strategic alliances with other firms possessing complementary skills and resources.

Consider, for instance, the international entry strategies of two companies that dominate the breakfast cereals business in the United States: Kellogg Company and General Mills, Inc. Over the past 70 years, Kellogg has on its own entered, nurtured, and achieved a dominant position in the market for breakfast cereals in a number of Western European countries. General Mills, on the other hand, which only recently began marketing its breakfast cereals in Western Europe, chose to enter a strategic alliance with Nestle S.A. Rather than developing its own distribution system from scratch, General Mills chose to take advantage of Nestle's extensive sales force and distribution infrastructure and its intimate knowledge of the Western European market (see Gibson, 1990; Knowlton, 1991). By pursuing this option, General Mills was also in a position to accelerate its pace of entry into the market for breakfast cereals in Western Europe.

Circumvent barriers to entering new international markets. When entering new international markets, firms often enter alliances to reduce economic risk. Moreover, by forming alliances with domestic firms that are familiar with the nuances of the local environment, a firm may also be in a position to circumvent legal, political, and/or regulatory barriers to entry as well as to reduce political risks. Furthermore, the alliance partner's experience in working with local advertising agencies, marketing research agencies, and mass communications media, as well as its in-depth knowledge of local markets, may enhance the effectiveness of the overall marketing effort.

Protect competitive position in the home market. By attacking a foreign competitor in its home market, and thereby necessitating diversion of resources away from expansion into new international markets and toward protection of its competitive position in its home market, a firm may be able to protect its share in the home market. Illustrative of the use of strategic alliances as a strategy to counter competition abroad in order to protect one's market position in the home market is Caterpillar's alliance with Mitsubishi of Japan (see Hout, Porter, & Rudden, 1982).

Broaden product line/fill product line gaps. The practice of firms entering into strategic alliances in order to broaden their product lines and/or fill gaps in their existing product lines is illustrated by alliances between U.S. auto manufacturers and their Japanese counterparts, such as GM's alliances with Isuzu and Suzuki of Japan and Chrysler's alliance with Mitsubishi of Japan.

Enter new product-market domains/gain a foothold in emerging industries. As industries mature, firms finding their traditional markets stagnating and their growth opportunities severely curtailed have entered into strategic alliances in attempts to diversify and take advantage of growth opportunities in other product-market domains. Also, foreseeing the emergence of alternative, substitute technologies, firms have entered into alliances with other companies on the leading edge of new technologies to gain a foothold in the emerging industries.

Shape industry structure. Strategic alliances that foster technological revolutions through the merging of heretofore divergent technologies and create dramatic changes in consumers' preferences can (a) significantly alter the bases of competition by eroding the existing sources of competitive advantage in an industry and (b) shape industry structure by raising barriers to entry, creating new technological standards, establishing new distribution channels, and developing new suppliers. Innovations such as new product designs, new production processes, and new marketing approaches can propel an entire industry into a higher rate of growth by stimulating primary demand.

Reduce potential threat of future competition. General Electric, by licensing its advanced gas turbine technology to foreign producers that GE viewed as potential major competitors, is reported to have not only created a captive market for its technology in these countries but eliminated the threat of future competition from these companies in the context of the U.S. market (see Watson, 1982).

Raise entry barriers. By joining forces to gain additional strength, alliance members might be able to erect entry barriers by denying competitors the base volume necessary to exploit economies of scale (Watson, 1982).

Overcome entry barriers. Strategic alliances can also enable firms to overcome entry barriers. For instance, the Canadian telecommunications industry, prior to its deregulation in 1992, was dominated by Northern Telecom, whose proprietary technology was in effect the industry standard. Subsequent to deregulation, AT&T, by forming a network of alliances with smaller Canadian firms such as Unitel Communications Inc., has been able to sell integrated technologies to large provincial utilities ("AT&T's Crucial Charge," 1993).

Enhance resource-use efficiency. Strategic alliances can enable partners to lower manufacturing costs by taking advantage of (a) scale, scope, and/or experience effects and (b) differences in factor costs. For instance, sharing manufacturing facilities may allow alliance partners to realize the benefits of economies of scale and experience effects. Similarly, using the sales force, distribution, and/or warehousing facilities of an alliance partner may allow a firm to market its offerings at a lower cost.

Resource extension. Strategic alliances are a viable alternative for any firm when internal developments or acquisitions are beyond its resource capabilities and a merger, which would entail the loss of the firm's corporate identity, is unacceptable. Alliances may be particularly attractive for smaller firms that lack the resources to invest in R&D, new products, and other competitive activities critical to gaining a foothold in the market or critical to defending or enhancing their market position. However, in the face of escalating costs of R&D and/or investments in capital equipment and facilities needed to serve a global market, even larger firms are increasingly being forced to enter into strategic alliances with partners willing to share in developmental costs and/or capital equipment outlay.

Acquire new skills. Firms often enter into alliances with the intent of learning from their alliance partners (Hamel, 1991). For instance, one of General Motors's key objectives in its alliance with Toyota was to learn Toyota's methods of managing and manufacturing. Learning to deal with labor and suppliers in the United States was reportedly among Toyota's major objectives. Interestingly, it has been pointed out that, as opposed to mutual learning, sometimes firms enter into strategic alliances with the intent of learning all they can from their partners (i.e., internalizing over time the distinctive capabilities/skills of the alliance partners) while at the same time safeguarding their own distinctive skills from being internalized by their partners. Strategic alliances have therefore also been characterized by many as a race to learn, and hence a new form of competition in which the partner that learns fastest will be able to dominate the relationship as well as to renegotiate the terms of the alliance in its favor (Main, 1990).

THEORETICAL PERSPECTIVES ON STRATEGIC ALLIANCES

A number of theoretical frameworks have been advanced to explain the motives underlying the entry of firms into strategic alliances, the conditions under which strategic alliances are likely to be formed, and the types of strategic alliances that are likely to be formed. These include the concept of domesticated markets (Arndt, 1979), theories of market attractiveness and organizational power (Kogut, 1988), interorganizational exchange behavior and resource dependence (Pfeffer & Salancik, 1978), and institutional economics (Day & Klein, 1987; Heide, 1994; Hennart, 1988; Oliver, 1990). Complementing these perspectives is the resource-based view of strategic alliances, which we discuss in a later section. Collectively, the various theoretical frameworks advanced to explain the evolution of strategic alliances suggest that market uncertainty, the drive for increased efficiency, resource dependence, skill and resource heterogeneity, and imperfect factor markets drive firms to form alliances in their quest for competitive advantage.

Kogut (1988) proposes that the motivations underlying the formation of joint ventures are reducible to three factors: (a) evasion of small-numbers bargaining, (b) enhancement of competitive position, and (c) provision of mechanisms for transfer of organizational knowledge. He compared the abilities of three theoretical perspectives (transaction costs, strategic behavior, and organizational theory) to explain the propensity of firms to enter into joint ventures rather than to select other modes of transacting. Kogut proposes that transaction cost theory is related to a firm's attempts, under conditions of asset specificity, to minimize costs by evading small-numbers bargaining and opportunism. Strategic motivation theory, on the other hand, according to Kogut, illuminates a firm's attempts to enhance its competitive position or market power to improve its overall profitability. Although uncertainty avoidance is central to both of these theories, product-market strategy is outside the domain of transaction cost theory but is central to strategic motivation theory. Kogut's third explanation of the formation of joint ventures is derived from organizational theory. This theory addresses a firm's attempts to transfer embedded organizational knowledge. Because organizational knowledge is tacit, experiential, and embedded, it is only through the melding of organizational structures (i.e., replicating organizational structures in the new joint-venture firm) that this knowledge can be transferred from one partner to another.

Resource dependence theory (see Pfeffer & Salancik, 1978) is based on the premise that few organizations are self-sufficient with respect to critical resources. Moreover, firms are heterogeneous, with asymmetric abilities to develop or acquire resources. This lack of self-sufficiency leads to dependence on other firms and introduces uncertainty into the firm's decision-making environment. The formation of strategic alliances is one means of creating governance mechanisms to reduce uncertainty and manage dependence. As Heide (1994) notes, a major implication of resource dependence theory is the identification of dependence and uncertainty as the key antecedent variables underlying the formation of interfirm relationships.

Underlying most theoretical bases of interfirm relations is the assumption that the environment in which firms operate is *not* characterized by perfect competition, where market-based exchanges are the most efficient means of consummating transactions. When imperfect conditions prevail, firms must choose between using market-based transactions governed by price mechanisms and the possibility of exploitation and internalizing transactions through either alliances (quasi-integration) or direct ownership (integration) and governing them through the firm's internal hierarchical control structure. Transaction cost theory thus parallels resource dependence theory in that it views nonmarket governance as a response to environmental uncertainty and dependence (Heide, 1994). Although in the original transaction cost framework (Williamson, 1975) complete vertical integration was identified as an appropriate response to governance problems (associated with [a] *safeguarding* transaction specific investments from subsequent opportunistic exploitation, [b] *adapting* to relevant external environmental contingencies that may be far too numerous or unpredictable to be specified *ex ante* in a contract, and [c] *evaluating* contractual compliance when facing performance ambiguity), recent theoretical extensions have shown that the governance features of internal organization can also be achieved within the context of interfirm relationships such as those found in strategic alliances (see Heide, 1994).

Oliver (1990) lists six determinants of relationship formation (necessity, asymmetry, reciprocity, efficiency, stability, and legitimacy), which she uses as contingencies to predict six types of interorganizational relations (trade associations, agency federations, joint ventures, social service joint programs, corporate-financial interlocks, and agency-sponsor linkages) that are likely to be formed. Although each of the factors may be sufficient to drive relationship formation, Oliver notes that they may also interact. The necessity factor, which refers to the legal or regulatory requirements governing business, is the only one used to explain why firms are mandated into relationship formation (i.e., the relationship is not voluntary). Oliver notes that asymmetry is important in explaining voluntary relationship formation, because firms have different resources and abilities that are not shared equally by all firms. Under conditions of asymmetry, Firm A seeks to exert power and control over another organization (Firm B) that possesses scarce resources Firm A depends upon. Reciprocity, on the other hand, explains the motivation of firms that seek control over resources through cooperation and collaboration rather than through domination. Efficiency motivations reflect the desires of firms to enter into relationships to reduce costs. When firms seek to adapt to uncertain environments, stability motives are believed to drive them to enter into relationships. Finally, Oliver proposes that the need for legitimacy incites a firm to enter into relationships if that will enhance the organization's ability to comply with prevailing norms or improve its reputation and image.

A closer examination of various theoretical explanations of the rationale underlying the entry of firms into strategic alliances, and/or the conditions under which firms are likely to enter into strategic alliances, suggests that, given their overlapping nature, it may be more appropriate to view them as complementing explanations rather than as competing explanations of the strategic alliance phenomenon. For instance, transaction cost and resource dependence concepts are the foundation of a theory of structure and governance, not one of strategy (Heide, 1994; Tallman, 1991). The focus of these theories is on the best responses to various environmental conditions, not on proactively seeking to change conditions through strategic thrusts. For instance, from a resource dependence theory perspective, the formation of interfirm links is seen as a strategic adaptation to environmental uncertainty and dependence (see Heide, 1994). Strategy, on the other hand, is a mechanism of change that reflects the power of idiosyncratic managerial intention and ability (Tallman, 1991), as exemplified by the concept of domesticated markets, which suggests that firms make conscious attempts to influence their environments through their exchange and interfirm relationships (see Arndt, 1979).

Industry, Geographic, and Functional Scope of Alliances

A framework for classifying alliances in terms of their industry scope (intra- versus interindustry), geographic scope (intra- versus international), and functional area scope (R&D, manufacturing, marketing, and so on) is presented in Table 10.3. A more detailed discussion of various types of strategic alliances follows.

INTRAINDUSTRY AND INTERINDUSTRY STRATEGIC ALLIANCES

Intraindustry Strategic Alliances:
The Case of Cooperation Among Rivals

A distinguishing feature of intraindustry strategic alliances is that the alliance partners tend to be rivals competing for market share in the same product class—in the same market segments, in different market

TABLE 10.3 Functional, Industry, and Geographic Scope of Strategic Alliances

| | Industry Scope and Geographic Scope of Alliance | | | |
Functional Area Scope of Alliance[a]	Intraindustry, Intranational	Interindustry, Intranational	Intraindustry, International	Interindustry, International
1. Technology exchange, licensing, and cross-licensing				
2. Joint exploration and development of sources of raw materials				
3. Joint R&D and technology development				
4. Joint product development				
5. Joint manufacturing				
6. Manufacturing-marketing alliances				
7. Joint marketing				
8. Reciprocal marketing				
9. Reciprocal after-sales service				
10. Franchising				

a. An alternative to delineating the scope of the alliance in terms of functional areas is to define the scope of the alliance in terms of the primary and secondary activities of the value chain. The scope of an alliance may either be limited to a specific functional area (value-chain activity) or encompass a number of functional areas (value-chain activities) listed in the first column.

285

segments, or in different geographic markets. The partners in an intraindustry strategic alliance can be market followers, market leaders, or a
market follower and a market leader.

Strategic alliance between market followers. When market followers in
an industry lack the resources to challenge the market leader or to defend
their market positions in the face of challenges posed by the market
leader, they may be in a position to compete effectively against the market
leader by pooling their resources and skills. It is conceivable that such
considerations might have provided the impetus for an alliance among
Honeywell of the United States, Group Bull of France, and NEC of Japan,
given the dominant position of IBM in the computer mainframe industry.

Strategic alliance between market leaders. Often, strategic alliances,
particularly in the international arena, are formed between firms with
strong competitive positions in their respective home markets. For instance, New United Motor Manufacturing Inc. (NUMMI) is an alliance between General Motors Corporation, the market share leader in the U.S.
automotive market, and Toyota Motor Company, the market share leader
in the Japanese automotive market. The output of this jointly owned,
U.S.-based passenger car manufacturing facility is marketed independently by GM and Toyota through their respective automotive dealership
networks under different brand names.

Strategic alliance between market leader and market follower. In certain
situations, the market leader in Country A may choose to enter into an alliance with a market follower in Country B. The market leader in Country
A may use such an alliance not only to challenge the market leader in
Country B but to drain the latter of its profits by forcing it to expend a substantial amount of resources to defend its leadership position in the home
market. This could possibly limit the amount of resources available to the
latter firm to enter new international markets, such as establishing a beach-
head in Country A. Thus pursuit of a potential foreign competitor's domestic
market through a strategic alliance with a market follower in that market
can help a firm protect its market position in its home market.

Table 10.4 provides an overview of alternative patterns of intraindustry
strategic alliances, some of which are currently in vogue and others of
which are suggestive of potential possibilities. Some of these alliances are
centered on *precompetitive resource sharing.* Such is the case when joint

TABLE 10.4 Intraindustry Strategic Alliances: An Overview of Prevailing Patterns and Potential Possibilities

---

Alliances with firms that currently compete with the focal firm in the same geographic market(s)
> Major competitor across the board or in a number of product-market segments
> Major competitor in certain product-market segments
> Minor competitor across the board or in a number of product-market segments
> Minor competitor in certain product-market segments

Alliances with firms that do not currently compete with the focal firm in the same geographic markets
> Firms perceived as potential competitors: firms contemplating entry and possessing the skills, resources, and ability to enter the served markets of the focal firm either across the board or in certain product-market segments
> Firms not perceived as potential competitors: firms that lack the skills, resources, and abilities needed to compete in the served markets of the focal firm

Alliances with other firms that the focal firm views as potential competitors
> Firms currently engaged in the development of products to compete with the focal firm's product offerings
> Firms not currently engaged in the development of products designed to compete with the product offerings of the focal firm, but that recognize the need to do so if other options (such as acquisition, merger, or strategic alliance) fail to materialize

---

exploration of raw materials is undertaken, R&D activities are pooled, or manufacturing facilities are constructed. Other alliances between firms within an industry entail one firm using some of its manufacturing capacity to produce goods for marketing by its alliance partner under the latter's brand name. For instance, General Motors Corporation, in addition to having a precompetitive resource sharing (manufacturing) alliance with the Toyota Motor Company of Japan, also has *manufacturing-marketing alliances* with Suzuki Motors and Isuzu Motors of Japan. Automobiles manufactured by Suzuki and Isuzu under these *production-by-proxy alliances* are marketed by GM under the Geo name through its Chevrolet automotive dealership network. Although Isuzu has its own (but much less extensive) dealer network in the United States, the alliance with GM allows it to benefit from economies of scale in manufacturing and experience effects. Precompetitive resource sharing might also be feasible in the context of supporting value-chain activities, such as the development and sharing of a computerized airline reservation system by a consortium of Asian, European, and North American airlines. In all of these types of alliances, some level of *postcompetitive resource sharing* might also be feasible. For instance, the alliance partners might be in a position to achieve cost savings by setting up a joint spare-parts inventory holding facility.

Interindustry Strategic Alliances

The pooling of R&D, manufacturing, and/or marketing resources by firms in an interindustry strategic alliance can often open up new product-market opportunities that neither firm would be able to exploit individually. Interindustry strategic alliances can involve firms competing in either related or unrelated industries. Potential opportunities for a firm to enter into alliances with firms in other industries include the following:

1. Alliances with firms whose product offerings complement the firm's product offerings
2. Alliances with firms in entrenched substitute industries
3. Alliances with firms in emerging substitute industries
4. Alliances with firms in new and evolving product markets in order to gain a foothold

Interindustry strategic alliances are often propelled by the convergence of industries and the complexity and multiplicity of technologies underlying the products of these emergent industries. As Ohmae (1989) notes, "Today's products rely on so many different critical technologies that most companies can no longer maintain cutting-edge sophistication in all of them" (p. 145). Similarly, a shift in customer buying patterns from the purchase of individual products to the purchase of integrated systems may necessitate a firm's entry into an interindustry strategic alliance, as well as a move away from stand-alone *product marketing* toward *integrated systems marketing.*

INTRANATIONAL AND INTERNATIONAL STRATEGIC ALLIANCES

Strategic alliances can be characterized as intra- versus international strategic alliances in reference to either the geographic scope of the alliance or the national identities of the alliance partners. An alliance such as the one between Pillsbury and Kraft, formed to market a specific line of products made by Pillsbury in the United States, is illustrative of an intranational strategic alliance in both respects (Varadarajan & Rajaratnam, 1986). Illustrative of alliances that are international in scope but formed by partners based in the same country are Japan's manufacturing and distribution *keiretsus,* which are complex groupings of firms with interlinked ownership and trading relationships (see Cutts, 1992; "For Bankrupt Companies," 1992; "Learning From Japan," 1992; Rapoport, 1991). The alliance between General Mills and Nestle discussed earlier (see Table 10.1) is illustrative of a strategic alliance that is international in terms of both scope and national identities of the alliance partners. In addition to the partners in this alliance being firms headquartered in different countries, the purpose of the alliance is to market a line of products in multiple national markets.

Firms competing in the triad markets (United States, Western Europe, and Japan) face similar problems—mature economies, escalating costs, dynamic technologies, and escalating R&D costs. International strategic alliances among triad firms are forged as partnerships among equals and are expected to supplant traditional joint ventures, which typically focus on a single national market (Ohmae, 1985). Also quite pervasive are strategic alliances between firms based in the triad markets and firms located in the Pacific Rim countries (Hong Kong, Malaysia, Singapore, South Korea, and Taiwan). Often these are designed to capitalize on the technological and marketing skills of the triad market firms and the relatively low cost of labor in these countries. Among the factors providing the impetus for triad market firms to enter into strategic alliances with firms in certain other countries (e.g., India, China) are the relatively large size of these markets, their proximity to one of the triad markets, and the sometimes restrictive policies of the host governments in regard to investments and ownership by multinational firms.

FUNCTIONAL SCOPE OF STRATEGIC ALLIANCES

Although certain strategic alliances tend to be extensive in scope, encompassing several functional areas or several activities in the value chain, others tend to be more limited in scope, restricted to a few functional areas or a single activity in the value chain. Understandably, the scope of any alliance is determined by the objectives of the alliance (Table 10.3). A brief discussion of some of the forms of alliances follows. *Joint product development alliances* (such as between Ford and Mazda) enable firms to spread the high costs of developing new products among alliance members, use limited resources to update a broader array of products, fill gaps in the product line, and learn new skills or enhance present skills. *Joint manufacturing alliances* (such as between Ford and Nissan) enable the cooperating firms to achieve scale economies in manufacturing yet maintain their distinct identities in the marketplace. Illustrative of a *reciprocal marketing alliance* is an international strategic alliance in which Firm A markets in its home country the product offerings of Firm B, and Firm B reciprocates by assuming responsibility for marketing in its home country the product offerings of Firm A (see Ohmae, 1989). A *joint marketing* or *comarketing alliance* is one in which the product and service offerings of the alliance partners are marketed together as a system (see Bucklin & Sengupta, 1993).

A forerunner to many of the emerging forms of strategic alliances is the type of alliance in which the special expertise or skills of one alliance partner complement the resources of the other alliance partner, as is the case with franchising types of alliances. For example, most international hotel chains generally do not own many of the hotels in various parts of the world bearing their names. Often, the strategic alliance partners in an international hotel chain tend to be investors/firms in individual countries. To these investors, the hotel chain initially offers its expertise in areas such as site selection, design and construction, financing, and training and human resources development. In some cases, it even assumes responsibility for the day-to-day management and operation of the facility. Using its infrastructural investments in communication and information systems, the franchisor handles reservations, billing, and other tasks for the affiliated hotels.

Internal and External Drivers of Strategic Alliances

Several factors may have impacts on the propensity of firms to enter into strategic alliances. Figure 10.1 provides a conceptual representation of a number of factors, grouped into three broad categories—firm, industry, and environmental characteristics—that influence the propensity of firms to enter into strategic alliances. For purposes of exposition and to spawn further research in this area, we present below a brief discussion relating to one factor from each of the three categories. It should also be noted that factors listed in Figure 10.1 are intended to be illustrative rather than exhaustive. Clearly, a potential direction for future research is the development and testing of a richer conceptual model delineating the

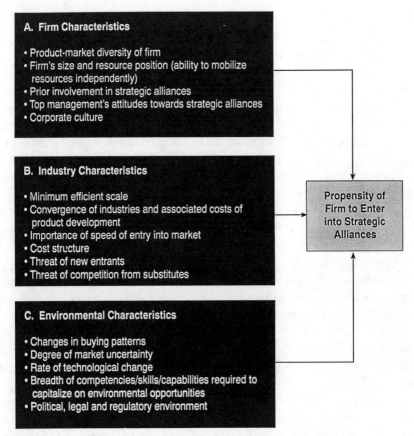

FIGURE 10.1. Factors Influencing the Propensity of a Firm to Enter Into Strategic Alliances

relationship between firm, industry, and environmental factors and a firm's propensity to enter into strategic alliances, as well as moderators and mediators of these relationships.

FIRM CHARACTERISTICS

Most firms face a trade-off between operating autonomy and resource constraints. All else being equal, firms possessing the financial where-withal to either acquire or internally develop the skills and resources needed to capitalize on a market opportunity are less likely to enter into strategic alliances. However, as competition becomes more global in scope and the cost of competing in key global markets continues to escalate, more and more multibusiness firms are likely to find themselves lacking in resources to compete effectively in multiple national markets and across multiple product categories. The broad options open to such firms are (a) to prune their product-market portfolios and concentrate on product markets that they believe they can dominate or (b) to maintain their product-market portfolios but broaden their resource bases by entering into strategic alliances. For instance, Toshiba Corporation, whose product portfolio ranges from power-plant equipment to refrigerators, has over the years made strategic alliances a cornerstone of its corporate strategy. Its strategic alliances with firms in Japan, the United States, Canada, South Korea, and a number of Western European countries span a broad array of product categories, including memory chips, color flat-panel displays, power-generating equipment, computers, fax machines and copiers, semiconductors, medical equipment, and home appliances. According to Fumio Sato, president and chief executive officer of Toshiba Corporation, this is the only workable strategy for high-tech companies with global ambitions. Sato contends that the technology has become so advanced and markets have become so complex that no single company is able any longer to dominate a technology or business alone or to be the best at the entire process (Schlender, 1993). Additionally, although a firm's prior involvement in strategic alliances and the outcomes of these alliances can be expected to influence its propensity to enter into future alliances, the firm's accumulated learning from its past involvement in strategic alliances is also likely to have an impact on the effectiveness of its future alliances.

INDUSTRY CHARACTERISTICS

Minimum efficient scale (MES) refers to the smallest volume for which unit costs are at a minimum. A firm is likely to demonstrate a greater propensity to enter into a strategic alliance if the base volume necessary to exploit scale economies (i.e., MES) is significantly greater than the scale of activity affordable given the firm's resource position. For a firm facing such a situation to be cost competitive, entering into a strategic alliance with another firm that is also in a similar situation may be imperative.

ENVIRONMENTAL CHARACTERISTICS

In the face of major discontinuities in the technological environment, firms are likely to find themselves lacking in the broader set of skills and resources they need to compete effectively in the changing marketplace and hence may demonstrate a greater propensity to enter into alliances with firms possessing complementary resources and skills. Recent alliances between firms in such industries as computer hardware, computer software, telecommunications, and television entertainment are cases in point.

Achieving Competitive Advantage
Through Pooling of Skills and Resources

Competitive positional advantages can be broadly classified as cost leadership and differentiation advantages. *Cost leadership* entails being able to perform value-chain activities at a lower cost than competitors while offering a parity product. *Differentiation* advantages entail being able to offer goods or services that customers perceive as consistently different with respect to important attributes relative to competitors' offerings (Porter, 1980, 1985). Two broad sets of factors underlying a firm's competitive positional advantages are its distinctive skills (capabilities) and its unique resources (assets). *Superior skills* are the distinctive capabilities of a firm's personnel that set them apart from the personnel of competing firms; *superior resources* are more tangible requirements for advantage that enable a firm to exercise its capabilities (Day & Wensley, 1988). Figure 10.2 lists a broad array of skills and resources that cooperating firms could conceivably pool in a strategic alliance. As shown in the figure, the pooling of resources and skills in a strategic alliance can lead to a competitive positional advantage by enabling the alliance partners to perform various value-chain activities at lower cost and/or in ways that lead to differentiation.

Strategic alliances can be broadly categorized in terms of (a) those that pool different and complementary resources and skills to create advantage and (b) those that pool similar resources and skills to lower costs

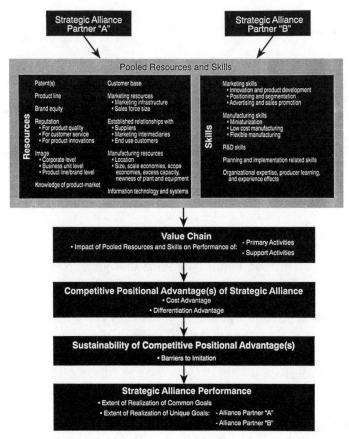

Figure 10.2. Achieving Competitive Advantage Through Strategic Alliances

(Ghemawat et al., 1986; Hennart, 1988; Nielsen, 1987). In effect, a firm entering into a strategic alliance may seek partners whose abilities either augment the firm's strengths or ameliorate its weaknesses. Complementarity represents "nonredundant distinctive competencies" brought by each member to the partnership. When firms have complementary abilities, each partner can concentrate on the part of the value chain where it can make the greatest contribution (Johnston & Lawrence, 1988). It is thus possible to envision the product-market offering of a strategic alliance enjoying a competitive positional advantage in the marketplace under two scenarios:

1. An alliance in which the individual partners focus on specific stages of the value chain where they can contribute the most toward cost and/or differentiation advantage given their distinctive skills and resources
2. An alliance in which the partners pool their skills and resources in order to perform jointly one or more value-chain activities (e.g., technology development; manufacturing, marketing) to achieve a competitive positional advantage

Building on the assumption that strategic resources are heterogeneously distributed across firms, the resource-based view of the firm examines the link between firm resources and sustained competitive advantage (Barney, 1991). Here the term *firm resources* is broadly construed to denote assets, capabilities, organizational processes, firm attributes, information, knowledge, and so on that are controlled by a firm and that enable it to conceive and implement strategies that enhance its efficiency and effectiveness (Daft, 1983). Given that each firm entering an alliance is a complex social system possessing heterogeneous resources and a distinct set of abilities (Tallman, 1991), the conditions under which the strategic alliance as a competitive entity in the marketplace is likely to enjoy a sustained competitive advantage (SCA) merits a brief explication. Barney (1991) lists four essential requirements for a resource to be a source of SCA:

- It must be *valuable*.
- It must be *rare* among a firm's current and potential competitors.
- It must be *imperfectly imitable*.
- There must not be any *strategically equivalent substitutes* for it.

The bundle of resources pooled in an alliance are valuable if they aid the partners in formulating and implementing strategies that improve efficiency and/or effectiveness (i.e., perform value-chain activities at lower cost or in ways that lead to differentiation). However, if competitors of the alliance also possess similar resources, or if those resources can be assembled by potential competitors entering into competing alliances, then the resources cannot be a source of SCA. For instance, when the number of firms possessing complementary skills and resources is limited to a small set, it is conceivable that the early entrants forming consortia of competing strategic alliances would enjoy a competitive advantage vis-à-vis firms that are locked out of opportunities for entering into similar alliances for

want of firms possessing complementary skills and resources. Valuable and
rare resources can enable an alliance to achieve SCA only if firms that do
not possess these skills and resources cannot obtain them (as a direct consequence of a capability gap [Coyne, 1985] or because the critical resources and skills are imperfectly imitable [Lippman & Rumelt, 1982]). Finally, an alliance can achieve sustained competitive advantage only if
strategically equivalent bundles of resources that can be exploited to implement the same strategy are nonexistent (Barney, 1991).

The Role of Marketing in Strategic Alliances

A study by Ernst & Young (reported in Kelly, 1990) that identifies (a)
achieving market growth and/or increasing sales and (b) gaining access
to new markets as the two most important reasons for entering into strategic alliances attests to the importance of the marketing function in strategic alliances. More generally, the extent of involvement of the marketing function in the planning and implementation of a strategic alliance is
contingent upon the nature and scope of the alliance. Guided by this
premise, the motives underlying the entry of firms into strategic alliances
are listed in Table 10.2 in an order that roughly corresponds to the likely
extent of involvement of the marketing function in the planning and implementation of the alliance. For example, marketing personnel can be expected to play (a) a *dominant* role in strategic alliances whose primary
motives are market related, such as gaining access to new international
markets or defending a firm's market position in its present markets; (b) a
participative role (in association with other functional areas such as R&D,
finance, and manufacturing) in alliances whose primary motives are related to product, product market, resource extension, or risk reduction;
or (c) an *advisory* role in alliances whose primary motives are related to
technology exchange, licensing, or cross-licensing.

Similarly, Table 10.3, which provides an overview of the functional area
scope, industry scope, and geographic scope of strategic alliances, shows
that marketing personnel can be expected to play a dominant role in strategic alliances that can be characterized as distinctively marketing in nature and scope (7 through 10 in Table 10.3), a participative role in strategic alliances that are multifunctional in scope and include marketing (4
and 6 in Table 10.3), and either an advisory or a limited role in some of the
other types of alliances listed.

Although the determinants of performance might vary across industries, very broadly they can be classified as efficiency- versus effectiveness-
related factors. Strategic alliances with an emphasis on efficiency (standardization, minimizing costs, and competing on price) will have relatively less of a marketing thrust than will those centered on effectiveness
(differentiation, target marketing, segmentation, and nonprice competition). Marketing activities are likely to be viewed as critical success factors in strategic alliances operating in competitive environments where
differentiation is an imperative and in markets undergoing rapid changes
in product technology, competitor activity, or consumer preferences. In
more stable markets, efficiency criteria are more likely to predominate
(Achrol, Scheer, & Stern, 1990).

The need for further refinement of the above normative viewpoints on
the role of marketing in strategic alliances is highlighted by some recent
and insightful observations of Webster (1992), McKenna (1991), and Day
(1992), among others. For instance, it has been suggested that the building of knowledge bases to serve customers and to integrate customers
into the marketing process, as well as to synthesize the specialized skills of
network partners, is often the leverage point of successful network strategies (McKenna, 1991). Webster (1992) notes that strategic alliances, with
their emphasis on improving a firm's competitive position, support the
notion that they are an important marketing phenomenon: "There are
multiple types of strategic alliances; virtually all are within the theoretical
domain of marketing as they involve partnerships with customers or resellers or with real or potential competitors for the development of new
technology, new products and new markets" (p. 8). In Webster's assessment, the key to understanding the changing role of marketing within
evolving corporations epitomized by new organizational forms such as
networks and strategic alliances is to recognize that (a) marketing operates at three distinct levels of strategy in organizations (corporate, business, and functional levels), and (b) there are three distinct dimensions to
marketing (marketing as a culture, marketing as strategy, and marketing
as tactics).

Day (1992) notes that in order for the field of marketing to make more
significant contributions to the theory and practice of strategy, marketing's competencies must be conceptualized in strategic terms. He notes
that such a broadened view of marketing's competencies would facilitate
distinguishing among three levels of potential contributions of marketing
to the theory and practice of strategy:

- *Distinctive competencies:* aspects of strategy content or process in which marketing as a function or discipline is the unchallenged expert
- *Integrative competencies:* aspects of strategy content or process that are primarily integrative in nature, in which marketing is equipped to take the lead role
- *Supportive competencies:* aspects of strategic content or process in which marketing is equipped to make a useful contribution, but not to provide the dominant perspective

Under this schema, one might view marketing's distinctive competencies in scanning the external environment to gather information and identify trends as critical to the success of strategic alliances from the vantage points of segmenting markets, anticipating consumer preferences, and assessing new technologies. These competencies may also be valuable in regard to the scanning of the internal environments of the alliance partners to understand more fully their strategic objectives, internalize their skills and knowledge bases, diffuse the acquired knowledge throughout the organization, and develop safeguards against unintended transfers of information (see Hamel, Doz, & Prahalad, 1989).

Limitations and Future Research Directions

In exchange for access to the resources, skills, or information of another firm, a partner in an alliance forgoes some flexibility and freedom of action or control over the scope of its activities. The merging of specialized organizations with diverse goals into an alliance inherently involves the management of conflict. Although in a strategic alliance a firm is required to pool its skills and resources and often must perform certain value-chain activities jointly with its alliance partner, the firm must also be concerned with safeguarding its proprietary skills from being appropriated by an opportunistic alliance partner. Conflict and the potential for opportunism are greater in alliances in which partners cooperate to serve one type of product market but compete in others (Bucklin & Sengupta, 1993).

Although a firm's forming alliances that enable it either to broaden its product line or to fill gaps in its product line through production-by-proxy agreements can indeed be beneficial, the perils of excessive dependence on such alliances must be borne in mind. A web of such alliances can conceivably lead to a gradual erosion of a firm's R&D and manufacturing capabilities and the transformation of the firm into essentially a marketer of products supplied by its partners.

Strategic alliances having been in vogue for the past several years, the corporate landscape abounds with case histories of successful as well as failed strategic alliances. Whereas, at one extreme, some firms seem to have been quite successful in establishing and maintaining webs of lasting alliances, a few firms at the other end of the continuum seem to have to their credit long lists of failed alliances. These realities illustrate the need for research that can shed some light on the factors underlying the success and failure of alliances, as well as on issues relating to systems, structures, and controls conducive to effective management of alliances. Representative of broad areas of research of particular interest to marketers are the roles of strategic alliances in managing innovation, in product and market development, in leveraging brand equity, and in delivering superior value to customers. Some specific research questions that merit investigation are the following:

1. Why are strategic alliances more pervasive in some industries than in others?
2. What factors explain some firms' being more proactive in forming strategic alliances than others within any industry?
3. Which objectives are best pursued using an alliance strategy?
4. How will traditional ways of organizing the marketing function have to be changed in light of the increasing incidence of alliances?

Conclusion

In periods of rapid change, decision makers face three strategic challenges: (a) *demand uncertainty,* which involves changing product specifications and technology; (b) *differentiation risks,* which relate to the inability to keep pace with competitors' changes and advances in research and development; and (c) *inefficiency risks,* which encompass the failure to keep up with cost savings technologies or processes of competitors (Child, 1987). In their attempts to survive and prosper in the face of these challenges, a growing number of firms have chosen to enter into strategic alliances with other firms possessing complementary skills and resources. Strategic alliances have come to be viewed more favorably in recent years in light of growing appreciation of (a) the scale-, scope-, and/or experience-related competitive cost advantages and (b) the multifaceted competitive differentiation advantages that firms can achieve by pursuing this option. It has been suggested that in environments characterized by scarce resources, large capital requirements, and rapid technological change, interorganizational cooperative strategies may be the best way for some firms to enhance their competitive position (Harrigan, 1984).

As organizations of the future become increasingly disaggregated and specialized, understanding alliance relationships and their market power is likely to become more important (Achrol, 1991). The significance of alliance relationships is also highlighted by the recent move toward a broader construal of relationship marketing as encompassing the entire network of organizations brought together on a continuing basis and monitored by governance mechanisms to serve particular product markets (see Anderson, Håkansson, & Johanson, 1994; Heide, 1994; Morgan & Hunt, 1994). Moreover, as Morgan and Hunt (1994) point out, relationship marketing is paradoxical in nature, in that in order to be more effective competitors, firms must learn and implement cooperative strategies.

References

Achrol, R. S. (1991). Evolution of the marketing organization: New forms for turbulent environments. *Journal of Marketing* 55 (October): 77-93.

Achrol, R. S., Scheer, L. K., & Stern, L. W. (1990). *Designing successful transorganizational marketing alliances* (Rep. No. 90-118). Cambridge, MA: Marketing Science Institute.

Adler, L. (1966). Symbiotic marketing. *Harvard Business Review, 45*(2), 59-71.

Anderson, J. C., Håkansson, H., & Johanson, J. (1994). Dyadic business relationships within a business network context. *Journal of Marketing, 58*(4), 1-15.

Ansoff, I. A. (1957). Strategies for diversification. *Harvard Business Review, 36*(1), 113-124.

Arndt, J. (1979). Toward a concept of domesticated markets. *Journal of Marketing, 43*(4), 69-75.

AT&T's crucial charge into Canada. (1993, August 14). *Financial Times of Canada*, pp. 4-5.

Badaracco, J. L., Jr. (1991). *The knowledge link: How firms compete through strategic alliances*. Boston: Harvard Business School Press.

Barney, J. B. (1991, March). Firm resources and sustained competitive advantage. *Journal of Management, 17*, 99-120.

Bleeke, J., & Ernst, D. (1991). The way to win in cross-border alliances. *Harvard Business Review, 70*(2), 127-135.

Bucklin, L. P., & Sengupta, S. (1993). Organizing successful co-marketing alliances. *Journal of Marketing, 57*(2), 32-46.

Buzzell, R. D., & Gale, B. T. (1987). *The PIMS principles: Linking strategy to performance*. New York: Free Press.

Café au lait, a croissant—and Trix. (1992, August 24). *Business Week*, pp. 50-51.

Child, J. (1987, Fall). Information technology, organization and response to strategic challenges. *California Management Review, 29*, 33-50.

Coyne, K. (1985, January-February). Sustainable competitive advantage—what it is, what it isn't. *Business Horizons,* pp. 54-61.

Cravens, D. W., Shipp, S. H., & Cravens, K. S. (1993, March). Analysis of cooperative interorganizational relationships, strategic alliance formation, and strategic alliance effectiveness. *Journal of Strategic Marketing, 1,* 55-70.

Cutts, R. L. (1992). Capitalism in Japan: Cartels and *keiretsu. Harvard Business Review, 70*(6), 48-55.

Daft, R. (1983). *Organization theory and design.* New York: West.

Day, G. S. (1992). Marketing's contribution to the strategy dialogue. *Journal of the Academy of Marketing Science, 20,* 323-330.

Day, G. S., & Klein, S. (1987). Cooperative behavior in vertical markets: The influence of transaction costs and competitive strategies. In M. Houston (Ed.), *Review of marketing* (pp. 39-66). Chicago: American Marketing Association.

Day, G. S., & Wensley, R. (1988). Assessing advantage: A framework for diagnosing competitive superiority. *Journal of Marketing, 52*(2), 1-20.

Dwyer, F. R., Schurr, P. H., & Oh, S. (1987). Developing buyer-seller relationships. *Journal of Marketing, 51*(2), 11-27.

For bankrupt companies, happiness is a warm *keiretsu.* (1992, October 26). *Business Week,* pp. 48-49.

Ghemawat, P., Porter, M. E., & Rawlinson, R. A. (1986). Patterns of international coalition activity. In M. E. Porter (Ed.), *Competition in global industries* (pp. 345-366). Boston: Harvard Business School Press.

Gibson, R. (1990, November 14). Cereal venture is planning honey of a battle in Europe. *Wall Street Journal,* pp. B1, B10.

Gupta, A. K., Raj, S. P., & Wilemon, D. (1986). A model for studying R&D: Marketing interface in the product innovation process. *Journal of Marketing, 50*(2), 7-17.

Hamel, G. (1991). Competition for competence and inter-partner learning within international strategic alliances. *Strategic Management Journal, 12,* 83-103.

Hamel, G., Doz, Y. L., & Prahalad, C. K. (1989). Collaborate with your competitors—and win. *Harvard Business Review, 67*(3), 133-139.

Harrigan, K. R. (1984, Summer). Multinational corporate strategy: Editor's introduction. *Columbia Journal of World Business, 19,* 2-6.

Harrigan, K. R. (1988). Joint ventures and competitive advantage. *Strategic Management Journal, 9,* 141-158.

Heide, J. B. (1994). Interorganizational governance in marketing channels. *Journal of Marketing, 58*(1), 71-85.

Hennart, J.-F. (1988). A transaction costs theory of equity joint ventures. *Strategic Management Journal, 9,* 361-374.

Hout, T., Porter, M. E., & Rudden, E. (1982). How global companies win out. *Harvard Business Review, 61*(1), 98-108.

How Ford and Mazda shared the driver's seat. (1992, March 26). *Business Week,* pp. 94-95.

Jarillo, J. C. (1988). On strategic networks. *Strategic Management Journal, 9,* 31-41.

Johnston, R., & Lawrence, P. R. (1988). Beyond vertical integration: The rise of the value-adding partnership. *Harvard Business Review, 66*(4), 94-101.

Kelly, M. (1990, Spring). Strategic alliances. *Investing in Canada, 3,* 1-3.

Knowlton, C. (1991, June 3). Europe cooks up a cereal brawl. *Fortune,* pp. 175-179.

Kogut, B. (1988). Joint ventures: Theoretical and empirical perspectives. *Strategic Management Journal, 9,* 319-332.

Learning from Japan. (1992, January 27). *Business Week,* pp. 52-58.

Lippman, S. A., & Rumelt, R. P. (1982). Uncertain imitability: An analysis of interfirm differences in efficiency under competition. *Bell Journal of Economics, 13,* 418-438.

Main, J. (1990, December 17). Making global alliances work. *Fortune,* pp. 123-126.

McKenna, R. (1991). Marketing is everything. *Harvard Business Review, 69*(3), 65-79.

Morgan, R. M., & Hunt, S. D. (1994). The commitment-trust theory of relationship marketing. *Journal of Marketing, 58*(3), 20-38.

Nielsen, R. P. (1987, July-August). Cooperative strategy in marketing. *Business Horizons,* pp. 61-68.

Ohmae, K. (1985, Spring). Becoming a triad power: The new global corporation. *McKinsey Quarterly,* pp. 2-25.

Ohmae, K. (1987, Spring). The triad world view. *Journal of Business Strategy, 7,* 8-19.

Ohmae, K. (1989). The global logic of strategic alliances. *Harvard Business Review, 67*(4), 143-154.

Oliver, C. (1990). Determinants of interorganizational relationships: Integration and future directions. *Academy of Management Review, 15,* 241-265.

Parkhe, A. (1993). Strategic alliance structuring: A game theoretic and transaction cost examination of interfirm cooperation. *Academy of Management Journal, 36,* 794-829.

Partners, The. (1990, February 10). *Business Week,* pp. 102-107.

Pfeffer, J., & Salancik, G. R. (1978). *The external control of organizations: A resource dependence perspective.* New York: Harper & Row.

Porter, M. E. (1980). *Competitive strategy: Techniques for analyzing industries and competitors.* New York: Free Press.

Porter, M. E. (1985). *Competitive advantage: Creating and sustaining superior performance.* New York: Free Press.

Porter, M. E., & Fuller, M. B. (1986). Coalitions and global strategy. In M. E. Porter (Ed.), *Competition in global industries* (pp. 315-343). Boston: Harvard Business School Press.

Rapoport, C. (1990, December 17). Mazda's bold new global strategy. *Fortune,* pp. 109-113.

Rapoport, C. (1991, July 15). Why Japan keeps on winning. *Fortune,* pp. 76-85.

Ruekert, R. W., & Walker, O. C. (1987). Marketing's interaction with other functional units: A conceptual framework and empirical evidence. *Journal of Marketing, 51*(1), 1-19.

Schlender, B. R. (1993, October 4). How Toshiba makes alliances work. *Fortune,* pp. 116-120.

Sheth, J. N., & Parvatiyar, A. (1992). Towards a theory of business alliance formation. *Scandinavian International Business Review, 1*(3), 71-87.

Spekman, R. E., & Sawhney, K. (1990). *Toward a conceptual understanding of the antecedents of strategic alliances* (Rep. No. 90-114). Cambridge, MA: Marketing Science Institute.

Tallman, S. B. (1991). Strategic management models and resource-based strategies among MNEs in a host market. *Strategic Management Journal, 12,* 69-82.

Terpstra, V., & Simonin, B. L. (1992). Strategic alliances in the triad: An exploratory study. *Journal of International Marketing, 1*(1), 4-25.

Varadarajan, P. R. (1986). Horizontal cooperative sales promotion: A framework for classification and additional perspective. *Journal of Marketing, 50*(2), 61-73.

Varadarajan, P. R., & Menon, A. (1988). Cause-related marketing: A coalignment of marketing strategy and corporate philanthropy. *Journal of Marketing, 52*(3), 58-74.

Varadarajan, P. R., & Rajaratnam, D. (1986). Symbiotic marketing revisited. *Journal of Marketing, 50*(1), 7-17.

Watson, C. M. (1982). Counter-competition abroad to protect home markets. *Harvard Business Review, 60*(3), 40-42.

Webster, F. E., Jr. (1992). The changing role of marketing in the corporation. *Journal of Marketing, 56*(4), 1-17.

Wells, J. (1984). *In search of synergy.* Unpublished doctoral dissertation, Harvard University.

Williamson, O. E. (1975). *Markets and hierarchies: Analysis and antitrust implications.* New York: Free Press.

11

Toward a Theory of
Business Alliance Formation

JAGDISH N. SHETH
ATUL PARVATIYAR

The popularity of business alliances has increased in recent years. The business press and academic researchers have reported thousands of alliances involving many international companies (Ellram, 1992; Ghemawat, Porter, & Rawlinson, 1986; Gross & Newman, 1989; Morris & Hergert, 1987). The importance of business alliances is illustrated by the fact that some of the world's largest companies—including AT&T, Philips, General Motors, Siemens, IBM, Ford, Boeing, Olivetti, General Electric, Xerox, Toyota, Mitsubishi, and General Foods—are involved in such relationships. A variety of patterns have also been observed, such as large-small company alliances (Doz, 1988; Hull & Slowinski, 1990), private (profit)-public (nonprofit) partnerships (Lynch, 1989), competitor alliances (Hamel, Doz, & Prahalad, 1989), and spider-web alliances (Gullander, 1975), wherein an intricate array of

NOTE: This chapter is reprinted from Jagdish N. Sheth and Atul Parvatiyar, "Towards a Theory of Business Alliance Formation," *Scandinavian International Business Review*, vol. 1, no. 3, pp. 71-87, copyright © 1992 by MCB University Press. Reprinted by permission.

interconnections exists among companies, often across international and industrial boundaries—as in the cases of networks and *keiretsu* (Ferguson, 1990; Håkansson & Johanson, 1988).[1]

The scope of these business alliances ranges from specific functional agreements—as in R&D, product development, distribution, logistics, and marketing—to full-scale joint ventures and/or consortia. This had led to several names and labels for business alliances, including *joint ventures, R&D consortia, minority participation, cross-licensing, cross-distribution, supply purchasing, franchising, comanufacturing, cross-marketing,* and *buying groups.* Some authors have begun to use *strategic alliance* as a common term to refer to all types of business alliances (Harrigan, 1986; Ohmae, 1989; Parkhe, 1991). This, however, is likely to cause confusion because, as we will show later in this chapter, not all business alliances are formed with strategic purposes. Furthermore, *strategic alliance* is a term borrowed from military and political science, where it has a specific connotation, namely, of a formal association of sovereign states for the use (or nonuse) of military force intended against specific other sovereign states, whether or not these sovereign states are explicitly identified (Snyder, 1991). As such, the use of the term *strategic alliance* in business is best suited for reference to competitive alliances; in our opinion, it should not be used as a generic term for all alliances. In this chapter, we will develop a typology of business alliances in order to reduce some terminological confusion.

Given the current popularity of business alliances, a comprehensive theory is needed to explain the purposes, properties, and governance of alliances. Although research in this area has been sparse, previous studies in strategic management and international business have developed constructs on the rationale for cooperation (Contractor & Lorange, 1988), alliance complexity (Killing, 1988), factors governing degree of cooperation in 50:50 equity joint ventures (Buckley & Casson, 1988), alliance characteristics and hybrid arrangements (Borys & Jemison, 1989), the influence of technological intensity and R&D intent of partners on the choice of alliance governance form (Osborn & Baughn, 1990), and social governance of dyadic networks (Larson, 1992). Although these conceptual frameworks and empirical observations have contributed significantly toward our understanding of some specific aspects of business alliances, what is lacking is a general theory of business alliances. Accordingly, this chapter represents our attempt to develop a theory of competitive and collaborative business alliances. It is based on a fusion of behavioral and economic constructs that underlie and determine the formation, governance, properties, and evolution of business alliances.

The theory is based on two constructs: purpose of the business alliance (strategic versus operations) and parties to the business alliance (competitors versus noncompetitors). We suggest that most forms of business alliances and their specific properties, governance structures, and evolution over time can be explained by these two constructs. Furthermore, we can provide a strong rationale for them based on several popular and powerful conceptual frameworks in industrial organization, behavioral science, and social science.

Theoretical Background on External Relations of Firms

It is important at the outset to define business alliances. A business alliance is an ongoing, formal business relationship between two or more independent organizations to achieve common goals. This definition encompasses any formalized organizational relationship between two or more firms for some agreed-upon purpose. It refers to the external relationships of a firm with other firms that are more than standard customer-supplier or labor-management relationships and more than venture capital investment or other stakeholder relationships, but fall short of outright acquisition or merger. Evident in our definition is that all business alliances have two underlying dimensions: purpose and parties. In this section we will develop theoretical support for the two underlying dimensions of alliances; in the following sections we will examine the characteristics of different types of alliances and their effects on governance structures.

The study of a firm's external relationships is grounded in four theories: transaction cost theory (Williamson, 1975, 1985), agency theory (Fama, 1980; Jensen & Meckling, 1976), relational contracting (Macneil, 1980), and resource dependence perspective (Pfeffer & Salancik, 1978). Whereas the common theoretical constructs in the first three approaches are the notion of contracts and transactions, the resource dependence perspective is concerned with organizational interdependencies and interorganizational power. An examination of the basic propositions of each theory will help identify the applicable constructs from these theories for an understanding of the nature and properties of alliances.

The primary concern of agency theory is the optimal incentive structure that will help avoid efficiency losses, given the conflicting interests of a principal and an agent (Fama & Jensen, 1983). Because agency theory presupposes a conflict of interests among interacting parties, it does not provide an appropriate perspective on the formation of business alliances. In other words, conflict of interest is not the basis for business alliances, but a potential context that may or may not exist in a specific business alliance.

The resource dependence perspective is anchored in two themes: that organizations are the primary social actors and that interorganizational relations can be understood as a product of interorganizational dependence and constraint (Pfeffer, 1987). From this perspective, the question of who controls the organization is both problematic and critical (Mintzberg, 1973). The issue of control is linked to apprehensions regarding the intent (trust) of each party. In essence, the issue of intent or trust can be considered to be the underlying dimension of such apprehensions. If each organization were certain about the other actor's actions and intentions, and, consequently, both parties trusted each other, the concern for control or internalization of interdependencies would be minimal. Thus trust is the underlying determinant of managerial action relating to control and acquisition of power. The more the actors trust each other, the less will be the intentional managerial action toward control of external interdependencies.

This notion of trust as in important dimension of a firm's external relationship is also supported in Macneil's (1980) relational contracting. There is a tacit assumption of trust in relationship contracting, unlike discrete contracts, wherein there is no room for tacit assumptions (Macneil, 1980). Other studies on alliances have also included trust as a significant variable in the analysis of partner relationships (Buckley & Casson, 1988; Larson, 1992; Schaan & Beamish, 1988).

Although recognizing the value of trust, transaction cost theorists have contended with the difficulties of operationalizing trust and hence have avoided it (Williamson, 1975, 1984, 1985). The basic proposition of transaction cost theory is that properties of transactions determine the governance structure and the institutional arrangements of firms (Reve, 1990; Williamson, 1985). Transaction cost economics provisionally identifies three key dimensions on which the properties of transaction differ: asset specificity (or the degree to which assets are dedicated to transacting with a particular economic partner), uncertainty (that is, ambiguity in transaction definition and performance), and infrequency (transactions that are rarely undertaken). Of the three, asset specificity is considered the most important and most distinctive (Williamson, 1990).

In our opinion, asset specificity and infrequency, which transaction cost theory treats as determinants, are really the consequences of managerial choice of specific institutional arrangements or alliance forms, and therefore they are consequent and not determinant variables. For example, the choice of joint venture or consortia as an institutional arrangement warrants commitment of specific assets to the project, whereas such degree of asset specificity may not be required in the case of cooperative agreements or cartel-type alliances. In fact, studies on joint ventures (Harrigan, 1985; Killing, 1983; Stuckey, 1983) have not indicated that joint ventures are not an inherent outcome in those cases where organizations have already committed specific assets to a project.[2] In short, asset specificity seems more an outcome, or a consequence, than a cause of business alliances. Given the fact that asset specificity can be a consequence of business alliances, we have decided not to use it as one of the determinants of business alliances.

Similarly, frequency of transactions is a managerially controlled decision that is influenced by the choice of particular institutional arrangements. For example, firms may choose to reduce or expand the frequency of transactions based on technical, physical, managerial, and financial considerations. One has only to look at the impact of on-line computerized systems on the frequency mix between alliance partners (say, between buyers and sellers). As we will show in subsequent sections, frequency of transaction is more a consequence of purpose and parties to business alliances. For example, operational purposes necessitate greater frequency than do strategic purposes.

Perhaps the most significant dimension of transaction cost theory that influences the selection of the type of institutional arrangement is uncertainty. Uncertainty plays a role in the supply of upstream products/services and the need for information by the downstream firm (Arrow, 1974). Uncertainty is a consequence of environment, and it largely has external origins in random acts of nature and unpredictable changes in customer preferences (Koopmans, 1957). Uncertainty, unlike asset specificity and infrequency, is not managerially controlled. On the other hand, organizations and managers have to cope with and deal with uncertainty. It is, therefore, an independent variables that determines managerial action. Based on the level of uncertainty with which they must cope, managers will choose an institutional form that helps reduce that uncertainty.

Hence we can infer from theories on external relationships of firms that there are two primary constructs that affect alliance relationships and their institutional arrangement: uncertainty and trust. The level of uncertainty and the level of trust are likely to have impacts on alliance characteristics. When there is high trust between partners, autonomy will be accorded to the alliance venture. Low trust among partners is likely to lead to high management control. It will also likely result in a greater degree of internalization of interdependence and the use of power as suggested by the resource dependence viewpoint. Similarly, when uncertainty is high, management will likely make assets specific to the transaction so that risk is delineated to the transaction-specific assets and partners are also locked in through designated commitment. In cases of low uncertainty, partners will be willing to rely on the market processes of buyers and sellers or to share the assets of the two firms.

Measurement of Uncertainty and Trust

Uncertainty and trust are not variables but constructs. Therefore, they need to be operationalized if they are to be linked with reality and empirical observation. Trust is a behavioral construct, thus it is often measured through self-assessment and perceptions of individual managers and decision makers involved in business alliances. Unfortunately, no one has yet fully developed a psychometric scale that measures trust with a sufficiently comfortable degree of reliability and validity (Andaleeb, 1992). Similarly, measures of uncertainty suffer from problems of ambiguity with respect to definition and observation.

In view of the fact that the traditional measures of trust and uncertainty are subject to measurement errors, we have adopted the econometric approach of identifying measurable indicators that can be good surrogates of these constructs. By measuring the purpose of a business alliance as operations versus strategic, we are able to capture the degree of uncertainty. Operations purposes are, by definition, more certain than strategic purposes because the latter are, by definition, anchored to the future.

Trust is a perceived notion regarding a partner's likely behavior. It is a perceived estimation of the behavioral "opportunism" (Williamson, 1975)

TABLE 11.1 Types of Alliances

| | Parties | |
	Competitors	Noncompetitors
Strategic	competitive alliances	collaborative ventures
Operations	cartels	cooperatives

NOTE: Purpose is a surrogate measure of uncertainty; parties is a surrogate measure of trust.

of the alliance partner. Such a perception of opportunistic behavior is likely to be associated more with partners who are competitors or are perceived as potential competitors. Guarding against competitors in an alliance relationship has thus been the concern of some studies (Hamel et al., 1989). We can therefore state that trust is manifested in parties to an alliance where the competitors are viewed with low trust and noncompetitors are generally viewed with greater trust.

Purpose and parties are, therefore, isomorphic dimensions of uncertainty and trust. Purpose and parties are easy to measure, hence we will use them. In the previous section, we defined business alliance with the two underlying dimensions of purpose and parties. This can be expressed notationally as follows:

$$\text{Business Alliance} = f \text{ (purpose, parties)}$$

The two dimensions can be easily dichotomized for a conceptual understanding of alliance types, its properties and governance structures. It is also possible to display the dimensions in the form of vectors representing the degree of strategic purpose and the degree of competitive rivalry among alliance partners. The dichotomous categorization of purpose and parties helps us to highlight the distinctive properties of each type of alliance and to make observations concerning the distinctive forms of governance structures associated with each type of alliance.

Table 11.1 presents a typology of business alliances based on the two dichotomies of purpose and parties. If a business alliance is formed for operations efficiency among competitors, it is called a *cartel*. If it is formed among noncompetitors (suppliers, customers, and noncompetitive businesses), it is called a *cooperative*. If a business alliance is formed for strategic purpose among competitors, it is called a *competitive alliance*. Finally,

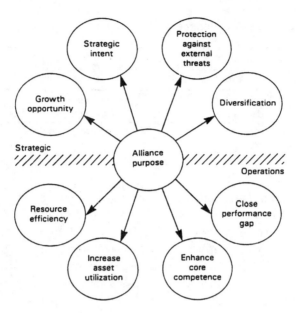

Figure 11.1. Purposes of Alliances

a business alliance formed among noncompetitors for strategic purpose is called a *collaborative venture*.

Purpose of and Parties to Business Alliances

Several factors drive companies toward entente. Some are related to macroenvironmental forces, such as globalization and integration of markets, rapid changes in technologies, high cost of R&D, increased global competition, and shortening of the period of competitive advantage (Badaracco, 1991; Collins & Doorley, 1991; Ohmae, 1989). Others are linked to corporate objectives and vision. The answer to the basic question of why companies form alliances can be found through a focus on the corporate purposes these alliances fulfill. As shown in Figure 11.1, eight corporate alliance purposes can be broadly identified. Four of these—growth opportunity, diversification, strategic intent, and protection against external threat[3]—reflect the future reasons for forming alliances. They are considered strategic because they have impacts on corporate effectiveness—that is, on the firm's future position and competitiveness. The other four

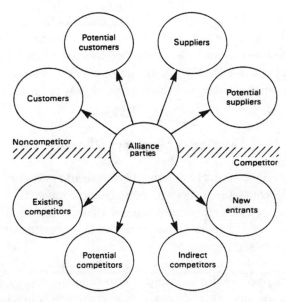

Figure 11.2. Alliance Parties

alliance purposes—asset utilization, resource efficiency, enhancement of core competence, and bridging of the performance gap—represent the operational purposes of alliances. They are operational because they affect corporate efficiency and improve the current position of the firm.[4] The strategic and operations purposes of alliances may overlap, but we can safely dichotomize alliances as predominantly strategic or predominantly operational in nature based on their primary purposes.

Along with the purpose of an alliance, also important to our conceptualization are the parties to the alliance and their role definition. The parties to an alliance can comprise those with whom a company already has ongoing relationships (customers, suppliers, or competitors)[5] or those with whom there is potential for relationships (potential customers, potential suppliers, and potential competitors). Potential customers, suppliers, and competitors may provide synergistic payoffs from complementary support and integrative linkages to business. Figure 11.2 shows at least eight parties with whom companies team up by forming business alliances.

On a broader level, customers, suppliers, and complementary consociates (potential suppliers and customers) can be considered as noncompetitors in an alliance, and existing competitors, new entrants, substitute producers (indirect competitors), and companies with similar future intent (potential competitors) can be grouped as competitors.[6] Thus we can categorize business alliances as those formed with either competitors or noncompetitors for either strategic or operations purpose. Based on these dichotomies, we can now develop a typology of business alliances.

Typology of Business Alliances

Given the two dimensions of alliance (purpose and parties) and their dichotomous levels (strategic versus operations, competitors versus noncompetitors), we can categorize business alliances into four types: cartels, cooperatives, collaborative ventures, and competitive alliances. The four alliance types are shown in Table 11.1.

Cartels are formal (or semiformal) agreements among competitors for an operations purpose, for example, controlling the supply of products, fixing prices, or sharing a common infrastructure. Cartels have been known to operate in the cases of petroleum, diamonds, semiconductor chips, and chocolate producers. They are more prevalent in Europe and Asia because existing anticompetitive laws allow these alliances to maintain industry efficiency.

Alliances between noncompetitors for operations purposes usually result in *cooperative* arrangements. Partners share costs and facilities with customers or suppliers or other consociates in order to introduce operating efficiency. Modification of the customers' or suppliers' systems or procedures, sharing of relevant information, and multiple-level two-way contacts are common in cooperative alliances. Examples include the cooperative marketing program between Wal-Mart and Procter & Gamble, Citibank's credit card and American Airlines's frequent-flier program, the cooperation between IBM and Sears to market Prodigy, and the warehouse service venture of Lever Brothers and Distribution Centers, Inc., for operation of a high-tech dedicated distribution center in Columbus, Ohio. The oldest forms of cooperative alliances are, of course, farmers' cooperatives and industrial buying groups.

Competitive alliances are business ventures between strong rival companies that remain competitors outside their alliance relationships. Most of these alliances have well-defined strategic objectives and are designed to serve global or regional markets. The firms involved see the virtue of leveraging their combined resources and each other's capabilities. Even the largest global companies, including General Motors, Toyota, Siemens, Philips, IBM, General Electric, and Mitsubishi, find the world too large and competition too strong for them to go it alone. General Motors and Toyota assemble automobiles; Siemens and Philips develop semiconductors; Canon supplies photocopiers to Kodak; France's Thomson and Japan's JVC jointly manufacture VCRs.

Competitive alliances are usually based on reciprocity—partners offering complementary products, facilities, skills, and technologies. Generally partnerships among equals, most competitive alliances are related to the core business of the partners. Their form is flexible to suit the needs of the project or program and the relative contributions of the partners.

Collaborative ventures are formed by noncompetitors for strategic purposes. Joint product, market, or technology development and joint marketing efforts are the hallmarks of collaborative enterprises. Usually the scope of such alliances is broad and encompasses many functional areas. The epitome of this kind of collaboration is a fusion of partner objectives and efforts. The most popular form of collaborative enterprise is the joint venture.[7]

Because uncertainty and trust are manifested in alliance purpose and parties, we can observe their incidence in different degrees in each alliance type. Collaborative ventures are likely to be formed when external uncertainty is high and partners trust each other significantly. When uncertainty is low and partners trust each other, cooperatives are most likely to be formed. Competitive alliances are most appropriate when uncertainty is high but partners do not trust each other enough. And cartels are the likely alliance form whenever there is low external uncertainty and a low or medium level of trust.

Organizational Properties of Business Alliances

Organizational properties of business alliances vary significantly depending upon the purpose of and parties to the alliance. Figure 11.3 displays a number of organizational properties that are directly linked to strategic versus operational purpose and to competitor versus noncompetitor parties to a business alliance. Most of the information in the figure is based on existing conceptual as well as empirical research.

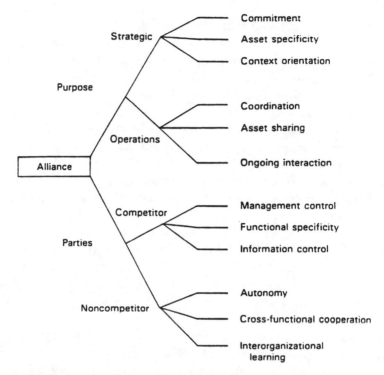

Figure 11.3. An Organizational Map of Alliance Properties

NOTE: The organizational properties of alliances are based on conceptual and empirical research in the disciplines of organizational psychology, interorganizational sociology, and industrial organization.

We know that strategic alliance purposes result in greater commitment and a higher level of asset specificity, and that such alliances are based more on context and on case-by-case analysis than are alliances with other kinds of purposes. Therefore, there is no real learning curve from one strategic alliance to the next. It is therefore unwise to rely on one successful strategic alliance as a guide for future alliances. This has been the experience of General Electric, AT&T, IBM, and Motorola in their global strategic alliances.

On the other hand, operational alliance purposes result in a high degree of coordination and asset sharing on an ongoing basis. This has been the experience of Whirlpool in appliances; buying groups in retailing, pharmaceuticals, and agriculture; and, more recently, joint quality efforts between suppliers and customers.

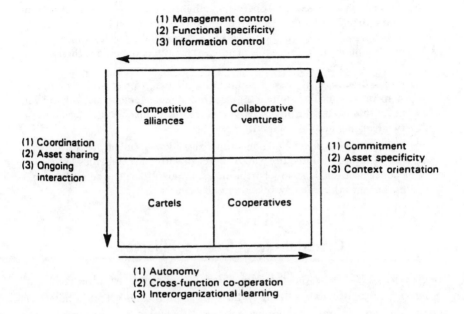

Figure 11.4. Properties of Alliances

If competitors are parties to an alliance, we know that there will be a high degree of management control and it will be limited to specific functions and tasks. Neither party will encourage an open-door policy even though each is interested in learning from the other. This is because there is lack of trust between the partners.

Finally, when noncompetitors get together in a business alliance, mutual trust is high. This encourages a high degree of autonomy for the alliance, free flow of information, and better cross-functional cooperation between alliance partners. This description leads us to state the following propositions (see Figure 11.4):

▓ *Proposition 1:* Successful strategic alliances (among competitors or noncompetitors) will require a high degree of commitment among alliance members and greater asset specificity dedicated to the alliance. Furthermore, strategic alliances will be context driven, and therefore each alliance must be organized as a unique business venture to achieve its strategic effectiveness.

- ▓ *Proposition 2:* A successful operations alliance (among competitors or non-competitors) will require a high degree of coordination and asset sharing on an ongoing basis. Furthermore, operations alliances will require reengineering of business processes of alliance members to achieve their operational efficiency.

- ▓ *Proposition 3:* A successful competitive alliance (for strategic or operations purpose) will require a high degree of management control and will be limited to specific functions. Furthermore, it must be organized for mutual learning among competitors.

- ▓ *Proposition 4:* A successful noncompetitive alliance (for strategic or operations purpose) will require a high degree of autonomy and cross-functional cooperation and learning. Furthermore, it must be organized in a way that encourages the free flow of communication.

Characteristics of Business Alliances

Each type of business (cartels, cooperatives, competitive alliances, and collaborative ventures) is likely to have its own unique set of behavioral, economic, and managerial consequences. Therefore, it is possible to use this profile as a benchmark against which to judge the performance of a specific business alliance in each category. Table 11.2 lists 10 benchmarks for each business alliance.

CARTELS

Operations alliances among competitors are likely to experience low entry barriers, especially in oligopolistic industries where business processes are standard and regulation allows sharing of resources for efficiency reasons. Conversely, it is relatively easy for a member to exit a cartel if economies of scale and scope justify the firm's doing so, rather than sharing in the cartel resources. Therefore, transaction cost theory (Williamson, 1975) and market governance are likely to determine the continuation of cartel alliances.

As a consequence, commitment to the cartel alliance by any member organization is likely to be low, and cross-functional cooperation will be bounded to specific functions, departments, and activities as specified in the cartel alliance. At the same time, management control and involvement will be high even though the cartel alliance is allowed to operate at arm's length in a semiautonomous manner. Finally, communications

TABLE 11.2 Characteristics of Business Alliances

Characteristics	Cartels	Cooperatives	Competitive Alliance	Collaborative Ventures
1. Entry barriers	low	moderate	high	high
2. Exit barriers	low	high	moderate	high
3. Alliance governance	market transaction	multilateral	bilateral	consortium
4. Asset specificity	low	moderate	high	high
5. Commitment to alliance	low	moderate	high	high
6. Management control	high	low	high	moderate
7. Autonomy of alliance	low	moderate	low	high
8. Cross-functional cooperation	limited	widespread	bounded	widespread
9. Information	guarded	open	proprietary	open
10. Interorganizational learning	incidental	widespread	focused	widespread

among the alliance members will be guarded, and interorganizational learning will be limited and focused on specific operations areas (R&D, manufacturing, marketing, logistics, customer service, and so on).

COOPERATIVES

Operations alliances among noncompetitors are likely to have low entry barriers because regulatory, emotional, and business processes will not inhibit their formation. However, once cooperative alliances are formed, they are likely to generate strong exit barriers due to operational alignment and each member's inability to justify economically its own dedicated resources to replace the shared operations. The governance mechanism will be multilateral or consortia.

Although firms' commitment to the cooperative alliance will be modest, and the members will dedicate only limited resources to it, there will be widespread cross-functional cooperation and sharing of information about one another through open communication. Consequently, cooperative alliances will result in widespread interorganizational learning.

COMPETITIVE ALLIANCES

Strategic alliances among competitors will experience high entry barriers, especially due to regulatory and emotional roadblocks. The historical rivalries among competitors will make them less comfortable with cooperating in the future. For example, it will be more difficult for General Motors and Ford Motor Company, or Coca-Cola and Pepsi, to get together in an alliance than it will be for them to get together with noncompetitors from other industries. Even if they do get together, let us say, at the urging of government policy or customer demands, the competitive alliance will be fragile and likely to dissolve quickly because the exit barriers are likely to be relatively low. The governance mechanism is likely to be bilateral, because it will be extremely difficult to bring together more than two competitors due to the possibility of coalition formation against any one member. For example, recently the computing industry tried to create a competitive alliance among Honeywell, Group Bull, and NEC, but it failed. Similarly, a consortium of U.S. memory chip makers (MCC) failed, probably for the same reasons.

Because the entry barriers are high and exit barriers low in a typical bilateral competitive alliance (GM-Toyota, IBM-Apple, GE-Thomson, Motorola-Hitachi, and so on), this kind of alliance will demand a high degree of commitment from the partners and greater allocation of resources on a dedicated basis (asset specificity). However, management control and involvement will be high, and the autonomy granted to the alliance will be limited. Finally, cross-functional cooperation will be bounded and limited, communication will be highly guarded, and interorganizational learning will be focused to the purpose and nature of the competitive alliance.

COLLABORATIVE VENTURES

Strategic alliances among noncompetitors will experience high entry barriers because strategic purposes may not be convergent or business processes cannot be utilized for future market or technology developments. This is especially true in joint ventures and technology transfers between advanced and developing nations, for example, between the United States and India or between Western Europe and Eastern Europe. Similarly, once a collaborative alliance is formed, it will be difficult for members to leave. This has been a common experience in many joint ventures, especially in the international context. The common governance structure is a trilateral or a small group consortium among noncompetitors for future business development. The recent formation of consortia in the telecommunications industry to participate in worldwide growth opportunities is a good example of this phenomenon.

Commitment to collaborative alliances will be high, and members will dedicate economic and physical resources to the alliance (usually by creating a joint venture). Such alliances will be given relatively high autonomy, and management control and involvement will be limited to financial performance, similar to the portfolio management approach. Finally, cross-functional cooperation will be widespread, communication will be open, and interorganizational learning will be high among the alliance partners.

Future Directions

In this chapter, we have attempted to present a theory of business alliance formation based on the purpose of alliance formation (strategic versus operations) and the parties to the alliance (competitors versus noncompetitors). Underlying these variables are the powerful constructs of uncertainty and trust. The uncertainty construct is anchored to risk assessment and risk sharing, whereas the trust construct is anchored to intent, opportunism, and self-interest. Because trust and uncertainty have not been operationalized satisfactorily in the fields of organizational psychology, industrial organization, and interorganizational sociology, we have chosen parties (competitors versus noncompetitors) and purpose (strategic versus operations) as surrogate indicators of trust and uncertainty.

Future research related to business alliances should address several issues. First, what are the specific operations and strategic purposes most common in the formation of alliances? Although we believe that most operations alliances (cartels and cooperatives) are formed for efficiency improvements, we do not know the specific areas of business inefficiency that may motivate organizations to get together for efficiency and productivity. We suspect that in the past this efficiency issue has focused on manufacturing operations, but as those operations have become more efficient, it may be more attractive for firms to form operations alliances for support functions (information systems, human resources, logistics, training, and the like) and for R&D, engineering, and customer service operations.

Similarly, the most common reasons for strategic alliances (competitive or collaborative) historically have been firms' desires to take advantage of international market opportunities and their need for domestic market protection. Once these goals have been reached, future strategic alliances may focus on reducing the technological, political, and economic barriers prevalent in particular industries. Also, we believe that future strategic alliances may be organized for process reengineering, the setting of global standards, and the development of new industries (for example, ecological business).

Another area for future research involves the governance principles of business alliances. What governance mechanisms are appropriate for each type of business alliance, and can we develop "best in practice" benchmarks that can be used as role models for similar types of business alliances? For example, which cartels, cooperatives, collaborative ventures, and competitive alliances are worth emulation by other cartels, cooperatives, collaborative ventures, and competitive alliances?

Finally, we know that business alliances, like all organizational arrangements, are dynamic and evolutionary. What is the evolution of a specific business alliance? Is there a life-cycle (birth-death) theory of business alliances? For example, competitor alliances (cartels and competitive alliances), as the members develop mutual trust, may behave more like noncompetitor alliances (cooperatives and collaborative ventures). On the other hand, if the members do not build mutual trust, the alliances are likely to be dissolved through exit or acquisition processes. Similarly, all operations alliances (cartels and cooperatives), once they achieve business efficiency, are likely to focus on strategic purposes and therefore are likely to evolve into strategic (competitive or collaborative) alliances. On the other hand, the operations alliance members may feel that there is no common strategic goal; thus the alliance may be dissolved by group consensus, and the members may allow it to die by not renewing the alliance agreement.

Notes

1. *Keiretsu* is a Japanese term for a society of business or group companies (Anchordoguy, 1990). Such industrial groups are not exclusive to Japan, however; they also exist in Europe and other Asian countries. Industrial groups such as Krupp and Axle-Johnson were dominant in Germany and Sweden not very long ago. Similarly, the Tata, Birla, and other industrial groups dominate the private sector in India.

2. Williamson (1985, pp. 118-119) cites evidence of asset specificity resulting in backward integration in the case of the aluminum industry, based on Stuckey's (1983) summary assessment. However, such evidence is not supported for joint-venture arrangements, and a true cause-and-effect relationship between asset specificity and institutional arrangement cannot be supported.

3. We state alliance purposes rather broadly here. In actuality, such purposes include many inflections. For example, firms can seek growth opportunities through new markets or through integration of technologies. Similarly, alliances may be formed for market diversification, product diversification, or technology diversification.

4. Examples of alliances formed to achieve one or more of these purposes can be found in Konsynski and McFarlan (1990), Bowersox (1990), Anderson and Narus (1991), Johnston and Lawrence (1988), Business International Corporation (1987), and Badaracco (1991).

5. The cooperative and collaborative paradigm of relationships with customers, suppliers, and competitors is a shift from the transactional or adversarial relationship orientation of the past (see Parvatiyar, Sheth, & Whittington, 1992).

6. The categorization of parties as competitors or noncompetitors is based on their role definition, rather than on any objective identification method. Role definition as competitor or noncompetitor is related to how partners view each other. It is largely based on intent and perspective.

7. The most common forms of collaborative enterprises include joint ventures and consortia. However, many traditional joint ventures fall short of being strategic collaborations, especially when companies do not enter into them as part of an overall strategic plan but limit them to dealing with specific problems, such as how to handle a single product or market. That is a tactical, short-term move, and at best a cooperative form of alliance. Some may view consortia as forms of competitive alliances, but we consider them as collaborative enterprises because the partners in these types of ventures do not view their role as that of competitors.

References

Anchordoguy, M. (1990). A brief history of Japan's *keiretsu*. *Harvard Business Review, 68*(4), 58-59.

Andaleeb, S. S. (1992). The trust concept: Research issues for channels of distribution. In J. N. Sheth (Ed.), *Research in marketing* (Vol. 11, pp. 1-34). Greenwich, CT: JAI.

Anderson, J. C., & Narus, J. A. (1991). Partnering as a focused market strategy. *California Management Review, 33*(3), 95-113.

Arrow, K. (1974). *The limits of organization*. New York: W. W. Norton.

Badaracco, J. L., Jr. (1991). *The knowledge link: How firms compete through strategic alliances*. Boston: Harvard Business School Press.

Borys, B., & Jemison, D. B. (1989). Hybrid arrangements as strategic alliances: Theoretical issues in organizational combinations. *Academy of Management Review, 14,* 234-249.

Bowersox, D. J. (1990). The strategic benefits of logistics alliances. *Harvard Business Review, 68*(4), 36-45.

Buckley, P. J., & Casson, M. (1988). A theory of cooperation in international business. In F. J. Contractor & P. Lorange (Eds.), *Cooperative strategies in international business* (pp. 31-53). Lexington, MA: Lexington.

Business International Corporation. (1987). *Competitive alliances: How to succeed at cross-regional collaboration.* New York: Author.

Collins, T. M., & Doorley, T. L. (1991). *Teaming up for the 90s: A guide to international joint ventures and strategic alliances.* Homewood, IL: Business One-Irwin.

Contractor, F. J., & Lorange, P. (1988). Why should firms cooperate? The strategy and economics basis for cooperative ventures. In F. J. Contractor & P. Lorange (Eds.), *Cooperative strategies in international business* (pp. 3-28). Lexington, MA: Lexington.

Doz, Y. L. (1988). Technology partnerships between larger and smaller firms: Some critical issues. In F. J. Contractor & P. Lorange (Eds.), *Cooperative strategies in international business* (pp. 317-338). Lexington, MA: Lexington.

Ellram, L. M. (1992). Patterns in international alliances. *Journal of Business Logistics, 13*(1), 1-25.

Fama, E. F. (1980). Agency problems and the theory of the firm. *Journal of Political Economy, 88,* 288-307.

Fama, E. F., & Jensen, M. C. (1983). Agency problems and residual claims. *Journal of Law and Economics, 26,* 327-349.

Ferguson, C. H. (1990). Computers and the coming of the US *keiretsu. Harvard Business Review, 68*(4), 55-70.

Ghemawat, P., Porter, M. E., & Rawlinson, R. A. (1986). Patterns of international alliance activity. In M. E. Porter (Ed.), *Competition in global industries* (pp. 345-366). Boston: Harvard Business School Press.

Gross, T., & Newman, J. (1989). Strategic alliances vital in global marketing. *Marketing News, 23*(13), 1-2.

Gullander, S. O. O. (1975). *An exploratory study of inter-firm co-operation of Swedish firms.* Unpublished doctoral dissertation, Columbia University.

Håkansson, H., & Johanson, J. (1988). Formal and informal cooperation strategies in international and industrial networks. In F. J. Contractor & P. Lorange (Eds.), *Cooperative strategies in international business* (pp. 369-379). Lexington, MA: Lexington.

Hamel, G., Doz, Y. L., & Prahalad, C. K. (1989). Collaborate with your competitors—and win. *Harvard Business Review, 67*(3), 133-139.

Harrigan, K. R. (1985). *Strategies for joint ventures.* Lexington, MA: Lexington.

Harrigan, K. R. (1986). *Strategic alliances: Form, autonomy and performance* (Working paper). New York: Columbia University.

Hull, F., & Slowinski, E. (1990, November-December). Partnering with technology, entrepreneurs. *Research and Technology Management,* pp. 16-20.

Jensen, M. C., & Meckling, W. H. (1976). Theory of the firm: Managerial behavior, agency costs, and ownership structure. *Journal of Financial Economics, 3,* 305-360.

Johnston, R., & Lawrence, P. R. (1988). Beyond vertical integration: The rise of the value-adding partnership. *Harvard Business Review, 66*(4), 94-101.

Killing, J. P. (1983). *Strategies for joint venture success.* New York: Praeger.

Killing, J. P. (1988). Understanding alliances: The role of task and organizational complexity. In F. J. Contractor & P. Lorange (Eds.), *Cooperative strategies in international business* (pp. 55-67). Lexington, MA: Lexington.

Konsynski, B. R., & McFarlan, F. W. (1990). Information partnerships: Shared data, shared scale. *Harvard Business Review, 68*(5), 114-120.

Koopmans, T. (1957). *Three essays on the state of economic science.* New York: McGraw-Hill.

Larson, A. (1992). Network dyads in entrepreneurial settings: A study of the governance of exchange relationships. *Administrative Science Quarterly, 37,* 76-104.

Lynch, R. P. (1989). *The practical guide to joint ventures and corporate alliances.* New York: John Wiley.

Macneil, I. R. (1980). *The new social contract: An inquiry into modern contractual relations.* New Haven, CT: Yale University Press.

Mintzberg, H. (1973). *The nature of managerial work.* New York: Harper & Row.

Morris, D., & Hergert, M. (1987). Trends in international collaborative agreements. *Columbia Journal of World Business, 22*(2), 15-21.

Ohmae, K. (1989). The global logic of strategic alliances. *Harvard Business Review, 67*(4), 143-154.

Osborn, R. N., & Baughn, C. C. (1990). Forms of interorganizational governance for multinational alliances. *Academy of Management Journal, 33,* 503-519.

Parkhe, A. (1991). Interfirm diversity, organizational learning and longevity in global strategic alliances. *Journal of International Business Studies, 22,* 579-601.

Parvatiyar, A., Sheth, J. N., & Whittington, F. B. (1992, April). *Paradigm shift in interfirm marketing relationships: Emerging research issues.* Paper presented at the Research Conference on Customer Relationship Management: Theory and Practice, Emory University, Atlanta, GA.

Pfeffer, J. (1987). A resource dependence perspective on intercorporate relations. In M. Mizruchi & M. Schwartz (Eds.), *Intercorporate relations: The structural analysis of business* (pp. 25-55). Cambridge: Cambridge University Press.

Pfeffer, J., & Salancik, G. R. (1978). *The external control of organizations: A resource dependence perspective.* New York: Harper & Row.

Reve, T. (1990). The firm as a nexus of internal and external contracts. In M. Aoki, B. Gustafsson, & O. E. Williamson (Eds.), *The firm as a nexus of treaties* (pp. 133-161). London: Sage.

Schaan, J. L., & Beamish, P. W. (1988). Joint venture general managers in LDCs. In F. J. Contractor & P. Lorange (Eds.), *Cooperative strategies in international business* (pp. 279-299). Lexington, MA: Lexington.

Snyder, G. H. (1991). Alliance theory: A neorealist first cut. In R. L. Rothstein (Ed.), *The evolution of theory in international relations* (pp. 83-103). Columbia: University of South Carolina Press.

Stuckey, J. (1983). *Vertical integration and joint ventures in the aluminum industry.* Cambridge, MA: Harvard University Press.

Williamson, O. E. (1975). *Markets and hierarchies: Analysis and antitrust implications.* New York: Free Press.

Williamson, O. E. (1984). The economics of governance: Framework and implications. *Journal of Theoretical Economics, 140,* 195-223.

Williamson, O. E. (1985). *The economic institutions of capitalism: Firms, markets, and relational contracting.* New York: Free Press.

Williamson, O. E. (1990). The firm as a nexus of treaties: An introduction. In M. Aoki, B. Gustafsson, & O. E. Williamson (Eds.), *The firm as a nexus of treaties.* London: Sage.

PART III

Partnering for Relationship Marketing

12

Relationship Marketing
in Mass Markets

C. B. BHATTACHARYA
RUTH N. BOLTON

There is considerable evidence that organizations are increasingly applying relationship marketing concepts in mass markets. The business press
abounds with examples, ranging from Citibank usage rewards to Saturn picnics (e.g., Aaker, 1994). These various approaches to developing stronger
bonds with customers are typically characterized as customer retention
programs, loyalty-based management, or one-to-one marketing strategies
(Peppers & Rogers, 1993; Reichheld, 1996). Many of these new marketing
practices have been enabled by advances in information and communications technology and the availability of new exchange forums such as the
World Wide Web and the Internet.

The focus of relationship marketing is frequently considered to be customer retention, because retention is less costly than acquisition (Fornell
& Wernerfelt, 1987; Reichheld, 1996) and small increases in retention
rates can have dramatic effects on the profits of a company (Fornell &

Wernerfelt, 1987, 1988; Reichheld & Sasser, 1990). For example, existing customers tend to purchase more than new customers (e.g., Rose, 1990), and, in most cases, there are efficiencies in dealing with existing customers compared with new customers (Reichheld, 1996). However, the term *relationship marketing* can refer to all marketing activities directed toward "establishing, developing and maintaining successful relational exchanges" (Morgan & Hunt, 1994, p. 22). Thus, following Berry (1983, p. 25), we define relationship marketing as marketing activities that attract, maintain, and enhance customer relationships.

In this chapter, we focus on relationship marketing in mass markets—that is, in markets in which customers (that is, potentially large numbers of end users) make exchanges involving goods or services with manufacturers or service providers. Our view of exchange is not restricted to economic resources alone—marketers have long recognized that exchanges can involve social and psychological resources as well as economic resources (e.g., Bagozzi, 1979). Specifically, exchanges can involve the transfer of psychological or social resources such as status, esteem, understanding, affect, information, and time as well as economic resources such as money, goods, and services (Foa & Foa, 1976).

In the remainder of this chapter, we address two questions:

1. What are the conditions under which relationship marketing will be effective in mass markets?
2. What marketing strategies will be most appropriate in influencing relationship processes and outcomes under these different conditions?

First, we discuss the conditions necessary for a relationship to develop between a customer and an organization. Next, given that the necessary conditions are satisfied, we describe the key product category characteristics that motivate customers to engage in relational behaviors. Third, we provide a model that outlines the evaluation process customers go through in deciding to withdraw from, maintain, or enhance particular relationships. Having outlined the model, we discuss the various strategies that marketers use to influence parts of this decision process and achieve desired relational outcomes. We finish the chapter with some suggestions regarding key research issues that need to addressed in the field of relationship marketing in mass markets.

Necessary Conditions for
Relationship Marketing

A relationship develops between a customer and an organization when there are benefits to both from one or more exchanges. For a profit-maximizing firm, the benefits of relationships with end users arise from the economics of retention (Reichheld, 1996), insulation from competition (Anderson & Sullivan, 1994), and so forth. For the customer, the benefits of a relationship with the organization include customization and decreased costs due to efficiencies in dealing with known suppliers, including lower search costs and risk reduction (Sheth & Parvatiyar, 1995). In this section, we discuss some necessary conditions for an exchange relationship to exist.

CUSTOMIZATION

Relationship marketing in mass markets requires that the market consist of different benefit segments that can potentially be served by differentiated products. In other words, for relationships to develop, customization must be possible within the product category—through products (including branding and image), people, or technology. Mass customization is generally considered to be a tool for building loyalty when mass-market quality is no longer a sufficient differentiator (Gilmore & Pine, 1997). Mass customization began in service industries, where customization is necessary due to simultaneity of production and consumption. Service operations or employees may customize the processes and/or the outcomes of the services for their customers. For example, a service organization can customize the process by offering a customer alternative appointment times when a visit to the customer's premises is required, or it can customize the outcome by offering a customer tailored product bundles. In manufacturing industries, mass customization entails the use of flexible processes, structures, and management to produce varied and even *individualized* products at the *low cost* of standardized, mass-production systems with *short cycle times*. For example, the IBM System/360 has modules for varied configuration needs, and Motorola manufactures a great variety of pagers.

At the extreme, many organizations desire one-to-one relationships with their customers (Peppers & Rogers, 1993). Technology has begun to make such customization possible through the use of multiple media such as telephone, electronic mail, and the World Wide Web for order taking and the handling of complaints. For example, the package tracking information available on the Federal Express and UPS Web sites can be customized to meet particular customers' information needs (Hoffman & Novak, 1996).

CUSTOMER INTIMACY

Relationships involve one or more exchanges over time. However, a key feature of relationship marketing is its explicit recognition that exchanges between organizations and customers extend beyond strict economic boundaries (Hunt & Morgan, 1994). For example, it recognizes that *emotions*—as well as cognition—play a role in the relationship between the buyer and the seller. In mass markets, relationship marketing can facilitate customer intimacy by invoking emotions in a variety of contexts. Broadcast media can create a sense of identification or affiliation with the organization. Organizational procedures can influence customers' perceptions of the fairness of the exchange relationship (Lind & Tyler, 1988). Substantively personalized service can influence customers' perceptions of the helpfulness and friendliness of the organization (Surprenant & Solomon, 1987). In favorable situations, these circumstances can evoke emotions such as happiness, pride, and achievement. In unfavorable situations, these same circumstances can evoke emotions such as anger and frustration. Customers and employees in organizations who engage in favorable relationships feel a sense of "commitment" or "connection" toward one another (Morgan & Hunt, 1994).

TWO-WAY INTERACTIONS

The very notion of an exchange relationship between the organization and the customer requires a (direct) two-way interaction. In mass markets, organizations typically have a variety of ways of contacting customers through the marketing mix. To practice relationship marketing in mass markets, managers must ask, Can customers contact the organization? In service organizations, customers frequently interact with the organization when they come in contact with service employees, such as salespersons, customer service representatives, or service providers (e.g., the claims taker at an insurance company). In manufacturing firms, customers interact with the organization by mail, through toll-free telephone numbers, through sweepstakes and contests, and via e-mail and the organization's Web site. Many organizations keep the addresses and/or phone numbers of their customers on file so that they can respond to customers who contact them by sending newsletters, information on upcoming events and appointments, and so forth—thereby fostering the relationship. In the case of computer-mediated environments, Hoffman and Novak (1996) have proposed a many-to-many communication model in which customers can actively take part in providing immediate, iterative feedback to the manufacturer or service provider. At the extreme, two-way interactions occur on a one-to-one basis. For example, Amazon.com is a virtual bookstore for customers with access to the World Wide Web. Two-way interactions can also reduce the propensity of customers to switch to new suppliers, as customers invest in educating their suppliers about their needs and realize that they will have to start all over again if they move to new suppliers (Hart, 1996).

EXTENDED TIME INTERVALS

The relationship between an organization and a customer occurs over a time interval that may encompass one or more exchanges. However, even if the interval includes a single monetary transaction, the exchange relationship often extends beyond the time of the actual sale. Because the exchange involves psychological/social resources as well as economic resources, the duration of the relationship includes the various stages of the selling process—prior to a particular sales transaction (e.g., interior decoration or real estate), during the sale (e.g., automobiles), or afterward (e.g., maintenance and repair of appliances). In the case of multiple exchanges, the relationship can include regular or intermittent transactions (e.g., hairdresser, dentist, massage therapist) or continuous transactions (e.g., telephone companies, electrical utilities, and cable television). Figure 12.1 provides a hypothetical illustration of the different stages of a relationship-building process that happens over time between a customer and a marketer. In contrast to the framework offered by Liljander and Strandvik (1995), note that each of the stages of relationship

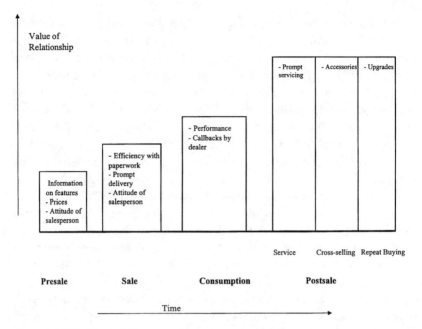

Figure 12.1. Typical Stages in the Relationship Marketing Process

building in our framework—such as presale, sale, and consumption—may involve multiple "episodes" or interactions.

Figure 12.1 could be used to explain how relationships develop between buyers and sellers in single exchanges that extend over lengthy periods of time, such as at automobile dealerships and insurance agencies. It highlights the role of elements that are *not* at the core of the product offering. In particular, social and psychological resources are exchanged between the buyer and seller in each stage and play an important role in determining the likelihood of the relationship's moving to the next stage. Thus an automobile salesperson at the presale stage may provide to the customer certain psychological/social resources (e.g., courtesy, respect) as well as economic resources (e.g., an opportunity to take a test drive, the provision of brochures), and these outcomes may (or may not) motivate a buyer to come back and make further inputs into the relationship—perhaps ultimately resulting in a purchase from the dealership. A valuable relationship may result in the buyer's purchasing accessories, upgrading his or her purchase, or recommending the dealership to friends and colleagues.

Conditions Facilitating Relationship Marketing

In the preceding section, we discussed the necessary conditions for organizations and customers to engage in relational behavior. However, even after the necessary conditions are satisfied, customers' proclivity to engage in relational behavior will vary across product categories. To take an extreme example, customers' propensity to switch brands in packaged goods may be quite different from their propensity to switch their primary care physician. In this section we describe three key product category characteristics that should influence customers' decisions to invest in, maintain, or withdraw from relationships. We also describe the various kinds of relational behaviors that may be observed in different product categories or situations.

PRODUCT CATEGORY CHARACTERISTICS

Product category heterogeneity. As discussed earlier, relationship marketing in mass markets is possible only when some degree of customization is possible. Customization is a major benefit to the customer and adds significant value to the exchange relationship. However, product categories differ in terms of the extent to which customization exists (or is possible) within them; this characteristic is called product category heterogeneity. Product category heterogeneity is associated with large numbers of alternatives in the category (e.g., shampoos), complex alternatives (e.g., computers), significant differences among alternatives (e.g., cars), and variance in retail operations (see Newman, 1977). Importantly, it may also be associated with perceived differences among alternatives (Dick & Basu, 1994)—these differences are mostly created through branding and image advertising. Customers tend to expand their consideration sets beyond existing exchange partners when they perceive a product category to be relatively homogeneous (e.g., Duncan & Olshavsky, 1982). Thus we propose that there is a positive relationship between perceived product category heterogeneity and the likelihood of customers' engaging in relational behavior. Analogously, contexts of high perceived heterogeneity are also those that are likely to have a greater degree of customization.

Perceived risk. Customers' decisions involve risk, in the sense that the decision to include/exclude an alternative from consideration will have consequences that cannot be predicted with certainty. Perceived risk is considered to be the probability of any loss that can occur as the result of the exclusion of an alternative from consideration, multiplied by the importance of that loss; it can include financial risk, performance risk, physical risk, and convenience risk (Peter & Tarpey, 1975; Srinivasan & Ratchford, 1991). Sheth and Parvatiyar (1995) propose that "the greater the perceived risk . . . , the greater will be the consumer propensity to . . . engage in relational market behavior" (pp. 258-259). Subsequently, they expand this notion beyond economic aspects of perceived risk and propose that "the greater the potential of a market choice to . . . reduce *social risks,* the greater the consumer propensity to adopt relational market behavior" (p. 260; emphasis added). For example, customers are likely to expand their consideration sets beyond existing exchange partners in product categories with intrinsically lower perceived risk of all types. Thus we propose that customers will be more likely to engage in relational behaviors when they perceive risk (financial risk, performance risk, physical risk, social risk, and so forth) to be high. Furthermore, Doney and Cannon (1997) emphasize that "trusting parties must be vulnerable to some extent for trust to become operational. In other words, decision outcomes must be *uncertain* and *important*" (p. 36; emphasis added). Thus we propose that perceived risk creates a context in which trust becomes an important influence on relational behaviors.

Switching costs. Switching costs are defined as the one-time costs that buyers encounter in switching from one supplier's product to another's (Porter, 1980). In addition to monetary costs, switching costs include search costs and nonmonetary costs (such as the cost of forming new relationships). These costs are frequently self-evident in business-to-business markets (e.g., the decision to perform a service in-house rather than outsource), but they are equally relevant in mass markets. For example, a customer who switches from an audiotape player to a compact disc player faces substantial monetary costs in replacing audiotapes with compact discs. Fornell (1992) proposes that repurchase intentions depend on customer satisfaction and switching costs (which vary across industries). In other words, customers are likely to value existing relationships more highly when search and switching costs are greater.

It is important to note that switching costs can include nonmonetary costs as well. Nonmonetary costs will be larger when customers face

	Low Risk		High Risk	
	Homogeneous	Heterogenous	Homogeneous	Heterogeneous
Low Switching Cost	Packaged goods, Telephone service	Retail merchandising, Restaurants	Airlines, Hotels, Package Delivery	Hair salons, Clothing, OTC medicines
High Switching Cost	Cable television, Car Insurance	Computers	Life Insurance	Housing, Child care, Financial services

Figure 12.2. Product Category Characteristics Facilitating Relationship Marketing

NOTE: Customers' propensity to engage in relational behaviors will be higher in categories characterized by higher perceived switching costs, higher levels of perceived risk, and greater heterogeneity among alternatives. Higher propensity to engage in relational behaviors is indicated by heavier shading within cells.

mental processing costs, social costs of forming relationships with the employees of new suppliers, and so forth. Mental processing costs will tend to be high when customers have little knowledge of the product class. Punj and Staelin (1983) found a negative correlation between cost of search (nonmonetary) and amount of search. Sheth and Parvatiyar (1995) propose that "the greater the need for information, knowledge, and expertise in making choices, the greater will be the consumer propensity to engage in relational market behavior" (p. 258). Thus we propose that customers will be more likely to engage in relational behaviors when they perceive monetary and nonmonetary switching costs to be high.

JOINT EFFECTS OF HETEROGENEITY, SWITCHING COSTS, AND PERCEIVED RISK

We propose that customers will have a greater propensity to engage in relational behaviors in categories characterized by greater heterogeneity among alternatives, higher perceived switching costs, and higher levels of perceived risk. This typology, with some product category examples, is shown in Figure 12.2. The shading in the cells of the figure indicates greater propensity to engage in relational behaviors and (consequently) potentially greater payoff from relationship marketing expenditures.

In developing our typology, we have discussed these three characteristics separately. However, it is important to note that they are not independent. Customers may perceive switching costs to be higher in a category where product heterogeneity is high. Similarly, in certain contexts, perceived risk and switching costs are also likely to be positively correlated. That is, in addition to the main effects, the interactions among these variables may also affect customers' propensity to engage in relational behavior. Thus, with reference to Figure 12.2, the heterogeneity in computer systems may inflate customers' perceptions of the high switching costs in that product category, or the risk perceptions of switching hairdressers may influence perceptions of heterogeneity in their capabilities.

Furthermore, our typology does not imply that when heterogeneity, switching costs, and perceived risk are high, customers will persist with the same providers or products forever. Depending on the product category and situational and personal characteristics, customers may have a need to seek variety (McAlister, 1982). In contexts where variety seeking is likely to be high, relationship marketers offer a wider assortment of goods and services or develop networks of providers (see Iacobucci, 1996) to enhance customer retention.

Modeling the Customer's Decision to Maintain, Build, or Withdraw From a Relationship

In this section we present a model of the customer's decision to maintain, build, or withdraw from an existing relationship with an organization. In the model, the customer's decision to build, maintain, or withdraw from a relationship is viewed from a cost-benefit perspective, rather than from a perceptual or processing perspective. Consistent with prior research (De-Sarbo & Jedidi, 1994; Hauser & Wernerfelt, 1990; Roberts & Lattin, 1991), the model represents the customer's informal, heuristic process for evaluating decision alternatives (i.e., build/maintain/withdraw) as a trade-off between costs and benefits/utility.[1] Specifically, we consider the customer's decision to engage in a relational behavior using the classic maximization of utility framework—but with an expanded conceptualization of utility.

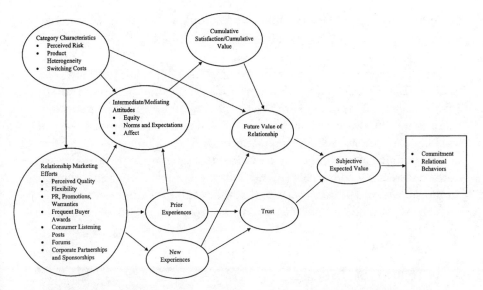

Figure 12.3. A Model of the Consumer's Decision to Maintain, Build, or Withdraw From a Relationship

THE SUBJECTIVE EXPECTED VALUE
OF RELATIONAL BEHAVIORS

Our model of the antecedents of customers' relational behaviors is depicted in Figure 12.3. Following Winer (1985), the model assumes that a customer seeks to maximize his or her subjective expected value from a relational behavior. The subjective expected value from a relational behavior depends on the customer's assessment of the behavior's *long-run future value,* weighted by the customer's *trust* in the organization.

Long-run future value. We postulate that the customer assesses the long-run future value arising from a relational market behavior (e.g., purchasing from an organization) where alternatives with greater benefits (including customization of economic, psychological, and social exchange elements) or lower costs (including mental processing costs, search costs, and opportunity losses) are more likely to be considered.[2] In this conceptualization, building or maintaining an existing relationship is more likely when the future value of a particular relational market behavior is high—that is, there are high perceived benefits/utility (due to customization,

personalization, product bundling, and so on) or low costs (due to reduced mental processing, search costs, and the like) in the long run.

Trust. In our model, the customer weighs the long-run future value of a
relational market behavior by his or her *trust* in the organization to obtain
an assessment of his or her subjective expected value. This expected-value
calculation implicitly assumes that trust is defined as "confidence in an
exchange partner's reliability and integrity" (Morgan & Hunt, 1994,
p. 23)—emphasizing that trust is a probabilistic belief. In this respect, we
follow Anderson and Narus's (1990) definition of trust as a belief that an
organization "will perform actions that will result in positive outcomes . . .
as well as not take unexpected actions that result in negative outcomes"
(p. 45).

ANTECEDENTS OF LONG-RUN
FUTURE VALUE AND TRUST

Both the customer's assessment of the long-run future value of a relational behavior and the customer's trust in an organization are considered
to be similar to belief, attitude, or cumulative perception. Following Hogarth and Einhorn's (1992) theory of belief updating, we postulate that
customers update these beliefs though a sequential anchoring and adjustment process in which the individual's current belief (i.e., the anchor) is
adjusted by the impact of succeeding *new experiences*. For example, the
customer's perception of the future long-run value of a relational behavior
is postulated to depend on his or her perception of the current value of the
relationship, updated by any new experiences (e.g., through advertising,
newsletters). The customer's trust in the organization is updated in a
similar fashion. Hence relational marketing efforts create prior experiences (for existing customers) and new experiences (for both new and existing customers) that influence long-run future value and trust through
their antecedents.

The antecedents of the long-run future value of a relationship to a customer are relatively straightforward. In an existing relationship, we expect
that the customer's perception of the future long-run value of the relationship will depend heavily on his or her cumulative satisfaction with the
prior experiences, updated by any new experiences. This notion is consistent with prior research concerning the linkage between satisfaction and

commitment (see Brown & Peterson, 1993; Gruen, 1995). Consequently, consistent with the customer dis/satisfaction research (Oliver, 1996), we consider that cumulative satisfaction depends on customers' perceptions of norms and expectations, equity and affect. Research on the antecedents of trust is less well developed, but it has included prior experiences that influence shared values and communications (Morgan & Hunt, 1994).

HOW RELATIONSHIP MARKETING VARIABLES INFLUENCE
THE ANTECEDENTS OF SUBJECTIVE EXPECTED VALUE

In categories in which there are greater heterogeneity among alternatives, higher perceived switching costs, and/or higher levels of perceived risk, there is an opportunity for relationship marketing variables to influence customers' assessments of the subjective expected value of the relationship. As shown in Figure 12.3, relationship marketing variables may create new experiences that directly increase customers' assessments of long-run future value and trust. (We describe these relational marketing efforts in greater detail in the next section.) For example, an organization may customize its product or decrease costs to the customer (such as by lowering search costs); these marketing efforts should attract new customers as well as retain existing customers. It is important to note that when a customer has prior experience with an organization, relationship marketing variables will frequently operate through cumulative satisfaction and its antecedents. In other words, relationship marketing variables create experiences that operate through mediating variables—such as affect, equity, cumulative satisfaction, long-run future value, and trust—to influence relational behaviors. Dwyer, Schurr, and Oh (1987) describe some potential subprocesses through which relationship marketing efforts may operate to deepen customer commitment and encourage relational behaviors. Unfortunately, there has been little research on the nature of this process. Peterson (1995) notes that *affect* seems to offer great promise for explaining customers' perceptions of satisfaction and long-term value. Bagozzi (1995) argues that reciprocity is a core feature of a marketing relationship—implying that the role of equity is particularly important. Both constructs are likely to be important for explaining how relationship marketing influences customer behavior.

For example, traditional equity theory proposes that parties to an exchange will feel equitably treated if the ratio of their outcomes to inputs is "fair"—that is, when the outcome-to-input ratio is proportionate for participants in the exchange (Adams, 1965; Deutsch, 1975). In other words, the customer is believed to apply an integration rule in which he or she compares own outcomes to inputs, compares other participants' outcomes to inputs, and finally compares the two ratios or differences (Oliver & Swan, 1989a, 1989b). If the customer's ratio of outcomes to inputs exceeds the ratios of the other parties in the exchange, he or she will attempt to restore balance in the exchange by increasing his or her own inputs. This notion suggests that it may be useful for the organization to engage in relational marketing efforts that provide positive outcomes to the customer in anticipation that the customer will attempt to restore balance within the exchange relationship by increasing his or her inputs—that is, by engaging in commitment behaviors (see Gruen, 1995, p. 457; Peterson, 1995, p. 280). For example, Bolton and Lemon (1997) found that customers adjusted their service usage levels in response to service provider changes in price and service levels to maintain equity in their relationships with an interactive television service provider and a cellular communications provider.

RELATIONAL BEHAVIORS

In maximizing their subjective expected value, customers may decide to engage in a variety of relational behaviors. A repeat purchase (that is, an additional identical exchange) can be considered a behavior consistent with maintenance of the relationship. The decision to build a relationship with an organization will be associated with behaviors such as increased usage, positive word of mouth, multiproduct purchases, and customer advocacy.[3] The decision to withdraw from a relationship with an organization will be associated with behaviors such as decreased usage or no purchase or interaction (i.e., relationship severance), negative word of mouth, and boycotts.

Commitment has been a central construct in studies of customer behavior within exchange relationships (e.g., Crosby, Evans, & Cowles, 1990). Morgan and Hunt (1994) define commitment as "an exchange partner believing that an ongoing relationship with another is so important as to warrant maximum efforts at maintaining it" (p. 23). Thus it can be viewed as an attitude or belief that coincides with a variety of relational behaviors—that is, behaviors associated with the customer's decision to maintain, build, or withdraw from a relationship with an organization. Furthermore, although many authors have suggested that these behaviors form a partnership hierarchy (Payne, Christopher, Clark, & Peck, 1995), we prefer to consider relational behaviors as an related "bundle" of decisions by the customer—where each of these decisions may be determined by many of the same factors (although with different weights). In other words, we view a behavior bundle as a portfolio in which some of the exhibited behaviors are positive (from the standpoint of the provider) and others may be negative. For instance, customers who participate in airline frequent-flier programs sometimes exemplify our notion of a bundle of relationship behaviors—they fly a particular airline because of the frequent-flier points, but they do not hesitate to bad-mouth the organization on every possible score. Jones and Sasser (1995) use the term "false loyalty" to describe such customers.

The Role of Marketing Variables

Because relationship marketing in mass markets is a relatively new topic for research, very little is known about how organizations' relational marketing efforts affect mediating variables—such as equity, norms, expectations, and affect[4]—to influence customer satisfaction, the perceived future value of the relationship, trust, and relational behaviors. In the preceding section, we discussed how the relationship marketing efforts of firms are influenced by the characteristics of the product category and how, in turn, these efforts affect customers' intermediate/mediating attitudes and ultimately relational behaviors. In this section, we discuss specific relationship marketing variables, the processes through which they operate, and their relational behavior outcomes.

We discuss relational marketing variables under four broad categories: product, pricing and promotions, distribution, and communications.[5] However, our discussion of relationship marketing variables is not intended to be exhaustive. We focus on variables that exploit the necessary conditions underlying exchange relationships (namely, customization, customer intimacy, two-way interactions, and extended time intervals) as well as product category characteristics that facilitate exchange relationships (namely, heterogeneity, switching costs, and perceived risk). We identify these marketing variables and explain how they operate, invoking a variety of theoretical disciplines, such as cognitive psychology and social psychology (e.g., Fiske & Taylor, 1991), network approaches (Iacobucci, 1996), economic perspectives on pricing and signaling (e.g., Eliashberg & Robertson, 1988), behavioral decision theory, and operations research.

PRODUCT VARIABLES THAT
FACILITATE RELATIONSHIPS

Perceived quality. The notion that customer satisfaction and perceived value depend on perceived quality is central to the marketing literature (e.g., Kotler, 1997) and appears prominently in the service quality literature (e.g., Parasuraman, Berry, & Zeithaml, 1991) and the relationship quality literature (e.g., Crosby et al., 1990). Perceived quality (including the consistency and reliability with which it is delivered) constitutes the "core" of a product. Thus delivery of a high-quality product can strengthen relationships with customers in mass markets. Moreover, "augmented" product attributes—which may include customized product attributes—signal product quality and thereby increase customer satisfaction and the perceived future value of the relationship. More specifically, customers may use the physical landscape, symbols used by the organization, the attitudes and behavior of employees, and brand name as signals of product quality (e.g., Bitner, 1990; Hartline & Ferrell, 1996). Hence these augmented product attributes can also influence customer satisfaction, value, and relational behaviors such as repeat purchasing and purchasing other products from the organization.[6]

Warranties. Warranties, guarantees, and return policies are signals that create customer expectations about product performance as well as reduce perceived risk (e.g., Bolton & Drew, 1995). The length of the warranty helps define the customer's perception of the time interval of the relationship. Warranties increase trust in the organization as well as improve the customer's perception of the future value of the relationship, so there is a dual effect on the customer's subjective expected value. Furthermore, warranties encourage two-way interactions between the customer and the service organization, facilitating proactive complaint management and continuous improvement efforts while reinforcing employees' use of relationship marketing practices.

PRICING AND PROMOTION PRACTICES
THAT FACILITATE RELATIONSHIPS

Usage rewards. Rewards from the organization to the customer that are related to the level of usage have become a common phenomenon. Airlines have frequent-flier programs, supermarkets have frequent-buyer programs, and restaurant chains have frequent-diner programs. These programs create an incentive for customers to stay with the same organizations to collect the rewards, thereby directly influencing purchase behavior. However, participation in many of these programs (e.g., paying for credit card usage but getting airline miles for every dollar charged) is strictly an economic decision for the customer; such participation may have no influence—or even a negative influence—on other relational behaviors, such as word of mouth. To steer the customer toward noneconomic usage and evaluation of the program, marketers use behavioral decision theory principles such as mental accounting (see Thaler, 1985) in their advertising. In general, as Dowling and Uncles (1995) suggest, rewards that directly support the product's value proposition (e.g., price promotions by a retailer) are better from a loyalty standpoint than are indirect rewards (e.g., raffle tickets offered by a retailer). Similarly, rewards that are relatively immediate (e.g., price discounts) are better than rewards that are delayed (e.g., frequent-shopper points).

Tailored promotions. Marketers also deploy tailored promotions using direct mail, telemarketing, and regional events. These variables create perceived heterogeneity within the product category. Personalization and customization increase the customer's perception of the future value of the relationship and increase perceived switching costs. Furthermore, certain tailored promotions (e.g., regional events) create positive affect that influences cumulative satisfaction with the organization and thereby perceptions of the future value of the relationship. Other promotions (e.g., giveaways, sweepstakes) may cause customers to perceive advantageous inequity in the relationship (i.e., they have received outputs from the organization that are disproportionate to their inputs), which may lead to relational behaviors intended to restore the balance.

DISTRIBUTIONAL VARIABLES THAT FACILITATE RELATIONSHIPS

In recent years, networks of purposeful cooperating firms have emerged to increase the value delivered to the customer. For example, Wal-Mart and Procter & Gamble cooperate to create value for the customer through their merchandising efforts. Campbell and Wilson (1996) call these value-creating networks "managed networks" and claim that their ultimate goal is to manage relationships. However, in the following paragraphs we focus on organizations' relationships with customers, rather than with other firms.

Flexibility. Flexibility in product delivery and distribution is another critical marketing variable used by organizations to strengthen relationships with customers. Flexibility leads to customization, which increases customer satisfaction and the perceived value of the relationship. With the advent of information technology, customization and personalization are increasingly evident in mass markets. For example, travel agents keep customers' idiosyncratic preferences on flights, hotels, and car rentals on file. The Ritz Carlton maintains a database of its guests and can provide them with their favorite newspapers, breakfasts, and so on without being asked (Hart, 1996). Direct marketers such as L. L. Bean enable customers to shop through catalogs or the World Wide Web and keep records of customers' sizes and preferences. In many contexts, astute relationship marketers even "tailor" products or services to customers at prices far lower than traditional custom-made models (Wiersema, 1996). For example, Federal Express provides its customers with software to update real-time information on the status of packages (McKenna, 1995).

People. Even in mass markets, products are frequently delivered by service employees. These interactions may take place face-to-face (e.g., retailing), over the telephone (e.g., customer care centers in insurance or telephone companies), or by mail (e.g., order fulfillment employees in direct-mail companies). Interactions between service employees and customers are, to some extent, always customized and personalized two-way interactions. They frequently entail the exchange of psychological/social resources as well as economic resources. To be successful in stimulating relational behaviors, effective human resource management (hiring, training, supporting, retaining policies) is critical to ensure that service employees can create customer satisfaction, develop personal trust, and so forth (Bowen & Lawler, 1992). For example, an important component of Starbucks Coffee Company's growth strategy is an innovative, comprehensive employee benefits package for both full-time and part-time employees (Berry, 1995, p. 172). By creating employee satisfaction, Starbucks is able to retain friendly and courteous employees, thereby creating customer satisfaction and increasing the future value of the relationship with Starbucks to the customer.

COMMUNICATIONS STRATEGIES
THAT FACILITATE RELATIONSHIPS

Communications strategies that facilitate relationships are likely to be frequent, two-way interactions, via personal rather than impersonal modes, with customized information content (Mohr & Nevin, 1990). These strategies are in direct contrast to typical mass-market communications strategies. In order to be effective, the elements of these strategies must be consistent in enhancing the customer's subjective expected value of the relationship. For example, to attract new customers, corporate advertising employing celebrities helps to develop a sense of affiliation between the customer and the organization and/or may signal the firm's reputation to the customer, both of which enhance the likelihood that the customer will buy products from the firm. In existing relationships, there are many opportunities to use communications strategies to enhance the customer's cumulative customer satisfaction and trust in the organization.

Public relations. On the one hand, public relations and corporate advertising create norms and expectations regarding product performance. On the other hand, such activities help develop a sense of affiliation between the organization and the customer (Peter & Olson, 1995) and influence overall attitudes. For example, advertising sports shoes using a well-known celebrity such as Michael Jordan may enable customers to develop a social identity for the sponsoring organization and subsequently a sense of identification with that organization. In turn, identification engenders positive affect and influences customer satisfaction and perceived value.

Customer listening posts. Listening is an important aspect of the organization-customer relationship that creates two-way interactions.

Listening has many benefits. For example, 3M claims that more than two-thirds of its product improvement ideas come from listening to customer complaints (Kotler, 1997). Organizations listen to their customers through a variety of media: letters, toll-free telephone numbers, e-mail, videotape, and marketing research. According to Reese (1996), availability of customer listening posts also raises customer expectations and may affect customer perceptions about a company and its products. Moreover, customers feel "wanted" and "taken care of" when organizations listen to them, which reduces disconfirmation in the instance of complaints and could even induce positive affect if the context is one of suggestions for improvement. In support of this notion, Fornell and Wernerfelt (1988) suggest that firms should even encourage complaints from customers because such complaints give them the chance to retain these customers.

Forums. Recently, organizations have sought to develop "connections" or relationships with customers through both electronic and personal interaction forums. Tenets of social psychology—social identity theory (Tajfel & Turner, 1986) in particular—help us to understand how forums help strengthen relationships. Increased contact with an organization leads to a sense of "identification" whereby customers start to define themselves in terms of the attributes and values of the organization (Bhattacharya, Rao, & Glynn, 1995). The Saturn picnics (Aaker, 1994), the Harley-Davidson rallies (Reid, 1989), and Reebok forums on the Internet (McKenna, 1995) are examples of personal interaction forums that lead to identification. In electronic forums, individual customers have established Web pages for automobiles, toys, and television shows (Hoffman & Novak, 1996). Identification has both cognitive and affective dimensions (Bergami & Bagozzi, 1996) and has been shown to be positively related to customer satisfaction. Not surprisingly, identification has desirable relational outcomes—in the context of employees, identification has been shown to lead to lower turnover (O'Reilly & Chatman, 1986), and in the context of alumni of educational institutions, it leads to increased donations (Mael & Ashforth, 1992).

Moreover, customers are also using the Internet to form "brand communities" around organizations such as Saab, Disney, and Lego (Winer et al., 1996). Organizations can facilitate and influence these customer-to-customer encounters by encouraging group formation, controlling the environments in which customer-to-customer encounters take place, and so forth. Research in business-to-business marketing contexts has shown that frequency of information exchange (facilitated by such forums) is positively associated with global relational behaviors (Boyle, Dwyer, Robicheaux, & Simpson, 1992). Not surprisingly, organizations have seen opportunities to exploit the extensive social networks among customers (e.g., MCI's Friends and Family program; Martin & Clark, 1996) to obtain desired relational behaviors.

Corporate partnerships and sponsorships. Corporations have always been associated with sporting and cultural events. The Virginia Slims women's tennis tournament and the Winston Cup in car racing are examples of organizations' trying to influence customer attitudes and behavior through associations. Typically, such associations are both cognitive and social in nature. In recent years, there has also been an increase in organizations' developing alliances with worthy causes and/or nonprofit organizations (Andreasen, 1996; Brown & Dacin, 1997; Varadarajan & Menon, 1988). Such partnerships and sponsorships seem to serve as "idiosyncratic investments" or pledges that influence the commitment of both parties to the relationship (see Anderson & Weitz, 1992). They also signal to the customer that the organization is "socially responsible," which is another dimension that enhances the value of the relationship for the customer.

MEASURING THE EFFECTIVENESS
OF RELATIONAL MARKETING VARIABLES

Measures of the effectiveness of relationship marketing variables should include individual or aggregate measures of customers' relational behaviors: share of purchases, customer retention rates or lifetime durations, purchase or usage levels, multiproduct sales, and so forth. However, the effectiveness of relationship marketing efforts is also reflected in measures of attitudes (e.g., service quality) and underlying predispositions (e.g., loyalty). For example, prior research has shown that relationship marketing efforts can influence interpurchase durations for goods and services (e.g., Crosby & Stephens, 1987). Furthermore, the elasticity of purchase intentions with respect to customer satisfaction is lower for organizations with high levels of satisfaction (Anderson & Sullivan, 1994), implying a long-run reputation effect insulating organizations that practice relationship marketing. In addition, more-satisfied customers have longer relationships with their service providers (Bolton, 1996) and higher usage levels of services (Bolton & Lemon, 1997). Typically, as the duration of the relationship increases, so do the benefits of the relationship for both the organization and the end user. Ultimately, we expect the effectiveness of relationship marketing variables to be reflected in financial/economic measures of the organization's performance (e.g., market share, share of customer, and profits).

Research Questions

Relationship marketing in mass markets is a fruitful topic for additional conceptual and empirical research. In the conceptual domain, the extant literature has focused almost exclusively on relational outcomes as a function of customer, firm, and product characteristics. However, the lateral relationships or networks that develop among groups of users are important determinant of relational outcomes. The popular MCI Friends and Family campaign may be one example of such a network. We need to understand how an individual customer's decision to withdraw from, build, or maintain a relationship is affected by relevant others' decisions to do the same, and, conversely, what strategies firms can use to enhance customer loyalty by strengthening the ties within these networks. The literature on organizational demography will be valuable for advancing such an understanding (e.g., Pfeffer, 1983).

In the empirical domain, there is much need for studies that use surveys, experiments, and longitudinal analysis of data collected from consumer panels. For instance, one area that is ripe for study is that of cross-category variation in the effectiveness of relational marketing efforts. Cross-sectional data on a number of different categories would make it possible for researchers to investigate how product category characteristics affect marketing mix effectiveness and subsequently relationship value. The same analysis could also shed some light on interdependencies in the perceptions of product heterogeneity, perceived risk, and switching costs (which we discussed above), and hence enable us to assess how the payoffs from relationship marketing efforts change with changes in product category characteristics.

Because relationships develop over time, there is also a need for dynamic models that explain how marketing mix variables influence relational behaviors via mediating constructs (e.g., trust). One approach to these issues is to conduct longitudinal research using data collection techniques, such as customer panels, that provide ongoing attitudinal and behavioral data for specific product categories. Such research could answer questions about the nature of the "value function" and its antecedents. For example, how is equity maintained in relationships over time? We can empirically test for the integration rule and extend Bolton and Lemon's (1997) work to investigate the types of mechanisms customers use over time to restore equity in their relationships. Furthermore, we can also investigate how equity affects the customer's assessment of the future value of the relationship.

Finally, experimental research could be undertaken to address a number of interesting issues. First, there is the whole area pertaining to the practice of using both brand and organization-level attributes to influence customer retention. We need to understand how customers process information about the organization and how they integrate that information with brand-related information. Relatedly, under what conditions does information pertaining to the organization affect brand/service purchase behavior? How is such information processing mediated by a customer's identification with the organization and strength of brand preference? Second, we need to understand how different sets of marketing mix conditions and product characteristics result in specific behavior bundles, such as repeat purchase, positive word of mouth, and multibrand loyalty. Computer-based experimental settings (e.g., Burke, 1996) are appropriate for this purpose because they allow researchers to create many different market conditions with relative ease. Third, it is important to understand whether there are asymmetries between relationship-building and relationship-withdrawal types of behaviors. If relationship withdrawal is interpreted by the customer as a loss of sorts, it is possible that psychological theories that speak to loss aversion (e.g., Kahneman & Tversky, 1979) may be useful for our understanding of whether customers are more likely to engage in behaviors such as negative word of mouth compared with the commensurate positive word of mouth expected in a relationship-building context.

Notes

1. This approach is similar to Sheth and Parvatiyar's (1995) suggestion that "consumers engage in relational market behavior to achieve greater efficiency in their decision making,

to reduce the task of information processing, to achieve more cognitive consistency in their decisions, and to reduce the perceived risks associated with future choices" (p. 256). However, our model concerns a multiplicity of relational behaviors; we do not focus, as Sheth and Parvatiyar do, on choice reduction.

2. The benefits for customers go beyond the routinization of purchase behavior to using the organization as a means of self-expression and self-identity. However, these features can also be considered "benefits" in our framework. This definition of value is similar to the definition suggested by Anderson, Jain, and Chintangunta (1993).

3. According to Webster (1992), one of the ultimate goals of relationship marketing is to have customers be advocates for the organization.

4. For a useful framework from which to view how firms can manage customer expectations, see Sheth and Mittal (1996).

5. This approach is similar to that of Rosenberg and Czepiel (1995), who describe a "customer keeping marketing mix" that consists of five elements: product extras, reinforcing promotions, sales force connections, specialized distribution, and postpurchase communication.

6. For example, based on self-report data, Keaveney (1995) found that negative attitudes and behaviors by employees were responsible for 34% of customer service switching behavior in her sample.

References

Aaker, D. A. (1994). Building a brand: The Saturn story. *California Management Review, 36*(2), 114-134.

Adams, J. S. (1965). Inequity in social exchange. In L. Berkowitz (Ed.), *Advances in experimental social psychology* (Vol. 2, pp. 267-299). New York: Academic Press.

Anderson, E., & Weitz, B. A. (1992). The use of pledges to build and sustain commitment in distribution channels. *Journal of Marketing Research, 29,* 18-34.

Anderson, E. W., & Sullivan, M. W. (1994). The antecedents and consequences of customer satisfaction for firms. *Marketing Science, 13,* 125-143.

Anderson, J. C., Jain, D. C., & Chintangunta, P. K. (1993). Customer value assessment in business markets: A state-of-practice study. *Journal of Business-to-Business Marketing, 1,* 3-29.

Anderson, J. C., & Narus, J. A. (1990). A model of distributor firm and manufacturer firm working partnerships. *Journal of Marketing, 54*(1), 42-58.

Andreasen, A. R. (1996). Profits for nonprofits: Find a corporate partner. *Harvard Business Review, 74*(6), 47-59.

Bagozzi, R. P. (1979). Toward a formal theory of marketing exchanges. In O. C. Ferrell, S. Brown, & C. Lamb (Eds.), *Conceptual and theoretical developments in marketing* (pp. 431-447). Chicago: American Marketing Association.

Bagozzi, R. P. (1995). Reflections on relationship marketing in consumer markets. *Journal of the Academy of Marketing Science, 23,* 272-277.

Bergami, M., & Bagozzi, R. P. (1996). *Organizational identification: Conceptualization, measurement and nomological validity* (Working paper). Ann Arbor: University of Michigan.

Berry, L. L. (1983). Relationship marketing. In L. L. Berry, G. L. Shostack, & G. D. Upah (Eds.), *Emerging perspectives on service marketing* (pp. 25-38). Chicago: American Marketing Association.

Berry, L. L. (1995). *On great service: A framework for action.* New York: Free Press.

Bhattacharya, C. B., Rao, H., & Glynn, M. A. (1995). Understanding the bond of identification: An investigation of its correlates among art museum members. *Journal of Marketing, 59*(4), 46-57.

Bitner, M. J. (1990). Evaluating service encounters: The effects of physical surroundings and employee responses. *Journal of Marketing, 54*(2), 69-82.

Bolton, R. N. (1996). *Linking customer satisfaction to the duration of customer provider relationships and revenues* (Working paper). College Park: University of Maryland.

Bolton, R. N., & Drew, J. H. (1995). Factors influencing customers' assessments of service quality and their invocation of a service warranty. In D. Bowen, S. W. Brown, & T. A. Swartz (Eds.), *Advances in services marketing and management* (Vol. 4, pp. 195-210). Greenwich, CT: JAI.

Bolton, R. N., & Lemon, K. N. (1997). *Customers' usage of services: Implications for equity and satisfaction* (Working paper). College Park: University of Maryland.

Bowen, D. E., & Lawler, E. E., III. (1992). The empowerment of service workers: What, why, how and when. *Sloan Management Review, 33*(3), 31-39.

Boyle, B., Dwyer, F. R., Robicheaux, R. A., & Simpson, J. T. (1992). Influence strategies in marketing channels: Measures and use in different relationship structures. *Journal of Marketing Research, 29*, 462-473.

Brown, T. J., & Dacin, P. A. (1997). The company and the product: Corporate associations and consumer product responses. *Journal of Marketing, 61*(1), 68-84.

Brown, S. P., & Peterson, R. A. (1993). Antecedents and consequences of salesperson job satisfaction: Meta analysis and assessment of causal effects. *Journal of Marketing Research, 30*, 63-77.

Burke, R. R. (1996). Virtual shopping: Breakthrough in marketing research. *Harvard Business Review, 74*(4), 120-131.

Campbell, A. J., & Wilson, D. T. (1996). Managed networks: Creating strategic advantage. In D. Iacobucci (Ed.), *Networks in marketing*. Thousand Oaks, CA: Sage.

Crosby, L. A., Evans, K. R., & Cowles, D. (1990). Relationship quality in services selling: An interpersonal influence perspective. *Journal of Marketing, 54*(3), 68-81.

Crosby, L. A., & Stephens, N. (1987). Effects of relationship marketing and satisfaction, retention, and prices in the life insurance industry. *Journal of Marketing Research, 24*, 404-411.

DeSarbo, W. S., & Jedidi, K. (1994). *A latent structure vector multidimensional scaling model for censored data: Market segmentation via consideration set compositions* (Working paper). Ann Arbor: University of Michigan.

Deutsch, M. (1975). Equity, equality, and need: What determines which value will be used as the basis of distributive justice? *Journal of Social Issues, 31*(3), 137-149.

Dick, A. S., & Basu, K. (1994). Customer loyalty: Toward an integrated conceptual framework. *Journal of the Academy of Marketing Science, 22*, 99-113.

Doney, P. M., & Cannon, J. P. (1997). An examination of the nature of trust in buyer-seller relationships. *Journal of Marketing, 61*(2), 35-51.

Dowling, G. R., & Uncles, M. D. (1995). *Customer loyalty programs: Should every firm have one?* (Working paper). Bradford, England: Bradford Management Centre.

Duncan, C. P., & Olshavsky, R. W. (1982). External search: The role of consumer beliefs. *Journal of Marketing Research, 19*, 32-43.

Dwyer, F. R., Schurr, P. H., & Oh, S. (1987). Developing buyer-seller relationships. *Journal of Marketing, 51*(2), 11-27.

Eliashberg, J., & Robertson, T. S. (1988). New product preannouncing behavior: A market signaling study. *Journal of Marketing Research, 25*, 282-293.

Fiske, S. T., & Taylor, S. E. (1991). *Social cognition*. New York: McGraw-Hill.

Foa, E. B., & Foa, U. G. (1976). Resource theory of social exchange. In J. W. Thibaut, J. T. Spence, & R. C. Carson (Eds.), *Contemporary topics in social psychology* (pp. 99-131). Morristown, NJ: General Learning.

Fornell, C. (1992). A national customer satisfaction barometer: The Swedish experience. *Journal of Marketing, 56*(1), 6-21.

Fornell, C., & Wernerfelt, B. (1987). Defensive marketing strategy by customer complaint management: A theoretical analysis. *Journal of Marketing Research, 24,* 337-346.

Fornell, C., & Wernerfelt, B. (1988). Model for customer complaint management. *Marketing Science, 7,* 271-286.

Gilmore, J. H., & Pine, B. J., II. (1997). The four faces of mass customization. *Harvard Business Review, 76*(1), 91-101.

Gruen, T. W. (1995). The outcome set of relationship marketing in consumer markets. *International Business Review, 4,* 447-470.

Hart, C. W. (1996). Technology is making it feasible to reach that market of one: Make sure that you're the first mover. *Marketing Management, 5*(2), 10-18.

Hartline, M., & Ferrell, O. C. (1996). The management of customer-contact service: An empirical investigation. *Journal of Marketing, 60*(4), 52-70.

Hauser, J. R., & Wernerfelt, B. (1990). An evaluation cost model of consideration sets. *Journal of Consumer Research, 16,* 393-408.

Hoffman, D. L., & Novak, T. M. (1996). Marketing in hypermedia computer mediated environments: Conceptual foundations. *Journal of Marketing, 60*(3), 50-68.

Hogarth, R., & Einhorn, H. (1992). Order effects in belief updating: The belief-adjustment model. *Cognitive Psychology, 24,* 1-55.

Hunt, S. D., & Morgan, R. M. (1994). Relationship marketing in the era of network competition. *Marketing Management, 3*(1), 19-28.

Iacobucci, D. (Ed.). (1996). *Networks in marketing.* Thousand Oaks, CA: Sage.

Jones, T. O., & Sasser, W. E., Jr. (1995). Why satisfied customers defect. *Harvard Business Review, 73*(6), 89-99.

Kahneman, D., & Tversky, A. (1979). Prospect theory: An analysis of decision under risk. *Econometrica, 47,* 263-291.

Keaveney, S. M. (1995). Customer switching behavior in service industries: An exploratory study. *Journal of Marketing, 59*(2), 71-82.

Kotler, P. (1997). *Marketing management: Analysis, planning, implementation, and control.* Upper Saddle River, NJ: Prentice Hall.

Liljander, V., & Strandvik, T. (1995). The nature of customer relationships in services. In D. Bowen, S. W. Brown, & T. A. Swartz (Eds.), *Advances in services marketing and management* (Vol. 4, pp. 141-167). Greenwich, CT: JAI.

Lind, E. A., & Tyler, T. R. (1988). *The social psychology of procedural justice.* New York: Plenum.

Mael, F., & Ashforth, B. E. (1992). Alumni and their alma mater: A partial test of the reformulated model of organizational identification. *Journal of Organizational Behavior, 13,* 103-123.

Martin, C. L., & Clark, T. (1996). Networks of customer-to-customer relationships in marketing. In D. Iacobucci (Ed.), *Networks in marketing.* Thousand Oaks, CA: Sage.

McAlister, L. (1982). A dynamic attribute satiation model of variety seeking behavior. *Journal of Consumer Research, 9,* 311-322.

McKenna, R. (1995). Real time marketing. *Harvard Business Review, 73*(6), 87-96.

Mohr, J., & Nevin, J. R. (1990). Communication strategies in marketing channels: A theoretical perspective. *Journal of Marketing, 54*(4), 36-51.

Morgan, R. M., & Hunt, S. D. (1994). The commitment-trust theory of relationship marketing. *Journal of Marketing, 58*(3), 20-38.

Newman, J. W. (1977). Consumer external search: Amount and determinants. In A. G. Woodside, J. N. Sheth, & P. D. Bennett (Eds.), *Consumer and industrial buying behavior* (pp. 79-94). New York: Elsevier-North Holland.

Oliver, R. L. (1996). *Satisfaction: A behavioral perspective on the consumer.* New York: McGraw-Hill.

Oliver, R. L., & Swan, J. E. (1989a). Consumer perceptions of interpersonal equity and satisfaction in transactions: A field survey approach. *Journal of Marketing, 53*(2), 21-35.

Oliver, R. L., & Swan, J. E. (1989b). Equity and disconfirmation perceptions as influences on merchant and product satisfaction. *Journal of Consumer Research, 16,* 372-383.

O'Reilly, C., III, & Chatman, J. (1986). Organizational commitment and psychological attachment: The effects of compliance, identification, and internalization on prosocial behavior. *Journal of Applied Psychology, 71,* 492-499.

Parasuraman, A., Berry, L. L., & Zeithaml, V. A. (1991). Understanding customer expectations of service. *Sloan Management Review, 32*(3), 39-48.

Payne, A., Christopher, M. G., Clark, M. K., & Peck, H. (Eds.). (1995). *Relationship marketing for competitive advantage: Winning and keeping customers.* Oxford: Butterworth-Heinemann.

Peppers, D., & Rogers, M. (1993). *The one to one future: Building relationships one customer at a time.* Garden City, NY: Doubleday.

Peter, J. P., & Olson, J. C. (1995). *Understanding consumer behavior.* Burr Ridge, IL: Irwin.

Peter, J. P., & Tarpey, L. X., Sr. (1975). A comparative analysis of three consumer decision strategies. *Journal of Consumer Research, 9,* 366-380.

Peterson, R. A. (1995). Relationship marketing and the consumer. *Journal of the Academy of Marketing Science, 23,* 278-281.

Pfeffer, J. (1983). Organizational demography. *Research in Organizational Behavior, 5,* 299-357.

Porter, M. E. (1980). *Competitive strategy: Techniques for analyzing industries and competitors.* New York: Free Press.

Punj, G. N., & Staelin, R. (1983). A model of consumer information search behavior for new automobiles. *Journal of Consumer Research, 9,* 366-380.

Reese, S. (1996, November). Toll-free, not hassle-free. *American Demographics,* pp. 24-25.

Reichheld, F. F. (with Teal, T.). (1996). *The loyalty effect: The hidden force behind growth, profits, and lasting value.* Boston: Harvard Business School Press.

Reichheld, F. F., & Sasser, W. E., Jr. (1990). Zero defections: Quality comes to services. *Harvard Business Review, 69*(1), 105-111.

Reid, P. C. (1989). *Well made in America: Lessons from Harley-Davidson on being the best.* New York: McGraw-Hill.

Roberts, J. H., & Lattin, J. M. (1991). Development and testing of a model of consideration set composition. *Journal of Marketing Research, 28,* 429-440.

Rose, S. (1990, Summer). The coming revolution in credit cards. *Journal of Retail Banking, 12,* 17-19.

Rosenberg, L. J., & Czepiel, J. A. (1995). A marketing approach for customer retention. In A. Payne, M. Christopher, M. Clark, & H. Peck (Eds.), *Relationship marketing for competitive advantage.* Oxford: Butterworth-Heinemann.

Sheth, J. N., & Mittal, B. (1996). A framework for managing customer expectations. *Journal of Market-Focused Management, 1,* 137-158.

Sheth, J. N., & Parvatiyar, A. (1995). Relationship marketing in consumer markets: Antecedents and consequences. *Journal of the Academy of Marketing Science, 23,* 255-271.

Srinivasan, N., & Ratchford, B. T. (1991). An empirical test of a model of external search for automobiles. *Journal of Consumer Research, 18,* 233-242.

Surprenant, C. F., & Solomon, M. R. (1987). Predictability and personalization in the service encounter. *Journal of Marketing, 51*(2), 86-96.

Tajfel, H., & Turner, J. (1986). The social identity theory of intergroup behavior. In S. Worchel & W. Austin (Eds.), *Psychology of intergroup relations* (pp. 7-24). Chicago: Nelson-Hall.

Thaler, R. (1985). Mental accounting and consumer choice. *Marketing Science, 4,* 199-214.

Varadarajan, P. R., & Menon, A. (1988). Cause-related marketing: A coalignment of marketing strategy and corporate philanthropy. *Journal of Marketing, 52*(3), 58-74.

Webster, F. E., Jr. (1992). The changing role of marketing in the corporation. *Journal of Marketing, 56*(4), 1-17.

Wiersema, F. (1996). *Customer intimacy.* Santa Monica, CA: Knowledge Exchange.

Winer, R. S. (1985). A price vector model of demand for consumer durables: Preliminary developments. *Marketing Science, 4,* 74-90.

Winer, R. S., Deighton, J., Gupta, S., Johnson, E. J., Mellers, B., Morwitz, V. G., O'Guinn, T., Rangaswamy, A., & Sawyer, A. G. (1996). *Choice in computer-mediated environments* (Working paper). Berkeley: University of California.

13

Membership Customers and Relationship Marketing

THOMAS W. GRUEN

Relationship Marketing in Membership Organizations

Although individuals rarely consider the pervasiveness of memberships in their lives, memberships in organizations serve important roles in the daily lives of almost everyone in developed countries. Membership organizations can provide their members access to desired services and preferential treatment, a sense of belonging and identity, and the ability to meet others with similar interests. Membership organizations are pervasive. In the United States, more than 23,000 national and 64,000 regional associations represent every industry, profession, cause, and interest. Seven out of ten adult Americans belong to at least one association, and one in four belongs to four or more associations (American Society of Association Executives, 1994). In addition, membership programs designed to maintain and enhance customer loyalty—typified by the airlines' frequent-flier programs—have flourished worldwide since the 1980s and show no signs of weakening. Loyalty-enhancing membership programs have become so institutionalized that for some industries these programs are an expected attribute of the service offer. For organizations, these membership programs are powerful tools for developing and maintaining relationships.

BASES FOR AND OBJECTIVES OF THIS CHAPTER

When an individual joins an organization as a member, that person makes a visible statement that he or she wishes to be in a relationship with that organization and the other members of the organization, and a formalized bond or linkage is established at a specific point in time. This visible and specific nature of member-organization relationships makes these relationships a rich area for relationship marketing to study, and it is this same nature that provides the three bases on which this chapter is included in this book. First, although membership organizations offer a potentially rich source for the study of relationship marketing, the research on these organizations to date has been scant and haphazard. A good theoretical model for studying these organizations—even if its primary purpose is to serve as a "straw man" for further theoretical development—needs to be available. Second, in spite of the natural and obvious opportunities that membership organizations have to practice relationship marketing, many organizations fail to utilize the full arsenal of relationship-building tools available to them. Those organizations that do a good job of building relationships have developed these skills through periods of trial and error, rather than through strategies built on sound theory. Thus marketing practitioners in membership organizations are in need of a strong model to guide their work. Third, whereas a strong discussion on relationship marketing in membership organizations will be enriched by studies of relationship marketing in other business areas (such as channel partnerships and other alliances), the opposite is also true. Relationship marketing research in other areas of business can be enriched by a solid theoretical base for relationship marketing to membership customers.

My four basic objectives in this chapter are as follows. First, I present a review of extant research on membership organizations. This is followed by an examination of the similarities and differences in the study of relationship marketing in a membership context as opposed to other contexts. Third, I propose a model that provides a comprehensive set of constructs that are applicable to practice as well as useful for further academic research. Finally, I suggest several avenues for additional research. The thoughts expressed in this chapter arise from my 15 years' experience in working with membership organizations, both as a manager and as a researcher.

DEFINITION AND DESCRIPTION OF MEMBERSHIPS

I restrict the use of the term *membership* in this chapter to a formalized relationship in which the member has made a formal application (which may or may not involve a fee), the member is recognized by the membership organization as a member (whereas others with similar characteristics or interests are categorized as nonmembers), and the organization maintains specific memory of the member (such as in a file—electronic or hard copy—or on a membership list). Although the entity that holds the membership may be an individual, a collection of individuals (e.g., a family), or an organization (e.g., a business that is a member of a trade organization), normally in this chapter I refer to members as individuals. It is worth noting that the definition of a membership used here is somewhat narrower than that used by Lovelock (1983, 1996) in the services marketing literature, where he describes almost any ongoing relationship between an organization and a customer as a "membership relationship."

MEMBERSHIP CATEGORIES

Governance and Management

Two important categories of memberships include (a) member-centric, in which members form and govern the organization in a cooperative sense (e.g., trade associations, country clubs, churches), and (b) organization-centric, in which members "join" to receive services but are not expected to participate in governing the organization (e.g., America Online, museums, Public Broadcasting Service, American Automobile Association, and company-sponsored loyalty membership clubs). In general, this distinction is made through an examination of the formation of the membership. Where the organization is formed prior to the memberships (such as in the case of loyalty membership programs), the membership is organization-centric. Where the organization has been developed and is governed by the members, it is member-centric. However, member-centric organizations often grow and become formalized, so that the distinction between these and organization-centric organizations is not always obvious. For example, the American Marketing Association would be categorized as member-centric, because members vote for directors, the directors are members, and members provide many of the most important services (e.g., put on conferences, write and review papers for journals, and network with each other). However, many members who do not actively participate may see the organization as organization-centric; this perspective could be stated as "I pay my dues and I get services in exchange."

Although the natural pattern of a membership organization that begins as a member-centric organization is to become more organization-centric as the organization becomes formalized, an additional phenomenon—the formation of identifiable member-centric subgroups to accommodate common interests among subsegments of an organization's members—frequently occurs. Continuing with the previous example, the American Marketing Association recently formed special interest groups within the association to meet the evolving needs of an increasingly diverse membership.

When such subgroups form in a membership organization, they play, to a certain extent, a role similar to that of strategic business units in a multibusiness corporation. From a relationship management perspective, the association faces a dual challenge of building and maintaining relationships directly with the individual membership customers, while at the same time managing relationships with the subgroups—a new type of membership customer. Ineffective management of the latter may lead to subgroups' breaking formal ties and forming their own membership organizations, thereby competing with rather than supporting the parent organization.

Other Categorizations

Another point of distinction is the membership that serves as an end in itself, as opposed to a membership that is formed as a means to an end. The latter case includes membership clubs that have been formed by organizations as a means of adding value to and building relationships with their members. Frequent-user programs (offered by many service and retail organizations), product loyalty clubs (e.g., Jenn Aire Grillmasters, Lego Maniacs), and some fan clubs are primary examples of membership organizations that have been formed by sponsoring organizations to enhance relationships with key customers. In addition, many nonprofit organizations, such as museums, zoos, educational institutions, and public broadcasting stations, create membership categories for their donors. These organizations tend to be formed and sustained by either benefactors or government funding (or a combination of the two) and then grow by soliciting donations from other interested parties. Creating membership status that provides recognition or preferential treatment (for example, a university "Partners" program for large donors) is a common means for rewarding these donors and sustaining loyal behavior. The important point here regarding such programs is that they are created as a means of enhancing the fundamental relationship rather than to serve as the fundamental relationship (Gruen & Ferguson, 1994).

Alternatively, many membership organizations are created as ends in themselves. Examples of these include most associations and interest groups. Although the purpose of such membership organizations is to enhance or promote common interests, these organizations also function as means through which individuals can obtain critical information and develop relationships with others who share their interests. Due to this characteristic, these organizations are more self-serving than are membership organizations that function as means of developing relationships.

Regardless of type, all membership organizations must establish and maintain portfolios of products and services (generally termed *benefits*) for their members that the members perceive as having sufficient value for them to retain their membership status. These benefits may be direct and tangible (e.g., a magazine), or they may be indirect and intangible (e.g., lobbying).

From a relationship marketing perspective, two general types of memberships can be derived from the above discussion. The first is membership in a loyalty or frequency marketing program, in which customers are offered membership by the selling organization. The second is the association-style membership, in which individuals with common interests join together. In the following section, I review the literature on both types of memberships, but in the discussion that follows the literature review, I focus mainly on marketing management of the association type of membership.

Review of the Literature on Marketing in Membership Organizations

In spite of the pervasiveness of membership organizations—both as associations and as relationship marketing drivers—few studies of these institutions have appeared in the marketing literature. The research that has been conducted tends to fall into five general areas: services marketing, categorizations, frequency marketing, identification, and benefits received.

In the area of services marketing, a study by Ferguson and Brown (1991) in which they focused directly on membership organizations provides a theoretical examination of the role of exchange in the prepayment of dues for member satisfaction. Most of the other services marketing literature focuses indirectly on memberships. For example, in Lovelock's (1983) classification of services, "membership relationship" is one of the forms of relationships that a service organization can have with its customers. Similarly, in his description of the three levels of bonds that a service organization can have with its customers—financial, social, and structural—Berry (1995) uses examples of membership organizations to describe each of the three levels of relationship marketing.

Although Lovelock (1983) has provided a crude categorization of membership types, there has been little formal categorization of membership types. Using a consumer choice perspective, in earlier work I proposed a categorization scheme in which membership is classified as (a) full-choice, (b) price-driven, (c) earned, or (d) access (Gruen, 1994). A *full-choice* membership is one in which the core good is available with or without the membership. Alternatively, in an *access* membership, the core good is available only through the membership. A *price-driven* membership is one in which there is little reason not to be a member due to the clear economic advantages, and an *earned* membership is restricted to those who have developed the relationship enough to qualify for membership. This scheme has been applied to various relationship management strategies (Gruen & Ferguson, 1994).

In spite of the pervasive nature and ongoing commitment of resources to frequency marketing programs by the transportation and hospitality industries, there has been little direct academic research of the value of frequency/loyalty promotional clubs. Two descriptive studies have been reported that examined the effectiveness of hotel frequent-guest programs. Toh, Rivers, and Withiam (1991) interviewed representatives of 31 hotels and 426 "steady sleepers" (industry lingo for frequent-guest program members) and found that the programs had only a small impact on hotel choice. McCleary and Weaver's (1991) mail survey showed that frequent-guest program members are willing to pay small premiums for a hotel's frequent-guest program, but only a small portion of the respondents indicated that they would switch to a chain that offers a frequent-guest program if their preferred chain dropped its program. Weaver and Oh (1993) conducted another descriptive survey of frequent travelers and again found that frequent-guest programs were of minor importance in determining hotel choice.

The applied business literature regularly reports on frequency- or loyalty-based membership programs. Literature searches through ABI-Inform and Lexis-Nexis databases provide many references to these programs. For example, Butscher (1996) has reported on the development of customer loyalty clubs in Europe. Trade books that focus on relationship marketing also discuss membership programs. Peppers and Rogers, in *The One to One Future* (1993), discuss the value of frequency marketing programs at length. Vavra, in *Aftermarketing* (1992), elaborates extensively on how to create a membership organization.

An area of emerging interest in relationship marketing is the role of social identification and memberships. Bhattacharya, Rao, and Glynn (1995) conducted an empirical study of the role that identification plays in the behavior of the members of a nonprofit museum. In a second study, Bhattacharya (1998) modeled the influence of member identification surrogates and then empirically tested the conceptual framework using a hazard rate model.

There has also been little research on the motivation of individuals to join membership organizations. In previous work, I have proposed five basic rationales for joining: social identification, exchange, desire for information, need for protection, and simplification (Gruen, 1994). Sheth and Parvatiyar (1995), although not directly addressing memberships, propose the desire of consumers to reduce choice. Gwinner, Gremler, and Bitner (1998) conducted an empirical study of consumers' perspectives on the benefits received by establishing relationships with service providers; they conclude that consumers receive "confidence benefits," "social benefits," and/or "special treatment benefits." Peterson (1995) obtained similar results in a preliminary study of benefits received by consumers in membership relationships; he classifies these as "economic," "convenience," and "recognition" benefits.

Commonalities and Unique Features of Relationship Marketing to Membership Customers and Other Customer Types

COMMONALITIES

Relationship marketing in membership organizations has several elements in common with relationship marketing in other customer situations. Because of these similarities, both relationship marketing theory and best practices developed in membership organizations can be used to "cross-fertilize" similar efforts in buyer-seller relationship domains. Five general similarities are outlined below: the asset nature of memberships, the requirement for core service performance, the availability and use of multiple types of bonds, mutual value creation, and the presence of psychological mediating constructs.

Asset nature of memberships. Memberships, as a form of a relationship, are assets, and they need to be managed in a manner similar to other buyer-seller relationships. This requires that measures of the value of relationships be utilized in the assessment of the performance of the asset. The common objective of relationship marketing in membership organizations as well as in other buyer-seller relationships is to build the asset, and this requires relationship marketing managers to place increased focus on customer (or member) retention while placing proportionally less focus on customer acquisition. A second common focus is that within the relationship, the selling organization is interested in the amount of business placed by each customer, which is commonly referred to as *share of customer* or, when individuals are the focus, *share of wallet.*

Requirement for core service performance. Regardless of the type of relationship, membership or otherwise, performance of the core good or service must—at a minimum—meet competitive offerings. Although the building of a relationship can provide a competitive advantage and immunity from competition even in an otherwise parity situation, an underlying premise is that the selling organization delivers fundamental value to the buyer. A membership program designed to create loyalty is based on a core good or service to which the member can be loyal. Similarly, individuals join cooperative associations because the value from the benefits exceeds the cost of acquisition of the benefits outside the associations.

Availability and use of multiple types of bonds. Similar to that proposed in the services marketing literature by Berry and Parasuraman (1991) and by Wilson and Mummalaneni (1986) in the distribution channels literature, the nature of the bond between the buyer and the seller can take various forms. The bonds used to cement membership relationships can take the form of financial or economic bonds, social bonds, or structural bonds.

Mutual value creation. In a member relationship as well as in other forms of relationships, the customer is expected to participate in value creation of the relationship. Even in organization-centric relationships, customers—by virtue of their ongoing exchanges with the organization—often take part in enhancing the design and delivery of services, become competent in accessing the services as they grow more intimate with the organization, and serve as advocates outside the organization (e.g., through word of mouth). The creation of value by the customer is a result of the nature of ongoing or "relational exchange," which is the nature of relationships, regardless of form (Gruen, 1995). The outcome of this mutual value creation is enhanced marketing effectiveness.

Presence of psychological mediating constructs. As with other customer types, research in relationship marketing in membership situations must work with such amorphous psychological mediating constructs as satisfaction, trust, and commitment (Gundlach, Achrol, & Mentzer, 1995; Morgan & Hunt, 1994). The relationship-building activities of organizations have impacts not only on desired behaviors but on psychological states. It is these psychological states that provide the motivations for ongoing exchanges between the relationship partners, and this results in marketing efficiency.

UNIQUE FEATURES

Although it shares much relationship marketing theory and practice with other customer types, relationship marketing with membership organizations is unique in several ways, even when compared with its closest customer type, service customers. Five unique characteristics are outlined below: the specific contractual period of a membership, the amount of coproduction often required by the members, the role of social identification, interdependence among members, and the linkage of the membership to the core service.

Specific contractual period of a membership. The issue of customer retention in relationship marketing is described above as common to all customer types. Some memberships may be open-ended (such as loyalty programs), but many membership relationships are formed for specific periods, normally for a year. Whereas most other relationship types have evolving and ambiguous starting, stopping, and renewal points, in a membership relationship there is a defining moment of becoming a member, a defining moment of membership renewal, and a defining moment of defection. In very few circumstances will a member defect at a point other than the membership renewal period. These defining moments of a membership relationship provide researchers with specific data points for measurement, and research using tools such as event history analysis become appropriate. Similarly, these moments provide managers with easily defined objectives, particularly retention rates.

Amount of coproduction often required by the members. The issue of value creation through coproduction by the member is described above as common to all relationship types. However, in association membership organizations, large portions of value creation may fall on the members. In a membership association, not only is the board of directors made up of members, but often much of the design and implementation of the core offering is accomplished by members. Even though coproduction occurs in other situations, in association-type memberships, coproduction is often the means of creating the fundamental value. As a result, the organization must consider the value the member receives from this extensive co-production effort and—if necessary—specifically reward that effort.

Role of social identification. The psychological constructs of trust, commitment, and satisfaction are described above as common to all customer types. However, an additional mediating psychological component, identification, plays a role in membership relationships. The description of the individual as a *member* naturally provides a piece of the social identification of that individual. Although commitment appears to play a major role in both individual member relationships and business-to-business relationships, the role of identification may be more important than commitment in membership relationships.

Interdependence among members. Another distinctive feature of membership relationships is the role that interdependence among the members plays. An important benefit provided by a membership organization is the ability of members to network with others with similar interests and concerns. The value of informal know-how trading among members (von Hippel, 1988) may be the most important service many members obtain from their affiliation. The importance of these internal relationships has both managerial and theoretical relationship marketing implications.

Linkage of the membership to the core service. In an examination of the nature of loyalty program memberships, an important distinction to be made is that of the membership being used to drive the primary relationship. As such, the process of managing the quality of the membership offering is likely to have an effect on the perceived quality of the core service. When managed well, the membership program can provide an effective means of enhancing the fundamental relationship. Alternatively, if run poorly, it can damage the fundamental relationship.

A Conceptual Model of Relationship Marketing of Membership Organizations

The above discussion outlines several of the important issues that are critical to relationship marketing of membership organizations. The next step is construct a conceptual model that synthesizes these critical issues. Such a model needs to incorporate three categories of constructs:

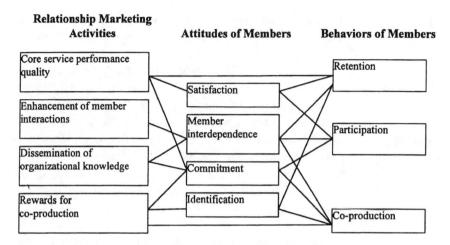

Figure 13.1. Overview of Conceptual Model Constructs

1. *Behaviors of the members that the membership organization is required to manage:* From the marketing manager's perspective, these include retention, share of customer (participation), and coproduction (both positive and negative).

2. *Important psychological attitudes of the members:* These constructs include satisfaction, commitment, identification, and interdependence (with other members). Several relationship marketing studies suggest that attitudinal constructs fully or partially mediate the link between relationship marketing antecedents and behaviors.

3. *Relationship marketing activities:* The model needs to provide a parsimonious yet comprehensive set of marketing activities that the membership organization can use to influence the attitudes and behaviors of members.

An overview of the proposed constructs for each category is shown in Figure 13.1, and these are delineated in the remainder of this section.

BEHAVIORS OF MEMBERS

In relationship marketing, as in all management situations, one needs to begin by understanding what one is managing toward. When a membership is considered as an asset, the management function can be considered as one of enhancing the long-term value of the asset. As shown in Figure

13.1, three key behaviors that indicate the value of the asset are retention (longer), participation/loyalty (more), and coproduction (more).

Retention

In associations, the number of members—regardless of their involvement—serves two basic purposes. The first indicates the extent to which the organization "speaks for" or represents the particular interest. The second is that the members form the base upon which all activities are built. All membership organizations suffer attrition, and to maintain membership they must respond by seeking new members and/or reducing the rate of attrition. By nature, relationship marketing focuses on keeping the members that the organization already has. Although obtaining new members is a critical part of the marketing strategy for any membership organization, keeping the members once they join the organization becomes an important objective.

Membership organizations ordinarily have a structural bond built into their relationships that creates a specific time period when members are most likely to leave: the time of dues renewal. The duration of the membership has a strong positive correlation with the likelihood of renewing membership (Bhattacharya, 1998; Gruen, 1997). Furthermore, the general consensus among those who study the management of individual relationships is that relationships become more profitable over time (Reichheld & Sasser, 1990).

Participation/Loyalty

Although the goal of retention is to keep members, an implicit subgoal is to increase the value of the members that the organization keeps. In general, an organization wants to increase participation in the organization, and where the membership organization competes with other organizations for its "share of the customer," the organization wants to increase loyalty to the organization. For example, an association normally wants its members to attend the annual convention/meeting not only because that is where the organization makes significant profits, but because it is where the member is most likely to experience directly the benefits of belonging to the organization.

Participation can take a negative form. Members can take advantage of the relationship in the form of opportunistic behaviors (Gruen, 1995). Members may, for example, "lend" their membership cards to nonmembers or provide nonmembers access to information normally reserved only for members. Since the inception of frequent-flier programs in 1991, members have often transferred their awarded free miles to others, in spite of airlines' policies restricting such transfers. However, since requirements have been instituted for photo identification of all airline travelers, such transfers have virtually been eliminated. Additionally, any form of prepaid subscription is susceptible to opportunistic behaviors. For example, a person may become a member of an Internet subscription service and then share the access password with friends who—as long as they do not simultaneously utilize the service—obtain the benefit for free.

Coproduction

Members coproduce many of the membership organization's services. Coproduction behaviors are important, as they create value to the organization and to the other members (Sheth & Parvatiyar, 1995). Coproduction behaviors can take many forms, the best known of which is word of mouth. However, in membership organizations, many opportunities for coproduction behavior exist. These include participation in leadership, voting, participation in public relations and/or political influence situations, making suggestions for the improvement of products and/or processes, proactive communication of anticipated problems, being flexible when the organization requires, and participation in research activities of the organization.

Like participation, coproduction can also take a negative form. The most obvious example is negative word of mouth. In addition, a member can make unreasonable demands on the leadership of the organization, sue the organization, or create other disruptions.

MEMBER ATTITUDES

Attitudes can be viewed as mechanisms through which behavioral outcomes are maintained (Wilson & Mummalaneni, 1986). Whereas the behaviors of members are outward indicators of asset value, the future value of the membership asset is stored in the attitudes—beliefs, feelings, and intentions—of the members. Four such attitudes that are crucial to relationship marketers are satisfaction, commitment, member interdependence, and identification.

Satisfaction

As the services marketing literature continually implores, customers (members) must be satisfied with the basic services of the organization or they will likely seek to find solutions to their needs elsewhere (Berry & Parasuraman, 1991; Gruen, 1995). Satisfaction is the member's assessment of the relative value of the basic exchanges in the relationship. Satisfaction is somewhat volatile, and it often depends on a member's most recent exchanges with the organization. Because of this, membership organization managers are continually besieged by members who ask, in effect, "But what have you done for me *lately*?"

The primary linkage between satisfaction and member behaviors is generally considered to be participation/loyalty. Satisfaction is likely to have some impact on retention and coproduction; however, the shorter-term perspective of satisfaction matches most closely with the choice of attendance or purchase of a good offered through the membership. Issues of the fundamental membership decision at dates of renewal are likely to be based on a longer-term perspective and may be constrained by other factors. However, the greatest losses in membership normally take place during members' initial few years with the organization, and decisions not to renew a membership are likely to be influenced by general satisfaction with the benefits received. Thus I offer the following propositions:

- *Proposition 1:* Increased levels of satisfaction will lead to increased levels of participation/loyalty.
- *Proposition 2:* During early years of membership, increased levels of satisfaction will lead to higher retention; however, this effect will diminish as the length of the relationship increases.

Commitment

A second key construct that regularly appears in the relationship marketing literature (e.g., Gundlach et al., 1995; Kim & Frazier, 1997; Morgan & Hunt, 1994) concerns the level of bonding or psychological attachment with the organization, commonly referred to as commitment (Gruen, 1997). The psychological attachment of the individual to the organization tends to be less volatile than satisfaction and explains why an individual maintains a relationship during periods of lower satisfaction (Gruen, 1995).

Commitment has been shown to take multiple forms, with three types commonly called *continuance, affective,* and *normative* (Allen & Meyer, 1990; Gruen, 1997). Continuance commitment is motivated by self-interest based on an individual's assessment of the cost of leaving a relationship, and has been shown to play a significant role in employee relationships. In marketing, continuance commitment has been examined in studies of manufacturer-distributor relationships (Kim & Frazier, 1997). However, the continuance form of commitment does not appear to play a role in individual membership relationships (Gruen, 1997). Affective commitment is based on an individual's overall positive feelings toward a relational partner (Allen & Meyer, 1990), and normative commitment is based on the individual's sense of felt obligation to the membership. In a membership relationship, both affective commitment and normative commitment are likely to play an important role. For example, in an association that represents an individual's profession, a member may feel an obligation to the organization because it works to maintain and enhance the individual's ability to produce a livelihood.

Commitment is frequently linked to increased retention, participation/loyalty, and coproduction (Mathieu & Zajac, 1990). However, two recent studies have raised questions regarding the linkage between commitment and retention (Gruen, 1997; MacKenzie, Podsakoff, & Ahearne, 1998). Whereas previous studies have examined the linkage between commitment and intentions to renew, these two studies used actual renewal/turnover data, and both failed to support the hypothesized relationship. One possible explanation for this surprising finding is that in early years, when most turnover occurs, performance quality (which is strongly linked to satisfaction) rather than commitment is the primary driver of retention (Gruen, 1997). In later years of membership, when the retention rates are higher, other factors aside from commitment are likely to drive the membership decision.

In a recent study of professional association memberships, affective and normative commitment were found to have positive effects on participation/loyalty and coproduction (Gruen, 1997). Thus I make the following proposition:

    ▓ *Proposition 3:* Increased levels of commitment will lead to increased levels of participation/loyalty and coproduction.

Identification

Whereas satisfaction and commitment have been examined in virtually all types of relationship marketing (e.g., business-to-business marketing), the concept of identification is generally reserved for relationship marketing situations involving memberships. Similar to commitment, identification is considered as a type of bond connecting the individual with the organization. The key difference between identification and commitment is that in the former organizational images are linked to members' self-concepts (Bhattacharya et al., 1995). By identifying with an organization, an individual defines her- or himself in terms of the organization (Ashforth & Mael, 1989).

The link between identification and member behavior is straightforward. As individuals identify more closely with the membership organization, positive effects on all three behaviors are anticipated. Bhattacharya et al. (1995) found a positive effect of identification on length of membership as well as on participation. Although they did not find a significant effect on donating behavior (coproduction), Mael and Ashforth (1992) did find alumni donations to be significantly related to levels of identification. Thus I offer the following proposition:

    ▓ *Proposition 4:* Increased levels of identification will lead to increased levels of retention, participation/loyalty, and coproduction.

Member Interdependence

Often a large portion of the value of belonging to a membership organization comes through the relationships that members establish with other members. Although the membership organization seeks to provide value to the individual members, they often obtain value through exchanges among themselves. The value created by members commonly comes through informal "know-how trading" (von Hippel, 1988), which occurs when members get to know each other and develop informal networks.

Relationship interdependence is viewed as the extent of the mutual value of the exchanges between members. This can be characterized by

		Low	High
Quantity of Exchanges	Many	*Broad and shallow* Interdependence: Moderate	*Extensive and deep* Interdependence: High
	Few	*Loners* Interdependence: Low	*Few but intimate* Interdependence: Moderate

Low   High
Quality of Exchanges

Figure 13.2. Characterization and Extent of Member Interdependence

both the breadth of the network and the quality of the exchanges. Figure 13.2 provides an overview of these two characteristics. Increased interdependence with other members in the organization is likely to correspond with higher levels of retention. Those who derive value through the organization—regardless of whether the source is another member or a benefit produced by the organization—will be motivated to remain in the organization. Similarly, members with higher levels of interdependence will also likely have higher levels of participation and coproduction because these are vehicles through which they can obtain the value of interdependence activities. Thus I offer the following proposition:

> ▓ *Proposition 5*: Increases in levels of member interdependence will lead to higher levels of retention, participation, and coproduction.

ACTIVITIES

The role of marketing is to have impacts on both the behaviors and the psychological states delineated above. The behaviors of interest may be affected by transactional marketing methods, such as membership retention campaigns, and by advertising and direct-mail campaigns to encourage participation and coproduction. Relationship marketing activities need to be designed to affect both the psychological states and the behaviors of interest. The advantage of affecting the psychological states is realized through an increasingly self-sustaining marketing process that becomes less dependent on external marketing impetus. This results in greater marketing efficiency, one of the goals of relationship marketing.

Below, I propose four general relationship marketing activities for membership organizations: performance of core services, rewards for contributions by members, enhancement of the relationships among association members, and enhancement of the members' organizational knowledge. Each of these activities can be directly influenced by those charged with managing the membership organization.

Performance of Core Services

Regardless of the context, the foundation for any long-term buyer-seller relationship is the ability of the supplying firm to deliver fundamental value to the customer, without which there is little reason even to consider a relationship. Several studies in services marketing have underscored this fundamental notion (Berry & Parasuraman, 1991). The performance of core services is defined as the extent of the quantity and quality of the planning and delivery of the membership organization's primary services.

Performance of core services is linked most directly with satisfaction (Berry & Parasuraman, 1991). Satisfaction is theorized to occur when expectations of value are met or exceeded. Thus the level of core service performance is likely to have a strong link with satisfaction with the organization. Additionally, the performance of core services is likely to affect member interdependence and commitment. Quality programming will draw members, which provides more opportunities to interact, thus enhancing member interdependence. Members enjoy being associated with a quality organization, and therefore the performance of core services is likely to affect commitment as well. Thus I make the following proposition:

> ▓ *Proposition 6:* Increased levels of core services performance will lead to higher levels of satisfaction, member interdependence, and commitment.

Rewards for Contributions

An important aspect of relationship marketing is the consideration of the mutual value creation of the buying and selling parties. In membership organizations, the value creation by the members can be the primary service delivered by the organization. For example, the National Association of Life Underwriters has more than 100,000 members and a large staff based in Washington, D.C. However, most of the programming is determined and managed by the members through 900 local association

TABLE 13.1 Five Areas of Rewards for Coproduction

Extrinsic rewards
  1a. Recognition within the organization: increased visibility and status by other
      organization members through internal public relations
  1b. Recognition outside the organization: increased visibility by community through
      public relations efforts by the organization
   2. Perks: rewards reserved exclusively for coproducers

Intrinsic rewards
   3. Sense of accomplishment: perception of short-term worthiness of coproduction
      efforts
   4. Perceived power/authority: perception of ability to influence the organization's
      goal setting, planning, and resource allocation
   5. Leaving a legacy: perception of the long-term worthiness of coproduction efforts

---

bodies, with the association staff playing an administrative and facilitating role. In this situation, models of relationship marketing need to account for the rewards members receive for these coproduction efforts. On the other hand, most services at the American Automobile Association are managed and delivered by the association staff, and rewards for contributions by members play a minor (if any) role because the contributions are of minor importance (if they occur at all).

Rewards for contributions are defined as the extent of the value received by the coproducing member for the efforts made on behalf of the membership organization. These rewards can be either intrinsic or extrinsic (a summary of these rewards is presented in Table 13.1). Although the membership organization is able to affect extrinsic rewards most directly, the organization needs to ensure that it has created an environment where intrinsic rewards can be realized.

The extent of rewards for contributions is likely to have a direct effect on members' future coproduction efforts. However, when the rewards are extrinsic in nature, a member's receiving a reward adds a psychological bond between the organization and the member, thus increasing the level of commitment. Additionally, if the motivation of the individual is the receipt of internal rewards for coproduction activities, this would affect the level of identification, as these rewards would assist in defining the individual in terms of the organization. Thus I present the following propositions:

- ▓ *Proposition 7a:* Increased levels of rewards for contributions will lead to higher levels of coproduction.
- ▓ *Proposition 7b:* Increased levels of rewards for contributions will lead to higher levels of commitment and identification.

Member Interaction Enhancement

In addition to the services created and delivered by the organization, member organizations can offer members the motivation, opportunity, and ability to build relationships with other members. Unlike the services that are created and delivered by the organization, this value is not directly supplied or controlled by the organization. Gummesson (1987) describes this situation, in which value is created among buyers who produce services among themselves if the seller provides the right systems, environment, and supporting personnel. He offers the example of a dance hall, where the primary service is not produced until the customers get up and dance with one another.

The use of Web sites greatly enhances membership organizations' ability to have their members interact. As SPSS president and CEO Jack Noonan stated as he announced the establishment of his company's Web site, "In addition to providing the latest information on our company and products, our web site gives SPSS users everywhere an open forum for the exchange of ideas and usage tips that can help them get the most out of data analysis tools" (SPSS, 1995, p. 7).

Because the membership organization does not directly produce member interdependence, it must develop tactics to provide members with the motivation, opportunity, and ability to exchange value with each other. Opportunity and ability are most often accomplished through membership directories, conventions/meetings where members congregate, and electronic meeting centers (e.g., Web sites). To motivate members to share know-how, membership organizations may need to "prime the pump" by providing testimonials of previous value creation among members.

As members increase their interactions with other members, they are likely to define themselves more as part of the organization and thus are likely to have higher levels of identification. In addition, increases in member interactions increase members' level of interdependence with other members of the organization. Thus I offer the following proposition:

▓▓ *Proposition 8:* Increased levels of activities that enhance the motivation,
ability, and/or opportunity of members to interact will have positive effects
on members' interdependence and identification.

Dissemination of Organizational Knowledge

Although there has been considerable emphasis on "getting close to
the customer," in relationship marketing there is a need for the reverse to
occur simultaneously: to get the customer closer to the organization. Individuals in a relationship have a need to feel competent in the relationship, desire to play their roles as required, and desire to know the appropriate scripts for their behavior. In membership situations this need for
customer (or member) socialization is critical because the member has
formally entered a relationship and knows that receiving the optimal
benefit from the membership involves getting to know the ropes. Chao,
O'Leary-Kelly, Wolf, Klein, and Gardner (1994) have identified six dimensions of socialization *content*: organization history, language, politics,
people, organizational goals and values, and performance proficiency. Applying these dimensions to a membership situation, I have identified three
primary content areas and have offered the following definition: Dissemination of organizational knowledge is the extent of the distribution of information to members about the organization's (a) goals and values, (b)
culture, and (c) politics/processes/personnel (Gruen, 1997).

Understanding the organization's goals and values helps to link individual members to the mission of the organization. Cultural knowledge includes the language, history, and traditions of the membership organization. Understanding the organization's politics/processes/personnel refers
to the member's understanding how the work of the organization gets accomplished. Membership organizations need to utilize the tools and tactics of integrated marketing communications to ensure that each of these
three primary content areas is clearly defined and then delivered through
all communications from the organization, regardless of the medium or
source.

As members get closer to the organization through the dissemination
of organizational knowledge, this enhanced level of bonding ought to lead
to an enhanced level of commitment to the organization. Although closeness with the organization does not necessarily provide the motivation for
identification with the organization, it does provide the opportunity to enhance identification. Based on this, I offer the following proposition:

▓ *Proposition 9:* Increased efforts in the dissemination of organizational knowledge will have positive effects on levels of member commitment and identification.

Research Directions

My final task in this chapter is to present a research agenda for those interested in furthering the knowledge of relationship marketing in the domain of membership organizations. I have offered nine propositions in the preceding pages, and each of these needs empirical testing. In addition, I suggest several additional research directions:

▓ *Enhanced classifications of memberships:* As the literature review presented above indicates, there has been only minimal classification of membership types. Enhanced classification of relevant membership types will assist researchers in developing theory as well as help practitioners to develop and manage membership programs.

▓ *Improved understanding of the role of psychological variables:* Amorphous terms such as *commitment, satisfaction, identification, interdependence,* and *trust* have all been described and used in relationship marketing research. However, the built-in ambiguity of these terms can lead to confusing conclusions on the part of both researchers and practitioners. Just what are the differences among identification, commitment, and interdependence? When is one phenomenon more important than another? How do concepts such as identification, commitment, and satisfaction interrelate in membership situations?

▓ *Improved understanding of the roles of variables in models:* Not only is further conceptual development of the psychological variables crucial, but the roles of these variables in models such as the one I have proposed in this chapter are uncertain. The key issue is how much the psychological variables mediate between marketing efforts and behaviors. Morgan and Hunt (1994) conclude that their fully mediating model is superior to a model that contains direct effects, with the psychological variables playing a partial mediating role. However, it is obvious that direct effects between marketing efforts and desired behaviors will occur. For example, I have noted above that increased knowledge of the organization is also likely to provide members with increased ability to take advantage of activities and coproduction opportunities. Thus increased knowledge of the organization plays the role of sales promotion (direct effect on behaviors) in addition to its relationship-building role (where psychological variable mediates the effect between marketing activities and customer behaviors). These differing roles need to be clarified.

■■ *Directionality of effects and reciprocal nature:* In relationship marketing research, the nature of the relationship is that it is built over time and through a series of interactions. As a result, static models and cross-sectional studies do not uncover the richness of the development of relationships. For example, although it is sensible that member interdependence would lead to participation, the opposite effect is also reasonable: The more one participates, the more one is likely to have opportunities to increase member interdependence. Thus research into the dynamic nature of the relationship is essential.

■■ *Definition of other determinants that lead to retention:* Aside from the factors proposed in this chapter, what else affects retention rates? Membership organizations that keep records of defections (nonrenewals) can assist researchers in building retention models. These models can be enriched through the availability of multiple-period retention data (e.g., over 3 or more years) and through the use of such analytic techniques as event history analysis.

■■ *Members-only offers:* When is it better to offer services exclusively to members, and when is it better to offer an option to obtain services through a member or nonmember offer? The impact of the former is that desirable casual business (and future membership business) could be "frozen out" (Lovelock, 1996). The impact of the latter is that the offer of services to nonmembers could lead to devaluation of the membership because it removes an important element of the membership.

■■ *Member selection:* Relationship marketing research has shown that many existing customers are not profitable to serve. When these customers are members, the organization may have less ability to "deselect" them than in a nonmember situation, from both a member relations perspective and an ethical perspective. What are the ethical issues? How can an organization deselect nonprofitable members in an ethical manner?

■■ *Role of the brand name:* What is the role of the brand name associated with a membership organization in terms of identification? For example, British Airways's Executive Club is an important brand name associated with the airline. What is the nature of the equity of this name? Does the club name function as a "brand extension" of the primary offering? Can branding be extended to other services as well, such as legal, accounting, and so on?

These are some research directions that should prove fruitful in this area of relationship marketing. There are likely to be several other research directions as well. One of my purposes in this chapter has been to summarize the current thought and knowledge in this area. A more important purpose has been to stimulate additional thinking and research in the membership relationship domain as well as in the broader arena of relationship marketing.

References

Allen, N. J., & Meyer, J. P. (1990). The measurement and antecedents of affective, continuance and normative commitment to the organization. *Journal of Occupational Psychology, 63,* 1-18.

American Society of Association Executives. (1994). *Associations: A family portrait.* Washington, DC: Author.

Ashforth, B. E., & Mael, F. (1989). Social identity theory and the organization. *Academy of Management Review, 14,* 20-39.

Berry, L. L. (1995). Relationship marketing of services—growing interest, emerging perspectives. *Journal of the Academy of Marketing Science, 23,* 236-245.

Berry, L. L., & Parasuraman, A. (1991). *Marketing services: Competing through quality.* New York: Free Press.

Bhattacharya, C. B., Rao, H., & Glynn, M. A. (1995). Understanding the bond of identification: An investigation of its correlates among art museum members. *Journal of Marketing, 59*(4), 46-57.

Bhattacharya, C. B. (1998). When customers are members: Customer retention in paid membership contexts. *Journal of the Academy of Marketing Science, 26,* 31-44.

Butscher, S. A. (1996, September 9). Welcome to the club: Building customer loyalty. *Marketing News,* p. 9.

Chao, G. T., O'Leary-Kelly, A., Wolf, S., Klein, H., & Gardner, P. (1994). Organizational socialization: Its content and consequences. *Journal of Applied Psychology, 79,* 730-743.

Ferguson, J., & Brown, S. (1991). Relationship marketing and association management. *Journal of Professional Services Marketing, 7*(2), 137-147.

Gruen, T. W. (1994). Exploring consumer behavior with respect to memberships. In J. A. Cote & S. M. Leong (Eds.), *Asia-Pacific advances in consumer research* (Vol. 1). West Hartford, CT: Association for Consumer Research.

Gruen, T. W. (1995). The outcome set of relationship marketing in consumer markets. *International Business Review, 4,* 447-469.

Gruen, T. W. (1997). *Relationship marketing and membership commitment among professional association members.* Unpublished doctoral dissertation, Indiana University.

Gruen, T. W., & Ferguson, J. (1994). Using membership as a marketing tool: Issues and applications. In J. N. Sheth & A. Parvatiyar (Eds.), *Relationship marketing: Theory, methods and applications* (pp. 1-10). Atlanta, GA: Emory University, Center for Relationship Marketing.

Gummesson, E. (1987). The new marketing: Developing long-term interactive relationships. *Long Range Planning, 20*(4), 10-20.

Gundlach, G. T., Achrol, R. S., & Mentzer, J. T. (1995). The structure of commitment in exchange. *Journal of Marketing, 59*(1), 78-92.

Gwinner, K., Gremler, D. D., & Bitner, M. J. (1998). Relational benefits in services industries: The customer's perspective. *Journal of the Academy of Marketing Science, 26,* 101-114.

Kim, K., & Frazier, G. L. (1997). Measurement of distributor commitment in industrial channels of distribution. *Journal of Business Research, 40,* 139-154.

Lovelock, C. (1983). Classifying services to gain strategic marketing insights. *Journal of Marketing, 47*(3), 9-20.

Lovelock, C. (1996). *Services marketing.* Upper Saddle River, NJ: Prentice Hall.

MacKenzie, S. B., Podsakoff, P. M., & Ahearne, M. (1998). Some possible antecedents and consequences of in-role and extra-role salesperson performance. *Journal of Marketing, 62*(3), 87-98.

Mael, F., & Ashforth, B. E. (1992). Alumni and their alma mater: A partial test of the reformulated model of organizational identification. *Journal of Organizational Behavior, 13,* 103-123.

Mathieu, J. E., & Zajac, D. (1990). A review and meta-analysis of antecedents, correlates, and consequences of organizational commitment. *Psychological Bulletin, 108,* 171-194.

McCleary, K. W., & Weaver, P. A. (1991, August). Are frequent guest programs effective? *Cornell Hotel and Restaurant Quarterly,* pp. 39-45.

Morgan, R. M., & Hunt, S. D. (1994). The commitment-trust theory of relationship marketing. *Journal of Marketing, 58*(3), 20-38.

Peppers, D., & Rogers, M. (1993). *The one to one future: Building relationships one customer at a time.* Garden City, NY: Doubleday.

Peterson, R. A. (1995). Relationship marketing and the consumer. *Journal of the Academy of Marketing Science, 23,* 278-281.

Reichheld, F. F., & Sasser, W. E., Jr. (1990). Zero defections: Quality comes to services. *Harvard Business Review, 69*(1), 105-111.

Sheth, J. N., & Parvatiyar, A. (1995). Relationship marketing in consumer markets: Antecedents and consequences. *Journal of the Academy of Marketing Science, 23,* 255-271.

SPSS, Inc. (1995). *Keywords.* Chicago: Author.

Vavra, T. G. (1992). *Aftermarketing: How to keep customers for life through relationship marketing.* Homewood, IL: Business One-Irwin.

von Hippel, E. A. (1988). *The sources of innovation.* New York: Oxford University Press.

Toh, R. S., Rivers, M. J., & Withiam, G. (1991, August). Frequent guest programs: Do they fly? *Cornell Hotel and Restaurant Quarterly,* pp. 46-52.

Weaver, P. A., & Oh, H. C. (1993). Do American business travelers have different hotel service requirements? *International Journal of Hospitality Management, 5*(3), 16-21.

Wilson, D. T., & Mummalaneni, V. (1986). Bonding and commitment in supplier relationships: A preliminary conceptualization. *Industrial Marketing and Purchasing, 1*(3), 44-58.

14

Affinity Partnering

Conceptualization and Issues

VANITHA SWAMINATHAN
SRINIVAS K. REDDY

In the wake of increasing competition, decreasing product differentiation, and declining customer loyalty, marketers are seeking ways of enhancing customer retention and providing added value to consumers. Marketing alliances have emerged as increasingly popular mechanisms for achieving these goals. For example, Fisher-Price and Compaq joined together to introduce a new range of children's video games. The Florida Orange Growers' Association uses the endorsement of the American Cancer Society in its advertising for Florida orange juice. H&R Block teams up with Excedrin and Alka Seltzer in a series of dual-signature ads.

The terms *strategic alliances, comarketing agreements,* and *symbiotic marketing* are used interchangeably in the literature to describe marketing alliances (Adler, 1966; Bucklin & Sengupta, 1993; Varadarajan & Rajaratnam, 1986). Adler (1966) defines symbiotic marketing as cooperation between companies other than those linked by the traditional

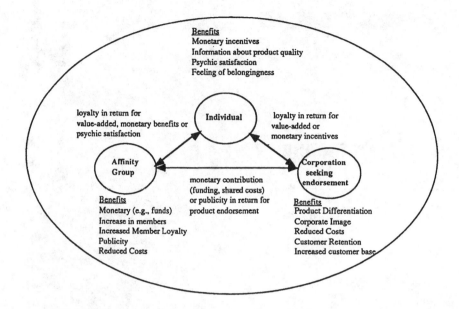

Figure 14.1. A Conceptual Framework of Affinity Partnering
SOURCE: Adapted from Macchiette and Roy (1992).

marketing-intermediary relationship. Varadarajan and Rajaratnam (1986) refine Adler's definition to include only those alliances in which the partners maintain separate identities. Bucklin and Sengupta (1993) describe comarketing alliances as lateral relationships between companies at the same level in the value-added chain. Although a number of studies have focused on strategic alliances in general and marketing alliances in particular, little has been written specifically about alliances in which the primary goal is to leverage the brand name or goodwill of a partner. The literature on strategic alliances typically focuses on the use of alliances for technology transfer, new product development, and market access (Spekman & Sawhney, 1990). There has been little discussion of the use of alliances to gain access to other companies' reputations. However, there is growing recognition that the value of an organization lies primarily in soft assets such as brand name capital, reputation, and customer relationships (Hunt, 1997). In this chapter, we investigate those strategic alliances in which the primary motive for partnering is to gain access to the brand

name capital or reputation of another company. We refer to these strategic alliances as *affinity partnering strategies.*

We define the affinity partnering strategy as a relationship marketing
strategy in which the primary goal of the partnership is to leverage the felt
affinity, goodwill, or brand name strength of a partner so as to enhance relational market behavior in existing or new market segments. Affinity
partnering strategies encompass a range of strategies, including affinity
programs and promotions, cause-related marketing, cobranding, dual-
signature or cooperative advertising, joint sales promotions, and dual
branding.

Affinity partnering strategies may be viewed as a special form of strategic alliance, but there are some factors that differentiate them from other
types of strategic alliances. In affinity partnering strategies, for instance,
unlike in other strategic alliances, explicit effort is made to *inform* the
consumer of the partnership. Also, whereas typical strategic alliances are
dyadic in nature, involving relationships between two partners, the affinity partnering relationship is of a triadic nature, involving the individual,
the affinity partner, and the corporation seeking endorsement (see Figure
14.1). By definition, although there is a demarcation between a corporation seeking endorsement and an affinity group (or corporation), in reality, both partners may seek each other's endorsements.

The overall success of the affinity partnering relationship depends on
the success of each of the three sets of relationships in the triad. Unlike in
a dyadic relationship, in affinity partnering relationships one partner may
direct contributions to one person but receive outcomes from another.
For example, an individual may engage in relational market behavior with
the corporation in return for the benefits provided to the affinity group by
the corporation. The differences between traditional strategic alliances
and affinity partnering relationships stem from the introduction of the individual consumer as an important element in the relationship between
two business entities. Therefore, we can best examine affinity partnering
relationships by utilizing relationship marketing frameworks from both
business-to-business and business-to-consumer contexts.

In this chapter, we review various types of affinity partnering strategies.
We first develop a typology of various forms of affinity partnering relationships and describe the benefits of the different forms to each of the partners. We then present a conceptual model of antecedents and outcomes of
successful affinity partnering relationships. Finally, we identify some topics for future research in this area.

Level of Integration

		Physical	Symbolic
	High	Affinity programs (e.g., Elvis Mastercard)	Affinity promotions
Level of Affinity	Moderate	Cause-related marketing programs	Cause-related marketing promotions
	Nominal	Cobranding Dual branding	Joint sales promotions Cooperative advertising

Figure 14.2. A Typology of Affinity Partnering Strategies
SOURCE: Adapted from Simonin and Ruth (1997) and Macchiette and Roy (1992).

A Framework of Affinity Partnering Relationships

TYPOLOGY

Affinity partnering relationships include a variety of strategies, ranging from affinity programs and promotions to cause-related marketing, co-branding, ingredient branding, cooperative advertising, and dual branding. What are the key differences among various types of affinity partnering relationships? Can they be classified based on the nature of the relationship and the manner in which the agreement is reached? Hunt (1983) suggests that organizing phenomena represent the first step in theory development. Based on an examination of various affinity partnering relationships observable in industry, these phenomena may be classified along two dimensions: the type of affinity partner (corporation or affinity group) and the nature of the partnership (physical integration or symbolic association). The classification framework of affinity partnering strategies based on these two dimensions is outlined in Figure 14.2. We now provide a brief description of these dimensions.

Type of Affinity Partner

The first dimension of this classification framework is the type of affinity partner: corporation or affinity group. Some alliances involve partnerships between two profit-making corporations. In cases where the affinity partner is a corporation, the individual's affinity is based primarily on ownership of product or service. In other partnerships, the partnering involves an affinity group, such as a professional association, personal-interest or hobby group, membership club, background or demographics-based affinity group, or value-centered affinity group (Macchiette & Roy, 1992). Here, the felt affinity derives from characteristics of the individual as opposed to product- or service-based affinity. Macchiette and Roy (1992) suggest that the felt affinity for affinity groups ranges from nominal affinity for product- or service-based groups to true affinity for hobby or interest groups. Some groups involve a combination of product-based affinity and affinity based on the interests of the individual. For instance, the Harley Owners Group comprises individuals who are Harley-Davidson owners but who also share an interest in motorcycling. To the extent that members' affinity for these groups derives from more than ownership of a product or service, these may be classified as personal-interest or hobby-based affinity groups.

Various affinity partnering relationships, such as cobranding, cooperative advertising, dual branding, and joint sales promotions, involve two marketing corporations. Other affinity partnering relationships, such as affinity programs, affinity promotions, and cause-related marketing, involve partnering with affinity groups.

Level of Integration

The second dimension on which affinity partnering strategies may be classified is the level of integration of the partners. Affinity partnering strategies may involve either physical integration of the product (e.g., IBM and Intel) or symbolic association that does not involve physical integration (Simonin & Ruth, 1998). Examples of affinity partnering relationships involving physical integration include cobranding, dual branding, and affinity programs. Affinity partnering strategies involving symbolic association include cooperative advertising, joint sales promotions, and cause-related marketing programs.

The physical integration of brand names in a joint product suggests investment in joint production or retail location facilities. When joint investment is accompanied by contractual safeguards such as relationship continuity, exclusivity, and exit barriers, it may lead to greater relationship longevity. In addition, when products are physically integrated, the product quality is dependent on the performance of both products. This implies a greater degree of interdependence between partners. The potential for negative publicity associated with one product's having spill-over effects on the partner is also likely to be greater when products are physically integrated. For instance, in the context of a partnership be-tween a computer manufacturer and a chip manufacturer, one may envision quality problems with the chip having a negative impact on perceived quality of the computer, because the performance of the computer is inherently linked with quality of the chip.

One of the major differences across various types of affinity partnering relationships resides in the benefits to partners in these relationships. Madhavan, Shah, and Grover (1994) suggest that there are a number of motivations underlying relationships in marketing, and these motivations may be present either uniquely or in combination. We elaborate below on various types of affinity partnering relationships, along with the benefits accruing to the partners in each type of relationship.

BENEFITS OF AFFINITY PARTNERING RELATIONSHIPS

Based on a comprehensive review of the marketing and organizational literature, Madhavan et al. (1994) outline the typical benefits accruing to partners in relationship marketing arrangements primarily in business-to-business settings. These benefits include control over market evolution (i.e., control), knowledge transfer (i.e., learning), improvement of input-output ratios (i.e., efficiency), stability of demand (i.e., stability), and enhancement of prestige through association with "elite" partners (i.e., legitimacy). In addition, in a business-to-consumer setting, Sheth and Parvatiyar (1995) outline various reasons individuals engage in relational market behavior. These include reduction of perceived risk, fulfillment of social aspirations, conformity to social norms, and reduction of negative consequences. The success of an affinity partnering strategy depends upon all partners benefiting from the relationship. Therefore, we evaluate various affinity partnering strategies in terms of benefits to the individual, to the corporation seeking endorsement, and to the affinity group.

Affinity Programs and Promotions

An affinity program is an alliance between a brand name and an affinity group involving physical integration (e.g., an Elvis Mastercard targeted to Elvis Presley fans). An affinity promotion is a promotion targeted to a well-defined affinity group, such as a demographic, professional, interest-based, product-based, service-based, or marketing group. Affinity promotions differ from affinity programs in that the associations are primarily symbolic in nature. One example of affinity promotion is the alliance between the publisher of the magazine *Modern Dad* and the National Center for Fathering, in which free copies of the magazine are distributed to members of the National Center for Fathering (Hochwald, 1997).

The benefits of affinity programs and promotions to the corporation include reduced demand fluctuations (i.e., stability), increased volume requirements (i.e., efficiency), and enhanced brand image (i.e., legitimacy). The benefits to the affinity group include increased contributions from private sources, improved stability of funding, and enhanced publicity. Participation in affinity programs and promotions provides individuals with a greater sense of belonging to the affinity group and creates psychic satisfaction from having benefited the group. Varadarajan and Menon (1988) suggest that affinity programs are popular primarily in markets characterized by little or no product differentiation (e.g., the credit card industry). In these categories, customers may be inclined to patronize a particular brand if its use entails no additional cost but benefits the affinity group.

Cause-Related Marketing

Cause-related marketing includes both promotional activities undertaken by a firm on behalf of a cause (e.g., distribution of promotional materials) and licensing of the name or logo of a nonprofit organization (Andreasen, 1996; Varadarajan & Menon, 1988). From the perspective of the corporation seeking endorsement, cause-related marketing enhances legitimacy. The legitimacy benefit stems from enhanced brand and corporate image, increased brand awareness, and improved national visibility (Cone, 1996; Ross, Patterson, & Stutts, 1992; Varadarajan & Menon, 1988). Cause-related marketing programs also enable companies to gain access to new market segments, promote new uses for product or service offerings, and promote multiple-unit purchases. The primary benefit to the nonprofit organization of alliance with a corporate partner is a stable source of funding (i.e., stability benefit). The benefits to individuals participating in cause-related marketing programs include both nonmonetary (e.g., psychic satisfaction from having contributed to a worthy cause) and monetary benefits (e.g., cents-off promotions).

There are, however, a number of risks associated with involvement in cause-related marketing programs. The risks to the nonprofit organization include increased reliance on a single source of funding, loss of organizational flexibility, and decreased contributions from private sources (Andreasen, 1996). From the perspective of individuals, cause-related marketing may lead to a perception that there is a commercialization of the cause and thus may erode appeal among traditional supporters, create an impression that the cause has "sold out" to the company, and reduce support for lesser-known causes (Varadarajan & Menon, 1988). To the corporation utilizing the cause-related marketing program, the challenges include a possible lack of support for corporate philanthropy within the organization and the difficulties associated with evaluating nonmonetary outcomes of the cause-related marketing activity.

Cobranding

Cobranding involves the combination of two brand names to create a new product (e.g., Healthy Choice with Kellogg breakfast cereal). Cobranding has evolved as an alternative strategy to brand extensions and individual branding strategies, especially in markets characterized by little or no product differentiation. One benefit to the consumer of purchasing a cobranded product is the reduction in perceived risk in terms of product quality on account of the signaling power present in two brand names (Rao & Ruekert, 1994). Therefore, in order for cobranding to succeed, at least one of the partners must possess the ability to signal quality. Another benefit to the consumer is attribute addition or enhancement of existing attributes due to the use of multiple brand names on one product. The benefits to the individual arise primarily from enhancement of the product or service offering. This may be contrasted with affinity programs and cause-related marketing, in which the benefits to the individual do not arise from enhancement of product or service but from the psychic satisfaction of having benefited the cause or the affinity group.

A special case of cobranding is the ingredient branding strategy. In ingredient branding, the final user promotes the use of a particular ingredient in its product (e.g., Diet Coke and Nutrasweet). Norris (1992) suggests that an ingredient branding strategy may be initiated by either the ingredient supplier (e.g., in the case of Nutrasweet and Diet Coke) or the manufacturer (e.g., Beechnut baby foods and Chiquita bananas). The manufacturer may benefit from the quality image (i.e., legitimacy) associated with an ingredient by advertising its use. Other benefits to the manufacturer are increased brand awareness, better access to distribution channels, and the efficiencies involved in cost sharing (Norris, 1992).

Benefits to the ingredient supplier include enhanced legitimacy through alliance with prestigious manufacturers, improved profit margins (i.e., efficiency), and increased stability of demand from customers (i.e., stability). Another benefit to the ingredient supplier is control over competition. For example, in order to differentiate itself from competitors in the chip market, Intel linked itself with brand name manufacturers such as IBM and Compaq. The "Intel Inside" campaign undertaken along with various computer manufacturers allowed Intel to enhance its legitimacy to end users (Arnott, 1994). The leapfrog strategy of marketing to end users also enabled Intel to control competition in the chip market.

Cooperative Advertising

Cooperative advertising may be defined as advertising communication for which costs are shared by more than one party (Young & Greyser, 1983). It is similar to cobranding in that it involves partnering by two profit-making organizations. However, the primary difference between cooperative advertising and cobranding is that the association between the partners is primarily symbolic. The benefits of this strategy to corporations include enhanced image (i.e., legitimacy) and cost efficiencies arising from the sharing of advertising expenditures (Young & Greyser, 1983).

Dual Branding

In dual branding, two or more companies share one retail location. This is increasingly a feature in service industries (e.g., KFC and Taco Bell). Dual branding provides benefits of cost reduction (i.e., efficiency) and increased customer traffic (i.e., stability). The greater variety of dual-branded locations as well as the convenience associated with one-stop shopping make it appealing to consumers. Dual branding typically involves sharing of investments (e.g., real estate) specific to the partnership.

Joint Sales Promotions

Joint sales promotions may be defined as the pooling of promotional resources by two or more companies in order to capitalize on joint promotional opportunities (Varadarajan, 1986). The primary benefit of joint sales promotions to partners is the efficiency that arises from pooling complementary resources and sharing advertising and promotional

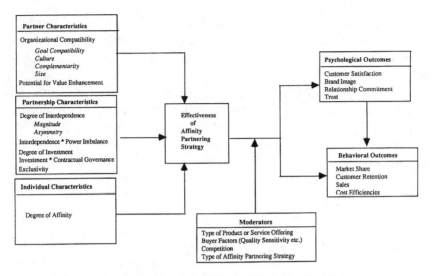

Figure 14.3. A Conceptual Model of Affinity Partnering Strategies

expenditures. Joint sales promotions stimulate demand by providing market access to new segments and by creating new usage occasions. Joint sales promotion is similar to cobranding in that it involves partnering by two profit-making entities. It differs from cobranding in that it does not lead to creation of a new product.

Conceptual Model

We provide here a conceptual model of success of affinity partnering strategies (see Figure 14.3). The dependent variable is the effectiveness of affinity partnering relationships and may be defined in qualitative as well as quantitative terms. A qualitative measure of performance, the perceived effectiveness of the relationship, has been used in a number of studies in the organizational literature (Bucklin & Sengupta, 1993; Ruekert & Walker, 1987; Van de Ven, 1976; Van de Ven & Ferry, 1980). Quantitative measures of alliance effectiveness include the number of new products introduced, sales volume of products, growth in sales, and alliance longevity.

Two streams of literature are relevant in identifying the antecedents of affinity partnering relationships. One of these focuses primarily on the factors influencing alliance effectiveness (Bucklin & Sengupta, 1993; Heide & John, 1990; Varadarajan & Rajaratnam, 1986). The second stream investigates factors influencing consumers' attitudes toward marketing alliances (Park, Youl Jun, & Shocker, 1996; Rao, Qu, & Ruekert, 1997; Simonin & Ruth, 1998). Based on our review of both streams of research, we propose a set of antecedents of effectiveness of affinity partnering relationships. We identify three broad categories of antecedents: partner characteristics, partnership characteristics, and individual characteristics. We also outline below some of the behavioral and psychological outcomes of affinity partnering relationships.

PARTNER CHARACTERISTICS

Partner characteristics are the features of potential partners that firms must evaluate before they enter into affinity partnering relationships. These characteristics may be broadly classified under two headings: compatibility and potential for value enhancement.

Compatibility

We posit that one of the primary characteristics of partners that influences the effectiveness of affinity partnering strategies is compatibility between partners. In the context of strategic alliances, compatibility has been defined as the degree to which exchange parties share norms and values, managerial style, and similar expectations regarding the goal of the alliance (Spekman & Sawhney, 1990). Lorange and Roos (1992) cite the example of Corning Glass, which has been successful in strategic alliances primarily due to four reasons: compatible strategy, comparable contribution, compatible strengths, and no conflicts of interest. Three aspects of compatibility are of particular importance: goal compatibility, culture compatibility, and complementarity.

Goal compatibility. One of the primary features of successful affinity partnering relationships is compatibility of goals. In the context of strategic alliances, some argue that it is important for partners to have similar expectations (Spekman & Sawhney, 1990), whereas others suggest that it is healthy for partners to have different strategic intents (Ohmae, 1989). Lorange and Roos (1992) suggest that both different and complementary goals are typical of many alliances and that the goals have to be sufficiently compatible to lead to cooperation. In the context of affinity partnering strategies, our review of benefits suggests that partners frequently have differing goals in mind when they enter into relationships. However, to the extent that the partners' goals are not incompatible, there is a greater likelihood that the affinity partnering strategy will be successful.

Culture compatibility. In the strategic alliances literature, culture match has been identified as a key variable influencing success (Bucklin & Sengupta, 1993; Harrigan, 1988). Incompatibility in cultures of alliances partners can prove detrimental to alliance formation and performance (Rao & Swaminathan, 1996). In the context of cause-related marketing programs, a number of authors have pointed out the role of corporate cultures in ensuring the success of the strategy. Andreasen (1996) suggests that differences in values and beliefs of partners may lead to negative perceptions of cause-related marketing programs among consumers. Varadarajan and Menon (1988) also suggest that a corporate culture that values ethical and social responsibility in addition to profit and efficiency is essential to ensuring the success of cause-related marketing programs.

Complementarity. A third important aspect of organizational compatibility is complementarity in terms of strengths and weaknesses of partners in an affinity partnering relationship. Complementarity has been identified as an important variable in both the business-to-business literature and the consumer behavior literature (Doz, 1988; Lorange & Roos, 1992; Park et al., 1996; Simonin & Ruth, 1998). The business-to-business literature focuses primarily on complementarity in terms of resource strengths and weaknesses. In the consumer behavior research on brand alliances, complementarity is defined as the "fit" between brands in an alliance. Simonin and Ruth (1998) discuss two aspects of perceived fit: product category fit and brand image fit. Product category fit is the extent to which consumers perceive the two product categories to be compatible. Simonin and Ruth suggest that brand image fit is the overall cohesiveness in the brand images of the partner brands.

Park et al. (1996) suggest that attribute-level complementarity between partners in a composite brand extension setting is important. Attribute-level complementarity is defined as follows: (a) Two brands have a common set of relevant (but not necessarily salient) attributes; (b) two brands differ in attribute salience such that attributes not salient to one are salient to the other; and (c) the brand for which the attribute is salient has a higher performance rating on that attribute than the brand for which the attribute is not salient.

Other important types of complementarity are use complementarity and user-group complementarity (Varadarajan, 1986). Use complementarity involves similarity in usage occasions (e.g., toothpaste and toothbrush). User-group complementarity is important in those instances where affinity partnering is undertaken with the objective of gaining access to new market segments (e.g., dual branding, joint sales promotions).

A number of examples suggest the importance of complementarity. In the cooperative advertising context, the partnership between H&R Block and Excedrin has been viewed as an alliance with potential negative consequences due to the association of H&R Block with migraine headaches ("H&R Block," 1991). Lack of attribute-level complementarity is cited as one of the primary reasons for failure of the alliance between Fisher-Price and McDonald's (Rao & Ruekert, 1994).

Thus complementarity in affinity partnering may be conceptualized in multiple ways. An interesting avenue for future research will be the investigation of various dimensions of complementarity in order to understand the roles these dimensions play in enhancing the effectiveness of affinity partnering strategies.

Size. The role of similarity in partner size has been discussed in both the strategic alliances literature and the consumer behavior literature. Size difference between partners has been identified as a key variable explaining the instability of collaborations in the context of strategic alliances (Doz, 1988; Harrigan, 1988). In the consumer behavior context, size manifests itself in a variety of brand-related factors, such as familiarity, reputation, and image (Simonin & Ruth, 1994). Rao and Ruekert (1994) suggest that an alliance between two equally reputable brands can be seen as one form of alliance, and an alliance between an established brand and a new brand can be seen as another. They also suggest that tensions arise when the less-reputed brand gains through association with the better-known brand and it is not in the interest of the better-known brand to let the lesser-known brand develop an identity of its own. Simonin and Ruth (1998) have found that brand familiarity is also significantly related to the amount of contribution to the alliance. Their findings indicate that two equally familiar brands contribute equally to the alliance. Based on the above discussion, we posit that asymmetries in brand familiarity and reputation influence both effectiveness of the affinity partnering strategy and the relative contributions of partners to effectiveness.

Potential for Value Enhancement

We have suggested above that complementarity may be a necessary condition for success of an affinity partnering strategy. However, complementarity alone may be insufficient to ensure success. Another variable that is frequently cited as an important characteristic is the potential value enhancement that the partner can provide (Rao & Ruekert, 1994). Complementarity is insufficient if the perceived value enhancement from a consumers' perspective is minimal. The perception of enhanced value is, in turn, a function of a number of factors, including buyers' quality sensitivity, buyers' ability to evaluate quality, degree of product differentiation in markets, product type (e.g., search versus experience good), and competitive offerings (Rao & Ruekert, 1994; Rao et al., 1997).

A number of alliances fail when the partners do not significantly enhance the perceived value of the product or service. One example of this is the Ford Citibank card, which offered rebates on purchases of Ford vehicles to cardholders. Urbanski (1997) reports that the card did little to increase balances for the bank. Most cardholders either used it as a charge card or simply transferred balances from other credit cards. Ford, in turn, found that the credit card did little to enhance loyalty. A careful evaluation of the partners' potential for value enhancement over and above the nearest alternative may have enabled both Ford and Citibank to reduce the risks of failure of this partnership.

The enhanced value provided by the partner must also be evaluated in terms of costs of the affinity partnering strategy. The costs of affinity partnering programs include royalty fees, licensing fees, advertising and communication costs, and the opportunity costs associated with allying with a particular partner. The costs of affinity partnering may also include those arising from risks of product failure and potential for negative publicity. To the extent that the affinity partnering strategy provides benefits that outweigh the costs, it may be preferable for a firm to enter into a brand alliance than to "make" the enhanced reputation or improved product offering within the organization.

PARTNERSHIP CHARACTERISTICS

We have outlined above various partner characteristics that impinge on the effectiveness of affinity partnering strategies. Organizations can evaluate these characteristics prior to initiating affinity partnering programs. There are, however, certain characteristics of partnerships that may influence their perceived effectiveness. Three characteristics of the partnership are important to the success of affinity partnering relationships: degree of interdependence, amount of investment, and exclusivity. We discuss each of these and its relationship to the effectiveness of the affinity partnering relationship below.

Interdependence

One of the primary factors influencing the effectiveness of affinity partnering strategies is the interdependence among partners in the relationship. Interdependence, a concept that has its origins in resource dependence theory, "exists whenever one actor does not control all of the conditions necessary for the achievement of an action or for obtaining the outcome desired from the action" (Pfeffer & Salancik, 1978, p. 40). For example, the affinity partnering between IBM and Intel, in comparison with an alliance between IBM and a manufacturer of computer monitors, entails a greater degree of interdependence because the chip is an important ingredient in computers. There are certain features of the manner in which agreement is reached among the partners that influence the degree of interdependence. For example, exit barriers and exclusivity constraints imposed on partners may serve to increase the degree of interdependence. Gundlach and Cadotte (1994) suggest that two aspects of interdependence are important: magnitude of interdependence and asymmetry of interdependence.

Magnitude of interdependence. Magnitude of interdependence is defined as the sum of dependence in an exchange. The magnitude of interdependence characterizes the amount of attention given to the relationship by each of the partners (Mohr & Nevin, 1990). Based on Pfeffer and Salancik's (1978) work, we may characterize the magnitude of interdependence as a function of two factors: the criticality of the resource and the concentration of control over a resource. To the extent that the partners in an affinity partnering relationship contribute critical resources and there are few alternative sources for these resources, there is likely to be a greater magnitude of interdependence. A greater magnitude of interdependence may create the need for contractual governance and bilateral expectations of continuity. This, in turn, will lead to greater effectiveness of the affinity partnering relationship.

This notion of interdependence is also echoed in the literature on brand alliances. Simonin and Ruth (1994) suggest that consumers can assess the degree to which one product is necessary to an alliance. As consumers' perceptions of "necessariness" increase, a type of halo effect is created. Consumers are more likely to believe that the quality or performance of the brand alliance is more closely linked to each of the brands in the affinity partnering relationship. Therefore, it is likely that there is a closer correspondence between independent brand evaluations and evaluations of the brand alliance where the brands are perceived to be more interdependent than when they are perceived to be less interdependent.

Asymmetry in interdependence. In the context of affinity partnering relationships, unlike in typical strategic alliances, the problem of asymmetric dependence is compounded by sequential patterns of interdependence. For example, when an individual makes a purchase from a corporation and is rewarded through contributions to the affinity group of which he or she is a part, it is likely that the individual may seriously underestimate the role played by the corporation in the affinity partnering relationship. Thibaut and Kelley (1959), in the context of the psychology of groups, suggest that when A gives to B but receives from C, A does not have firsthand knowledge of the kinds of contributions B makes to C. This leads to A's having inaccurate perceptions of B's contributions, and this may lead to greater perceptions of asymmetry in resource interdependence.

Another issue relating to resource interdependence in a triad is the need for balance in the amount of dependence across all three sets of relationships. For example, Thibaut and Kelley (1959) note that mutually attracted pairs within a triad create a problem for measurement of the cohesiveness of the group (how highly interdependent the members are). A triad is not very cohesive if most of its interdependence derives from a relationship between two of its members. Dependence in a triad, therefore, means each partner's dependence upon both the other partners—upon their joint actions of belonging to the triad (Thibaut & Kelley, 1959).

The challenges of managing asymmetric resource interdependencies are likely to be greater in an affinity partnering relationship than in a typical strategic alliance. Asymmetries between partners in an affinity partnering relationship may create power imbalances that reduce the effectiveness of the affinity partnering strategy.

Investment

The degree of investment in a relationship influences the perceived effectiveness of that relationship. A greater degree of investment of assets, time, and managerial resources suggests a greater commitment to the relationship. Investment in assets may, however, lead to opportunistic behavior and power imbalances. Power imbalances, in turn, may be negatively related to effectiveness of affinity partnering strategies.

When investment in a specific relationship is high, firms will also undertake measures to safeguard investments. One such safeguard is contractual governance (Bucklin & Sengupta, 1993). Another safeguard to prevent opportunism is the establishment of more durable, long-lasting relationships (Heide & John, 1990). Such durability, according to Heide and John (1990), can arise from explicit contractual terms or from a bilateral expectation of continuity. We posit that when investment in a relationship is accompanied by contractual safeguards and expectations of continuity, it is likely to lead to enhanced effectiveness of the affinity partnering strategy.

Exclusivity

The role of exclusivity has been highlighted in both the literature on strategic alliances and the consumer behavior literature. The notion of partner exclusivity concerns whether partners are engaged in relationships to the exclusion of other relationships. An exclusive agreement with a business partner will enable partners in an affinity partnering strategy to increase commitment to the relationship and will also reduce power imbalances (Bucklin & Sengupta, 1993). From a consumers' standpoint, an exclusive relationship with one partner may enhance the relationship's worth if the alliance is viewed as unique or novel (Simonin & Ruth, 1994).

However, it may also be argued that multiple affinity partnering relationships may be desirable because they increase brand presence. Intel, American Express, and Visa are examples of companies that have multiple affinity partnering relationships. In the case of Intel, the use of multiple alliances had two consequences. First, the widespread use of the Intel logo eroded the ability of the chip's manufacturers to charge a premium for its use (Arnott, 1994). However, Intel's presence in a computer became a signal of quality, so much so that it became essential for every computer manufacturer to use the Intel name to preserve parity with other manufacturers. The strategy of allying with multiple manufacturers also allowed Intel to establish its brand name presence among end users. One of the disadvantages of multiple alliances is the potential for brand dilution due to the variety of partners a brand is seen to be allied with. The relative merits and demerits of affinity partnering relationships with multiple partners versus a single "exclusive" arrangement depend on the context and the nature of competition; this represents an interesting avenue for future research.

INDIVIDUAL CHARACTERISTICS

We have summarized above the influences of partner characteristics and partnership characteristics on the perceived effectiveness of affinity partnering relationships. We have also suggested that the key difference between strategic alliances and affinity partnering relationships is the introduction of the individual as one partner in a triadic relationship among the individual and two corporations. Therefore, characteristics of the individual must be incorporated into the analysis of factors influencing the success of affinity partnering strategies. The degree of affinity felt by the individual toward the affinity group (or corporation providing endorsement) is an important individual characteristic influencing effectiveness.

Degree of Affinity

An individual's degree of affinity is his or her level of cohesiveness, social bonding, identification, and conformity to the norms and standards of a particular reference group (Macchiette & Roy, 1992). In affinity partnering programs, the affinity group or corporation provides guidance to individuals by endorsing a product or service. When a group or corporation endorses a product or service, a consumer with a greater degree of affinity toward the group will utilize the endorsement as a cue that the product is of acceptable quality. According to reference group theory, individuals are motivated to conform to group standards by their need to be socially integrated. The desire to be socially integrated has also been noted as one of the key motivations for engaging in relational market behavior (Sheth & Parvatiyar, 1995).

A number of factors have been identified that may enhance individuals' degree of affinity, including homogeneity of group members, level of structure of the group, degree of member interaction, type of affinity group, and reward factors. Some of these factors have been identified in the literature on groups (Gruen & Ferguson, 1994; Jewell & Reitz, 1981).

Homogeneity of group members. One of the primary factors influencing affinity toward a group is the homogeneity of group members. Individuals in groups in which the members share similar backgrounds and attitudes have greater affinity than do members of more heterogeneous groups.

Level of structure. Another important factor influencing affinity is the level of structure of the group, which involves the patterns of status, roles, authority, and communication that provide guidelines for group interaction (Jewell & Reitz, 1981). In some groups, the structure is highly formalized and relatively rigid. In others, it is quite informal and loose. A greater degree of structure is known to enhance group cohesiveness and member interaction. This, in turn, enhances the members' level of affinity toward the group.

Degree of member interaction. Another key factor for group affinity is the degree of member interaction. Both frequency and duration of interaction are potentially important variables. According to Jewell and Reitz (1981), frequency of contact, often an indicator of investment in a social relationship, does not always imply a high level of involvement in the relationship. Duration of contact is likely to be a better indicator of involvement, because it is a measure of the amount of time (a limited resource) that individuals spend with each other. Hence we posit that the degree of member interaction, in terms of both frequency and duration, will play an important role in enhancing the degree of affinity.

Type of affinity group. The type of affinity group also potentially has an important role to play in the degree of affinity. Macchiette and Roy (1992) identify various kinds of affinity, including professionally based affinity, socially based affinity (e.g., product- or service-centered affinity, customer-driven affinity, celebrity-centered affinity, activity- or interest-centered affinity), value-centered affinity, and demographic-based affinity. The degree of affinity is likely to vary based on the type of affinity group. For example, it is likely that a product- or service-based affinity group will have lower levels of affinity than will an interest-based affinity group. Macchiette and Roy (1992) suggest that professional and alumni associations may represent a higher degree of affinity than cause-related affinity groups. They suggest that cause-related affinity is in turn associated with a higher degree of affinity than is marketing-generated affinity. Therefore we suggest that the type of affinity group may influence the degree of affinity toward the group as a whole.

Reward factors. Rewards for coproduction and citizenship behaviors, or extrarole behaviors, are likely to enhance the degree of affinity. Coproduction involves the consumer's performance of some of the marketer's functions (Sheth & Parvatiyar, 1995). Citizenship behavior, or extrarole behavior, has been defined as helpful, constructive gestures exhibited by members that are valued or appreciated by the organization but are not related to requirements of the individual's role (Gruen, 1995). Rewards for citizenship behavior through appreciation or recognition are likely to enhance the individual's felt affinity toward the group.

Based on the above review of a number of factors that may influence the degree of affinity felt by an individual toward the affinity group, we posit that the degree of affinity felt by an individual toward the affinity group or corporation influences the effectiveness of the affinity partnering strategy.

OUTCOMES OF AFFINITY
PARTNERING RELATIONSHIPS

There is a long tradition in relationship marketing of examining both psychological and behavioral outcomes of business-to-business and business-to-consumer relationships (Gruen, 1995). Psychological outcomes typically include commitment, trust, and satisfaction, whereas behavioral outcomes include customer retention, allocated purchase share, opportunistic behavior, citizenship behavior, sales, and market share (Gruen, 1995).

Some of the key psychological outcome variables that may result from affinity partnering relationships are improved trust, enhanced relationship commitment of the consumer to the corporation, improved customer satisfaction, and better brand image. Some of the key behavioral outcomes are increased sales and market share, increased cost efficiencies, and enhanced customer loyalty. There are, however, a number of difficulties in relating success of marketing alliances directly to both behavioral and psychological outcomes. One issue for the measurement of outcomes is the cumulative effect of affinity partnering programs over time. Another issue is the interaction among various marketing mix variables, which poses a challenge to those attempting to isolate the effect of one element in the entire mix. A third issue is the assessment of outcomes on behalf of each member in the triad. Different members may gain differentially from the affinity partnering relationship. Figure 14.3 illustrates various outcomes of affinity partnering strategies. As the figure shows, based on past research, we have posited that psychological outcomes are antecedents to behavioral outcomes (Gruen, 1995). Because our focus is on managerial implications, the figure describes only outcomes to the corporation(s) involved in affinity partnering relationships.

The outcomes of various relationships may differ based on the type of affinity partnering strategy. For instance, the primary outcomes from cause-related marketing programs for the corporation are improved relationship trust and commitment, enhanced brand image, and increased customer loyalty. In the context of affinity programs and promotions, the outcomes for the corporation are primarily increased commitment and trust, customer loyalty, and market share. The key outcomes of cobranding are increased customer satisfaction, improved relationship commitment, enhanced customer loyalty, and increased market share. Joint sales promotions are aimed at increasing customer satisfaction and market share. Cooperative advertising and dual branding aim to create cost efficiencies as well as to improve brand image.

MODERATORS

We posit that the type of affinity partnering strategy, type of product or service offering, nature of the competition, and type of customer are important moderators of the role of the effectiveness of affinity partnering strategies in influencing the outcome variables. The extent to which these elements moderate the impact of perceived effectiveness on both behavioral and psychological outcomes needs to be investigated further. (The role of these moderating variables is graphically depicted in Figure 14.3.)

Summary and Discussion

We have discussed affinity partnering as a form of strategic alliance involving three partners: the individual, the affinity group, and the corporation seeking endorsement. One aspect that differentiates affinity partnering from other types of strategic alliances is the introduction of the consumer as an important partner in the relationship. Another unique feature is that an affinity partnering relationship is a triadic relationship among the individual, the corporation seeking endorsement, and the affinity group; this creates a unique set of challenges with respect to managing dependencies across all three sets of relationships in the triad.

One issue arising from the manner in which the affinity partnering relationship is organized is the sequential pattern of interdependence. The corporation may contribute to the affinity group but receive its benefits from the individual. This sequential nature of interdependence poses two challenges: (a) how to monitor the contributions made by each partner and (b) how to balance asymmetries across all three sets of relationships. How do the sequential patterns of interdependence influence power imbalances in affinity partnering relationships? What mechanisms serve to counterbalance these imbalances? How do partners evaluate each other's contributions to the relationship? What are the implications of sequential patterns of interdependence for communication patterns in triadic relationships? These are some issues that need to be investigated; research in these areas will serve to enhance our understanding of affinity partnering relationships and the factors influencing their effectiveness.

Another issue that should be investigated is the role of physical integration in influencing relationships among the partners as well as the consumers' perceptions of the alliance. It is likely that relationships involving physical integration entail a greater degree of investment in joint production. This may imply a greater degree of relationship continuity and a greater need for contractual safeguards than is the case in partnering involving only symbolic association. In addition, consumer perceptions of relationships may vary based on the degree of physical integration involved. It is possible that consumers may evaluate brands that are physically integrated more critically. In relationships involving physical integration, there are likely to be greater spillover effects of the partnering on individual brands. These spillover effects may influence brand image, associations, and perceived quality. The impact of physical integration on partner brands represents an interesting avenue for future research.

A third area for future research is exploration of the meaning of complementarity in affinity partnering relationships. Complementarity may be viewed in terms of competence match among the partners. It may also be viewed in a number of different ways from a consumers' perspective (e.g., use complementarity, user complementarity, image complementarity). An interesting topic for further research would be an investigation of the various dimensions of complementarity and the influence of each of these dimensions on the effectiveness of affinity partnering relationships.

A fourth area for future research is the role of moderators such as the nature of competition and type of product category: How do these variables moderate the impacts of effective affinity partnering strategies on key outcome variables? A summary of our conceptual model of successful affinity partnering relationships is provided in Figure 14.3. Future research should focus on testing the relationships outlined in the conceptual model, and thereby shed light on key factors influencing the success of affinity partnering strategies.

References

Adler, L. (1966). Symbiotic marketing. *Harvard Business Review, 45*(2), 59-71.

Andreasen, A. R. (1996). Profits for nonprofits: Find a corporate partner. *Harvard Business Review, 74*(6), 47-59.

Arnott, N. (1994). Inside Intel's marketing coup. *Sales and Marketing Management, 146*(2), 78.

Bucklin, L. P., & Sengupta, S. (1993). Organizing successful co-marketing alliances. *Journal of Marketing, 57*(2), 32-46.

Cone, C. L. (1996). Doing well by doing good. *Association Management, 18*(4), 103-108.

Doz, Y. L. (1988). Technology partnerships between larger and smaller firms: Some critical issues. In F. J. Contractor & P. Lorange (Eds.), *Cooperative strategies in international business* (pp. 317-338). Lexington, MA: Lexington.

Gruen, T. W. (1995). The outcome set of relationship marketing in consumer markets. *International Business Review, 4*, 447-469.

Gruen, T. W., & Ferguson, J. (1994). Using membership as a marketing tool: Issues and applications. In J. N. Sheth & A. Parvatiyar (Eds.), *Relationship marketing: Theory, methods and applications* (pp. 1-10). Atlanta, GA: Emory University, Center for Relationship Marketing.

Gundlach, G. T., & Cadotte, E. R. (1994). Exchange interdependence and interfirm interaction: Research in a simulated channel setting. *Journal of Marketing Research, 31*, 516-532.

H&R Block, Excedrin discover joint promotions can be painless. (1991, February 28). *Wall Street Journal.*

Harrigan, K. R. (1988). Strategic alliances and partner asymmetries. *Management International Review, 28*, 53-72.

Heide, J. B., & John, G. (1990). Alliances in industrial purchasing: The determinants of joint action in buyer-supplier relationships. *Journal of Marketing Research, 27,* 24-36.

Hochwald, L. (1997). Affinity for dads. *Magazine for Magazine Management, 26*(2), 54.

Hunt, S. D. (1983). *Marketing theory: The philosophy of marketing science.* Homewood, IL: Richard D. Irwin.

Hunt, S. D. (1997). Competing through relationships: Grounding relationship marketing in resource advantage theory. *Journal of Marketing Management, 13,* 431-445.

Jewell, L. N., & Reitz, H. J. (1981). *Group effectiveness in organizations.* Glenview, IL: Scott, Foresman.

Lorange P., & Roos, J. (1992). *Strategic alliances: Formation, implementation and evolution.* Cambridge, MA: Blackwell.

Macchiette, B., & Roy, A. (1992). Affinity marketing: What is it and how does it work? *Journal of Services Marketing, 6*(3), 47-57.

Madhavan, R., Shah, R. H., & Grover, R. (1994). Motivations for and theoretical foundations of relationship marketing. In *Proceedings of the 1994 AMA Winter Educators' Conference* (pp. 183-190). Chicago: American Marketing Association.

Mohr, J., & Nevin, J. R. (1990). Communication strategies in marketing channels: A theoretical perspective. *Journal of Marketing, 54*(4), 36-51.

Norris, D. G. (1992, Summer). Ingredient branding: A strategy option with multiple beneficiaries. *Journal of Consumer Marketing, 9,* 19-31.

Ohmae, K. (1989). The global logic of strategic alliances. *Harvard Business Review, 67*(4), 143-154.

Park, C. W., Youl Jun, S., & Shocker, A. D. (1996). Composite branding alliances: An investigation of extension and feedback effects. *Journal of Marketing Research, 33,* 453-466.

Pfeffer, J., & Salancik, G. R. (1978). *The external control of organizations: A resource dependence perspective.* New York: Harper & Row.

Rao, A. R., Qu, L., & Ruekert, R. W. (1997). *Brand alliances as information about unobservable product quality* (Working paper). Minneapolis: University of Minnesota.

Rao, A. R., & Ruekert, R. W. (1994). Brand alliances as signals of product quality. *Sloan Management Review, 36*(1), 87-97.

Rao, B. P., & Swaminathan, V. (1996). *Uneasy alliances: Cultural incompatibility or culture shock?* Paper presented at the 13th Annual Association of Management Conference, Vancouver.

Ross, J. K., Patterson, L. T., & Stutts, M. A. (1992). Consumer perceptions of organizations that use cause-related marketing. *Journal of the Academy of Marketing Science, 20,* 93-97.

Ruekert, R. W., & Walker, O. C., Jr. (1987). Marketing's interaction with other functional units: A conceptual framework and empirical evidence. *Journal of Marketing, 51*(1), 1-19.

Sheth, J. N., & Parvatiyar, A. (1995). Relationship marketing in consumer markets: Antecedents and consequences. *Journal of the Academy of Marketing Science, 23,* 255-271.

Simonin, B. L., & Ruth, J. A. (1994). Towards a better understanding of strategic alliances in marketing through observation of symbiotic relationships in nature. In J. N. Sheth & A. Parvatiyar (Eds.), *Relationship marketing: Theory, methods and applications.* Atlanta, GA: Emory University, Center for Relationship Marketing.

Simonin, B. L., & Ruth, J. A. (1998). Is a company known by the company it keeps? Assessing the spillover effects of brand alliances on consumer brand attitudes. *Journal of Marketing Research, 35,* 30-42.

Spekman, R. E., & Sawhney, K. (1990). *Toward a conceptual understanding of the antecedents of strategic alliances* (Rep. No. 90-114). Cambridge, MA: Marketing Science Institute.

Thibaut, J. W., & Kelley, H. H. (1959). *The social psychology of groups*. New York: John Wiley.

Urbanski, A. (1997). Learning from an auto accident. *Promo, 10*(12), 45-46.

Van de Ven, A. H. (1976). On the nature, formation, and maintenance of relations among organizations. *Academy of Management Review, 1,* 24-36.

Van de Ven, A. H., & Ferry, D. L. (1980). *Measuring and assessing organizations*. New York: John Wiley.

Varadarajan, P. R. (1986). Horizontal cooperative sales promotion: A framework for classification and additional perspective. *Journal of Marketing, 50*(2), 61-73.

Varadarajan, P. R., & Menon, A. (1988). Cause-related marketing: A coalignment of marketing strategy and corporate philanthropy. *Journal of Marketing, 52*(3), 58-74.

Varadarajan, P. R., & Rajaratnam, D. (1986). Symbiotic marketing revisited. *Journal of Marketing, 50*(1), 7-17.

Young, R. F., & Greyser, S. A. (1983). *Managing cooperative advertising: A strategic approach*. Lexington, MA: Lexington.

15

Relationship Marketing and Key Account Management

JOSEPH P. CANNON
NARAKESARI NARAYANDAS

Recent trends toward relationship marketing practices have been most pronounced in the business-to-business marketing arena. Over the past decade and a half, more than ever before, sellers have found that they have to reexamine their approaches to managing their largest and most important customers (Cohen, 1996). In most business markets, mergers and acquisitions have led to consolidation of firms that are very large and account for a major share of their sales volume (Shapiro & Moriarty, 1982). These firms not only possess enormous purchasing power by virtue of their size, they also have sophisticated information systems that enable them to monitor and manage seller performance more effectively (Cespedes, 1995; Shapiro & Moriarty, 1982). Using their newfound skills and power, firms are focused on improving their own competitiveness. They are looking for ways in which they can leverage their suppliers' capabilities to enhance the value that they deliver to their own customers. They are moving away from maintaining adversarial relationships with multiple suppliers for the same products and toward establishing close, long-term relationships with fewer suppliers (Spekman, 1988). In exchange for long-term volume commitments, these customers now expect the selected suppliers to provide greater coordination and collaboration in the form of specialized support and value-added services at lower prices.

These customer demands have forced suppliers to reevaluate traditional customer relationship management strategies. Typically, sellers have developed key account management (KAM)—sometimes called national account management or major account management—programs. The guiding principle is the 80/20 rule: When 20% of a firm's customers provide 80% of its business, that 20% merits special attention. At its heart, the concept is simple: Dedicate a sales force to the task of maintaining long-term profitable relationships with the top 20% of customers that account for 80% of the seller's total sales.

Although the concept of key account management is simple, sellers are finding out that designing, monitoring, and managing KAM programs are not easy tasks (Cespedes, Doyle, & Freedman, 1989). Overall, KAM involves a mind-set and an approach that differ from those associated with traditional sales management. KAM relationships involve significant costs (investments) and (often longer-term) benefits to the seller. In contrast to traditional selling approaches, effective KAM requires a seller to make extensive and expensive systems and processes. At the other end, the rewards to the seller from KAM go beyond the profitability of any single transaction in the relationship. Measuring the benefits derived from KAM relationships is not a trivial task. Without a clear understanding of what they need to put into KAM relationships and what they can get from these relationships, sellers will find it difficult to decide which customers to develop as key accounts and what services to provide each key account.

Our primary purposes in this chapter are to review these issues in greater detail, along with the extant literature relevant to each, and to point out opportunities for future research in the area of key account management. We view key account management as the embodiment and implementation of the relationship marketing paradigm for large business customers. Before we address these issues, we begin by more clearly contrasting traditional sales approaches with KAM. Subsequently, we identify some trends that we expect will play important roles in the evolution of KAM programs. We conclude by discussing some methodological challenges to empirical research in this area.

TABLE 15.1 Traditional and Key Account Selling Paradigms

	Traditional Selling Paradigm	*Key Account Selling Paradigm*
Sales volume	varies	large volume of product purchased by the customer, often across multiple divisions of seller
What is being bought/sold?	core product/service	the core + augmented product
Time horizon	relatively short-term	long-term
Benefits to sold customer	lower prices and higher quality	lower total costs, broader set of benefits
Sales force objectives	maximize revenue satisfied customers	obtain position of preferred supplier lower customer firm's total costs enhance learning in the relationship reduce uncertainty manage dependence
Information being shared	focus on price and product attributes	broader focus as firms share strategic intentions and longer-term goals
Selling firm interface	individual salesperson is primary, possibly only, customer interface	many people from the selling firms interact with the customer, usually involve multiple functional areas of the seller (emergence of team selling)
Buying firm interface	relatively few contacts in the buying organization	many people from the customer interact with the buying firm
Relative dependence	varies, often asymmetric in nature	higher level of interdependence

SOURCES: Cespedes (1995), Krapfel et al. (1991), Shapiro (1988), and Shapiro and Moriarty (1982).

The Key Account Paradigm

In this section, we compare and contrast the key account and traditional selling paradigms. These differences are summarized in Table 15.1, and we describe them briefly here. Key accounts typically purchase a very large volume from the supplier. Further, exchange between buyers and sellers extends beyond a "core product," as sellers augment the product to provide additional services and support not usually available to other customers (Kotler, 1997). Enhancing customer value through programs such as vendor-managed inventory, joint production planning and scheduling for just-in-time (JIT) inventory management, concurrent engineering, and collaborative quality improvement efforts requires significant commitments by a seller.

In key account relationships, the focus of exchanging parties is usually broader than that involved in traditional sales exchanges. Whereas traditional sales management objectives typically concentrate on increasing revenue, key account relationships involve more multifaceted goals. For example, firms may engage in closer relationships to lower total costs to both sides by reducing the seller's selling and servicing costs (Kalwani & Narayandas, 1995) and the buyer's acquisition and operations costs (Cannon & Homburg, 1997; Cespedes, 1995). Other benefits of KAM include the management of uncertainty and/or dependence and the establishment of control over the direction of an industry (Oliver, 1990). The nature of these objectives complicates (a) the choices of partners (i.e., selection criteria), (b) evaluation of relationship success, and (c) efforts to manage ongoing KAM programs.

In order to deliver a broader base of value effectively to large and important customers, the interpersonal contact between the buying and selling firms must extend beyond the salesperson-purchasing agent/decision maker relationship. In describing the complex relationship that Procter & Gamble has with Wal-Mart, Muccio (1997) uses a variation on Figure 15.1. The "bow tie" (Figure 15.1a) and "diamond" (Figure 15.1b) represent two approaches to buyer-seller interaction. In the bow-tie approach, the salesperson and purchasing agent have primary (if not exclusive) contact across the two firms' boundaries. The diamond reflects a situation in which a team of functional experts from both organizations regularly interact—allowing, for example, the seller's finance people to talk directly with the buyer's accounts payable, manufacturing, or information systems people. The diamond model allows for greater interaction between functionally or technically specialized personnel from both firms, creating situations in which these experts can cooperatively identify solutions that lower costs or enhance value in exchange.

Key account relationships are typically long-term, involve high interdependence, and demand high levels of commitment from both parties. The

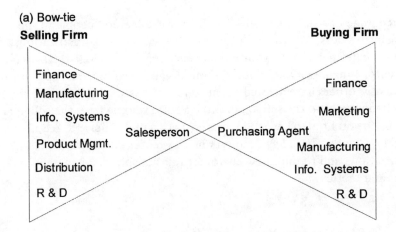

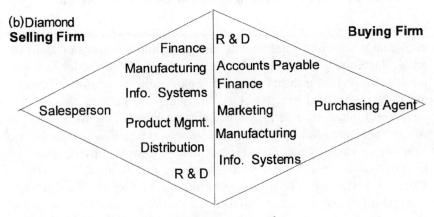

Figure 15.1. Two Forms of Supplier-Customer Interface
SOURCE: Based on Muccio (1997).

seller's dependence may initially emerge from the high purchase volume and demands placed by the customer. But if the seller learns more about the customer's operations, provides extra services, and effectively delivers a higher level of role performance, the buyer's switching costs and dependence are raised (Narayandas, 1994). One of the primary objectives of many key account management programs is to provide value and thus keep a buying firm from viewing the exchange as a commodity purchase.

The comparisons drawn here are consistent with definitions of key account management in the literature. Cespedes (1995) defines a key account as a customer who (a) purchases a significant volume as a

percentage of a seller's total sales, (b) involves several people in the purchasing process, (c) buys for a geographically dispersed organization, and
(d) expects specialized attention and services such as logistical support,
inventory management, price discounts, and customized applications.
Recently, others have defined key accounts as customers that have strategic importance to the seller, purchase a large volume from the seller, and
have the potential to lower a seller's costs (Krapfel, Salmond, & Spekman,
1991). Clearly, these key accounts place greater demands on selling organizations and require new customer relationship management strategies and tactics.

Directions for Research in Key Account Management

In this section we highlight some high-potential areas for theoretical and
empirical research in relationship marketing and key account management. Specifically, we discuss three areas that we believe offer rich avenues for future research and can make important contributions to emerging KAM theory and practice. First, we integrate perspectives on how
buyers and sellers interact. Here, our objective is twofold. We look at (a)
the management of investments in a key account relationship and (b) the
adaptations made by the two sides. Second, we examine pricing and cost-
to-serve issues that are critical to generating profits in KAM programs.
Third, we examine three systems and processes critical to effective KAM:
internal integration and coordination mechanisms; sales force organization; and control, evaluation, and compensation of key account personnel.

INTERACTING WITH KEY ACCOUNTS:
KAM AS INVESTMENT MANAGEMENT

A central process in commercial exchange relationships involves the extent and types of investments in relationship-specific adaptations made by
buyers and sellers (see Håkansson, 1982; Hallén, Johanson, & Seyed-
Mohamed, 1991). These adaptations are numerous, frequent, and central
to the coordination of buyer-seller exchanges. They may include customizing products, financial terms, information-sharing routines, pricing, inventory stocking policies, delivery schedules, and production processes to
meet the needs of a particular exchange relationship. Adaptations usually

involve investments of time and/or money for at least one of the parties. Firms typically invest in adaptations to lower costs, increase revenues or other benefits, or gain control in a relationship. The returns on these investments are usually long-run and difficult to anticipate and measure. Thus investments in relationship-specific adaptations represent key strategic decisions and are amplified in their importance in KAM programs.

Investments play a key role in several conceptual models of KAM. Although investments can be made by both parties, scholars have suggested that the primary responsibility for key account relationships as a critical corporate asset lies with the selling firm (McDonald, Millman, & Rogers, 1996; Spekman & Johnston, 1986).[1] A central element of McDonald et al.'s (1996) six-stage "key account relational development model" concerns the type and nature of investments made by the parties across the stages of the relationship development process. These authors indicate that investment strategy should depend on both the attractiveness of a customer and the stage of relationship development. Ford's (1980) relationship life-cycle model similarly emphasizes the importance of adaptations in building commitment and increasing the closeness between the two sides. Hallén et al. (1991) show that one party's adaptation encourages reciprocal adaptation, deepening the interdependence that is crucial to successful key account relationships. Mutual investments tie the two firms closer together and facilitate cooperation (Kumar, Scheer, & Steenkamp, 1995).

A customer's willingness to make such commitments may be a function of the customer's perception of the value received from the relationship. Pardo (1996) examined key account customers' perspectives on such relationships. Based on in-depth interviews with 20 customers, she categorizes customers' perceptions of their relationships with sellers along a continuum from low perceived added value to high. She calls these customers "disenchanted," "interested," or "enthusiastic" about the key account process. Clearly, any investment strategy in a key account relationship must recognize the customer's perspective and the likelihood of both sides making reciprocal investments in the relationship.

Focusing on the role of key account managers as "investment managers" directs attention to the types of investment decisions that must be made. At one level, a seller must make decisions about which customer relationships to invest in. This emphasizes the importance of proper and systematic selection of accounts for KAM programs and a well-thought-out process that details the nature and extent of subsequent investments. In addition to investments, decisions must be made about pricing. These decisions can be based on analysis of customers' cost-to-serve. In such analysis, the firm treats its customer base as a portfolio and chooses customers that will yield the highest return in the long run. We review the research in this area below.

Pricing and Cost-to-Serve Key Accounts

Shapiro, Rangan, Moriarty, and Ross (1987) recommend that sellers develop a price versus cost-to-serve matrix for all their major accounts to understand the health of their customer base. As they point out, in an ideal world, customers would line up along a value axis such that customers that demand higher levels of service would be willing to pay a higher price, and customers that require lower levels of service would pay a lower price. However, in the real world, the largest customers (which are usually the key accounts) end up getting lower prices while receiving the highest levels of services from sellers. Kaplan (1990) relates the case of a European manufacturer of heating wire and cable whose top two customers accounted for –150% of the total profits of the firm. This example highlights the fact that sellers can lose a significant amount of money serving the wrong set of customers as key accounts.

Rangan, Moriarty, and Swartz (1992) use customer trade-offs between price and service as a criterion to segment national accounts of a large industrial company. They link this approach to seller profitability and show how the seller can use this information to customize account management, redirect scarce seller resources, and effectively manage national accounts.

The link between price and cost-to-serve is very important to KAM programs. The management of key accounts involves high levels of relationship-specific investment in adaptations by a seller firm. Getting lower prices is always important to customers, especially when the purchases made in a relationship account for a significant portion of the customer's total purchases. Given that key accounts demand special services and are usually more costly to serve, it is important that sellers take great care in managing customer perceptions and expectations when it comes to pricing. Being able to extract the right price for the value created for the customer is very important. Implementing this approach is key to the success of a KAM program. Although this is easy to suggest, it can be difficult to implement because of several issues, which we discuss next.

First, key account customers are usually a seller's largest customers and account for a significant portion of the seller's total sales. This leads to asymmetry in power, with customers becoming more powerful over time and forcing the seller to reduce prices while keeping the level of service high. Second, the scope of these relationships is sometimes not very well defined, and sellers run the risk of providing a lot of support and services for which they are not adequately compensated. Finally, with key account customers, the level of service might vary across multiple locations, leading to situations in which the seller may not be able to realize higher prices for the higher levels of service provided. There are also other complications and constraints of which sellers need to be aware. For example, in the United States, the Robinson-Patman Act prohibits a seller from providing a better price or better services to one customer and not others, unless this action is justified by costs or other extenuating circumstances are present.

Overall, the decisions to be made concerning the level of service to provide, the extent of customization to be done, the level of investments to be made in the short and long run, and the appropriate link to be made with price are key aspects of KAM. It is difficult for sellers to negotiate these points in detail with their large customers *ex ante*. Sellers need to develop relationships that will enable them to receive fair returns for their services and that will prevent them from being held hostage and forced to give away the house.

At a more strategic level, sellers can use this type of information to develop portfolios of customers. A number of academic scholars have presented models for this purpose, which we review below.

Customer Portfolio Models

Fiocca (1982) presents a two-step process that is useful for developing a customer relationship management strategy. First, he suggests generating a graph that indicates the strategic importance of each customer to a seller and the difficulty faced by the supplier in managing that customer. In Fiocca's model, strategic importance can be determined using sales volume, future potential, prestige, account's market leadership, and several other factors. The difficulty of managing each account involves the product characteristics that deal with how customer needs can be met, account characteristics that deal with how customers need to be managed, and competition for the account. The next step is an in-depth analysis of each important account. This enables the seller to develop marketing strategies and estimate profitability for each account considered.

Using the research approach of the IMP Group, Campbell and Cunningham (1983) have developed a three-step process for managing large customers that includes understanding the life-cycle stage of customer relationships, analyzing competition in each relationship/segment, and conducting a portfolio analysis of key customers on whom the seller is most likely to expend a significant amount of resources.

Krapfel et al. (1991) offer a strategic approach to managing buyer-seller relationships based on the relationship value and commonality of interests. Relationship value is defined as a function of the criticality of a relationship to the two sides, the quantity or volume of business involved, the replaceability or switching costs involved, and the ability to reduce costs in the relationship. As these authors point out, unless the right set of conditions exists, sellers might not benefit from trying to develop close collaborative relationships with all customers. Further, they suggest different approaches to managing relationships based on the level of relationship value.

In all these studies, the basic recommendation is that sellers conduct detailed analyses of customers, the environment, competition, and their own skills before making investments of significant resources.

In contrast to financial investment theories, which provide methods for evaluating a risk-adjusted rate of return on investments, the marketing area is far from understanding how to estimate the costs, risks, and rewards of the types of investments typically pondered by key account managers. In addition to customer portfolio models, recent research in accounting and control on activity-based management and activity-based costing (Johnson & Kaplan, 1987) may provide useful tools. Firms can also apply these new cost accounting approaches to get a better handle on individual customer profitability. Many of the softer benefits incurred in key account relationships—new product ideas, learning about new markets, and test marketing ideas—also need to be included in any cost-benefit analysis. In our opinion, quantifying (on a relationship-by-relationship basis) the unique costs and benefits incurred and linking them to a KAM program's overall profitability is a critical opportunity for academic research to provide guidance for management practice. We suggest that marketing scholars consider drawing more from theories in other areas, such as cost accounting and financial investing, and adapting these concepts for application in the key account context.

THE SELLER'S INTERNAL SYSTEMS
AND PROCESSES

Central to any organization's ability to deliver value to customers is having its internal systems in order. This is particularly critical with key accounts. KAM places new challenges on selling firms that have typically relied entirely on traditional sales/account management approaches. KAM places a premium on delivering excellent customer service, which "requires internal coordination and more attention to . . . the structures and systems that customers rarely see or care about" (Cespedes, 1992, p. 66). Below, we discuss three structures and systems central to KAM effectiveness: integration and coordination across internal boundaries; team selling; and control, evaluation, and compensation.

Internal Integration and Coordination

The delivery of value to key account customers comes through more than just providing a quality product, delivering it on time, and charging a reasonable price. As discussed before, key accounts demand and expect more, often in the form of customized services and support from their sellers, including vendor-managed inventory, joint product development, unique ordering systems (JIT II), and customized products. These programs and initiatives require the involvement and cooperation of multiple functional areas of both firms. When a firm has multiple divisions selling to the same customer, it must leverage its economies of scale by implementing supply-chain management programs, requiring high levels of cooperation across multiple sales divisions (Cespedes, 1995). Finally, as customer firms become more geographically dispersed, it is increasingly necessary for selling organizations to coordinate the efforts of different international units (Yip & Madsen, 1996). Implementing KAM places new demands on multiple functions in a seller firm, and new forms of internal coordination are necessary for success (see Cespedes, 1995; Cohen, 1996).

Research into mechanisms that facilitate internal (cross-functional, cross-divisional) coordination and integration has been conducted primarily by organizational behavior scholars. For example, in their classic research, Lawrence and Lorsch (1967) found that the most successful firms in the three industries studied had higher levels of formal integration mechanisms (formal rules and plans, authority/hierarchy, and decision-making committees). Integration was defined as the quality of collaboration across interdependent units. In marketing, Menon, Bharadwaj, and Howell (1996) examined the effectiveness of marketing strategy and found that formal rules and higher levels of interdepartmental connectedness increased levels of *functional* conflict, which subsequently resulted in better marketing strategies. These results emphasize the role of formal procedures in facilitating intraorganizational coordination.[2]

Another mechanism is to create functional interdependence to foster greater coordination efforts (Ruekert & Walker, 1987). Timely and effective communication can also be very important to the success of KAM programs, as are patterns and forms of communication. Recent research by Maltz and Kohli (1996) has shown the impact of effective and timely coordination of market information across members of an organization.

Informal mechanisms can also be developed to enhance coordination. March and Simon (1958) describe the informal structures in organizations as those interpersonal linkages that do not appear on an organization chart. Key account managers often rely on unofficial channels to help their customers, and these types of contacts can be efficient and effective. Managers can foster them in simple ways, by encouraging different divisions to attend each other's training seminars or by not segregating offices by functional area. An organization can also foster a culture and norms whereby coordination is expected.

Here we propose a number of additional directions for future research. A first step might include the development of a taxonomy of different types of mechanisms that enhance internal coordination efforts. Although concepts such as formalization and planning have received considerable attention in the broader literature, more informal mechanisms have received relatively sparse attention. For theoretical insights, it might also be useful to draw on research into coordination in the interorganizational context, where theory appears to be better developed. For example, similar to Bradach and Eccles's (1989) perspective on interorganizational governance mechanisms, we believe that internal coordination mechanisms might be conceptualized as building blocks. Efforts at determining which combinations of these mechanisms work most effectively together, and under what circumstances, would provide considerable insight for theory development and practice.

Although an emerging literature is being developed, the important role of information technology as a coordinating mechanism suggests that more attention is warranted. Cespedes (1995) discusses how appropriately designed databases can foster greater cooperation across functional areas. It should be noted that practitioners are beginning to use intranets (e.g., Lotus Notes) to facilitate interaction. If properly developed and implemented, information systems have the power to enhance internal coordination efforts. Given the relatively recent development of these technologies, academic research could help guide managers in applying them in the KAM context.

Research should also consider the situational factors that might have direct, moderating, or mediating effects on the relationship between coordination mechanisms and performance. For example, when investments involve changing formal processes such as delivery procedures and interfirm information systems, formal integration and communication mechanisms may be most effective. On the other hand, for processing complex orders or getting answers to particular customer queries, the use of informal mechanisms may be more effective and less costly.

As a final comment, we believe that enhanced coordination comes at a cost. Greater coordination will result in increased conflict, will involve more management time, and will usually involve significant financial investments. It is important for researchers to understand the broad range of potential costs and benefits that might accrue from enhanced coordination efforts.

Team Selling

Team selling offers a specific method for interacting with customers that enhances both internal and interorganizational coordination. It reflects a response to the complex service demands of key accounts. A first step in understanding team selling is to describe the phenomenon. Fortunately, over the past 15 years a number of scholars have refined our understanding of the selling process. Inspired by the buying center concept (Robinson, Faris, & Wind, 1967), Hutt, Johnston, and Ronchetto (1985) describe a selling center as "organizational members who are involved in initiating and maintaining exchange relationships with industrial customers" (p. 33). In refining this concept, Moon and Armstrong (1994) distinguish between selling centers, which have fluid membership (some members brought in only to assist with a particular transaction), and core selling teams, which have permanent members assigned to a particular customer to implement strategic plans. Smith and Barclay (1990) provide a broad review of theoretical perspectives relevant to team selling.

Descriptive studies like these provide a foundation upon which theory can be built and empirically tested on larger samples.

Recently, a few empirical studies concerned with team selling have appeared in the literature. Smith and Barclay (1997) examined a unique selling team in which the members are employed by different firms selling complementary products. Their results indicate that trusting behaviors by partners have a strong influence on the parties' satisfaction and a lesser impact on task performance. Gladstein (1984) studied task group effectiveness in a sample of sales teams in the communications industry. She found that dimensions of group composition, group structure, intragroup processes, and boundary management were related to self-reported group effectiveness but not sales performance. Moon, Perreault, and Armstrong (1997) found that team effort and group norms for high performance were the most powerful predictors of sales performance.

The team selling area is wide open with opportunities for future research. Although several empirical studies have been conducted on factors related to the effectiveness of individual salespeople (Churchill, Ford, Hartley, & Walker, 1985), very few have examined these factors in the team selling environment. Many issues that are now well understood at the level of the individual salesperson may not be so clear in the KAM/team context. One set of issues revolves around individuals in selling centers. For example: What types of individual behaviors enhance team performance? How do role conflict and role ambiguity operate in the team selling context? A second set of issues focuses on teams as the unit of analysis. For example, there is debate on whether teams are best composed of functional experts or generalists. Like Cespedes (1995), we believe that the nature of KAM requires members to have in-depth functional expertise to be able (a) to evaluate and assess investment opportunities and (b) to help with implementation. Such an assertion needs to be empirically tested. Answers to these questions and others will provide valuable contributions to the theory and practice of team selling—the new selling mode for many KAM programs.

Control, Evaluation, and Compensation

Control systems are typically put in place to align employees' objectives with those of the organization. Oliver and Anderson (1994) note that a sales management control system involves "levels of monitoring and directing, as well as methods for evaluating and compensating salespeople" (p. 54). In part because salespersons' activities are performed outside a manager's observation, control systems are particularly important for employees in this role. Control systems are often categorized as behavioral or outcome based. In the sales context, behavioral control includes monitoring salespeople's behavior (e.g., direct observation, completed call reports); outcome-based methods rely heavily on commission-based compensation or quotas that are based on measured outputs (typically sales revenue).

Research in marketing has identified factors favoring the relative use of behavioral versus outcome-based controls (Basu, Lal, Srinivasan, & Staelin, 1985; Cravens, Ingram, LaForge, & Young, 1993; John & Weitz, 1989), but these approaches typically assume that (a) the selling firm's objective is to maximize revenue, (b) the selling task is performed by an individual, and (c) it is possible to monitor and evaluate performance by monitoring outputs or behavior. These assumptions are often not valid in the key account selling context. First, in many key account selling scenarios, a seller's objective is to build a long-term relationship, not necessarily to maximize short-term revenues. This objective has led many firms to focus on other relational outcomes, such as lowering transaction costs, building trust, enhancing customer satisfaction, and developing and testing new products. The processes by which these benefits can be achieved are not standardized or universal. It is often the expertise embedded in an individual key account manager or the key account team that determines a seller's ability to generate these benefits. Team selling also increases the complexity of evaluating the performance of individual team members, making the use of outcome-based control mechanisms particularly problematic (John & Weitz, 1989).

Traditional behavioral or output-based control mechanisms fail when it is difficult to measure outputs and knowledge about the transformation process is imperfect (Ouchi, 1979). Under these circumstances, Ouchi (1979) suggests that "clan" control offers the superior alternative. Clans use socialization to eliminate goal incongruence between individuals and the organization. This type of control mechanism relies heavily on the firm's selecting appropriate people for the position and training them in both the skills and the values of the organization.

A variety of other factors may influence a firm's choice of control systems. One is the historical tradition within the organization. For example, because the clan mechanism relies on socialization, one might expect that key account managers are promoted from the firm's regular sales force. If that sales force is controlled largely by outcome-based controls, then the key account manager may be most motivated by this type of reward. On the other hand, the use of team selling complicates performance measurement and socialization, suggesting a need for behavioral controls. For these reasons, we find that in practice, control involves a hybrid approach; that is, behavioral, output-based, and clan mechanisms may be combined (Jaworski, 1988). It has been shown that each of these three general control categories includes many specific types of control that researchers have only recently begun to understand (see Bradach & Eccles, 1989; Challagalla & Shervani, 1996; Jaworski, 1988; Jaworski, Stathakopoulos, & Krishnan, 1993).

We believe that a fruitful endeavor for researchers would be to provide a better understanding of the effects of each control mechanism and the simultaneous use of multiple controls. In addition, because we do not expect incentive-based compensation to be eliminated, future research will need to address (a) the time frame for compensation payout and performance evaluations in team selling situations, (b) the division of sales credit among salespeople supporting the same key account, and (c) the unit(s) of measurement that should drive incentives in these situations. Researchers might also extend the work of others who have begun to identify and explore particular forms of behavioral control (e.g., Challagalla & Shervani, 1996; Jaworski, 1988; Jaworski et al., 1993). There is also a need to understand how firms might best develop clan-based control mechanisms. Aside from the theoretical approaches reviewed here, managerial perspectives may offer additional insights that could complement and extend developing theory (e.g., Johnson, 1993; Saunier & Hawk, 1994).

Future Trends and Implications for Key Account Management

A number of future trends promise to challenge KAM, including the tiering of sellers, globalization of customers, increased interaction of firms with customers using the Internet, and increased sales, marketing, and service efficiencies using automation tools. Although relatively little academic research has examined these issues, their emergence creates new challenges for the implementation of KAM programs. We briefly discuss each in an attempt to stimulate future research in these emerging areas.

Over the past decade and a half, there has been an evolution in supplier-base management. In the first stage of supplier-base reduction, customers focused on buying the same components or parts from fewer suppliers. Now, customers are further reducing their supplier bases by tiering their suppliers and dealing directly with only their designated primary suppliers. They expect these primary suppliers, in turn, to take on the responsibility of monitoring and managing secondary/other smaller suppliers. In order to continue being suppliers to their key accounts, primary suppliers have to redefine significantly the scope of these relationships, taking on additional roles and responsibilities. For example, one industrial customer now expects its electrical component supplier also to manage the customer's physical plant service operations. Sellers need to make conscious decisions about whether it is worthwhile for them to take on these additional responsibilities, and they must understand how these decisions could affect their ability to serve other customers.

A second trend involves the emergence of global customers. Global customers expect their suppliers to provide coordinated sales and service efforts in locations around the world (Shapiro & Moriarty, 1982; Yip & Madsen, 1996). In most cases, global customers want to make procurement decisions centrally but expect the products, services, and other value-added activities to be provided locally. These customers are interested in dealing only with suppliers that are willing to make substantial global investments, which can exacerbate internal coordination problems for the suppliers. Once again, a key issue that arises is whether the benefits to the seller exceed the investments made. Understanding the implications of developing global service will be a very critical area for sellers. It would be a mistake to assume that going global is just a scaling up of national-level KAM programs. At a time when most sellers have regional sales forces to sell in different parts of the globe, creating global teams dedicated to supporting key accounts will not be an easy task. Sellers also need to account for differences in regulations, market conditions, and competitive threats across different markets. An additional wrinkle in the implementation of these programs is the significant variance in customer service needs across regions and the price the seller is willing to pay. All of this will increase the complexity of the KAM process.

The third trend is increased use of the Internet, which represents an omnipresent factor for all aspects of marketing. The Internet has the potential to redefine interactivity in various stages of buyer-seller transactions. For example, customers can now use the Internet to access any information that is archived on-line by the seller. In addition, they can place orders electronically and monitor the entire order cycle. Finally, after-sales service can also be provided effectively over the Internet. Sellers will need to develop the skills and technologies needed to harness the power of the Internet to provide better service to their key accounts on a timely and cost-effective basis. This does not mean that the role of personal selling will diminish in the future, but we believe that its scope will be significantly redefined. Sellers will need to reorganize their selling efforts to strike the right balance between the new modes of interaction and conventional person-to-person interactions.

Finally, recent advances in the power of computing hardware and software and the availability of communications technologies have already had a significant impact on sales force management. Comprehensive automation solutions are now available that allow sellers to link their marketing, sales, and service operations. Using these systems, sellers can provide integrated services to manage customers through all stages of the purchase cycle.

Each of these trends places new challenges on KAM programs. Sellers have new investment opportunities with customers, but these trends make costs and benefits more difficult to evaluate and predict. They will further exacerbate coordination problems and require more sophisticated organizational structures, making KAM programs more complex and challenging to manage. Researchers in marketing will be challenged to integrate their research with the work done in the international business, information technology, organization theory, and human resources areas.

Challenges of Conducting Empirical Research in Key Account Management

There are a number of issues involved in conducting empirical investigations in the area of KAM. First, we need to think about research design. Of course research in this area (where feasible and useful) should be longitudinal or cross-sectional. By their very nature, customer relationships develop gradually over time (Dwyer, Schurr, & Oh, 1987; Ford, 1980; McDonald et al., 1996). The roles of the key account team and the key account manager and the way the seller interacts with various parts of a customer's buying organization can be expected to vary across the life cycle of the relationship. McDonald et al. (1996) suggest a number of different stages to the key account relationship process. Anderson (1995) points out that although longitudinal studies are a must, the reality is that most studies will continue to be cross-sectional or pseudolongitudinal at best. Like Anderson, we suggest that rather than conducting large-scale one-time surveys, it would be better for researchers to investigate fewer relationships over time and in more detail.

A second issue is the use of single-informant versus multiple-informant studies, particularly where survey data are being collected. Although many key account relationships clearly involve multiple parties that may have multiple perspectives on the relationships, conducting research using multiple informants can create difficulties in both data collection and data analysis. This does not validate the use of single informants, however. There is a clear need for research that examines the shortcomings of using single informants and provides better guidelines to clarify conditions under which the use of multiple respondents is imperative.

The third issue that researchers need to consider concerns the use of dyadic information versus information collected from just one side in the relationship. Any research on buyer-seller relationships can benefit from data collected from both sides of the dyad. Although this approach is optimal, the collection and interpretation of dyadic data can be very difficult. Traditionally, research has examined buying organizations' trust of sellers (e.g., Doney & Cannon, 1997; Kumar et al., 1995). We are currently engaged in a study that examines how a national account manager's trust of a customer is related to the way in which he or she manages the relationship and performance outcomes (Cannon, Gundlach, & Narayandas, 1997). Future research might continue by examining both sides' perspectives (e.g., Anderson & Narus, 1990).

Research in this area must also be cognizant of the multiple levels at which a relationship may exist. Although interpersonal relationships provide the basis for relationships between firms, there is clearly a component of the relationship that exists between organizations (see Doney & Cannon, 1997). It is important for researchers to recognize this issue and study KAM relationships at multiple levels.

In addition to the above, there is a need for greater understanding of other factors that moderate the effectiveness of key account practices. For example, we believe that the nature of the product/service, the relationship objectives, and the relative dependence of the two parties are important antecedents or moderators of the effectiveness and success of various key account practices. All of the issues raised above have serious implications for what needs to be researched, how it is researched, and research designs. Together, these factors will also raise the bar for scholars conducting KAM research in the future. Unless they are addressed, the usefulness of research in this area will be greatly restricted, as it has been in the past.

Conclusion

KAM continues to be the predominant strategy for business marketers attempting to manage relationships with their largest and most important customers. In this chapter we have suggested a particular perspective from which to approach key accounts: viewing key accounts as investment opportunities. This perspective has strategic implications for the evaluation of costs and benefits incurred in key account management. Effective implementation of KAM also requires changes in the processes and systems of selling organizations. Although we have reviewed important research in this area, significant opportunities for understanding KAM remain. We hope that our review provides interested scholars with some insights into and inspiration to pursue these opportunities.

Notes

1. For an alternative perspective, see Leenders and Blenkhorn (1988); these authors place the responsibility with the purchasing organization.

2. Another formal approach to this problem has been the use of cross-functional teams. We examine team selling in the following subsection.

References

Anderson, J. C. (1995). Relationships in business markets: Exchange episodes, value creation and their empirical assessment. *Journal of the Academy of Marketing Science, 23,* 346-350.

Anderson, J. C., & Narus, J. A. (1990). A model of distributor firm and manufacturer firm working partnerships. *Journal of Marketing, 54*(1), 42-58.

Basu, A. K., Lal, R., Srinivasan, V., & Staelin, R. (1985). Salesforce compensation plans: An agency theory perspective. *Marketing Science, 4,* 267-291.

Bradach, J. L., & Eccles, R. G. (1989). Price, authority, and trust. *Annual Review of Sociology, 15*, 97-118.

Campbell, N. C. G., & Cunningham, M. T. (1983). Customer analysis for strategy development in industrial markets. *Strategic Management Journal, 4*, 360-380.

Cannon, J. P., Gundlach, G. T., & Narayandas, N. (1997, April 29). *Issues of trust in customer-supplier partnering.* Paper presented at the meeting of the National Account Management Association, Ft. Lauderdale, FL.

Cannon, J. P., & Homburg, C. (1997). *Buyer-supplier relationships and customer firm costs* (Working paper). Ft. Collins: Colorado State University.

Cespedes, F. V. (1992, March-April). Once more: How do you improve customer service? *Business Horizons*, pp. 58-67.

Cespedes, F. V. (1995). *Concurrent marketing: Integrating product, sales and service.* Boston: Harvard Business School Press.

Cespedes, F. V., Doyle, S. X., & Freedman, R. J. (1989). Teamwork for today's selling. *Harvard Business Review, 67*(4), 44-58.

Challagalla, G. N., & Shervani, T. A. (1996). Dimensions and types of supervisory control: Effects on salesperson performance and satisfaction. *Journal of Marketing, 60*(1), 89-105.

Churchill, G. A., Jr., Ford, N. M., Hartley, S. W., & Walker, O. C., Jr. (1985). The determinants of salesperson performance: A meta-analysis. *Journal of Marketing Research, 22*, 103-118.

Cohen, A. (1996, April). A national footing. *Sales and Marketing Management, 148*, 76-80.

Cravens D. W., Ingram, T. N., LaForge, R. W., & Young, C. E. (1993). Behavior-based and outcome-based salesforce control systems. *Journal of Marketing, 57*(4), 47-59.

Doney, P. M., & Cannon, J. P. (1997). An examination of the nature of trust in buyer-seller relationships. *Journal of Marketing, 61*(2), 35-51.

Dwyer, F. R., Schurr, P. H., & Oh, S. (1987). Developing buyer-seller relationships. *Journal of Marketing, 51*(2), 11-27.

Fiocca, R. (1982). Account portfolio analysis for strategy development. *Industrial Marketing Management, 11*, 53-62.

Ford, D. (1980). Introduction to special issue on industrial marketing. *European Journal of Marketing, 14*, 235-238.

Gladstein, D. L. (1984). Groups in context: A model of task group effectiveness. *Administrative Science Quarterly, 29*, 499-517.

Håkansson, H. (Ed.). (1982). *International marketing and purchasing of industrial goods: An interaction approach.* New York: John Wiley.

Hallén, L., Johanson, J., & Seyed-Mohamed, N. (1991). Interfirm adaptation in business relationships. *Journal of Marketing, 55*(2), 29-37.

Hutt, M. D., Johnston, W. J., & Ronchetto, J. R., Jr. (1985, May). Selling centers and buying centers: Formulating strategic exchange patterns. *Journal of Personal Selling and Sales Management, 5* 33-40.

Jaworski, B. J. (1988). Toward a theory of marketing control: Environmental context, control types, and consequences. *Journal of Marketing, 52*(3), 23-39.

Jaworski, B. J., Stathakopoulos, V., & Krishnan, H. S. (1993). Control combinations in marketing: Conceptual framework and empirical evidence. *Journal of Marketing, 57*(1), 57-69.

John, G., & Weitz, B. A. (1989). Salesforce compensation: An empirical investigation of factors related to the use of salary vs. incentive compensation. *Journal of Marketing Research, 26*, 1-14.

Johnson, H. T., & Kaplan, R. S. (1987). *Relevance lost: The rise and fall of management accounting.* Boston: Harvard Business School Press.

428   PARTNERING FOR RELATIONSHIP MARKETING

Johnson, S. T. (1993, March-April). Work teams: What's ahead in work design and rewards management. *Compensation and Benefits Review,* pp. 35-41.

Kalwani, M. U., & Narayandas, N. (1995). Long-term manufacturer-supplier relationships: Do they pay off for supplier firms? *Journal of Marketing, 59*(1), 1-16.

Kaplan, R. S. (1990). *Kanthal (A)* (Case No. 9-190-002). Boston: Harvard Business School.

Kotler, P. (1997). *Marketing management: Analysis, planning, implementation, and control.* Upper Saddle River, NJ: Prentice Hall.

Krapfel, R. E., Jr., Salmond, D., & Spekman, R. E. (1991). A strategic approach to managing buyer-seller relationships. *European Journal of Marketing, 25*(9), 22-37.

Kumar, N., Scheer, L. K., & Steenkamp, J.-B. E. M. (1995). The effects of perceived interdependence on dealer attitudes. *Journal of Marketing Research, 32,* 348-356.

Lawrence, L., & Lorsch, J. (1967). *Organization and environment.* Boston: Harvard Business School Press.

Leenders, M. R., & Blenkhorn, D. L. (1988). *Reverse marketing: The new buyer-supplier relationship.* New York: Free Press.

Maltz, E., & Kohli, A. K. (1996). Market intelligence dissemination across functional boundaries. *Journal of Marketing Research, 33,* 47-61.

March, J., & Simon, H. (1958). *Organizations.* New York: John Wiley.

McDonald, M., Millman, T., & Rogers, B. (1996). *Key account management: Learning from supplier and customer perspectives.* Cranfield, England: Cranfield University, School of Management.

Menon, A., Bharadwaj, S. G., & Howell, R. (1996). The quality and effectiveness of marketing strategy: Effects of functional and dysfunctional conflict in intraorganizational relationships. *Journal of the Academy of Marketing Science, 24,* 299-313.

Moon, M. A., & Armstrong, G. M. (1994, February). Selling teams: A conceptual framework and research agenda. *Journal of Personal Selling and Sales Management, 14,* 17-30.

Moon, M. A., Perreault, W. D., Jr., & Armstrong, G. M. (1997). *A task group model of selling team performance* (Working paper). Knoxville: University of Tennessee.

Muccio, T. (1997). Procter and Gamble: Allocating resources. In G. Conlon (Ed.), *Unlocking profits: The strategic advantage of key account management* (pp. 61-70). Chicago: National Account Management Association.

Narayandas, N. (1994). *Essays on the management of long-term manufacturer-supplier relationships by supplier firms.* Unpublished doctoral dissertation, Purdue University.

Oliver, C. (1990). Determinants of interorganizational relationships: Integration and future directions. *Academy of Management Review, 15,* 241-265.

Oliver, R. L., & Anderson, E. (1994). An empirical test of the consequences of behavior- and outcome-based sales control systems. *Journal of Marketing, 58*(4), 53-67.

Ouchi, W. G. (1979). A conceptual framework for the design of organizational control mechanisms. *Management Science, 25,* 833-848.

Pardo, C. (1996). *Key account management in the business to business field: The key accounts point of view.* Paper presented at the 12th IMP Group Conference, University of Karlsruhe, Germany.

Rangan, K. V., Moriarty, R. T., & Swartz, G. S. (1992). Segmenting customers in mature industrial markets. *Journal of Marketing, 56*(4), 72-82.

Robinson, P. J., Faris, C. W., & Wind, Y. (1967). *Industrial buying and creative marketing.* Boston: Allyn & Bacon.

Ruekert, R. W., & Walker, O. C., Jr. (1987). Marketing's interaction with other functional units: A conceptual framework and empirical evidence. *Journal of Marketing, 51*(1), 1-19.

Saunier, A. M., & Hawk, E. J. (1994, July-August). Realizing the potential of teams through team-based rewards. *Compensation and Benefits Review,* pp. 24-33.

Shapiro, B. P. (1988). *Close encounters of the four kinds: Managing customers in a rapidly changing environment* (Working Paper No. 9-589-015). Boston: Harvard Business School.

Shapiro, B. P., & Moriarty, R. T. (1982). *National account management: Emerging insights* (Rep. No. 82-100). Cambridge, MA: Marketing Science Institute.

Shapiro, B. P., Rangan, V. K., Moriarty, R. T., & Ross, E. B. (1987). Manage customers for profits (not just sales). *Harvard Business Review, 66*(1), 101-108.

Smith, J. B., & Barclay, D. W. (1990). Theoretical perspectives on selling center research. In D. Lichtenthal, R. E. Spekman, D. T. Wilson, P. F. Anderson, H. P. Root, W. J. Johnston, J. A. Narus, J. C. Anderson, M. J. Ryan, F. V. Cespedes, T. Bonoma, G. E. Hills, & T. Reve (Eds.), *Proceedings of the American Marketing Association Winter Educators' Conference* (pp. 5-12). Chicago: American Marketing Association.

Smith, J. B., & Barclay, D. W. (1997). The effects of organizational differences and trust on the effectiveness of selling partner relationships. *Journal of Marketing, 61*(1), 3-21.

Spekman, R. E. (1988, July-August). Strategic supplier selection: Understanding long-term buyer relationships. *Business Horizons,* pp. 75-81.

Spekman, R. E., & Johnston, W. J. (1986). Relationship management: Managing the selling and buying interface. *Journal of Business Research, 14,* 519-531.

Yip, G. S., & Madsen, T. L. (1996). Global account management: The new frontier in relationship marketing. *International Marketing Review, 13*(3), 24-42.

16

Horizontal Alliances for Relationship Marketing

DAVID W. CRAVENS
KAREN S. CRAVENS

There is perhaps no management paradigm that has generated more interest from scholars and managers than the strategic alliance. Although it is not a recent development, extensive adoption of alliances by many companies on a global basis highlights alliances' escalating importance. Horizontal alliances are popular strategies for leveraging the distinctive competencies of two or more companies for the purposes of developing new technologies, expanding product portfolios, and entering new markets. These strategic partnerships between competitors or other firms at the same level in the value-added system offer opportunities for firms to enhance and accelerate their value offerings to customers. The annual growth rate of domestic and cross-border alliances during the first half of the 1990s was in excess of 25% (Bleeke & Ernst, 1995). This trend is expected to continue into the 21st century.

"Strategic alliances, a manifestation of interorganizational cooperative strategies, entail the pooling of specific resources and skills by the cooperating organizations in order to achieve common goals, as well as goals specific to the individual partners" (Varadarajan & Cunningham, 1995,

p. 282). Although horizontal alliances share certain characteristics with joint ventures, the former involve agreements to collaborate on strategic projects, whereas joint ventures result in the formation of new independent organizations by the venture partners. It is this melding of two or more distinct organizational units that makes the alliance relationship so powerful yet so complex to manage and evaluate. From a research perspective, it is often difficult to distinguish the achievement of alliance objectives from the achievement of overall organizational objectives unless the strategic project can be clearly defined and its outputs measured. Because the two types of objectives can be similar, participants in an alliance may not attribute results directly to the alliance.

Horizontal alliances are best viewed as components of business strategies rather than as complete and independent strategies. Alliances are part of the management control systems of organizations. It is the management control system that executes the corporate strategy. In the process of becoming market oriented, providing customers with superior value, and leveraging the organization's distinctive capabilities, an alliance contributes to the management control process by gaining access to markets, enhancing customer value, and complementing the organization's distinctive capabilities. The alliance's strategic role is to provide a way for the firm to collaborate with other organizations toward the objective of creating superior customer value. Depending on the nature and extent of the alliances developed, alliances may substantially alter the design of an organization.

In this chapter we first consider the context of horizontal alliance relationships. We then develop a horizontal alliance process model and examine the major constructs that constitute the model. Finally, we explore several emerging issues concerning the conceptualization of horizontal alliances and the research examining such alliances.

The Context of Horizontal
Alliance Relationships

Because the term *strategic alliance* is often used to describe various interorganizational relationships, it is important that we indicate the context of our discussion of horizontal alliance relationships. At the basic level, an alliance is a collaborative relationship among two or more independent organizations joining together to pursue a strategic project. A company may have several alliances that together form a network, with the organization serving as the network coordinator (Cravens, Piercy, & Shipp, 1996). The characteristics of a horizontal alliance include the following (Cravens, Shipp, & Cravens, 1993; Parkhe, 1993; Sheth & Parvatiyar, 1992; Varadarajan & Cunningham, 1995; Yoshino & Rangan, 1995):

- Collaboration on a strategic project of mutual interest although the partners remain independent organizations
- Pursuit of common strategic objectives as well as specific objectives for each company
- Sharing of the benefits of the alliance and control over the performance of assigned tasks
- Utilization of interlinked organizational processes that employ resources and/or governance structures from the alliance participants
- Membership in the same industry or value-chain level for participating organizations (horizontal linkages)
- Commitment to long-term strategic involvement rather than short-term tactical linkage

RATIONALE FOR FORMING A HORIZONTAL ALLIANCE

Organizations sometimes seek partners and form alliances because they lack the skills or resources needed to pursue particular projects independently; in other instances, the incremental advantages of partnering are sufficient justification for forming alliances. Motivations for forming alliances may include skill/resource gaps and/or high environmental turbulence/diversity (Cravens et al., 1993). Varadarajan and Cunningham (1995) point to market uncertainty, skill and resource differences, and imperfect factor markets as reasons for the formation of alliances to gain competitive advantage. Hagedoorn (1993) discusses similar motivations for alliance formation in technology partnering.

Horizontal alliances are more complex than supplier-producer and other vertical relationships (Day, 1995). The former involve integrating an alliance process into the partners' organizational structures, whereas vertical relationships build on existing supplier-producer linkages and processes. Organizations' decisions regarding how to craft alliance strategies and structure alliance relationships are difficult due to the complexity of integrating the competencies and the internal and linking processes of two or more organizations. In light of these complications, we consider below various attributes that distinguish the domain of horizontal alliances from other partnerships.

DOMAIN OF HORIZONTAL ALLIANCES

Differing from Varadarajan and Cunningham (1995), we exclude joint ventures and supplier-producer collaborations (and other vertical distribution channel relationships) from the domain of strategic alliances; instead, we include alliances between firms at the same level in the supplier-end user chain. This is consistent with Sheth and Parvatiyar's (1992) definition of competitive alliances. There is a major base of theoretical and empirical support from channel of distribution and organizational buyer-seller research that applies to vertical relationships, and it does not necessarily transfer directly to horizontal relationships. Moreover, although some authorities consider joint ventures to be strategic alliances, we believe it is appropriate to distinguish between the two organization forms. Although joint ventures share certain characteristics of horizontal alliances, a joint venture results in the formation of a separate organization with its own mission, personnel, resources, and structure. We also exclude licensing and franchising from the alliance domain. None of these alternative collaborate arrangements possesses the same degree of interorganizational integration as do horizontal alliances. In essence, the horizontal alliance integrates an external entity directly into the management control systems of the partner firms.

It is unfortunate that much of the research and literature concerning alliances makes no distinctions among horizontal (competitor) alliances, vertical collaborative relationships, and joint ventures. Thus readers should exercise caution in interpreting the conceptual foundations and empirical findings of these studies.

Horizontal Alliance Configuration

Although others propose a broad definition of strategic alliances, portraying all interorganizational cooperative relationships between two firms as strategic alliances may mask the unique features of different alliances as well as the challenges of understanding and evaluating them. Because of this, we propose that an alliance configuration should involve horizontal collaboration between organizations at the same level in the value chain. Thus two competing or complementary manufacturers might form an alliance to develop a new technology (or product) or to market each other's products in different geographic markets. Similarly, two direct marketers such as Amway and Tupperware might form an alliance in which Amway markets Tupperware's products in international markets. Amway competes in many countries, whereas Tupperware has a limited international presence. Burgers, Hill, and Kim (1993) have analyzed the global auto industry and empirically tested motivations for horizontal alliance formation (including joint ventures).

Successful horizontal alliances involve partners that bring complementary contributions to the partnership that, when coupled together, have the potential to create customer value greater than either could achieve alone. Horizontal alliances are normally project oriented rather than ongoing supplier-customer linkages (e.g., Procter & Gamble and Wal-Mart). It is important to note that horizontal alliances may have success characteristics that are different from those in supplier-producer relationships. For example, power and dependence are more balanced between the partners in horizontal alliances compared with vertical relationships among suppliers, producers, and marketing channel members (Buffington & Farabelli, 1991). Moreover, organizational learning may be an important objective in the horizontal alliance, and transaction cost savings and short-term performance may not be as essential as gaining technical competencies, tacit knowledge, or market understanding (Osborn & Hagedoorn, 1997).

Characteristics of Alliance Projects

An alliance has a project or program orientation in which the partners perform interlinked activities, such as joint development of a new product or process, joint manufacturing, joint exploration and development of sources of raw materials, and joint marketing (Varadarajan & Cunningham, 1995). Specific activities included in the alliance are performed by each of the partners and involve shared information, resources, and personnel. The resulting processes become very complex when the activities performed are closely interrelated and certain activities are dependent on the completion of related activities by the partner.

In describing Corning Inc.'s successful alliances, Day (1995) comments on the difficulty outsiders have in gaining an understanding of Corning's alliance processes and approaches. He points to the problem of overcoming the barrier of "causal ambiguity" because the "essential skills

and knowledge are embedded so deeply into the people, the tacit knowledge about alliances, the cultures, and the supporting processes that they
cannot be directly observed" (p. 299). Interlinked processes constitute an
important distinction between horizontal alliances and joint ventures.
The joint venture results in the creation of a new organization whose functions and processes are much more visible and clearly defined than are intercompany horizontal alliance processes. Similarly, the management of
the independent joint venture process is also more clearly defined and less
complex.

From Alliances to Networks

Closely paralleling the adoption of alliance strategies is the formation
of complex networks of interorganizational relationships (Cravens et al.,
1996). Globalization and networking promise to alter the traditional concept of the organization, presenting new opportunities and complex management challenges (Yoshino & Rangan, 1995). Whereas networks may involve both collaborative and transactional relationships, horizontal alliances
are often popular strategies for linking network participants. The firm serving as the network coordinator may develop several strategic alliances to
gain the distinctive capabilities of the partners. Research indicates that
when competencies of alliance partners are complementary with respect
to interest and organizational fit, the alliances are more likely to be successful (Bucklin & Sengupta, 1993).

Alliances and Customer Value

Horizontal alliances offer firms the potential to add value to customer
relationships by leveraging the competencies and assets of the alliance
partners to lower cost, differentiate the product offer, or provide a combination of lower cost and differentiation. For example, Intuit Corp. (Quicken
Software) has alliances with a large group of financial services companies,
including American Express and Chase Manhattan Bank. The objective is
to offer on-line banking services to handle customer inquiries and through
which customers can transfer funds, make payments, and obtain financial
products. The value to the customer is an integrated financial service
package accessed by computers.

The customer obtains superior value when the relative benefits exceed
the relative costs (Day & Wensley, 1988). Day (1995) stresses the importance of the partners' working together to create a new bundle of value

rather than providing a straight exchange of value. Through such techniques as strategic cost analysis (Shank & Govindarajan, 1992), the alliance participants can consider potential partners to facilitate cost savings and/or product differentiation.

Horizontal alliances involve collaboration in performing value-chain activities that enhance the value offering made to the customer. The intent is for each partner to contribute complementary resources and skills (Varadarajan & Cunningham, 1995). Customer benefits arising from alliances may include availability (in a market not previously served), development of unique products, faster delivery of value offerings, and/or lower prices. For example, the objective of the proposed alliance between American Airlines and British Airways is to offer frequent flights across the Atlantic as well as to expanded gateway cities in the United States and simplified transfers between the two carriers (Ayling, 1997). Cost savings are anticipated that, if translated into lower prices, will also enhance the value offering to the customer. A similar strategy was employed by one of the firms seeking the British Airways advertising account. One of the finalist agencies in the selection process did not possess worldwide capabilities and sought to form an alliance with another firm to fill the gap (Goldman, 1995).

ALTERNATIVE ALLIANCE PATHS

Drawing from McKinsey & Company's consulting experience with more than 200 alliances, Bleeke and Ernst (1995) discuss the different alliance paths that may be pursued in strategic partnerships. Although their categories include joint ventures, the classifications offer important insights concerning the strategic nature of alliances:

1. *Collisions between competitors:* These partnerships between direct competitors, involving their core businesses, do not have a good success record.
2. *Alliances of the weak:* This alliance path is intended to produce synergy, but coupling two weak companies typically does not produce positive results.
3. *Disguised sales and bootstrap alliances:* These relationships involve a weak and a strong partner, and often result in acquisition by the stronger partner.
4. *Evolutions to a sale:* Partnering by two strong companies may achieve initial objectives, although eventually one partner is acquired by the other partner.

5. *Alliances of complementary equals:* These alliances have a good record of
   success. Both partners are strong, and they bring unique competencies and
   assets to the relationship.

Thus the McKinsey experience suggests that alliances of complementary equals offer the greatest promise for success. Other research evidence indicates the importance of clear definition of objectives and equivalency in the contributions of the partners in determining the success of the relationship (Gupta & Tannenbaum, 1991). Within the context of organizational learning, Parkhe (1991) proposes that less similar partners in global alliances require more adjustments to facilitate learning. Nonetheless, "the once central notion of strategic compatibility seems to be fading in popularity" (Osborn & Hagedoorn, 1997, p. 267). Organizational learning can have a positive effect on alliance stability and outcome and can counter many problems inherent in difficult alliances. Thus dissimilar partners faced with a particularly challenging set of alliance requirements are further burdened by the nature of their partnership. Parkhe (1991) also suggests that the degree and type of interfirm differences will affect how management invests in the alliance in terms of particular activities.

Horizontal Alliance Process Model

Many researchers have indicated that alliances should be defined and studied as processes rather than as outcomes (Doz, 1996; Mohr & Spekman, 1994; Ring & Van de Ven, 1994; Varadarajan & Cunningham, 1995). Nonetheless, although scholars acknowledge that studying the evolutionary processes through which alliances move is an important research priority, research attention has been centered on explaining how alliances are formed and on examining relationships between alliance outcomes and initial characteristics of the alliance (Doz, 1996).

A process perspective is useful for portraying alliance constructs and interrelationships. A view of the alliance process as a combination of evolutionary stages appears useful as a guide for conceptual development and empirical research. A horizontal alliance process model is shown in Figure 16.1. Below, we examine each stage in the process model, indicating relevant constructs, the current state of knowledge, research questions, and related issues.

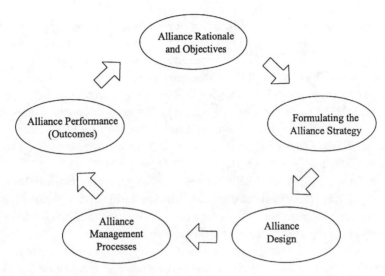

Figure 16.1. Horizontal Alliance Process Stages

ALLIANCE RATIONALE AND OBJECTIVES

Varadarajan and Cunningham (1995) provide an excellent review of various conceptual frameworks that seek to explain the motives of organizations in considering the formation of strategic alliances. Osborn and Hagedoorn (1997) provide an important state-of-the-art prospective evolutionary dynamics of alliances. The motives for forming alliances can be placed into two major categories: opportunism and resource dependence.

Hagedoorn (1993) considers these two general categories in a slightly different categorization relating to the motives for formation of strategic technological alliances. Hagedoorn provides an extensive overview of the literature related to general technological motivation, acquisition of concrete innovation processes, and access to markets and opportunities. However, an evaluation of motivation relating to opportunism and resource dependence includes these factors. Most important, Varadarajan and Cunningham (1995) emphasize the need to recognize that the rationale for strategic partnering is likely to include a combination of factors rather than a single theoretical justification. The specific drivers of the alliance may include opportunistic factors (e.g., organizational learning) as well as resource dependence factors (e.g., gaps in distinctive capabilities and assets). These motivations will in turn affect the specific objectives that the alliance seeks to achieve. From a research perspective, the diffi-culty arises in determining whether or not the alliance is suitable for a sin-gle objective or a combination of specific objectives.

Osborn and Hagedoorn (1997) indicate that the very large number of alliances formed in the 1980s and early 1990s argues against their having been formed as the result of negotiations among senior executives and subsequent direct command and control by these executives. Instead, many of these alliances appear to be linked to business strategy rather than to overall corporate strategy.

Osborn and Hagedoorn (1997) also question the logic of strategic com-patibility as an important predictor of alliance formation, operation, and success. The alliance record indicates that many organizations forming al-liances display quite discrepant characteristics. Osborn and Hagedoorn observe that in the many alliances that are formed, either strategically compatible partners are involved or this dimension is not particularly im-portant. Because compatibility has strong support in the alliance litera-ture, the questioning of its role has important implications for alliance research.

Opportunism

As Kogut (1988) notes, an alliance provides an avenue for increasing competitive advantage, increasing organizational learning, and improv-ing efficiency. Although Kogut's research considers joint ventures, his findings may also be relevant for explaining alliance motives. An oppor-tunistic firm recognizes the potential benefit of seeking one or more part-ners with which to collaborate in achieving the firm's strategic objectives. A firm may be much more successful in offering superior customer value by working with a strong partner than by competing alone. The relation-ship may also offer the firm an opportunity to learn from the partner, and better efficiencies may be gained by both partners. For example, oppor-tunism benefits are present in the proposed American Airlines and British Airways strategic alliance.

One recent study examined the effects of knowledge transfers on tech-nological capabilities of strategic alliance partners (Mowery, Oxley, & Sil-verman, 1996). The research results indicate that equity joint ventures ap-pear to be more effective in transferring complex capabilities than are contract-based alliances. The researchers also found support for lower levels of transfer occurring in unilateral contracts compared with bilateral contracts.

Resource Dependence

The underlying logic of resource dependence is that few companies are self-sufficient concerning all of the essential capabilities and assets needed to execute their strategies (Varadarajan & Cunningham, 1995). Skill and resource gaps and environmental risks and uncertainties cause organizations to seek collaborative relationships with other organizations. Accordingly, interorganizational dependence and uncertainty constitute potentially important antecedent constructs in the formation of strategic alliances.

The primary research stream concerning strategic alliances has centered on the rationale for and objectives of such alliances. Doz (1996) has reviewed several studies conducted during the past decade that have examined the patterns of alliance formation. He indicates that most of the studies involve cross-sectional analysis and concern (a) the determinants of cooperation and/or (b) contractual versus relational forms of cooperation.

FORMULATING THE ALLIANCE STRATEGY

When reaching the strategy formulation stage of the alliance process, the initiating organization will have decided to pursue an alliance because of one or more opportunism and resource dependence antecedents and will have identified the objectives to which the alliance is expected to contribute. Formulating the alliance strategy includes analyzing and reconfiguring the value chain, deciding which partner(s) to select, and anticipating future challenges in maintaining strategic options (Yoshino & Rangan, 1995, pp. 75-77).

Analyzing and Reconfiguring the Value Chain

Analysis of each value-chain activity helps to determine where partnering may be beneficial. The organization benefits by concentrating on internal activities that add substantial and distinctive value, whereas opportunities for partnering center on the activities that can be performed better or at lower cost by the alliance partner. Reconfiguring is the result of allocation of the value-adding activities among the partners for the strategic project. Shank and Govindarajan (1992) provide an overview of the value-chain analysis process from a cost-reduction perspective. However, this is an excellent illustration that includes strategic motivations and can be applied to collaborative relationships. Several companies have adopted a value-chain approach that has resulted in significant cost savings from a variety of methods. For example, in its 1994 annual report, Toyota publicized the specifics of an overall value-chain analysis that resulted in a cost savings of $1.5 billion. Unfortunately, the reconfiguration of the structures of companies involved in alliances has received no apparent research attention.

The strategy of competing on capabilities offers considerable conceptual direction to value-chain activity analysis and reconfiguration (Cravens, Greenley, Piercy, & Slater, 1997; Day, 1994). The process of mapping and analyzing capabilities provides direction as to which activities will be performed by each partner and how activity linkages will be accomplished. The concepts and methods guiding total quality management offer a basis for analysis and reconfiguration of the value chain. Porter (1995) provides important guidelines and applications for developing activity-system maps.

Partner Selection

A substantial amount of research has been conducted on the desirable characteristics of alliance partners (Harrigan, 1988). Although the match with a partner that can contribute complementary value-enhancing activities is a necessary selection criterion, commitment and trust between the partners are also critically important factors in the choice of alliance partners (Morgan & Hunt, 1994).

Bucklin and Sengupta (1993) also document the benefits resulting from the presence of complementary partners in an alliance, but Parkhe (1991) suggests an additional dimension of the partnership that should be considered. According to Parkhe, interfirm diversity and its related effects on organizational learning will also affect alliance longevity and effectiveness. Parkhe has developed a process model of longevity that considers different types of interfirm diversity. This model provides a useful framework that enhances the consideration of alliance partners from a research perspective.

Based on alliance studies of 37 companies from 11 regions of the world, Kanter (1994, pp. 99-100) identifies three important partner selection criteria:

1. Self-analysis aimed at self-understanding and industry analysis coupled with experience in evaluating alliance partners
2. Chemistry—that is, positive feelings between the partners, including personal and social interests
3. Compatibility on common experiences, values and principles, vision, and the future

Interestingly, these criteria center on people rather than on financial and strategic analyses, suggesting that such analyses are necessary but not sufficient bases for partner selection. Kanter's research has also identified different global views about relationships. She found North American companies to be the most opportunistic and Asian companies to be very positive toward relationships; European companies were positioned between the other two groups.

Burgers et al. (1993) consider more traditional criteria, such as performance and firm size, and the affect on partner selection within the global auto industry. Their results indicate that large and small firms seek alliance partners from a smaller, related subnetwork. Intermediate-size firms do not concentrate on partner selection from a subnetwork. Burgers et al. also show that larger firms tend to seek alliances with smaller firms and vice versa, rather than forge alliances with firms of comparable size. In discussing the trade-offs between reducing uncertainties through networks of alliances and losing strategic flexibility, Burgers et al. point to a firm's joining a subnetwork that is not interlinked to other subnetworks involving the same organizations.

Gulati's (1995) research provides support for a close relationship between social structure and alliance formation. His data cover a 9-year time span and involve 4,543 alliance dyads in 166 firms representing new materials, industrial automation, and automotive products sectors. The findings indicate that companies are more likely to form alliances with partners with which they have greater interdependence. These findings are generally consistent with those of Kanter (1994).

Anticipating Future Challenges

At the strategy-formulation stage of the alliance, studies of alliance experiences point to the need for the firm to develop mechanisms for coping with future relationship situations, including the possibility of the partner's becoming an adversary (Yoshino & Rangan, 1995, pp. 76-77). Also important is the organization's anticipating possible failure of the partner to meet its responsibilities in the relationship. This may have serious negative consequences with customers, whose expectations have been elevated by the potential alliance results.

ALLIANCE DESIGN

Alliance design and structure have received some research attention. The findings support a relationship between alliance structure and success of the partnership (Hamel, Doz, & Prahalad, 1989; Ohmae, 1989; Yoshino & Rangan, 1995). Research evidence and management experience suggest that managers allocate substantial time and effort to deciding how to structure their alliances. Moreover, lack of attention to this stage of the alliance process may indicate a risk of poor performance.

Two factors appear to be important in the choice of alliance structure: the compatibility of the alliance structure with an organization's competitive strategy and the operational efficiency of the alliance structure (Yoshino & Rangan, 1995). Studies of alliance structure will benefit from a longitudinal or evolutionary process perspective, and, as Doz (1996) notes, such studies are scarce. Although not specifically focusing on structure, Doz's research concerning learning processes in alliances provides useful descriptive insights about the operational aspects of alliance structures.

Day (1995), in commenting on the durability of alliances through mutual commitment of the partners and citing Kanter's (1994) analyses of specific alliance commitments, offers useful insights into alliance structure. Day discusses the specific investments of the partners; the nature and scope of information sharing; the development of people linkages at different organizational levels and across functions; defined authority, responsibilities, and decision process; and integrity in the relationship indicated by behaviors that enhance mutual trust. The examination of these alliance design and structure elements presents major research challenges, including the need to design and conduct longitudinal studies.

Parkhe (1993) has addressed strategic alliance structuring and its relationship to the opportunity for cheating, high behavioral uncertainty, and poor stability, longevity, and performance. His sample consisted of 111 interfirm alliances. The structure-related constructs in Parkhe's model include the "shadow of the future" (trade-off between the gains of cheating and the possible sacrifice of future gains by violating an agreement) and the "pattern of payoffs" (changes that may alter the initial payoff conditions). Parkhe did not find a significant relationship between alliance performance and the shadow of the future, but the relationship between performance and the pattern of payoffs was significant. Although Parkhe's research is relevant to alliance structure, it provides only limited insight into the design and structure of alliances. Additional research into this stage of the alliance process is needed.

Yoshino and Rangan (1995) observe that competitive strategy considerations are likely to have more impact on the choice of the alliance structure than are operational efficiency factors. Included in the former are the perceived impact of the alliance on competitive success over the long term, the strategic interdependence of the partners, and the opportunities for learning. Even though less important than strategy considerations, the operational costs related to production aspects, marketing interfaces, and operating characteristics of the partners are also potentially relevant determinants of structure.

ALLIANCE MANAGEMENT PROCESSES

Ring and Van de Ven (1994) make a persuasive argument for taking a process view in the study of cooperative interorganizational relationships (IORs):

> As agents for their firms, managers need to know more than the input conditions, investments, and types of governance structures required for a relationship. These process issues also have important temporal implications for performance. The ways in which agents negotiate, execute, and modify the terms of an IOR strongly influence the degree to which parties judge it to be equitable and efficient. (p. 91)

They also acknowledge the importance of the inputs, structure, and desired outputs of a relationship, and they highlight the role of processes in continuing or aborting the relationship over time. The ongoing interaction processes may create positive, negative, or neutral perceptions of the relationship.

Process Framework

Ring and Van de Ven (1994) have developed a process framework that includes the stages of negotiations, commitments, and executions, as well as assessments of each of these process stages. Included in the negotiations stage are partners' motivations, possible investments, and uncertainties about the relationship. Negotiation involves formal bargaining processes and choice behavior of the alliance members. The commitments stage resolves the terms and governance structure of the relationship. In the executions stage the commitments and rules of action are implemented. Assessment occurs throughout these management process stages.

Empirical Research on Process

Ring and Van de Ven (1994) present seven propositions based on their process framework, but do not conduct empirical tests, although they conducted an earlier process study concerning the structuring of cooperative relationships (Ring & Van de Ven, 1992).

Doz's (1996) study of learning processes in strategic alliances provides empirical findings concerning how learning across several dimensions (environment, task, process, skills, goals) mediates between the initial conditions and the outcomes of alliances. Employing case studies of alliance projects, Doz provides support for the positive impact of learning on alliance success.

INFLUENCES ON HORIZONTAL ALLIANCE PERFORMANCE

Much of our understanding of the determinants of successful strategic alliances is experience based rather than the result of empirical studies (see, e.g., Bleeke & Ernst, 1991, 1995; Collins & Doorley, 1991). Experience suggests that alliance success depends on (a) the underlying logic for forming the alliance, (b) the process of implementing the alliance strategy, and (c) the activities and people involved in managing the alliance to achieve successful outcomes. However, there is limited empirical evidence that suggests an additional determinant of alliance success: the complexity of the alliance objective.

Assessing the Logic of the Alliance

Assessing the logic of the alliance involves considering whether the project corresponds well with the features of a horizontal alliance. Day (1995) indicates that the sustainability of competitive advantage through a strategic alliance depends on whether the relationship offers (a) mutual value to the partners, (b) durability through mutual commitment, and (c) barriers to imitation. These characteristics play key roles in the success of an alliance. Osborn and Hagedoorn (1997) point also to the relevance of national and industry considerations as factors in alliance formation while emphasizing the need for increased understanding of how (and to what extent) these factors affect alliance processes and performance.

Implementing the Alliance Strategy

Day (1995) indicates that an advantageous alliance depends, in part, on the positioning of the alliance within a broader network of collaborative relationships. Even if the logic is sound, success of the alliance is very dependent on effective implementation (Collins & Doorley, 1991; Day, 1995). Studies of successful alliances indicate that several considerations affect the implementation process, including choosing the right partner, developing comprehensive plans, establishing a leadership structure, identifying the contributions of each partner, and balancing trust with self-interest. Analysis of the alliance formation process guided by comprehensive planning appears to be an important success factor. Nonetheless, most of the findings are the result of case histories rather than the consequence of rigorous conceptual and empirical research.

Managing the Alliance

Various aspects of the management processes of the alliance may affect alliance success. Considerations identified through analysis of the experiences of alliance partners include anticipating and providing guidelines for conflict resolution, recognizing the interdependence of the partners and providing for flexibility to adjust for changing conditions, and accommodating cultural differences (Collins & Doorley, 1991). Parkhe (1991) echoes these challenges and emphasizes the increased difficulties associated with global alliances in terms of cross-cultural negotiations, management procedures, corporate culture, and national setting.

Complexity of the Alliance Objective

Hagedoorn (1993) provides indirect support for the consideration of complexity as a determinant of alliance success. This, of course, has a high degree of intuitive appeal. In addition to the selection of projects that correspond to the features of an alliance, the eventual success of the alliance may be a function of the complexity of the project. Clearly, firms form alliances in response to needs that they cannot fulfill as independent entities. It is logical that alliances that seek to fulfill complex objectives along several dimensions will extract more effort from the partners and will be more difficult to manage. In a study exploring the motivations for the formation of more than 4,000 strategic technology alliances, Hagedoorn (1993) found that the more complex forms of alliances are created when firms seeks to satisfy wider sets of objectives. More simple and one-dimensional forms of alliances are selected when the objective is to improve innovation, such as applied research cooperation. Thus this research suggests that the alliance form may be derived from the complexity of the objective of the alliance. This complexity is likely to translate to difficulties in governance and execution that may influence the potential for success of the alliance. Questioning the uniqueness of this aspect of alliances, Osborn and Hagedoorn (1997) note that complexity is not unique to alliances; many internal organization forms present complex integration and management challenges.

Measurement of Alliance Performance

Parkhe (1993) has developed scales to measure alliance performance. Two factors were produced, with one loading on major strategic needs (e.g., when needs are satisfied, the alliance is performing well). The second factor, indirect performance, includes benefits for the parent firms, relative profitability, and overall performance assessment. Parkhe found fulfillment of major strategic needs to be significantly correlated with behavioral transparency, frequency of interaction, length of time horizon, opportunistic behavior (negative), cooperative history, and nonrecoverable investments. Indirect performance is significantly correlated with frequency of interaction, length of time horizon, opportunistic behavior (negative), cooperative history, nonrecoverable investments, and firm size. Parkhe's data were obtained from a judgmental sample of 111 executives in firms with alliance experience.

Performance Issues

Several alliance performance issues require attention in the planning and conduct of strategic alliance research. Performance should be examined from both partners' perspectives, because an alliance is intended to achieve joint and individual objectives. Assessment at different alliance evolution stages is also necessary to determine changes and capture the entire process. In a complex network organization, determining overall alliance performance may require examining performance across various alliance dyads.

Kanter (1994) emphasizes that alliances are living systems that evolve over time and need to (a) yield benefits for the partners, (b) create new value rather than exchange value, and (c) involve a complex network of interpersonal connections and internal infrastructures that enhance learning. Performance assessment requires the development of relevant measures of these complex living systems of interlinked organizations.

Saxton (1997) employed a longitudinal research design to examine the effects of partner and relationship characteristics on alliance outcomes. Performance studies have typically used cross-sectional samples. One interesting finding is that a prior relationship among the partners was linked to initial satisfaction but not to the longer-term alliance benefits gained by the partners.

Emerging Issues in Horizontal Alliance Research

Strategic alliance research will expand in the future due to the escalating importance of this element of business strategy. Acknowledging that there are many issues to be resolved in planning alliance research, we discuss below some that we believe are particularly important.

RELEVANT CONSTRUCTS AND RELATIONSHIPS

The conceptual logic of viewing strategic alliances as evolutionary processes is clearly acknowledged, and researchers point to various constructs that are related to one or more process model stages. We have discussed several constructs of potential importance in alliance research, including objectives, commitment, trust, structural linkages, distinctive capabilities, cooperation, adaptability, reputation, and compatibility. What is less apparent is how these constructs and the process stages fit together into a conceptual framework that can guide future research.

The alliance model conceptualizations that have been developed consider only a few constructs and process stages (Doz, 1996; Parkhe, 1993; Ring & Van de Ven, 1994). Ring and Van de Ven (1994) outline a research approach for studying their propositions that tracks alliance events (critical incidents related to the development of the participants' relationship) from the beginning of the alliance to a conclusion, such as the completion of a project.

The reality is that our knowledge concerning alliance processes and the constructs that operate in the context of these processes is very limited. One issue to be addressed in our attempts to advance the state of knowledge is whether we should seek to expand our conceptual understanding of alliance processes or, instead, work toward building empirical findings guided by the present limited conceptual foundations. The evidence seems to favor the pursuit of both research avenues. The objectives would be to expand the conceptual foundations through empirical research and to make incremental additions of potentially relevant constructs to the conceptual models guiding the empirical research.

UNIT(S) OF ANALYSIS

Another important alliance research issue is the question of what unit(s) of analysis to employ. Several options for the unit of analysis in the study of strategic analysis are shown in Figure 16.2. Possibilities for research focus include the executive(s) responsible for the alliance in each organization, the dyad relationship between two partners, the alliance project, the business strategy to which the alliance is intended to contribute, and the organization's entire network of relationships. For example, we could consider the alliance between Organization E and the network coordinator. The unit of analysis would be the dyad. Alternatively, the alliance project might be the focus of research and might involve A, C, and D. From a different perspective, an alliance project could be examined in terms of its role in business strategy. Doz (1996) proposes combining

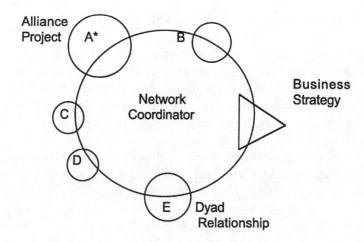

Figure 16.2. Units of Analysis for Studying Horizontal Alliances

*Interorganizational relationships between the network coordinator and organizations A-E.

units of analysis at multiple levels of aggregation. This approach would consider expectations and behaviors of specific individuals and interpersonal relationships for specific alliance projects. Additionally, a third level of analysis would involve organizational and strategic contexts.

The research approaches used in various channel of distribution studies may offer insights for the study of horizontal strategic alliances (e.g., Burgers et al., 1993; Dwyer, Schurr, & Oh, 1987; Mohr & Spekman, 1994). A typical limitation of alliance empirical studies is the use of only one partner as the source of data. A complete view of the alliance process requires that researchers obtain information from individuals in both partner firms and examine the organizational characteristics of both partners.

Several empirical studies have included different interorganizational relationships in their samples. Researchers may include joint ventures, horizontal alliances, and supplier-manufacturer collaboration in their samples. As discussed initially, we believe the alliance designation should be restricted to horizontal collaborative relationships. Regardless of the strategic alliance designation employed, the combining of data from different interorganizational forms has the potential to generate misleading results unless the researcher pays attention to the effects of the different organization forms.

OBTAINING SAMPLES FOR EMPIRICAL STUDIES

Identifying companies participating in strategic alliances may require qualifying respondents through initial contacts to determine their extent of involvement in collaborative interorganizational relationships. The use of the term *strategic alliance* to designate various horizontal and vertical relationships requires a clear operational definition of the relationship being studied.

There are alliance databases available such as the Cooperative Agreements and Technology Indicators (CATI) database, which has information on more than 9,000 alliances involving more than 5,000 companies representing various industries and countries (Mowery et al., 1996). The CATI database was developed from secondary information. INSEAD in Fontainebleau, France, maintains a large database on cooperative arrangements between organizations. Organizations such as the Conference Board conduct studies of alliances and publish the results in their reports to members.

Our research with *Fortune* 1000 companies indicates that about half of them participate in one or more strategic alliances. This estimate is probably low, considering the expanding use of alliances. Alliances are most likely to be used by large companies competing in global markets.

NETWORK ORGANIZATIONS AND ALLIANCES

Because alliances often are part of network organizations, it is important for researchers to examine issues involving alliance networks. Two areas in particular warrant attention: (a) identification and study of network linkages, structures, and configurations in different types of networks; and (b) the examination of how environmental and industry characteristics affect the formation and stability of network linkages as well as the resulting distinctive organization sets and networks (Cravens et al., 1996).

Two network forms are likely to employ collaborative relationships involving strategic alliances. The *flexible network* utilizes specialists working with an organization that is the network coordinator. It possesses market knowledge and provides product design expertise. The *virtual network* utilizes both vertical and horizontal collaborative relationships, with the network coordinator providing product innovation and production skills (Cravens et al., 1996).

Alliance research involving network organizations needs to take into account how alliance dyads fit into the network structure. Utilizing only a dyad focus may not reveal relevant network linkages that influence the dyadic relationship being studied. Developing a complete perspective may require the use of the network as the unit of analysis.

Burgers et al. (1993) discuss the dilemma confronting firms involved in complex networks. Such relationships reduce uncertainty but also decrease long-term strategic flexibility. A possible strategy for coping with this situation is the formation of a network organization comprising several subnetworks (Aldrich & Whetten, 1981). Depending on an organization's objectives, it may form such a network or join a particular subnetwork. A firm can use either strategy to increase strategic flexibility. The subnetwork can be altered or disbanded more easily than can a complex interlinked network.

Summary and Conclusions

Strategic alliances have been very popular during the past decade and will continue to be employed in the 21st century as companies increasingly align with partners and create networks of interorganizational relationships. The incidence of alliances has surged ahead of conceptual and empirical research, creating a rapidly expanding array of research needs. The opportunities for research are extensive, although there are major research challenges involved in the study of these complex relationships.

Many research questions are suggested in our discussion of the alliance model (Figure 16.1) and the constructs linked to various stages of the model. Varadarajan and Cunningham (1995) also point to several research topics, including assessing the extensive use of alliances in certain industries, determining the underlying reason for the proactiveness of certain companies (such as Corning and General Electric) in pursuing alliances, deciding the objectives that are particularly appropriate for alliance strategies, and considering the implications for organizing the marketing function in organizations employing alliance strategies. Similarly, in their state-of-the-art examination of interorganizational alliances and networks, Osborn and Hagedoorn (1997) identify many research opportunities and challenges.

A major hindrance to the advancement of our understanding of alliances has been the failure of researchers to recognize different classifications or types of alliances. Sheth and Parvatiyar (1992) provide a classification, but many researchers do not acknowledge the impact of the alliance form on the results of empirical studies. This dimension may account for some of the contradictory findings of alliance research.

Strategic alliances will expand in importance in the future for those organizations seeking to leverage their capabilities with partners in order to create superior customer value. The low success record of alliances, the potential opportunities for gaining competitive advantage, and limited understanding of the use and effectiveness of strategic alliances present major research challenges for both scholars and managers.

More important, research may also need to consider the extent to which firms employ alliances actually to assist in the development of strategy, rather than merely to implement strategic objectives. Simons (1990) describes this sort of phenomenon in a general sense. Ultimately, strategic alliances are most effective when they are used in a truly proactive and "strategic" manner. However, research on alliances must first progress to a more complete understanding of alliance attributes and execution before a more complex analysis can be conducted.

References

Aldrich, H. E., & Whetten, D. A. (1981). Organizational sets, action sets, and networks: Making the most of simplicity. In P. C. Nystrom & W. H. Starbuck (Eds.), *Handbook of organizational design* (pp. 385-408). New York: Oxford University Press.

Ayling, B. (1997, January 30). Britain's sky wars: We're benefiting the consumer. *Wall Street Journal*, p. A16.

Bleeke, J., & Ernst, D. (1991). The way to win in cross-border alliances. *Harvard Business Review, 70*(2), 127-135.

Bleeke, J., & Ernst, D. (1995). Is your strategic alliance really a sale? *Harvard Business Review, 73*(3), 97-105.

Bucklin, L. P., & Sengupta, S. (1993). Organizing successful co-marketing alliances. *Journal of Marketing, 57*(2), 32-46.

Buffington, B. L., & Farabelli, K. F. (1991). Acquisitions and alliances in the telecommunications industry. In H. E. Glass (Ed.), *Handbook of business strategy* (3rd ed.). New York: Warren, Gorham, & Lamont.

Burgers, W. P., Hill, C. W. L., & Kim, W. C. (1993). A theory of global strategic alliances: The case of the global auto industry. *Strategic Management Journal, 14*, 419-432.

Collins, T. M., & Doorley, T. L. (1991). *Teaming up for the 90s*. Homewood, IL: Business One-Irwin.

Cravens, D. W., Shipp, S. H., & Cravens, K. S. (1993, March). Analysis of cooperative interorganizational relationships, strategic alliance formation, and strategic alliance effectiveness. *Journal of Strategic Marketing, 1*, 55-70.

Cravens, D. W., Piercy, N. F., & Shipp, S. H. (1996). New organizational forms for competing in highly dynamic environments. *British Journal of Management, 7*, 203-218.

Cravens, D. W., Greenley, G., Piercy, N. F., & Slater, S. (1997). Strategic management as a business philosophy. *Long Range Planning, 30*, 493-506.

Day, G. S. (1994). The capabilities of market-driven organizations. *Journal of Marketing, 58*(4), 37-52.

Day, G. S. (1995). Advantageous alliances. *Journal of the Academy of Marketing Science, 23*, 297-300.

Day, G. S., & Wensley, R. (1988). Assessing advantage: A framework for diagnosing competitive superiority. *Journal of Marketing, 52*(2), 1-20.

Doz, Y. L. (1996). The evolution of cooperation in strategic alliances: Initial conditions or learning processes? *Strategic Management Journal, 17*, 55-83.

Dwyer, F. R., Schurr, P. H., & Oh, S. (1987). Developing buyer-seller relationships. *Journal of Marketing, 51*(2), 11-27.

Goldman, K. (1995, April 19). Bartle Bogle is seeking alliance to win British Airways account. *Wall Street Journal*, p. B12.

Gulati, R. (1995). Social structure and alliance formation patterns: A longitudinal analysis. *Administrative Science Quarterly, 40*, 619-653.

Gupta, U., & Tannenbaum, J. A. (1991, December 2). Small drug firms break through with research deals. *Wall Street Journal*, p. 32.

Hagedoorn, J. (1993). Understanding the rationale of strategic technology partnering: Interorganizational modes of cooperation and sectoral differences. *Strategic Management Journal, 14*, 371-385.

Hamel, G., Doz, Y. L., & Prahalad, C. K. (1989). Collaborate with your competitors—and win. *Harvard Business Review, 67*(3), 133-139.

Harrigan, K. R. (1984, Summer). Multinational corporate strategy: Editor's introduction. *Columbia Journal of World Business, 19*, 2-6.

Harrigan, K. R. (1988). Joint ventures and competitive advantage. *Strategic Management Journal, 9*, 141-158.

Kanter, R. M. (1994). Collaborative advantage. *Harvard Business Review, 72*(6), 96-108.

Kogut, B. (1988). Joint ventures: Theoretical and empirical perspectives. *Strategic Management Journal, 9*, 319-332.

Mohr, J., & Spekman, R. E. (1994). Characteristics of partnership success: Partnership attributes, communication behavior, and conflict resolution techniques. *Strategic Management Journal, 15*, 135-153.

Morgan, R. M., & Hunt, S. D. (1994). The commitment-trust theory of relationship marketing. *Journal of Marketing, 58*(3), 20-38.

Mowery, D. C., Oxley, J. E., & Silverman, B. S. (1996). Strategy alliances and interfirm knowledge transfer. *Strategic Management Journal, 17*, 77-91.

Ohmae, K. (1989). The global logic of strategic alliances. *Harvard Business Review, 67*(4), 143-154.

Osborn, R. N., & Hagedoorn, J. (1997). The institutionalization and evolutionary dynamics of interorganizational alliances and networks. *Academy of Management Journal, 40*, 261-278.

Parkhe, A. (1991). Interfirm diversity, organizational learning and longevity in global strategic alliances. *Journal of International Business Studies, 22,* 579-601.

Parkhe, A. (1993). Strategic alliance structuring: A game theoretic and transaction cost examination of interfirm cooperation. *Academy of Management Journal, 36,* 794-829.

Porter, M. E. (1995). What is strategy? *Harvard Business Review, 74*(2), 61-78.

Ring, P. S., & Van de Ven, A. H. (1992). Structuring cooperative relationships between organizations. *Strategic Management Journal, 13,* 483-498.

Ring, P. S., & Van de Ven, A. H. (1994). Developmental processes of cooperative interorganizational relationships. *Academy of Management Review, 19,* 80-118.

Saxton, T. (1997). The effects of partner and relationship characteristics on alliance outcomes. *Academy of Management Journal, 40,* 443-461.

Shank, J., & Govindarajan, V. (1992). Strategic cost management and the value chain. *Journal of Cost Management, 5*(4), 5-21.

Sheth, J. N., & Parvatiyar, A. (1992). Towards a theory of business alliance formation. *Scandinavian International Business Review, 1*(3), 71-87.

Simons, R. (1990). The role of management control systems in creating competitive advantage: New perspectives. *Accounting, Organizations and Society, 15,* 127-143.

Varadarajan, P. R., & Cunningham, M. H. (1995). Strategic alliances: A synthesis of conceptual foundations. *Journal of the Academy of Marketing Science, 23,* 282-296.

Yoshino, M. Y., & Rangan, U. S. (1995). *Strategic alliances.* Boston: Harvard Business School Press.

17

Supplier Partnering

JOHN T. MENTZER

In Porter's (1985) value chain, one of the four support activities (procurement) directly involves supplier management, and all of the five primary activities either directly involve (inbound logistics and operations) or are indirectly affected by (outbound logistics, marketing activities, and service) the focal firm's suppliers and their performance. The fact that these value-chain functions are so important and inextricably linked to the suppliers of the focal firm suggests that increased focus should be placed on effective coordination of their interaction with the performance of suppliers.

The marketing value of exploiting supplier partnership competence is demonstrated by the positional advantage (Day & Wensley, 1988) available as a result of the linking of firms and their suppliers into strategic alliances and partnerships. The past decade has witnessed the growth of vertically integrated marketing systems in a behavioral or relational sense (Dwyer, Schurr, & Oh, 1987; Frazier, Spekman, & O'Neal, 1988; Narus & Anderson, 1986; Shamdasani & Sheth, 1995; Sheth, 1996b; Sheth & Parvatiyar, 1995). The strategic alliances that have evolved are broader in scope than simple outsourcing (Sheth & Parvatiyar, 1995) because they include risk and reward sharing. The efficient and effective performance of suppliers produces benefits shared by both partners. As Frazier et al. (1988) note, the emphasis in such relationships is on "the notion of 'total cost of ownership' and the array of value-added services provided" (p. 53). Finally, the past several years have witnessed increasing efforts by firms to reduce their supplier bases and move into single-source relationships with key suppliers (Bertrand, 1986; "Buyers Keep Trimming," 1989; Frazier et al., 1988). These trends underscore the need to refocus strategic thinking on the role suppliers play in establishing positional advantage for the focal firm.

This quest for positional advantage, which has been addressed by numerous authors (Day & Wensley, 1988; Porter, 1985), involves the search for unique value-added services the focal firm can provide to its customers—services that cannot be duplicated readily by competitors. Positional advantage is achieved when the services are unique to the focal firm, cannot be duplicated by the competition, and are readily recognized by customers. Integral to this quest for positional advantage are the values perceived by the customer to emanate from the focal firm, regardless of whether they are actually created by that firm or not. In fact, one of the cornerstones of supplier partnering is functional value sharing—the joint creation of value-added services that benefit both suppliers and customers of the focal firm (Sheth, 1996a). As long as the supplier relationship (not necessarily the supplier or the focal firm) creates these values, the relationship has the potential to achieve positional advantage in the marketplace. Achievement of this potential is dependent upon whether competitors can duplicate these values and whether customers perceive them as benefits emanating from the focal firm. Such successful positional advantage should result in improved supply-chain performance.

My purpose in this chapter is to examine this potential for positional advantage through supplier partnering. To accomplish this, I will first examine the various dimensions of supplier partnering. I will then develop a model of positional advantage through supplier partnering. Finally, I will discuss the research and managerial implications of these dimensions and the model.

Dimensions of Supplier Partnering

Several attempts have been made to identify the factors that are critical to successful partnerships (Bowersox, Daugherty, Dröge, Germain, & Rogers,

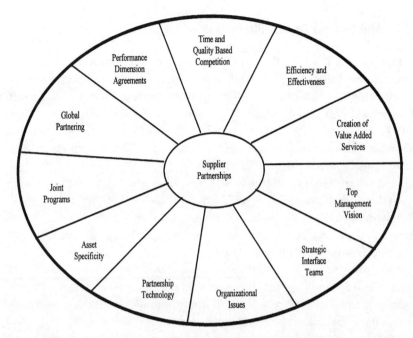

Figure 17.1. The Managerial and Research Dimensions of Supplier Partnering

1991; Monczka, Callahan, & Nichols, 1995; Sheth, 1996a; Tate, 1996). Although there is no general agreement on what these "critical factors" are, a number of dimensions appear to be components of successful supplier partnering and, as a result, are prime candidates for future managerial and research endeavors. These dimensions include competition based on timeliness and quality, efficient and effective performance, the creation of value-added services, the vision of top management, strategic interface teams, organizational issues for both members of the partnership, partnership technology, assets committed specifically to the partnership, joint programs, global partnering, and agreement on partnership objectives, performance measures, and reward structures. These dimensions are illustrated in Figure 17.1, and I discuss each of them below. I will present the apparent impetus for each dimension in supplier partnering, along with a review of the research and managerial thinking on that dimension to date. In addition, I will address the future managerial and research implications of each dimension.

TIME-AND-QUALITY-BASED COMPETITION

Time-and-quality-based competition focuses on achieving positional advantage by eliminating waste in the form of time, effort, defective units, and inventory in manufacturing-distribution systems (Larsen & Lusch, 1990; Schonberger & El-Ansary, 1984; Schultz, 1985; Sheth, 1996a; Wafa, Yasin, & Swinehart, 1996; Waters-Fuller, 1996). The most popular time-and-quality-based concepts are just-in-time (JIT), quick response (QR), and vendor-managed inventory (VMI).

JIT has many facets and touches almost all aspects of a business enterprise (Bartholomew, 1984; Daugherty & Spencer, 1990; Frazier et al., 1988; Rosenberg & Campbell, 1985). As a result, marketing, purchasing, transportation, inventory, and manufacturing personnel all consider JIT to be indigenous to their performance (Yanacek, 1987). In reality, all these areas of the business enterprise are affected by the adoption of a JIT system, and the focus of all these areas is upon supplier performance—purchasing must negotiate and maintain the supplier relationships, transportation must rethink its operations to meet the quick response needs of a JIT system, inventory must be managed more closely, and manufacturing depends upon the performance of all these areas and the supplier to increase efficiency.

Importantly, significant marketing-oriented value-added benefits can result from the establishment of JIT competence with a supplier. For example, higher customer satisfaction from better-quality products with zero defects, more consistent availability, and faster product delivery from the supplier all allow the focal firm to pass similar benefits on to its customers. Typically, such benefits can by fully exploited for positional advantage only if a long-term-oriented partnership exists between the firm and key suppliers. Sheth (1996a) refers to this long-term orientation as "structural bonding," "value bonding," and "reputation bonding." The result of the first of these is that managers are more attuned to supply-side systems and cost control, whereas value and reputation bonding are the result of integrating supplier value-added benefits with the focal organization's marketing programs and customer requirements.

QR and VMI systems are similar to JIT programs (i.e., the requisite integration of marketing with supplier-oriented purchasing, transportation, inventory, and manufacturing) but differ in that they deal with the distribution of finished products from manufacturers and wholesalers to retailers (Larsen & Lusch, 1990). That is, the focal organization in a QR or VMI system is the retailer, and the supplier is a wholesaler or manufacturer. Many of the principles of successful QR and VMI are similar to the logic that drives JIT. However, because QR typically deals with finished-product distribution, supplier performance is an even more integral part of total customer service (Dumaine, 1989). Because a VMI system turns over the management of retailer inventory to a key supplier, supplier performance is not only integral but crucial to retailer customer service (Achabal & McIntyre, 1987; McKinnon, 1990). However, the primary drivers that make most existing QR and VMI programs successful are inventory velocity and total cost reduction. Only a limited number of firms have begun to manage QR programs (Daugherty & Spencer, 1990) or VMI systems (Achabal & McIntyre, 1987) toward the goal of achieving competitive advantage through value-added benefits. The competitive impetus for such coordination of inventory velocity and cost control with customer satisfaction serves as a catalyst for retailer partnering with suppliers, but the potential of value-added benefits leading to positional advantage will be the driving force of such relationships in the future.

The combined effect of time-and-quality-based systems has been to emphasize the need for supplier partnering as a competitive advantage. Whereas JIT, QR, and VMI thrive on long-term supplier partnering, such arrangements must be driven by a desire to reduce cost, improve asset utilization, and service customers more effectively. Future research in this area seems likely to involve investigation of the antecedents and consequences of time-and-quality-based system forms of supplier partnerships. The search for antecedents should focus upon the competitive market environment (i.e., changes in competitive structure, technology, or government regulation), whereas the consequences should follow such established measures of performance as return on investment (ROI), return on assets (ROA), market share, sales growth, and customer satisfaction. Also of particular interest is the management of customer and supplier expectations as retailers and suppliers focus on a narrower range of potential partners (Sheth & Mittal, 1996).

In particular, Sheth (1996a) provides a valuable starting point for the investigation of the antecedents of time-and-quality-based supplier partnering. In his model of partnering enhancement processes, Sheth suggests 10 antecedents to the structural, reputation, and value bonding that leads to enhanced partnering processes: a quality obsession, responsiveness, competence and professionalism, value engineering, mass customization, proactive innovation, frontline information systems, supplier focused teams, supplier involved marketing, and supplier retention compensation. In addition to the competitive market environment factors mentioned in the preceding paragraph, quantification of these antecedents and the testing of their effects on supplier partnering offer a rich avenue for future research.

EFFICIENCY AND EFFECTIVENESS

The supplier perspective on partnership performance is, by its nature, primarily a quantitative measurement of efficiency—delivery time, product quality, the number of short orders, inventory levels, and similar operational activities can be measured readily. As a result, supplier-performance-oriented practice and research has been more operationally oriented and has tended to focus more on economic, or efficiency, measures of performance (Ellram & Krause, 1994; Morash, Dröge, & Vickery, 1996; Murphy, Pearson, & Siferd, 1996). The absolute magnitude of operations cost in the partnership has directed many suppliers to focus on controlling the expense side—that is, to manage the process to achieve a level of efficiency. Unfortunately, from the perspective of the focal organization, it is not the level of efficiency (operational performance) of the supplier that is of primary concern, but rather the level of supplier effectiveness (customer service to the focal firm).

Although there has been considerable research concerning how supplier operational activities affect customer service (for reviews, see Bienstock, Mentzer, & Bird, 1997; Mentzer, Gomes, & Krapfel, 1989), only recently have protocols for measuring customer responsiveness to supplier service levels begun to emerge (Bienstock et al., 1997; Walton, 1996). Further, the traditional focus of supplier research on economic (efficiency) issues rather than behavioral issues has not brought the attention of behavioral researchers in marketing to bear on this problem. Although much research in marketing has been devoted to the behavioral implications of service quality and customer satisfaction/dissatisfaction for final customers (for a review, see Zeithaml, Berry, & Parasuraman, 1993), little such research has addressed the behavioral implications of changes in service quality as part of an overall supplier partnering strategy (Mentzer,

Bienstock, & Kahn, 1993; Mentzer, Rutner, & Matsuno, 1997; Shamdasani & Sheth, 1995; Walton, 1996).

However, cost control (efficiency) without recognition of customer service requirements (effectiveness) will doom any aspect of a supplier partnering effort to eventual failure. An important dimension of the strategic implications of supplier partnering relationships, and a viable avenue for future research, encompasses the need for clearly defined linkages among supplier operational performance, the service needs of the focal organization, and the service needs of the focal organization's customers; the behavioral consequences of all three; and the impacts of all these upon positional advantage.

Traditional research that focuses on a single key informant in either the supplier firm or the focal organization will not fully tap all these elements. Research to address these issues and increase our understanding of the dynamics of supplier partnerships will have to utilize matched-pair dyadic units of analysis to compare and contrast the perceptions of focal organizations and their suppliers of service needs, service performance, operational efficiency, and degree of relationship strength.

CREATION OF VALUE-ADDED SERVICES

The exploitation of supplier relationship competence offers a meaningful way to create value-added services not achievable in other ways (Andraski, 1994; Cooke, 1990; Gentry, 1996; Mentzer, 1993; Wittersdorf, 1991). Such competence requires defining critical focal firm business processes from the perspective of the entire supply chain (Dumand, 1996). This is a challenge not only for the specific supply chain, but for the research community as well. Valuable research questions include the following: What environmental and structural conditions define the types of critical process and supply-chain competencies? When do these competencies lead to channel differential advantage?

The focus on these value-added processes in specific supply chains has spawned the development of new channel institutions—that is, new types of suppliers. Logistics facilitation companies are among the most rapidly growing of these institutions (Bowersox, 1990). Such facilitators do not view themselves as traditional suppliers, such as wholesalers, retailers, warehousers, or transportation companies (Bowersox, Mentzer, & Speh,

1995). They envision themselves as service organizations that satisfy specific value-added service niche requirements. They provide economies of scale, essential services (Lieb & Randall, 1996), and time-and-quality-based delivery. Research concerning the antecedents that lead to the spawning of these institutions, and therefore the ability to predict their advent, would prove valuable to the business community.

The combination of more effective delivery and lower cost translates to increased value. Thus what have traditionally been supplier operational cost drivers are becoming supplier partner-based drivers of differentiation (Day & Wensley, 1988; Porter, 1985). Again, the shift from cost driving activities to drivers of differentiation requires a partnership relationship with key suppliers. Important future research questions include the following: What are these drivers of differentiation? How do they change the roles of traditional suppliers (Gentry, 1996)? How do these drivers of differentiation create new forms of suppliers? How can these drivers of differentiation be turned into positional advantages?

TOP MANAGEMENT VISION

Top management must fully understand and embrace the real and significant operational and market impacts that result from supplier partnerships. Recent history has demonstrated that many of the successes achieved by large consumer goods mass merchandisers have resulted from their suppliers' ability to lower costs while increasing service, resulting in increased final consumer satisfaction combined with reduced retailer inventory (Andraski, 1994). These drivers of differentiation were accomplished only through the vision of top management for the potential of these supplier partnerships and a commitment to leverage these partnerships for the ultimate customers.

Top management vision will result in successful supplier partnering only if the following elements are in place:

1. The supplier's top management applies resources to bring supplier expertise to the focal organization on a customer-by-customer basis (Davis & Manrodt, 1991)
2. The attitude that the satisfaction of the focal organization's customers can result only from a view of the supplier partnership as a corporate core com-

petency is nurtured by top management throughout the entire focal organization

3. The benefits of the supplier partnership are communicated directly from the supplier CEO to the focal firm CEO

An important task for future research is to test the relative importance of these top management perspectives on supplier partnering success in terms of efficiency, effectiveness, and longevity. Specifically, to what degree is the success of supplier partnering driven from the top down?

STRATEGIC INTERFACE TEAMS

Supplier partnering as a driver of differentiation can be achieved only when all parties in both organizations are integrated in terms of the basic concept of customer satisfaction, the potential for supplier performance to aid in obtaining focal firm customer satisfaction, how the message of supplier partnership-based customer value needs to be communicated, and to whom this message should be delivered. Team approaches, with teams typically comprising marketing, sales, logistics, finance, and production representatives, are commonplace and the norm in some industries, with significant resultant advantages (Hutt & Speh, 1984). However, the norm of such teams is to focus on the company's customers, not its suppliers. Sheth (1996a) suggests that one of the key drivers to enhanced partnering processes is teams that are focused on the suppliers to the focal organization.

To achieve this differential advantage through supplier partnering, marketing, sales, and finance from the focal firm must recognize the roles that operations and marketing (in both the focal firm and the supplier) play in the achievement of ultimate customer satisfaction. Without this recognition, the related promotional, pricing, and "service package" strategies to market the customer service advantages of the supplier partnership to the customers of the focal firm will not be achieved. It falls to the supplier, in partnership with the focal firm, to develop and deliver the operational excellence that marketing has identified as important to customers. It falls to the marketing area of both the supplier and the focal organization to leverage this operational excellence with the ultimate customer of the supply chain. It falls to future research to establish more strongly the links between partnership operations and marketing effectiveness, strategic interface teams, and positional advantage.

ORGANIZATIONAL ISSUES

Competence can be created through supplier partnering, but unless both the supplier and the focal firm are positioned to exploit it jointly, little strategic significance (i.e., positional advantage) will result. One way to leverage supplier excellence is to establish hierarchies and reporting relationships, both within each organization and between the two companies, that maximize the potential of the partnership. When marketing, sales, purchasing, and logistics personnel in either company in the partnership report to separate vice presidents, each with his or her own organization, more effort will be required to break down the inherent internal organizational barriers so that the intercorporate integration discussed above can be achieved.

Customer teams and matrix management are commonly used to overcome organizational inflexibility (Clark & Wheelwright, 1992; Gibson, Ivancevich, & Donnelly, 1988; Lawrence, Kolodny, & Davis, 1977). However, because supplier partnering is a function that affects customer satisfaction and has significance as a competitive marketing tool, the value of aligning supplier management more closely organizationally with marketing is a valuable issue for future research. Rather than a team approach, if supplier management reports directly to marketing, the potential for maximum market impact of supplier partnerships may be increased. This will be a radical managerial suggestion in most firms. Typically, supplier management (or procurement/purchasing) is a stand-alone function or reports within the operational hierarchy (i.e., to manufacturing or to logistics). Treating this function as a marketing (customer-value-generating) activity will not be well received by many firms. However, the potential competitive advantages of such an organizational move—and the fact that such a change cannot be quickly duplicated by competitors, resulting in positional advantage—should make for dramatic success stories for the first firms that try it. The role of future research in this area will be to document the performance of firms that try this approach and, eventually, to test the effects on supplier partnership performance of marketing-oriented purchasing functions, as opposed to more traditional operations-oriented purchasing functions or matrix team approaches.

PARTNERSHIP TECHNOLOGY

Improvements in the performance of supply-chain functions (order transmission, order processing, order shipping, and order tracking) are often the key to the success of supplier partnerships. Without success in these functions, there is little impetus to form or maintain a supplier partnership. For the most part, improvements in these functions are technology based and include such technological innovations as electronic data interchange (EDI), bar coding, scanning, advance shipment notices, and sales forecasting (Fojt, 1995).

EDI has been examined extensively in the literature (Daugherty, Germain, & Dröge, 1995; Dearing, 1990; Emmelhainz, 1988; O'Callaghan, Kaufmann, & Konsynski, 1992). Although originally including the simplest fax transmissions of orders to suppliers, EDI has come to refer to direct computer linkages of information concerning orders, demand, and order status. Customer-order-based supplier production scheduling and VMI by the supplier based on customer point-of-sale (POS) information are common features of extant EDI systems. These sophisticated recent manifestations of EDI cannot be achieved without investment in such technologies as universal bar coding and scanning. With all products carried in the supply chain bar coded and scanned at the point of sale to obtain instantaneous, accurate demand information, suppliers can receive accurate, real-time demand information that is directly translatable into the inventory in all the suppliers' and the focal firm's facilities.

Because EDI provides the supplier with information on the focal firm's customer demand far in advance of the supplier's needing to ship product, more precise (and lower-cost) planning of supplier operations can result. Advance shipping notices sent electronically from the supplier to the focal organization allow for similar improved operations planning in the focal firm. Taken together, all of these elements significantly reduce the incidence of producing and/or shipping of the wrong product to the focal organization's facilities as well as reduce the overall levels of inventories in the supply chain. The final result is a lower partnership cost of providing the product and lower incidence of customer service failures due to stock outs.

A technological cornerstone to such inventory-coordinated supplier partnering that has only recently received attention is partnership sales forecasting (Kahn & Mentzer, 1996). In traditional channels of distribution, the retailer orders inventory based upon forecasts of final customer demand. The wholesaler, in turn, orders inventory based upon forecasts of all its retail customers' demand, and the suppliers to the wholesaler do the same. Because each level in the channel is trying to anticipate the demand of the next lower level, each adds some "safety stock" to its orders to account for forecasting errors. Each subsequent level back up the channel sees this safety stock as demand, causing a pattern of overordering and overproduction that magnifies as it moves back up the channel (Kahn & Mentzer, 1996). This phenomenon has been called the bullwhip or whiplash effect (Lee, Padmanabhan, & Whang, 1997).

In supplier partnerships, however, the retailer is the only member of the channel who actually forecasts future final customer demand and carries safety stock to account for forecasting error. Each supplier in the partnership is electronically (through EDI) provided with the retailer forecast and POS demand as it occurs. Each member of the partnership, in turn, uses this real-time information to plan inventory policy. In more advanced forms of this relationship, VMI is instituted and the supplier actually manages the focal organization's inventory based upon the focal organization's forecast. It has been estimated that such supplier partnering can potentially reduce supply-chain inventories by as much as 40% (Kahn & Mentzer, 1996), but no actual empirical evidence of the magnitude of these savings has yet been presented in the literature. An important area for future research would be to provide empirical support for this form of partnering.

ASSET SPECIFICITY

Although the technology-based programs discussed above provide considerable potential for value-added services among the supplier, the focal organization, and the focal organization's customers, organizations must invest in joint technology to achieve these value-added services. Considerable attention has been paid to the impact of transaction-specific assets on the dynamics of strategic channel partnerships (Achrol, Scheer, & Stern, 1990; Anderson & Weitz, 1992; Anderson & Narus, 1990; Dant & Schul, 1992; Dwyer et al., 1987; Gundlach, Achrol, & Mentzer, 1995; Heide & John, 1992; John, 1984; Kaufmann & Stern, 1988; Noordewier, John, & Nevin, 1990).

As noted above, much of the impetus for forming supplier partnerships is technology based, and thus the formation of such partnerships requires investment in assets by suppliers and/or the focal organization that may be idiosyncratic—that is, these assets may be of little value in other partnerships. In addition, these assets may not be fungible, or of any real value if the relationship dissolves. Consider, for example, a supplier that invests in an EDI system that makes the supplier's production scheduling and inventory control software compatible with the ordering software of its customer partner. If the relationship breaks down, the supplier may be left with millions of dollars of investment in communications hardware and software that are not compatible with the systems of any other potential customers. Thus the investment is idiosyncratic (cannot be used with other customers) and nonfungible (cannot be sold to any other company at any appreciable price). Such an investment presents a considerable initial and ongoing risk for the company making the investment.

In particular, this has been the stumbling block for the implementation of EDI in many channels—the reluctance of each organization to embrace the (often idiosyncratic and nonfungible) computer technology of the potential partner. Such embracing involves considerable investment in computer hardware and software, all with little hope of the system being compatible with the EDI systems of other suppliers. Further, once the investment has been made, the investing company is at a considerable disadvantage to the other partner in negotiations (i.e., the investing company now "needs" the partnership to recoup its investment).

The transaction cost analysis paradigm (Macneil, 1980; Williamson, 1975, 1985) has seen considerable application to this problem in the marketing channels literature. One research area ripe for investigation involves the application of this paradigm to the particular manifestations of idiosyncratic, nonfungible investments in supplier partnering, with examination of its impact on the negotiation behaviors of both the supplier and the focal organization and on long-term relationship success.

JOINT PROGRAMS

As the level of technology in supplier partnerships—and the concomitant level of asset specificity—increases, the need for a balancing of dependence and trust in the relationship increases. Research has repeatedly demonstrated that unbalanced investment and dependence lead to opportunistic behavior, which is ultimately a threat to relationship survival (Gundlach et al., 1995; John, 1984). Further, several authors have argued that the existence of reciprocal obligations ameliorates the unbalanced nature of the relationship (i.e., balances dependence) and acts as a deterrent to opportunistic behavior (Kogut, 1988a, 1988b; Pfeffer & Salancik, 1978).

The key research question regarding supplier partnerships is, What kind of joint ventures are best at balancing specific types of idiosyncratic investments? One can envision factorial design research in which various joint ventures with suppliers are crossed with the different types of investments in technology discussed in the two preceding subsections, with trust, relationship satisfaction, and perceived and objective relationship performance as the dependent variables. ROI, ROA, market share, return on sales, and profitability of the supplier, the focal organization, and the overall partnership would all constitute objective measures of relationship performance. Conclusions from such research would provide considerable managerial guidance for supplier relationship balancing as well as valuable insights into the nature of channel relationships in general.

GLOBAL PARTNERSHIPS

Many firms today face decisions regarding whether to use domestic suppliers, global suppliers, or a combination of both. Regardless of the host country for the focal organization, global sourcing often brings with it lower costs but much longer and more variable order cycle times. Further, the cultural differences that arise when two companies from divergent cultures try to conduct business can be astronomical.

Conventional wisdom argues that the savings in product cost from global sourcing ameliorate the costs of increased inventory levels for the focal company. However, little research has been conducted into the ability to leverage global supplier partnering to reduce product costs *and* systemwide inventory levels. What are the leverage points to overcome long and uncertain order cycle times that drive up focal company inventory levels? What are the key cultural, technological, investment, and operational impediments to achieving these leverage points? What are the driving factors that cause a company to choose domestic supplier partnerships over global partnerships or a combination of both? These are all intriguing research questions, the answers to which will have profound value to practitioners and international marketing researchers alike.

AGREEMENT ON PERFORMANCE DIMENSIONS

Finally, any relationship involving joint programs will eventually fail without some definition of the performance dimensions of the partnership. What are the objectives of the relationship? What are the performance measures of each objective? What are the rewards that accrue to achieving performance against these measures? How often will performance be reviewed and rewards allocated? All of these questions are critical to the establishment of trust and a sense of fairness in the relationship with a supplier, both of which are crucial for long-term relationship survival.

Fojt (1995) suggests that the two primary dimensions of channel partnership performance are lowering costs (i.e., financial performance) and improving customer service (i.e., nonfinancial performance), where the financial measures include return on investment and direct product profit and nonfinancial measures include time between order generation and restocking, POS data accuracy, reliability of order lead times, proportion of merchandise sold at full price, and customer satisfaction scores.

Given the discussion of the idiosyncratic, nonfungible assets that are endemic to the technological investments of suppler partnerships, the ROI measure seems particularly important. Further, I have suggested a number of additional measures above, including return on assets, return on sales, and overall perceptions of partnership satisfaction. An important avenue for future research is the investigation of the level of sophistication in performance appraisal in supplier partnerships (i.e., How well are the four questions at the beginning of this subsection defined in the performance evaluation programs with the supplier?), the degree of correlation between performance and rewards, and the relationship of both to perceived partnership success.

A Model of Positional Advantage Through Supplier Partnering

The dimensions just discussed can be viewed as the antecedents to positional advantage for a particular supplier partnership. As such, the existence of these dimensions should lead to the characteristics of positional advantage presented by Day and Wensley (1988)—services that are

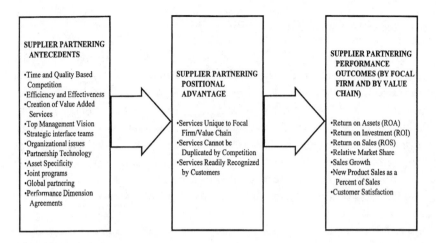

Figure 17.2. A Model of Positional Advantage Through Supplier Partnering

unique to the focal firm (or supply chain), cannot be duplicated by the competition, and are readily recognized by customers. The existence of these characteristics, in turn, should lead to improved overall performance of the focal firm and the value chain as a whole, as measured by ROA, ROI, return on sales, relative market share, sales growth, new product sales as a percentage of sales, and customer satisfaction. These relationships are presented in Figure 17.2.

I have discussed above a number of preexisting conditions to the establishment of the antecedents in the model. However, without the causal linkages illustrated in Figure 17.2, the worth of supplier partnering is problematic. Beyond the future research directions I have mentioned for each antecedent, the true research challenge is to test this model and establish the efficacy of these linkages. The managerial challenge is, on a partnership-by-partnership basis, to begin measuring and documenting the impact of supplier partnering on the performance outcome dimensions in Figure 17.2. Of course, the challenge for both management and research is the operationalization of measures for each of the constructs in Figure 17.2.

Conclusion

Current developments in the business environment and the marketing literature suggest that the supplier partnering dimensions discussed above are having considerable impacts on relationship management. There are increasing examples of firms such as Wal-Mart, Target, and Kmart establishing alliances with manufacturers to jointly reduce costs and leverage performance. Although less well publicized, similar supplier partnerships are developing between participants further up the consumer channels and in industrial channels.

Further, the recent interest in the marketing literature concerning relationship marketing (Anderson & Weitz, 1992; Anderson & Narus, 1990; Dant & Schul, 1992; Dwyer et al., 1987; Frazier et al., 1988; Heide & John, 1992; Larsen & Lusch, 1990; Sheth & Parvatiyar, 1994) suggests progress (in both theory and methodology) in researchers' examination of the strategic management impact of building relationships, both with customers and with suppliers.

Results of such alliances in practice and increased research scrutiny suggest that the issues raised above can be jointly resolved and that superior supplier performance can be integrated into mainstream marketing strategy and research. The reality of such dimensions and the potential to be gained from them argue strongly for in-depth examination of supplier partnership effectiveness in overall marketing strategy and a searching consideration of the key role that supplier relationships play not only in reducing costs, but in creating customer value and satisfaction. To accomplish this, more documentation of extant supplier partnerships and their resultant benefits is needed. From a managerial perspective, such increased documentation is necessary to convince management of the value of such partnerships and to serve as a guide to their effective implementation. From a research perspective, such increased documentation will serve as further antecedent justification for the operationalization of the model presented in Figure 17.2.

The challenge to the research community is twofold. First, researchers must address the dimension-specific issues raised throughout this chapter. The results of such research will establish the conditions under which each dimension does and should exist. Second, researchers need to operationalize and test the model of positional advantage through supplier partnering presented in Figure 17.2. The first step must be a thorough review of existing measures for each of the constructs contained within the model. The next step will be the development of new scales/measures for those constructs not previously addressed in the literature. Finally, the testing of the model through structural equation modeling should provide both researchers and practitioners with considerable insight into the nature of positional advantage through supplier partnering.

As relationship management moves more toward upstream as well as downstream partnering, a program of research to examine individually the dimensions presented in this chapter, to test collectively the model in Figure 17.2, and eventually to move beyond the model with consequent research questions will make timely, interesting, and insightful contributions to the relationship management body of knowledge.

References

Achabal, D. D., & McIntyre, S. H. (1987). Information technology is reshaping retailing. *Journal of Retailing, 63,* 321-325.

Achrol, R. S., Scheer, L. K., & Stern, L. W. (1990). *Designing successful transorganizational marketing alliances* (Rep. No. 90-118). Cambridge, MA: Marketing Science Institute.

Anderson, E., & Weitz, B. A. (1992). The use of pledges to build and sustain commitment in distribution channels. *Journal of Marketing Research, 29,* 18-34.

Anderson, J. C., & Narus, J. A. (1990). A model of distributor firm and manufacturer firm working partnerships. *Journal of Marketing, 54*(1), 42-58.

Andraski, J. C. (1994). Foundations for successful continuous replenishment programs. *International Journal of Logistics Management, 5*(1), 1-8.

Bartholomew, D. (1984). The vendor-customer relationship today. *Production and Inventory Management, 2,* 106-121.

Bertrand, K. (1986, June). Crafting "win-win situations" in buyer-seller relationships. *Business Marketing, 71,* 42-50.

Bienstock, C. C., Mentzer, J. T., & Bird, M. M. (1997). Measuring physical distribution service quality. *Journal of the Academy of Marketing Science, 25,* 31-44.

Bowersox, D. J. (1990). The strategic benefits of logistics alliances. *Harvard Business Review, 68*(4), 36-45.

Bowersox, D. J., Daugherty, P. J., Dröge, C. L., Germain, R. N., & Rogers, D. S. (1991). *Logistical excellence: Its not business as usual.* New York: Digital.

Bowersox, D. J., Mentzer, J. T., & Speh, T. W. (1995, Spring). Logistics leverage. *Journal of Business Strategies, 12,* 36-49.

Buyers keep trimming supplier base despite tight supplies. (1989, February 23). *Purchasing, 104,* 18.

Clark, K. B., & Wheelwright, S. C. (1992, Spring). Organizing and leading "heavyweight" development teams. *California Management Review, 34,* 9-28.

Cooke, P. N. C. (1990). Value-added strategies in marketing. *International Journal of Physical Distribution and Logistics Management, 20*(5), 20-24.

Dant, R. P., & Schul, P. L. (1992). Conflict resolution processes in contractual channels of distribution. *Journal of Marketing, 56*(1), 38-54.

Daugherty, P. J., Germain, R. N., & Dröge, C. L. (1995). Predicting EDI technology adoption in logistics management: The influence of context and culture. *Logistics and Transportation Review, 31,* 309-324.

Daugherty, P. J., & Spencer, M. S. (1990). Just-in-time concepts, applicability to logistics/transportation. *International Journal of Physical Distribution and Logistics Management, 20*(7), 12-18.

Davis, F. W., Jr., & Manrodt, K. B. (1991). Principles of service response logistics. In Council of Logistics Management (Ed.), *Annual conference proceedings* (pp. 339-355). Chicago: Council of Logistics Management.

Day, G. S., & Wensley, R. (1988). Assessing advantage: A framework for diagnosing competitive superiority. *Journal of Marketing, 52*(2), 1-20.

Dearing, B. (1990, January-February). The strategic benefits of EDI. *Journal of Business Strategy, 11*, 4-6.

Dumaine, B. (1989, November). P&G rewrites the marketing rules. *Fortune*, pp. 34-48.

Dumand, E. J. (1996). Applying value-based management to procurement. *International Journal of Physical Distribution and Logistics Management, 26*(1), 5-24.

Dwyer, F. R., Schurr, P. H., & Oh, S. (1987). Developing buyer-seller relationships. *Journal of Marketing, 51*(2), 11-27.

Ellram, L. M., & Krause, D. R. (1994). Supplier partnerships in manufacturing versus non-manufacturing firms. *International Journal of Logistics Management, 5*(1), 43-54.

Emmelhainz, M. A. (1988). Strategic issues of EDI implementation. *Journal of Business Logistics, 9*(2), 55-70.

Fojt, M. (1995). Strategic logistics management. *International Journal of Physical Distribution and Logistics Management, 25*(7), 5-70.

Frazier, G. L., Spekman, R. E., & O'Neal, C. R. (1988). Just-in-time exchange relationships in industrial marketing. *Journal of Marketing, 52*(4), 52-67.

Gentry, J. J. (1996). The role of carriers in buyer-supplier strategic partnerships: A supply chain management approach. *Journal of Business Logistics, 17*(2), 35-56.

Gibson, J. L., Ivancevich, J. M., & Donnelly, J. H., Jr. (1988). *Organizations: Behavior, structure, and processes* (6th ed.). Plano, TX: Business Publications.

Gundlach, G. T., Achrol, R. S., & Mentzer, J. T. (1995). The structure of commitment in exchange. *Journal of Marketing, 59*(1), 78-92.

Heide, J. B., & John, G. (1992). Do norms matter in marketing relationships? *Journal of Marketing, 56*(2), 32-44.

Hutt, M. D., & Speh, T. W. (1984). The marketing strategy center: Diagnosing the industrial marketer's interdisciplinary role. *Journal of Marketing, 48*(4), 53-61.

John, G. (1984). An empirical investigation of some antecedents of opportunism in a marketing channel. *Journal of Marketing Research, 21*, 278-289.

Kahn, K. B., & Mentzer, J. T. (1996). EDI and EDI alliances: Implications for the sales forecasting function. *Journal of Marketing Theory and Practice, 4*(2), 72-78.

Kaufmann, P. J., & Stern, L. W. (1988). Relational exchange norms, perceptions of unfairness, and retained hostility in commercial litigation. *Journal of Conflict Resolution, 32*, 534-552.

Kogut, B. (1988a). Joint ventures: Theoretical and empirical perspectives. *Strategic Management Journal, 9*, 319-332.

Kogut, B. (1988b). A study of the life cycle of joint ventures. In F. J. Contractor & P. Lorange (Eds.), *Cooperative strategies in international business*. Lexington, MA: Lexington.

Larsen, P. D., & Lusch, R. F. (1990, October). Quick response retail technology: Integration and performance measurement. *International Review of Retail, Distribution and Consumer Research, 1*, 17-34.

Lawrence, P. R., Kolodny, H. F., & Davis, S. M. (1977). The human side of the matrix. *Organizational Dynamics, 6*(1), 47-62.

Lee, H. L., Padmanabhan, V., & Whang, S. (1997). Information distortion in a supply chain: The bullwhip effect. *Management Science, 43*, 546-558.

Lieb, R. C., & Randall, H. L. (1996). A comparison of the use of third-party logistics services by large American manufacturers, 1991, 1994, and 1996. *Journal of Business Logistics, 17,* 305-320.

Macneil, I. R. (1980). *The new social contract: An inquiry into modern contractual relations.* New Haven, CT: Yale University Press.

McKinnon, A. C. (1990). Electronic data interchange in the retail supply chain: The distribution contractor's role. *International Journal of Retail and Distribution Management, 18*(2), 39-42.

Mentzer, J. T. (1993). Managing channels in the 21st century. *Journal of Business Logistics, 14*(1), 27-42.

Mentzer, J. T., Bienstock, C. C., & Kahn, K. (1993). Customer satisfaction/service quality research: The defense logistics agency. *Journal of Consumer Satisfaction, Dissatisfaction and Complaining Behavior, 6,* 43-49.

Mentzer, J. T., Gomes, R., & Krapfel, R. E. (1989). Physical distribution service: A fundamental marketing concept? *Journal of the Academy of Marketing Science, 17,* 53-62.

Mentzer, J. T., Rutner, S. M., & Matsuno, K. (1997). Application of the means-end value hierarchy model of understanding logistics service quality. *International Journal of Physical Distribution and Logistics Management, 27*(9-10), 230-243.

Monczka, R. M., Callahan, T. J., & Nichols, E. L., Jr. (1995). Predictors of relationships among buying and supplying firms. *International Journal of Physical Distribution and Logistics Management, 26*(10), 45-59.

Morash, E. A., Dröge, C. L., & Vickery, S. K. (1996). Strategic logistics capabilities for competitive advantage and firm success. *Journal of Business Logistics, 17*(1), 1-22.

Murphy, D. J., Pearson, J. N., & Siferd, S. P. (1996). Evaluating performance of the purchasing department using data envelopment analysis. *Journal of Business Logistics, 17*(2), 77-92.

Narus, J. A., & Anderson, J. C. (1986). Turn your distributors into partners. *Harvard Business Review, 64*(4), 66-71.

Noordewier, T. G., John, G., & Nevin, J. R. (1990). Performance outcomes of purchasing arrangements in industrial buyer-vendor relationships. *Journal of Marketing, 54*(4), 80-93.

O'Callaghan, R., Kaufmann, P. J., & Konsynski, B. R. (1992). Adoption correlates and share effects of electronic data interchange systems in marketing channels. *Journal of Marketing, 56*(2), 45-56.

Pfeffer, J., & Salancik, G. R. (1978). *The external control of organizations: A resource dependence perspective.* New York: Harper & Row.

Porter, M. E. (1985). *Competitive advantage: Creating and sustaining superior performance.* New York: Free Press.

Rosenberg, L. J., & Campbell, D. P. (1985). Just-in-time inventory control: A subset of channel management. *Journal of the Academy of Marketing Science, 13,* 124-133.

Schonberger, R. J., & El-Ansary, A. (1984, Spring). Just-in-time purchasing can improve quality. *International Journal of Purchasing and Materials Management, 20,* 1-7.

Schultz, D. P. (1985, April). Just-in-time systems. *Stores,* pp. 28-31.

Shamdasani, P. N., & Sheth, J. N. (1995). An experimental approach to investigating satisfaction and continuity in marketing alliances. *European Journal of Marketing, 29*(4), 6-23.

Sheth, J. N. (1996a). Becoming a world-class customer. In *Strategic purchasing: Sourcing for the bottom line* (Rep. No. 1157-96-CH, pp. 11-13). New York: Conference Board.

Sheth, J. N. (1996b). Organizational buying behavior: Past performance and future expectations. *Journal of Business and Industrial Marketing, 2,* 7-24.

Sheth, J. N., & Mittal, B. (1996). A framework for managing customer expectations. *Journal of Market-Focused Management, 1,* 137-158.

Sheth, J. N., & Parvatiyar, A. (Eds.). (1994). *Relationship marketing: Theory, methods and applications.* Atlanta, GA: Emory University, Center for Relationship Marketing.

Sheth, J. N., & Parvatiyar, A. (1995). The evolution of relationship marketing. *International Business Review, 4,* 397-418.

Tate, K. (1996). The elements of a successful logistics partnership. *International Journal of Physical Distribution and Logistics Management, 26*(3), 7-13.

Wafa, M. A., Yasin, M. M., & Swinehart, K. (1996). The impact of supplier proximity on JIT success: An informational perspective. *International Journal of Physical Distribution and Logistics Management, 26*(4), 23-34.

Walton, L. W. (1996). Partnership satisfaction: Using the underlying dimensions of supply chain partnership to measure current and expected levels of satisfaction. *Journal of Business Logistics, 17*(2), 57-76.

Waters-Fuller, N. (1996). The benefits and costs of JIT sourcing: A study of Scottish suppliers. *International Journal of Physical Distribution and Logistics Management, 26*(4), 35-50.

Williamson, O. E. (1975). *Markets and hierarchies: Analysis and antitrust implications.* New York: Free Press.

Williamson, O. E. (1985). *The economic institutions of capitalism: Firms, markets, and relational contracting.* New York: Free Press.

Wittersdorf, R. G. (1991). Adding value through logistics management. *International Journal of Physical Distribution and Logistics Management, 21*(4), 6-8.

Yanacek, F. (1987, May). One more just-in-time. *Handling and Shipping Management, 28,* 47.

Zeithaml, V. A., Berry, L. L., & Parasuraman, A. (1993). The nature and determinants of customer expectations of service. *Journal of the Academy of Marketing Science, 21,* 1-12.

PART IV

Enablers of Relationship Marketing

18

Relationship Marketing and Marketing Strategy

The Evolution of Relationship Marketing Strategy Within the Organization

ROBERT M. MORGAN

Over the past three decades the study and practice of business strategy—marketing strategy in particular—has experienced a number of dominant approaches. Some of these approaches have been so widely diffuse and conceptually discontinuous from predecessors that they were labeled new "paradigms" by observers. Strategic planning, portfolio approaches, population ecology, and business process reengineering are all examples of these

AUTHOR'S NOTE: I wish to thank Barry Mason, Ron Dulek, Sharon Beatty, Robert Robicheaux, Tammy Crutchfield, and Beverly Brockman (all of the University of Alabama), Shelby Hunt (Texas Tech University), and Jagdish Sheth (Emory University) for very helpful comments offered during the development of this chapter.

once-dominant approaches to strategy. Although many of these and other approaches to strategy might best be thought of as fads or fashions, others that are no longer dominant continue to offer insights to scholars of strategy and useful guidance for practitioners of strategy. For example, many consulting firms and businesses are once again recognizing the value of strategic planning, now mindful of the pitfalls that accompany its misuse ("Strategic Planning," 1996).

More recently, relationship marketing has emerged in the academic and trade literature as a useful approach to "doing business." It has been argued that relationship marketing is not new (Peterson, 1995; Weitz & Jap, 1995), as businesspeople have long held and practiced business philosophies that promote treating customers and suppliers courteously and working to build corporate cultures that encourage high levels of customer satisfaction through social interaction. However, many scholars and observers of relationship marketing imply, if not express, that relationship marketing can be more than a business philosophy, that it can go beyond a customer-friendly corporate culture: It can be a part of the firm's overall means of achieving its goals and objectives (Morgan & Hunt, in press). In short, relationship marketing can be a major part of the firm's business strategy. Relationship marketing provides the firm with a guiding strategy for a wide variety of decisions, including (a) choices of transactional, recurrent, and relational exchange with customers, suppliers, and others; (b) methods for building competitive advantages based on relationships, where resources are shared through relationships; and (c) structure and selection of cooperative value nets that the firm will participate in so that it may compete in increasingly competitive environments.

In this chapter, I will explore the implications of relationship marketing as part of the firm's marketing strategy. I will take some initial steps to identify what relationship marketing has to offer the study and practice of strategy and what approaching relationship marketing as strategy offers scholars and practitioners of relationship marketing. Moreover, I will trace the evolution of relationship marketing strategy within the organization as it becomes increasingly embedded in the overall strategy of the firm. To achieve this, I begin by revisiting and expanding on the Morgan and Hunt (1994) commitment-trust theory of relationship marketing, which I then use to introduce the strategic nature of marketing relationships. Next, I will explore the relationship-based competitive advantages (RBCAs) that can arise from these relationships as they solidify and mature. I will address how firms combine and manage resources to achieve

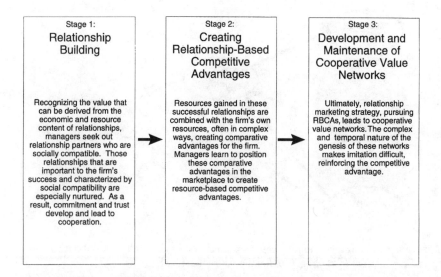

Stage 1: **Relationship Building**	Stage 2: **Creating Relationship-Based Competitive Advantages**	Stage 3: **Development and Maintenance of Cooperative Value Networks**
Recognizing the value that can be derived from the economic and resource content of relationships, managers seek out relationship partners who are socially compatible. Those relationships that are important to the firm's success and characterized by social compatibility are especially nurtured. As a result, commitment and trust develop and lead to cooperation.	Resources gained in these successful relationships are combined with the firm's own resources, often in complex ways, creating comparative advantages for the firm. Managers learn to position these comparative advantages in the marketplace to create resource-based competitive advantages.	Ultimately, relationship marketing strategy, pursuing RBCAs, leads to cooperative value networks. The complex and temporal nature of the genesis of these networks makes imitation difficult, reinforcing the competitive advantage.

Figure 18.1. The Evolution of Relationship Marketing Strategy Within the Organization

advantages—recognizing the role of relationship marketing in the overall strategy of the firm. Finally, with this theoretical foundation in place, I will close by discussing cooperative value nets, which represent the highest level of sophistication of relationship strategy. Cooperative value nets illustrate the importance of practicing relationship marketing principles suggested by the expanded commitment-trust and RBCA theories. This evolutionary process of relationship marketing as marketing strategy is illustrated in Figure 18.1.

Relationship Marketing and the Economic, Resource, and Social Contents of Marketing Relationships

Morgan and Hunt's (1994) commitment-trust theory of relationship marketing holds that commitment and trust are essential to the process of building cooperative marketing relationships. We recognize, however, that the explanatory power of our theory—an initial attempt to explain

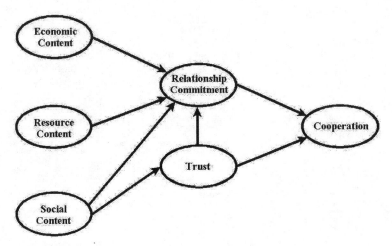

Figure 18.2. The Economic, Resource, and Social Contents of Relationships in the Commitment-Trust Theory of Relationship Marketing

relationship marketing—is limited in some respects. Perhaps most conspicuous is the lack of a theoretical framework for the antecedents of commitment and trust. It seems that to understand more fully the strategic nature of relationship marketing, we need an expanded commitment-trust theory that includes such a framework, because such a framework would shed light on the processes and motivations of relationship building.

The development of commitment, trust, and effective cooperation in marketing relationships depends on three intertwined sets of conditions. First, relationships that provide participants with superior economic benefits will foster effective cooperation and, thus, relationship preservation and success. These economic benefits and costs constitute the *economic content* of marketing relationships. Although economic benefits are necessary, they are insufficient to ensure effective cooperation. A second condition is that parties require the resources of their partners in order to achieve positions of competitive advantage. Indeed, the impetus for each party to enter relationships is to improve its competitiveness by obtaining the resources that it does not already have (Van de Ven & Walker, 1984) or cannot acquire otherwise. Thus the *resource content* of marketing relationships combines the interdependence and strategic explanations for marketing relationship existence and identifies the partner's resources that, when combined with the firm's own unique resources, promote effective cooperation within marketing relationships and result in heightened competition across marketing relationships. Third, marketing relationships must, over time, be characterized by a social environment that encourages effective cooperation. Partners must view past interactions with their partners favorably and believe that future actions by their relationship partners will be constructive—they must perceive that they and their partners are, and will continue to be, compatible. Compatibility results from, for example, partners' sharing similar cultures and communicating openly (Mohr & Spekman, 1994; Morgan & Hunt, 1994). As relationships develop, these factors, the *social content* of marketing relationships, establish norms that guide partner behavior. I propose that, together, the economic, resource, and social contents of relationships constitute the categories of antecedents of commitment and trust, which lead to cooperation and other positive outcomes for marketing's interorganizational relationships (see Figure 18.2).

To establish the underpinnings of an expanded commitment-trust theory of relationship marketing, I first discuss the economic content of marketing relationships, focusing on termination costs and relationship benefits. Second, turning to the resource content, I examine the interdependence and strategic explanations for why firms are inclined to participate in marketing relationships. Finally, looking to the relationship literatures of marketing, management, and sociology, I theorize that, although firms initiate marketing relationships to gain needed resources, several cognitive and behavioral variables—components of the social content of relationships—must be present for marketing relationships to develop and continue.

THE ECONOMIC CONTENT OF MARKETING'S INTERORGANIZATIONAL RELATIONSHIPS

In market-based transactions, participants focus exclusively on the economic benefits of the exchange. Even though in relational exchange the focus widens, economic benefits remain important to all of the partners in marketing relationships. For example, manufacturers desire distributors who require minimal selling support and can move the largest volume of their products (Campbell & Cunningham, 1983); distributors want suppliers whose goods and services provide attractive profit margins, minimize their own selling expenses, and offer superior value to their own customers (Moody, 1993); and alliance partners in symbiotic relationships desire to reduce production and marketing costs (Mody, 1989).

As a relationship becomes increasingly attractive economically for the relationship's partners, it becomes prudent for them to cooperate, as the long-term total costs of doing business are lower *because of* the relationship (Jarillo, 1988). Furthermore, as a relationship moves from market based to episodically recurrent to relational—and hence is characterized as more cooperative—the economic benefits of continuing the relationship increase, as do the economic costs of terminating it. The importance of the economic content of relationships has been illustrated in (a) total quality theory (Anderson, Rungtusanatham, & Schroeder, 1994; Dean & Bowen, 1994; Kalwani & Narayandas, 1995), emphasizing that firms must continually seek out products, processes, and technologies that add customer value to their own offerings, and that collaboration is essential to this process; (b) the costs of cooperation (Porter & Fuller, 1986), where relationships characterized by trust and commitment inherently have lower collaboration costs (including monitoring costs) than those based solely on legal contracts (Astley & Brahm, 1989); and (c) the related concepts of switching costs (Heide & Weiss, 1995; Morgan & Hunt, 1994) and customer retention, widely recognized as providing the firm with marketing efficiency—an economic benefit (Sheth & Parvatiyar, 1995).

THE RESOURCE CONTENT OF MARKETING'S INTERORGANIZATIONAL RELATIONSHIPS

In discussing the resource content, I address three facets of the role of resources in establishing marketing relationships: the interdependence that arises between organizations that exchange resources; the complementarity, and thus the strategic implications, of resources owned, acquired, or needed; and reciprocity, or the degree of equity in commitment of resources to the relationship (Ring & Van de Ven, 1994).

Resources and Interdependence

More than 35 years ago, Levine and White (1961) observed that if resources were in "infinite supply there would be little need for organizational interaction and for subscription to cooperation as an ideal. Under actual conditions of scarcity, however, interorganizational exchanges are essential to goal attainment" (p. 587). Their seminal observations have influenced many social science approaches to exchange, including resource dependence theory (Beder, 1984; Pfeffer, 1981). This theory has centered on the control and autonomy, or power, that organizations surrender by entering into relationships in order to gain needed resources (Aldrich, 1979). Oliver (1991) observes that "resource dependence theorists, in particular, propose that organizations 'seek to avoid being controlled' in exchange relations and that an organization's aversion to establishing interorganizational connections will be proportional to the loss of autonomy anticipated to result from relationship formation" (p. 943). In simpler terms, resource dependence theory maintains that firms are relationship averse.

Oliver (1991) conducted the first empirical test of this tenet of resource dependence theory and failed to find support for it. At least three reasons account for this failure. First, managers realize that the fully integrated firm cannot adapt quickly and lacks flexibility (Powell, 1990). Second, partners realize that specialization of partners, although increasing interdependence, also increases efficiency and effectiveness. As Jarillo (1988) notes, "The network is economically feasible because the specialization of each supplier makes the final total cost lower" (p. 39). Third, the need for resources among *partners* in long-term relationships is ultimately bilateral. Exchanges between firms often begin as market-based transactions, where one party exchanges resources for currency. Eventually resources, both tangible and intangible, are shared as the partners become involved in more complex, shared programs. For these reasons, interdependent firms often seek, rather than avoid, cooperation. Indeed, resources have a strategic role in relationships.

The Strategic Role of Resources

Reviewing the interdisciplinary interorganizational literature, Pennings (1981) observes that "strategic interorganizational behavior has been the primary concern of economics, while sociology and other social sciences have contributed little" (p. 433). Although resource dependence theory captures the *immediate* motivation for forming relationships—to acquire needed resources—it fails to grasp the *strategic* purposes for forming those relationships. Varadarajan and Cunningham (1995) and

Powell (1987), respectively, propose several strategic motivations for forming strategic alliances and partnering more generally. In all instances, the firm is seeking *resources*, including technology, markets, complementary research or production resources, financing, human skills, and competencies.[1] The strategic goal is to achieve a sustainable competitive advantage through long-term relationships (Ganesan, 1994; Varadarajan & Cunningham, 1995) based on complementary resources.

A recent stream of literature in strategic management emphasizes the strategic importance of the firm's *own* resources in the creation of sustainable competitive advantages. Known as the *resource-based view* of the firm (Barney, 1991; Wernerfelt, 1984), this theory maintains that it is the comparative advantage in resources that leads to a position of competitive advantage in the marketplace and, thereby, superior financial performance. As turbulence arising from rapid changes in technology and markets forces organizations to strive for flexibility in their product-market strategy, relational exchanges—collaborations—give strategic meaning to resources (Astley & Brahm, 1989; Morgan & Hunt, in press; Walker, 1988). The resulting competitive advantages derived from a partner's resources serve to sustain strong relationships (Sethuraman, Anderson, & Narus, 1988). Thus resource-based theory explains the *strategic motivation* for the initiation and maintenance of cooperative relationships.

Reciprocity and Equity

The importance of equity (Ring & Van de Ven, 1994) or, more generally, reciprocity (Larson, 1992; Powell, 1987) of resources exchanged in relationships has been stressed frequently. Rooted in exchange theory, equity requires equality in exchange, whereas reciprocity requires only that benefits be proportional to investments (Leventhal, 1980; Ring & Van de Ven, 1994). For relationship success, partners must believe that exchanges of resources are "fair" in the long run. Dodgson (1993) has observed that "at any one time one partner will be a net gainer in a collaboration. The disincentive to cut and run is based on the view of future gains which can only be achieved through continuity of collaboration" (p. 92). In true cooperative relationships, a long-term perspective is taken; short-term sacrifices are outweighed by the prospect of long-term gains. Therefore, partners anticipate that eventually they will have either equal contributions and rewards or rewards proportional to contributions. This is especially true of networks (Larson, 1992).

Commitment Arises From the Economic and Resource Contents of Marketing Relationships

In successful marketing relationships, partners that deliver superior economic benefits—on such dimensions as product profitability, customer satisfaction, and product performance—are highly valued, and firms will commit themselves to establishing, developing, and maintaining relationships with such firms. Furthermore, expected termination costs arising from relationship-specific investments lead to the ongoing relationship's being viewed as *important,* thus generating *commitment* to the relationship (Blau, 1964; Cook, 1977).

Possessing resources that are strategically important to marketing relationship partners leads those partners to become committed to the relationship (Buckley & Casson, 1988). Moreover, possessing resources that are unique can bestow a competitive advantage on a firm (Barney, 1991). Sethuraman et al. (1988) propose that when this advantage is derived from a relationship with another organization, it results in a "partnership advantage." As a consequence, they hold, as do I, that such a partnership advantage gives rise to commitment on the part of the exchange partner. When these exchanges of resources are seen as reciprocal, commitment is enhanced (Buckley & Casson, 1988; Saxenian, 1991).

THE SOCIAL CONTENT OF
INTERORGANIZATIONAL RELATIONSHIPS

Simply acquiring resources per se neither requires nor engenders cooperation. Spot transactions in which cooperation amounts to nothing more than one party providing a good or service and the other providing remuneration occur daily between buyers and sellers. In such transactions neither party anticipates future exchanges. Thus simply needing another's resources is a necessary but insufficient condition for effective cooperation in marketing relationships (Van de Ven, 1976). What other conditions are required? The answer lies in the social content of marketing relationships.

Scholars studying interpersonal relationships emphasize the importance of *compatibility* in relationships (Murstein, 1970; Ort, 1950; Vinacke, Shannon, Palazzo, Balsavage, & Cooney, 1987). Similarly, the social content of a marketing relationship centers on partners' compatibility. Compatible relationships are those in which partners (a) have *similar* attitudes, values, beliefs, and goals; and (b) play *complementary* roles (Murstein, 1970; Vinacke et al., 1987). As Jarillo (1988) notes, firms should choose partners carefully, "searching explicitly for people the entrepreneur can 'relate to,' i.e., with similar values" (p. 37). Likewise, in international joint ventures the domestic partner often acts as the marketplace liaison and the foreign partner provides technological know-how. Thus the parties' roles are identified as complementary.

Compatibility assessments rely on both the words and the actions of potential and current partners. As marketing relationships develop, relational norms are created by which behavior is judged (Heide & John, 1992). Thus compatibility in marketing relationships often involves Ring and Van de Ven's (1994) notion of "congruent expectations" (p. 100). Compatible partners will share views on the relationship norms, their mutual responsibilities, and leadership. Partners jeopardize relationship health and create conflict by violating norms or acting inconsistently within their prescribed roles. Conversely, relationship stability results from partners' abiding by relationship norms and fulfilling accepted roles.

Over time, through communication and observing partners' behaviors, organizations assess the compatibility of themselves and their marketing relationship partners. Compatible strategies (Contractor & Lorange, 1988), goals (Bucklin & Sengupta, 1993; Ruekert & Walker, 1987), managerial and organizational styles (Bucklin & Sengupta, 1993; Porter & Fuller, 1986), operating environments (Galaskiewicz & Shatin, 1981), cultures (Bucklin & Sengupta, 1993), values (Morgan & Hunt, 1994), norms (Gundlach & Murphy, 1993; Heide & John, 1992), and personal characteristics of firm members (Galaskiewicz & Shatin, 1981) contribute to building relationships. In so doing, they decrease the costs of cooperating (Whetten, 1981).

Underlying the social content of most interorganizational relationships are the *interpersonal* relationships that develop among individuals in the partner firms. Moody (1993) studied a variety of interorganizational partnerships and concludes, "At their heart, *partnerships are made by people* working to create an entirely new level of enterprise advantage" (p. 15). These interpersonal relationships form the foundation for establishing beliefs of compatibility, commitment, and trust (Metcalf, Frear, & Krishnan, 1992) and result in a decreased propensity for interorganizational relationship dissolution (Seabright, Levinthal, & Fichman, 1992).

Commitment and Trust Arise From the Social Content of Marketing Relationships

When marketing relationship partners share values and cultures and have established relationship norms, they establish a basis for commitment to develop. Combining these conditions with complementarity of skills and roles gives the relationship added value and commitment is enhanced. Furthermore, as Powell (1990) notes: "Networks should be most common in work settings in which participants have some kind of common background—be it ethnic, geographic, ideological, or professional. The more homogeneous the group, the greater the trust. . . . When the diversity of participants increases, trust recedes and so does the willingness to enter into longterm collaborations" (p. 326). Similarly, Galaskiewicz (1985) holds that managers trust those who are like themselves. Managers base many of their judgments of compatibility on the behavior of their partners. Communication that is frequent, timely, and meaningful fosters trust by resolving disputes and aligning perceptions and expectations (Anderson & Narus, 1990; Dodgson, 1993). When marketing relationship partners are compatible on these indicators, as well as others, they tend to be more trusting of one another and more committed to their relationships (Bucklin & Sengupta, 1993).

Through this extension of Morgan and Hunt's (1994) original commitment-trust theory, we better understand the motivations for firms to engage in relationships. Furthermore, the framework provides us with a way to organize conceptually the multitude of variables that relationship marketing research continues to identify as important to building and maintaining relationships. This understanding gives us a firm foundation for exploring further the strategic implications of relationships and the outcomes that are expected when relationship marketing is included as a component of the organization's marketing strategy. In the section that follows, these implications become very clear, as we see the organization realize the true benefits of relationship marketing that is practiced deliberately and successfully: Relationships become a contributor to the organization's competitive advantage(s).

Resources and Relationship-Based
Competitive Advantages

The resource content of interorganizational relationships identifies the motivations for partnering and the strategic nature of relationships. Simply, firms engage in interorganizational relationships to gain resources, resources that when secured through long-term relationships will ultimately fuel competitive advantages. Regarding the choosing of partners whose shared resources will lead to these relationship-based competitive advantages, several questions must be asked, including the following: What resources need to be gained from relationships? Which partners will contribute most to the firm's sustainable competitive advantage(s)? What are the obstacles to superior management of resources gained in relationships? We can begin to answer these questions by drawing again on the resource-advantage theory of competition (Hunt & Morgan, 1995, 1996, 1997).

Drawing on several streams of literature from strategy and economics, Hunt and Morgan (1995) propose that firms' resources can be separated into seven categories: financial, physical, legal, human, organizational, relational, and informational. An illustration of how this typology of resources could be applied to marketing's cooperative relationships can be found in Table 18.1. Morgan and Hunt (in press) have critically analyzed these categories of resources and propose that comparative advantages created from resource combinations that include complex, intangible resources—that is, organizational, relational, and informational resources—are the most likely candidates to lead to competitive advantages that are sustainable. Although there are many instances in which financial, physical, legal, and human resources are sought by firms in the process of choosing relationship partners, organizational, relational, and informational resources are the most sought-after resources because they are much more difficult to imitate, duplicate, or purchase and are less vulnerable to substitutes. Furthermore, firms possessing those resources will be the most attractive candidates for partnering. By possessing these unique, valuable resources, they offer potential partners the building blocks of competitive advantages.

Understanding these resource issues helps to answer the first two questions raised above. A resource perspective reinforces the view that

TABLE 18.1 Resources Potentially Gained in Cooperative Relationships

Resource	Specific Resource Examples	Relationship Marketing Applications
Financial	venture capital, cash and securities, and borrowing capacity	franchising, financing, leasing
Legal	patents, contracts, and licenses	licensing complementary products
Physical	geographic coverage of markets, plants and equipment, access to raw materials	distribution and logistics decisions
Human	selling skills and breadth of sales personnel, research scientists, visionary leadership, management skills	merchandise selection, training, distribution outlet decisions, compensation for relational exchange
Technological	computer-aided design, unique manufacturing processes, information systems	new product development partnering
Organizational	corporate culture and climate, valued brands, processes for organizational monitoring and quality control systems	high-quality customer service driving choices of partners for foreign market entry
Relational	loyal patrons, committed partners (including employees, suppliers, and intermediate customers), global alliances	retailers' relationships with ultimate customers driving manufacturers' choice of retailers for their products
Informational	knowledge of the unique needs and requirements of segments of customers and the strengths and weaknesses of competitors	foreign market entry partnering decisions; manufacturers' relationships with EDI and ECR partnering retailers and wholesalers

SOURCE: Adapted from Morgan and Hunt (in press).

relationship partners should not be selected by chance. Managers must identify the resources that will best complement their own resources and identify which potential partners have the resource profiles that best fit those needs and lead to true RBCAs. Partner candidates that hold strengths in complementary organizational, relational, and informational resources should be prized above others. However, as emphasized earlier, choosing partners without considering the economic and social content of the resulting relationships can have disastrous outcomes.

Our third question requires us to gain a deeper understanding of *resource management*. Relationship managers must realize that simply acquiring valuable resources from compatible partners is not sufficient to ensure RBCAs and superior relationship performance (Morgan & Hunt, in press). First, the resources must have been or continue to be *efficiently acquired*. A major tenet of resource-based theory is that for a resource to provide value in the process of building advantages, competition for the resource must be limited (Peteraf, 1993), otherwise, the gains of employing the resource would be outweighed by the cost of acquiring it. Relatedly, managers—particularly relationship managers—must also contend with the issue of asset mass efficiencies. For some resources, incremental increases in resource stock acquisition become easier as levels of existing stocks of the resource become large. Dierickx and Cool (1989) point to the example of establishing a dealer network in a new geographic area. Commonly, the first dealerships are the hardest to establish, but they pave the way for the dealerships that follow.

Second, resources are most valuable when they are *combined* in ways that provide effectiveness that is superior to competitors' resource combinations. For many observers of strategy, the process of combining resources is central to explanations of firm success and failure (Hofer & Schendel, 1978; Prahalad & Hamel, 1990). As Hunt and Morgan (1995, 1996) point out, higher-order resources, formed from bundles of two or more resources, are often more difficult to imitate than are single resources. Further complicating the management of relationships, RBCAs, and their attendant resources is the *timing* of managers' efforts to combine resources (Dierickx & Cool, 1989). For extremely valuable resources, the firm's strategy must allow time for relationships to mature—for commitment and trust to be built—so that partner firms will be willing to share those resources.

Third, valuable resources and resource combinations must be properly *positioned* to yield competitive advantages for relationship partners. A task that is daunting in the context of a single firm and its own resources (Hunt & Morgan, 1995), the positioning problem becomes extremely difficult when the roles and actions of two or more relationship partners must be determined and coordinated (Morgan & Hunt, in press). It is in this relationship management task that the value of cooperation, built on commitment and trust, can determine the success or failure of a firm's relationship marketing strategy. For the relationship manager, knowing when and how to deploy the resources of the combined parties is difficult, and when that is combined with the task of implementing that deployment in the face of multiple relationship partners, it is easy to see why so many relationships fail to perform to managers' expectations.

Finally, resources must be *maintained and protected*. Resource flows must be safeguarded, through dutiful relationship nurturing, to maintain resource stocks at adequate levels (Dierickx & Cool, 1989). As with the other duties of relationship managers described above, this proposition becomes much more difficult in a multifirm relationship context. Managers must be aware of the time-dependent nature of relationships while understanding the resource heritage, stocks, and flows of the partner firm(s).

In summary, to achieve competitive advantages, managers must learn to manage the firm's various resources. Managers who are also charged with managing the firm's relationships (e.g., marketing managers) have a much more challenging task. We saw that in the implementation and practice of the first stage of relationship marketing strategy, relationship managers must recognize which potential partners offer the resources most needed by their firm, understand what social factors will contribute to or harm those relationships, and understand the economic costs and benefits of various alternative partners. As organizations advance to the second stage of relationship marketing strategy, they must manage those relationships—nurture, develop, and maintain them—while they concomitantly manage the resources gained from those relationships to produce competitive advantages. We can see that although these relationship-based competitive advantages are complex and demand time and resources to develop, this complexity adds to their sustainability. In the third stage of relationship marketing strategy, we will see how the relationships grown by the organization and its partners further cement competitive advantages as multiple dyads become a network.

From Value Chains to Cooperative Value Nets: Relationship Marketing and Customer Value Creation

Ultimately, marketing strategies, including relationship marketing, must enable the organization to provide superior value to the end customer. Strategists and strategy scholars have therefore been concerned with identifying the value that is added by each member of the supply chain and the source of this value (Aaker, 1995; Abell & Hammond, 1979). A popular approach to mapping the process of value created by, and flowing between, firms has been Porter's (1985) value-chain concept. The value chain represents individual firms performing nine general types of activities that add value to a product as it moves through the production and distribution process. Under Porter's illustration, these value-adding activities—inbound logistics, operations, outbound logistics, marketing and sales, service, procurement, technology development, human resource management, and infrastructure management—are manipulated to provide differentiation in outputs or to achieve a position of low cost for the firm.

The value chain has been a useful tool for mapping the value production process. Textbook writers in marketing (Aaker, 1995; Czepiel, 1992; Kotler, 1988), management (Ivancevich, Lorenzi, Skinner, & Crosby, 1994), and strategy (Thompson & Strickland, 1995) have included it in discussions of value creation and value mapping. However, given many recent developments in relationship marketing, strategy, and the general practice of business, the value chain presents at least three problems. First, the value-chain approach to understanding value creation fails to recognize that, at the most basic level, *value arises from the firm's resources and how those resources are managed.* Drawing on the previous discussion of resource management, value is created when resources are (a) acquired efficiently, (b) bundled with other resources to create unique combinations of resources that provide superior effectiveness, (c) thoughtfully positioned in the marketplace in ways that take advantage of the uniqueness of these combinations, and (d) diligently protected and maintained to ensure customers that the value flow is uninterrupted. The activities identified in Porter's value chain could be recast into the resource management framework. However, the point is that for these activities to produce superior value in the long term, the firm must possess—or have access to—unique, valuable resources and must recognize the fundamental importance of those resources. Rather than taking the existence of these resources as given, resource-advantage theory emphasizes the heterogeneous nature of the distribution of firms' resources and their primacy (Hunt & Morgan, 1995).

Second, as constructed, the value chain encourages a focus on the functional areas or disciplines of business (e.g., marketing, logistics, manufacturing, and human resources) and their tasks, rather than on the resource management activities that should be the focus of all managers. Instead of encouraging firms to organize their efforts along traditional disciplinary boundaries, superior performance under resource-advantage theory requires that managers be versatile, having a more complete picture of the firm and its environment than what a narrow, discipline-based understanding would allow. Responsibility for resource management must cut across all functional areas of the firm. In this respect, resource management under the resource-advantage approach to competition is similar to relationship marketing. Gummeson (1991) has argued that, to be successful, relationship marketing must diffuse throughout the organization and be practiced by *all* employees—indeed, relationship resources are the responsibility of the entire organization.

Third, in an age of increasing dependence on networks of firms, the value chain fails to reflect truly the flow of value to customers. Porter (1985) allows for "coalitions," multidivisional firms, and multiple suppliers and buyers for any focal firm, where the product of one firm's value chain is passed along to the next. However, network organizations (a) go beyond mere multiple linkages; (b) require reciprocation of resources, including complex resources such as information about markets, product design, and technology; and (c) emphasize the importance of the social content of relationships, both direct and indirect. Portions of the value produced by these activities and processes commonly flow *back* through the supply chain, failing to be captured by the value-chain concept. Furthermore, the flow of value in the network is commonly circuitous, and may occur both laterally and vertically, where two members of the network who have direct interaction actually receive indirectly the value created by each other. Moreover, in all networks, social factors often facilitate or impede the flow of value.

Using this approach to value creation, in an effort to illustrate the flow of value in networks characterized by cooperative relationships between the members of the network, value creation by an individual firm can be represented by the model shown in Figure 18.3. Here, the firm manages its resources—acquiring, bundling, positioning, maintaining, and protecting them—as discussed above. Often, individual business processes, such as new product development or segmentation, involve more than one of these four resource management activities. Hopefully, as resources are managed competitive advantages are produced and, consequently, value is realized.

Figure 18.4 expands the scope of our view to include multiple firms and illustrate the cooperative value net as it might appear when the focal firm is a pharmaceutical manufacturer.[2] The partner categories developed by

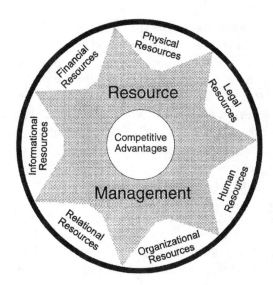

Figure 18.3. Value Creation From a Resource-Advantage Perspective

Morgan and Hunt (1994) are used to provide a framework for the various types of firms that may be involved.[3] Close, cooperative relationships—characterized by high levels of commitment and trust—are indicated by short linkages between partner firms. Weaker relationships—where exchanges tend to be only recurrent—are indicated by longer linkages. Furthermore, the volume of value transferred is proportional to the width of the linkages.

The cooperative value net emphasizes several important departures from the value-chain approach to mapping value flow between organizations. First, drawing on the resource-advantage discussion supporting the value creation model illustrated in Figure 18.3, the cooperative value net emphasizes the fundamental importance of resources and their management to the creation of competitive advantages. Second, the cooperative value net approach abandons the focus on the traditional disciplines of business and emphasizes that managers of the modern firm must be reasonably cognizant of the firm's array of resources—especially those that are the source(s) of competitive advantage(s). Third, the cooperative value net approach allows for the reciprocated, indirect, reverse, and circuitous flows of value between networks of firms. Finally, drawing further on relationship marketing theory, the cooperative value net approach

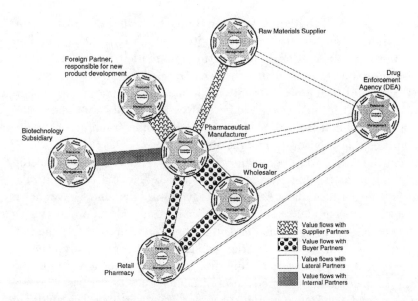

Figure 18.4. Value Flows Within Cooperative Value Nets Involving a Pharmaceutical Manufacturer

recognizes the importance of the social content of exchange relations to the ultimate delivery of customer value.

The development of these cooperative networks of smaller, dyadic relationships represents the evolution of the organization's use of relationship marketing-oriented strategies from the simple objective of securing a stable source of a needed resource to a strategy for gaining resources—often resources that would never have been conceived of—through complex, slowly developing networks of cooperative firms.

Discussion

The pace of conceptual and empirical contributions to the developing relationship marketing literature has been gratifying. Marketing scholars and practitioners continue to be interested in learning more about building, maintaining, and nurturing relationships, as well as the outcomes of relationship marketing. However, early practice and research have

commonly ignored the larger strategic impacts of adoption of relationship marketing for the firm. In this chapter I have attempted to build on
existing theory in relationship marketing and marketing strategy to increase our understanding of how the two may inform each other. I have offered an evolutionary view of relationship marketing strategy to explain
how the organization's goals and objectives for relationship marketing
can evolve and mature with an ever-increasing understanding of the opportunities that relationship marketing provides.

An initial step toward better understanding of the role of relationship
marketing in marketing strategy is to integrate existing theory in relationship marketing and marketing strategy. Toward that end, I have shown
how an existing model of relationship marketing—Morgan and Hunt's
(1994) commitment-trust model—might be expanded to clarify the role
of relationship marketing in marketing strategy. Future research should
certainly be directed toward testing this expanded model across multiple
relationship contexts. The model presented in Figure 18.2 is based largely
on theory and experience in industrial marketing settings. The ability of
the model to explain relationships in consumer marketing contexts is in
need of further exploration and testing.

Competitive advantage, the cornerstone of strategy, is not typically
mentioned in discussions of relationship marketing. However, trends in
the competitive nature of business today require managers to seek out resources beyond the boundaries of the firm. Resource-advantage theory
(Hunt & Morgan, 1995, 1996, 1997) would lead observers of relationship
marketing to believe that, because of the complexity of interorganizational relationships, relationship-based competitive advantages—derived
from these complex relationships—should be safe from imitation. Scholars and practitioners of relationship marketing need to understand more
fully the resource issues of their relationships. Which resources are most
highly valued? What combinations of partners' resources are most common? What combinations are unique? What types of controls are used to
secure these resources across different types and levels of relationships?
Couched within the context of the earlier discussion of resource management, it is likely that we are somewhat knowledgeable of resource acquisition and resource maintenance issues in relationship marketing, but resource coupling and resource positioning in this context remain largely
mysteries. Further development of resource management in an interorganizational context is needed.

Finally, perhaps nowhere is the discussion of value mapping more pertinent than in the theory and practice of relationship marketing. However, current practices of value mapping, especially Porter's (1985) value chain, leave much to be desired when discussed in the context of relationship marketing. I have offered an initial attempt at providing a practical tool for mapping the creation and flow of value among members of networks of firms that are involved in relational exchange. This approach, diagraming cooperative value nets, acknowledges recent advances in relationship marketing and competitive strategy theory. However, a call for alternative approaches and critical evaluation is warranted.

Notes

1. In addition to cooperating in order to receive resources, firms may cooperate because of government mandate to do so (Oliver, 1990) or to influence the competitiveness of a market by, for instance, setting entry barriers (Porter & Fuller, 1986).
2. Figure 18.3 is, of course, simplified for the purposes of explanation. The true value net of such a firm would involve many more firms than can be illustrated here.
3. Morgan and Hunt (1994) propose 10 types of relational exchange partners, which are grouped into four categories: supplier partnerships (goods suppliers and service suppliers), lateral partnerships (competitors, nonprofit organizations, and government), buyer partnerships (ultimate customers and intermediate customers), and internal partnerships (functional departments, employees, and business units).

References

Aaker, D. A. (1995). *Strategic market management*. New York: John Wiley.

Abell, D. F., & Hammond, J. S. (1979). *Strategic market planning*. Englewood Cliffs, NJ: Prentice Hall.

Aldrich, H. E. (1979). *Organizations and environments*. Englewood Cliffs, NJ: Prentice Hall.

Anderson, James C., & Narus, J. A. (1990). A model of distributor firm and manufacturer firm working partnerships. *Journal of Marketing, 54*(1), 42-58.

Anderson, John C., Rungtusanatham, M., & Schroeder, R. G. (1994). A theory of quality management underlying the Deming management method. *Academy of Management Review, 19*, 472-509.

Astley, W. G., & Brahm, R. A. (1989). Organizational designs for post-industrial strategies: The role of interorganizational collaboration. In C. S. Snow (Ed.), *Strategy, organization design, and human resource management*. Greenwich, CT: JAI.

Barney, J. B. (1991). Firm resources and sustained competitive advantage. *Journal of Management, 17*(1), 99-120.

Beder, H. (1984). Interorganizational cooperation: Why and how? In H. Beder (Ed.), *Realizing the potential of interorganizational cooperation*. San Francisco: Jossey-Bass.

Blau, P. M. (1964). *Exchange and power in social life*. New York: John Wiley.

Buckley, P. J., & Casson, M. (1988). A theory of cooperation in international business. In F. J. Contractor & P. Lorange (Eds.), *Cooperative strategies in international business* (pp. 31-53). Lexington, MA: Lexington.

Bucklin, L. P., & Sengupta, S. (1993). Organizing successful co-marketing alliances. *Journal of Marketing, 57*(2), 32-46.

Campbell, N. C. G., & Cunningham, M. T. (1983). Customer analysis for strategy development in industrial markets. *Strategic Management Journal, 4,* 360-380.

Contractor, F. J., & Lorange, P. (1988). Why should firms cooperate? The strategy and economics basis for cooperative ventures. In F. J. Contractor & P. Lorange (Eds.), *Cooperative strategies in international business* (pp. 3-28). Lexington, MA: Lexington.

Cook, K. S. (1977). Exchange and power in networks of interorganizational relations. *Sociological Quarterly, 18,* 62-82.

Czepiel, J. A. (1992). *Competitive marketing strategy*. Englewood Cliffs, NJ: Prentice Hall.

Dean, J. W., Jr., & Bowen, D. E. (1994). Management theory and total quality: Improving research and practice through theory development. *Academy of Management Review, 19,* 392-418.

Dierickx, I., & Cool, K. (1989). Asset stock accumulation and sustainability of competitive advantage. *Management Science, 35,* 1504-1511.

Dodgson, M. (1993). Learning, trust, and technological collaboration. *Human Relations, 46*(1), 77-95.

Galaskiewicz, J. (1985). Interorganizational relations. *Annual Review of Sociology, 11,* 281-304.

Galaskiewicz, J., & Shatin, D. (1981). Leadership and networking among neighborhood human service organizations. *Administrative Science Quarterly, 26,* 434-448.

Ganesan, S. (1994). Determinants of long-term orientation in buyer-seller relationships. *Journal of Marketing, 58*(2), 1-19.

Gummesson, E. (1991). Marketing-orientation revisited: The crucial role of the part-time marketer. *European Journal of Marketing, 25*(2), 60-74.

Gundlach, G. T., & Murphy, P. E. (1993). Ethical and legal foundations of relational marketing exchanges. *Journal of Marketing, 57*(4), 35-46.

Heide, J. B., & John, G. (1992). Do norms matter in marketing relationships? *Journal of Marketing, 56*(2), 32-44.

Heide, J. B., & Weiss, A. M. (1995). Vendor consideration and switching behavior for buyers in high-technology markets. *Journal of Marketing, 59*(3), 30-43.

Hofer, C. W., & Schendel, D. (1978). *Strategy formulation: Analytical concepts*. St. Paul, MN: West.

Hunt, S. D., & Morgan, R. M. (1995). Marketing and the comparative advantage theory of competition. *Journal of Marketing, 59*(2), 1-15.

Hunt, S. D., & Morgan, R. M. (1996). The resource-advantage theory of competition: Dynamics, path dependencies, and evolutionary dimensions. *Journal of Marketing, 60*(4), 107-114.

Hunt, S. D., & Morgan, R. M. (1997). Resource-advantage theory: A snake swallowing its tail or a general theory of competition? *Journal of Marketing, 61*(4), 74-82.

Ivancevich, J. M., Lorenzi, P., Skinner, S. J., & Crosby, P. B. (1994). *Management: Quality and competitiveness*. Burr Ridge, IL: Irwin.

Jarillo, J. C. (1988). On strategic networks. *Strategic Management Journal, 9,* 31-41.

Kalwani, M. U., & Narayandas, N. (1995). Long-term manufacturer-supplier relationships: Do they pay off for supplier firms? *Journal of Marketing, 59*(1), 1-16.

Kotler, P. (1988). *Marketing management: Analysis, planning, implementation, and control* (6th ed.). Englewood Cliffs, NJ: Prentice Hall.

Larson, A. (1992). Network dyads in entrepreneurial settings: A study of the governance of exchange relationships. *Administrative Science Quarterly, 37,* 76-104.

Leventhal, G. S. (1980). What should be done with equity theory? New approaches to the study of fairness in social relationships. In K. J. Gergen, M. S. Greenberg, & R. H. Willis (Eds.), *Social exchange: Advances in theory and research* (pp. 25-55). New York: Plenum.

Levine, S., & White, P. E. (1961). Exchange as a conceptual framework for the study of interorganizational relationships. *Administrative Science Quarterly, 5,* 583-601.

Metcalf, L. E., Frear, C. R., & Krishnan, R. (1992). Buyer-seller relationships: An application of the IMP interaction model. *European Journal of Marketing, 26*(2), 27-46.

Mody, A. (1989). *Staying in the loop: International alliances for sharing technology.* Washington, DC: World Bank.

Mohr, J., & Spekman, R. E. (1994). Characteristics of partnership success: Partnership attributes, communication behavior, and conflict resolution techniques. *Strategic Management Journal, 15,* 135-153.

Moody, P. E. (1993). *Breakthrough partnering: Creating a collective enterprise advantage.* Essex Junction, VT: Oliver Wright.

Morgan, R. M., & Hunt, S. D. (1994). The commitment-trust theory of relationship marketing. *Journal of Marketing, 58*(3), 20-38.

Morgan, R. M., & Hunt, S. D. (in press). Relationship-based competitive advantage: The role of relationship marketing in marketing strategy. *Journal of Business Research.*

Murstein, B. I. (1970). Stimulus-value-role: A theory of marital choice. *Journal of Marriage and the Family, 32,* 465-481.

Oliver, C. (1990). Determinants of interorganizational relationships: Integration and future directions. *Academy of Management Review, 15,* 241-265.

Oliver, C. (1991). Network relations and loss of organizational autonomy. *Human Relations, 44,* 943-961.

Ort, R. S. (1950). A study of role-conflicts as related to happiness in marriage. *Journal of Abnormal and Social Psychology, 45,* 691-699.

Pennings, J. M. (1981). Strategically interdependent organizations. In P. C. Nystrom & W. H. Starbuck (Eds.), *Handbook of organizational design* (Vol. 1). New York: Oxford University Press.

Peteraf, M. A. (1993). The cornerstones of competitive advantage: A resource-based view. *Strategic Management Journal, 14,* 179-191.

Peterson, R. (1995). Relationship marketing and the consumer. *Journal of the Academy of Marketing Science, 23,* 278-281.

Pfeffer, J. (1981). *Power in organizations.* Marshfield, MA: Pitman.

Porter, M. E. (1985). *Competitive advantage: Creating and sustaining superior performance.* New York: Free Press.

Porter, M. E., & Fuller, M. B. (1986). Coalitions and global strategy. In M. E. Porter (Ed.), *Competition in global industries* (pp. 315-343). Boston: Harvard Business School Press.

Powell, W. W. (1987). Hybrid organizational arrangements. *California Management Review, 30*(1), 67-87.

Powell, W. W. (1990). Neither market nor hierarchy: Network forms of organization. In B. M. Staw & L. L. Cummings (Eds.), *Research in organizational behavior* (Vol. 12). Greenwich, CT: JAI.

Prahalad, C. K., & Hamel, G. (1990). The core competence of the corporation. *Harvard Business Review, 68*(5), 71-91.

Ring, P. S., & Van de Ven, A. H. (1994). Developmental processes of cooperative interorganizational relationships. *Academy of Management Review, 19,* 80-118.

Ruekert, R. W., & Walker, O. C., Jr. (1987). Marketing's interaction with other functional units: A conceptual framework and empirical evidence. *Journal of Marketing, 51*(1), 1-19.

Saxenian, A. L. (1991). The origins and dynamics of production networks in Silicon Valley. *Research Policy, 20,* 423-437.

Seabright, M. A., Levinthal, D. A., & Fichman, M. (1992). Role of individual attachments in the dissolution of interorganizational relationships. *Academy of Management Journal, 35*(1), 122-160.

Sethuraman, R., Anderson, J. C., & Narus, J. A. (1988). Partnership advantage and its determinants in distributor and manufacturer working relationships. *Journal of Business Research, 17,* 327-347.

Sheth, J. N., & Parvatiyar, A. (1995). Relationship marketing in consumer markets: Antecedents and consequences. *Journal of the Academy of Marketing Science, 23,* 255-271.

Strategic planning. (1996, August 26). *Business Week,* pp. 46-50.

Thompson, A. A., & Strickland, A. J., III (1995). *Strategic management* (8th ed.). Burr Ridge, IL: Irwin.

Van de Ven, A. H. (1976). On the nature, formation, and maintenance of relations among organizations. *Academy of Management Review, 1,* 24-36.

Van de Ven, A. H., & Walker, G. (1984). The dynamics of interorganizational coordination. *Administrative Science Quarterly, 29,* 598-621.

Varadarajan, P. R., & Cunningham, M. H. (1995). Strategic alliances: A synthesis of conceptual foundations. *Journal of the Academy of Marketing Science, 23,* 282-296.

Vinacke, W. E., Shannon, K., Palazzo, V., Balsavage, L., & Cooney, P. (1987). Similarity and complementarity in intimate couples. *Genetic, Social, and General Psychology Monographs, 114*(1), 77-96.

Walker, G. (1988). Network analysis for cooperative interfirm relationships. In F. J. Contractor & P. Lorange (Eds.), *Cooperative strategies in international business.* Lexington, MA: Lexington.

Weitz, B. A., & Jap, S. D. (1995). Relationship marketing and distribution channels. *Journal of the Academy of Marketing Science, 23,* 305-320.

Wernerfelt, B. (1984). A resource-based view of the firm. *Strategic Management Journal, 5,* 171-180.

Whetten, D. A. (1981). Interorganizational relations: A review of the field. *Journal of Higher Education, 52*(1), 1-28.

19

Organizing for Relationship Marketing

IAN GORDON

The preceding chapters in this volume have considered different types of relationships and their implications for relationship marketing and the company more generally. In this chapter, I discuss how relationship marketing can affect the entire enterprise and describe how a company can organize to capture the inherent opportunities. I first consider how relationship marketing changes the environment within which the company must succeed. I then explore the implications of relationship marketing for organizational redesign.

Relationships Determine Future Success

Relationships are the fundamental asset of the company. More than anything else—even the physical plant, patents, products, or markets—relationships determine the future of the firm. Relationships predict whether new value will continue to be created and shared with the company. If customers are amenable to a deepening bond, they will do more business with the company. If employees like to work there, they will continue down their learning curve and produce more and better. If investors and bankers are happy with their returns, they will continue to keep their funds in the company

and help secure its financial underpinning. And so on for other stakeholders. Relationships are predictive. All else is history. Yet organizations continue to approach relationship marketing using the same structures that
were appropriate for the marketing era, a time when product, price, promotion, and distribution channels were discrete, preestablished, and one-
way. In short, today's organization is often designed for the technologies
and processes appropriate for transactions, not relationships.

A relationship exists while there is mutual value to be created and
shared. When the relationship cannot deliver this value to both parties, it
erodes. In the 1990s, the rate of relationship formation and erosion has
been accelerating. Organizational design must be sufficiently flexible to
recognize and facilitate this change.

Connections will become more fluid.

In the relationship marketing era, connections between customers and
suppliers, and among the entities that create end-customer value, form
and collapse more rapidly. Much is fluid. In the "dirty thirties," the unem-
ployed rode freight cars across the United States and Canada in search of
work. They gave up their roots and connections in small towns across the
land to find food and a future. Now, it will not take an economic catastro-
phe to send people on their way. With computers, the Internet, videoconferencing, modems, and telephone lines, people will more rapidly make
and break connections to shape value for customers and find meaning for
themselves. In short, connections have the potential to change on a more
frequent basis, within the company, between enterprises, among clusters
of companies that have chosen to associate, between the company and individuals beyond its borders, and among individuals outside the company.
Only value-creating relationships will hold connections in place. Organizational design needs to accommodate and enable the internal and external connections that will be made and broken in support of creating customer value.

Relationships can extend
the duration and value of connections.

Recognizing this, companies have just two choices. They can go with
the flow and build the capabilities needed to enhance relationships, or
they can go against the flow and seek to lock down every current and

valuable connection by increasing exit barriers or by making contracts and then enforcing those contracts to protect the embedded value. In this way, they can profit from their past investments and use the funds to buy into other, similar situations. For example, some U.S. utilities are considering imposing exit charges for customers switching to other energy suppliers, to compensate the original utility for investments made in expensive nuclear plants or other costs that are now harder to recover—so-called stranded costs. Other utilities are considering instead how to bond more tightly with their customers and increase customer retention in this way. It will not be easy for utilities to raise exit barriers and increase customer bonding simultaneously. They will need to do one or the other.

A relationship marketing company must be structured differently from one organized according to traditional marketing principles.

Relationship marketing draws from traditional marketing principles, yet is quite different. Marketing can be defined as the process of identifying and satisfying customers' needs in a competitively superior manner in order to achieve the organization's objectives. Relationship marketing builds on this, but has six dimensions that differ materially from the historical definition of marketing. Taken together, these differences have the potential to transform a company's view of the marketing it undertakes and almost everything about the enterprise, from the work it does to the technology it employs to the products it produces to the structure by which it achieves its objectives. The transformation requires a design for the organizational structure that recognizes how relationship marketing differs from conventional marketing and allows for the issues noted previously and below.

- Relationship marketing seeks to create *new* value for customers and then to *share* the value so created between producer and consumer.
- Relationship marketing recognizes the key role *individual* customers play, not only as purchasers, but in *defining* the value they want. Previously, companies would be expected to identify and provide this value in what the company would consider a "product." In relationship marketing, the customer helps the company provide the benefit bundle that the customer values. Value is thus created *with* customers, not *for* them.
- Relationship marketing requires that a company, as a consequence of its business strategy and customer focus, *design and align* its business pro-

cesses, communications, technology, and people in support of the value individual customers want.

- Relationship marketing is a *continuously cooperative* effort between buyer
and seller. As such, it operates in *real time.*

- Relationship marketing recognizes the value of customers over their purchasing *lifetimes,* rather than as individual customers or organizations that
must be resold on each purchasing occasion. In recognizing lifetime value,
relationship marketing seeks to bond progressively more tightly with customers.

- Relationship marketing seeks to build a *chain of relationships* within the organization to create the value customers want and between the organization and its main stakeholders, including suppliers, distribution channel
intermediaries, and shareholders.

Implications of Relationship Marketing for the Organization

Among the implications of relationship marketing for the marketing function are the technology it uses to drive its processes, the processes themselves (which can be affected by such issues as the scope of the business,
selection and rejection of customers, and relationships with stakeholders
in addition to those with customers), and human resource considerations,
including teams composed of internal and external stakeholders—nota-
bly including customers and the distribution channel intermediaries who
are to ensure that the processes perform. Below, I address selected issues
relevant to relationship marketing in the context of organizational design.

Technology enables relationship marketing.
Its design must be integrated with that
of organizational design.

Relationship marketing suggests that the company can focus on the ultimate market segment and serve customers as individuals. Companies
can give individual customers, or logical groups of customers (where serving the individual uniquely makes no sense to either customer or supplier),
the value each wants by using technology appropriately and throughout
the value chain. Often this means taking apart existing business processes
and inserting technology into them. For example, when the Internet is
used for on-line ordering, the process for purchasing has been redesigned

and technology has been injected to "disintermediate" the process for introducing technology between customer and supplier (which can result in distribution channel intermediaries being bypassed) and to mass customize. Companies doing this have the potential not only to get closer to their individual customers, but also to gain competitive advantage, a particular opportunity for the innovator.

Technology is clearly a major factor in organizational design, as it is a key enabler of customer relationships. The information technology (IT) department cannot be left to engineer its solutions in a functional silo while the rest of the organization waits for solutions to appear, so that processes can be engineered around the new technologies and people can be assisted through the transition to the new reality. IT design and implementation must have close and ongoing links to the users, either through process reengineers or through participation in stakeholder teams geared to achieving performance improvement through technology.

Relationship marketing means competing on scope, often through partnering. This changes processes, with profound implications for organizational design.

Companies serving customers as they wish to be served may find they have to do things they have never done before. Some companies may need to expand the scope of their products or services, providing customers with more than just what the companies make. In the process, firms increasingly will distribute the products or services of others, or work with companies with stronger or more-relevant customer relationships to distribute their own products or services. This represents a marked departure in strategy for those companies that have built their businesses through economies of scale. It may also require that firms reorient their relationship focus, from serving customers to seeing other firms as their primary customers or as their collaborative partners.

Many companies consider how to improve their supply chains, configuring processes to supply products and services within specific time, quality, and cost guidelines. It may be more appropriate for companies to consider how the needs and behaviors of customers can drive procurement, production, and logistics, among other considerations. For this to work effectively, the firm needs to develop and align a chain of relationships to provide for changing demands. This chain comprises stakeholders such as resellers and retailers, employees, suppliers, bankers, and investors. Each of these will have different needs and each will want to benefit from the creation and sharing of the value developed by the company with its end customers. This is a reversal of traditional thinking in the area of supply-chain management.

Competing on scope means deciding what categories of products and services are to be provided, which will be made by the company and which will be outsourced, in part or in whole. Associated with scope are considerations of the roles and responsibilities of an expanded array of stakeholders and the processes by which they are to interact in the entire value chain. Organizational designs in most companies currently do a poor job of facilitating nontraditional stakeholders, some of which may be "competitors," in a virtual value chain.

Customer choice affects organizational design.

The company competing on scope typically also partners with a narrower range of customers. The basic idea is to put more of your eggs in a few baskets and to watch the baskets very closely. This means selecting some customers and rejecting others—yes, even firing customers. Employing this principle, firms will focus on customers appropriate to their strategies and reject others that no longer fit. A major accounting/consulting firm has recently been through an account review and has decided to focus on a limited subset of companies, narrowing its worldwide priority-focus customer list from several thousand firms to fewer than 100. Although the move initially met stiff opposition among the firm's partners, the firm is now achieving record sales and profits. Associated with these changes has been significant change in processes, with account manager and staffing pools replacing the more traditional pyramidlike structure associated with craft work teams. The firm has yet to address the issue of staff mentoring and skill development, but this will surely be a requirement as the processes become more mature.

The four Ps of marketing do not describe the nature of marketing well in this relationship marketing era.

Below, I discuss the impacts of relationship marketing on the "four Ps" of marketing (product, price, promotion, and placement/distribution) as well as on organizational design.

Product. Relationship marketing, when appropriately implemented, results in products' being cooperatively designed, developed, tested, piloted, provided, installed, and refined. Products are not developed in the historical way, with the company conceiving of product concepts, researching these with customers, and then engaging in various research and development initiatives, leading to product rollout sometime later. Rather, relationship marketing involves real-time interaction between the company and its priority customers as the company seeks to move more rapidly to meet customer requirements. The product is therefore the output of a process of collaboration that creates the value customers want for each component of the product and associated services. Products are not bundles of tangible and intangible benefits that the company assembles because it thinks this is what customers want to buy. Rather, products comprise an aggregation of individual benefits that customers have participated in selecting or designing. The customer thus participates in the assembly of an unbundled series of components or modules that together constitute the product or service. The "product" resulting from this collaboration may be unique or highly tailored to the requirements of the customer, with much more of the customer's knowledge content incorporated into the product than was previously the case. Consider how General Electric works with airframe companies such as Boeing, from the outset of the concept for the plane, to make jet engines capable of meeting Boeing's specifications. GE's engine for one Boeing plane differs from the engine for another, in part because Boeing's knowledge and direction are incorporated in the design and development process.

Price. Traditional marketing sets a price for a product and offers the product/price set in the market, perhaps discounting the price in accordance with competitive and other marketplace considerations. The price seeks to secure a fair return on the investment the company has made in its more or less static product. In relationship marketing, the product varies according to the preferences and dictates of the customer, with the value varying commensurately. So when customers specify that a product should have specific features and that certain services should be delivered before, during, and after the sale, they naturally want to pay for each component of the value bundle separately. Just as the product and services are secured in a process of collaboration, so too will the price need to reflect the choices made and the value created from these choices.

Business-to-business marketers, especially for larger capital goods and installations, have typically engineered the products and services to customer requirements and negotiated the prices of their services. But customers have not often been involved in all aspects of the value chain and the price/performance trade-offs that vendors have deemed necessary. Relationship marketing invites customers into the pricing process, and all other value-related processes, giving customers an opportunity to make any trade-offs and to further develop trust in the relationship.

Promotion. Traditional marketing sends smoke signals for all within a specific market segment to see. "Buy me," the signals say to all who can see them. Relationship marketing instead gives individual customers an opportunity to decide how they wish to communicate with the enterprise, using smoke signals or other media, how often, and with whom. Mass promotion becomes support to build equity in the firm or brand, rather than a means to influence purchase directly. So when Motorola sponsors a racing car, it has the opportunity not only to claim that its onboard telemetry is an important ingredient in the vehicle's success, it can develop the multiple impressions of its umbrella brand to an audience that may include customers for each of its individual products.

Technology can make promotion become communication because technology can engage individual customers when and how they wish to relate. For the producer of capital goods, this communication may involve opportunities for supplier and customer to interact at the strategic level—considering each other's plans, customers, strategies, and initiatives—so that both can consider how best to be interdependent over the planning horizon. It may also tie in the customer's and supplier's information and communications systems, letting staff in each firm feel as though they work with the other in an integrated way. In this way, the lines between supplier and customer can be further blurred. For producers of consumer products, they could relate and communicate in much the same way with their channel intermediaries, such as the retailers. And now, with technology, individual end customers can be interactively and uniquely engaged. Using technologies such as the Internet, computer-telephony integration at call centers, intelligence at point of sale, kiosks, smart cards, and interactive voice response, companies can give customers a host of options for communicating with the company and have information on hand to engage, inform, and direct each customer with complete knowledge as to the customer's preferences and behaviors.

Placement/distribution. Current marketing thinking focuses on distribution channels as the mechanism to transfer a product or its title from producer to consumer. That is, marketing sees distribution as the channel that takes the product from producer to consumer. In the case of the computer industry, Dell sees distribution as a direct sales approach, primarily using telephone sales and order placement, whereas IBM uses many approaches to distribution, including its own stores, a direct sales force, and retailers that resell the firm's personal computers. Relationship marketing instead considers distribution from the perspective of the customer, who decides where, how, and when to buy the combination of products and services that constitute the vendor's total offering. Seen this way, distribution is not a channel but a *process*. The process allows customers to choose where and from whom they will obtain the value they want. Continuing the computer example just mentioned, the customer can choose whether to buy an off-the-shelf model from a reseller and take it home immediately, order one to be built to individual preferences at the factory and shipped within a week or so, or have one configured in-store that will be available within a few days. It thus may be more accurate to think of distribution as "placement," giving customers choices with regard to the locations at which they will specify, purchase, receive, install, repair, and return individual components of the products and services. That is, whereas traditional marketing considers a product as a bundled package of benefits, relationship marketing unbundles the product and service and allows the customer to initiate a placement decision for each element.

Additionally, relationship marketing affects organizational design in a number of other ways.

By changing much about the processes and capabilities of the company, relationship marketing should also change how the company organizes. Some of the main changes to the company's processes are found in the areas addressed below.

Customer mix. By reconsidering their customer mix, deciding with which customers they should do business, with which they should not, and what to do about those in between, firms can fundamentally alter their nature.

Having identified best, average, and worst customers, companies will develop strategies to build profitability from each category. Firms will research and analyze their best customers to explore how they can bond even more tightly with those customers and become yet more strategic to the accounts. Firms will examine the behaviors of best customers and derive insights from their purchases and actions, with the data warehouse supporting much of the analysis. Among other benefits, the warehouse and associated mining and visualization tools can help firms to be ready to sell when customers are ready to buy.

Whereas some customers will require investment for a deepening of bonds, others should be fired because they are not profitable today, never will be, and have no influence on the firm's market success. Customers who are in between—average customers—will need to be managed and disciplined to build company profitability. Many will follow the lead of the banks that push consumers out the doors to the automatic teller machines (ATMs) for routine transactions. If they will not be managed, they will be disciplined, just as the banks charge higher service fees at the counter for standard deposits and withdrawals that could have been handled by ATMs.

Banks are also deploying new technologies, such as on-line banking, for their average customers. This not only expands the range of services for which technology can substitute for people, it deepens the bond between consumer and company once the consumer has invested time in learning the software.

Focus. Focus has historically been seen as the holy grail of management. To those who are financially trained, focus often means cutting products or markets and bringing the organization into alignment to cater to the remaining most profitable or strategic sectors. This can lead to scale economies and improved profitability. This is an approach that works well in companies with too much complexity and those with too little competition. But now most companies have reengineered much of the complexity out of their businesses. The overly busy people who remain do not have too much appetite for further complexity. And no business today is immune from brutal competition, so simple focus and business alignment often open the door to those who are happy to have less focus and more business. Now the word *focus* should be redefined to mean focusing on the best customers and giving them everything they want, whether individual products or services are profitable or not. This will lead to an increase in scope—more products and services, rather than fewer—and lead some to charge that the firm is not focused.

Access. In the relationship marketing era, competition will be primarily for customer access. Those companies that have access will be able to benefit from an increase in scope. Those that do not will become suppliers to those that do, or perish. Companies that today identify the best customers and pursue their business with passion will be better able to earn access and to put in place the processes that will enable them to become kingpins.

A few years ago, a small company printed forms and communications materials for its customers. Then it focused on its best accounts. It began to manage customer inventories of its own products. In so doing, it reduced the costs of the processes for ordering while improving service. In turn, the printer received opportunities to supply much of the new business in the account, whether it could actually print the products or not. Now, other printers that want to deal with these accounts must go through the lead supplier. This situation is making this small firm much bigger and vastly more profitable, challenging the basis for competition in the industry.

Bonding. Every relationship could benefit from increased bonding. This means that all suppliers need to know where they stand with their customers, where they want to be, and how they plan to get there. Bonding is a continuum, and it makes more sense for companies to think in terms of advancing a relationship to the next level than to consider vaulting all the way to the end of the spectrum. Who gets married on the first date? The parties must speak to one another first. Enjoy one another's company. Seek common ground. Hold hands. And so on. A company needs a bonding objective and a strategy to achieve this—with every account and customer.

Collaboration. Relationships, whether business or personal, fizzle without continuous reinvestment to create new value. Collaboration is a key to building this new value, and the closer this collaboration is to real time, the more opportunity there is to bond. One way to secure real-time or near-real-time interaction is to use technology at the customer interface. Another is to blur the lines between customer and supplier, eventually inviting the customer into the innermost sanctum of the company, just as one might expect to be invited in by the customer. Work teams properly structured, governed, managed, and geared to mutual learning can help drive collaboration throughout the processes by which value is made. Companies need strategies for collaborating. But first, they need to overcome the notion that there is an "us" (our firm) and a "them" (the customer). Companies need not think of customers as kings, but they do need to think of them as peers in a process by which both customer and supplier are to benefit.

Chain of relationships. Great customer value requires that even more value be created with suppliers. Some of the value the customer wants is lost along the way in the form of learning curves, inefficiency, profit margins, and errors. This friction means that companies have to work even harder to align with all their stakeholders to eliminate the friction that customers do not want. Technology helps. Process design and formalization help. But more than these, strategy is required to frame approaches to creating and sharing mutual value with every category of stakeholder, without incurring the friction for which customers should not pay.

Novelty. Some years ago, a company was rescued from the brink of bankruptcy by a banker sympathetic to its plight. And 30 years later, the firm was still doing business with the same bank. The only trouble was, the bank had long since stopped investing in the relationship with this, by now, very successful company. The company president asked himself, "They got me to where I am, but will they get me to where I want to be?" The answer caused him to switch banks. This true story exemplifies the idea that companies must create current and strategic value. They need novelty and a strategy for giving this to their customers. Novelty means more than innovation. You can innovate the process for counterbalancing rotating camshafts in car engines and still be irrelevant to the customer. Novelty means giving the customer new, strategic value.

Customer's customer. It is no longer enough to have strategies to add value with the customer. The company seeking an enduring bond will need to help its customers develop relationships with their customers, further extending the chain of relationships mentioned earlier. In short, the company needs an understanding of its customers' customers and the strategies of the customers in respect to each end customer, and a strategy for advancing its customers' relationship marketing interests with their customers.

Dependence of relationships on flexible capabilities. Those companies seeking to build relationships and create new value will need to build flexible capabilities into their technologies, processes, people, and knowledge/insight. Their technologies must allow for virtually any shift that can be foreseen—in areas such as technology and industry structure, considering scenarios for industry evolution; and in areas such as the formation of buying groups, concentration of ownership or the disappearance of classes of trade, such as wholesalers. Technology must be open to customers and other stakeholders and must be secure from competitors and predators. Databases must be broad and deep, and companies should continue to make investments in data through good times and bad, for it will be the data that provide the new ideas, insights, and sources of increased earnings. Data can be mined only if the ore body is rich.

Customer and stakeholder data. The customer data warehouse is only the beginning. Databases should not be limited to customer transactions. They should cover customers more extensively, considering their various interactions with the company and the communications of the company with them, whether or not actual purchases or returns have been made. And databases should be maintained for stakeholders in addition to customers, so that knowledge and insight can be developed and new value continuously developed with each. Although some companies have put in place data warehouses for customer data, the relationship marketing company of tomorrow will have data warehouses for other stakeholders as well, and will manage these databases to create new value with all, be they investors, employees, channel intermediaries, or suppliers. In many firms, databases are spread throughout the company. An opportunity exists to reuse many of the existing transaction, behavior, and research data to create more value. The tools are here today to manage existing data more effectively.

Companies should seek new ways to exploit the data, such as cross-linking the various databases so that any resulting relationships can be even deeper. How deep would be the bonding between the company and its stakeholders if the bonding occurred at multiple levels? Companies already encourage employees to become investors. Could customers be encouraged to become investors, or could employees also be customers, or customers employees?

User involvement in process design. Processes, too, should be open, flexible, and continuous. Processes should be mapped and framed by the users of the outputs and by those who manage the processes. For example, strategic planning should not be a 2-day exercise for the executives at a comfortable retreat. It should be a continuous process—one in which all stakeholders and best customers, in particular, participate. There is an implicit warning here that Karl Marx might have issued. If processes are designed without the input of those tending them, and if we, the means of production, find the processes to be alienating, then we have a situation far more devastating than the worker alienation seen by Marx. We will become alienated from ourselves. Companies whose workers are alienated in this way will find that they are the most alienated of all. Employees disgruntled with the processes of the U.S. Postal Service who return with shotguns have been categorized as having "gone postal." In the future, and without user involvement in the design of the processes they must tend, widespread alienation may result in more business for therapists, pharmacists, gunsmiths, and prisons—the extreme outcomes of really bad relationships with one another and ourselves.

Structure follows strategy and process.

Structure follows strategy. Thus one cannot engineer an organizational design before framing an appropriate relationship marketing strategy. Yet many companies have skimped on the strategies at the front end, moving quickly to the implementation of many fragmented, unaligned programs. Management puts more and more pressure on existing organizational designs to accommodate the changed technologies and associated processes. Strategy is needed before a firm can move forward with organizational design. Management in a company where there is apparent lack of focus and execution, and where organizational changes occur very frequently, might well ask about the coherence and applicability of their strategies and the extent to which these are used as touchstones for the business.

If strategy and processes are to determine structure, companies organized according to the mass-marketing paradigm now need to reorganize around customers and other stakeholders. One way of thinking about this

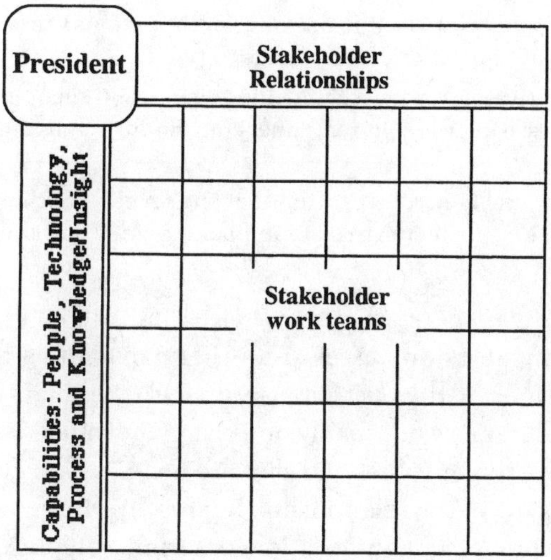

Figure 19.1. Capabilities and Relationships as Cornerstones in Organizational Design

is illustrated in Figure 19.1, which suggests the need for two main thrusts in organizing the company: capabilities and relationships with stakeholders. Work teams are created to address the key capability and relationship dimensions the company has determined to be important in its strategic assessment. Membership in the work teams is multifunctional, reflecting a process view of the organization. Thus the team focused on customer acquisition will include individuals from such areas as marketing, sales, advertising, research, operations, and finance.

The President's Role

The company president's role includes five main components in the context of such structure:

1. To integrate—the capabilities with one another, relationship-focused work teams with one another, and the capabilities with the work teams
2. To resource—ensuring that a sufficient flow of people, time, money, and knowledge goes to the areas that need these

3. To balance and prioritize the demands of the various work teams and the capabilities and initiatives each wishes to pursue

4. To lead, motivate, provide a compelling vision, and keep the organization focused on creating value in real time, continuously and mutually with stakeholders

5. To organize and control, ensuring that the results are there and that financial and operational controls are in place to limit any abuse of trust

Relationship managers, whatever their titles, will be in charge of integrating the company's processes and other capabilities that create customer value—right at the customer interface. The relationship manager should be a leader on a work team comprising individuals who manage the processes the customer values and that are necessary to develop, nurture, and control aspects of the relationship. Representatives could have responsibility for such processes as innovation, ordering, shipping and billing, and customer service.

Other work teams could be organized to address the needs of other categories of stakeholders, such as employees, suppliers, and channel intermediaries. Representatives on these teams would have responsibility for the principal capabilities, including processes, that develop value for and with these stakeholders.

Working with the relationship managers would be capability managers in charge of planning and implementing flexible and high-performance capabilities to supercharge the customer relationship. There should be a capability manager for each of people, process, information technology, and knowledge and insight systems. Process capability managers could be further classified according to the specific processes for which they are responsible.

Benefits of This Approach

A company organized along the lines described above will have a structure that does the following:

1. Organizes the company around its stakeholders, with the customer being first among equals.

2. Integrates stakeholders into the business processes and seeks to work continuously with them to create the value each wants.

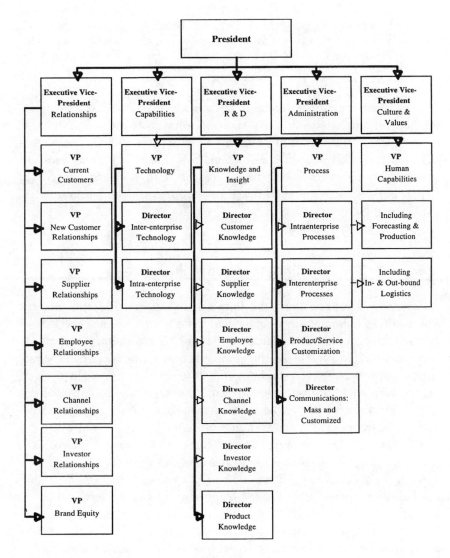

Figure 19.2. Organizing for Relationship Marketing

3. Understands the importance of specific capabilities in advancing relationships with stakeholders and that these capabilities should be key areas for investment.
4. Creates a series of trust-based relationships, which rely on the company's capabilities to indicate departure from the norm. If trust is abrogated, the

various processes, people, and IT systems should bring the company back into line. A manager of culture and values would be responsible, in this structure, for ensuring that codes of conduct are appreciated and enshrined.

This approach is modular. It allows the company to add work teams for different categories of stakeholders, such as for investors and government. It lets the firm structure teams for specific best customers and other teams to handle remaining customers. The same hold true for best employees and others. It even permits the company to blur its borders and to incorporate virtual work teams, some of which it may not directly lead but in which it could participate.

Stop Along the Road to the Future

A company organized along the lines I have described in this chapter would differ fundamentally from most of today's companies. A quick reaction to the organization recommended above, therefore, may be that it is complex and unworkable. As the company moves from its current structure to one more closely resembling that describe above, it will likely need some intermediary steps to allow for employee adjustment to the changes and to learn what works and what should be avoided as the firm proceeds. The structure described above should therefore be seen as a destination on the way to which the company will likely need interim structures. Perhaps Figure 19.2—a more formal organization chart—could serve as a starting point for discussion in a company that seeks to make relationship marketing its cornerstone and to structure itself accordingly.

The traditional functional roles change in a company organized primarily by capability and relationship. Some of the most important functional areas seen in today's company structures are underplayed or roles are changed by the suggested structure, especially for sales and marketing, but also for product management, plant operations, and research and development. Sales and marketing will increasingly be divided into two main roles, one associated with identifying, securing, and forming initial relationships with new accounts, and one associated with retention, penetration, and new value creation with existing accounts. Sales and marketing with new customers can include the traditional roles and current structures most organizations use while incorporating selected processes from relationship marketing, such as identifying prospects from the profiles of the company's best accounts. Reporting of sales and marketing can be through the executive vice president of relationships to help ensure an orderly transition in the management of an account when it is designated as a current customer.

Are companies organized this way today? Some are going down this road, taking breathers along the way. One new media company has a structure substantially similar to that described here, for example, and attributes much of its success to that fact. It has an internal relationship manager whose sole purpose is to manage connections, culture, and values and overcome any internal friction. Other firms, such as Hewlett-Packard, have senior management in charge of relationship marketing.

Clearly, a company serious about relationship marketing will need to consider how its organization must change to reflect this new strategy. A firm could give consideration to a structure such as that presented above in the context of the firm's culture, leadership, and other business strategies as it seeks to create mutual value continuously with customers and other stakeholders.

20

Information Technology

*Its Role in Building, Maintaining,
and Enhancing Relationships*

RAJENDRA S. SISODIA
DAVID B. WOLFE

Information is the lifeblood of all marketing, but effective relationship marketing demands a more highly enriched stream of information than does traditional product- or transaction-driven marketing. Having the right information in timely fashion, in the appropriate amount, and delivering it in the right style and at the right tempo are critical to marketers' maintaining satisfying relationships with customers.

In this chapter, we pointedly deal less with the technical side of information technology (IT) than with certain behavioral concepts, knowledge of which we believe is critical to reaping maximum benefits from IT in marketing applications. There is an abundance of literature about IT systems design, processes, applications, and potentials, but little on the human aspects of IT applications—perhaps because "too many organizations have spent too much time obsessing on the information they want their networks to carry and far too little time on the effective relationships that those networks should create and support . . . *a grave strategic error"* (Schrage, 1997, p. 3).

Drawing from their experiences in consumer research, Clancy and Shulman (1991) argue that for surmounting the biggest challenges marketing faces today, "neither the data (in IT systems) nor the computer is the solution." In this chapter we therefore approach the subject of the relationship marketing applications of IT from a behavioral rather than from a technical perspective, giving more attention to the behavior of marketers and consumers than to IT systems per se. In this context, we see IT as an agent of surrogacy to be enlisted to help marketers re-create the operating styles of yesterday's merchants, who diligently cultivated individual relationships with their customers. (Although our primary focus is on the application of IT in consumer marketing, much of what we discuss applies to channel marketing as well.) Such an idea begins to shift the focus of IT in marketing from information management to relationship management.

Relationship marketing requires more complex information systems than does product-driven or transaction marketing because of increased intimacy among providers, channel clientele, and consumers. In transaction marketing, consumer information is typically gathered on a sampling basis and "averaged" into marketing messages that are generalized for a broad market. In relationship marketing, information about consumers and players in marketing channels is gathered on an individual basis and used to tailor products, product distribution, and marketing messages.

In transaction marketing, suppliers to marketing channels often "push" distributors and retailers into taking their products, with limited concern for channel clients or consumers' preferences. In relationship marketing, suppliers collaborate with distributors and retailers on an individual basis. Key to this is an alignment of the information systems between suppliers and their channel customers.

In recent years, the marketing profession has been undergoing considerable self-examination and internal debate. The overriding emphasis in "traditional" marketing is on acquiring as many customers as possible by assembling the marketing mix most likely to result in that outcome. Evidence is mounting, however, that traditional marketing is becoming too expensive and is less effective over time. For example, an analysis of 20 industries revealed that half had selling, general, and administrative costs (SG&A) of more than 40% of every sales dollar, and all had SG&A of more than 30%. For the perfume, cosmetics, and toilet preparation industry, SG&A represented 53% of every sales dollar (Herremans & Ryans, 1995, p. 51).

Many leading marketing scholars and practitioners have concluded that marketing needs to jettison many of its long-standing practices and operating modes, and move toward a relational paradigm that is based on repeated market transactions and mutual gain for buyers and sellers alike (McKenna, 1991; Mitchell, 1996; Sheth, Gardner, & Garrett, 1988; Sheth & Parvatiyar, 1995).

At the same time marketing has been experiencing its internal conceptual revolution, a parallel revolution has been under way in the field of information technology. Starting in the early 1980s, the revolution in computing has delivered unprecedented improvements in price performance for information storage, processing, and delivery. The ability to store and process information locally rather than at remote sites and the availability of highly intuitive user interfaces have spurred managers to make much greater use of marketing information. Rapid developments in database technology, particularly better front-end applications for query and manipulation, have enabled marketers to provide individualized attention to ever-increasing proportions of their customers.

As a result of the ongoing information technology revolution, knowledge is replacing natural resources and money as capitalism's basic resource. Ready access to virtually unlimited amounts of information is shifting the balance of power away from marketers and toward consumers. The new power that consumers enjoy is reshaping marketing from mass marketing to one-to-one marketing, and from monologue to dialogue. Marketing dynamics are moving from *push* (product-driven) marketing to *pull* (consumer-driven) marketing, which involves more intimate and intense relationships among provider, channel clientele, and consumers. All marketing is therefore evolving toward relationship marketing.

This parallelism between the forces of technological change and radically new thinking in marketing has been highly fortuitous; new technologies (such as the World Wide Web) have emerged "just in time" to allow marketers to implement many essential aspects of relationship marketing. Other technologies have become more affordable, enabling marketers to deploy them more widely across a broader spectrum of customers (for a comprehensive but largely pre-Internet treatment of the impact of information technology on marketing, see Blattberg, Glazer, & Little, 1994).

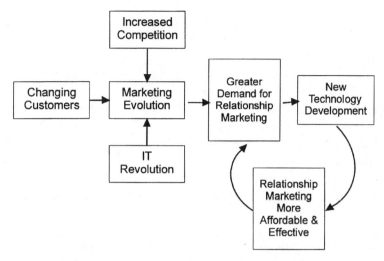

Figure 20.1. "Virtuous Cycle" Between IT and Relationship Marketing

As Figure 20.1 depicts, there is a symbiotic relationship—a "virtuous cycle"—between technology advances and the change in marketing paradigms toward relationship marketing. The impetus for relationship marketing comes only partly from developments in information technology; it has been driven primarily by the dysfunctionality of traditional marketing, the rising expectations of customers, and greater competitive pressures. Both push (from technology) and pull (customer expectations) effects are thus at work. The proliferation of relationship marketing approaches is in turn giving rise to the development of technological innovations specifically geared toward improvements in relationship marketing. For example, Webcasting (or push technology) facilitates relationship marketing by enabling marketers proactively to push relevant information to customers. "Content-focused matchmakers" use "deep interviewing" techniques to match customers with exactly the right products—and thus initiate relationships with a high likelihood of success and endurance. Communities of users with similar interests in books, music, movies, and so on congregate at sites such as Firefly, which is able to make use of that information to make recommendations to users on products and services that they might find of interest. The more successful such recommendations, the more likely users are to sustain and strengthen the relationship.

Relationship Marketing:
Back to the Future

As is often noted, relationship marketing is not a new idea. In earlier times (before the advent of mass production and mass media), relationship marketing was the norm; sellers usually had firsthand knowledge of buyers, and the successful ones used this knowledge to help keep customers for life.

In today's high-volume sales environments, however, it is not possible to know much about individual customers without sophisticated IT systems in place. But even this is inadequate to fulfill the higher promises of relationship marketing. There are aspects of our humanness that simply cannot be integrated into IT systems. Only the human mind deals effectively with the murky zones of unquantifiable subjectivity that are part of human behavior in every waking moment.

No matter how "smart" an IT system is, the quality of its information will be inferior in important respects to what merchants knew about their customers when oral exchange was the primary source of customer information and databases were index cards. Silicon chips now take the place of index cards, but that has not changed a basic fact: Information *is not* knowledge. Information is but "discrete little bundles of fact, sometimes useful, sometimes trivial, and never the substance of thought" (Roszak, 1994, p. 87). The storekeeper of yore who knew his customers well could intuit much about their needs because, in addition to objectively measurable information, he had intuitive (subjective) knowledge of his customers. No IT system developed to date can match the storekeeper in this. Nevertheless, undue attention given to the objective information aspects of IT is compromising its potential in marketing, as implicitly suggested in a recent research report issued by Merrill Lynch:

> In reality, viewing these technologies through the lens of "information" is dangerously myopic. . . . The so-called "information revolution" itself is actually, and more accurately, a "relationship revolution." Anyone trying to get a handle on the dazzling technologies of today and the impact they'll have tomorrow, would be well advised to re-orient their world view around relationships. . . . The coin to this new realm isn't data and information; it's the value and priority that people place on the quantity and quality of their relationships. (Schrage, 1997, p. 1)

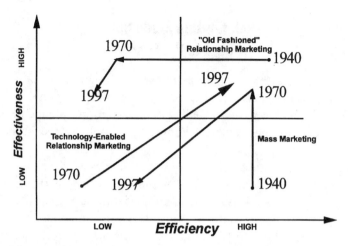

Figure 20.2. Productivity of Different Modes of Marketing

In contemplating the role of IT in relationship marketing, we can benefit from recalling how a major IT development more than 500 years ago led to radical changes in how people related to each other. Gutenberg's movable type press "wasn't merely about producing compendia of information. It was about transforming traditional relationships between the People, their Church and the State. . . . Here may lie the irony of our so-called Information Age: Information itself offers value only when presented in the context of relationships" (Schrage, 1997, p. 1).

Grant and Schlesinger (1995) point out that in the past we lacked the technological capability to be able to maximize profitability from customer relationships. New information and technology tools enable companies to link their investments in customer relationships more directly to the returns that customers generate. Companies can thus "optimize the value exchange, which is the relationship between a company's financial investment in customer relationships and the return that customers generate in responding to that investment."

Figure 20.2 shows how mass marketing and "old-fashioned" relationship marketing have become unproductive (in a relative sense) forms of marketing while technology-enabled relationship marketing has improved both its efficiency (through falling costs of technology) and its effectiveness (new and improved capabilities) to become the preferred mode of doing business.

Larson (1996) suggests that mass marketing is "cold" because it "deals in generalizations, and the audience has to work to complete the connection between itself and the message." On the other hand, good relationship marketing makes use of information about each customer that is "complete, specific, and pertinent—so that the message can't help but resonate" (p. 31).

There is increasing evidence to suggest that product attributes are becoming less important in determining customer preferences (Larson, 1996). This is not to suggest that customers no longer care about product quality or capabilities. Rather, it reflects the reality that most new attributes can be readily copied and improved upon by competitors. As a result, marketing success in the future will increasingly come from a company's proximity to its customers and its ability to understand their changing needs. Technology will play a central role in enabling firms to achieve this. However, the technology itself can be readily duplicated and bestows no long-term competitive advantage. What cannot be duplicated as easily is the totality of how the firm views and pursues relationships with its customers and how it continues to enrich those relationships over time by leveraging its constantly growing base of knowledge about its customers.

Procter & Gamble, widely regarded as the world's preeminent consumer products company, has recognized the need to design new marketing templates in a recently launched major restructuring of its distribution policies and practices (Narisetti, 1997). It has adopted relationship marketing as its benchmark for the future, beginning with careful nurturing of relationships with its distributors and retailers.

P&G has long been the archetypal transaction marketer. Transactions, not customers' circumstances, dominated the firm's thinking—true as much for channel customers as for consumer customers. P&G pushed products into the marketplace as fast and as hard as they could be pushed, in a kind of "damn the torpedoes, full speed ahead" mentality. Relationships between retailers and consumers alike were of relatively little concern to the company, inspiring retailers to refer to P&G as "Procter & God" (Narisetti, 1997). Lately however, the company has tempered its brute-force approach. It is paying more attention to retailers' circumstances and increasing efforts to secure consumer input. P&G has widely aligned its IT systems with its channel customers' IT systems in what some are calling "virtual integration," a reference to shared ground between two different companies' IT systems. When a Wal-Mart clerk records the purchase of a P&G product at a checkout station, information about the sale is transmitted immediately to IT centers in both companies. This enables precise knowledge of a product's sales velocity and leads to more economical and efficient inventory management. P&G is in the forefront of companies that are changing the direction from which marketing decisions develop: from the bottom up, through continuous dialogues with everyone in the value-creation chain, including consumers.

ONE-TO-ONE MARKETING

Rogers and Peppers (1997) suggest that "instead of selling one product at a time to as many customers as possible in a particular sales period, the one-to-one marketer uses customer databases and interactive communications to sell one customer at a time as many products and services as possible, over the lifetime of that customer's patronage" (p. 63). In contrast to traditional marketing's focus on getting the largest possible number of customers, one-to-one marketing emphasizes retaining the most valuable customers and growing them. Rogers and Peppers advocate "learning relationships" that can enhance customer convenience by maintaining a memory of customer preferences and tastes. Customer dialogues are ongoing from encounter to encounter, creating a growing "barrier of inconvenience" that serves as a powerful reason for customers not to want to do business with other providers—provided they continue to receive quality products and services at fair prices.

Rogers and Peppers (1997) suggest that the transition to one-to-one marketing be done customer by customer, rather than by product or division. A company should identify a handful of its most valuable customers and assign them to some of the most talented employees in the company (from marketing, sales, or customer service), who would be designated as "customer managers." Gradually, the company should expand the number of customers served in this manner. Because technology is a heavy component of costs in the one-to-one mode, declining IT costs make it affordable for a company to transition more and more customers over time. "If the cost of information technology continues to fall by 50% every 18 months or so, then it's no great leap to figure out that many of the programs and policies that make sense for today's MVCs will make sense in about 18 months for customers worth only half as much" (Rogers & Peppers, 1997, p. 64).

CUSTOMERS AS ASSETS

After decades of marketing based on pushing products into the market-place with limited concern for the circumstances of individual consumers, customers are coming to be seen as assets that need to be carefully husbanded. Interestingly, at the same time businesses all over have abandoned lifelong employment philosophies, there has been a surge of interest in the adoption of lifelong customer philosophies. However, there is strong evidence that a stable employee base goes hand in hand with a stable customer base. Says one specialist in customer loyalty, "We found that there was a cause-and-effect relationship between the two; that it was impossible to maintain a loyal customer base without a base of loyal employees; and that the best employees prefer to work for companies that deliver the kind of superior value that builds customer loyalty" (Reichheld, 1996, p. 2).

Reichheld's studies show that relationship marketing is essentially *holistic* marketing—marketing that operates within a total economic ecosystem in which dwell numerous categories and specimens of interdependent human beings who generate something of value for each other. He details how customer husbandry in an economic ecosystem makes bottom-line sense. His studies show that the cost of generating a dollar of income from new customers is greater than the cost of generating a dollar of income from existing customers. Collaterally, income from long-term customers generally is markedly higher than income from new customers. Although all this seems like common sense, it has been only since the advent of extensive IT systems used in tracking individual sales that detailed measurement of the economics of customer acquisition and maintenance have been broadly charted.

Technology Impact on Relationship Marketing: Scale and Scope Economies

The use of technology changes both scale and scope economies of relationship marketing. Scale economies are changed in that individualized attention now becomes possible for a much larger number of customers, each representing a much smaller transaction volume. Scope economies reflect the fact that technology enables a broadening of the geographic scope of relationships; it also expands the time scope and the range of offerings that can be made available to a particular customer.

SCALE ECONOMIES

Although it is possible to practice relationship marketing on a small scale without the extensive use of information technology, it is impossible to do so effectively on a larger scale. The rapidly escalating affordability and capabilities of IT augur well for marketers' ability to deploy more and more of these capabilities to an ever-increasing proportion of customers.

Traditionally, relationship marketing was practiced locally; small merchants had personal knowledge of each of their customers and leveraged this knowledge to provide each customer with individualized attention. As the geographic scope of businesses and the numbers of customers both expanded, it soon became impossible for merchants to maintain the same level of one-on-one relationships. Although some merchants adopted a variety of information management approaches to help them keep track of the burgeoning customer information, the mechanical nature of this process made it too expensive to maintain and too cumbersome to use.

This situation persisted for decades; despite continuous advances in the power and affordability of information technology, it remained basically infeasible for marketers to collect, store, and leverage information on individual customers. In the past several years, however, the affordability of information-processing and storage capabilities has improved to such an extent that individualized relationships based on detailed customer information are now economically and operationally viable for the vast majority of customers for the vast variety of marketers. Today, IT enables, on a mass scale, the kind of individualized attention that marketers routinely bestowed on customers several generations ago.

SCOPE ECONOMIES

Along with the scale economies described above, technology has enabled the expansion of scope economies, expanding the domain of customer relationships over time, space, and different product categories. Economies of scope are those characteristics of a process that make it easy to produce multiple products because they use similar components and are made in similar ways. Information technology endows relationship marketing with tremendous scope economies. It provides a tool to organize all relevant information around individual customers; this information can be used to provide customers with a broad range of products and services. Many of these offerings may in fact be produced by other entities; they are assembled into a package by the company managing the relationship.

The domain of technology-enabled relationship marketing extends well beyond marketing; it includes operational and technological linkages between companies that create a strong structural bond between them. For example, the Internet can facilitate connections between the company and the customer such as inventory management links, referral systems, and automatic ordering processes; all of this can be done on a scale previously unimaginable.

Drivers of Technology-Enabled Relationship Marketing

SUPPLY SIDE: TECHNOLOGY EVOLUTION AND REVOLUTION

Technological developments in the information industry over the past 15 years have been truly epochal, as we describe below. The sheer magnitude of these developments has had important consequences for every major industry and business function, including marketing.

Technology Changes

Processing. As postulated by Moore's Law, the circuit density of computer chips—and hence their computing power—is doubling, on average, every 18 months. The costs of computer hardware, relative to capabilities, declined dramatically during the 1980s and early 1990s, reflecting Moore's Law as well as experience-based cost reductions and aggressive pricing strategies adopted by producers in order to expand their markets. Already, the current generation of $200 video game machines puts in schoolkids' hands the graphics power of a 1980s-vintage Cray supercomputer.

At the heart of the processing revolution is, of course, the microprocessor. The first microprocessor, Intel's 4004, was developed in 1971. Because it was a single chip, the 4004 was the first processor that could be made in bulk. Over time, by enlarging the wafer and shrinking the transistors, more and more processing power has been stamped out in chip factories. Intel's Pentium Pro (P6) chip contains 5.5 million transistors, compared to the 4004's 2,300 transistors. The rate of improvement in microprocessor technology has risen from approximately 35% a year in the mid-1980s to about 55% a year in the mid-1990s. Processors are now three times as fast as predicted in the early 1980s (Patterson, 1995).

Data storage. The trends in data storage are toward greater capacity, easier access, and lower cost. Paralleling the improvements in computer hardware, data storage capabilities are expanding, and their costs are declining. In 1956, IBM introduced the first disk drive, with five megabytes of storage at $10,000 a megabyte. Since 1991, the average capacity of disk drives sold has increased 18-fold (from 145 megabytes to 2.65 gigabytes) while the price per megabyte has dropped 52-fold (from $5.23 to 10 cents), according to *Disk Trend.*

Contemporary systems are designed to accommodate video images of ever-higher resolution, along with rapidly growing amounts of alphanumeric data. CD-ROMs provide much greater storage capacity than earlier modes, but are now being rendered obsolete by DVDs, which provide 6 to 30 times as much storage capacity.

Communications. At the same time computing power and affordability are expanding at a dramatic rate, they are doing so in a relatively steady fashion. On the other hand, advances in telecommunications promise even greater change of a discontinuous nature: We are likely to see an explosion of bandwidth in coming years that will dwarf anything seen in the past. Technologically, it is a virtual certainty that over the next decade, computer speeds will rise about a hundredfold and bandwidth will increase a thousandfold or more.

Thus far, improvements in bandwidth to end users have been slow and steady. Whereas the past 10 years have seen a 10-fold improvement in typical modem speeds, for example, this increase pales in comparison with developments in microprocessor technology. As Bill Gates commented recently to *Fortune*:

> The original insight for Microsoft was this: What if computing was free? The answer: Individuals could use computers as a tool, and software standards would become the critical element in making this happen. . . . You could say that the big insight for the next ten years is this: What if digital communications were free? The answer is that the way we learn, buy, socialize, do business and enter-

tain ourselves will be very different, and that we hope software and software standards will be important. (quoted in Schlender, 1995, p. 35)

The new explosions of bandwidth will enable interactive multimedia and video information to come into every household in various ways—through the air from satellites and terrestrial wireless systems, through fiber-optic cables and cable TV and phone company coaxial cables (Gilder, 1994, p. 162).

Display. Displays will have greater resolution, less bulk, and less cost. Key developments in display technology include improvements and cost reductions for so-called active matrix color LCDs, which are used in laptop and notebook computers. Other technologies still in development include various types of flat panel displays and digital high-definition television (HDTV).

Key Properties of Digital Electronic Information Technology

Information technology based on digital electronics has several unique properties: It is convergent and versatile, boundaryless and global, affordable, and addictive.

Convergent and versatile. Ever since the invention of programmable computers, the promise, and the pure genius, of information technology has been its sheer plasticity. Getting the computer to do previously unimaginable things is simply a matter of developing the right software and perhaps adding some peripherals. Software programs in multipurpose computers can replace dedicated hardware systems, causing dramatic shifts toward "virtuality." This first happened decades ago, when computers started replacing adding and tabulating machines. The PC and its peripherals are gradually taking over many office and shop-floor tasks previously performed by stand-alone devices: typewriters, telephone answering machines, fax machines, typesetting machines, filing cabinets, copying machines, drafting boards, painting easels, and even foundries (through stereolithography, PCs are now churning out physical prototypes of new products in minutes). Today, chips can perform functions once handled by mechanical switches, motors, and other moving parts. Information technology is thus versatile and highly convergent—the same component technologies can be used in myriad ways to perform diverse tasks.

Boundaryless and global. The organizing principle of the information revolution is the opposite of the spirit that guided the Industrial Revolution two centuries ago, which was separation—the breaking up of work into its component parts to allow mass production. The central tenet of the information revolution is unification; networks of computers allow company departments to fuse, and enterprises grow so closely allied with customers and suppliers that boundaries between them seem to dissolve. This unification can make a division or a company across the world seem as if it is down the hall, transforming our conception of distance as radically as the supplanting of stagecoaches by railways in the 1840s. Information technology is thus essentially unbound by geographic limitations. It is distance-irrelevant and available "anytime, anyplace." For example, the Internet knows no global boundaries; individuals from around the world, regardless of location and time difference, have created virtual communities to discuss and share information on subjects from hobbies to politics.

Affordable. Volume production rapidly drives down the incremental costs of producing electronic products. This is evidenced in the falling prices and costs of products such as calculators in the past and microprocessors currently. Volume production can be achieved only through aggressive penetration pricing and targeting of the broadest possible market.

Addictive. An important property of electronic information technologies is that they are extraordinarily addictive to users. Because they offer such significant improvements in price performance and convenience over alternative means, and because they affect vital areas of human activity, such as work, socialization, and entertainment, these technology-based enhancements represent a one-way street for adopters. From a marketing standpoint, this property is significant and fortuitous.

Easy and fun to use. Over time, technology evolves to hide its inner complexity. For example, television sets used to have relatively simple technology inside, but they had complicated interfaces, requiring users to control tuning, vertical hold, contrast, color saturation, and so on. Today's televisions are highly sophisticated on the inside but have extremely easy interfaces. This transition has already occurred (to a large extent) with Web technology, accounting for its explosive growth.

The quality of the interface is critical to the adoption of any new technology. Any technological interaction that users regard as dehumanizing will be shunned; it will be imperative, therefore, that high-tech companies pay great attention to "high-touch" issues. The same technology that is seen as dehumanizing one aspect of life can also be used to increase the human quotient; videoconferencing and work-at-home technologies are two recent examples. Each can be pushed as a time-and-money-saving substitute for physical human contact or can be positioned as a way to improve the quality of life by adding flexibility and visual connection.

Consumer-oriented systems will have to be extraordinarily easy and fun to use. Further, designers will have to pay attention to the crucial high-touch or human dimension when designing these "high-tech" systems. They will have to incorporate these human characteristics in the design of the interfaces as well in advertising and marketing. Designers will have one great advantage in trying to create natural interfaces: an abundance of computing power. Even today, 80% of a typical microprocessor's capability in a graphical user interface (GUI) personal computer is used to create the interface; only 20% is needed to "do the work." When capabilities expand manyfold, designers will be able to use vast amounts of computing and communications power to hide the complexity of the system from the user. Rather than the user having to learn the interface, the interface will evolve to learn the user's preferences. Capabilities such as voice recognition (and, to a lesser extent, handwriting recognition) will be key in this regard.

The above is clearly illustrated today in the exploding popularity of the World Wide Web on the Internet. The Web presents users with a multimedia GUI and instantaneous linkages to related information anywhere in the world. Even in the current narrowband mode, the potential of the technology is clearly apparent, especially for electronic shopping applications. Virtual shopping malls will permit consumers to choose the mode of shopping with which they are most comfortable. Impulse-oriented shoppers are likely to want to "stroll" visually down the various aisles of a virtual supermarket (which may look exactly like their preferred stores or could be custom designed by them) and click on their desired items. Others may wish to place standing orders and review them periodically. Over time, the application of more virtual-reality technology will permit consumers to "try out" numerous products electronically, from their homes.

The Internet

Interactive media such as the Internet allow marketers to deliver real-time, personalized information to one consumer at a time. Such media allow marketers to provide better service at lower cost. For many services (such as information, software, education, medical advice, legal advice), the Internet can also be used as a delivery channel (Kierzkowski, McQuade, Waitman, & Zeisser, 1996).

Relationships are one of the defining qualities of marketer-customer interaction over the Internet. Marketers can use the medium to collect market data and to question, listen to, and respond to customers (Jones, 1996). Foskett (1996) describes automated relationship building as that resulting from the computer-to-computer interactions that take place on-line: "Online marketers communicate instantly and directly with prospective customers—and can provide instant fulfillment as well" (p. 38). This requires that the customer come to the marketer, reversing the traditional process of marketers trying to reach customers.

Web-based commerce is still in its infancy, although it is growing at an exponential rate. For the most part, it is serving as an adjunct to traditional "bricks and mortar"-based commerce (e.g., Autobytel.com and other automobile purchase services refer customers to traditional dealers), although some "pure" Internet-based players are starting to emerge (e.g., Amazon.com, the on-line bookseller). The key is that the Web-based commerce must be significantly better than traditional commerce for a widespread transition to occur. The state of the technology currently is inadequate for this; despite all the extraordinary advances over the past several years, it is still too slow, difficult, and expensive. Web commerce will be ready for "prime time" with the advent of digital HDTV, reliable availability of large amounts of bandwidth, more affordable computers, and easier-to-use software. This will greatly enhance the "naturalness" of the interface, with real-time exchange of high-fidelity audio and video information.

Marketers tend to focus narrowly on consumers' needs within the parameters of their own product categories. They will have to expand their horizons as "electronic communities" emerge. In many cases, emerging electronic communities will threaten the existing distribution channels of dealers, brokers, and retailers (Deighton, 1996). In fact, Hagel and Armstrong (1997) suggest that Internet commerce will be driven primarily by on-line communities. Companies could take the lead in establishing on-line communities around particular interests, such as travel. They could provide chat rooms and bulletin boards for users to share experiences and answer each other's questions. They could also provide information that is useful and interesting to the community, such as travel-related articles about different locales. Users would develop personal relationships with each other, which would prompt them to come back repeatedly to the site. The site sponsor also could provide users with the ability to purchase goods and services related to the community interest, such as on-line booking of hotels, airline seats, tours, and rental cars. It is important that the sponsor of such a site establish an atmosphere of trust with its community members, working with them to meet their various needs rather than overtly selling to them. As Hagel notes:

> Community precedes commerce. In earlier network environments, there was a notion that commerce and community were somehow at odds with each other, that as soon as you introduced commerce, you undermined community. Certainly, that can be true if abused, but if it's thoughtfully done, commerce can actually reinforce community and extend value to members. (quoted in Kelly, 1997)

Web sites enable companies to provide to a virtually unlimited number of customers and prospects information and services that they could previously provide to only a few. In the past, responding to customer inquiries about product problems, features, or upgrades required companies to invest heavily in customer hot lines, follow-up calls, and large sales and customer service departments. Now, through the Web, companies can respond to most such needs at very little cost. In addition, each customer "visit" becomes an opportunity for the company to provide additional services and sell more products.

Two important elements in the establishment of relationships with customers over the Internet are privacy and security. Marketers must demonstrate to customers that the information they provide is to the customers' benefit and will not be used in any detrimental way. A rather ingenious means of delivering customized information and services to customers is the use of "cookies." Cookies are files of information that reside on the user's machine; these files contain information about sites visited by the customer. Marketers can use this information to determine the user's preferences and can provide advertisements and make special offers based on those preferences. Customers, however, tend to view the use of cookies as a violation of their privacy; it is up to marketers to convince them that cookies will be used only to enhance value and reduce "noise" to the consumer.

Security issues are also prominent obstacles to Web commerce. Customers feel that the information they provide sellers is not secure and could be intercepted by others. For the most part, these concerns are overblown, and they are already being addressed in multiple ways (e.g., the use of encryption technology).

CAROL: "a personal docent for cyberspace." A key technology that is likely to play a major role in Internet commerce is agent technology. Wolfe (1996) describes a unique type of "agent" that could be designed to perform on behalf of consumers. CAROL (not yet commercially deployed) is unique in that it preserves consumer privacy while enabling marketers as well as consumers to enjoy the benefits of tailored, targeted offerings.

CAROL (Consumer's Anonymous Reporting Omnibus Link) is an agent that travels throughout cyberspace on behalf of her client users. The same as any agent whom a person might engage, CAROL needs information about her clients to best represent them. Of course, how much information a person is willing to share with an agent depends on how much the agent can be trusted. CAROL's integrity is beyond reproach. She operates with the silence of the confessional and is bonded against distributing any client information without the express permission of the client.

CAROL does not build databases for marketers; she locates and retrieves information for consumers. In fact, vendors do not have any need for a database on CAROL's individual clients. For a licensing fee, vendors are linked to CAROL, who knows what products are suited to her clients.

CAROL bases her information-gathering activities for clients on both explicit and implicit reports her clients make about themselves. With that information, CAROL goes on forays throughout cyberspace, gathering information for her clients that is increasingly relevant to their situations, because she acquires more knowledge about her clients with each on-line encounter.

Firefly: harnessing the power of word-of-mouth marketing. Thus far, the Web has provided less satisfying buying experiences for many than paper catalogs and toll-free calls. A technology called *collaborative filtering* may change that. Companies gather and pool information volunteered by customers. Computers can then predict what products or services people may like and can guide their shopping based on the experiences of their peers.

An interesting example of how this new technology can be used to marketing advantage is a new service called Firefly (http://www.firefly.com), which is one of the first commercial services to attempt to harness the power of peer recommendations or word-of-mouth marketing (Judge, 1996). Firefly works by building detailed psychographic profiles of members based on their answers to scores of questions. Using this information, it then identifies individuals' "psychographic neighbors"—other individuals who appear to have similar predispositions. It then makes recommendations for products and services based on what others have reported liking. Although currently limited to music and movies, Firefly is planning to add mutual funds, restaurants, and books. Firefly also uses the information gathered to pinpoint advertising messages to individuals.

Going beyond facilitating transactions, Firefly also enables user-to-user communications, with communities based on shared interests. Corporate users of the service so far include Merrill Lynch, MCI, Dun & Bradstreet, Reuters, Yahoo, and ZD Net.

Importantly, Firefly has "aggressively" sought to maintain user privacy; it does not require users to provide real names and addresses unless they choose to. The company has gone so far as to hire Coopers & Lybrand to conduct audits twice a year to ensure that it is adequately safeguarding user privacy. Firefly's privacy policies have earned it plaudits from the Electronic Frontier Foundation, a group that advocates privacy for Internet users.

Database Marketing

Database marketing can make every customer contact more meaningful and more profitable than the one before (Harrison, 1995). In database marketing, communications are directed to individuals, households, or organizations by name. According to Cespedes and Smith (1993), database marketing involves "three Ts": *targeting* messages to specific types of customers or prospects (and not others), *tailoring* messages to customers' interests or other characteristics, and the development of *ties* or long-term relationships with preferred customers.

Although database marketing methods have long been employed by direct marketers such as catalog houses and magazine publishers, improvements in IT have made the approach increasingly practical for mass marketers as well since the mid-1980s. Rapp and Collins (1990) describe numerous examples of database marketing programs carried out by marketers of automobiles, cigarettes, alcoholic beverages, foods, personal care products, and services.

Bickert (1992) describes several types of customer databases that are used in marketing. The simplest is one that includes a company's own customers, ideally with their transaction histories. Many kinds of marketers have always had this type of information, although their ability to store and analyze the data was limited until computer systems became sufficiently inexpensive and user-friendly. More recently, marketers that do not deal directly with end users have begun collecting customer names in order to assemble databases.

External household customer databases include customer or subscriber lists rented from direct marketers or publishers, special-purpose lists derived from public records such as auto registrations and births, and multisource compiled databases that are derived from a wide variety of sources. Another type of database is assembled from voluntary consumer responses to questionnaires published in newspapers. Business and institutional customer databases are derived primarily from directories, updated by periodic telephone surveys. Very large-scale databases can be stored on CD-ROMs and utilized on desktop computers or local area networks, making database marketing much easier to implement than in the past.

At times, the terms *relationship marketing* and *database marketing* have been used interchangeably, evidencing the close information-focused connection many people make between IT and relationship marketing. However, most database marketing is essentially automated transaction marketing. Its main distinction from traditional transaction marketing is that it is more targeted because of information about individual consumers either bought from others or captured in previous transactions. But the dynamics tend to be basically the same as in "old-fashioned" transaction marketing: products are pushed toward consumers without their active collaboration or any semblance of the two-way communications that have been called critical to relationship marketing scenarios. The push aspect of most database marketing to consumers ignores the role of collaboration in building trust, something most researchers agree is essential in relationship marketing.

IT can play an invaluable role in capturing and crudely sorting data on individual consumers, but determining the real meaning of those data still requires human judgment. Thus alert systems need to be built into IT systems to trigger human involvement at critical junctures. Despite all the confidence being placed in contemporary database marketing systems, strongly bonded, emotionally satisfying relationships require periodic human presence that achieves some qualitative threshold for the parties involved. Absent human involvement on the supply side, authenticity is compromised in customers' perceptions.

Neural Networks

Neural networks look for unusual patterns in marketing data. They can help spot new sales opportunities, reduce customer churn, and forecast demand more accurately. Neural network-based software is now available for the identification and tracking of opportunities, postsales customer service, and the generation of new leads using geographic and demographic databases (Bird, 1995).

DEMAND SIDE

Changing Customers

On the demand side of the equation, a major impetus for relationship marketing comes from customers, whose needs and expectations have changed to the point that traditional marketing solutions simply do not satisfy them anymore. Today's customers are increasingly heterogeneous; they do not fit into traditional stereotyped categories, and they certainly do not respond to "mass-market" approaches. Much has been written on this in recent years, and we will not belabor the point. Suffice it to say that without a heavy dose of information technology, it is impossible for companies to maintain individualized relationships with large numbers of customers economically and effectively.

From the marketer's viewpoint, customers have become, in many ways, quite capricious. This is a natural reaction on their part to decades of marketing overindulgence. Through long experience with never-ending promotions and a long history of overpromising and underdelivering, customers have become highly deal-prone and cynical about marketing claims. They have little or no tolerance for underperformance and switch suppliers at the smallest provocation. This is evidenced by the extremely high churn rates found in many industries; in the telecommunications industry, for example, churn rates range from 30% to 50% a year in sectors such as cellular telephony and small-business long-distance service.

This reflects an interesting dichotomy that is developing: Today's customers appear to have lower expectations for "one and done" transaction-oriented purchases (e.g., from McDonald's) and higher expectations for long-term (longitudinal) purchases (e.g., from dentists). Ironically, many of the companies offering the former tend to practice relationship marketing, whereas too many of the firms offering the latter fail to do so. The payoffs from relationship marketing are the greatest in these circumstances, as are the penalties associated with failure to practice it.

Customers today have far more knowledge, and thus power, than they ever did in the past. In part, this is due to their cynicism; lacking trust in marketers, they feel they must arm themselves with as much information as possible. It is also due to the sheer availability of more objective information (much of it from new third-party providers) than before. For traditional marketers, all this knowledge is a threat; it allows customers to "get a better deal" with them each time around. For more enlightened marketers practicing relationship marketing, customer knowledge is seen as an advantage; such customers may be more demanding in terms of quality and value, but they are less demanding in terms of customer service and support. Provided a company is capable of delivering good quality and value, it can leverage its customers' knowledge and expertise to mutual advantage.

Stone, Woodcock, and Wilson (1996) suggest that in the future, customers will increasingly seek to manage the relationship themselves, using new technologies, and that companies need to prepare themselves for this world.

Increasing Competition

Competitive intensity in most industries today is higher than it has ever been, despite extensive consolidation. Most open markets today are home to the best players the world has to offer, the hardy survivors of Darwinian battles that raged on for decades. The greater the competitive intensity, the higher the performance bar for satisfying and thus retaining customers. For traditional companies, this is clearly a major challenge. New competitors often have better weapons at their disposal; unencumbered by "legacy systems" or traditional practices, they are able to deploy highly cost-effective and powerful technologies to aid in customer acquisition and retention. Most new competitors are unburdened by stranded or uneconomic assets, such as extensive physical inventory management or distribution infrastructures. For example, Amazon.com is a formidable competitor to Barnes & Noble because its cost structure is not saddled with huge real estate costs. It can operate as a pure virtual presence. Figure 20.3 summarizes the drivers of technology-enabled relationship marketing.

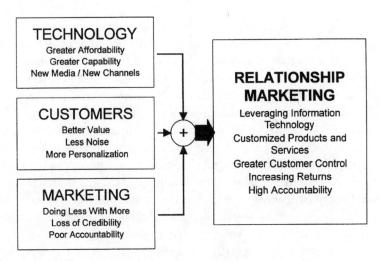

Figure 20.3. Drivers of Technology-Enabled Relationship Marketing

Characteristics of Technology-Enabled Relationship Marketing

With the above as prologue, in this section we discuss some of the salient characteristics of technology-enabled relationship marketing. In broad terms, the intelligent use of information technology in relationship marketing will lead to a truer customer focus. It will be characterized by respect for customers' time and intelligence and by understanding and empathy for their priorities.

THE ROLE OF INFORMATION TECHNOLOGY IN REHUMANIZING MARKETING

In traditional research, differences between individual consumers tend to become blurred in statistical representations of consumers, which are arrayed in clusters or typologies that contain benchmarks for developing standard, one-size-fits-all, nonrelationship approaches to marketing. In contrast, relationship marketing not only requires real information about real consumers on an individual basis, it also often requires such information on a real-time basis, especially in marketing in cyberspace.

Operating at a novice level of understanding of human behavior, legions of marketers have been coconspirators in business's move away from viewing consumers as individuals. In effect, modern consumers have been largely dehumanized, turned into phantoms of sorts. Big business has replaced the real consumer with a *statistical* consumer who resides not on Main Street, but in mathematical models and marketing planning scenarios. However, like the amputated limb that continues existence as a phantom to agitate the mind periodically, the shadows of real consumers lurk on the sidelines of failed marketing programs everywhere. The focus on illusionary consumers has led real consumers to lower steadily their degree of brand loyalty. *Real* consumers do not abandon brands for others; brands (or rather the companies and marketers behind them) abandon them.

The phantom consumer syndrome haunts business journals and trade media, which prefer dealing with "tangibles"—things that can be measured, such as technology, units manufactured, and units sold, and "case studies," lessons from which can rarely be applied elsewhere because of cultural differences in companies—to dealing with matters as yeasty and nebulous as human behavior. To the degree that behavior is addressed in trade media, it often is in sweeping generalizations about broadly defined demographic groups, such as "Generation X'ers," "Boomers," "Seniors," and "Hispanics," or in generalizations about groups of consumers that researchers have relegated to so-called psychographic categories or typologies, often under the questionable presumption that personality per se is the major causative force in consumer behavior.

It is noteworthy that although great sums have been invested in consumer typologies, none has broadly gained the confidence of decision makers in business. Perhaps this is because consumer typologies are inherently statistical fictions; they do not capture the essence of the *real* behavior of *real* consumers in *real* marketplaces. Mitchell's VALS (values, attitudes, and lifestyles) typology, first released in the 1970s, relegates all consumers to nine "lifestyle" categories. Mitchell saw strong correlations if not causative relationships between personality attributes and buying behavior. Many major consumer product companies signed on as VALS subscribers, eventually finding that VALS failed to meet expectations. This led to a "more advanced model" called VALS II. But it also turned out to be far from the magic bullet marketers are hoping for (Wolfe, 1990). Such attempts to link personality with buying behavior have been astonishingly unproductive, yet this fact "hasn't seemed to have reached many marketing executives" (Clancy & Shulman, 1991). This speaks poorly of efforts to consign consumers to categories based on personality traits. It also frames a warning to designers of IT expert systems that analytic protocols based on personality typologies alone will not be very productive.

These ideas are critical to a full understanding of the potential of IT in relationship marketing and how IT can be harnessed to increase marketing effectiveness dramatically. It is a matter of IT facilitating a shift from thinking about consumers en masse in mathematical representations to thinking about them in real form as real individuals. This presents the marketing profession with a gut-wrenching paradigm shift in analytic methodologies. If IT is more about relationships than about information, promoting major change in how marketers view consumers will be IT's biggest contribution to relationship marketing.

It helps to remember that relationship marketing revolves around *real* consumers, beginning in the analytic and conceptual stages of marketing. In contrast, transaction marketing revolves around imaginary or illusory relationships with *statistical* consumers—mathematical representations of *real* consumers used in devising marketing plans. But in slavish dependence on such models, "the vocabulary of the mathematical fiction inexorably becomes the vocabulary with which we describe the reality"—a truism captured many centuries ago in Plato's dictum that computations speak only to appearances, not realities (Bailey, 1996, p. 107). How does one market to a computation? However it is done, it is a practice growing in obsolescence because of the rising use of relationship marketing techniques that owe much to advancements in IT.

IT is reaching levels of sophistication that permit marketers to set aside mathematical fictions about consumers and begin developing "a computational model of the individual human being that reflects how that human being actually behaves. 'The ideal would be algorithmic behavior that could pass the Turing test. . . . Calibration ought not to be merely a matter of fitting parameters, but also one of building human-like qualitative behavior into the algorithmic specification itself' " (Bailey, 1996, p. 107).[1]

Such a model stands to change the face of marketing research and practice radically. For example, population sampling becomes largely unnecessary when marketers have real information on real consumers on an individual basis. For similar reasons, the use of focus groups for testing marketing concepts—a practice that is continuously put to question—loses value. The virtually unlimited power of IT systems to store, retain, and process data describing *real* consumers on an *individual* basis erodes the value of traditional research methods and activities for many analytic functions of marketing. To the degree that IT becomes capable of *virtual* intuition about consumers' situations, this will be even more so.

Many argue that IT will never be able to emulate and deal with human subjectivity as competently as the human mind does. Nevertheless, IT information flow can boost marketers' intuitive insights and creativity into higher orders of effectiveness simply because of superiority in speed and volume of *quantifiable* (objective) information processed. And that is the most productive role of IT—not replacement of human faculties, but the amplification of them.

IT promises service of mutual benefit to business and consumers by restoring the phantom consumer to corporeal form and giving business a platform for rendering customized attention to each customer. However, before this can come to pass, a deeper understanding of human behavior than is required in transaction marketing must emerge throughout the marketing profession.

"Forced" objectivity drives companies to market to statistical consumers, ignoring real consumers, who respond by not developing deep emotional bonds with companies and their brands. Real consumers are emotional creatures who easily feel abandoned. Statistical consumers are different. They are more even-tempered denizens of hypothetical universes created by researchers for purposes of planning and predicting. Because statistical consumers are imaginary, it is relatively easy for them to acquire some of the characteristics of their sponsors (marketers) and their creators (researchers). Scientific research protocols, following Cartesian tradition, supposedly bar that from happening in the creation of statistical consumers and the manipulation of their values and behavior. But, as practitioners of deeper sciences are increasingly realizing, it is impossible for any product of human effort not to reflect something of the producer's or analytic observer's unique self.

THE CENTRALITY OF DIALOGUE
IN RELATIONSHIP MARKETING

In pull marketing models (IT mediated or otherwise), customer retention depends largely on the human qualities of the relationship between supplier and consumer, and the durability of the relationship depends on the consumer's subjective measures of satisfaction. Healthy, satisfying relationships depend on meaningful bilateral communications; thus a major challenge in IT-mediated marketing activities is facilitation of credible and responsive dialogue. Satisfying dialogues (and satisfying relationships) depend on the quality of four conditions:

1. Bilateral or reciprocal empathy (ability to identify with and understand another person's conditions, feelings, and motives)
2. Bilateral or reciprocal vulnerability (lowering of defenses, a prerequisite of enduring, satisfying relationships)
3. Bilateral or reciprocal faith (confidence that the relationship will meet expectations)
4. Bilateral or reciprocal trust (belief that parties to the relationship will morally work to its benefit

Dialogue is the most essential psychosocial element in relationship marketing. Without dialogue there can be no continuing, satisfying relationship. This does not matter much in transaction marketing, but in relationship marketing, dialogue is critical.

Getting the most out of IT applications for managing customer relationships requires an understanding of the role of dialogue in relationships. This starts with knowing what a dialogue is. Simply stated, a dialogue is a collaborative exchange of information. The state of the art in managing dialogue in consumer-based relationship marketing is still fairly primitive in comparison with what it likely will be in the future. Most marketers still need to negotiate a transition of thought from marketing philosophies that have been averse to dialogue between sellers and buyers. This attitude has been fortified by lawyers, who have traditionally discouraged marketers from forming close relationships with consumers on the grounds that this broadens company liability and risk of litigation.

IT and Reciprocal Empathy

There is a common view, frequently developed in the relationship marketing literature, that "trust" is the foundation of lasting relationships. We propose that trust is as much a result as an antecedent of relationships—and much of the time, it is more of a result. Whether or not a relationship brings pleasure and satisfaction may be a better index to consult in assessing relationships with consumers. The experiential core of relationships revolves around subjective interactions between people in what is often referred to as *chemistry*. Implicit in that term is that "good chemistry" means good feelings. Perhaps as much as anything else, relationship marketing in consumer markets is about good feelings.

IT offers the opportunity to shift marketing back to the subjective dimensions of human existence, where good feelings are experienced and consumers' decisions are really made. This requires a unique synergism between human and machine in which the machine (computer) processes objective information and the human (the marketer) integrates subjective information with the machine's content and output to come to a robust understanding of the real, individual consumer. To do this effectively, the marketer needs to know how consumers make decisions. With this knowledge, subjective interchanges between sellers and buyers can take place in an atmosphere of *reciprocal empathy,* a necessary ingredient of long-lasting healthy relationships.

The dehumanization of consumers in statistical models has contributed in a major way to a massive decline in the incidence of reciprocal empathy in consumer marketing. We believe this has played a large role in raising marketing costs while other costs of business operations have fallen dramatically (Sheth & Sisodia, 1995a, 1995b). It also seems likely that a large measure of consumer litigation stems directly from the dehumanizing of consumers in research, marketing planning, and marketing practice. People simply are not as inclined to sue persons or organizations to which they are bonded. Unfortunately, the cost of decline in reciprocal empathy in provider-consumer relationships is an unexamined issue in terms of marketing because in the era of transaction marketing and statistical consumers, such fuzzy matters as empathy are a bother. It is too much of an immeasurable for standard statistical modeling and marketing planning, so why think about it? Yet it is well-nigh impossible to mount a credible argument against the proposition that empathy is a critical ingredient of enduring, satisfying relationships.

IT can increase human effectiveness in many marketing tasks because of computer superiority in storage capacity and data-processing speed, but reciprocal empathy in provider-consumer relationships must be supplied by humans. Moreover, the greater amount of information IT makes available to marketers does not convert directly into more effectiveness. However, more information from IT systems often leads to major changes in knowledge requirements—in what it takes to use advantageously the larger body of information flowing through IT systems today.

If, as Schrage (1997) notes, "Information itself offers value only when presented in the context of relationships" (p. 2), many marketers need to sharpen their knowledge bases about what makes for enduring, satisfying relationships. The protocols of transaction marketing that seek minimal contact with consumers often lead companies into marketing failure because of a lack of relationship contexts. The emotional, empathic dimensions of provider-consumer relationships cannot be assessed in conventional modeling of consumer behavior, because Cartesian traditions call for barring entry of such influence in scientific analysis. The much-heralded potentials of relationship marketing must change that perspective in order to be realized. The argument that IT is about relationships, not information, also calls for major changes in the mind-set of marketing, from academe to Madison Avenue—changes that could be referred to collectively as "the rehumanizing of marketing."

RELATIONSHIP MARKETING
AND MASS CUSTOMIZATION

A combination of events, including the development of advanced IT systems and an older population that is more demanding of personal attention, are behind the near-oxymoronic term *mass customization*. Mass customization heralds a new era in product design, manufacturing, and marketing, as well as in marketing communications. For many products, customization now can be accomplished on a mass basis for little or no more cost than standardized production. The Internet has been particularly influential in driving marketing toward mass-customized messaging. BroadVision of Palo Alto was one of the pioneers in developing technology that allows marketers to change messages "on the fly" as consumers surf the Net. Information is captured as a user surfs, and that information is analyzed to make best-guess judgments regarding what products and services the user would likely be interested in.

In the heyday of mass production, standardized products, and formulaic marketing messages, anything resembling customization was seen as too expensive. Now, customized attention to customers' individual circumstances is being seen not only as an efficient way to manage and control inventory costs (little or no waste and no carrying costs) but as a way to lower marketing costs. Customized attention encourages stronger customer loyalty, which leads to greater income from existing customers than from new customers (Reichheld, 1996).

Advancements in IT make it possible to know much about consumers on a mass basis yet communicate with them on an individual basis. IT has played a major role in making it economically possible for firms to custom design a wide range of products that less than a decade ago would not seem likely subjects for mass customization at basically off-the-shelf prices. Examples of this include Levi-Strauss (jeans), the *Wall Street Journal* (newspapers, on-line), Seiko (watches), Motorola (pagers), and a Japanese bicycle company that can produce more than 11 million variations of racing, road, and mountain bikes.

IT applications in business have reached dazzling levels of sophistication, enabling such recent developments as mass customization and the individualized customizing of messages on the Internet and in the U.S. mails. But for relationship marketing to warrant the claims many make about its future, it must be seen as more than technological processes based on sophisticated usage of databases for mass customization.

The Need for Authenticity in Relationship Marketing

Information technologies clearly have a critical role to play in surmounting one of the biggest challenges in business today: the development of protocols to support more intimate and intense provider-consumer relationships than have generally prevailed since the end of World War II. However, if the promise is the attention of a personal relationship, but the delivery is impersonal (think of automated telephone answering systems that force callers to go through too many menus before reaching a live person), customers will have a hard time feeling human presence in the relationship, and the marketers will be back in the era of transaction marketing and phantom consumers.

Few database-driven marketing programs are truly collaborative or cooperative, thus few qualify at this time as a form of relationship marketing if relationship marketing is "marketing which centers around relationships, network and interactions" (Gummesson, 1995, p. 6). Often, database marketing is little more than manipulation of consumer data in ways intended to create an illusion that the provider is presenting a customized response to an individual consumer's needs. This is fundamentally an inauthentic play for a consumer's attentions—it brings to mind Woody Allen's famous advice (paraphrased here) that sincerity is the most important thing in relationships; if you can fake that, you have it made.

Lack of authenticity is seen in direct-mail pieces that awkwardly begin with the equivalent of "Dear Terry M. Brown." The addressee's full name is used to avoid the mistake of calling a person "Mr. Brown" when Terry happens to be female. Also, by not using honorifics, such openings avoid ego-offending mistakes. The result is an unnatural salutation that severely compromises the letter designer's intentions of persuading the addressee that he or she is getting individual attention. The presumptuous discussion about the addressee's needs and desires that usually follows further reveals the inauthentic and manipulative character of the letter. Consumers want relationships with providers that are authentic, empathic, and positioned in *mutual vulnerability*—a reciprocal openness on the part of both parties. This speaks to the "symmetry . . . in the behavioral constructs that underlie the relationship" (Anderson & Narus, 1990).

When consumers are invited into the marketing process—which is what symmetrical collaboration with consumers means—the irregularities in human behavior cannot be ignored, as they are in transaction marketing. More flexible protocols than are customary in transaction marketing are demanded. The mechanistic frameworks of traditional marketing theory and practice must be replaced with more organic frameworks that acknowledge consumers' individuality and foster corporate recognition in humanistic terms of the interdependence between company and consumer. This ethos is implicitly recognized in Cumby and Barnes's (1996) observation that "the challenge for relationship marketers is to determine if and when it may be appropriate . . . to transform exchange-oriented relationships into communal ones, and the role that a database can play in facilitating such decisions."

Ultimately, if the relationship is to be long, strong, and productive, an automated relationship-building process using IT systems needs to shift from being technically competent to being humanistically competent. Absent such a shift, consumers may be prone eventually to regard the relationship as inauthentic—as being less in reality than implied or promised in marketing communications.

Authenticity in relationships has long been regarded in adult development psychology as achieving greater importance with age (Erikson, 1959; Hall & Nordby, 1973; Maslow, 1971). According to Jung, in the first half of life the influence of authenticity in our lives is compromised by what he terms the *persona* (from the Latin for *mask*). We cover the visages of our innermost selves with masks that we have configured in hopes of promoting our prospects for social acceptance (Hall & Nordby, 1973).

However, for normally developing personalities, this becomes a less urgent need in the second half of life, resulting in increased respect for (indeed, the need for) authenticity.

Authenticity is more than a matter of ethics in relationship marketing. Trust, on which satisfying and enduring relationships depend, is built on the foundations of authenticity. This is not a major concern in transaction marketing, where the main objective is to consummate transactions rather than to build relationships. Authenticity in marketers' behavior has not received much attention among advocates of relationship marketing, probably because "academic marketing theory has yet to define consumer expectations for consumer-brand marketing relationships" (Hess, 1996, p. 86). It is commonly asserted that the marketing profession has in the past been overly focused on consumer markets at the expense of business markets. In fact, for more than four decades, marketing theory and practice have given far greater attention to the expectations of business than to those of consumers; the latter have been dealt with only superficially and with a view to manipulating consumers' behavior to suit the ends of marketers. Thus much of marketing has been about "staging" product performances on business's behalf, with the issue of "genuine" authenticity (redundancy required in view of the frequent incidence of "staged" authenticity) regarded as being more interesting to ethicists than to marketers.

Impacts of Technology-Enabled Relationship Marketing

With all of the characteristics described above, the adoption of technology-enabled relationship marketing will have several major impacts. First, it will greatly increase the velocity at which commerce occurs. Better knowledge and anticipation of customer requirements (so that, for example, order forms are already 90% filled out) can reduce time demands on customers. In a time-poor society, this is extremely valuable. With linkages to operational systems in place, order fulfillment can readily be expedited as well. As the Mobil advertisement for its Speed Pass service (a good example of using technology to facilitate concentrated, long-term relationships) goes, its "like buying time without paying for it."

Equally as important, technology-based relationship marketing is highly efficient in its use of all resources, not just time. Business processes can be streamlined to take advantage of new modes of doing business. Far better targeting results in very little wasted marketing expenditure. As Peppers and Rogers (1995) point out, although mass marketing might be less expensive per person reached, it is almost always cheaper per sale completed to communicate individually with a valued customer and solve a problem for him or her. The value of targeted marketing efforts is also readily seen when one considers how concentrated consumption in many industries truly is; for example, about .02% of the U.S. population accounts for 25% of all car rentals in the country.

Traditional marketing operates in a "just-in-case" mode, with huge amounts of inventory in the distribution channel "in case" a customer decides to show up. Technology-enabled relationship marketing truly moves the company toward "just-in-time" marketing. This achieves an equally high level of availability with a mere fraction of the inventory in traditional systems, especially when it is coupled with a JIT production system.

In addition to efficiency improvements, technology-enabled relationship marketing will also lead to higher levels of marketing effectiveness. One dimension of this is the ability not only to respond quickly to customer needs, but to anticipate those needs. Freid and Freid (1995) suggest that, to be successful at maintaining long-term relationships, companies will have to learn how to anticipate what customers want and need. They suggest that there are three steps involved in this anticipation: surveying, detecting, and simulating. The first step is to understand the drivers of customer buying decisions. The second is the ability to detect patterns of change, to understand relationships between customer values and external forces. The third step is to simulate customer behavior.

Another compelling dimension of effectiveness in marketing is the ability to routinize or automate certain kinds of consumption. Time poverty and the availability of an abundance of information technology will lead to a greatly increased level of automated transactions between consumers and marketers. Akin to "automatic replenishment" as practiced in the business-to-business marketing arena today, such arrangements will become increasingly commonplace in the future. They may happen directly between consumers and manufacturers for larger purchases and through intermediaries for smaller purchases. Suppliers of large items or major services will have opportunities to become the suppliers of choice for an ever-widening array of goods and services.

Technology-enabled relationship marketing will lower systemwide costs and improve value delivery to customers. This should result in higher overall profits; a well-honed relationship marketing approach will make previously unprofitable customers profitable and will lead to large amounts of new value creation generally. Consider the benefits that accrue from Baxter's ValueLink system, which allows a hospital to convert inventory warehousing space to clinical space. The hospital thus replaces a cost center with a revenue center while improving the overall level of availability of supplies to its clinical departments.

The value that is thus created should be shared with customers; indeed, savvy consumers will increasingly demand that corporations share the benefits of cost cutting with them. Just as Wal-Mart demands that P&G lower its costs and then share the benefit with Wal-Mart, so too will customers with high lifetime value demand and receive similar considerations. Smart companies will do this without being forced; they will proactively invest resources in those relationships with the greatest long-term value. Currently, investment in customers usually stops after they have become customers; spending on customer retention activity is much lower than spending on acquisition. Further, loyal customers tend to subsidize those who are less loyal, as well as the acquisition of new customers. Overall, the economics of customer acquisition and retention require and will receive much more understanding and attention than they do currently.

Implementation Issues

Companies making the transition toward technology-enabled relationship marketing must keep several implementation issues in mind. First, significant early-mover advantages will accrue to companies that make the transition sooner rather than later. Each new generation of technologies builds upon the learning curves associated with the previous generation. Although it is possible in some cases to leapfrog generations of technology, this happens only when there is revolutionary change. When technology changes in a more evolutionary (albeit still rapid) manner, early adoption is crucial. Rather than wait for the perfect moment to

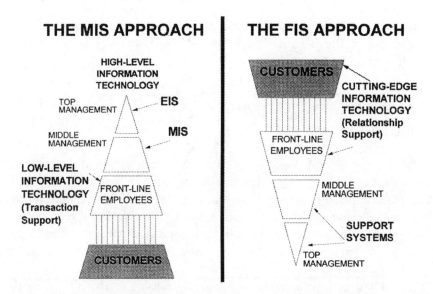

Figure 20.4. Frontline Information Systems for Relationship Marketing

enter, companies need to jump in and start deploying the new technologies as early as possible. They need to accumulate institutional experience with the technology and develop the ability to customize it to suit their purposes. Early-mover advantages tend to persist for a long time, provided that the company keeps abreast of rapid technological changes.

When a business gets redefined around customer relationships, and when the process of managing those relationships gets thoroughly reengineered, companies need to make significant changes in how they organize their activities. First, they must define the entire business in service terms. They must greatly elevate the role and importance of the customer service function, in recognition of its role in customer retention and thus profitability. Both customer service (retention) and sales (customer acquisition) must report to the marketing function. The company should also enable self-service by developing easy-to-use customer-focused tools.

A vital component of success in this arena is the provision of cutting-edge information technology to sales, customer service, and other frontline personnel. Figure 20.4 depicts the importance of the frontline information system (FIS). As it shows, the companies that are the most successful at achieving dramatic impacts through information technology are those that deploy it at the front lines, where it can directly affect customer satisfaction. The information that companies need for management control purposes (the domain of traditional MIS and EIS) is collected as a by-product of doing the work.

DANGERS OF TECHNOLOGY-ENABLED RELATIONSHIP MARKETING

There are several dangers inherent to a strategy predicated upon technology-enabled relationship marketing. First, a lack of authenticity can make a mockery of attempts to operate in a "one-to-one" marketing mode. As discussed earlier, authenticity is an elusive quality. It requires periodic intervention by humans, extremely sophisticated and self-learning systems, and in-depth understanding of the experiential elements of service design and flow.

If mismanaged, technology-intensive relationship marketing can easily degenerate into an impersonal and faceless experience for customers. The result: no referrals, no loyalty, only a relentlessly price-driven customer who uses the power of technology to obtain the best price on each transaction.

Discussion and Areas for Future Research

In moving toward technology-enabled relationship marketing, there are three possible scenarios:

- *High-tech marketer and high-tech customer:* This is the best situation; it has the maximum potential for new value creation and sharing.
- *Low-tech marketer and high-tech customer:* From the marketer's perspective, this is the worst situation. Customers can cherry-pick and play one marketer against another. The marketer becomes a sitting duck and margins disappear. In this situation, it is imperative that the marketer acquire technological savvy as soon as possible.
- *High-tech marketer and low-tech customer:* This is a middle situation; its primary drawback is that it is inefficient. The marketer must continue to make expensive low-technology modes of doing business available. This situation calls for the marketer to become adept at marketing the technol-

ogy itself. As discussed earlier, the marketer must pay careful attention to so-called high-touch issues.

There are several important research areas that relate to the interface between information technology and relationship marketing:

- ▦ *How to speed up customer adoption of new IT-based relationship marketing processes:* With employees, companies can simply mandate the adoption of new business processes; even then, implementation is fraught with problems. Companies certainly cannot mandate that customers reengineer their purchasing and consumption habits. What are the psychological and tangible switching costs, and what is their relation with perceived benefits? What are the benefits and drawbacks of persuasion versus coercion?

- ▦ *Mechanisms for sharing new value created:* Companies that seek to appropriate all of the new value created in a relationship will soon see their customers defect. Clearly, there needs to be value sharing between company and customer. The question is, How best can this be done? For example, should companies set up customer business development accounts and fund them based on some formula that incorporates customer-derived revenues and directly attributable costs?

- ▦ *The development of authenticity in relationship marketing:* As discussed earlier, this is a key element but one that appears elusive in definition and thus management. What exactly constitutes authenticity in relationship marketing? How important is it? Are there segments that do not care about it?

- ▦ *Extent to which strong customer relationships can translate into the provision of unrelated products:* This is related to the assertion that information technology leads to an expansion in the scope of offerings that can be made to a given customer. Individual customers presumably want to reduce the number of suppliers, just as corporations have done. Is this true? Are co-marketing relationships an effective mechanism to enable this?

- ▦ *Creation of shared infrastructures to enable relationship marketing in a cost-effective manner:* To make relationships effective and affordable, certain infrastructures have to be developed. The Internet is one such infrastructure; it would clearly have been prohibitively expensive, if not operationally impossible, for one company to have developed this infrastructure. Infrastructure costs are always prohibitive when borne by a single player. New infrastructures that may be needed include one for the frequent delivery of small packages, a clearinghouse to address privacy concerns, and an infrastructure to enable small payments. Research is needed to flesh these out and identify other elements of shared infrastructure, as well as to develop insights into how these infrastructures should be designed, constructed, and managed.

Note

1. In this test, which is named after Alan Turing, people type messages to an unseen correspondent who answers. If the correspondent (a computer) fools the person into believing that the correspondent is another person, the computer has earned the right to be called intelligent.

References

Anderson, J. C., & Narus, J. A. (1990). A model of distributor firm and manufacturer firm working partnerships. *Journal of Marketing, 54*(1), 42-58.

Bailey, J. (1996). *Afterthought: The computer challenge to human intelligence.* New York: Basic Books.

Bickert, J. (1992). Database marketing: An overview. In E. L. Nash (Ed.), *The direct marketing handbook* (2nd ed.). New York: McGraw-Hill.

Bird, J. (1995, February). Logical guides to marketing. *Management Today,* pp. 58-62.

Blattberg, R., Glazer, R., & Little, J. D. C. (1994). *The marketing information revolution.* Boston: Harvard Business School Press.

Cespedes, F. V., & Smith, H. J. (1993). Database marketing: New rules for policy and practice. *Sloan Management Review, 35*(1), 7-22.

Clancy, K. J., & Shulman, R. S. (1991). *The marketing revolution.* New York: Harper Business.

Cumby, J., & Barnes, J. G. (1996). Relationship segmentation: The enhancement of databases to support relationship marketing. In A. Parvatiyar & J. N. Sheth (Eds.), *Contemporary knowledge of relationship marketing.* Atlanta, GA: Emory University, Center for Relationship Marketing.

Deighton, J. (1996). The impact of electronic commerce on marketing. *Harvard Business Review, 74*(5), 137.

Erikson, E. (1959). *Identity and the life cycle.* New York: International Universities Press.

Foskett, S. (1996). Online technology ushers in one-to-one marketing. *Direct Marketing, 59*(7), 38-40.

Freid, C., & Freid, S. (1995). Beyond relationship marketing: Anticipating what customers want. *Planning Review, 23*(4), 40-41.

Gilder, G. (1994, December 5). Telecosm: The bandwidth tidal wave. *Forbes ASAP,* pp. 162-173.

Grant, A. W. H., & Schlesinger, L. A. (1995). Realize your customers' full profit potential. *Harvard Business Review, 74*(1), 59-72.

Gummesson, E. (1995). *Relationship marketing: From 4Ps to 30Rs.* Malmö, Sweden: Liber-Hermods.

Hagel, J., III, & Armstrong, A. G. (1997). *Net gain: Expanding markets through virtual communities.* Boston: Harvard Business School Press.

Herremans, I. M., & Ryans, J. K., Jr. (1995, September). The case for better measurement and reporting of marketing performance. *Business Horizons,* pp. 51-60.

Hall, C. S., & Nordby, V. J. (1973). *A primer of Jungian psychology.* New York: New American Library.

Harrison, J. (1995, June). Database marketing breakthroughs. *Target Marketing, 18,* 14-15.

Hess, J. S. (1996). An investment model of consumer-brand relationships. In A. Parvatiyar & J. N. Sheth (Eds.), *Contemporary knowledge of relationship marketing.* Atlanta, GA: Emory University, Center for Relationship Marketing.

Jones, N. (1996). Talking pages. *Marketing Week, 19*(18), 37-40.

Judge, P. C. (1996, October 7). Why Firefly has Madison Avenue buzzing. *Business Week,* p. 100.

Kelly, K. (1997, August). It takes a village to make a mall. *Wired* [On-line], p. 5.

Kierzkowski, A., McQuade, S., Waitman, R., & Zeisser, M. (1996). Marketing to the digital consumer. *McKinsey Quarterly, 2,* 180-183.

Larson, M. (1996). In pursuit of a lasting relationship. *Journal of Business Strategy, 17*(6), 31-33.

Maslow, A. H. (1971). *The farther reaches of human nature.* New York: Penguin.

McKenna, R. (1991). *Relationship marketing: Successful strategies for the age of the customer.* Reading, MA: Addison-Wesley.

Mitchell, A. (1996). P&G slams inefficient marketing. *Marketing Week, 19*(33), 26-27.

Narisetti, R. (1997, January 15). P&G, seeing shoppers were being confused, overhauls marketing. *Wall Street Journal,* p. A1.

Patterson, D. A. (1995, September). Microprocessors in 2020. *Scientific American, 273.*

Peppers, D., & Rogers, M. (1995). A new marketing paradigm: Share of customer, not market share. *Planning Review, 23*(2), 14-18.

Rapp, S., & Collins, T. (1990). *The great marketing turnaround: The age of the individual—and how to profit from it.* Englewood Cliffs, NJ: Prentice Hall.

Reichheld, F. F. (with Teal, T.). (1996). *The loyalty effect: The hidden force behind growth, profits, and lasting value.* Boston: Harvard Business School Press.

Rogers, M., & Peppers, D. (1997, January). Making the transition to one-on-one marketing. *Inc.,* pp. 63-65.

Roszak, T. (1994). *The cult of information.* Berkeley: University of California Press.

Schlender, B. (1995, January 16). What Bill Gates really wants. *Fortune,* pp. 35-47.

Schrage, M. (1997). *The relationship revolution.* Paper presented at the Merrill Lynch Forum, New York.

Sheth, J. N., Gardner, D. M., & Garrett, D. E. (1988). *Marketing theory: Evolution and evaluation.* New York: John Wiley.

Sheth, J. N., & Parvatiyar, A. (1995). Relationship marketing in consumer markets: Antecedents and consequences. *Journal of the Academy of Marketing Science, 23,* 255-271.

Sheth, J. N., & Sisodia, R. S. (1995a). Feeling the heat: Part I. *Marketing Management, 4*(2), 8-23.

Sheth, J. N., & Sisodia, R. S. (1995b). Feeling the heat: Part II. *Marketing Management, 4*(3), 19-33.

Stone, M., Woodcock, N., & Wilson, M. (1996). Managing the change from marketing planning to customer relationship management. *Long Range Planning, 29,* 675-683.

Wolfe, D. B. (1990). *Serving the ageless market.* Englewood Cliffs, NJ: Prentice Hall.

Wolfe, D. B. (1996). A behavior model for imparting empathy to relationship marketing in cyberspace. In A. Parvatiyar & J. N. Sheth (Eds.), *Contemporary knowledge of relationship marketing.* Atlanta, GA: Emory University, Center for Relationship Marketing.

21

Customer Profitability

Analysis and Design Issues

KAJ STORBACKA

My purpose in this chapter is to discuss, within a relationship marketing context, analysis and relationship design issues in relation to customer profitability.[1] Profitability issues have traditionally not been focal for marketing scholars or for the practitioners (Sheth & Sisodia, 1995). The traditional marketing management approach focuses on creating single- or multiple-exchange transactions, and the profitability of these have been determined by product cost and pricing. Marketing management thus measures the efficiency of marketing based on products. Measures such as product cost, market share, sales volume, and gross margin indicate a company's ability to market specific products in a given market.

But as marketers' relationships with customers become complex, the cost structure of these relationships also becomes complex. In such an environment a customer who purchases only profitable products may end up being unprofitable, due to the company's inability to account for all the nongoods components connected to maintaining the relationship.

Several definitions of relationship marketing exist, but my discussion in this chapter is based on a definition offered by Grönroos (1997): "Relationship marketing is the process of identifying and establishing, maintaining, enhancing, and when necessary terminating relationships with customers and other stakeholders, at a profit, so that the objectives of all parties involved are met, where this is done by a mutual giving and fulfillment of promises." The interesting part of this definition is the small sub-sentence "at a profit." Despite the obvious importance of valuation of relationships and its immediate applicability in terms of both research and management, little research has been carried out within the domain of relationship marketing with respect to profitability. Much of the research has been directed toward an understanding of the nature of relationships and relationship marketing.

Levels of Analysis

In service management and marketing, research has largely focused on the "moment of truth" (Normann, 1991) or the "service encounter" (Solomon, Surprenant, Czepiel, & Gutman, 1985). In a relationship context such encounters can be called episodes (Strandvik, 1994). Episodes are events that represent complete functions from the customer's point of view. Examples of episodes are a visit to a restaurant, staying overnight at a hotel, and a trip to a city on an airline. The word *relationship* implies that the link between the provider and the customer lasts longer than one episode. A long-term relationship with one provider can be described as a string of episodes, and the total benefit or value that the customer receives during the relationship is not provided in one episode. Rather, the benefits are delivered in "smaller portions" during the relationship.

Some relationships are built from series of discrete episodes in which customers make repetitive purchase decisions. There are, however, also relationships that are continuous, in which customers make contracts (implicit or explicit) with providers and receive offerings on demand. Examples of such relationships include those involving telephone, maintenance, and banking services (Liljander & Strandvik, 1995; Strandvik & Liljander, 1994). In a continuous relationship context, customers by definition use a large variety of different episode types, ranging from simple routine episodes (such as cash withdrawals from an ATM) to complex episodes (such as loan negotiations).

As the calculation of customer profitability is dependent on the availability of relevant information about relationships, much of the research in this area has been carried out within industries that have continuous relationships with their clients. This bias will also be clearly present in this chapter.

In order to understand the anatomy of a relationship, one has to understand its configuration of episodes. Different customers generate different types of episodes, use different variations of each episode type, and use different amounts of them. Each and every relationship is thus configured differently. Whatever typology is chosen, it is obvious that the different categories of episodes have their own specific impacts on customer profitability. Some of the episodes are costly to produce, whereas others are inexpensive; some of the episodes occur often, whereas others occur seldom; and so on. The episodes are clearly very disparate, from both the customer's and the provider's point of view. In a bank, an episode related to the buying of a house is a very special occasion to the customer, occurring perhaps once or twice in his or her lifetime. Thus the customer has little or no experience of how to behave in the episode or what the issues are in which he or she should be interested. On the other hand, the withdrawal of funds from an ATM is an episode with which the customer is very familiar, and thus the customer can be expected to assume a greater role in the production of the episode.

Provided that a typology of possible episodes can be created, relationships can be depicted using an episode configuration matrix such as that shown in Figure 21.1. The horizontal axis describes the customer relationship and shows the types of episodes (not the number of episodes) the provider has had with the customer. The matrix can be analyzed from the provider's perspective or from the customer's perspective. From the provider's point of view, the number of episodes needs to be added. The total number of episodes is the sum of the demand of all customers who have chosen the specific type and variation of discrete episodes.

The building blocks of a customer base can now be defined: The customer base consists of customer relationships, and each customer relationship is configured of a specific pattern of episodes. Each episode is, in its turn, built out of a specific set of activities. Profitability can thus be analyzed on four levels: the customer-base level, the relationship level, the episode level, and the activity level. Different aspects of profitability become important on the different levels. In this chapter, I focus on the first two levels.

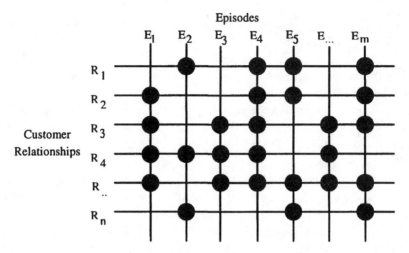

Figure 21.1. Episode Configuration Matrix
SOURCE: Storbacka (1994).

Analyzing Customer Bases

As customer bases can be regarded as assets, the key questions on a customer-base level relate to the choice of customer relationships and the creation of portfolios of relationships (Grant & Schlesinger, 1995; Storbacka, 1994). On a customer-base level, the questions are more of a strategic nature, the key question being how to allocate resources in an optimal way. Investments in the customer relationship can be regarded as long-term, and therefore customers could be viewed as a fixed asset. Thus the provider has to choose the "right" customer relationship in which to invest in order to ensure productivity of the capital employed.

Typical questions on a customer-base level would include the following: How is the profitability of a company distributed among customers? How should customers be grouped? Where are the biggest profitability potentials? What is the retention rate for different parts of the customer base? Is the provider losing customers in a certain part of the business? How should resources be allocated among different customer groups? Could the processes toward different parts of the customer base be differentiated?

On a customer-base level, the key tool for analysis is the distribution of profitability within the customer base. The distribution can be used to measure the sensitivity of the customer base because it indicates how dependent the company is on a few customers and shows the cross-subsidizing effect in the customer base. This, in turn, can be used to compare different customer bases as to their potential value and risk profile.

THE DISTRIBUTION OF PROFITABILITY

As several researchers have argued, the dispersion of customer profitability in a customer base is evidently vast in all industries (Connell, 1995; Foster, Gupta, & Sjoblom, 1996; Reichheld & Sasser, 1990; Shapiro, Rangan, Moriarty, & Ross, 1987; Storbacka, 1993; Storbacka & Luukinen, 1994). Thus some relationships in every customer base are profitable and others are unprofitable. The proportion of profitable customers obviously varies among providers. Cooper and Kaplan (1991) suggest that in certain industrial markets, 20% of the customers account for 225% of the total customer-base profitability. Empirical evidence from retail banks has shown that 20% of these banks' customers account for between 130% and 200% of the total profits (Storbacka, 1994).

As the distributions of profitability in customer bases are very skewed, they are best analyzed as ordered distributions. I have created the Stobachoff curve to be used in comparisons of ordered distributions of customer bases (Storbacka, 1994). The Stobachoff curve, shown in Figure 21.2, is drawn as follows. The vertical axis shows the cumulative profitability of the customer base as a fraction of the aggregated customer-base profitability. The customers are ranked on the horizontal axis according to their profitability so that the most profitable customer is to the far left of the axis. The profitability of the second customer is added to the profitability of the first customer, and the sum is compared with the aggregated profitability of the customer base.

The logic in the figure reveals that some of the customer relationships are much more important to the provider than others. The 25% or so most profitable customers are basically the provider's "lifeline." On the other hand, one might conclude that the 25% or so of unprofitable customers that erode the profitability to the final level are unimportant. It is, however, important to note that these customers may be unprofitable because of high relationship costs. Because there is a large proportion of fixed cost allocated, these customers account for a major part of the provider's fixed-cost mass. Removing these customers would in fact mean that the fixed cost would have to be redistributed among the remaining

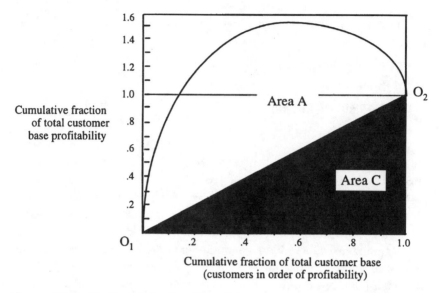

Figure 21.2. The Profitability Distribution of a Customer Base: The Stobachoff Curve

customers—something that certainly would make some of the currently profitable customers unprofitable.

THE STOBACHOFF INDEX

If every customer were equally profitable (and all customers were profitable), the Stobachoff curve in Figure 21.2 would not be a curve but instead a linear function (a straight line between the points O_1 and O_2). The curve's shape correlates with the equality of the distribution and thus with the degree of subsidizing between the profitable and unprofitable customers.

Based on the above discussion, an index (the Stobachoff index) for the distribution of profitability can be developed. Let the profitability distribution be represented by a vector $(p_1, p_2, \ldots, p_n)$, where p_i is the profitability of the ith customer $(i = 1, 2, \ldots, n)$. In the curve drawn in Figure 21.2 the profitability is arranged according to size:

[1] $$p_1 \mid p_2 \mid \ldots \mid p_n.$$

If the total profitability of a customer base is P, the points in the Stobachoff curve correspond to the following coordinates:

[2] $(0, 0)$; $(1/n, p_1/P)$; $(2/n, (p_1 + p_2)/P)$; . . . ; $(1, 1)$.

The area of the curve above the O_1-O_2 line (area A) compared to the total area of the curve above the x axis (area A + area C) can then be used as a measure of the distribution. The bigger area A is in comparison with area C, the more unequal the distribution and the more extensive the subsidizing effects. The Stobachoff index is thus based on the comparison of these areas.

Let the area under the Stobachoff curve (between the curve and the x axis) be T ($T = A + C$). The area of T can be estimated using the trapezoid rule

[3] $$T = \frac{1}{2n}\sum_{i=0}^{n-1} (\dot{p_i} + \dot{p}_{i+1}), \text{ where } \dot{p_i} = \dot{p}_{i-1} + \frac{P_i}{P} \text{ and } \dot{p_0} = 0.$$

The area A above the O_1-O_2 line can be expressed as follows (by noting that area $C = 1/2$):

[4] $$A = \frac{1}{2n}\sum_{i=0}^{n-1} (\dot{p_i} + \dot{p}_{i+1}) - \frac{1}{2}$$

The Stobachoff index (S) can thus be calculated as a quota of A and T:

[5] $S = A/T$.

The Stobachoff index is actually a measure of the studied customer base's deviation from an "ideal" customer base. When the Stobachoff index is zero, the profitability is equally distributed (i.e., all customers are equally profitable) and all customers are profitable. As soon as the index is greater than zero, the profitability is unequally distributed. The theoretical maximum value for the index is 1, and this value is reached only if there is one profitable customer with infinite profitability, a large number of customers with zero profitability, and an unprofitable customer with infinite negative profitability.

The Stobachoff index is a measure of the cross-subsidizing between customers in the provider's customer base. Hence the provider can use the Stobachoff index as a management instrument that can facilitate the assessment of different customer bases over a period of time.

In an analysis of the different theoretical shapes that the Stobachoff curve could have, it becomes obvious that an additional measure is needed in order to show the skewedness of the curve. In an extreme customer base a hypothetical situation could exist in which there is one extremely profitable customer and the rest of the customers in the customer base are unprofitable (or close to zero). The Stobachoff index for this customer base can be the same as for a customer base with a larger proportion of profitable customers. Given the same Stobachoff index, the customer base with the greater proportion of profitable customers would obviously be preferred.

A measure to help us to deal with this need could be the profitability proportion. Let n_u be the number of unprofitable customers in the customer base and n the total number of customers. The profitability proportion (P) can then be expressed as follows;

[6] $$P = (n - n_u)/n.$$

The higher the proportion of profitable customers, the better (given the same Stobachoff index).

CUSTOMER-BASE PORTFOLIO ANALYSIS

The Stobachoff index, combined with the proportion of profitable customers, can be used in several ways. It can be used to follow the development of a certain customer base over time, and it can also be used to grade customer bases within the same company. In companies where, for instance, customers are affiliated administratively to different geographic areas, the index may be used in making comparative studies of the customer bases in each area. The indexes will give information on the

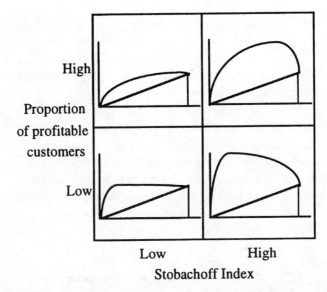

Figure 21.3. Customer-Base Portfolio Analysis (Verbal and Graphic Depictions)

sensitivity of the profitability of the customer bases and thus on the risk involved in the management of the customer relationships in the particular area.

Based on the index, one can analyze the generic development situations of a customer base by combining the two dimensions. The generic situations are valid when one compares profitable companies with the same level of aggregated profitability. The combination is depicted in Figure 21.3. The best situation would be that the Stobachoff index is 0 and the proportion of profitable customers is 1. In this situation the risks involved in dealing with the customer base are proportionally smaller as the company is not as dependent on a small number of customers. The need to segment the customer base grows smaller as P approaches 1 and S approaches 0. Thus there would be no need to find ways to group the customer base in the ideal situation.

Having a high Stobachoff index combined with a high proportion of profitable customers would indicate that there are a small number of very unprofitable customers eroding the aggregated profitability. Thus the unit under investigation may radically improve its profitability by identifying the unprofitable customers and influencing the reasons behind the unwanted economic results. In a situation where the unit's total cost is to a large extent variable, it may be an interesting alternative for the company to try to terminate its relationship with the most unprofitable customers and thus radically improve the aggregated profitability of the unit. This would not be the case, however, in most retail banks, where total cost is to a high degree fixed.

A low proportion of profitable customers combined with a low Stobachoff index indicates that there probably are no extremely unprofitable customers and thus—even though there are only a small number of profitable customers—the risks involved with the customer base are fairly low. As the profitability is equally distributed, there is probably little need for a differentiated strategy toward different customers. Hence it is unlikely that there is a great need to segment the customer base.

Having a high Stobachoff index combined with a low proportion of profitable customers is the worst case. This would indicate that the company is essentially dependent on a small number of customers, a state that makes it vulnerable to competitive action and to potential customer defections. The power positions of the profitable customers can be such that they may negotiate terms that will make them less profitable very soon. This would force the unit to have an extremely differentiated strategy based on a clear segmentation of the customer base.

SEGMENTING CUSTOMER BASES

There are two distinct segmentation needs in maintaining and enhancing customer relationships. First, there is a need to determine the state of the existing customer base in terms of the degree of homogeneity over a number of variables describing both the documented patronage behavior of the customers and background data on the customers. This type of analysis can be labeled *retrospective* because it is based on historical data. The retrospective analysis is more of a strategic tool as it makes possible decisions regarding product and price positioning and discrimination. It also allows for systematic evaluation of the state of the customer base in terms of possible risks and possibilities within the customer base.

The second type of analysis can be labeled *prospective* because it deals with the provider's ability to enhance existing customer relationships. The prospective analysis is operative or tactical in nature because the key issue is to find ways to enhance a particular relationship or a group of relationships. Such analysis is oriented toward creating practical solutions as to how to approach customers, how to communicate with them, and how to influence their behavior. These solutions are transitory because they are used basically for a "campaign" of different activities.

In this chapter, I focus only on segmentation based on retrospective customer-base analysis. The need for segmenting the customer base is a function of the differences between customers in terms of preferences, sales volume, transaction intensity, and customer profitability. The key attribute to be used in determining the need to segment the customer base is the distribution of profitability within the customer base.

Several ways of segmenting the customer base are evidently possible. Based on the literature (Bellis-Jones, 1989; Foster et al., 1996, Howell & Soucy, 1990; Shapiro et al., 1987; Storbacka, 1994), there are four basic ways to segment customer bases: (a) based on relationship revenue, (b) based on combining relationship revenue and relationship cost, (c) based on customer profitability, and (d) based on combining relationship revenue and customer relationship profitability. Examples of all these segmentation solutions using empirical data from retail banking can be found in Storbacka (1994).

The grouping of customers is static and therefore requires additional analysis in which customers are followed over time, so that migration patterns can be identified (Shapiro et al., 1987). Migration patterns are important when it comes to following both profitable and unprofitable customers. In analyses of migration, the focus should be on the turnover of customers (i.e., the defection rate; Reichheld & Sasser, 1990), the migration of unprofitable/profitable customers, and the degree of migration.

Designing Customer Relationships

Cultivating relationships is the core of customer management. On a relationship level, there are three key design issues, relating to (a) the revenue that the provider gets from the relationship (relationship revenue; RR), (b) the cost incurred by the relationship (relationship cost; RC), and (c) the length of the relationship with a specific customer (relationship longevity; RL). Typical questions would be as follows: How can the provider get the customer interested in concentrating his or her business—that is, how can the provider get a bigger customer share? Can new price carriers for services be identified in order to increase revenues? How could the provider change the customer's configuration of episodes (i.e., the customer's buying behavior) and still produce the same value for the customer? How can customer loyalty be ensured?

INCREASING RELATIONSHIP REVENUE

The relationship revenue of a particular customer is only a share of the total volume that the customer spends in the particular industry—the total industry volume (TIV). The total industry volume, in turn, is only a share of the total amount of money that the customer has at his or her disposal, the customer's total volume (CTV). Customers have certain amounts of money at their disposal, and they divide this money among many different sectors of their lives, including savings, housing, food, clothes, and hospitality services. Money spent in other sectors is not readily available to the providers in other industries.

It would seem interesting, from a relationship marketing perspective, to measure the provider's share of TIV. The RR/TIV ratio is called *patronage concentration,* as it measures the actual patronage behavior of the customer. The bigger the quota, the stronger the provider's position is and the stronger the relationship can be argued to be. It is important to note that when RR < TIV, the customer has other relationships to other providers in the same industry; the customer is only a partial customer. Partial customers obviously constitute a key potential when a company is trying to increase relationship volume and thus relationship revenue.

Based on the above logic, there are basically three ways for a company to increase relationship revenue: (a) by raising prices, (b) by increasing the patronage concentration of the customer under consideration (i.e., increasing RR/TIV), and (c) by increasing the RR/CTV ratio (i.e., by trying to cross-sell products other than the company's own to the customer).

A particularly interesting aspect of increasing relationship revenue is price bundling. Several researchers have discussed price bundling from different perspectives (Channon, 1986a, 1986b; Guiltinan, 1987; Normann, Cederwall, Edgren, & Holst, 1989; Normann & Ramirez, 1995; Storbacka, 1993). Price bundling relates to the fact that the offering always consists of a number of components (Grönroos, 1990; Normann, 1991) that are difficult to separate from each other—they are sold as a bundle. The bundle is often sold at a price that makes it impractical for customers to purchase the components separately. According to Guiltinan (1987), price bundling is used as a tool to regulate demand. Bundling a service that the customer might not be interested in paying for with a very attractive service may increase the demand for the less attractive service. Price bundling can thus increase the customer's patronage concentration. At the same time, there are obviously risks that the bundling activity will create resentment from the customer's side as the customer is "forced" to buy something he or she might not need or want.

The demand for different components in an offering is often dependent on the type of offering under consideration. This dependence can be divided into intraindustry dependence and interindustry dependence. Intraindustry dependence indicates that several elements in a provider's offering depend on each other. For instance, in a bank this means that a customer who has an account usually uses miscellaneous transaction instruments. Interindustry dependence between different services and goods is also common; financing is often offered bundled to different types of household appliances, cars, and so on.

Price bundling can be used to enhance the attractiveness of a specific service. It is common for retail banks to bundle accounts with some sort of debit or ATM card, or to bundle a loan with a life insurance policy. Bundling banking services and insurance services creates a situation that enables the provider to increase its share of the customer total business potential. Many banks have created price-bundled offerings (often called service packages) that model the buying behavior (as to the accounts, episode configuration, and access channel used) of ideal customer archetypes.

DECREASING RELATIONSHIP COSTS

To decrease relationship costs, the provider has to influence the episode configuration of the customer relationship. A number of changes are relevant: (a) decreasing the intensity of episodes (i.e., Is it possible to affect the customer's behavior in such a way that fewer episodes are needed in order to generate the same amount of business?), (b) changing to cheaper episode variants (i.e., Are there any substitutes for this type of episode?), and (c) changing the cost structure of the present episode type in order to make it cheaper to produce (Foster et al., 1996; Manning, 1995).

In order to achieve these objectives, as they design relationships, providers have to take into consideration the complexity and divergence of the processes, the potential roles of the customers, and how to script these in an appropriate manner. They also need to define how to regulate the customer's access to certain episode types (see also Cooper & Chew, 1996).

Relationship Cost as a Function of Complexity and Divergence

The design and execution of episodes is a focal area of interest in the analysis of relationships. Two dimensions are especially important in this analysis: complexity and divergence. Complexity can be seen as a technical description of the number of activities that need to be carried out owing to or during the episode. Every activity carries a production cost—that is, is a cost carrier. Adding activities to the episode thus increases the costs.

From the perspective of both employees and customers, complexity is also a cognitive issue. Episodes that are technically simple can be regarded as complex if the employees or customers are unfamiliar with the type of episode and are thus inexperienced performers of their tasks.

Both technical and cognitive complexity drive costs. Adding new activities to the episode will add to the direct costs of the relationship. Cognitive complexity adds indirect costs in that both employees and customers spend more time in the actual production process, owing to the cognitive problems associated with the episode.

Design and execution of episodes can also be analyzed on the basis of divergence in the process. Divergence pertains to the amount of adaptation that is allowed during the process. Divergence can also be divided into technical and cognitive divergence. Technical divergence relates to the idea that there are several options from which the customer can choose during the episode process, options that are built into the process. Making selections available means that the process is different for each discrete episode. Divergence increases as a function of both the number of decision points involved in the process and the range of potential choices available at each decision point.

Surprenant and Solomon (1985) call technical divergence "option personalization." They argue that there are two other ways of personalization of delivery that relate to the process. In "programmed personalization," there are elements scripted into the process that acknowledge the customer as an individual (using the customer's name, greeting the customer, and so on). In "customized personalization," the employee makes

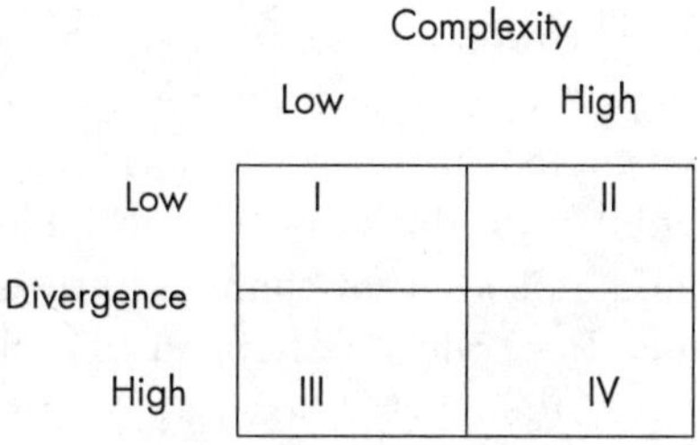

Complexity

Low	High

Low	I	II

Divergence

High	III	IV

Figure 21.4. Combining Complexity and Divergence

a cognitive effort to assist the customer. Both of these can be called cognitive divergence, because they involve the connotation experienced by the customer.

Divergence drives both indirect and direct costs. Divergence requires more competence from the performers during the episode. The production process is also longer and more complicated. Shostack (1987) concludes that complexity and divergence are separate dimensions that may be combined into a matrix (see Figure 21.4). On the basis of the above reasoning, the episodes in quadrant IV of Figure 21.4 are the most expensive to produce and thus generate high relationship costs. The episodes in quadrant I are the cheapest to produce and thus generate a lesser amount of relationship costs. Providing that the same benefits (perceived by the customer) can be produced, it seems reasonable to propose that providers should try to reduce the divergence and complexity of relationships.

Decreasing Relationship Cost Through Customer Participation

The concept of customer management implies that customers are regarded as the provider's partial employees (see Mills & Morris, 1986). Several researchers within services marketing and management have viewed customer participation as important (Eiglier & Langeard, 1987; Lehtinen, 1983, 1988; Lovelock & Young, 1979). The increased interactivity in all industries generates more interest in how to create value jointly (Normann & Ramirez, 1995; Sheth & Parvatiyar, 1995a).

Role theory is a promising model for understanding how customers and employees perform during episodes. Both the provider's employees (contact resources) and the customer have certain (learned) role behaviors in an episode, and they try to act out their roles to their own satisfaction. The "code" that influences the role-playing is called a script. Both parties to the encounter have their own scripts. The more experienced the role player is, the more elaborate the script is and the less explicit it is to the role player. This would indicate that changes in the script should encounter greater resistance from the experienced role player. Discrepant role expectations decrease efficiency. When role players read from different scripts, communication is inhibited and considerable confusion results. This has a negative effect on the productivity of the episode.

All relationship processes can be said to consist of scripted activities and discretionary activities. The discretionary activities have to be "invented" as they become necessary in order to produce the episode. The script consists of (a) explicit codes in the form of work standards, directives, and written or oral instructions on how to behave in the episode; and (b) implicit rules or norms that direct behavior. In many episodes, implicit scripts dominate.

Fox and Bender (1986) suggest that the behavior setting influences customers in the episode. The setting program "sets the stage" for the customer and the contact resource ("the human components") and thus tells them how to perform different roles in the setting.

Episodes are highly scripted either because they have been designed to have a very low level of discretionary activities (low level of divergence) or because the encounter in question is an old type of encounter in which experienced role players participate (there is a strong setting program). Changing scripts requires many learning activities, both for the contact resources and for the customers, and should include changes in both the explicit scripts and the implicit scripts. The "learning organization" has developed capabilities to create new scripts and to change the relationship process.

Using Access Barriers to Decrease Relationship Cost

Limiting access to different types of episodes is one way to influence customer behavior. Access barriers are used primarily in relationships of a continuous nature. Access barriers can be used to differentiate between customer groups.

The concept of access barriers is related to the concept of price discrimination, but the former is a larger construct. Channon (1986a) identifies the following possibilities for price discrimination in banking: (a) customer discrimination, meaning that customers pay different prices for the same services or are provided with different service packages at the same prices (typical examples are student programs and senior citizen programs); (b) product-form discrimination, meaning that different versions of the same product are priced differently but not proportionally to their respective costs (typical examples are the "gold" and "platinum" versions of different debit or credit cards); (c) access channel discrimination, meaning that prices differ according to the access channel used (a typical example is the ATM transaction that is cheaper than a teller-performed transaction); and (d) time discrimination, meaning that prices vary according to when services are provided.

Access barriers can be built as volume barriers, as behavioral barriers, or as a combination of the two. If the customer achieves a certain volume, he or she gains access to certain services (such as a personal relationship manager) or discounts. Behavioral barriers relate to both the number of episodes and the types of episodes used by the customer. Some providers use barriers of this type to force customers to use self-service channels, the idea being that approval for a lower price requires that the customers not use personnel-intensive services. Customers who pass the barrier usually get discounted prices.

INCREASING RELATIONSHIP LONGEVITY

Relationship longevity is of great importance to the provider from an efficiency point of view. Longevity can originate in relationship-extrinsic and relationship-intrinsic factors. Examples of relationship-extrinsic factors include the market structure (competitive situation and market concentration) in which the relationship exists and possible geographic limitations (the customer moves to a location where the provider does not have a presence). The number of alternative providers the customer has to choose from influences the customer's interest and his or her possibility of evaluating alternatives. A relationship in a monopolistic market is evidently different from a relationship in a highly competitive market.

In this chapter, my focus is on designing relationships, and thus relationship-intrinsic factors are more important. According to Storbacka, Strandvik, and Grönroos (1994), longevity can be said to originate in relationship strength. Relationship strength is a function of relationship-intrinsic factors such as the relationship history, the volume and relative importance of the relationship (for both parties), the customer's commitment and satisfaction, the bonds developed during the history of the relationship, and the provider's ability to handle critical episodes.

In any analysis of relationship-intrinsic factors, relationship inertia has to be considered. Every relationship acquires inertia based on mutually positive history. Thus a customer who has used the provider for a longer period of time, involving many and important episodes during which strong social bonds have developed with key individuals in the provider's organization, may remain a customer for a long time without ever seriously contemplating the existing alternatives.

An important relationship-intrinsic factor is the relative worth of the relationship to both parties in the dyad. Low-volume customers have little power in the relationship because the provider's survival does not depend on their business. High-volume customers, on the other hand, have considerable power, which they exercise especially in price negotiations.

There is obviously also an economic dimension to relationship strength. A relationship with a customer cannot be regarded as strong as long as the patronage concentration is low (see Sheth & Parvatiyar, 1995b). Strength thus also has to indicate that the customer prefers to concentrate a major part of his or her business with the provider under consideration. Additionally, the number of relationships that a customer has with other providers in the same industry is inversely proportional to his or her patronage concentration. Thus a customer with a low level of patronage concentration probably has a number of relationships (or at least one more) with other providers and is in a position to compare the performance of the providers. A customer who has concentrated all business with one provider is not as knowledgeable about the alternatives and can be expected to be more loyal. As a conclusion, patronage concentration can be regarded as a switching barrier.

It is important to note that every episode does not carry the same importance or weight in the customer's evaluation of the relationship. Some episodes can be labeled as routine, whereas others can be labeled as critical (Storbacka et al., 1994). The routine episodes usually represent the larger proportion of all episodes. Low levels of mental involvement and routinized behavior characterize these episodes. The customer usually has a clear script guiding his or her behavior during the routine episode.

The script is acquired either through experience of the same or similar episodes or through distinct guidance during the episode.

A critical episode can be defined as one that is of great importance for the relationship. The importance of the episode is partly a function of the economic significance the particular episode has for the relationship. Economic significance can be described according to three dimensions: (a) the volume of the exchange (i.e., how big the exchange of money involved in the episode is relative to the parties' resources), (b) the cost of the episode (i.e., what the costs of producing the episode are, for both provider and customer), and (c) the risks involved (i.e., what the risks are relative to the episode and the mutual commitments binding the parties on the basis of the episode).

The continuation of the relationship is dependent, in both negative and positive ways, on critical episodes. A successful critical episode can strengthen the relationship so that it may withstand several unsatisfactory routine episodes. On the other hand, an unsuccessful critical episode may end the relationship abruptly even though it may have been preceded by years of satisfactory routine episodes. An important part of relationship longevity is thus the "art" of service recovery—that is, the provider's skill in escalating activities in cases where critical episodes have occurred.

Future Research Agenda

Further research on customer profitability is needed especially in the three areas noted below.

Longitudinal studies. The most important thing that future researchers can do in examining customer profitability is to pursue longitudinal studies. It is clearly a limitation to most research carried out that in each study all the available data on customer profitability concern only one fiscal year. Hence very little research is available that describes migration patterns of customers between segments in customer bases. Obviously, studies of profitability on a yearly basis can be dangerous if they lead to management actions that are perceived in a negative way by customers who at present are unprofitable but have great potential to become key customers.

The pursuit of longitudinal studies will probably require the development of new constructs. Payne and Rickard (1993) have developed some interesting ideas related to longitudinal studies. Their approach is based on the calculation of net present values for customer relationships, which makes it possible to evaluate the value of customer bases (and companies). Although their model—and its depiction, the "retentiongram"—builds on a number of difficult assumptions, they have still been able to draw some interesting conclusions as to the importance of customer relationship longevity.

The valuation of relationships. Researchers concerned with valuation have mostly focused on customer profitability. But the value of a customer relationship is not only a question of the profits the relationship generates to the company. There are other equally important dimensions (Storbacka, 1993), such as the reference value of a customer (customers may be used systematically as references, and both the positive and negative word-of-mouth effect of customers has to be considered), competence value of the customer (customers may bring important competencies to the relationship and may force companies to learn, which may be valuable to the company in other relationships), and the potential value of a customer relationship (a relationship that is unprofitable may be valuable because it has major potential to improve profitability in the future). Additionally, relationship strength may be regarded as an important dimension in the evaluation of relationships because it is obvious that a company's likelihood of enhancing a relationship is dependent on the relationship's existing strength.

Analysis of relationship profitability. Another important area for future research concerns the usage of customer profitability information. How can information be utilized? What kinds of analyses can be carried out on that information? What insights can be gained from the results of such analyses? How can the profitability of relationships be enhanced?

As the strength of the relationship is of utmost importance to the design of action programs for customer relationship enhancement, we need a good understanding of what constitutes relationship strength and how it can be affected. This, of course, relates to the relationships among customer satisfaction, customer loyalty, and relationship profitability (Hallowell, 1996; Reichheld, 1993, 1996; Storbacka et al., 1994).

Note

1. Customer profitability is defined as the profits generated by a customer relationship during one fiscal year.

References

Bellis-Jones, R. (1989, February). Customer profitability analysis. *Management Accounting*, pp. 26-28.

Channon, D. F. (1986a). *Bank strategic management and marketing*. New York: John Wiley.

Channon, D. F. (1986b). *Cases in bank strategic management and marketing*. New York: John Wiley.

Connell, R. (1995). *Measuring customer and service profitability in the finance sector*. London: Chapman & Hall.

Cooper, R., & Chew, B. W. (1996). Control tomorrow's costs through today's designs. *Harvard Business Review, 74*(3), 88-97.

Cooper, R., & Kaplan, R. S. (1991). Profit priorities from activity-based costing. *Harvard Business Review, 69*(5), 130-135.

Eiglier, P., & Langeard, E. (1987). *Servuction: Le marketing des services*. Paris: McGraw-Hill.

Foster, G., Gupta, M., & Sjoblom, L. (1996, Spring). Customer profitability analysis: Challenges and new directions. *Cost Management*, pp. 5-17.

Fox, K. F. A., & Bender, S. D. G. H. (1986). Behavior-settings analysis to improve bank service delivery. In M. Venkatesan, D. M. Schmalensee, & C. Marshall (Eds.), *Creativity in services marketing: What's new, what works, what's developing*. Chicago: American Marketing Association.

Grant, A. W. H., & Schlesinger, L. A. (1995). Realize your customers' full profit potential. *Harvard Business Review, 74*(1), 59-72.

Grönroos, C. (1990). *Service management and marketing*. Lexington, MA: Lexington.

Grönroos, C. (1997). Value-driven relational marketing: From products to resources and competencies. *Journal of Marketing Management*.

Guiltinan, J. (1987). The price bundling of services: A normative framework. *Journal of Marketing, 51*(2), 74-85.

Hallowell, R. (1996). The relationships of customer satisfaction, customer loyalty, and profitability: An empirical study. *International Journal of Service Industry Management, 7*(4), 27-42.

Howell, R. A., & Soucy, S. R. (1990, October). Customer profitability—as critical as product profitability. *Management Accounting*, pp. 43-47.

Lehtinen, J. R. (1983). *Asiakasohjautuva palvelujärjestelmä—käsitteistö ja empiirisiä sovelluksia* [The customer-oriented service system: Terminology and empirical applications]. Tampere, Finland: University of Tampere, Department of Business Economics and Business Law.

Lehtinen, J. R. (1988). *Asiakasyrittäjä—liiketoiminnan resurssi* [Customer entrepreneur: The resource of business activity]. Helsinki, Finland: SMG Kustannus Oy.

Liljander, V., & Strandvik, T. (1995). The nature of customer relationships in services. In D. Bowen, S. W. Brown, & T. A. Swartz (Eds.), *Advances in services marketing and management* (Vol. 4, pp. 141-167). Greenwich, CT: JAI.

Lovelock, C. H., & Young, R. F. (1979). Look to customers to increase productivity. *Harvard Business Review, 57*(3), 168-178.

Manning, K. H. (1995, January). Distribution channel profitability: ABC concepts can help companies make strategic decisions. *Management Accounting,* pp. 44-48.

Mills, P. K., & Morris, J. H. (1986). Clients as "partial" employees of service organizations: Role development in customer participation. *Academy of Management Review, 11,* 726-735.

Normann, R. (1991). *Service management: Strategy and leadership in service business* (2nd ed.). New York: John Wiley.

Normann, R., Cederwall, J., Edgren, L., & Holst, A. (1989). *Invadörernas dans—eller den oväntade konkurrensen* [The dance of the invaders]. Malmö, Sweden: Liber.

Normann, R., & Ramirez, R. (1995). *Designing interactive strategy.* New York: John Wiley.

Payne, A., & Rickard, J. (1993). *Relationship marketing, customer retention and service firm profitability.* Unpublished manuscript.

Reichheld, F. F. (1993). Loyalty-based management. *Harvard Business Review, 71*(4), 64-73.

Reichheld, F. F. (with Teal, T.). (1996). *The loyalty effect: The hidden force behind growth, profits, and lasting value.* Boston: Harvard Business School Press.

Reichheld, F. F., & Sasser, W. E., Jr. (1990). Zero defections: Quality comes to services. *Harvard Business Review, 69*(1), 105-111.

Shapiro, B. P., Rangan, V. K., Moriarty, R. T., & Ross, E. B. (1987). Manage customers for profits (not just sales). *Harvard Business Review, 66*(1), 101-108.

Sheth, J. N., & Parvatiyar, A. (1995a). The evolution of relationship marketing. *International Business Review, 4,* 397-418.

Sheth, J. N., & Parvatiyar, A. (1995b). Relationship marketing in consumer markets: Antecedents and consequences. *Journal of the Academy of Marketing Science, 23,* 255-271.

Sheth, J. N., & Sisodia, R. S. (1995). Improving marketing productivity. In J. Heilbrunn (Ed.), *Encyclopedia of marketing for the year 2000.* Chicago: American Marketing Association/NTC.

Shostack, L. G. (1987). Service positioning through structural change. *Journal of Marketing, 51*(1), 34-43.

Solomon, M. R., Surprenant, C. F., Czepiel, J. A., & Gutman, E. G. (1985). A role theory perspective on dyadic interactions: The service encounter. *Journal of Marketing, 49*(1), 99-111.

Storbacka, K. (1993). *Customer relationship profitability in retail banking* (Research Rep. No. 29). Helsinki, Finland: Swedish School of Economics and Business Administration.

Storbacka, K. (1994). *The nature of customer relationship profitability: Analysis of relationships and customer bases in retail banking* (Research Rep. No. 55). Helsinki, Finland: Swedish School of Economics and Business Administration.

Storbacka, K., & Luukinen, A. (1994). Managing customer relationship profitability: Case Swedbank. In ESOMAR (Ed.), *Banking and insurance: From recession to recovery.* Amsterdam: ESOMAR.

Storbacka, K., Strandvik, T., & Grönroos, C. (1994). Managing customer relationships for profit: The dynamic of relationship quality. *International Journal of Service Industry Management, 5*(5), 21-38.

Strandvik, T. (1994). *Tolerance zones and perceived service quality* (Doctoral Dissertation No. 58). Helsinki, Finland: Swedish School of Economics and Business Administration.

Strandvik, T., & Liljander, V. (1994, June). *Relationship strength in bank services.* Paper presented at the annual Research Conference on Relationship Marketing, Atlanta, GA.

Surprenant, C. F., & Solomon, M. R. (1985). Dimensions of personalization. In T. M. Bloch, G. D. Upah, & V. A. Zeithaml (Eds.), *Services marketing in a changing environment* (pp. 56-61). Chicago: American Marketing Association.

PART V

Teaching and Research Implications of Relationship Marketing

22

Developing a Curriculum to Enhance Teaching of Relationship Marketing

JOSEPH P. CANNON
JAGDISH N. SHETH

In recent years, business schools have increasingly become targets of criticisms from students and the business community. These criticisms have focused on curriculum content (Byrne, 1993; Mason, 1992; Porter & McKibbin, 1988; Sheth, 1988), teaching methods and pedagogy (Hotch, 1992), and the relevance of academic research (Behrman & Levin, 1984; Byrne, 1990; Stanton, 1988; Walle, 1991). In response to these criticisms, many

NOTE: This chapter is reprinted from Joseph P. Cannon and Jagdish N. Sheth, "Developing a Curriculum to Enhance Teaching of Relationship Marketing," *Journal of Marketing Education*, vol. 16, Summer 1994, pp. 3-14, copyright © 1994 by the *Journal of Marketing Education*. Reprinted by permission.

AUTHORS' NOTE: The program described in this chapter was developed through the cooperative efforts of the marketing faculty and students at Emory Business School and encouraged by many business executives. Their numbers are too great to list here, but we would like particularly to acknowledge the contributions of Sundar Bharadwaj, Chitrabhanu Bhattacharya, Terry Clark, Michael Cummins, Nick DeBonis, Chip Frame, Ron Frank, Ed Leonard, Jack McSweeney, Mike Milligan, Atul Parvatiyar, Todd Reale, and Brown Whittington.

business schools have radically changed their curricula (Bongiorno, 1993; Byrne, 1992; Mason, 1993).

During this same period, a rapidly changing competitive environment, the total quality management (TQM) movement, advances in information technology, and increasing globalization of industries have changed the ways firms market their products. Many firms are shifting their attention from the single-minded acquisition of new customers to a greater focus on the *retention* of current customers (Liswood, 1990; Vavra, 1992). These trends point to the emergence of a new paradigm or school of marketing thought: relationship marketing (Kotler, 1992; McKenna, 1991; Parvatiyar, Sheth, & Whittington, 1992; Sheth, Gardner, & Garrett, 1988).

Our purpose in this chapter is to describe an innovative curriculum being developed at the Emory Business School at Emory University. The curriculum at Emory is being revised to address the concerns of its customers (students and business) and to place a greater emphasis on relationship marketing. The enhanced curriculum and supporting structures create a three-way partnership among students, faculty, and the business community. These changes are creating an environment that enhances the relevance and quality of teaching and research in relationship marketing.

We begin by briefly expanding upon the criticisms of teaching and research in graduate management education. In the second section of the chapter, we describe and discuss relationship marketing. Given the shortcomings of current business education and the emergence of relationship marketing, we next develop and elaborate a set of objectives governing curriculum development. We then describe the proposed curriculum and its supporting structures. We close with a discussion of the implications of the program for students, faculty, the business school, and business practice as well as some proposed directions for future development.

Criticisms of Business Schools

Business schools have come under attack for failing to teach students the subject matter and skills they need to be effective managers and for spending too much time conducting "fuzzy" and/or "irrelevant" research (Byrne, 1990). Criticism of the education and research provided by graduate business schools falls into three general categories (see Table 22.1). Some have criticized the content of management education, noting the lag in bringing leading-edge management practices to the classroom (Byrne,

TABLE 22.1 Criticisms of Education and Research in Business Schools

Criticisms of the content of the education provided to MBA students	Curricula are failing to keep up with leading-edge management practice (Byrne, 1993; Hotch, 1992; Mason, 1992; Porter & McKibbin, 1988).Traditional curricula do not focus on the cross-functional nature of business, and courses do not integrate across functional areas (Mason, 1992; Sheth, 1988).
Criticisms of the pedagogy employed in graduate business schools	Current teaching practices do not train students in the key skills necessary to manage in today's environment. Skills needed but not being developed include communications, leadership, and team building (Mason, 1992).Students are not being provided with adequate real-world experiences (Hotch, 1992).
Criticisms of the research being conducted by business school faculty	The research does not address issues of relevance for today's managers (Byrne, 1990; Chonko & Caballero, 1991; Porter & McKibbin, 1988; Stanton, 1988; Walle, 1991).Business schools need to bring the results of research into classrooms more quickly (Byrne, 1990; "Wharton Business School," 1991).

1990; Hotch, 1992) and failure to focus on the cross-functional nature of business practice (Mason, 1992; Sheth, 1988). Others indict the pedagogy or process of management education, saying that typical teaching methods have not helped students develop requisite skills (Byrne, 1993) or provided students with adequate real-world experience (Hotch, 1992).

Aside from knowledge dissemination, a key role for business school faculty is to develop in students the knowledge relevant for managers (Berry, 1993). Yet business school research does not tackle problems important and relevant to today's managers (Byrne, 1990; Chonko & Caballero, 1991; Stanton, 1988). Furthermore, relevant research takes too long to get into the classroom ("Wharton Business School," 1991). The lengthy journal review and publication process means that research conceptualized and conducted now may not be in print for 2 to 3 years, or more. It might be 2 more years before such findings make it into textbooks.

The criticisms outlined above suggest that business schools need to balance research and education among three criteria: relevance, process, and rigor. Managers (current and future) require faculty to provide them with knowledge that is relevant and useful to guide their decisions. Students desire that the pedagogy help them to develop skills and provide them with hands-on experience. Faculty value research and education that is rigorous and, therefore, valid. The criticisms of business and marketing education outlined above suggest that in some ways we have gotten away from these criteria. In the following section we describe how relationship marketing provides a relevant umbrella for our curriculum.

Relationship Marketing

The development of marketing theory and practice is undergoing a paradigm shift from a transactional to a relationship orientation (Arndt, 1979; Dwyer, Schurr, & Oh, 1987; Kotler, 1992; McKenna, 1991; Sheth et al., 1988). The curriculum described below places a great emphasis on the role of marketing in building and managing relationships with a company's many stakeholders, which could include suppliers, competitors, governments, and employees as well as customers (Morgan & Hunt, 1994; Webster, 1992). In this section we briefly describe the emergence of relationship marketing in marketing research and practice.

Relationship marketing reflects a strategy and process that integrate customers, suppliers, and other partners into the company's design, development, manufacturing, and sales processes (Sheth & Parvatiyar, 1993). Relationship marketing emerged from dissatisfaction with existing paradigms. In their evaluation of different schools of marketing thought, Sheth et al. (1988) suggest the need to focus on ongoing, collaborative exchange that creates value (win-win) for both parties (see Figure 22.1). Indeed, many marketing theories tend to focus on exchanges as ad hoc transactions based on conflict (zero-sum, win-lose).

Observing that theory does not match up with current practice, academic researchers in marketing have begun to pay greater attention to ongoing relationships. Drawing on theories from economics (e.g., transaction cost analysis; Williamson, 1985), social psychology (e.g., social exchange theory; Thibaut & Kelley, 1959), sociology (Macaulay, 1963), and law (e.g., relational contracting; Macneil, 1980), many marketing scholars have started to focus on ongoing buyer-seller relationships (Anderson & Narus, 1984; Arndt, 1979; Crosby, Evans, & Cowles, 1990; Dwyer et al., 1987; Håkansson, 1982; Heide & John, 1990; Kaufmann & Stern, 1988).

The practice of relationship marketing is spreading across many markets and industries. Manufacturing organizations build closer relationships with their suppliers to manage total quality and inventory costs

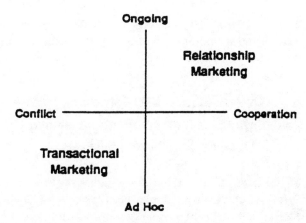

Figure 22.1. Forums of Customer-Marketer Interaction

more efficiently and to facilitate new product development (Burt, 1984; O'Neal, 1989; von Hippel, 1988). Several packaged goods firms have built closer relationships with retailers to mutually reduce costs and increase sales (Tosh, 1993). Many organizations are now seeking methods for building closer relationships with consumers through the management of brand equity (Keller, 1993) and database marketing (Copulsky & Wolf, 1990; Shaw & Stone, 1990). Firms are discovering that directing more marketing resources toward consumer retention (as opposed to acquisition) may prove more efficient (Liswood, 1990).

Practicing relationship marketing requires a different set of skills and tools. For example, personal selling traditionally involves identifying prospects, persuading them of the benefits of the product or service, handling objections, and closing the sale. Relational selling requires a salesperson to build trust and to teach, as well as learn from, customers (Shapiro, 1988). In such selling, one builds databases with information about consumer needs and preferences, ultimately developing an ongoing dialogue with consumers (Peppers & Rogers, 1993). Consumers benefit from customized products and services. Relationship marketing changes the way a firm looks at other marketing mix elements as well. Customer service gains new importance and customer satisfaction becomes an increasingly important measure of marketing effectiveness.

We are still learning a great deal about the theory and practice of relationship marketing. The emerging paradigm promises to redefine marketing practice and the role of marketing in the firm (Webster, 1992). The curriculum and supporting structures outlined below are designed to enhance the research and teaching of relationship marketing synergistically.

Objectives for a New Curriculum: Enhancing Exchange Relationships Among Students, Faculty, and Business

The critics of business schools cited above suggest three areas for improvement. Interestingly, each of these areas represents a key interest for each of the main stakeholders of business schools—students, the business community, and faculty. Students have the most to gain from improvements in the teaching *process*—the way that business schools disseminate knowledge. The business community seeks to influence teaching and research into topics *relevant* to today's marketing manager. Finally, business school faculty seek to maintain sufficient *rigor* to assure the validity of new knowledge.

In developing a new curriculum, our overarching goal is to enhance the value of the exchanges among all of the parties. We have sought to balance the main desires of each of these parties by focusing on developing a curriculum that addresses both teaching and research while emphasizing relevance, process, and rigor. In addition, the emerging relationship marketing paradigm suggests an area where students, faculty, and business can benefit from the development and dissemination of new knowledge. The following were our primary objectives in developing the new curriculum:

1. Relationship marketing must be a theme that runs through all of the classes in the new curriculum. Although not abandoning the critical role of marketing in acquiring new customers, a new curriculum must place a greater emphasis on the role of marketing in *retaining* current customers through relationship marketing.

2. Individual courses and support structures should foster increased student and faculty linkages with the business community to provide more opportunities for students to study and solve real-world problems.

3. To enhance the value and timeliness of the educational product being delivered, the curriculum must create opportunities for faculty to bring the most recent research findings into the classroom.

4. The curriculum must provide students with many opportunities to build and develop their leadership, team-building, and communication skills.

The Program: Curriculum and Support Structures

Addressing the objectives outlined above necessitated changes in pedagogy, course content, and the development of supporting structures. We begin this section by describing the specific marketing courses that make up the core of the curriculum development. Next, we discuss changes to the pedagogy that cut across most of the courses. In the last subsection, we explain the role of two supporting structures, the student-run Emory Marketing Association and the Center for Relationship Marketing

MARKETING COURSES

Developing a new curriculum requires modification or elimination of existing courses and the development of new courses. Decisions on changes to course content reflect the need to place greater emphasis on relationship marketing. These changes resulted in the 17 courses represented graphically by the wheel of relationship marketing depicted in Figure 22.2. At the hub of the wheel is our core course, Marketing Management. In the first ring around the core are secondary-level courses that deal with key marketing skills. These first-ring courses have titles familiar to many marketing curricula, but each focuses attention on the role of relationship marketing in building and managing relationships with key constituencies. The outer-ring courses are more advanced electives that focus on developing and implementing relationship marketing strategies.

This section is organized according to the wheel of relationship marketing. We begin with Marketing Management, then move clockwise around the first-ring courses and then around the outer-ring courses. Many of the courses described below are up and running, whereas others are currently being developed.

Marketing Management: A Relationship Perspective. This is the core and introductory course in the marketing curriculum. As with traditional courses of this type, this class introduces students to concepts and principles of marketing management and develops their skills in analyzing marketing issues. During the first week of class, students are exposed to the basic principles of relationship marketing. The class discusses conditions under which relationship strategies are most appropriate. As concepts regarding situation analysis, the marketing mix, and marketing strategy are presented, we highlight differences between relationship and transac-

Figure 22.2. Curriculum Wheel of Relationship Marketing

tional orientations. In the discussion of marketing communications, for example, communications with current customers receive as much attention as do communications with prospective customers (Vavra, 1992). Differences among the messages, media, and measures used in these types of communications are discussed as well. Students also spend a week specifically examining relationship marketing and its application and implementation in consumer and business markets.

Marketing Research. The Marketing Research course teaches students methods for collecting, analyzing, and interpreting data relevant to managerial decision making. Yet different research questions and methodologies are employed when the goal is customer retention as opposed to acquisition. Because both of these topics are essential for today's manager, this course identifies research techniques appropriate for each objective. For example, significant time is spent on the complex but important issues of measuring customer satisfaction and brand equity.

Customer Behavior. Customer Behavior reflects more than a name change to the traditional Consumer Behavior course. This course emphasizes that marketplace choices are made by a broad spectrum of internal and external customers. Students examine the behavior of different types of customers—consumers, businesses, resellers, and governments—as well as suppliers, employees, stockholders, and other stakeholders of the firm. The course develops a common framework based on the values that influence market choices (Gross, Newman, & Sheth, 1991). This course, which makes the assumption that customer satisfaction provides a critical source of sustainable competitive advantage, helps students determine the sources of satisfaction for various types of customers.

International Marketing. Aside from the traditional four Ps, the International Marketing course adds two more Ps: government policy and public opinion processes. Firms must develop relationships with suppliers, customers, competitors, and governments. Today's dynamic and complex environment for international commerce increases the need for firms to develop closer relationships (Klein, Frazier, & Roth, 1990). Closer buyer-seller relationships are a method for managing and reducing uncertainty, but cultural differences can hinder relationship building. Therefore, this course teaches the mechanics involved in developing, managing, and maintaining relationships across cultural boundaries.

Marketing Strategy. This course builds on the Marketing Management course and emphasizes the development and implementation of marketing plans. The course provides the students with a better understanding of marketing strategy as they examine the evolution of strategy. The past two decades have seen a number of frameworks: strategic planning, portfolio models (Haspeslagh, 1982), and Porter's (1980) model. This course reviews these frameworks and develops a relationship framework that focuses on using relationships with suppliers, distributors, competitors, and customers to build a sustainable competitive advantage. Customer

˙ ʌey issue, and students learn methods for assessing a firm's ᴄustomer mix and strategies for retention and deletion.

Foundations of Relationship Marketing. This course is an introduction to the emerging relationship marketing paradigm. The course brings together skills essential to the practice of relationship marketing and discusses their application to building and maintaining both inter- and intra-organizational relationships. The course integrates student learning on TQM, information technology, team building, theories and concepts of cooperation, and project management, and demonstrates how these concepts apply to building and managing relationships.

Measuring Customer Satisfaction. Building on what students learn in Marketing Research, Measuring Customer Satisfaction is a minicourse (one-third or one-half semester long) that focuses on the evaluation of customer satisfaction. Keeping close tabs on customer satisfaction is key to customer retention. Currently, many organizations are struggling with developing customer satisfaction measures that can be used to compensate salespeople, evaluate managers, and assess changes in marketing strategy. This course introduces students to the theories and methodologies used by organizations attempting to measure the level of satisfaction of their various customer groups. The assessment of satisfaction trends and effects of particular interventions are also discussed. By comparing and evaluating methods used by different firms in different industries, students are expected to gain an appreciation of the importance and complexity of assessing customer satisfaction.

Database Marketing. Advances in computing power and database management (e.g., scanner data and direct-marketing databases) create unique analytic and strategic opportunities for marketing managers (Shaw & Stone, 1990). These databases allow organizations to build, manage, and evaluate relationships with individual consumers efficiently (Peppers & Rogers, 1993; Schultz, Tannenbaum, & Lauterborn, 1992). This course presents methods for building, managing, and analyzing databases for sustainable competitive advantage.

Key Account Management. For many companies, the old 80:20 rule is no longer valid. For many firms, less than 5% of customers provide more than 90% of their business. Further, principles of total quality management,

ISO 9000, supply-chain management, and process reengineering (when the process includes customers) demand that firms build and maintain closer relationships with fewer customers and suppliers. These realities require firms to develop new sales and purchasing tactics. Team selling (Cespedes, Doyle, & Freedman, 1989) may require a salesperson to work with cross-functional teams from the buyer and seller, developing custom systems to maximize the efficiency and effectiveness of exchange. This minicourse requires students to interact with local businesses to learn and assess how these firms manage their interactions with key accounts.

Integrated Distribution Management. The focus of this course is supply-chain management, including aspects of purchasing, manufacturing, logistics, customer service, and relations with other channel members. Advances in information technology allow for increased integration across these functions to allow the order cycle to be managed as a single process. This allows a firm to compete on key attributes of customer service, time, and cost (Gopal & Cypress, 1993). In this course, students are exposed to methods for managing the intra- and interorganizational relationships necessary to make this process work effectively.

Direct Marketing. Building relationships with smaller sales-volume customers requires firms to employ direct-marketing techniques. Through the creative use of databases, telemarketing, direct mail, and direct sales, many firms are finding low-cost methods for building and maintaining relationships with customers. This minicourse exposes students to strategies and tactics necessary to the successful employment of direct marketing for the purpose of building closer customer relationships.

Global Sourcing. A recent trend in business has been a focus on core competencies. This has led many firms to outsource not only manufacturing but also services (e.g., data management) and personnel. Some firms are finding that firms or employees in other countries are more effective or efficient. Procuring these services leads to long-term commitments and unique relationship management needs. This minicourse examines this trend and discusses methods for managing these external sourcing relationships under a cross-cultural and cross-national context.

Global Alliances. Most business schools are currently placing increasing emphasis on their international offerings. As noted above, the com-

plexity and dynamics of the international marketplace require closer relationships, but cultural differences can complicate their management.
This course allows students interested in the international arena to examine these issues further. The nature of the course might allow for codevelopment or team teaching with faculty in the policy area.

Integrated Marketing Communications. Integrated marketing communications (IMC) recognizes that mass advertising by itself does not seem
to work (Schultz et al., 1992). IMC takes a customer-focused view of how
customers learn about products and services. This course looks beyond
advertising and personal selling and examines controllable (e.g., direct
marketing, customer service, and packaging) and uncontrollable (e.g.,
word of mouth, competitive activities, and retail merchandising) communications. IMC manages these communications sources under one umbrella to present a unified message. IMC also emphasizes the importance
of using communications to develop a dialogue with customers to enhance the development and management of customer relationships.

Marketing Planning and Implementation. This advanced-level elective
focuses on the cross-functional requirements necessary to implement a
marketing strategy. The success of a marketing strategy requires close relationships and integration across functional areas. This course exposes
students to the need for cooperation and collaboration with other functional areas and suggests methods for enhancing the ability to implement
marketing strategies.

Customer Business Development Track. This course provides an educational experience that is unique in both content and process and represents a new model for business education. The course examines a number
of key issues important to developing, managing, and maintaining relationships with business customers, including developing information systems, determining how to utilize multifunctional resources to support a
customer strategy, and managing the change to a new method of selling.

The process of the course is also unique. The first phase begins with
summer internships at one of the sponsoring companies. Students inter-
view for internships that allow each of them to work in the marketing area
of one of the companies. The summer internship is monitored and supported by a faculty member. This interaction not only assures that the student's experience is meaningful, but allows the faculty member to gain

contacts and insight into current practice. The faculty member may discover potential research topics and research sites.

The process continues into the fall through a symposium series. The symposia bring the students, cross-disciplinary faculty, and executives of sponsoring companies together to discuss the topics outlined above. Students' preparation involves reading key articles dealing with the day's topic. Each of the parties shares ideas and experience relevant to the day's readings under the guidance of a lead faculty member. The three-way partnership that drives this course is designed to ensure that the issues and research discussed are timely.

Internal Relationships. Some important types of relationships occur within the firm. The nature of these internal relationships is critical to the competitive effectiveness of an organization and to its ability to develop external relationships. This includes the concept of internal marketing but goes beyond relationships among employees. This course includes discussion of relationships between divisions, between functional units, and between revenue centers (such as marketing and sales).

PEDAGOGY

The courses outlined above are taught using many of the traditional methods, including mixes of cases, texts, and outside readings as well as simulations, lectures, and classroom discussion. A number of educators have cited the benefits of group learning ("For Many Teachers," 1989; Johnson & Johnson, 1987; Williams, Beard, & Rymer, 1991). One of the objectives of the curriculum described above is to enhance students' teamwork, communication, and leadership skills. Group projects offer a method for advancing student skills in each of these areas. Working in teams simulates work groups, which are becoming increasingly common in business practice (Cespedes et al., 1989; Williams et al., 1991). Group interaction, as well as writing and presenting the results of their projects, enhances students' communication skills (Henke, Locander, Mentzer, & Nastas, 1988). Finally, effective accomplishment of group work requires students to assume particular roles and practice leadership skills.

Two further objectives of our curriculum are to enhance student and faculty relationships with the business community and to foster the study of real-world issues. Many of the group projects involve students working with local businesses. Field projects in the Marketing Management course have included designing a marketing communications program for a community recycling center and developing marketing plans for several local charitable organizations. International Marketing requires each student to write a case study of an international marketing problem at a real company. The Marketing Research course employs field projects in which students perform research for nonprofit organizations. These activities enhance the school's legitimacy within the community. More than one of these field projects has led to faculty research.

Another pedagogical tool that has been introduced to the curriculum is team teaching. Many of the courses employ team-teaching techniques, either with other marketing faculty or by employing expertise that exists in another functional area.

SUPPORTING STRUCTURES

Two additional organizations support and enhance the exchange relationships among students, faculty, and business. The Emory Marketing Association and the Center for Relationship Marketing complement and help to integrate the changes to the curriculum, and both provide field experience for students to enhance the principles learned in class.

Emory Marketing Association. The Emory Marketing Association is a student-run organization that enhances the overall marketing education of Emory Business School students. The association does this by providing opportunities for experiential learning through greater interaction with faculty and the business community. This is accomplished through the organization's sponsoring of speakers, faculty-student mixers, and a major event—the Marketing Competition.

For the Marketing Competition, each sponsoring company pays a participation fee and provides a marketing-related challenge to be solved by teams of students. The student teams develop and carry out research proposals in conjunction with faculty and their sponsoring companies. Student groups work on the projects for several months, with the process culminating in competitive presentations. Executives of the sponsoring companies and the faculty judge the projects, and the winning teams receive cash prizes.

Center for Relationship Marketing. The Center for Relationship Marketing has been created as an interdisciplinary hub for coordinating and managing a full range of research and education activities designed to create and disseminate breakthrough knowledge of relationship marketing principles and practices. The center is also designed as a prototype for a new model of business research and education that incorporates a three-way partnership process among business, faculty, and students as the core of all center activities. This partnership concept represents a relationship approach to concurrent knowledge engineering that fuses together the historically disparate strands of scholarly research, teaching students, and the broader dissemination of new learning to the business community.

The innovative Customer Business Development Track specialization in the MBA program (described above) has established the three-way partnership among business, faculty, and students to provide value added in education. This program will be housed in the Center for Relationship Marketing, and its underlying partnership model is currently being extended to include basic and applied research.

The center is currently undertaking an international benchmarking study of "best practices" methods of relationship marketing, which will provide scholars with a rich source of primary data to analyze. It will also provide guidance to industry regarding which relationship marketing practices are most effective in enhancing organizational performance. In addition, the Center for Relationship Marketing funds support for PhD dissertations and faculty research projects that focus on relationship marketing issues. In 1994, the center hosted the American Marketing Association's Faculty Consortium on Relationship Marketing, and every 2 years the center sponsors a research conference on relationship marketing that draws academic scholars and professional researchers from around the world to share their latest research on the subject.

Discussion

The curriculum described in this chapter is still evolving and is being implemented gradually. Significant change does not come easily in any organizational setting. We begin this section with a discussion of challenges that may face a school attempting to implement this curriculum and the situations in which implementation may be most successful. We conclude this section by describing how the curriculum may be modified for an undergraduate program.

IMPLEMENTING THE RELATIONSHIP MARKETING CURRICULUM

Implementing the relationship marketing curriculum described above requires good working relationships among the marketing faculty as well as good relationships of marketing faculty with faculty across other disciplines, with the school's administration, and with the business community. Thus far, we have benefited by having a group of faculty who share a common worldview and believe in relationship marketing as an emerging school of thought. Our shared vision allows us to agree more easily on a new direction. We expect that schools where faculty have more diverse opinions regarding pedagogical emphasis and the most appropriate marketing paradigm will have greater difficulty in implementing the curriculum we suggest.

Gaining faculty cooperation is critical to the success of the new curriculum. The changes in course content will require many faculty members to revise completely their well-developed course preparations. The new courses often have no precedents, models, or textbooks to follow. Faculty members must invest time in researching the topics and preparing new courses. Further, because relationship marketing concepts are not well understood, faculty must stay current on theory and practice and be prepared to update course content constantly to reflect the latest thinking. Finally, courses involving fieldwork may place additional burdens on faculty members to manage the logistics of contact with local business organizations. Making these changes may be particularly challenging in schools that do not place a high value on teaching relative to research.

Many of the classes will require cooperation and coordination with other disciplines in the school. For example, the Foundations of Relationship Marketing course employs guest faculty from management to discuss team building, from operations to discuss TQM and information systems, and from accounting to discuss activity-based costing. Because many of the more advanced elective classes require knowledge acquired in other disciplines, faculty must be aware of the content of courses in other areas.

Another challenge for many schools will be developing appropriate linkages with the business community. Student internships and executive participation in the symposia are key aspects of the Customer Business Development Track. For businesses to make this kind of commitment, they must have confidence in the school and its students and be convinced of the value of relationship marketing.

With the curriculum being focused more heavily on relationship marketing, our faculty had to decide what aspects of marketing required less emphasis. We chose to place less emphasis on courses dealing with the traditional elements of the marketing mix. Therefore, the curriculum does not include many traditional marketing courses in advertising, sales management, pricing, and product management. This is not to say that these elements of the marketing mix are not included in other courses, only that we have given them less attention by making them parts of other courses. In replacing a traditional Consumer Behavior course with Customer Behavior, we provide students with a broadened perspective on "customers" at the expense of the in-depth analysis of consumers. We made these trade-offs consciously, and we chose to limit the depth in areas where students were likely to receive additional training and knowledge in their first jobs.

ADAPTING THE CURRICULUM TO AN UNDERGRADUATE PROGRAM

Although our emphasis here has been on describing our curriculum for the MBA program, we plan to include many of these courses in the undergraduate program. Many of the courses focus on basic tools that have equal application to undergraduate education. This is particularly true for Marketing Management (titled Principles in the undergraduate class), Customer Behavior, Marketing Research, Marketing Strategy, and International Marketing.

On the other hand, some of the courses are specifically designed to prepare students for more advanced positions, and we do not have plans to offer Key Account Management or Global Alliances to undergraduates. Finally, the Customer Business Development Track, with its internships and symposia, appeals to companies looking to hire and benefit from advanced students. This type of program may be possible at a school with an established internship program and strong links with the business community.

Conclusion

Many of the criticisms being directed at business schools today are valid. These represent comments from our key customers—students and the business community—and they should not be ignored. The failure of many business schools to address these criticisms is causing a growing number of our customers to reassess the value of graduate business education.

Emory Business School's marketing area seeks to increase the school's value simultaneously to the students, faculty, and the business community. This goal is being addressed through the establishment of a new curriculum and associated structures that provide a program bringing rigor and relevance to *both* teaching and research.

The program described here is in a state of evolution. Rapidly changing technology and competition do not allow any organization to sit still. The TQM philosophy suggests that we need to emphasize "concurrent knowledge engineering," whereby we constantly improve our educational offerings to reflect the latest thinking, technology, and practice. The curriculum has been designed to allow for evolution. This is accomplished primarily through the flexible outer-ring courses and the close relationships the marketing area has with students and practitioners.

References

Anderson, J. C., & Narus, J. A. (1984). A model of the distributor's perspective of distributor-manufacturer working relationships. *Journal of Marketing, 48*(4), 62-74.

Arndt, J. (1979). Toward a concept of domesticated markets. *Journal of Marketing, 43*(4), 69-75.

Behrman, J. N., & Levin, R. I. (1984). Are business schools doing their job? *Harvard Business Review, 62*(3), 140-147.

Berry, L. L. (1993, Fall). Our roles as educators: Present and future. *Journal of Marketing Education, 15,* 3-8.

Bongiorno, L. (1993, November 15). A case study in change at Harvard. *Business Week,* p. 42.

Burt, D. N. (1984). *Proactive procurement.* Englewood Cliffs, NJ: Prentice Hall.

Byrne, J. A. (1990, October 29). Is research in the ivory tower fuzzy, irrelevant, pretentious? *Business Week,* pp. 62-66.

Byrne, J. A. (1992, October 26). The best B-schools. *Business Week,* pp. 60-70.

Byrne, J. A. (1993, July 19). Harvard B-School: An American institution in need of reform. *Business Week,* pp. 58-65.

Cespedes, F. V., Doyle, S. X., & Freedman, R. J. (1989). Teamwork for today's selling. *Harvard Business Review, 67*(4), 44-58.

Chonko, L. B., & Caballero, M. (1991, Spring). Marketing madness, or how marketing departments think they're in two places at once when they're not anywhere at all (according to some). *Journal of Marketing Education, 13,* 14-25.

Copulsky, J. R., & Wolf, M. J. (1990, July-August). Relationship marketing: Positioning for the future. *Journal of Business Strategy, 11,* 16-20.

Crosby, L. A., Evans, K. R., & Cowles, D. (1990). Relationship quality in services selling: An interpersonal influence perspective. *Journal of Marketing, 54*(3), 68-81.

Dwyer, F. R., Schurr, P. H., & Oh, S. (1987). Developing buyer-seller relationships. *Journal of Marketing, 51*(2), 11-27.

For many teachers, classroom lecture is giving way to projects that students tackle in small groups. (1989, August). *Chronicle of Higher Education,*p. A9.

Gopal, C., & Cypress, H. (1993). *Integrated distribution management: Competing on customer service, time, and cost.* Homewood, IL: Business One-Irwin.

Gross, B. L., Newman, B. I., & Sheth, J. N. (1991, March). Why we buy what we buy: A theory of consumption values. *Journal of Business Research, 22,* 159-170.

Håkansson, H. (Ed.). (1982). *International marketing and purchasing of industrial goods: An interaction approach.* New York: John Wiley.

Haspeslagh, P. (1982). Portfolio planning: Uses and limits. *Harvard Business Review, 60*(3), 60-73.

Heide, J. B., & John, G. (1990). Alliances in industrial purchasing: The determinants of joint action in buyer-supplier relationships. *Journal of Marketing Research, 27,* 24-36.

Henke, J. W., Jr., Locander, W. B., Mentzer, J. T., & Nastas, G., III. (1988, Spring). Teaching techniques for the new marketing instructor: Bringing the business world into the classroom. *Journal of Marketing Education, 10,* 1-10.

Hotch, R. (1992, February). This is not your father's M.B.A. *Nation's Business,* pp. 51-52.

Johnson, D. W., & Johnson, R. T. (1987, Spring). Conflict in the classroom: Controversy and learning. *Review of Educational Research, 49,* 51-70.

Kaufmann, P. J., & Stern, L. W. (1988). Relational exchange norms, perceptions of unfairness, and retained hostility in commercial litigation. *Journal of Conflict Resolution, 32,* 534-552.

Keller, K. L. (1993). Conceptualizing, measuring, and managing customer-based brand equity. *Journal of Marketing, 57*(1), 1-22.

Klein, S., Frazier, G. L., & Roth, V. J. (1990). A transaction cost analysis model of channel integration in international markets. *Journal of Marketing Research, 27,* 196-208.

Kotler, P. (1992). Marketing's new paradigm: What's really happening out there. *Planning Review, 21*(1), 50-52.

Liswood, L. (1990). *Serving them right: Innovative and powerful customer retention strategies.* New York: Harper Business.

Macaulay, S. (1963). Non-contractual relations in business: A preliminary study. *American Sociological Review, 28,* 55-67.

Macneil, I. R. (1980). *The new social contract: An inquiry into modern contractual relations.* New Haven, CT: Yale University Press.

Mason, J. C. (1992, September). Business schools: Striving to meet customer demand. *Management Review,* pp. 10-14.

Mason, J. C. (1993, July). Learning beyond the classroom. *Management Review,* p. 7.

McKenna, R. (1991). *Relationship marketing: Successful strategies for the age of the customer.* Reading, MA: Addison-Wesley.

Morgan, R. M., & Hunt, S. D. (1994). The commitment-trust theory of relationship marketing. *Journal of Marketing, 58*(3), 20-38.

O'Neal, C. R. (1989). JIT procurement and relationship marketing. *Industrial Marketing Management, 18,* 55-63.

Parvatiyar, A., Sheth, J. N., & Whittington, F. B. (1992, April). *Paradigm shift in interfirm marketing relationships: Emerging research issues.* Paper presented at the Research Conference on Customer Relationship Management: Theory and Practice, Emory University, Atlanta, GA.

Peppers, D., & Rogers, M. (1993). *The one to one future: Building relationships one customer at a time.* Garden City, NY: Doubleday.

Porter, L. W., & McKibbin, L. E. (1988). *Management education and development: Drift or thrust into the 21st century?* New York: McGraw-Hill.

Porter, M. E. (1980). *Competitive strategy: Techniques for analyzing industries and competitors.* New York: Free Press.

Schultz, D. E., Tannenbaum, S. I., & Lauterborn, R. F. (1992). *Integrated marketing communications.* Lincolnwood, IL: NTC Business Books.

Shapiro, B. P. (1988). *Close encounters of the four kinds: Managing customers in a rapidly changing environment* (Working Paper No. 9-589-015). Boston: Harvard Business School.

Shaw, R., & Stone, M. (1990). *Database marketing: Strategy and implementation.* New York: John Wiley.

Sheth, J. N. (1988). Changing demographics and the future of graduate management education. *Selections,* pp. 22-27.

Sheth, J. N., Gardner, D. M., & Garrett, D. E. (1988). *Marketing theory: Evolution and evaluation.* New York: John Wiley.

Sheth, J. N., & Parvatiyar, A. (1993, May). *The evolution of relationship marketing.* Paper presented at the Sixth Conference on Historical Thought in Marketing, Atlanta, GA.

Stanton, W. J. (1988, Summer). It's time to restructure marketing in academia. *Journal of Marketing Education, 10,* 2-7.

Thibaut, J. W., & Kelley, H. H. (1959). *The social psychology of groups.* New York: John Wiley.

Tosh, M. (1993, May 10). E.C.R.'s guiding principal. *Supermarket News,* pp. 1-28.

Vavra, T. G. (1992). *Aftermarketing: How to keep customers for life through relationship marketing.* Homewood, IL: Business One-Irwin.

von Hippel, E. A. (1988). *The sources of innovation.* New York: Oxford University Press.

Walle, A. H. (1991, February 4). Practitioners are getting fed up with business schools. *Marketing News,* p. 4.

Webster, F. E., Jr. (1992). The changing role of marketing in the corporation. *Journal of Marketing, 56*(4), 1-17.

Wharton Business School: A New M.B.Age. (1991, December 14). *Economist,* pp. 72-74.

Williams, D. L., Beard, J. D., & Rymer, J. (1991, Summer). Team projects: Achieving their full potential. *Journal of Marketing Education, 13,* 45-53.

Williamson, O. E. (1985). *The economic institutions of capitalism: Firms, markets, and relational contracting.* New York: Free Press.

23

Relationship Marketing

Paradigm Shift or Shaft?

JAGDISH N. SHETH

Relationship marketing, at least at the practice level, is recognized as a major paradigm shift in marketing comparable to what the marketing concept in the 1960s, with its focus on customer needs and wants, and more recently the quality concept, with its focus on customer satisfaction, did in transforming business practices and philosophy. Indeed, at Procter & Gamble, the company that pioneered the modern marketing organization and integration of the four Ps of marketing (product, place, promotion, and price) has just renamed its marketing department Customer Business Development and has shifted focus toward its immediate customers such as large retailers and supermarkets. Similarly, many business-to-business

AUTHOR'S NOTE: The title of this chapter was originally created by Lou Pelton, University of North Texas, for a session on relationship marketing at the meeting of the Academy of Marketing Science, May 1996.

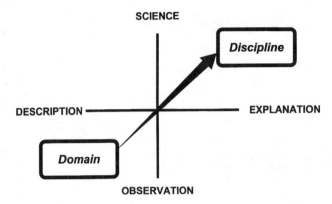

Figure 23.1. Domain Versus Discipline

companies, such as Xerox, IBM, and Citicorp, are investing in global account management processes to serve their key accounts more uniformly
across national and cultural boundaries. Finally, with databases, many service companies such as airlines, banks, and insurance, telephone, and
direct-marketing companies, including catalog companies, have begun to
implement one-to-one marketing and loyalty programs with their end-user
customers.

Relationship marketing with a focus on customer retention and commitment as well as on share of the customer business instead of market
share has also generated enormous research interest. Hundreds of papers
have been presented at dozens of conferences. Several papers have been
published in top journals and many books have been written on this topic,
as indicated by the literature reviews presented in this volume.

Journey From Domain to Discipline

Will relationship marketing create a paradigm shift? Will it become a discipline out of a domain? Nobody knows for sure. However, to me this is
"déjà vu all over again." Therefore, we can learn some key lessons from
situations in the past in which new concepts or domains either succeeded
or failed to become distinct disciplines of marketing.

In order for a domain to become a discipline, it needs to go beyond description and into explanation of the phenomenon by providing hypotheses and theory; at the same time, it needs to go beyond observation and

become a science by utilizing methodological rigor. In the past three decades, there have been at least three successes and three failures in the move from domain to discipline in marketing. By analyzing and understanding why each of these domains failed or succeeded in becoming a discipline of marketing, we may gain some insights and even engage in intervention to make sure that relationship marketing becomes a distinct marketing discipline.

CONSUMER BEHAVIOR VERSUS
INTERNATIONAL MARKETING

In the 1960s, consumer behavior made a successful transition from domain to discipline whereas international marketing did not. Research on consumer behavior quickly focused on only the buying behavior of consumers and attempted to provide explanations for the systematic preferences of consumers as they choose particular brands within a product class. At the same time, researchers began to utilize the operations research techniques of stochastic processes (Markov chains) and underlying theory of learning over time to measure quantitatively the degree of brand loyalty exhibited by household customers.

Unfortunately, for whatever reason, international marketing did not or could not generate its own focus or theory. The debate about standardization versus adjustment of marketing mix across cultures and countries did not result in any well-accepted theory. Also, researchers in this area did not use scientifically accepted methodologies, especially statistical analysis and inferences, to rise above observation.

A number of other factors also contributed toward consumer behavior's becoming a discipline. First, it attracted scholars trained in economic, behavioral, and quantitative sciences to devote their time and talents on this domain. This enhanced the respectability of the domain. Second, most marketing curricula in schools of business developed separate courses on consumer behavior as part of marketing core knowledge. Third, a separate journal, the *Journal of Consumer Research* (*JCR*), was established with the blessings of several disciplines and organizations. *JCR* now ranks among the top three journals in marketing. Third, consumer behavior researchers had the good fortune of having access to longitudinal household panel data from the *Chicago Tribune* and MRCA, which enabled access to significant amounts of empirical research without the usual enormous cost and time constraints. In some sense, this is also what happened in finance and accounting with the availability of Compustat databases on publicly held companies. Finally, several theories of consumer behavior—some very simple, such as Bauer's (1960) theory of risk reduction and Festinger's (1957) theory of cognitive dissonance, and some very comprehensive, such as Howard and Sheth's (1969) theory of buyer behavior—added legitimacy to the transition of consumer behavior from a domain to a discipline.

Unfortunately, none of these factors was available to international marketing. On the contrary, there were traditional scholars who believed at that time that international marketing is strictly a contextual phenomenon requiring no unique constructs or theory, and therefore it should not be a distinct discipline. Marketing departments had a tough time creating separate courses in international marketing, although such courses are now more prevalent.

MARKETING STRATEGY VERSUS
SOCIAL MARKETING

The decade of the 1970s saw a similar race between two other domains in their aspiration to become disciplines: marketing strategy and social marketing. Marketing strategy became a discipline but social marketing did not. A number of enabling events were very helpful to marketing strategy. First of all, business strategy was mandated by the accreditation process of the American Assembly of Collegiate Schools of Business as part of core business education. This resulted in an evolution of academic journals in business strategy similar to the evolution of management science and operation research journals in the 1960s. Second, and perhaps more important, the Strategic Planning Institute allowed academic institutions to license and use the industry benchmarking data called the PIMS, which proved to be a gold mine of exploration and discovery. Also, the PIMS advocates discovered several lawlike generalizations anchored to the impact of market share and customer satisfaction on financial performance.

The transition of marketing strategy from a domain to a discipline was further propelled by the impact of Porter's (1980) book on competitive strategy and its links to market strategies of differentiation and focus. Also, a number of alternative theories, such as population ecology and transactions cost, became popular in marketing strategy as explanations

for market behaviors. Finally, most marketing curricula developed cap-
stone courses anchored to marketing strategy. This was further enhanced
by several computer simulation games, such as the MarkStrat and the
Beer Game, that encouraged a more analytic approach to education and
learning.

In contrast, social marketing suffered, right at its inception, from definition debate. Is it marketing of nonprofit and social services (education,
health care, population control) or is it the malpractices of marketing,
such as the misrepresentation, deception, and ecological and cultural
harm that marketing practices create? Even today, this debate has not
been resolved. At the same time, there was a strong movement toward con-
sumerism and a "consumer bill of rights," including truth in lending and
truth in advertising. Even public policy research could not provide a focus
for this domain. Unfortunately, there was also advocacy—or evangelistic
fervor—among well-known marketing scholars who braved the research in
this area. This made objective scientific inquiry untenable. Finally, as was
the case for international marketing, most scholars believed that social
marketing is an extension of marketing theory and practice, and therefore
needed no unique constructs or its own theory. It is unfortunate that despite good scholars publishing in top journals, social marketing could not
make the transition from a domain to a discipline.

SERVICES MARKETING VERSUS
BUSINESS MARKETING

The decade of the 1980s saw a similar parallel between services marketing and business-to-business marketing. The former has begun to become
a discipline, whereas the latter continues to be a domain. What is the difference? First of all, by the 1980s, the economy had become predominantly a services economy, and the total quality management philosophy,
with its focus on customer service, had become very popular. Both the government and the industry were willing to commit money to improve product and service quality, especially in consumer mass markets. This led to
the emergence of government quality awards (Malcolm Baldrige Award)
and private quality awards (J. D. Power), and to performance metrics such
as airline on-time arrival and baggage delivery, to rate superiority of one
company over others. Soon thereafter, the Marketing Science Institute
supported major research funding that led to the development of SERVQL,

a methodology to measure service quality. At about the same time, several books were published to articulate how and why services are different from products. This led to the conceptualization of several unique properties of services, such as intangibility, interactivity, perishability, and proximity. A number of universities and schools of business started separate centers of research and education in services marketing in addition to offering separate courses.

Services marketing has started the journey toward becoming a discipline by establishing its own scholarly journal, by focusing its research on services as unique and distinct from products, and by having access to large-scale databases related to customer support services.

Business-to-business marketing in the United States has not enjoyed the same benefits. Although there are some research centers and some focus, it is not a significant phenomenon. On the other hand, in Europe research in business-to-business marketing has led to multicountry, multi-industry consortia and has now become the IMP school of thought, with an emphasis on networks of alliances and relationships both vertically and horizontally. Unlike the rest of the world, U.S. marketing is focused more on consumer marketing than on industrial marketing. Industrial marketing, therefore, has not attracted as many scholars. Also, business-to-business marketing is closely related to organization behavior and management, which employs comparable concepts and research techniques. In other words, business-to-business marketing has not been able to create its own distinct domain and still remains synonymous with marketing activities in business-to-business companies. Those marketing activities are predominantly sales support activities, and do not have the degree of centrality that brand management enjoys in a packaged goods company.

Lessons for Relationship Marketing

What lessons can relationship marketing learn from the above examples? How can it evolve into a discipline of marketing? I believe it needs to focus on the following eight areas.

Delimit the domain. The concept of relationship and relational behavior is universal. It is in physical, animal, plant, and human sciences. There-

fore, every discipline has applications and implications of relational behavior. Indeed, it is so universal that the most widely used statistical technique is correlation, or the relationship between two or more phenomena,
whether bivariate or multivariate in nature. Therefore, it is not only easy
but also tempting to extend the concept of relationship beyond marketing
and beyond business—but then it would lose its identity and uniqueness.
This is analogous to consumer behavior, which is only one subset domain
of all human behaviors—that is, the behavior and the roles people manifest as consumers in contrast with the roles of producers or middlemen or
citizens or kinship. In short, relationship marketing must be limited to
the discipline of marketing, which is focused on understanding and managing customers and their buying, paying, and consuming behaviors.

Furthermore, not all marketing can be relationship marketing. Relationship marketing has to be a subset of marketing. In other words, not all
marketing relationships are relationship marketing. Just as we have services marketing, international marketing, and social marketing, there is or
should be a unique domain called relationship marketing whose objectives, processes, performance, and governance are unique with respect to
organizations' marketing and nonmarketing resource allocations. The objective of relationship marketing is to increase customers' commitment
to the organization through the process of offering better value on a continuous basis at a reduced cost. This can be achieved partly within the organization and partly through partnerships with suppliers and even competitors. The measure of success is the growth of the share of a customer's
business and its profitability.

Agree on a definition. Relationship marketing has proliferated with
many definitions and many programs. It includes affinity marketing, loyalty marketing, cobranding, comarketing, and customer-supplier partnering. In professional services, it includes personalized one-to-one relationships with individual clients and dedication of the organization's resources
to the individual relationship. In business-to-business marketing, it includes key account management and solution selling.

Analogous to social marketing, there is already a definitional debate
about relationship marketing. Some have argued that it is an old concept already incorporated in existing schools of marketing thought, and therefore
needs no separate identity; others have suggested that it overlaps with so

many domains of marketing (services, channels, global, and direct marketing) that it needs no separate identity. Still others believe that relationship marketing is synonymous with direct marketing, and thus it is more appropriate in business-to-business marketing and services marketing.

What we need is a definition that will articulate the uniqueness of the concept with its own distinct properties, similar to what services marketing has done. There are at least three aspects unique to relationship marketing. First, it is a one-to-one relationship between the marketer and the customer. In other words, relationship cannot be at an aggregate level; it has to be at an individual-entity level. Second, it is an interactive process and not an exchange. This is a fundamental distinction, because marketing is founded on the principle of exchange and transactions. Relationship marketing, however, is all about interaction and activities; it is coproduction and coconsumption in which the time, location, and identity boundaries between the supplier and the customers are blurring into one extended supply-and-demand chain of management. At the same time, each member in the value chain is a distinct and independent organization with its own capital and management; therefore, it is a virtually integrated network of organizations and not a traditional vertically integrated organization.

The third, and equally important, uniqueness of relationship marketing is that it is a value-added activity through mutual interdependence and collaboration between suppliers and customers. Just as hardware and software create a symbiotic value addition, and one without the other is less useful to users and consumers, relationship marketing must add value through collaborative and partnering mind-sets and behaviors of suppliers and customers. This is very obvious in services industries, where the user must cooperate and collaborate with the provider, whether it is a doctor, accountant, lawyer, or teacher. It is becoming more the case with automated services such as automatic teller machines, telephone answering systems, and gasoline pumps. Finally, with electronic ordering and Internet commerce, it is also becoming prevalent for traditional product offerings, especially in business-to-business marketing.

Build respectable databases. Perhaps the single biggest lesson we can learn from marketing strategy involves the access to PIMS databases with measures of financial performance. I believe that relationship marketing needs to access similar data from corporations and service bureaus. It was the availability of household panel data on more than 200 consumer products that led to quantitative performance measures of brand loyalty in consumer behavior. Today, it is the availability of scanner data through IRI and A. C. Nielsen that is propelling scientific research on brand equity.

In my opinion, this is very possible, especially in the United States. For example, we can utilize the Compustat database on publicly traded companies and collect information on an ongoing basis with respect to relationship marketing practices of these companies. This will then allow us to correlate relationship marketing with financial performance similar to the PIMS or the IRI databases. At the Center for Relationship Marketing at Emory University, we have attempted to collect these databases and hope to create a database for anyone to use for research purposes. The IMP's success in Europe in understanding relationships and networks in industrial purchasing and marketing is further testimony that this can be done.

Develop performance metrics. It is equally important that we develop some standardized metrics to measure relationship marketing's performance as well as antecedents that are likely to be its determinants. For example, SERVQL, a standardized instrument used to measure service quality, is now utilized across national boundaries, similar to the Briggs-Myers scale in personality or 360-degree feedback for management performance.

It is not sufficient to develop scales to measure constructs such as trust, commitment, and long-term orientation; it is equally important to measure performance outcomes using well-accepted financial and accounting methods. Recent studies by several scholars concerning the merging and purging of existing public financial and customer-supplier databases and utilizing them to examine the impact of relationship marketing on the performance of the firm are very encouraging. However, we need to do more. I do not believe that psychological instruments, not matter how well validated, will be sufficient. What we need to know is not what informants say or believe in, but rather what organizations do. This is equally true for household customers. It is therefore encouraging to see that many direct-marketing service companies (such as telephone and insurance companies, airlines, and utilities) have begun to analyze actual behavioral or usage data on their customers through billing and customer service and to develop standardized performance measures by linking them to the cost of serving each customer.

Employ longitudinal research methods. Relationship marketing, like product life and diffusion of innovation, is a time-centric process. It is an evolutionary and dynamic phenomenon over time. Therefore, it is important that we utilize research techniques such as longitudinal panels, which measure changes over time; we need time-series data similar to what psychologists use in measuring learning or econometricians use to measure business cycles and trends.

Although it is easy to use cross-sectional data as surrogates, this method is not as legitimate as the use of longitudinal data. I believe the need for longitudinal data will create more difficulties for young scholars, who have to publish quickly to get tenure and promotions. It was the access to longitudinal household panel data that enabled consumer behavior scholars to analyze brand loyalty relatively quickly. Similarly, it is the time-series data obtained from government agencies or the stock market that enable scholars in economics, finance, and accounting to test time-centric concepts in their respective disciplines. The point I am trying to make is that we should not compromise the integrity of research methodology because of the urgency of publishing. There is a solution, and it is involves access to longitudinal data from commercial and government sources.

Publish in top journals. The medium is the message. Therefore, it is very important for an emerging discipline's researchers to publish in first-tier journals of the main discipline. These journals provide source credibility and legitimacy. Unfortunately, it is also not easy to get published, especially if the emerging discipline is part of a paradigm shift. Resistance to changing or challenging a discipline's lawlike generalizations is pervasive, and it takes strong editorial leadership or revolt by a journal's readership to encourage innovation. There are two alternatives to publishing in mainstream first-tier journals. The first is to create a new journal devoted to the emerging discipline, but the success of this strategy depends to a large extent on the new journal's gaining the same level of academic reputation as the traditional journals of the discipline. This is precisely what happened in consumer behavior with the successful creation of the *Journal of Consumer Research* and, more recently, with *Marketing Science* for modeling scholars.

The second alternative is to publish a seminal book on the topic. Indeed, there are numerous examples of this in all disciplines. Books and monographs have often had greater impacts on disciplines than have journals, probably because of their wider reach and distribution. Most journals have very limited circulations when compared with books. This is what happened with the publication of the Howard and Sheth (1969) theory book, and it was also the case with Michael Porter's *Competitive Strategy*

(1980). More recently, even such popular professional books on management as *In Search of Excellence* (Peters & Waterman, 1982) and *Reengineering the Corporation* (Hammer & Champy, 1993) have had significant impacts on business disciplines.

Encourage respected scholars. We must learn from the consumer behavior discipline in marketing as well as from finance and accounting about this reality. Finance became even more respectable when well-trained and well-known economists became interested in finance. Similarly, rural sociology became more respectable when top sociologists began to focus on that area, which led to seminal theories, such as diffusion of innovation. Similarly, both behavioral concepts and psychometric methodology enhanced accounting to a discipline from a double-entry system of practice. And consumer behavior became respectable when psychologists, modelers, and economists began to focus their time and talent on the issues of consumer behavior.

Relationship marketing needs a similar infusion of respected marketing scholars, especially those who can add conceptual and methodological rigor to the domain. Because relationship marketing is very popular, at least in practice, I believe it is likely to attract respected scholars.

Develop explanatory theory. No domain has ever become a discipline without some explanatory theory, or at least the development of some constructs. Fortunately, relationship marketing has a good start in this direction. A number of constructs, including trust, commitment, and long-term orientation, have emerged as building blocks of a theory. Also, even if we cannot develop a theory, it is important that we develop at least some lawlike generalizations comparable to product life cycle, diffusion of innovation, and PIMS research. However, no matter what we do, it is important that we make sure that the constructs as well as the lawlike generalizations are unique and distinctive to relationship marketing. In this regard, trust may not be unique, because even for a one-time transaction, there must be a minimum level of trust between the seller and the buyer. On the other hand, the concept of commitment is more likely to be unique to relationship marketing. Similarly, the concept of collaboration is unique because it is not appropriate in other types of marketing relationships.

Fortunately, it should be possible to develop a theory of relationship marketing because of the richness and universality of relationship as a phenomenon. We already have a number of theories (social contract, agency, and transaction cost theories) from other respected disciplines. Also, there is a growing and interesting body of knowledge on cooperation, collaboration, and competition.

Conclusion

Will relationship marketing become a well-respected, freestanding, and distinct discipline in marketing? My belief is that it certainly has the potential; my wish is that it should happen, because marketing will benefit enormously from it.

The lessons learned from previous efforts, both successful and unsuccessful, of various marketing domains that have tried to become disciplines provide a good road map for how to evolve relationship marketing into a distinct discipline. As an intervention strategy, it would be highly desirable for relationship marketing researchers to organize their own association and their own scholarly journal.

References

Bauer, R. A. (1960). Consumer behavior as risk taking. In R. S. Hancock (Ed.), *Dynamic marketing for a changing world* (pp. 389-398). Chicago: American Marketing Association.
Festinger, L. (1957). *A theory of cognitive dissonance.* Stanford, CA: Stanford University Press.
Hammer, M., & Champy, J. (1993). *Reengineering the corporation: A manifesto for business revolution* (Rev. ed.). New York: Harper Business.
Howard, J. A., & Sheth, J. N. (1969). *The theory of buyer behavior.* New York: John Wiley.
Peters, T. J., & Waterman, R. H., Jr. (1982). *In search of excellence: Lessons from America's best-run companies.* New York: Harper & Row.
Porter, M. E. (1980). *Competitive strategy: Techniques for analyzing industries and competitors.* New York: Free Press.

Index

About the Contributors

Leonard L. Berry (PhD, Arizona State University) holds the J. C. Penney Chair of Retailing Studies, is Distinguished Professor of Marketing, and is Director of the Center for Retailing Studies at Texas A&M University. He is a former national president of the American Marketing Association. His research interests are in the areas of services marketing, service quality, and retailing strategy. He has published numerous journal articles and books, including *Discovering the Soul of Service: The Nine Drivers of Sustainable Business Success* (1999), *On Great Service: A Framework for Action* (1995), and *Marketing Services: Competing Through Quality* (1991).

C. B. Bhattacharya is Associate Professor of Marketing at the School of Management at Boston University. He received his PhD in marketing from the Wharton School of the University of Pennsylvania in 1993 and his MBA from the Indiana Institute of Management. He is currently working on measuring brand loyalty and brand health using scanner data, determinants of customer retention, and the roles of corporate social responsibility and organizational identification and disidentification in the design of marketing strategy. He has published in a number of scholarly journals, including the *Journal of Marketing, International Journal of Research in Marketing, Journal of the Academy of Marketing Science, Marketing Letters,* and the *Journal of Retailing and Consumer Services.*

Ruth N. Bolton is Thomas Henry Carroll Ford Foundation Visiting Associate Professor at the Harvard Business School. She is visiting the Harvard Business School from the Robert H. Smith School of Business at the University of Maryland, where she is Associate Professor of Marketing and Harvey Sanders Professor of Retailing and Services Marketing. Her current research is concerned with high-technology services sold to business-to-business customers. She is a frequent speaker on services, marketing, customer satisfaction, customer retention, and quality management topics. She currently serves on the editorial boards of the *Journal of Retailing, Journal of Marketing, Marketing Science, Marketing Letters, Journal of Marketing Research,* and *Journal of Service Research.*

Joseph P. Cannon is Assistant Professor of Marketing at Colorado State University. He received his PhD from the University of North Carolina. His primary research interests involve the issues related to the effective management of business-to-business buyer-seller relationships in domestic and international markets. His research has appeared in the *Journal of Marketing, Journal of the Academy of Marketing Science, Academy of Management Review,* and other academic journals.

David W. Cravens, PhD, holds the Eunice and James L. West Chair of American Enterprise Studies at Texas Christian University. He is internationally recognized for his research on marketing strategy and sales management, and he has contributed more than 100 articles, monographs, books, and proceedings papers. His textbook *Strategic Marketing* (1997) is widely used in strategy and management courses.

Karen S. Cravens is an Arthur Anderson Faculty Fellow and Associate Professor of Accounting at the University of Tulsa. She is a licensed certified public accountant and holds a PhD from Texas A&M University. Her work has been published in *Business Horizons, International Business Review, International Journal of Accounting, Journal of Financial and Strategic Decisions, Journal of Strategic Marketing, Managerial Auditing Journal, Managerial Finance, Oil & Gas Tax Quarterly,* and *Research in Accounting Regulation.*

Margaret H. Cunningham (PhD, Texas A&M University, College Station) is Associate Professor of Marketing at Queen's University in Kingston, Ontario. Her major research interests are in the areas of marketing alliances, social partnerships, and marketing ethics. Her research has been published in the *Journal of the Academy of Marketing Science, Social Marketing and Fundraising, Journal of International Marketing, Festival Manage-*

ment & Event Tourism Journal, and the *Philanthropist,* as well as in a number of marketing textbooks.

Ian Gordon is President of Convergence Management Consultants, Toronto, a firm providing strategic marketing services to executive management. His interest is in helping companies bond with chosen customers and ensuring that they do so better than their competitors. He has authored books on relationship marketing and competitive intelligence and strategy, as well as more than 50 articles. He lectured in undergraduate and graduate business programs at York University, Toronto, for 15 years.

Christian Grönroos, Dr. Econ., is Professor of Service and Relationship Marketing and Chairman of the Board of the Research and Knowledge Center, CERS Center for Relationship Marketing and Service Management, at Hanken Swedish School of Economics, Finland. His research interests include service management, services marketing, service quality, and relationship marketing in both consumer and business-to-business environments. His book *Service Management and Marketing* (first edition 1990) has been published in eight languages. His work has been published in the *Journal of the Academy of Marketing Science, Journal of Business Research, Journal of Marketing Management, International Journal of Service Industry Management, European Journal of Marketing, Journal of Business and Industrial Marketing, Journal of Services Marketing, Integrated Marketing Communication Research Journal,* and *Asia-Australia Marketing Journal.*

Thomas W. Gruen (PhD, Indiana University) is Assistant Professor of Marketing at the Goizueta Business School at Emory University. His research interests cover three areas of relationship marketing: memberships, team selling, and category management. His work has been published in the *Journal of Business Research, Business Horizons,* and *International Business Review.*

Håkan Håkansson (PhD, Uppsala University) is Professor of Industrial Marketing at Uppsala University in Sweden. Aside from industrial marketing, his two complementary research interests are technical development and purchasing. He is the author or coauthor of a number of books and has published articles in the *Journal of Marketing, Journal of Marketing Re-*

search, *Journal of Business-to-Business Marketing, International Journal of Research in Marketing, European Journal of Management,* and *Industrial Marketing Management.*

Sandy D. Jap is Assistant Professor of Marketing at the Sloan School of Management at the Massachusetts Institute of Technology. Her research interest is in collaboration in the distribution channel and supply chain. Her work has been published or is forthcoming in the *Journal of Marketing Research, Journal of the Academy of Marketing Science, Journal of Business Research,* and *Sloan Management Review.*

John T. Mentzer is the Harry J. and Vivienne R. Bruce Excellence Chair of Business Policy in the Department of Marketing, Logistics and Transportation at the University of Tennessee. He has published more than 120 articles and papers in the *Journal of the Academy of Marketing Science, Journal of Marketing, Journal of Business Logistics, Journal of Business Research, International Journal of Physical Distribution and Logistics Management, Transportation and Logistics Review, Transportation Journal, Columbia Journal of World Business, Industrial Marketing Management, Research in Marketing, Business Horizons,* and other journals.

Robert M. Morgan is Associate Professor of Marketing and Reese Phifer Faculty Fellow of Marketing at the University of Alabama. His research focuses on marketing strategy and relationship marketing, particularly on understanding how strategies centering on relationship building develop and their impacts on the firm, its constituencies, and its partners. His research has been published in the *Journal of Marketing, Academy of Management Journal, Marketing Management,* and *Journal of Advertising.*

Narakesari Narayandas is Assistant Professor of Business Administration at the Harvard Business School. He received his PhD in marketing from the Krannert Graduate School of Management, Purdue University. His research interests are in the area of customer management. His work has previously been published in the *Journal of Marketing, Journal of Service Research,* and *Journal of Business-to-Business Marketing.*

Atul Parvatiyar is Assistant Professor of Marketing at Goizueta Business School, Emory University. He received his MBA and PhD from Banaras Hindu University, India. He has authored a number of articles in the areas of international marketing, business alliances, and environmental marketing. His previous research has been published in the *Journal of the Academy of Marketing Science, International Business Review, Research in Marketing,* and *Journal of Business Research.* He is coeditor of *Research in Marketing* and serves on the editorial review board of *International Marketing Review* and the *International Journal of Customer Relationship Management.*

Adrian Payne is Professor of Services and Relationship Marketing and Director of the Center for Relationship Marketing at the Cranfield School of Management, Cranfield University. His research interests include customer retention and relationship marketing. His books include *Relationship Marketing: Strategy and Implementation* (1999), *Advances in Relationship Marketing* (1995), *Relationship Marketing for Competitive Advantage* (1995), and *Relationship Marketing* (1991).

Srinivas K. Reddy (PhD, Columbia University) is Professor of Marketing and Sanford Research Fellow at the Terry College of Business, University of Georgia. His research interests are in marketing strategy, particularly in the areas of brand management and pricing. His research has been published in the *Journal of Marketing Research, Journal of Marketing, Management Science, Journal of the Academy of Marketing Science, Journal of Business Research, Journal of Advertising Research,* and *Multivariate Behavioral Research.*

Jagdish N. Sheth is the Charles H. Kelistadt Professor of Marketing at Emory University. He has published more than 200 books and research papers in different areas of marketing. His book *The Theory of Buyer Behavior* (1969), with John A. Howard, is a classic in the field. He has recently published two scholarly books: *Marketing Theory: Evolution and Evaluation,* with D. M. Gardner and D. E. Garrett (1988); and *Consumption Values and Market Choices,* with B. I. Newman and B. L. Gross (1991). He is on the editorial boards of at least a dozen scholarly journals in marketing, international business, and quantitative methods; he is also series editor of *Research in Marketing.* In 1989, he received the Outstanding Educator Award from the Academy of Marketing Science, and in 1992 he received the P. D. Converse Award from the American Marketing Association. He is also a Fellow of the American Psychological Association and Past President of the Association for Consumer Research.

Rajendra S. Sisodia is Trustee Professor of Marketing at Bentley College. Previously, he was Associate Professor of Marketing and Director of Executive Programs at George Mason University and Assistant Professor of Marketing at Boston University. He has a PhD in marketing from Columbia University. He has published approximately 50 articles in journals such as the *Harvard Business Review, Journal of the Academy of Marketing Science, Journal of Business Strategy,* and *Marketing Letters and Marketing Management,* as well as several book chapters. He has also authored about two dozen cases, primarily on strategic and marketing issues in the telecommunications industry, as well as a number of telecommunications industry and company analyses.

Ivan J. Snehota (PhD, Uppsala University) is Associate Professor of Marketing at Stockholm School of Economics. His research interest is in market strategy in business markets. He is coauthor of *Developing Relationships in Business Networks* (1995) and *Managing Business Relationships* (1998).

Kaj Storbacka has worked on strategy formulation as a management consultant to major Scandinavian service companies for 15 years. In 1991 he founded CRM Customer Relationship Management Ltd., a consulting company that specializes in developing customer-oriented strategies. He is also one of the founders of CRM International, a network of consulting companies. He has held various positions (researcher, lecturer, and professor) at the Swedish School of Economics and Business Administration in Helsinki, Finland. Currently he is affiliated with the Center for Relationship Marketing and Service Management at the Swedish School of Economics and Business Administration. He has written a number of research reports on marketing issues, several articles and working papers on relationship marketing and service management, a book on leadership in service organizations, and a book about relationship management, which won a Scandinavian award for best business book 1994-1997.

Vanitha Swaminathan is Assistant Professor of Marketing in the Isenberg School of Management at the University of Massachusetts at Amherst. Her research interests center on branding strategies such as brand alliances and extensions and on branding issues in the emerging electronic media. She has published in the *Journal of Marketing Research* and *Advances in Consumer Research,* and in the proceedings of conferences held by the

American Marketing Association, the Academy of Management, and the Center for Relationship Marketing.

P. Rajan Varadarajan is Professor of Marketing and Jenna and Calvin R. Guest Professor of Business Administration at Texas A&M University. His research interests are in the areas of corporate, business, and marketing strategy; marketing management; and global competitive strategy. His research has been published in the *Journal of Marketing, Journal of the Academy of Marketing Science, Academy of Management Journal, Strategic Management Journal, Sloan Management Review, California Management Review, Business Horizons,* and other journals. He is coauthor of the textbook *Contemporary Perspectives on Strategic Market Planning.* He served as an editor of the *Journal of Marketing* from 1993 to 1996, and he currently serves on the Board of Governors of the Academy of Marketing Science, as chair of the Marketing Strategy Special Interest Group of the American Marketing Association, and on the editorial review boards of the *Journal of Marketing, Journal of Strategic Marketing,* and *Journal of International Marketing.*

Barton A. Weitz is Chairman of the Marketing Department, the J. C. Penney Eminent Scholar Chair, and Executive Director of the Center for Retailing Education and Research at the University of Florida. He is a member of the board of directors of the National Retail Federation and former editor of the *Journal of Marketing Research.* His research interests focus on the development of long-term relationships between firms in a channel of distribution (retailers and vendors), between firms and their employees, and between salespeople and their customers.

David T. Wilson (PhD, University of Western Ontario) is Alvin H. Clemens Professor of Entrepreneurial Studies at the Smeal College of Business Administration at the Pennsylvania State University. His research interest is in value creation and measurement in value-creating networks of business-to-business firms. He has published widely in leading national and international journals.

David B. Wolfe heads Wolfe Resources Group, a consumer behavior consultancy located in Reston, Virginia. His client list includes American Express, Bausch & Lomb, Ford Motor Company, General Motors, MetLife, and Marriott, as well as other major U.S. companies. His work has taken him to Africa, Asia, and Europe. He frequently guest lectures at major universities on a new marketing model called *developmental relationship marketing*. He has authored more than 20 articles in the past 10 years and is author of a book on marketing to middle-aged and older consumers, *Serving the Ageless Market*.